The Rioplatense Guitar

The Bold Strummer Guitar Study Series No. 3

The Rioplatense Guitar

Volume I:

The Early Guitar and Its Context

in Argentina and Uruguay

by

Richard Pinnell

with

Ricardo Zavadivker

The Bold Strummer, Ltd.
Westport, Connecticut

ISBN No.
0-933224-42-7 Hard
0-933224-43-5 Paper

Library of Congress No. 93-079324.
The history of the guitar
in Argentina and Uruguay.

Distributed to Libraries and Institutions of learning by
Pro/Am Music Resources, White Plains, NY

Published by
The Bold Strummer Ltd.
20 Turkey Hill Circle, PO Box 2037, Westport, CT 06880-2037

Bold Strummer Guitar Study Series No. 3

Dedication

For Piedad and the People of

Argentina and Uruguay

with affection

[Para Piedad y la Gente de

la Argentina y el Uruguay

con cariño]

Acknowledgments

In 1961 I made my first trip to the *Río de la Plata* (River of Silver) as a guitarist and lived on both sides of the river, in Argentina and Uruguay. Then I made additional trips to bring my total residence there to over three years. However, once returned to the States after my first trip, I married an Uruguayan, Piedad Yarza of Melo, enabling my contact with a circle of friends, associates, and even relatives from the Plata region to remain continuous now for over three decades. All this, plus foreign residence in other Latin republics and Spain, has enabled me to amass the stockpile of materials and information from which this volume emanates.

Any scholarly book enlists the forces of past and present experts in its subject matter. Documentation in this study musters advocates of bygone days, but present-day guitarists, teachers, musicologists, and even scholars from allied fields have also contributed directly. For instance, Ricardo Zavadivker of Buenos Aires, who always insisted on the *"intercambio de datos"* [the free exchange of data] in my dealings with him, has made a major contribution to this volume as author of Part V—although it represents only a sample of his expertise. Special thanks are due to editor Roberto Lara as well as the heirs of Abel Fleury and Editorial Lagos of Buenos Aires, Argentina for their authorization to publish the sensitive *Ausencia*. Bonifacio del Carril has kindly contributed plates of the *media caña* and *cielito* dances as well as the gaucho ballad in the *pulpería* (Plates VII–IX, used by permission of Emecé Editores S.A., Buenos Aires). Likewise innumerable associates over the decades have made contributions to or influenced this investigation, but the mere enumeration of names would fill a whole chapter. Instead I am dedicating this volume to them as a token of my high esteem and heartfelt appreciation.

The project of writing *The Rioplatense Guitar* would have been impossible without financial support from many sources. Foremost among them was the Fulbright Senior Research Fellowship to Buenos Aires and Montevideo with which I updated the inquiry. (I am grateful to Prof. Robert Stevenson [UCLA] for the Fulbright connections.) Moreover, institutional grants from the University of Wisconsin–La Crosse (UW–L) funded travel to collections or release from teaching in order to complete the work. I received several grants from the Research Committee and a sabbatical leave with the support of the Faculty Development Committee; numerous smaller grants came from the College of Arts, Letters and Sciences, Foundation, and International Education at UW–L, and from the Center for Latin America at UW–Milwaukee.

Many colleagues advanced the work with their expertise. Jean Bonde of UW–L's Interlibrary Loan imported a plethora of source materials. Some UW–L faculty members read portions of the text or furnished translations—professors like Sonja Schrag, Leslee Poulton, and Gary Kuhn. However, I am most indebted to my colleagues who perused the entire manuscript in order to provide additions or corrections: Professors Richard Hudson (UCLA), Thomas Heck (Ohio State), Clare Callahan (CCM, University of Cincinnati), William Katra (UW–Eau Claire), and Stanley Rolnick (UW–L). Thanks go to Dave Faulkner and Tom Lewis for help on formatting, and to Nicholas Clarke for inspiration.

Despite this unflagging support, however, as principal author, editor, and translator, I alone carry the burden of any inadvertent errors of commission or omission. My only justification is that throughout the writing, the availability of sources determined the shape of the product.

—Richard Pinnell
University of Wisconsin–La Crosse

The Rioplatense Guitar

Volume I:
The Early Guitar and Its Context in Argentina and Uruguay

Table of Contents

xii

Special Features
A. Figures

B. Musical Examples

C. Tables

Foreword

Towards the end of 1963, I was taking guitar lessons from maestro Samuel de León del Río in Uruguay. He would always come from Durazno every Saturday to a private home in the neighboring town of Paso de los Toros to give the lessons. By then I was just starting to play the concert-worthy folk dances of Abel Fleury. After a certain lesson that summer, the maestro took me into the dining room and explained that he had a special treat for me, inasmuch as one of his best students had come along to perform. After introducing us, he said of his guest, *"El es un estudiante bien serio,"* with latent implications. Indeed, the student did appear quite serious, although he was only in his mid-teens. Being strikingly handsome, he gazed up but momentarily from dark, deeply set eyes, and commenced to play with confidence. He led off with the first étude of Villa Lobos, and with it he made it a marvelous outpouring of spirit. He played it fast: even with all the repeats, it surely took no more than two minutes. The student made it sound rather like the speed and polish of Manuel Barrueco's 1976 recording of the same piece. It was so well played that it caused a turning point in my life: "How could it be?" I asked myself. "What untold forces were operative upon and within this young prodigy?"

As I have pondered explanations over the decades since then, that same young man has returned again and again to the fore. It was Baltazar Benítez, who subsequently won Segovia's Santiago de Compostela competition to launch a career of recordings and recital performances throughout the world.

That experience and many others like it have precipitated the present study, a volume on the early guitar in Argentina and Uruguay. The Introduction describes the main theme (the guitar of those countries) and its countersubject (the guitar's cultural context there). However, the volume is comprised of five main parts, the first of which sets the stage and introduces the characters. The geographical gamut of the Plata region comes into full view, and with it the great cultural clash that the Europeans brought with the conquest. Spaniards came by the thousands in search of gold and silver, initially, bringing along, as part of their predominantly Andalusian culture, the guitar. Simultaneously it was becoming known as "the Spanish guitar" as it invaded popular and aristocratic lifestyles of Europe (Part II). Starting in the 16th century, the guitar of the Río de la Plata emerged in full bloom, revealing its appearance and construction as well as its use in society. It was a five-course, double-strung guitar, sometimes characterized by fancy shell inlays or black filigree ornamentation. It was played by women almost as often as men, and it belonged to all social ranks and in every context—even in church! It was thus the national instrument from the earliest times (Part III). Even so, owing to its pervasive popularity, the guitar was not without its infamous associations: it was as typical of the flamenco dance called the fandango as the rowdy *pulpería* taverns where it was performed (Part IV). After independence in Argentina and Uruguay, the guitar's repertoire began to subdivide into popular and classical categories, as documented by the testimony of numerous foreign observers in the 19th century (Part V by Ricardo Zavadivker of Buenos Aires). Consequently, according to a wealth of new sources, the Rioplatense guitar ran parallel with the history of the European guitar. Yet in the Plata, the prestige of playing it lasted longer than it did in Europe—a partial explanation for the Plata's outstanding school of guitar players, which has lasted undiminished until the present day.

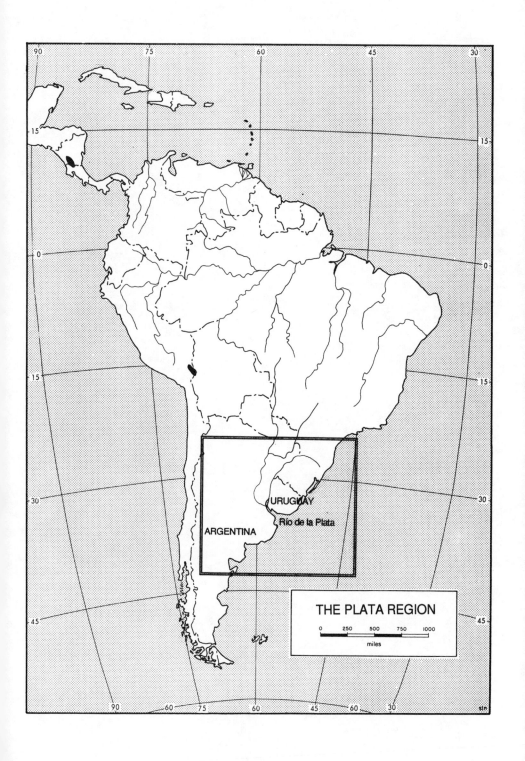

THE PLATA REGION

0   250   500   750   1000
miles

URUGUAY
Río de la Plata
ARGENTINA

Introduction

𝕿𝖍𝖊 𝕽𝖎𝖔𝖕𝖑𝖆𝖙𝖊𝖓𝖘𝖊 𝕲𝖚𝖎𝖙𝖆𝖗 is the story of the Hispanic peoples of the Río de la Plata and their favorite instrument. This volume, being the first of several in a projected series, explains the yet untold origin and development of the instrument which the Spanish conquerors introduced into the Americas, and how it evolved to become the magnificent guitar of Argentina and Uruguay.

The Spanish key word *Rioplatense* (Ree-oh-plah-ten-say) derives from a contraction of *Río de la Plata*. This "River of Silver" flows between present-day Argentina and Uruguay, and other South American republics border on the shorelines of its tributaries. Explorers in the 16th century named the great River of Silver for its access to the ancient treasure of the Andes. In fact, by mid-century, the Plata's river system had led the conquerors directly into the silver mining district of the Bolivian highlands, validating the designation. Yet ironically, the name endured over the centuries despite the fact that the inhabitants on the Atlantic side never controlled the mining operations. The Hispanic invasion of South America developed simultaneously on both the east and west sides of the continental divide; then the mines, at the top of it,

1

happened to become subject to the Pacific flank of the invasion. As the conquest continued, the court began the mining operations and soon thereafter established the Viceroyalty of Peru, centered at Lima, to oversee them and to govern the rest of the South American continent. Under the rule of Lima, the silver exports from Buenos Aires constituted either minuscule or contraband shipments. Thus the term "Río de la Plata" came to be associated with the peoples who settled around the so-called River of Silver, on the Atlantic side of the continent, even though they never saw the extent of the treasure.

From the time of the European conquest, the Plata region remained a hotbed of guitar playing. Ranging historically from the pioneer settlements around the Plata estuary to the world's concert halls of the present day, whether in the classical or popular style, some guitarists of Argentina and Uruguay have achieved world-class quality. This achievement was due to their heritage and their environment. They inherited the predilection for the guitar from the Spaniards who brought it to the Americas in the first place and who provided the population base for subsequent generations. However, the Plata colony became unique in the Hispanic conquest because of its isolation. The guitar came to the Americas at the peak of its prestige. At the time of conquest, it was not only connected to the populace but also to the aristocracy, for guitar playing was held in high esteem. It was a lofty privilege, just as worthy of the prince as the princess. Meanwhile the Spaniards had become resigned to the fact that the Plata did not have the nearby precious metals of their quest, so the monarchy left the region to dwindle in isolation from the rest of Hispania during the distractions of a remarkable Golden Age. Consequently the archaic, pre-Golden Age norms of Rioplatense life went unchanged for centuries—suspended in time. The high regard for the guitar during colonial times endured. The Rioplatense guitar never declined; it was never superseded.

Playing the guitar in the Plata region has ever been a matter of pride and prestige. Its guitarists, whether from Argentina or Uruguay, have always been confident of their prowess. For them, playing the guitar is somewhat like playing soccer, their favorite sport, because they need an audience to deliver a peak performance.

Soccer is a national pastime, and admittedly, like the guitar, it may be played to excess. But put a team before an audience, and the game becomes at once a compelling, passionate expression and a striving for excellence. Such pride and intensity of focus on soccer led the Argentines to two World Cup championships. The Uruguayan teams also proved to be fierce contenders in the international arena: representing a republic of a mere three million inhabitants, they captured twice the World Cup and twice the Olympic gold.

The prestige of playing the guitar there has even been more consequential. Ever since the days of conquest, guitarists have commanded respect and esteem for their work. They have enjoyed all the rewards for achievement that a society can supply. For example, in a short story that appeared in Argentina at the turn of the century, Martín Gil, scientist and guitarist, author and associate of Segovia, wrote a piece about a friend's personal experience. It was memorable because of the guitar's importance in resolving a difficult situation.

The protagonist of the story was a young man of Buenos Aires who had grown tired of the hustle and bustle of the capital city and yearned for fresh air and a change of scene. He went far inland to the hills of Córdoba, and stayed briefly in a hotel until he was able to relocate to a cheaper *pensión*—essentially a boarding house on the outskirts of town which was run by a family. A Doña Liboria was in charge, and her daughters Nicomedes and Pepa served the food and changed the bedding. All was well except for one glaring inconvenience: some university professors there, known collectively as *los doctores,* were getting all the attention. They were attended first in every circumstance, and they enjoyed the best meals. They dined on quail while everyone else had *mazamorra* (cornmeal mush), and so on. The young man was soon aggravated so he asked if the venerable professors paid more room-and-board than everyone else—but no was the answer. While they were paying exactly the same, they deserved better service because of their pre-eminence! Well, flabbergasted, he decided to check out of the establishment the following day. Then at the height of boredom and hunger, he turned to his guitar, which he had been neglecting up to that moment, and began to play:

Ref. 1 *La guitarra y los doctores*   Martín Gil

[The first thing that came to my fingers was a romance by
Mendelssohn, a sensitive little piece full of arpeggios. Even
though my instrument was excellent—a concert guitar—, I
was quite surprised at its sonority. It must have been due to the
dryness of the air.... I looked towards the doorway and saw the
silhouette of the patroness with her cooking spoon in hand.
Then another break in the light: it was one of the young ladies
with a serving plate; and finally there was a total eclipse.

Only a cluster of immovable heads remained visible in the
doorway. I realized instantly what was happening so I started
to vary the repertoire without stopping....

About then, all of a sudden some shouts of dialogue were
overheard from far in the background:

—¡Nicomedes! ¡Peeepa!

—Nicomedes! Pe-e-epa!

*—Che, te están llamando
los doutores—dijeron a media voz.*

—Hey, the doctors are calling
you—said someone in a whisper.

*—¡Mentís! ¡Es a vos que
estás con la fuente!*

—You lie! They want you: you're
the one with the serving plate!

—¡Cállense, chinitas...!

—Be quiet, you little kids!—

*Para evitar desbande entré
de lleno en el repertorio criollo.
A los primeros compases de un gato
punteado, se volcó la fuente de
Nicomedes.*

To avoid confusion, I went
straight into the popular repertoire.
At the first measures of a plucked
gato, Nicomedes' serving plate was
turned over.

—¡No empujen, oh!

—Don't push, OH!—

*El cuarto se saturó de un
perfume exquisito.*

Then the room became saturated
with an exquisite perfume.

*—¡Se quema el asao,
misia Liboria!*

—The barbecue meat is burning,
Doña Liboria!

—¡Cállate! Andá, dalo güelta.

—Shut up! You go, turn it over.

*Los gritos de auxilio de
los doctores seguíanse oyendo.
De pronto sentí un vozarrón que
decía:—¿Y qué significa esto?
¡Hace una hora larga que
esperamos la comida!
Ya estamos roncos de gritar....*

Meanwhile the doctors' cries for
help continued in the background.
Finally I heard a deeply resonant
voice that said:—What is the meaning of this? It has been a long hour
that we have been waiting for dinner!
Now we are all hoarse from yelling....

(Throughout the next day, the guitarist received repeated demonstrations of respect well into the afternoon, whence he continued his story:)

At that time Doña Liboria arrived to request a list of my preferred meals, because she wanted to get to know my taste...and if I would be able to play the guitar that night in honor of her brothers who were coming from a distance of some three leagues (10 miles) away. I responded that I would be delighted....

That night I played the guitar in honor of Doña Liboria's relatives, not to mention the entire complement of her neighborhood. The following day it began to rain cheeses, apples, tunas, goats, cantaloupes, and watermelons.

—In the end—said my friend and protagonist of this adventure, —out in the countryside the six strings of a well-played guitar are worth more than six years at the university] (Gil 1907:149–53).

Thus ends the story, without mention of the prestige of guitar playing in the capital cities. To be sure, in Buenos Aires or Montevideo, the rewards for guitar playing are different from those of the vast interior regions, but traditionally they are not less effusive. Rather than receive the countryside's best produce, guitarists are rewarded in more cosmopolitan ways, as we shall see.

1. The Knowns and the Unknowns

Since the foregoing particulars of the Rioplatense guitar originate from the internal perspective, they are undoubtedly new to readers in the Northern Hemisphere. Yet certain other aspects about their guitar are already well known. Essentially from our northern perspective, we have a fragmented view of their guitar: there remain knowns and unknowns.

Given the distance between us and the Plata republics, and the inevitably poor communications resulting from our linguistic and other cultural differences, it is surprising how much we already know. What understanding we have acquired is largely a product of the international dialogue established by the eminent guitarists of Argentina and Uruguay. They have gone out to the world. For the greater part of the twentieth century, we have been on the receiving end of their communications through performances, recordings, and publications.

Of all their achievements, the guitarists of the Plata have excelled most notably in performance. In fact for several decades, they have been in conspicuous demand as recitalists throughout the world, and they continue to dominate international guitar competitions. For instance, considering both first and second prizes of the Radio France competition in Paris prior to 1988, Argentina had produced five winners and Uruguay, four. Then Pablo Márquez of Argentina and Juan Carlos Amestoy of Uruguay took to the stage: they won, respectively first and second place (Heck 1988: 156). Thus were they thrown into the limelight of external, critical acclaim as they followed in the footsteps of their compatriots.

Without realizing it themselves, these performers reveal a great deal about the guitar in their locale. They form the tip of the proverbial iceberg, and their performances bespeak the enormous underlying structure of their achievement. Obviously they could not have won without experiencing high standards of performance excellence, quality teaching, and a stimulating environment in which to perform throughout their ascent to perfection. Yet all of this underlying structure has remained hidden from our view. Obscured by distance, time, and cultural barriers, most of the Rioplatense guitar's internal aspects have remained well beyond the northern perspective.

Nevertheless, during the past decade or so, better communications have developed between us. Dialogue has begun to emanate steadily from the north, for a change. Several European and American guitar periodicals have established a regular feature on Latin America (as in the columns cited in the References, below by Richard Stover, Jury Clormann, Brian Hodel, and Francisco González). Guitar methods such as those of Argentine Julio Sagreras or Emilio Pujol (that written in Buenos Aires), have begun to appear in English translation. The boom in Latin American fiction (Gray 1988) has demonstrated the viability of quite another market: our music publishers are vesting new interest in music for the guitar with the Latin tinge. Enfin, owing to political turmoil in the Plata during the 1970s, numerous expatriate Argentines and

Plate I Abel Carlevaro in Uruguay, 1987

Maestro Carlevaro features here a guitar of his own design. Manuel Contreras built it in Madrid according to new specifications. Without the sound hole, the top has more area and mass than usual. Contreras mounted the top, like some 19th-century precedents, to the sides with invisible wedges in order to allow the sound to escape from a narrow opening between the top and sides. The resulting sound is rich in volume and tone.

Uruguayans exiled themselves to European or U.S. locations, revealing thus their personal and musical style before an expanded audience. Jorge Morel has been exemplary in this regard, for he was trained at the Conservatory of Music in Buenos Aires, yet he has resided in New York as a base for a career of recitals, recordings, and publications that reach out to both sides of the Atlantic.

In recent years, however, the most notable statesman of the Rioplatense guitar has been Abel Carlevaro. Being Andrés Segovia's oldest and most accomplished student, Carlevaro has assumed his mantle of leadership not by any personal gesture but, rather, by the acclamation of innumerable classical guitarists across the globe because of his instrumental mastery. His performances have received steady acclaim, yet he has also taught with empathy in numerous master classes in his home town of Montevideo and abroad. He wrote a carefully reasoned method and then followed up with instructive booklets containing both technical exercises and an approach to some difficult spots of the standard repertoire. Moreover, Carlevaro's own compositions juxtapose the 20th-century harmonic idiom and his own frame of reference, whether for ensemble or guitar solo. His Chanterelle recording of some of these has now become available in the U.S.

Therefore, although the unknowns of the Rioplatense guitar far outnumber the knowns, we can take confidence in fact that, at long last, a real understanding of the guitar in Argentina and Uruguay is beginning to take shape. Recent two-way dialogue has already precipitated a healthy climate for the subject at hand.

2. Why the Cultural Context?

Here in the north, we have a basic appreciation of the external, international aspects of the Rioplatense guitar. After all, the world impact of Argentina's and Uruguay's guitarists, like that of their soccer teams, is not a debatable issue. But unavoidably, whenever we confront the guitarists of that faraway place on their own terms instead of ours, whenever we probe their unique, internal culture, we have heretofore met with either partial understanding or none at all. From our northern perspective, their part of the world remains curious and exotic. This impression is normal. The formative centuries of the Plata's development occurred in distant isolation from the monarchy and its designated viceroyalties, so even Spanish speakers from other parts of the world find the Plata unique and different. In this day and age of global awareness when we have come to relish cultural diversity, this uniqueness is beautiful. Yet it was not always so well received.

While in the Northern Hemisphere we can certainly enjoy a fine concert performance or a recording by one of the Río de la Plata's world-class recitalists, while we can be entertained with the folk dances of Argentina or Uruguay, or even dance a tango, we cannot claim a complete understanding of their music. Cultural barriers still stand in the way of our understanding, like the language of the region or unfamiliar musical forms or styles. Suppose for instance that we are attending a guitar recital which features Alfonso Broqua's "creole suite" (Pujol-Llobet edition of 1929). We discover that the program includes a *Vidala,* a *Chacarera,* and *Milongeos,* from Uruguay. Are these dances or songs? Fast or slow? Do they contain traditional melodic formats or merely rhythm patterns of typical dances? Our Spanish-speaking friends in attendance offer no help because the vidala, chacarera, and milongeos are, frankly, unknown in Spain or Mexico. Obviously here in the north, a basis for understanding this music is sorely needed.

Our situation is portrayed in a story—admittedly the sort of thing heard around guitar shops and music stores. About twenty years ago the Ernie Ball guitar shop in Los Angeles became a clearinghouse of Rioplatense guitar music. Somehow the buyers for the shop had collected some five hundred titles of Argentine and Uruguayan guitar music, both folk and classical pieces, to be sold on the retail market. Their library became a treasure-trove of beginning, intermediate, and recital-level pieces, with what appeared to be all the available titles of two Buenos Aires publishers: Romero y Fenández and Ricordi—though small companies were also represented. The recital pieces were fingered or transcribed by the likes of Miguel Llobet (a Spaniard residing in Buenos Aires), or Argentines Julio Sagreras, María Luisa Anido (a dozen titles alone), and Antonio Sinópoli for the concert stage. There were also solos, duets, and even trios of the colorful Rioplatense folk dances

composed or arranged by such celebrated guitarists as Andrés
Chazarreta, Pedro Antonio Iparraguirre, Nicodemo Casuscelli,
Juan Alais, Domingo Prat, L.Vicente Gascón, Tomás Pomilio, Carlos Vega, Jorge Martínez Zárate, and many others, not to mention
a few tango arrangements for guitar solo. However, there was a
hitch; it would not sell. In L.A. or thereabouts, guitarists did not
know what to do with it. Despite their long-standing exposure to
Latin culture from the California borderlands, somehow they
could not relate to this music. Business was so poor that shop proprietors had to liquidate the stock. Finally the entire collection
faced donation at a total loss! But the story ends with this happy
twist: the owners donated the complete repertoire to UCLA's
Music Library in Schoenberg Hall, where proper filing enabled it
to remain perfectly accessible to future generations.

To open our understanding we do not need more music or more
musical analysis. Instead, Rioplatense guitar music requires description once and for all within its own cultural context in order to
assess the guitar's role in that society. As we study their history, we
can learn not only what happened but why it happened. Thereby
we may discover their concepts of excellence and begin to make
aesthetic judgements by their standards. Ultimately we may even
comprehend and appreciate their music according to the intentions of its composers and performers. Therefore, the authors of
the present volume cannot assume that the reader has a background in Rioplatense culture. Enough of the cultural context
needs to be provided so that the music and its history make sense
as they come into focus.

The present undertaking is the first of several projected volumes on the Rioplatense guitar. As part of a chronological series, it
treats the early guitar in detail. Unavoidably it remains rather
complex, with its own unprecedented content and unique form.
Since it is devoted mostly to the guitar of the colonial era, its complexity grows out of the three arenas of the Hispanic domination.
Owing to the fact that initially everything about the guitar was
imported, when dealing with any one of its aspects, that aspect
must be accounted for in Spain during the Golden Age, then in its
westward transition to Latin America, and finally in its southward
expansion into the Río de la Plata. Naturally the presentation

could be made simpler by excluding all mention of these stages, but then all the external accountability would be lost. The Rioplatense guitar's external relationships would thus continue to languish without connections, as untied loose ends. However, if the three stages are understood and the connections can be made between them, then a slow but sure footing is established as the network of these tie-ins develops into the emerging tapestry. The goal is to produce a study reflecting the perfect likeness of its object, a chronological tapestry, as it were, that reproduces the major events and salient features of the guitar and its cultural context in the Plata.

In this first tome of the chronology, the information about the guitar's cultural context looms nearly as substantial and voluminous as that concerning the guitar itself. The guitar is indeed the principal theme, but Rioplatense culture is its foil, the contrasting, subordinate theme. Even so, the cultural context must be presented first, then it gives way gradually. The design of this relationship can be illustrated with a pair of coordinated *crescendo* and *decrescendo* marks, the one on top of the other. Here the guitar is the crescendo; though scarcely heard in the beginning it increases in volume until dominating the entire mass. The cultural context is the simultaneous decrescendo which gradually and proportionately diminishes throughout the volume.

In addition to the changing emphasis of Volume I, it also has its own specific architectural layout in the shape of an arch. Its form is dictated by the relationships between the theme and its countersubject. Arch form is neither new nor novel in architecture, but rather, common to nature, literature, and the arts in all parts of the world. Among members of the Rioplatense intelligentsia, for instance, the arch-form arrangement is known as the *esdrújula*, and it occurs in word games as in the following maxim:

> *Daba le arroz a la zorra el abad*
> [—Dr. Julio Pose].

(Disregarding its perfect symmetry, it means—The abbot was giving rice to the fox.)

Composers have been attracted to arch form because it always insures variety in the continual appearance of new material in its first half, and unity in its gradual resolution of the materials in the second. Arch form has been used as a simple, straightforward layout for either a multi-movement composition, as in a Haydn divertimento where the slow movement is central in the layout, or as the format for a single movement. Beethoven used the arch form as an underlying dramatic scheme in the finale to the *Eroica Symphony*. Here the movement known for its superficial form of "theme and variations" has in fact several contrasting, interactive themes placed around the calculated center of the movement. The result is a more intense and engaging form than one in which there is the mere re-orchestrated, verbatim repetition of sections. The formal focus of the *Eroica* finale is revealed in its changing tonality: its home key is Eb, but the keystone of the movement is the exotic "Hungarian march" at midpoint in the key of G minor. Beethoven surrounded it with contrapuntal fugatos of unstable tonality. Then he enveloped the fugatos with the theme he borrowed from his own ballet *Prometheus* (1801, Op. 43), in each case in the stable key of Eb. The result is almost paradoxical: he creates a unique form which seems ever-spontaneous, yet ever-cohesive.

The reason for elaborating on the formal structure of the *Eroica* finale is that its layout is identical to that of the present volume. The subject at hand is not less inclusive than the "national instrument" of the Río de la Plata in relation to its pan-social impact during the early centuries. This theme and countersubject correspond precisely, without contrivance, to the succession of themes and sections of the *Eroica* finale, as shown in the comparative chart on the next page.

The chart demonstrates some comparable factors between Volume I and the finale. Both are organized like the Spanish/English word ROTOR, essentially a palindrome with a focal point at the center. The keystone of Volume I's arch is at Part III, the centerpiece. Its epigraph is taken from the wisdom of one of the most distinguished historiographers of Argentine music: "the guitar is the musical instrument most our own." Parts II and IV deal with the impact of Andalusian culture, at first generally, then specifically with reference to the fandango. Parts I and V are related by antithesis, and they must obviously provide a point of departure and an ending. Even though there are other structural similarities between Volume I and the finale, the most important one is related to

Fig. 1 Plan of the First Volume		
Volume I:		Beethoven, Eroica, IV movement:
List of Contents		Prologue (scale flourish)
Intro to Theme	(Forethought)	Bass Theme in Eb
(R) PART I	The Conquest (no guitar)	Prometheus Theme
(O) PART II	Andalusian Culture	Fugato
(T) PART III	La guitarra es el instrumento musical más nuestro	HungarianMarch in G minor
(O) PART IV	Andalusian Fandango	Fugato
(R) PART V	Foreign Perspectives (all guitar)	Prometheus Theme poco andante in Eb
Appendix	(Afterthought)	transition
Source List		Coda, presto (scale flourish)

Beethoven's bass theme. At first it masquerades playfully as the
main theme of the movement; later it becomes subservient to the
Prometheus tune as its bass line. But rather than make the bass
theme the prima donna of the movement, Beethoven has given it a
supportive role after disclosing its identity. Similarly in Volume I,
despite the initial prominence of the cultural context, its role becomes subservient; it provides the point of departure as well as the
recurring basis of the chronology. Just like Beethoven's bass
theme, the cultural context pales in the presence of the composition's main theme.

The strength of the arch lies in its simplicity. In Volume I, the
arch binds together its various parts into a plain geometric design.
Knowing its layout in advance is like hearing a diverse symphonic
movement and at once detecting the themes, their relationships,
and sections, rather than being tossed inevitably by waves of information with no apparent order as though it were a great, chaotic
storm without purpose, direction, or hope of resolution. With a
memorable layout for Volume I, its form remains evident from the
very beginning. The advance knowledge of the presentation's balance will not inhibit the reader's understanding of it, for, like the
listener who can actually hear contrasting themes and relate
them by antithesis to the perception of the whole, the reader here is
sure to perceive the theme and its countersubject in the beginning,
carry through their give-and-take across a vast field of documentation and chronology, and arrive at their resolution with maximum understanding.

Moreover, a description of the Rioplatense guitar's sociology is
intrinsic and inseparable from its own history, for it had a stagger-
ing impact on the region. It was not only an important musical instrument there, it was a socio-cultural phenomenon. Obviously the
instrument itself was an object of the past, hence the need for describing its appearance, stringing, fretting, and construction as
well as its repertoire. However, the people who were performing
with it, and listening or dancing to it were not less worthy of note.
The players and their audience have long needed classification according to gender, race, and socio-economic status. Naturally social forces shaped its history, yet the Rioplatense guitar gave back
in return a rich heritage of folk, classical, and even religious music

to the Hispanic society whence it came. Its picturesque or polished functions belonged to every musical category: it was the first instrument in popular serenades, dances, and taverns, as well as in the refined aristocratic salons and pious churches of Plata territory. The guitar may indeed have been the national instrument of Spain during its Golden Age. Yet simultaneously, owing to the diverse, colorful, and pervasive use of the guitar among men and women of all the various Rioplatense classes, it was even more of a national instrument there than it had been in the country of its origin! Therefore an empirical approach to the Rioplatense guitar must remain pragmatic enough to encompass its sociology.

Given the many faces and functions of the guitar in Rioplatense society, the methodological approach to the subject must remain closer to ethnomusicology than to historical musicology—with which European or American musics are usually studied. Even though *The Rioplatense Guitar* is a history by definition, an ethnomusicological approach permits a broad scope of access to its subject. If we are to overcome the linguistic impasse between us and the people of the Plata region, if we are to discover the unknowns of their music on their terms, within their frame of reference, what choice do we have but to face the problems head-on? Ethnomusicology offers the advantages of providing practical and diverse methods of collecting information, of addressing folk and popular expressions as well as art music, and of bringing a high priority onto the cultural context of the music in question so that it may be fully comprehended, even by a faraway audience.

3. Precedents

Scholarly surveys often precede intensified specialist work like the calm before the storm. This has already been in evidence among guitar specialists in Argentina and Uruguay, and it has certainly been the case with English-language research on the guitar ever since 1969. That was the year Frederic Grunfeld published *The Art and Times of the Guitar*. Being the first substantial history of the guitar in English, well-documented and profusely illustrated with iconographical evidence, it was soon followed by the histories

of Alexander Bellow and Harvey Turnbull. While their surveys
were obviously not the sole cause of the fission/fusion explosion in
English-language research on the guitar, they were certainly precipitating factors in showing the way to fascinating specializations.
Since then we have enjoyed such a landslide of research, master's
and doctoral dissertations, articles, new guitar periodicals and so-
cieties, and specialized books that anyone would agree: guitar
scholarship has blossomed right along with the guitar's renaissance. Now areas of guitar performance and composition, guitar
construction, flamenco guitar, the guitar in early music, etc., are
flourishing alongside research into all aspects of the instrument.

The last frontier of guitar research is Latin America, particularly in English-language historiography. This is due to an enormous gulf left in our previous coverage of the subject. The gulf has
a name: *the Atlantic*. While the renaissance in guitar scholarship
has been addressed to every historical period in Europe, the Latin
American guitar has continued to beckon English readers to no
avail, as summarized by Peter Sensier:

> Every time I read some 'History of the Guitar' I find the same
> inexplicable gap.... From the early 16th century, from that day
> in 1519 when Cortés and his followers set foot on Mexican soil,
> the scene was set for the guitar to become *the* instrument of a
> whole continent stretching from Mexico in North America to
> Tierra del Fuego in the far south of Argentina (1975:16).

Fortunately, since the publication of his article, the editors of
guitar periodicals have heeded the signs, and the Latin American
guitar is now a regular feature in many of them. Even so, and
most unfortunately, the book-length regional studies on the Latin
American guitar which have already helped to fill in the gap have
remained obscured by distance, time, and the continuing lack of
real two-way communication between the English-speaking and
Spanish-speaking audiences. To conclude the analogy, what was
once a sea without so much as an island of respite across it is now
dotted with intermittent stations.

Even so, there is not a single precedent for *The Rioplatense
Guitar* in any language. However, several substantial histories of

the guitar in that region have already appeared in Spanish. Two were written by Argentines as follows:

Ricardo Muñoz, *Historia de la guitarra* (Buenos Aires: n.p., 1930), 423 pp.

Segundo N. Contreras, *La guitarra argentina* (Buenos Aires: Castro Barrera, 1950), 77 pp.

In addition, an Uruguayan recitalist wrote another guitar history during the 1960s primarily in the Republic of Uruguay. However, because of the Uruguayan political upheaval of the 1970s during the military regime, he had to polish the manuscript in Mexico and publish it in Argentina:

Cédar Viglietti, *Origen e historia de la guitarra* (Buenos Aires: Albatros, [1973]), 271 pp.

Muñoz's history antedates our English-language guitar histories by more than a generation. Viglietti's is also a general history, yet he and Muñoz address the Rioplatense guitar in the second half of their books. The account by Contreras is less enterprising, less comprehensive, and less documented than the others, but is the most accessible of all. Each history was a monumental, single-handed achievement in its time, and each of the authors went on to further distinction by following up with additional guitar-related publications. All three authors directed their histories to an audience that was understood: they wrote and published where all the particulars of Plata life were common knowledge. Yet inasmuch as the cultural background must accompany the Rioplatense guitar's history for English readers, this additional burden explains why the project has never been attempted.

Given the fact that scholars of the Plata have surveyed the guitar in their midst every twenty years or so in Spanish, the latest directions in guitar research there have been towards musicological studies of an intentionally narrow focus. Generally they have been either historical or ethnomusicological in nature. The historical treatises have probed such subjects as iconography, organology, and the review of the early witnesses of the guitar in the Plata region. One of these is especially noteworthy, however, inasmuch as it came from France. It is the organology of Bruno Montanaro entitled *Guitares hispano-américaines*. It treats the origin, models, and types of unique guitars that have developed in Hispanic America—those of either European or American provenance. Montanaro went to the Río de la Plata during the past decade and gathered his information there on location. The portions devoted to the Río de la Plata contain accurate descriptions of the tuning, stringing, and construction of *charangos, requintos,* and *tiples* as well as guitars of a more traditional appearance. Max Peter Baumann published a similar study at Stockholm in 1985.

Ethnomusicological studies of great worth to the history of the guitar have appeared during the past several decades in Argentina and Uruguay. These are valuable not for their overview of the guitar, but rather for their wealth of detail about it. Most of them are synchronic; they disregard historical origins. Their purpose is to document the musical practices of a specific time and place. They often treat the folklore of a certain region. Ercilia Moreno Chá, director of the Instituto Nacional de Musicología "Carlos Vega" in Buenos Aires, completed an exemplary project of this type. Her work proceeded from the method developed by her illustrious teachers Carlos Vega and Lauro Ayestarán, who made extensive field recordings to serve as original sources for their independent research and many publications. Her project, entitled *Documental folklórico de la Provincia de La Pampa* [Documentary on the Folklore of La Pampa Province], is comprised of two long-play recordings and copious accompanying notes about them. There she presents copies of her field recordings (professionally mastered), her photographs of some of the performers, precise documentation, and an analysis of her findings. Nearly all of her thirty-five authentic recordings, made on location between 1973 and 1975, feature the guitar. It is heard either as a solo instrument or as an accompaniment to the voice or other instruments.

Despite the significance of these studies or the earlier general histories of the Rioplatense guitar, the present volume is in no way a duplication of effort or a mere translation of their contents. It emanates from the viewpoints of more recent scholarship and experience, and it is a product of the discoveries and methods of the present. Its emphasis is different as well, with a new focus on the earlier periods so as to achieve a more balanced coverage than ever before. This is in keeping with the need for attention to the colonial era of the Río de la Plata. The current predicament of the Plata's early history was described in a review by Carmen García Muñoz, then the director of the other Vega institute in Buenos Aires, the Instituto de Investigación Musicológica "Carlos Vega" housed at the Catholic University:

[We share and applaud the idea of bringing out specialized publications based on original sources so that little by little the stages of our music history may be reconstructed. The colonial period of Argentine territory needs them urgently] (1989:187).

4. The Early, Popular Guitar

The Hispanic conquest and domination of the Río de la Plata was a long, difficult process. The first, 1536 settlement of Buenos Aires was destroyed by Indians, so its few survivors went far upstream to found the fortified city of Asunción (now Paraguay). From there the *conquistadores* established Plata towns downstream, among them the second settlement of Buenos Aires. Then they traversed the Andes from the east side; gradually over the centuries they built interior towns between the mountains and the Atlantic.

The conquerors and settlers were predominantly Andalusian, bringing their lineage, language, and learning from southern Spain to the Plata region. Many of them hailed from Seville inasmuch as it was Spain's principal port and governing seat of the Americas, as well as their capital. Once the immigrants began to settle the basin, they had to maintain their Hispanic identity to rule, to purchase or inherit land, and to keep an upper hand in business, so their Andalusian culture was vigorously cultivated and preserved. More than by simple majority, the settlers standardized the Andalusian dialect and customs in the Plata region out of necessity and choice despite the faraway rule of Madrid. During more than two centuries, trade restrictions and neglect of the court compounded the Río de la Plata's distance from the rest of

Imperial Spain, leaving there a society and culture that remained little changed from the outside. Like its population, it had grown primarily from within. Meanwhile, Spain's Golden Age had come and gone with relatively little impact on the Rioplatense colony until 1776 when the crown established the Plata Viceroyalty.

The *conquistadores* brought the guitar to America. They used the guitar aboard their ships to help relieve the tension or boredom of the transatlantic passage. It was already the most popular instrument in Spain because there the lute had been rejected owing to its Arabian (Moslem) associations, and early on, the four-course *guitarra* had thus become a more suitable instrument with which to accompany the popular songs and dances of Christendom. In the 16th century the larger, six-course, *vihuela* served for contrapuntal effusions, yet as the century wore on, the distinctions between it and the *guitarra* began to fade. Eventually an instrument of compromise, the five-course *guitarra española* which Vicente Espinel and Joan Carles Amat helped to popularize, superseded the other plucked strings and became the Baroque guitar.

Whether *guitarra* or *vihuela*, it did not matter throughout early Hispanic America because settlers used the terms indiscriminately from the moment of contact. Even so, of the two, *guitarra* gradually became the more common and enduring term as *vihuela* faded into the background to remain the more nostalgic when employed as a device to evoke the past. The guitar served to attend secular songs and dances, as before, yet in the Americas it also accompanied the mass or vespers, sometimes with the harp, until priests installed pneumatic organs in their churches. Artists portrayed pretty musical angels in 17th-century religious paintings with a five-couse guitar in hand at three South American locations: in Coro, Venezuela, the Franciscan Convent, Santiago de Chile, and the Jesuit Church in Córdoba, Argentina. Meanwhile, since the guitar was portable and capable of local fabrication, it became diffused in several sizes and configurations of strings among the populace of the Americas. It enjoyed wide use among the folk—as among cowboys, for instance, the *llaneros* of Venezuela or the *huazos* of Chile. Yet the upper class women of Chile, Peru, and Venezuela were also fine performers. Given the guitar's universal popularity, however, it became a bone of contention among members of polite society. The monastic orders of Lima banned it around 1600; thereafter, in cities across Hispanic America, the guitar was subject to curfews imposed by religious and secular authorities alike in order to curtail late-night serenading, wild parties, and lascivious dances such as the *fandango*.

The Rioplatense guitar had a similar if a more isolated development in its first few centuries. Settlers assiduously cultivated its use along with the other traits of Hispanic identity. Their lurking threat was always that the Hispanic dominion could diminish, either by loss of control to another power, or by subtle erosion from within—particularly with the widespread intermarriage of the first settlers that at worst had the potential of leading back to the state of nature which they found there in the first place. When the dissolution of Hispanic character was threatened for whatever reason in the New Land, the settlers depended on the guitar to invoke the past heritage better than any other remedy. Long before churches or other institutions would dot the settlements, the guitar connected the player with a world of bygone yet indispensable cultural associations. In addition to the immediate gratification of the senses, the guitar brought the player in contact with Spain and the rest of Hispania as it renewed the player's personal identity.

According to surviving evidence in the Plata region, the guitar persisted longer and more frequently in church services than anywhere else in the world, even though Rome had banned all instruments except for the organ. By mid-16th century, the Council of Trent, was advocating a cappella music. Even so, the expense accounts of some early churches around the Plata have preserved dated payments for guitar strings, instruments, and fees paid to guitarists. The Jesuit fathers also taught guitar along with other instruments, because they used music to good advantage in attracting and retaining the faithful during their prolific missionary period in Paraguay and northern Argentina, from 1607 to 1767. And they too used the guitar in the mass.

Initially the Rioplatense guitar was small by our standards. As the name *guitarra* began to predominate over *vihuela* late in the 17th century, however, larger sizes gained preference, often as imports from Brazil. They were eventually strung singly with gut strings—also imported, for the most part. After the shift to single

stringing, however, the number of strings increased from four or
five on smaller guitars to six on the larger ones. The range of prices
for the guitar and its variegated materials of construction disclosed
the identity of its players. The guitar was popular among all
classes: the best instruments were characterized by imported
ebony components and mother-of-pearl inlays; others were rather
crudely made of pine or local willow wood.

The guitar, like *Rioplatense*—the regional dialect, pervaded the
activities of all classes. It continued to be acceptable as an aristocratic instrument, counting liberators and dignitaries among its
aficionados. During the English invasion of Argentine territory in
1806, for instance, Major Alexander Gillespie noted that the waltz
was certainly in vogue among the elites and danced to the piano
with guitar accompaniment. Later a certain Captain Belgrano
invited the Major to dine at home; after dinner the Captain's wife
and her lady-friends entertained the men by singing songs in both
English and Spanish to the guitar (Gillespie 1818:67–69). Liberator José Artigas and President Bernardo P. Berro were guitarists
in Uruguay; General San Martín was a student of Fernando Sor
in Paris; in Argentina Manuelita Rosas (daughter of the dictator)
performed in the salons and political philosopher Juan Bautista
Alberdi wrote a guitar method (Prat 1934:330). Thus, like Rioplatense—the "national language," the guitar became the national
instrument as advocated from the top of the social ladder.

The guitar was frequently the only musical instrument found
among the folk, and as always, it was used either for solos or to accompany songs and dances. On the one hand, the songs were lyrical and extremely sad like the *yaraví, triste,* or *vidala.* On the
other, the gaucho *cantor* or *payador* [singer or bard] specialized in
lengthy ballads and performed them for his living like a medieval
minstrel. The texts of his ballads were partly or totally improvised,
but the music had a set pattern. The vocal line and the accompaniment had to be memorized, and they remained unchanged during the verses. Over the pattern of strums or arpeggios, the singer
was free to create spontaneous, rhymed verses of extraordinary
wit and daring. The tour de force of gaucho balladry was to sing
contrapunto between two musicians. Both musicians simultaneously accompanied the verses on their guitars, but they sang

alternately in rhymed, <u>improvised dialogue</u>. Contrapunto was essentially a competition; since the first to hesitate was the loser, the contests among the best performers went on, uninterrupted sometimes for several hours if not all day. As unique as these practices seemed, there were precedents in Spain and other parts of the Americas.

Because of isolation in the Plata colony and because of severe clerical opposition, the Andalusian dances died away despite their sensational early popularity. In their place, many lively, colorful "creole" dances developed among the Hispanic population. Then during the era of independence, they flourished all the more as part of the celebration. While some like the *malambo* were danced solo as a showcase of difficult steps and spectacular moves like the flamenco *zapateado,* the norm was to dance in couples if separated, without touching except for the hands. The couple dances were upbeat and showy, with flying handkerchiefs or finger snapping in place of castanets. They were usually notated in a duple 6/8 to accommodate the frequent syncopations of a superimposed 3/4 meter. Sometimes the couples exchanged improvised verses in public, as in the promenade of the *aires* and *pericón,* the latter of which became the national dance of Uruguay with the publication of Gerardo Grasso's version in 1887. As more dancers participated, so did more guitarists. Two or three had to perform in order to provide sufficient volume for loud merrymaking. In spite of the inroads of other popular musics on life in the Plata during the 20th century, the old folk dances remained quite popular up to the "boom folklórico" of the 1960s.

Centuries ago, popular dances of the Plata were accompanied on the guitar with techniques of strumming or plucking inherited from Europe. Chordal strumming entailed the use of fingernails. Guitarists called it *rasgueado* (also *rasgueo* or *rasgado*) just as they did formerly in Spain, and they even played it in a manner similar to that described in some of the 17th-century Spanish and Italian guitar methods. They eventually developed catchy strums which involved simultaneous left-hand damping for a rhythmic tick. Just the same, advanced performers always added an embroidery of intricate, plucked solo passages to the texture, especially if two or more of them shared in the accompaniment of dance or song.

Plate II Carlos Gardel, after an old press photo, c. 1930

Around 1900 the final flowering of Hispanic popular music took root in Plata territory: the tango began to bloom in Buenos Aires. The tango was a cultural fusion of the old *milonga* and the new tastes of a largely immigrant population in the lurid taverns and brothels around the port—and thus a development parallel to the history of jazz. In the *guardia vieja* or first phase of the new dance, guitarists either strummed, *rasgueado* style, the accompaniment of its lyrical melody or plucked, finger style, the introductions, interludes, and counter melodies as in the folk dances. At first the guitar was the only, later the principal chordal instrument. The most memorable performances—heard even today in recordings on either side of the Plata—were those of Carlos Gardel, initially the tango's matinee idol and ultimately its world-wide ambassador. Gardel was himself a guitarist who toured and recorded early with Uruguayan guitarist José Razzano. Gardel added more guitars as he concentrated on his gift of vocal expression: for his international tours, he depended on three guitarists for supporting accompaniment. He travelled to Paris and to the States, but not without his "brooms." He referred to them affectionately as his *escobas* because of the brushing style of their *rasgueado* strumming! Gradually, however, following the sudden death of Gardel in a plane crash in 1935, the older styles of the tango faded away and the guitar with it. An early pioneer of the new sound was Roberto Firpo; his claim to fame was that he, being a pianist, had replaced the guitarist in his own quartet. Julio de Caro, a child prodigy on the violin who performed with Firpo, also excluded the guitar in his tango ensembles. The avant-garde style demanded ever more volume on the ballroom floor for dancers of the tango, waltz, and *milonga*. It was accomplished with a *bandoneón* (the strident button accordion) or sometimes violins in the lead, and a background of piano and double bass as essential. In the end, an entire orchestra, the *orquesta típica* became necessary as the tango conquered the world between the World Wars. Hence the popular expression:

> *Guarango como guitarra en tango*
> [Awkward as a guitar in a tango]!

As the Rioplatense guitar developed, a particular phenomenon occurred regularly. The guitarists of the popular medium became known as exemplary soloists. Typically they took popular materials of songs or dances, removed them from their original context, and transformed them into exciting solos—a practice similar to the preparation of a flamenco solo, but obviously in quite a different style. Naturally no form of popular music in its initial stage was ever intended for recitals, but the result of such continual focus and accomplished performances of Plata guitarists often made their solos recital-worthy. Some of the 19th-century dances of Juan Alais already fit into this category of native music. Throughout the 20th century, classical guitarists were drawn to the popular medium (despite the opposition of some purists), including the more ecumenical of the classical teachers there. Atilio Rapat, for instance, collaborated with Ariel Ramírez across the Plata in a transcription of *La tristecita*. For an introduction to the folk guitar solo, one could begin by performing the catchy Uruguayan dances of José Pierri Sapere which have an engaging, authentic sound. Eduardo Falú and the late Atahualpa Yupanqui are deservedly the most renowned Argentine folk guitarists, yet their recordings are sure to feature the voice as prominently as the instrument. Notwithstanding, folk guitarists occasionally publish guitar solos of their songs, such as Falú's melancholy zamba *Trago de sombra* [A Drink of Shade]. As for the duo recital, Antonio Sinópoli's arrangement of the *Pericón* by Gerardo Grasso for two guitars has strong audience appeal because of its exciting finale on a high tremolo in both parts. This published regional repertoire of solos and duets is precisely what is most likely to appeal to guitarists north of the equator. As a matter of fact, many editions of these pieces remain in circulation, and sometimes recordings are available, as well.

Abel Fleury (1903–1958) was particularly adept at the Argentine folk style, and his guitar solos have remained accessible up to the present day. They have endured because in them he achieved a delicate balance between facility, style, and regional character. He was a fine classical guitarist in the first place, yet throughout his teaching and recital tours he gradually created his own solo repertoire (García Martínez 1987). In the wake of popular demand, he proceeded to publish and record his solos himself in Buenos Aires. He composed in the various Rioplatense lyrical and dance forms of the region, as in Example 1 on the following pages.

The example is taken from Roberto Lara's new edition of *Ausencia* [Absence], a nostalgic milonga. After a sprightly, major-key introduction, it flows into C minor with a plaintive, sequential melody orchestrated darkly with some doublings of an octave below. The melody remains melancholy and continuous in tone, as it is played on the inside strings initially to give the piece its somber character. Moreover, vibrato is readily possible on every beat of the descending, mournful motive as it plays out its sequences. Then the higher range comes into play, yet without any loss of its chordal sonority. At the same time, *Ausencia* is not overly difficult because, as usual, it remains so idiomatic to the guitar, and the popular rhythm patterns are quite steady under its memorable lines. Fleury wrote more difficult pieces, but *Ausencia* has plenty of character and invites an emotional interpretation.

Fleury's solos are continually reappearing in new editions and recitals. In 1987 Roberto Lara edited the first volume of a projected performing edition of all the Fleury solos. Example 1, from that volume, is here published with authorization from the heirs of Abel Fleury and from Editorial Lagos, Buenos Aires, Argentina. Lara has carefully added all the fingerings, which are rather scarce in the original editions. Best of all, Lara has recorded six delightful solos from his first volume (including *Ausencia*) along with a dozen others, and they are available in the U.S. on Lyrichord 7253. The album is recorded well, and Lara's versions are refined and sensitive, ever faithful to the tradition of performance excellence.

The same old practice of re-orchestrating or re-composing popular dances also came to bear upon the tango. As the tango ascended to a pinnacle of popularity among dancers at home and abroad, specialized guitarists were creating tangos for guitar solo. Whether original or transcribed, some solos were so stylized that they became objects of art; they were no longer intended for dancing. Three Argentine exponents of the medium were born in the same year—1879, and they flourished between the World Wars: Julio Sagreras, Pedro Antonio Iparraguirre, and Mario Rodríguez Arenas. Sagreras composed original tangos along with pieces in the folk style to accompany his multi-volume guitar method. Iparraguirre and Rodríguez Arenas arranged and published some of the best dance hits of their day (e.g., see References).

Al Dr. Ramón Melgar

AUSENCIA
MILONGA

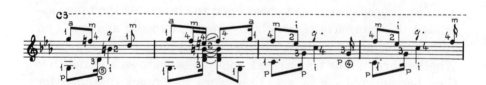

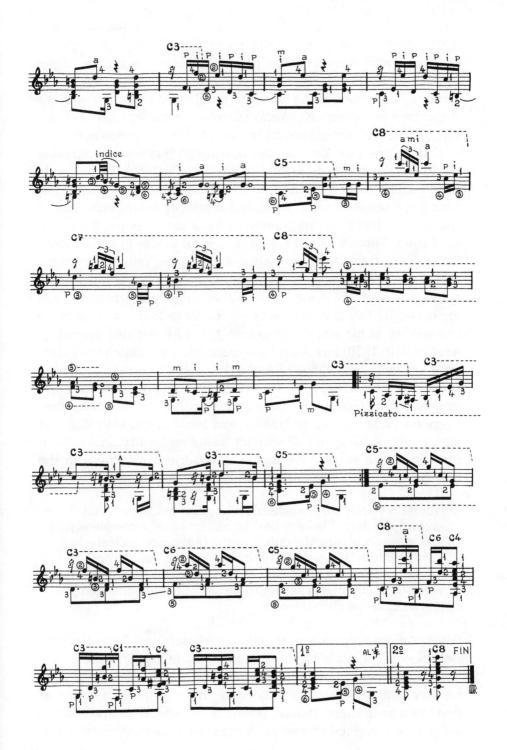

After World War II, foreign dances and styles began an eclipse of the tango's popularity. But such guitar transcriptions as the Uruguayan standard *La cumparcita* (Díaz Losa, arr.) and the Argentine evergreen *El choclo* (Escobar, arr.) witness that the tango's solo medium did not die out as it fell from the limelight.

During the past decade, the solo tango has made a striking world-wide resurgence among guitarists. Cacho Tirao has published some tango solos and recorded others; Jorge Oraisón has recorded a sensitive set by Argentine composer Astor Piazzolla, but the dean of the idiom continues to be Agustín Carlevaro, the brother of Abel. Though he pursued a successful career in architecture and retired from it, he was always arranging tangos for guitar solo. From this pursuit, his "first love," he developed nonetheless another career. He made innumerable public performances during his entire life, and left plenty of recordings that bear witness to the quality of his work. For example, his LP entitled *Marrón y Azul* (Vol. 3, 1976) has three interpretations that match the extraordinary emotional range of Astor Piazzolla's originals, including the title track. Piazzolla's tangos are extremely chromatic and expressive, so Carlevaro's considerable challenge is to interpret them with a maximum of dynamic and tonal range, with tinges of vibrato and rubato, and all without losing continuity. Piazzolla in turn published superlative approval of Carlevaro's efforts in the newspaper *El País*—in Carlevaro's hometown of Montevideo:

[Agustín Carlevaro is another of the great musicians that there are around here. I believe that he has invented a completely new way of utilizing the guitar in the tango, and inclusively I have told him this personally that what he is doing would interest Europeans a great deal as well as people elsewhere. His versions of my pieces, as also those of Troilo and other composers, seem to me stupendous.]

Some of these tango arrangements have become available through Dale Needles, Agustín's agent at Guitar Solo in San Francisco.

In conclusion, the Rioplatense musicians and audience of 20th century popular music have been far from isolated in terms of their own awareness. Indeed, people of Buenos Aires and Montevideo have remained abreast of change and quite in touch with the

Western World. They receive, for instance, most American and European films in standard or video format as well as some of our television serials with over-dubbed Spanish dialogue. Our technologies, including the electric guitar (since 1960), continue to impact on their society. With the gradual decline of folklore and the tango, however, foreign contacts and communications have brought in the popular music of other countries. Expert musicians there have learned to perform all of the imported styles, but unavoidably the foreign imports have diluted the impact and focus on national music. In some cases, as in the recent recordings of renowned guitarists Daniel Viglietti (son of Cédar) or Jaime Roos, there has even been a fusion with the imported styles. In the face of a tremendous influx of jazz, tropical, Brazilian, and rock, the interest in their popular music has become diffused and diminished: they too have their own anarchic *rock nacional* (Vila 1989). Currently the imports and fusions threaten the extinction of national music altogether among teen-age youth. The authentic music of the Plata may have enough of a following to permit anyone of our generation to hear the tango and folklore performed live. But if not, at least their recordings and sheet music are destined to be around for a long time.

5. The Classical Guitar after Independence

Argentine classical guitarists did not cultivate their art as a specialty until after becoming independent of Spanish rule in 1810. An immediate consequence of independence was that the Plata region began to attract foreign settlers from several European countries. Throughout two decades under the leadership of Rivadavia, the guitar flourished in the salons of Buenos Aires alongside the other arts from 1810 to 1830. A few expatriate Italians came during this period to transplant the guitar repertoire that was then current in the salons of Paris, Vienna, and numerous cities of Italy and Spain. The major light of this period was Esteban Massini; he left a wake of successful concerts and a long list of students who would carry on in his stead. There was no change in this development until poet Esteban Echeverría had finished his European sojourn which was centered at Paris. On his return to the Plata in 1830, he brought not only the literary Romanticism of Victor Hugo's circle back to Buenos Aires, but also the new styles and techniques of the Spanish virtuosi Fernando Sor and Dionisio Aguado. From this point forward, the basic approach to guitar playing and composition in Argentina became decidedly Spanish, though it was to lie fallow along with the other arts around mid-century during the dictatorship of Juan Manuel de Rosas because the intelligentsia of Buenos Aires went en masse into a self-imposed exile.

With the downfall of Rosas, the exiled artists, musicians, and intellectuals returned to Buenos Aires in the company of an exodus of guitarists from Spain. Foremost among the Spaniards were José Iparraguirre y Velardi and Gaspar Sagreras, who after their respective arrivals in 1858 and 1860, professed the art through performance, composition, and teaching on the guitar. Whereas the Europeans had emphasized the performance of their Italian or Spanish repertoire, few Argentines were able to distinguish themselves as composers, except for those who imitated the graces of the Continental style. Gradually, however, Argentine guitarists began to follow the lead of their literary compatriots, and composers such as Juan Alais (1844–1914) incorporated folklore or other national strains into their works. Most of his output was European salon music, primarily dances for the guitar, but he orchestrated the Argentine folk dances with the same, facile classical technique. Alais composed them within the forms and rhythmic patterns of the *pericón, gato, milonga, zamacueca*, or *güeya* which were popular at the time.

Meanwhile in Spain at the close of the 19th century, Francisco Tárrega was developing the well-known classical guitar technique of today. Although he never ventured to cross the Atlantic, his pupils established his school more firmly in the Plata than anywhere else in the world. As they travelled to perform guitar recitals, they discovered the mecca of the guitar at Buenos Aires. Such footloose performers as Miguel Llobet and Emilio Pujol resided there temporarily, but Domingo Prat made the Argentine capital his new base of operations. Apart from their performing abilities, the disciples of Tárrega were all accessible teachers, yet they had their own specialties, as well. Llobet performed with sensational acclaim,

Prat wrote the longest, most detailed encyclopedia ever devised for the guitar, and Pujol published the comprehensive method on his teacher's technique, four monumental volumes with Ricordi of Buenos Aires. Once this diverse expertise came to the Argentine capital, brought fresh from the leading edge of European studios, the next generations of Argentine performers included world-class recitalists such as Julio Sagreras (son of Gaspar) and María Luisa Anido. In the meantime, Spanish instruments had already set the tone of the era among recitalists. José Yacopi was merely a late arrival in a long line of Spanish luthiers who settled in Buenos Aires and advocated the construction of fine instruments. Today Argentines remain at the forefront of the world's performers with the likes of Roberto Aussel, Eduardo Castañera, and Víctor Pellegrini, all of whom were first-prize winners of the "International Alirio Díaz Competition" held in Venezuela for the consecutive years of 1976, 1977, and 1979. (There was none in 1978.)

All artistic distinction in Uruguay was to remain contingent upon its own lagging independence. The Uruguayans never conceded to subject themselves to the superpowers on the north or the southwest. War was thus inevitable with Argentina, Brazil, and even some European interests following their independence in 1825. Once they proved capable of self-defense, however, they finally achieved a sense of direction with the election of Fructuoso Rivera as the first President of the Uruguayan Republic in 1830.

Even so, the classical guitar's tradition in Uruguay, focused in Montevideo, was often closely related to that of Buenos Aires. While Antonio Saenz of Sevilla may have been a respected classical professor in Montevideo starting in 1829, a sudden boost to the art arrived with the foremost guitarists of Buenos Aires who came as part of the mass exile of the intelligentsia during the mid-century dictatorship across the Plata. The notable Argentines were pupils of Massini, for instance Dr. Nicanor Albarellos, who concertized in Montevideo. Eventually some Uruguayans would also study with maestro Massini in turn by crossing the delta. But after this substantial beginning, so many Spaniards settled in Montevideo that they dominated the scene until the advent of Argentine folklorist Juan Alais, composer of *La perezosa* [The Lazy One]. It was so well accepted in Uruguay that Cédar Viglietti has asked:

¿Qué aficionado no la tocó entonces, lo mismo que La ñatita,
*desde su aparición en 1880 hasta la segunda o tercera década
de este siglo* (1973:165)?
[What aficionado hadn't played it back then—the same with
La ñatita (The Baby-Faced Girl)—since its appearance in 1880
up until the second or third decade of this century?]

The first century of the classical guitar in Montevideo may be
represented with the figure below, which summarizes the major
developments preceding the organization of the *Centro Guitarrístico del Uruguay* and the new, permanent residence of Andrés
Segovia (both of which began in 1937):

Fig. 2 The First Century of the Classical Guitar in Uruguay

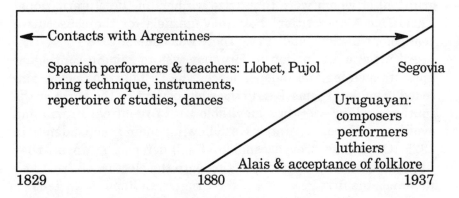

Not until after World War I did the Uruguayan guitarists become independent of foreign dominance altogether and come into
their own. Naturally Montevideo continued to be counted among
the stops for South American tours, as those of Llobet and Pujol.
But solid teaching established concert-worthy technique, as in the
case of Conrado Koch, professor of Isaías Savio who eventually left
on tour and made a home and considerable fame in Brazil. Then
Julio Martínez Oyanguren toured the United States and brought
the sensitive Latin style before the east-coast audience, including a
stop at the White House. Confident Uruguayan nationalism now
surfaced among composers. Alfonso Broqua portrayed some typical styles in his *Siete evocaciones criollas* [Seven Creole Evoca-
tions], edited by Llobet and Pujol for the Paris firm of Max Eschig

in 1929. Then Carlos Pedrell, nephew and pupil of the Catalan musicologist of the same surname, published three pieces in Segovia's Schott Editions. Luthiers came to the fore, namely Antonio Pereira Velazco and Juan Carlos Santurión, to win yet more distinctions, this time in guitar construction.

The formation of the *Centro Guitarrístico del Uruguay* in 1937 set the final stage in Uruguay's guitar history. The Center began as an association of aficionados who paid a membership fee; it never received support from a government agency. Nevertheless, its members were the avant garde of the instrument in Uruguay, and a few became international artists. The function of the club was to advocate guitar music by presenting a forum for guitar recitals—about 75 to 100 a year! Musicality, not age, was the criterion of excellence, with child prodigy Antonio Pereira Arias performing his debut as a pupil of maestro Atilio Rapat at the age of thirteen. Its performers who found international acceptance were Oscar Cáceres (a student of Rapat and Ramón Ayestarán) who subsequently recorded several albums for the Musical Heritage Society, and Abel Carlevaro who recorded three award-winning albums during the 1960s in Montevideo before launching his illustrious career of compositions, performances, recordings, and master classes in the cities of the Western World.

Some of the best Rioplatense talents have moved on to excellent but faraway careers, becoming a credit to themselves and their country, yet, like Isaías Savio, losing ties back home. After performing recitals at home and abroad as a guitar prodigy, Pereira Arias played double bass in the Plata orchestras, and then went to the Low Countries as an associate conductor in the early 1960s, but apparently never performed again in Montevideo. Likewise, some Argentines moved away: Jorge Morel made New York his center of activity; Jorge Fresno went to Spain to become an exponent of early music, concertizing on the authentic Baroque guitar and vihuela. Even though the Argentines Ernesto Bitetti (see Irving 1985) or Jorge Cardoso (Clinton 1986) moved away in the 1970s, thereby avoiding completely the Argentine military regime, they have some interesting parallels in their careers. Their former guitar teachers, Graciela Pomponio, Jorge Martínez Zárate, and María Herminia Antola all continued on at the Conservatory

"Juan José Castro." Meanwhile, both Bitetti and Cardoso had gravitated to opportunities in Spain, settling there in order to develop their busy schedule of international tours and recording contracts. Most of their albums went out to Europe instead of the United States; Cardoso recorded 10 on various labels and Bitetti, 22 on Hispavox, alone. Now Bitetti teaches at Indiana University.

Today many of the top classical guitarists of Argentina and Uruguay have either conceded to the leadership of Abel Carlevaro's school or they are simply his former students. His method appeals as rational, even scientific, yet unlike some other teachers, he has accommodated brilliant students of differing styles. Among his young compatriots, for instance, Baltazar Benítez won first prize at the Segovia competition at Santiago de Compostela in 1971, and then recorded Carlevaro's five *Preludios americanos* on Nonesuch in 1976. José Fernández Bardesio plays with soaring, expressive phrases (hence his prizes at Caracas in 1983 and at Segovia competitions in 1984 and 86). Yet Eduardo Fernández has a ready technique for the 21st century, as set forth in his many London and Decca recordings. Eduardo, particularly at home with Bach and Brouwer's virtuosic Cuban style, appears yearly in the U.S. with Shaw Concerts. Among the Argentines, Abel Carlevaro encouraged Eduardo Egüez's inclination to fuse classical technique with folklore, tango, or early music. Carlevaro also helped Roberto Aussel and Miguel Angel Girolet towards their awards at the annual international competition of Radio France.

> (On a recent occasion, the top four contestants in the Paris competition were Carlevaro disciples.) All are noted for being technically at ease and having an extremely varied tonal palette (Hodel 1985:21).

Credit is also due to many Rioplatense women who have made splendid achievements, particularly as teachers, for the guitar has always been a widely acceptable medium of expression for them. Prominent guitar schools of women have produced artists of note on either side of the Plata. To cite but two in Montevideo: (1) Olga Pierri taught her nephew Alvaro Pierri, winner of numerous competitions including that of Radio France, and coached the

youthful duo of Regina Carrizo and Ana Zeballos; (2) Lola Ayestarán, who continued with the guitar studio established by her late
husband Ramón Ayestarán, taught Radio France medalist and
Etcetera recording artist Jorge Oraisón as well as Leonardo Palacios who won the 1979 Canals competition in Barcelona. In Buenos
Aires, Irma Costanzo (another disciple of Carlevaro) met a multitude of guitarists as artist-in-residence of the Conservatory "Juan
José Castro," even though her performance tours and recording
dates kept her intermittently away. For her, there was never any
question of "gender equity" with the Rioplatense guitar, and her
Conservatory administration provided a good example. On one
occasion, Costanzo participated in an interview during the course
of which she was asked who was teaching at the Conservatory.
She responded with a perfectly balanced answer, as follows, by
referring unconsciously to women and men mixed with a bit of
history:

> [There is lady María Herminia Antola. Her husband, now de-
> ceased, was Jorge Gómez Crespo, a man at the forefront of the
> intellectuals and musicians of Buenos Aires, who for many
> years was head of the guitar department of the Buenos Aires
> Conservatory. Whenever Segovia would arrive in Argentina
> and had to recommend a teacher, he always mentioned this
> married couple because they were then the best guitar teachers
> in the republic.
>   Also, there are Jorge Martínez Zárate and his wife, Graciela
> Pomponio, to whom I have referred in some of these (previous)
> conversations; Horacio Zeballos, member of the Martínez Zár-
> ate quartet, and the excellent pedagog Nelly Menotti, who also
> studied with my teacher, Vicente Gascón, and who is the pro-
> tégé of María Luisa Anido] (Camps 1978:78).

The triumphs on the Rioplatense guitar have been so exemplary, diverse, and numerous that it would be impossible to name
them all in a sketch of highlights such as this is. The major
triumphs, moreover, were local achievements. But some special
attention must be given to Segovia's impact there, inasmuch as it
was nearly as significant in the Río de la Plata as it was in the
United States.

Segovia

Plate III Andrés Segovia in Argentina, after 1920

Ricardo Zavadivker is providing Plate III. It is taken from an old postcard
dating back to the time of Segovia's first recitals in the Plata. On the back
it says, in translation—"Carmicino Bros. Music Company, successors of R.
Carmicino, 1936 Cabildo St., telephone 73-6629. For Pirastro [strings],
the artist's best collaborators."

Andrés Segovia (1893–1987) was the outstanding Andalusian guitarist who eventually captured world-wide leadership in his specialty. When he came to the fore at the beginning of the 20th century, the Catalan students of Tárrega were foremost in the field, so Segovia's achievement was no easy feat: it entailed not only a matter of public recognition but also another approach. As he developed his well-known, assertive style with fingernails, he found that his volume was louder than that of Tárrega's devotees who played without nails. Thereby he ventured to fill larger halls than ever before—in fact those built for orchestra concerts. In the process, he transformed the intimate classical guitar recital into a full-scale public concert. His many trips to the Río de la Plata and his eventual residence of a decade there would prove critical to the success of his project. Simultaneously his technique appealed in the Plata where guitarists had always used fingernails to play popular music. Even so, his time there, the middle period of his career, has remained the least understood.

According to his own testimony, Segovia was already performing recitals in the Plata region by 1919 or 1920 (Zavadivker 1979: 50). Newspapers confirmed this in Buenos Aires: his management advertised two recitals in *La Nación*'s column, "Los conciertos de la semana," one for the Salón "La Argentina" to be given on 16 June, and another for the Teatro Odeón on 19 June of 1920. At first the young Segovia found it difficult to achieve any special distinction, for he was merely one of a cavalcade of foreign guitarists marching across the stages of Buenos Aires, Montevideo, and the larger interior towns—what with competition from the leading students of Francisco Tárrega as well as the eminent Paraguayan Agustín Barrios. At one point in Montevideo, Segovia and Barrios were scheduled for performances on consecutive nights, and they happened to stay in the same hotel. Olga Pierri recalled that one night there was even a mix-up with their rooms! With his characteristic wit before a group of avid fans who had followed him into the hotel, Segovia settled the misunderstanding at once. He made a gesture to the room of Barrios, and then, in no uncertain terms, he claimed that it was definitely not his own:

No. ¡Este es del alambrado!

[No. This one belongs to the wire fence!]

In a hasty, twice-condescending metaphor referring to Barrios's innovation of wire strings in place of gut, and associating them with the fencing of the rural countryside (thus insinuating Barrios's origins) he made an inside joke of several meanings.

Segovia's intermittent ties to the Río de la Plata since 1920 were made continuous with his permanent residence in Montevideo. Like so many Spanish artists of his generation, the likes of Pablo Casals or Pablo Picasso, Segovia found the European wars intolerable. He decided to leave Spain during the Spanish Civil War, and he chose to make "Montevideo *simpático*" his new residence in 1937. Then within the year, he married the Catalan pianist Paquita Madriguera, whereupon they settled in the elite suburb of Pocitos. They stayed throughout the Spanish Civil War and then World War II; their daughter Beatriz was born there. They were within perfect access to the downtown area of Montevideo, and in touch with its lively performances of operatic superstars (on tour from La Scala), orchestra concerts, and naturally guitar recitals.

Segovia coached some area guitarists, including Abel Carlevaro. However, given their own achievements on the guitar, the Uruguayans were always reluctant to concede any undue glory to Segovia, despite his long residence in their midst. In Segovia's mind, Carlevaro was his protégé; in Carlevaro's, Segovia was only a friendly advisor and consultant at a time when he was developing his own rational approach to the guitar and its repertoire. In 1942, after five years of study with Segovia, Carlevaro presented his inaugural recital at the SODRE, no less, the brand new orchestral auditorium downtown which carried the logo of the National Broadcasting System and which seated several thousand. Segovia published his paternal blessing on the very day of the concert in the announcements of *El Día*. Subsequently Carlevaro studied another four years with him before Segovia moved away.

Being in his prime, and having reached a technical zenith, Segovia immersed himself in innumerable creative projects. He found time to perform several recitals a year in Montevideo, either at the historic five-tier opera theatre called *el Teatro Solís,* or at the SODRE auditorium. His performances in town were an excellent test for the music he was preparing for his international tours, most of which, owing to the climate of war in Europe, were then directed to Latin American cities. He devoted plenty of effort to study and rehearsal. It was there that he completed more of the Schott editions begun on the Continent. His collaborations with Mexican composer Manuel Ponce continued also, the highlight of which was the completion and première of the *Concierto del Sur*. Segovia had to work piecemeal at the few pages Ponce was able to send by air mail. Despite poor health, Ponce came to Montevideo to make the final adjustments under Segovia's advice and then to hear its splendid first performance on 4 Oct. 1941 by Segovia and the SODRE orchestra (see reviews in Otero 1983:69).

The manner in which Segovia dealt with the Ponce concerto exposed the aggressive strategy of his career at mid-point. He developed an interpretation at Montevideo by playing to one of the large halls. If successful, he would engrain his approach in more concert-hall performances in Latin America; then finally he was ready for any hall of Europe or the United States. His process of bringing a piece to full artistic fruition was evident in a review from Havana, which emanated from the Cuban Guitar Society:

> [In his different interviews with the President, Secretary, and other members of the Board, Segovia demonstrated above all his great enthusiasm for the guitar concerto which his favorite friend Manuel Ponce, the notable Mexican composer, dedicated to him. This concerto premièred in Montevideo, the city where the guitarist now resides, and then he performed it in Santiago de Chile, Colombia, Peru, and in the Teatro Colón of Buenos Aires, with the orchestra under the direction of the famed Argentine conductor Juan José Castro. Later it would be heard in Mexico City] (Botet 1945:11).

Segovia was thus preparing and performing the repertoire he would later publish and record, the music that would perpetuate his fame for many years to come. After the wars, however, he needed a change of scene. The investment of countless creative hours in his professional work over the course of nearly a decade of residence in Montevideo enabled him to launch the next phase of his career. Segovia moved directly to New York where he had already earned acceptance with numerous performances, including the U.S. debut of Ponce's *Concierto del Sur*.

6. References Cited in the Introduction

A. Books, Articles, and Teaching Materials

Baumann, Max Peter
  1985   "Saiteninstrumente in Lateinamerika," in *Studia instrumentorum musicae popularis* VIII, Erich Stockmann, ed. Bericht über die 8. Internationale Arbeitstagung der Study Group on Folk Musical Instruments...in Piran, Jugoslavien, 1983. Stockholm: Musikmuseet.

Bellow, Alexander
  1970   *The Illustrated History of the Guitar.* Rockville Centre, NY: Franco Colombo, Belwin/Mills.

Botet, María Emma
  1945   "Apuntes sobre la última visita de Andrés Segovia a La Habana," *Guitarra* (Havana) V (Jul.), 11–12.

Camps, Pompeyo
  1978   *Reportaje a la guitarra con Irma Costanzo.* Buenos Aires, etc.: El Ateneo.

Carlevaro, Abel
  1978   *Escuela de la guitarra: Exposición de la teoría instrumental.* Montevideo: Dacisa, Buenos Aires: Barry. English ed., Jihad Azkoul and Bartolomé Díaz, trans. New York: Boosey and Hawkes, 1984.

  1967–present *Serie didáctica* [explanations in Eng. and Sp.]:
    No. 1, Escalas diatónicas, B & C 4006.
    No. 2, Técnica de la mano derecha, B & C 4007.
    No. 3, Técnica de la mano izquierda, B & C 4009.
    No. 4, Técnica de la mano izquierda (conclusión), B & C 4013.
    Buenos Aires: Barry.

  1985–present *Técnica aplicada* [clases magistrales]:
    Vol. 1, 10 estudios de Fernando Sor.
    Vol. 2, Sobre 5 Preludios y el Choro No. 1 de H. Villa Lobos.
    Montevideo: Dacisa. English editions forthcoming from Heidelberg: Chanterelle.

Clinton, George
  1986   "Jorge Cardoso," *Guitar International* (London—formerly *Guitar*), Dec., 40–43.

Clormann, Jury
  1985   "Music from Argentina" [the first of a series dealing with traditional folk dances and songs], *Guitar International* (London), Dec., 23–26.

"Los conciertos de la semana,"
1920 *La Nación* (Buenos Aires) 13 Jun. (Sunday).

Contreras, Segundo N.
1950 *La guitarra argentina: Apuntes para su historia y otros artículos.* Buenos Aires: Castro Barrera.

García Martínez, Héctor
1987 *Abel Fleury: El poeta de la guitarrra.* Fasc. No. 1. Buenos Aires: by the autor.

García Muñoz, Carmen
1989 "[Review of] Waldemar Axel Roldán, *Música colonial en la Argentina: La enseñanza musical* (Buenos Aires: El Ateneo, 1987)" in *Latin American Music Review* (Austin, TX) X, 186–87.

Gil, Martín
1907 "La guitarra y los doctores" in *Una novena en la sierra.* Buenos Aires: Espasa-Calpe, 1944.

Gillespie, Major Alexander
1818 *Gleanings and Remarks: Collected during Many Months of Residence at Buenos Aires and within the Upper Country... until the Surrender of the Colony of the Cape of Good Hope....* Leeds: Whiteley.

González, Francisco
1988 "La guitare en Amérique Latine," *Les Cahiers de la Guitare* (Paris) No. 25, 20–22.

Gray, Paul
1988 "Bridge over Cultures: A Translator Gives Latin Writers a New Home," *Time* (New York) CXXXII (11 Jul.), 75.

Grunfeld, Frederic
1969 *The Art and Times of the Guitar: An Illustrated History of Guitars and Guitarists.* London: Macmillan, Collier-Macmillan.

Heck, Thomas
1988 "The *Concours International de Guitare:* A View from the Juror's Box," *Soundboard* (Palo Alto) XV, 155–57.

Hodel, Brian
1985 "Abel Carlevaro: Master Teacher," *Guitar Review* (New York) No. 62 (summer), 20–23.

1986 "The Guitar in Latin America" [the first in a series of articles on this theme], *Guitar Review* (New York) No. 65 (spring), 27.

Irving, Darrel
1985   "Ernesto Bitetti in New York," *Guitar* (London), Apr., 12–15.

Montanaro, Bruno
c.1983 *Guitares hispano-américaines*. Aix-en-Provence: Edisud.

Muñoz, Ricardo
1930   *Historia de la guitarra*. Buenos Aires: n.p.

Otero, Corazón
1980   *Manuel Ponce and the Guitar*, John D. Roberts, trans.
        Shaftesbury, Dorset, Eng.: Musical New Services, 1983.

Piazzolla, Astor
1986   "Agustín Carlevaro," *El País* (Montevideo), 6 Apr. (Sunday).

Prat, Domingo
[1934] *Diccionario biográfico, bibliográfico, histórico, crítico de
        guitarras (instrumentos afines) guitarristas (profesores,
        compositores, concertistas, lahudistas, amateurs) guitarreros
        (luthiers)....* Buenos Aires: Romero y Fernández.

Pujol, Emilio
[1933] *Escuela razonada de la guitarra basada en los principios
        de la técnica de Tárrega*. 4 vols. [Prologue signed by Manuel
        de Falla in 1933.] Buenos Aires: Ricordi. Eng. trans. of Vols.
        I and II by Brian Jeffery. Boston & Columbus: Editions
        Orphée, 1983.

Sagreras, Julio S. (1879–1942)
1955   *Las primeras lecciones–Las sextas lecciones* [method-books
        for guitar based on the Tárrega technique in 6 vols., with many
        original compositions in the folk style of the Plata]. Buenos
        Aires: Ricordi. Eng. trans. of Vol. I. Milwaukee: Hal Leonard.

Sensier, Peter
1975   "A Gap in the Story of the Guitar," *Guitar* (London), Oct.,
        16–17.

Stover, Richard
1982   "Guitarra Americana," [the first installment of a quarterly
        column lasting over two years that featured South America,
        especially the music of Agustín Barrios] *Soundboard* (Palo
        Alto) IX (summer), 150–53.

Turnbull, Harvey
1974   *The Guitar, from the Renaissance to the Present Day*. New York:
        C. Scribner's Sons. Westport, CT: The Bold Strummer, 1992.

Viglietti, Cédar
[1973] *Origen e historia de la guitarra*. Buenos Aires: Albatros.

Vila, Pablo
  1989   "Argentina's Rock Nacional: The Struggle for Meaning,"
          Latin American Music Review (Austin, TX) X, 1–28.

Zavadivker, Ricardo
  1979   "Andrés Segovia, entrevista," *Notas* (Buenos Aires) XXII,
          50–51.

                        B. Scores and Sheet Music

    The music literature and recordings cited in the text are intended as
    a sampler of the excellence and diversity of the Rioplatense guitar.
    A comprehensive checklist would fill another volume. (In Buenos
    Aires, the guitar catalogue from Editorial Lagos now has 17 pages,
    that of Ricordi, nearly 100, etc.) The music and recordings which
    are available in the Northern Hemisphere receive emphasis here.

Alais, Juan
  n.d.   *La ñatita,* N. Casuscelli [ed.] para una o dos guitarras. B.A.
          9903. Buenos Aires: Ricordi, printed 1957.

  n.d.   *La perezosa,* N. Casuscelli [ed.] para una o dos guitarras. B.A.
          9904. Buenos Aires: Ricordi, printed 1954.

Beethoven, Ludwig van
  1803   *Symphony No. 3 in Eb Major, Op. 55 ("Eroica")* in Paul Henry
          Lang, ed., *The Symphony, 1800–1900.* New York: Norton, 1969.

Broqua, Alfonso (b. Montevideo, 1875)
  1929   *Evocaciones criollas* a María Luisa Anido *(Ecos del paisaje,*
          Vidala, Chacarera, Zamba romántica, Milongeos, Pampeana,
          Ritmos camperos). Edited and fingered by Miguel Llobet and
          Emilio Pujol, Bibliothèque de Musique...pour Guitare Nos.
          1209–15. Paris: Max Eschig.

Carlevaro, Abel (compositions:)
  1958   *Preludios americanos.* B & C 4010–4018, passim.
          1. Evocación, 2. Scherzino, 3. Campo, 4. Ronda, 5. Tamboriles.
          Buenos Aires: Barry.

  1978   *Concierto del Plata: para guitarra y orquesta,* reducción
          para guitarra y piano. B & C 4027. Buenos Aires: Barry.

  1983   *Introducción y capricho.* Heidelberg: Chanterelle. The
          Introducción, alone appeared in *Guitar Review* (New York)
          No. 62 (summer), 24–26.

  1986   *Arenguay...*"identifies the spirit and people of Argentina
          and Uruguay by combining the two names," *Duo Concertante*
          for 2 Guitars. Heidelberg: Chanterelle.

Carlevaro, Agustín, arr.
1968   *Serie del ángel: Astor Piazzolla, Milonga del ángel, La muerte
        del ángel, La resurrección del ángel...para guitarra.* Buenos
        Aires: Lagos.

1970   *4 Estaciones porteñas...música: Astor Piazzolla, arreglo
        para guitarra: Agustín E. Carlevaro.* Buenos Aires: Lagos.

1979   *Album de tangos* [no. 1]: *Griseta, La muela cariada, La copa
        del olvido, El cachafaz.* B.A. 13260. Buenos Aires: Ricordi.

1985   *Adios nonino: Tango by Astor Piazzolla....* Dale Needles, ed.
        San Francisco: Guitar Solo.

1986   *Album de tangos* [no. 2]: *Nunca tuvo novio, La última cita,
        ¡Qué noche! Gallo ciego, El baquiano.* B.A. 13402. Buenos
        Aires: Ricordi.

Díaz Loza, F.M., arr.
n.d.   *La cumparcita, tango de G.H. Matos Rodríguez, arreglo
        fácil para guitarra.* B.A. 6272. Buenos Aires: Ricordi,
        printed 1963.

Escobar, P.C., arr.
1940   *El choclo, tango de A.G. Villoldo para guitarra.* Buenos Aires:
        A. Perroti, printed 1962.

Falú, Eduardo
1962   *Trago de sombra, zamba para guitarra.* B.A. 12200. Buenos
        Aires: Ricordi.

Fleury, Abel
n.d.   *Ausencia, milonga.* Buenos Aires: Antigua Casa Núñez.

1987   *Obras para guitarra,* revisión y digitación: Roberto Lara.
        Vol. I. [Contents: *Ausencia, Vidalita, Tonada, A flor de
        llanto, La cimarrona, Chamamé, Estilo pampeano, Pegando
        la vuelta, Te vas milonga, Milongueo del ayer, Pago largo,
        Real de guitarreros, Relato.* See Lara's recording of these,
        below.] Buenos Aires: Lagos.

Iparraguirre, Pedro A. (b. Buenos Aires, 1879), arr.
        [The following transcriptions for guitar solo by Iparraguirre
        are kept in the "Sala Uruguay," Biblioteca Nacional, Montevideo,
        along with the tango transcriptions of other guitarists. None have
        dates of copyright or imprint.]

        Como te quiero, tango de Francisco Canaro. Buenos Aires:
        H.N. Pirovano.

        Confesión, tango de Enrique S. Discépolo. Buenos Aires: Pirovano.

Cruz de palo, tango de Guillermo D. Barbieri. Buenos Aires:
Pirovano.

Pelele, tango de Pedro M. Maffia. Buenos Aires: Pirovano.

Sacudíme la persiana [Shake my Shutter!], *tango de V. Loduca.*
Buenos Aires: Núñez.

Sufra, tango de Francisco Canaro. Montevideo: Editorial
Montevideo.

Un tropezón, tango de Raúl de los Hoyos. Buenos Aires:
Pirovano.

Morel, Jorge
   1981   *Virtuoso South American Guitar...Guitar Solos.* [Morel is
            composer of three items, arr. of three others.] Gateshead,
            Eng.: Ashley Mark.

Pierri Sapere, José
   1975-86 [The following appear in Pierri Sapere's easy series for guitar,
            edited by his daughter Olga Pierri. These pieces sound authentic,
            yet since they lack the complexities of higher positions or difficult
            rhythms, they provide a means of introducing the style. Many
            pieces in the folk style are available in Buenos Aires, as well.]
            Vidala, Milonga, Rancherita, Estilo No. 8, Gato, Vidalita, Ma-
            zurca, Pericón, Milonga No. 3. Montevideo: Palacio de la Música.

Rapat, Atilio, arr.
   1954   *La tristecita, zamba de Ariel Ramírez...transcripción para*
            guitarra. B.A. 10970. Buenos Aires: Ricordi.

Sagreras, Julio S.
   n.d.   *Don Julio, tango criollo para guitara.* Buenos Aires: Antigua
            Casa Núñez.

Santorsola, Guido
   1976   *Suite all'antica para dos guitarras.* Horacio Ceballos, revisión
            y digitación. B.A. 13172. Buenos Aires: Ricordi.

Sinópoli, Antonio, arr.
   n.d.   *Pericón de Gerardo Grasso, transcripción para una o dos*
            guitarras. B.A. 6962. Buenos Aires: Ricordi, printed 1952.

   n.d.   *Pericón de Gerardo Grasso...arreglo fácil* [easy] *para*
            guitarra. B.A. 8416. Buenos Aires: Ricordi, printed 1955.

Tirao, Cacho, arr.
   1981   *La puñalada, milonga tangueada de Pintín Castellanos;*
            Derecho viejo, tango de Eduardo Arolas para guitarra.
            B.A. 13300. Buenos Aires: Ricordi.

C. Recordings

Benítez, Baltazar
1977   *Latin American Music for the Classical Guitar* [by Manuel
        Ponce, Agustín Barrios, and Abel Carlevaro: *5 Preludios ame-*
        ricanos.] Stereo, long-play, H 71349. New York: Nonesuch.

Cáceres, Oscar
n.d.   *Masters of the Lute and Guitar.* Stereo, long-play, MHS 1055.
        New York: Musical Heritage Society.

1973   *Oscar Cáceres Interprets Leo Brouwer.* Stereo, long-play,
        MHS 3777. New York: Musical Heritage Society.

Carlevaro, Abel
n.d.   *Recital de guitarra* [Manuel Ponce, Moreno Torroba, Isaac
        Albéniz]. Hi-fi, long-play, ALP 1002. Montevideo: Antar.

n.d.   *2o. Recital de guitarra* [J.S. Bach, A. Barrios, Abel Carlevaro,
        Camargo Guarnieri]. Hi-fi, long-play, ALP 4002. Montevideo:
        Antar.

n.d.   *Guitarra: Domenico Scarlatti, Fernando Sor* [respectively,
        sonatas & studies]. Long-play, ALP 4014. Montevideo: Antar.

1980   *Compositores americanos del siglo XX.* Stereo, long-play,
        S44-120. Montevideo: Sondor.

1986   *Carlevaro plays Carlevaro* [five *Preludios americanos,*
        Introducción y capricho, Cronomías (Sonata I)]. Stereo,
        long-play, CR 1000. Heidelberg: Chanterelle. The score for
        Introducción appeared in *Guitar Review* (New York) No. 62
        (summer 1985), 24–26.

Carlevaro, Agustín
1976   *Marrón y Azul, Agustín Carlevaro interpreta versiones para*
        guitarra de Agustín Carlevaro [tangos]. Volumen 3. Stereo,
        long-play, A/E 8. Montevideo: Ayuí.

1984   *Piazzolla y Gershwin.* Stereo cassette, LBC 026. Montevideo:
        La Batuta.

Falú, Eduardo
1977   *Tiempo de partir* [incl. V. Sojo/Alirio Díaz, *Cinco temas*
        venezolanos, A. Chazarreta (arr.) *Zamba de vargas,* and five
        originals]. Stereo cassette, P 7126268. Montevideo: Philips.

1984   *Recuerdos.* Digital stereo, long-play, ACON 5050. Grafenau,
        Ger.: Aconcagua.

Fernández, Eduardo
1985   *Legnani, Giuliani, Sor, Diabelli, Paganini.* Digital CD,

DH 414-160-2. [London:] Decca. [This and the other CDs listed below are also available on London LP records.]

n.d.   *Rodrigo, Falla, Granados, Albéniz, Turina, Torroba.* Digital CD, DH 414-161-2. Decca.

n.d.   *Villa Lobos: Preludes, Etudes. Ginastera: Sonata.* Digital CD, DH 414-616-2. Decca.

1986   *Rodrigo: Concierto de Aranjuez, Fantasía para un gentil- hombre. Castelnuovo-Tedesco: Guitar Concerto No. 1, Op. 99...*[with the] English Chamber Orchestra, Miguel Gómez Martínez. Digital CD, DH 417-199-2. Decca.

r.1986 *Mauro Giuliani: Guitar Concerto in A Major, Op. 30. Antonio Vivaldi: Concerto in D Major RV93, Concerto for Guitar and Viola d'amore in D Minor RV540, Concerto in A Major RV82* [=Trio Sonata in C Major].... Norbert Blume, viola d'amore, English Chamber Orchestra, George Malcom. Digital CD, DH 417-617-2. Decca.

Fleury, Abel and Atahualpa Yupanqui
1971   *Guitarras en el tiempo.* Stereo, long-play, DMO 55612, Serie Azul. Buenos Aires: Odeón.

Gardel, Carlos
[1970] *Selección 35 aniversario: Gardel con acompañamiento de guitarras.* [A re-mastered long-play of old hit recordings with José Razzano, guitar.] P 1065. New York: Parnaso.

Lara, Roberto
n.d.   *Argentina: Guitar of the Pampas.* [18 compositions in the folk style by Abel Fleury.] Stereo cassette, L 7253. New York: Lyrichord.

Morel, Jorge
1981   *Virtuoso South American Guitar.* Stereo, long-play GMR 1002. Leeds: Guitar Masters.

Moreno Chá, Ercilia, ed.
1975   *Documental folklórico de la Provincia de La Pampa, graba- ciones, textos y fotografías de Ercilia Moreno Chá.* Long-play recording, QF 3015/16. New York/Buenos Aires: Qualiton.

Oraisón, Jorge
1982   *Castelnuovo Tedesco: Guitar Concerto No. 2, Tarantella, Capriccio, Rondo,* with Adam Gatehouse conducting the Concertgebouw Chamber Orchestra. Stereo, long-play ETC 1001. Amsterdam: Etcetera [dist. in New York: Qualiton].

1984   *Astor Piazzolla: Death of the Angel, Songs and Tangos for*

Guitar. Stereo, long-play, ETC 1023. Amsterdam: Etcetera.

1987   *Leo Brouwer: Tres apuntes, Elogio de la danza, Canticum,*
       Tarantos, Temas populares cubanos, El decamerón negro,
       Variaciones sobre un tema de Django Reinhardt. Digital
       stereo, long-play, ETC 1034. Amsterdam: Etcetera.

Roos, Jaime
1982   *Siempre son las cuatro.* Stereo cassette, SCO 90689. [Monte-
       video:] Orfeo.

Segovia, Andrés
1973   *Manuel Ponce: Concierto del Sur, Rodrigo: Fantasía para*
       un gentilhombre. Enrique Jordá, conducting. Long-play,
       MCA 2522. Universal City, CA: MCA Records. (This record-
       ing originally appeared on Decca, DL 710027.)

Tirao, Cacho
1975   *Momento musical* [includes Astor Piazzolla, *Verano porteño*].
       Stereo cassette CBS 90.011. Buenos Aires: Discos CBS-SAICF,
       1975–1985.

Viglietti, Daniel
1973   *Trópicos* [in collaboration with Cuban composer Leo Brouwer].
       Stereo cassette, SCO 90.575. [Montevideo:] Orfeo.

Part I

The Hispanic Domination
of the
Río de la Plata

The vast, grassy plains around the basin lay scarcely disturbed by their unique flora, small game, and several Indian tribes. Then, early in the 16th century, the Spaniards discovered the Plata region in their transatlantic voyages. Innumerable followers came in search of El Dorado, sailing up the Plata, its tributaries, or even making the thousand-mile trek across the plains in order to reach the fabled treasure. Time and time again the legend proved to be true: the mines at the fountainhead of the rivers, high in the Andes, had already provided precious metals for the hoard of the Incas. The mines would produce yet another magnificent golden age— Spain's *Siglo de Oro*.

In their quest for treasure, or for land or slaves, the Spaniards met with extraordinary opposition. As soon as they took to the land, lives were lost. Juan Díaz de Solís led the first European party of exploration into the Plata environs: he was killed himself in a skirmish with the Charrúa tribe. At that moment, he scarcely

5 1

could have realized that he set in motion one of the momentous cultural clashes of all time. In spite of their firepower and other military technologies, the Spaniards were far outnumbered by the natives. Both sides displayed great heroism, and both suffered irreparable losses. The Indians destroyed Buenos Aires, the first city on the basin's shoreline, so its few survivors had to flee far upstream to take refuge. From the town they called *Asunción,* the Spaniards were finally able to make peace because the Guaraní Indians there were generally hospitable, unlike most of the other tribes they encountered. As the Spaniards gained a foothold in Asunción, they slowly established towns downstream despite the continuing opposition. In the early years of those towns, the settlers barely survived as countless courageous men and women lost their lives in the ensuing battles.

In order to help reinforce their establishments, the Spaniards brought black slaves along for the manual labor. Most of their servants were purchased from the Portuguese, who alone held the rights of access to the land east of the papal *Line of Tordesillas.* The division gave the Portuguese absolute control of all the territorial claims east of Brazil (including all parts of Africa and the Orient). Nevertheless the Spaniards dominated in their territory, west of the line, in spite of their juxtaposition against African and Amerindian races, and the occasional intervention of other nations.

The Spanish conquest kept momentum because of several singular strengths of the *conquistadores* [conquerors]. In the beginning their search for treasure, sparked by fantasies of mythical El Dorado, brought clear purpose to their project. Motivation soared and in fact grew in proportion to the size of their task: at first it was dominating the Caribbean Indians with Columbus, then the Aztecs with Cortés, then South America! Had they seen the size of their project initially, they might have turned away from it. If finding treasure was the primary purpose of the conquest, then secondary was the acquisition of lands and servants, both of which were abundant in the Americas. Immediate rewards of domination and substance awaited the conqueror.

Another of their strengths was the absolute unity of their faith. The Spaniards were conservative Roman Catholics in the Old World; in the New, whether devout or not, they all either professed or acknowledged the faith. In their eyes, the conquest was partly religious, or at least a crusade in the medieval sense. They carried the cross against the heathen, knowing that Church leaders would follow in their footsteps to erect buildings with local labor and then provide other benefits of the religious establishment with European support. Their organization called for the development of several monastic orders filled with European priests. Among the religious orders, the most visible was that of the Jesuits, which, for 160 years, led in the conversion of Indians. But inevitably, for every conversion to Christianity, there were religious and political implications. Every *converso* was subject to Spanish rule and also to the *encomienda* system of Indian farm labor that built the estates and harvested the crops of the land barons.

Yet another of their strengths was the European horse. The Spanish officers won their battles on horseback, so naturally they took care to breed their own livestock. To their delight, the animals that they carried painstakingly across the Atlantic and up the Plata tributaries flourished on the humid plains around them called the *pampa*. Over the centuries, some of their cattle and horses escaped from domestic subjection and proliferated on the pampa to roam in wild, teeming herds by the thousands.

During the search for El Dorado in the Plata region, the Spaniards located the treasure from the Peruvian side. Subsequently as they mined the treasure of the Andes, they nearly forgot the Río de la Plata, leaving it fallow for more than two centuries. Since the Plata did not have precious metals nearby, it was deemed too far south to be included in either the route of the Spanish fleet or in direct communication with the monarchy. Not until 1776 did the Spanish court turn the southernmost, outback territory into a viceroyalty—a literal extension of the court of Madrid. The court's officials created the Plata Viceroyalty in an attempt to arrest the contraband of cowhides and tallow. Even so, as royalists began to arrive with the new political establishment, independence was only a generation away. The strength of Imperial Spain abroad was diminishing in proportion to Napoleon's threat of invasion at home. When it was imminent, Spain lost her dominion over the Plata. A new order superseded the empire—independence in the Republics of Argentina, Paraguay, and finally Uruguay.

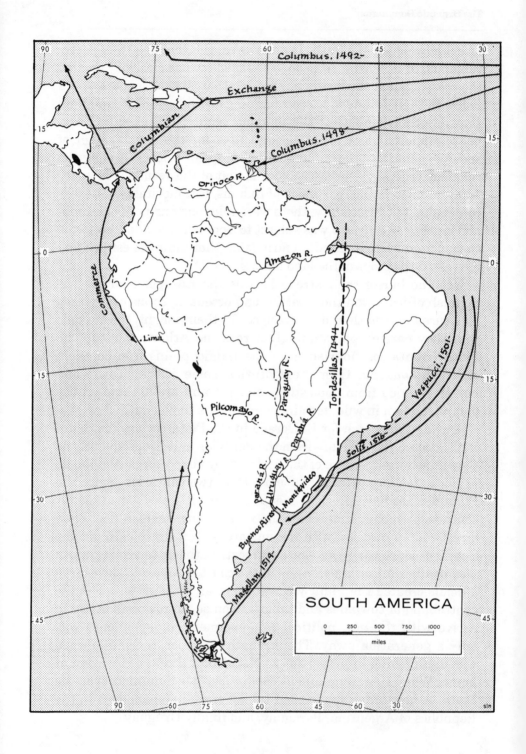

SOUTH AMERICA

0 250 500 750 1000
miles

1. Geography

After Columbus landed in America while searching for a passage to the Indies by heading west, his followers continued his quest. He had made his initial discovery on the hypothesis that land remained on the west side of the Atlantic; subsequently he discovered South America. Likewise his followers chanced to come upon the Río de la Plata. Solís and others merely crossed the Atlantic on his route to the Caribbean and then continued exploring the South American coastline until suddenly, they swung around northwest and headed into a huge freshwater flowage.

The *Río de la Plata* [River of Silver], located on the present boundary between Argentina and Uruguay, is an estuary formed at the inland collision of the Paraná and Uruguay Rivers. The Paraná is by far the larger of the two: initially it carries the drainage of the magnificent *Iguazú Falls* which alone are two miles in width and contain some twenty cataracts averaging 200 feet in height along the Brazilian border. Then the Paraná gathers more volume from the Paraguay River, which joins it later at the southern tip of the Republic of Paraguay. The Plata's elaborate drainage system of lands and rivers is even larger than the combined river systems of the Mississippi, Ohio, and Missouri. Where the Paraná and the Uruguay end, their confluence begins the Río de la Plata which flows southeast some 180 miles as it heads out towards the Atlantic Ocean. The Plata gradually increases in width from about 30 to 130 miles in its trajectory. It is thus the widest river in the world and second only to the Amazon River in drainage area.

The elaborate waterways of the greater Plata river system provided the Spaniards with immediate access to desirable areas for settlement. Their invasion, followed by centuries of development, resulted in the colonization of three republics. After initial contacts on the waterways, they completed settlements first at Asunción, Paraguay, then along the river banks and the north-central part of Argentina, and last on the Uruguayan shore. As they grew, these settlements became, along with Bolivia, the great republics to the south of Brazil, which in and of itself is larger than the contiguous United States, but the republics below it are also of impressive size—especially Argentina. To paraphrase Francis Bond Head, a 19th-century British mining expert who traversed it many times on horseback, the extent of the Argentine pampa is so stupendous that it is bound on the north by forests of palm trees and on the south by eternal snows. From the Bolivian border to Tierra del Fuego, Argentina measures some 2,300 miles as the crow flies.

It was inevitable, of course, that the peoples or governments around the Plata basin would intervene in its development. The basin descends eastward from Argentina's formidable Andean rim: the highest peaks in the Western and Southern Hemispheres (21 surpass Mount McKinley). On the Atlantic side, southern Brazilian ports provided occasional stops for navigators during the age of discovery. Yet of greater consequence, the boundaries of the Plata republics became firm with their independence, which left Uruguay set against Brazil, and Argentina due south of the inland republics of Bolivia and Paraguay. In terms of colonial administration, all of these territories, except for Brazil, had been part of the greater Río de la Plata, which (lacking autonomous authority of its own) was subject to the Viceroyalty of Peru. Thus communications were rather slow to come across the continental divide or around Cape Horn! Worse yet, the viceroyal administrators had little reason to favor the faraway Rioplatense colony. The Plata had viable ports on the Atlantic that threatened to compete for European trade, so Lima's export/import restrictions were the norm rather than favors that might have spurred the economy.

The climate of the Plata basin is mild and humid because the waterways draw the temperate Atlantic zone inland for hundreds of miles. Montevideo is on the 35th degree south, so its temperatures are every bit as balmy as those of Sidney, Australia or Santa Barbara, California, which lie on the same degree. In consequence, many a sailor considered it perfect for early retirement:

> [Everything about the place entices the sailor to it...it is that one lives there almost without working. In fact, how can one resist... sliding along in the lap of idleness on tranquil days, under a delicious climate?] (Bougainville 1769:54).

The rather unique flora and fauna of the Plata fascinated the European travellers. One early description of the region appeared in English despite the fact that its author was a Jesuit priest. In his book on Patagonia, Father Thomas Falkner was writing at some length about the environs of the Paraná River:

> Some of the islands of the Paraná are two or three miles in length; they have great quantities of timber on them, and afford both food and shelter to great numbers of lions, tigers, stags, capivaras, or river-hogs, river-wolves (which I take to be of the same kind as our otter in England) aquaraquazúes, and many alligators. The aquaraquazú is a very large fox, with a very bushy tail; aquara (in the Paraguay tongue) signifying fox, and quazú, great. Their common little fox they call aquarachay.
> This river abounds in fish of many kinds, both with and without scales; some of which are known, and others unknown in Europe. Those that have scales, are the dorado or gold fish, the packu, corvino, salmon, pequarey, lisa, boga, savala, dentudo, and other lesser fry. Those that have no scales, are the mungrullú, zurubí, patí, armado, raya or ray, erizo or water hedgehog, many river tortoises, bagres [catfishes], etc. (Faulkner 1774:56–57).

Félix de Azara, emissary of the Spanish government in the Plata region from 1789 to 1801, also made some sweeping observations about the fauna in the 18th century, if for a different purpose. He was to survey the land in terms of its potential economic development. Azara offered the following advice concerning the fur-bearing animals and fowl, in confirmation of Father Falkner's observations:

> [Finally it is a matter of the country to take advantage of the fine furs, which are those of the tiger, cougar, deer, (wild) dogs, river wolves, foxes, skunks, ferrets, weasels, hares, (mink-like) nutrias, large prairie dogs, bison(?); and the plumes of ostriches, swans, cranes, and crested screamers] (Azara 1801 MS:f. 12v).

Although not at first perceived by the Spaniards, none of the natural resources surpassed the potential of the *pampa,* the limitless grassland that grew in response to the temperate, humid

climate. Even without rain, the heavy dew enabled prairie grasses
to sink deep roots into the deposits of silt that had formed during
eons of geological time. The growth of the grasses was so pro-
digious that, just as in the Midwest plains of the U.S. before the
advent of the modern plow, farming was next to impossible, except
on higher ground above the wetlands. The pampa was full of
magnificent animals, some unique in the world, despite the fact
that there were neither horses nor cattle to graze on on the pasture
before the arrival of the Spaniards:

> The country of Buenos-Ayres, the antient [sic] habitation of the
> Chechehets, is situated on the south side of the River of Plata.
> The coast here is wet and low, with many bogs and marshes.
> The waterside is covered with wood, which serves for fuel.
> These marshes reach, from the banks, till you come to the ris-
> ing grounds; which are also in some parts very boggy; being a
> clay, with very little depth of soil to cover it, till you go farther
> into the country.... The country is everywhere flat, with small
> rising grounds; and it is very surprising, that in all this vast
> jurisdiction, in that of Santa Fe, and of St. Jago del Estero, there
> is not to be found one stone, which is the natural produce of the
> country: and this is the case as far as the mountains of Vuul-
> can, Tandit, and Cayrú, to the south east of Buenos-Ayres.
>   The country which is between Buenos-Ayres, and the river
> Saladillo...is entirely a plain, without so much as one tree or
> rising ground till you come to the banks of this river (Falkner
> 1747:51–52).

The Spaniards discovered a dangerous territory, indeed—it was
already inhabited. Numerous tribes of Indians occupied the Plata
region. Most of them were warlike and comprised of fearless defenders of their homeland. Solís was killed by the Charrúa tribe of
Uruguayan territory, the Timbúes destroyed one of the forts and
its inhabitants established by Sebastian Cabot on the Paraná islands, and the Pampa Indians continuously ambushed the settlers
on the grassy plain beyond Buenos Aires. Nevertheless, some tribes
were sensitive to the music and mission of the Jesuits, like the
Lules. Even so, the one outstanding tribe of Plata Indians was the
Guaraní. They were a large, often friendly tribe in the northern

parts of the region, and were it not for their kind hospitality, the Spaniards might never have survived the conquest. The Guaraní eventually made peace with the Spanish conquerors and even adapted somewhat to the ways of Hispanic society in the colony. Many of these Indians were converts of the Jesuit missionaries.

As for the origins of the colonial immigrants, all of Spain's regions were represented in the Río de la Plata, but the Region of Andalusia predominated. Cultural ties to the southernmost Spanish region were everywhere in evidence and continue to the present day. Yet the impact of Seville, both a province and the capital of Andalusia, was most notable of all. Seville was not only the major port to the New World but also the eastern terminal of the Columbian Exchange; its customs offices were like a great funnel through which the cargo, crew, and every passenger of the Spanish fleet had to pass. Thus many of the workers whose skills supported the voyages, such as the sailors, soldiers, and tradesmen bound for the New World were Andalusian, and their style, dialect, and culture soon set the tone of colonial life. Though Spain was eventually ruled from Madrid, from the centrally located Region of New Castile, it was Seville and generally the southern Region of Andalusia that provided the typical genetic and cultural heritage in the Plata.

2. The Conquest and Its Bounty

The first European encounters with the great estuary of the Río de la Plata were on the northeast (Uruguayan) side. The Spaniard Juan Díaz de Solís, sailing on behalf of the Spanish crown, claimed it in 1516. Although he was killed by Charrúa Indians as he explored its environs, his men returned to Spain with the news of his discovery. In his honor, it was named the *Río de Solís*. The Portuguese explorer Fernando de Magalhães (Magellan) followed with another Spanish fleet, and in 1520 sailed into the natural port that is now Montevideo. As his ship approached the lone hill alongside the port, either he or one of his Portuguese sailors exclaimed, *"Monte vide eu!"* [I saw a mountain!], hence the port's name. But after a brief layover, Magellan continued on to the south with his project of circumnavigating the globe.

The news of Solís's discovery spread fast, for one of his ships, when returning to Spain, wrecked at the Brazilian Island of Santa Catarina. Several of its survivors, including Enrique Montes and Melchor Ramírez, circulated among the inhabitants of the island and discovered the whereabouts of treasure. According to the report that one Luis Ramírez completed in 1528, there was a place in the Andes above the tributaries of the Paraná River where the Indians were mining great quantities of gold and silver. The island inhabitants gave them clear instructions on how to find it:

> [Entering by way of the Río de Solís, we would come upon a river that they call the Paraná which is of extremely great volume and it flows into this one of Solís...because the aforementioned Paraná River and the others that come down to it lead to a jagged mountain range whereinto many Indians are accustomed to go and to come. It was in this place that there were many kinds of metal, and in it there were gold and silver in abundance.... The crest of this jagged range crossed more than two hundred leagues (600 miles) by land, and in the lap of it there were likewise many mines of gold, silver, and other metals.]

With such a roadmap at their disposal and bright prospects of discovering treasure, Montes and Melchor Ramírez lost no time in preparing a trip to the region thereafter called the *Sierra de la Plata,* in other words, the Sawtooth Range of Silver. Their instructions implied that several of the western tributaries of the Paraná River pointed in the direction of the mining district, and the Pilcomayo River (the present border between Argentina and Paraguay) led straight into it. So Montes and Ramírez prepared an expedition by land with a handful of other surviving crewmen of their ship and obtained the services of Indian guides and porters. They started out and became the first Europeans to cross the territory of present-day Paraguay. They arrived at the outskirts of the silver range, but they were not able to explore any of the principal mines because of their situation. At least they spent time with the Indians thereabouts and gathered facts to guide new searches:

[Although they had not reached the mines, at least they had conversed with some Indians of the vicinity next to the Sierra who wore on their heads some crowns of gold, and hung from their necks and ears some plates of gold, which they also contrived to wrap around their waists. They sent a dozen (Indian) porters with samples of the metal that they said would demonstrate how in that land there was a great deal of treasure, and that the people there had already gathered plenty of metal. However, even though they invited them to go farther with them, the Spaniards did not wish to do so because the others (of their expedition) had passed through much danger.... Afterwards the Spaniards received news that their companions were returning to where the group was, but were killed by a tribe of Indians called the Guaraní who had come to rob the slaves that were laden with the metal] (L. Ramírez 1528).

Thus, despite the discoveries of Montes and Ramírez, their mission was unsuccessful; they had to relinquish their treasure along with their porters and return with only scant evidence. They finally made it back to the Portuguese settlements along the Brazilian coastline with no more than a few precious trinkets and their lives (Díaz de Guzmán 1612:41). Their lack of substantial evidence notwithstanding, the adventure of Montes and Ramírez became sufficiently known to their followers that it incited visions of the fabled treasure of El Dorado to all who dared to search for it.

Many Spanish and Portuguese expeditions followed their lead, but none was as significant as Cabot's. In 1526 Sebastian Cabot (son of Venetian navigator Giovanni Caboto) had agreed to sail for the Spanish crown to the Orient by heading west along the route of Magellan. He left Seville with several ships and hundreds of men on 3 April 1526. Yet once underway, his activities suggested the obvious intention of neglecting his charge. He made a long delay in the settlements along the Brazilian coastline so as to discover all that he could about the treasure of the Río de Solís. In fact, he took the trouble of interviewing both Enrique Montes and Melchor Ramírez concerning the Sierra de la Plata (Madero 1939:98). Then he resumed his voyage south but proceeded off course just as soon as he arrived at the Río de Solís. He led his fleet inland on the Solís, straight to the confluence of the great Paraná and Uruguay rivers and established a base camp on an island at the north end of the estuary in 1527.

The clear purpose of Cabot's presence in the Río de Solís was revealed in the memoirs of one of his own passengers. Though Cabot had indeed sailed on behalf of the Spanish crown, he had brought along an Englishman by the name of Roger Barlow, who became not only the first British visitor to the region but also its first British chronicler. Barlow's diary confirmed the report of treasure in the Andean Sierra de la Plata, even though the extant account was written over a decade after his visit there. The Spaniards, during this interim, had already reached the Sierra from the western or Peruvian side:

> And the helthfullest contre [country] it is that ever men came in, for when we came thider manye of or. company were sicke of divers grevous deseases and of the pockys, and here thei recouvered every man his healthe, for the cliere aire and the fysshe of this rever was so holsome that God and it restored them to ther healthe. On the west parte of this river wtin. the lond toward the mountains 150 leges of, is a serra or mount wheras thei saie is a king where is a grete abounbance of gold and sylver and al his vesseles and stoles that he sitteth on is of gold and sylver, and among thes indies by this revers side we had golde and silver wch. the women were [wear] upon ther brestes and about the armes and legges, and by ther eares. This lond and the lond of pirro [Peru], wch. is in the southside that the Spaniards have dyscouered of late, is all one lond, wheras thei had so grete riches of gold and sylver (Barlow 1541:fol. 89v).

Although Sebastian Cabot etched his name in history by being the first European navigator to sail up the Paraná and the Paraguay Rivers, he was unable to find either the fabled king or the source of precious metals among the Indians. The hard evidence of his discovery consisted of the few pieces of jewelry for which he too exchanged the lives of some of his men in battle. During his maneuvers, he chanced to meet other competitors. In spite of the competition and other pressures to succeed, Cabot had no choice but to turn back for lack of rest and provisions. Finally, he made his way back to Spain, and though he was punished with temporary exile for disobeying his orders, the tales and trinkets of silver that he brought back gave rise to the new official name of the *Río de la Plata* [River of Silver] in place of the designation it had been given in honor of its discoverer, Solís. But the Portuguese, who had obvious interests in the region, were much happier with the new name, in place of one honoring a representative of the Spanish crown. Ever since the shipwreck of Solís's men in Brazilian territory, on the Island of Santa Catarina, they had been circulating stories about the supposed silver in the inland mountain range. Whether the Spanish or the Portuguese standardized the new name was of no consequence; either way, it bore news of treasure.

Meanwhile, after the Spanish discovery of the Pacific Ocean in 1513, Francisco Pizarro continued the conquest by exploring Inca territory on the west side of the continent. Sailing ever southward along the Pacific coast (1530–1532), he found the Incas divided in civil war. So he landed, grouped his men, and made a devastating sweep east, towards the Andes which brought the Incas under complete subjection. Then in 1534 he sent word of victory back to Spain along with a bounteous shipment of gold and silver. The announcement of his escapades corroborated stories that were circulating on the Atlantic side about treasure in the Andes.

Therefore, only a few months after this sensational news, Pedro de Mendoza had agreed to try to get to the Andes by land, entering by way of the Río de la Plata. His plan was to establish a colony there as a base camp. Owing to extensive preparations with the help of the court's ministers, Mendoza brought eleven ships laden with some 1200 men plus unnumbered women, 200 slaves, 70 horses, and all their provisions from Spain; they landed on the west bank of the Plata in 1536. There Mendoza built and fortified the port called Buenos Aires. The name stuck for two reasons: (1) the early histories of Schmidl and Díaz de Guzmán confirm that the men commented on the *good airs,* or pleasant breezes of the place on their arrival; (2) in Seville there was a well known home and hospital for sailors known as *Nuestra Señora del Buen Aire* (Madero 1939:148–51). Whether to please the men or to cast a good omen, Mendoza established the complete, official name as *Nuestra Señora Santa María de Buenos Ayres.* Despite the good omen and the pleasant breezes, the environment proved inhospitable and food was scarce. Juan de Ayolas, second in command, was sent upstream and others elsewhere for provisions during a siege enforced by neighboring Indians. While some of the Spanish ships were away, the Indians of several tribes banded together and set fire to the fort and the remaining ships anchored at Buenos Aires!

Disregarding these hardships, Ayolas went upstream again, but this time in search of gold or silver. His strategy was to take two ships, with Domingo de Irala in command of the second, and to leave that one and its crew waiting at a refuge point called Candelaria for four months. Thereby Ayolas could penetrate farther north along the waterways and then on foot with an experienced Indian guide. Ayolas followed again to the edge of the Sierra de la Plata, but his return to Candelaria was long overdue. When he finally went back to the refuge point, thirteen months had passed! By now Irala had of course returned to Buenos Aires, and though Ayolas and his crew had collected treasure, all was lost in a last-minute Indian ambush during March of 1538. Having thus died with his men, he was never to know of the end of Pedro de Mendoza who died at sea en route to Spain and who had bequeathed to him both his estate and command of the colony.

Meanwhile, in order to gain improved access to the Sierra de la Plata, the Spaniards had established another fortress high on the Paraguay River. It was alongside a natural harbor they called *Asumpción*—obviously named for the holiday of the Assumption—but later the word was contracted to *Asunción,* with the modern spelling.

Domingo de Irala inherited the command from Ayolas, whom he was supposed to have met in Candelaria. As a result, Irala became the first governor of the territory and ruled from 1539 to 1542. He resided safely in Asunción by fortifying the shoreline and town, and in 1540, by ordering the remaining souls in Buenos Aires to abandon their position and to come to Asunción for protection. Thus consolidated, the Spanish survived; then, thanks to the peace made with the Guaraní Indians and the considerable intermarriage between them and the Spaniards, Asunción became both the founding city of the Plata region and its population base. Several major cities downstream including Santa Fe, Corrientes, and the second Buenos Aires, as well as many small towns were eventually founded by the Spanish and Spanish/Indian settlers of Asunción (Torre Revello 1970:Ch. II).

In 1542 the swashbuckling explorer Alvar Núñez Cabeza de Vaca came from Spain to be the second governor but failed to win over the populace. So Domingo de Irala accepted the position again and held it from 1544 to 1546. With his new rise to prominence, Irala undertook yet another expedition to the Andean Sierra de la Plata. Under his popular leadership and with a sufficient body of men to bypass any obstacle, he set out to satisfy the dreams and expectations of his men and his predecessors. He planned to follow the same route that Montes and Ramírez had undertaken by land and that Cabot and Ayolas had tried to duplicate upon the maze of rivers. Given their previous disappointments, Irala brought along 350 Spanish soldiers, no less, and 2,000 Guaraní warriors to clinch his success. They marched westward towards the Andes, crossing the tropical, green wilderness of the *Gran Chaco* where Spanish settlements were altogether unknown. Then they ascended into the slopes. At last they reached the highlands of the Sierra de la Plata but were dumbfounded with what they encountered: they were greeted in Spanish on the other side! The Indians there had only just begun to work the mines under the founder of Chuquisaca, Pedro Anzures. He and Irala corresponded formally by letters which the troops could scarcely understand, for Anzures was understandably threatened by the size and intent of Irala's army. The troops became painfully aware that they were late: the conquest had already been made. The treasure and other spoils of their long-sought victory were lost forever. In no time, the men grew impatient with all the protocol and rebelled, deposing their leader in a full retreat to Asunción. Finally, in order to handle the many skirmishes with the tribes of the *Chaco* jungle on their return, Irala took charge again. After reaching Asunción, he ruled once more as governor from 1552 until his death in 1556 (Schmidl 1567:Chh. 42–50).

In South America, the dream of El Dorado was realized primarily in the mining districts of present-day Bolivia. Once the conquerors had taken the available treasure from their subjects as the spoils of war, they found the sources of their wealth at the mines in the adjoining districts of Chuquisaca and Potosí. Using Indian labor, they extracted silver, for the most part, and sent it to Spain. The process was accomplished by private enterprise because the court demanded only a fifth of the profits of favored aristocrats. Besides, revenues on either end of the Columbian Exchange and other taxes were maintaining the richest country in the world. Whether for the court or for the coffers of the mining barons, the ingots were loaded on mules and carried to the ports below Lima and thence by ship to the Isthmus of Panama. The Spanish fleet was waiting on the Atlantic side to receive them, but they had to be transported overland again by mules. Because of this awkward arrangement through the jungles of the Darien Gap, the Peruvian Viceroyalty jealously guarded the rights of shipment; its ministers permitted neither the development of the excellent ports of the Río de la Plata nor the standardized shipment of bullion through its channels. The threat was always that the bullion could be sent across the *Gran Chaco* by land or by rafts on the Bermejo or Pilcomayo Rivers which connected the mining district and Asunción directly; from there it was downstream on enormous waterways to the Atlantic, and off to Europe without further ado. But the standard route ran west through Lima and thence by transshipment of mules again to the Caribbean. The route was observed several times after 1659 by Acarete du Biscay:

> They use divers ways of carriage, to transport all the silver that is annually made about *Potosí* for *Spain,* first they load it upon mules, that carry it to *Arica,* which is a port on the South-Sea, from whence they transport it in small vessels to the fort of *Lima,* or *Los Reyes,* which is a fort upon the same sea, two leagues from *Lima;* here they embark it with all that comes from other parts of *Peru,* in two great gallions that belong to his Catholick Majesty, each of which carry 1000 tuns, and are arm'd each with 50 or 60 pieces of canon; these are commonly accompanied with a great many small merchant ships as richly loaded, which have no guns but a few petareroes to give salutes; and take their course towards *Panama* (du Biscay 1698:54).

With other motives now, Juan de Garay continued the difficult conquest of the Río de la Plata: he established Santa Fe on the

Paraná River in 1573, and then re-established Buenos Aires on higher ground in 1580. Finally at the end of the 16th century an American-born governor was elected. Hernando Arias de Saavedra, *Hernandarias,* as he was affectionately known, was the first of the governors to survey the domain on the southeast of the River Uruguay (what is now the Uruguayan Republic), and to recommend it to the court for colonization because of its fertility and its ability to sustain livestock.

Thanks to the undaunted enterprise of the *conquistadores* of the 16th century, the court could finally observe the fact that the conquest of the Río de la Plata would be neither quick nor lucrative. Since the conquest of Peru had been such a sweeping victory and it had preceded the conquest of the Plata, if by only a few years, the Viceroyalty of Peru was able to dominate the Hispanic development of South America for the ensuing centuries. Inevitably the more sensational conquests of Peru and Mexico occupied the attention of the faraway Spanish court as the expenses of the *Siglo de Oro* were being met with foreign bounty, and as the Plata region was falling ever more into the background. Once the land passage into the Bolivian highlands from the east side proved useless in either the extraction or shipment of precious metals, the Plata conquerors lost much of the motivation for their quest. As a result, the settlers who followed them into the vast, uncharted region had no choice but to begin the search for other objectives as they languished for want of independent jurisdiction. The southern colony's natural geographic isolation ensured a libertine existence for its inhabitants, but it also left the Plata in hopeless competition with Peru on the open market, resultant trade restrictions, and neglect of the court throughout the 17th and most of the 18th centuries.

The Plata's story was not without an ironic twist. The river/ estuary was aptly named because of the evidence of silver which the earliest navigators obtained, and because the river system did indeed access its source. The legend of the mountain range of silver was verified over and over again, and its proverbial king was indeed the Inca. The Spaniards found tremendous motivation for the conquest in their search for the Plata's treasure, but then it was located and accessed from the other side of the continent. This dramatic turn of events left the Plata conquerors without the least part in the discovery of the mountain hoard. Now they had no choice but to seek other resources and interests in the region. For those who remained, what proved capable of further development came from its land, its colonists, and the wild herds of livestock.

3. The Colonization

The transition from the initial conquest to colonization was gradual, and the pivotal figure between them was Hernandarias. He was elected to three terms as governor near the beginning of the 17th century. Therefore, the period of colonization ran from about 1600 to 1776, the start of the Viceroyalty of the Río de la Plata.

Even though the Europeans had reached the Uruguayan and Argentine shores of the Plata initially, they ultimately populated same shorelines from the interior—from the upstream region of Paraguay. Asunción had been the center of Hispanic colonization in the 16th century because of its safety among the Guaraní and because of its proximity to the mines. But its dominance diminished as colonists began to settle and prosper in new towns downstream. Although the white population of the second Buenos Aires did not exceed 500 in 1602, it was designated as the capital of the *Gobernación del Río de la Plata* already in 1617, and thus it became equated politically with Asunción (Torre Revello 1970:166).

It was also remarkable that such a small white population could have dominated the Indians that had proven to be such valiant opponents in the conquest. Part of the explanation remained in the formation of an unofficial Spanish-Guaraní alliance. The *conquistadores,* who did not hesitate to lead the Guaraní into battle against their enemies, also mixed their blood liberally with that of the native residents. While their mestizo children attempted to repeat the pattern again, the intent was prohibited for only whites could rule. American-born whites, known as *criollos* [creoles] like Governor Hernandarias, could rule provided that both sides of the lineage could be traced back to Europe. Therefore, the members of the elite ruling class took new care to preserve the lineage, especially in the capital:

[At Buenos Aires...starting in the 17th century, mixed unions were carefully guarded. The racial fusion of the initial stages was diminishing as the mestizo element fell from the elevated proportion of the first epoch] (Torre Revello 1970:172).

By the middle of the 17th century in Buenos Aires, with the conquest out of the way, there was no more fighting except for Indian raids on the outskirts. Thus Hispanic men had already taken to a more sedentary way of life, particularly with the increasing population of women:

> They are also marry'd and masters of families, and consequently have no great stomach to fighting. They love their ease and pleasure, and are entirely devoted to Venus; I confess they are in some measure excusable in this point, for most of their women are extreamly pretty, well shaped, and clear skin'd; and withal so faithful to their husbands, that no temptations can prevail with them to loosen the sacred knot: But then if their husbands transgress, they are often punish'd with poison or dagger. The women are more in number than the men (du Biscay 1698:23).

The Hispanic, Christian identity was of paramount importance, especially for males. It virtually guaranteed aristocratic life, and the Spaniards of all classes aspired to attain and maintain it. For, even as Pedro de Rada said in 1781, "[Every Spaniard has left and continues to leave for the New World with the object of obtaining the comforts which he does not have in his own country] (Torre Revello 1970:32)." Consequently the white European or creole males developed domineering attitudes that in this period of growth allowed them to lead the settlements which included Hispanics, mestizos, and peaceful natives. The Indians of the colony, who far outnumbered the whites, were responsible for food production or other domestic service in exchange for education, religion, supervision, and protection.

The main crops of the colonial period were at first harvested by Indian subjects. They worked on *encomiendas,* the early, sprawling estates particularly those near Salta and Tucumán, but during the 17th century the encomiendas were largely replaced by the

missions because the Indians gravitated towards the Jesuit ideals
by the thousands. On the encomienda plantations the Indians
harvested both European and native products that flourished in
specific regions, namely wheat in Córdoba, cotton and fruit in
Tucumán, wine in Mendoza, and tobacco and *yerba* in Paraguay.
The latter, an herb for Indian tea (*ilex paraguayensis*; see Appendix II), became the principal export of the Jesuit missions.

Slavery was practiced from the beginning of the European invasion but not always legally. Already in 1538, authorities confiscated two slaves from Captain León Pancaldo's ship which
chanced to dock in Buenos Aires during a storm (Musso Ambrosi
1976:107). The conquerors usually enslaved the Indians who remained their prisoners of war (Díaz de Guzmán 1613:II, Ch. XIV).
Later during the colonization, laws prohibited exploitation of the
Indians while specifying the details of their participation and
workload on the encomiendas. However, the colonists also imposed
legal slavery on African blacks. Indeed, the first sub-Saharan
colonists of the Plata came with Pedro de Mendoza. When the
King empowered him with its colonization on 21 May 1534, he
asked Mendoza to carry *doscientos esclavos negros*—half men,
half women—as part of his entourage (Madero 1939:408). After
that the Portuguese, masters of both the African and Brazilian
coastlines, brought innumerable slaves to sell in the Plata. Captain
Lope Váez provided an early example when, travelling from Brazil
to Buenos Aires in 1588, he imported six black slaves on behalf of
the Bishop of Tucumán. Again on the slave route from Brazil to the
Plata, customs officers confiscated 51 slaves in 1596 (Torre Revello
1970:78–79). By around 1730 the incoming Jesuits estimated
among a population of 5,000 whites in Buenos Aires, more than
20,000 blacks who lacked all instruction because they did not know
Spanish (Mühn 1946:41, 145).

Azara put the three great races of the Río de la Plata into clear
relief, though at the moment he was only describing American-
born Spaniards:

[As soon as they are born, the Spaniards of mention are delivered to mulata—or black or mestizo—wet nurses, which care
for them ordinarily until the age of six or more years.... The

repugnance toward work (among adults), which is greater in America than anywhere else, reinforces the inclination all the more in children.... The Spaniards of all these countries believe themselves to be of a much higher class than that of the Indians, of the blacks, and of the people of color. Yet amongst themselves there reigns the most perfect equality, without distinction of either noble or plebeian] (Azara 1801:220–22).

In their domination of the Plata, the Spaniards also prevailed against the Portuguese, but not without a papal decree. Since the Portuguese navigators had been just as active worldwide as the Spanish, their oft-disputed claims finally reached Pope Alexander VI, who being Spanish, brought special empathy to the impasse. The Pope resolved in the *Treaty of Tordesillas*, 1494 that the world be divided in half—into Hispanic and Portuguese domains. He and his geographers drew a hypothetical line from the north to the south poles of the globe passing roughly along the 49th parallel. Then, all past and future discoveries made east of the line would belong to Portugal, and those west of it would belong to Spain. Consequently every part of the Americas, its discoverer or patron notwithstanding, would belong to Spain, except for the European settlements of Brazil which went east of the line and thus belonged to Portugal (see map above).

Despite their exclusion from the Plata, officially an Hispanic territory, the Portuguese had an enormous impact on it. Although only a handful of families from Buenos Aires founded Montevideo in 1726, and they were reinforced by settlers from the Canary Islands, it was an effort to deter further encroachment by the Portuguese—who had named it in the first place. Besides, the Portuguese supplied, if unwittingly, the first cattle to the pampa.

4. European Livestock on the Pampa

The Spaniards can scarcely be blamed for their neglect of the Plata colony, especially in the light of their achievements of the same period. Their landfall in the Americas, including the Río de la Plata, may have been accidental, yet it also sparked an era of incomparable prosperity. They had come upon two continents in exchange for the support of their navigators, and they certainly remained masters of their territory. However, the empire became untenable like Rome, except that it was ten times larger and farther away. The Plata region was left to prosper on its own, without a systematic plan and precious little supervision, for it had slipped into oblivion during a remarkable Golden Age. Although it had to fend for itself, its time would come. As the mines became lean and other powers threatened an inglorious end to Imperial Spain, cattle hides and tallow became increasingly important to Europe— and so did the Plata.

Most of the Plata's domestic meat and animal by-products (such as hides for leather, tallow for candles, lubricants, cosmetics, etc.) had origins in imported livestock. Mendoza brought over the first horses in 1536, about 70 in all, even though many had escaped into the pampa after the fire and sieges of the first Buenos Aires. Other horses were imported, as well, such as the 26 that survived the trip with Governor Núñez Cabeza de Vaca which remained domesticated. Yet whatever their state, the horses proliferated, as confirmed by Azara:

> [Many horses are found in a wild state. However, although they descend from the Andalusian race, it seems to me that they do not have the size, elegance, strength, or agility of the Andalusian horse. I attribute this difference to selective breeding, which has no place in America. Here the horses live in complete liberty on the plains, in herds of several thousands each] (Azara 1801:132).

The domestic sheep and goats of the Plata may have had European origins, but they did not come initially through the Plata ports. They were brought over the Andean route. They were present in Asunción as early as the middle of the 16th century and the return of Irala's troops from across the *Gran Chaco*.

Soon thereafter the first cattle were brought with extraordinary effort yet little expense from Brazil. Rui Díaz Melgarejo and two Portuguese brothers obtained cattle at São Vicente, Brazil in 1555. But rather than take all the trouble of importing the cattle themselves, they appointed as their driver a man by the name of Gaete:

[These men were the first to bring cattle into this province, making the animals walk many leagues by land, and later (travel) up the river on rafts; there were seven cows and a bull in the charge of a certain Gaete, who arrived with them in Asunción with great effort and difficulty all for the interest of a cow, which was directed to him for salary, whence remained in that land the proverb that says: "They cost more than the cows of Gaete"] (Díaz de Guzmán 1612:II, Ch.XV).

The Portuguese certainly confirmed the story, with the added twist that the cows were stolen in the first place! Among the witnesses in the territory of Brazil was one who signed his testimony in 1564: "[The only intention that the said Rui Díaz had, with those of his company, was to go and rob the cows that the Portuguese were keeping in the fort of São Vicente, where he witnesses that he was living] (Coni 1925:14)."

Once on the pampa, the cattle proved to be even more prolific than the horses; many of them escaped into the wild for the lack of fences or were stolen at night in spite of precautionary measures. At length they filled the Argentine pampa beyond all expectations. Then thanks to Hernandarias, European livestock also reached the east side of the Plata, known at the time as the *Banda Oriental*. Following his expedition to survey it at the beginning of the 17th century, Hernandarias sent over a shipment of cattle and horses to multiply in the wild over on the East Bank. Some decades later, a merchant named Acarete du Biscay travelled to the Plata on a business trip; then in 1657, he remarked on the prolific quantity of livestock which had already become the major Plata resource:

All the wealth of these inhabitants consists in cattle, which multiply so prodigiously in this Province, that the plains are quite cover'd with'em, particularly with bulls, cows, sheep, horses, mares, mules, asses, swine, deer and others, insomuch that were it not for a vast number of dogs, who devour the calves and other young beasts, they would over-run the country. They make so great profit of the skins and hides of these animals, that a single instance will be sufficient to shew how far it might be improv'd by good hands: The 22 Dutch ships that we found at Buenos Aires were each of them laden with 13 or 14,000 bull-hides at least (du Biscay 1698:20).

By 1700 the number of cattle hides had escalated to 50,000 on every cargo ship headed for Spain (Mühn 1946:56). Finally Azara, speaking about the livestock of both the east and west sides of the Plata, concluded the following around 1800, after the new viceroyalty had been established in the Río de la Plata:

[There are numerous wild and domestic cattle, which are not differentiated from those of Andalusia and Salamanca, except that they are less ferocious. About a million hides a year are exported to Spain.... The color of the domestic cattle is quite varied, and that of the wild is invariably constant: they are dark red over the top part of the body, and over the rest, black] (Azara 1801:134).

During the Hispanic colonization, the mule was another domestic resource. In his description of Córdoba's livelihood, Acarete du Biscay singled out the importance of the mule trade at the end of the 17th century in the Argentine towns:

The inhabitants [of Córdoba] are rich in gold and silver, which they get by the trade they have for mules, with which they furnish *Peru* and other parts; which is so considerable, that they sell about 28 or 30,000 of 'em every year, which they breed up in their farms. They usually keep'em till they are about two years old, then expose'em to sale, and have about six *Patagons* a piece for'em. The merchants that come to buy'em, carry'em to *St. Jago,* to *Salta* and *Xuxuí,* where they leave'em for three years till they are well grown and become strong, and afterwards bring'em to *Peru,* where they presently have vent for'em because there as well as in the rest of the western part of *America,* the greatest part of their carriage is upon mules. The people of *Córdoua* also drive a trade in cows, which they have from the countrey of *Buenos Ayres,* and carry to *Peru,* where without this way of subsistence 'tis certain they would have much ado to live (du Biscay 1698:31).

In the next century, mules continued to be a major Plata resource in crossing the continental divide. This was because mules were a natural monopoly in the Plata towns: they could not be bred in the Andes, where they were needed most:

This country affords little for exportation to Europe, except bull and cow hides, and some tobacco, which grows very well in Paraguay; but it is of the greatest importance to the Spaniards because all the mules, or the greatest part of them, which are used in Peru, come from Buenos-Ayres and Córdova, and some few from Mendoza; without which they would be totally disabled from carrying on any traffic, or having any communication with the neighbouring countries; as the high and rugged mountains of Peru are impassable but by mules, and in that country they cannot breed these animals (Falkner 1774:48).

5. The Missions

The marriage of Ferdinand and Isabella consolidated Spain for the first time with the virtual wedding of their vast domains of Castile and Aragón. Then, after the retaking of southern Spain in 1492, they became the patrons behind the voyages of Columbus. However, despite such memorable achievements, they were known as *los Reyes Católicos* [the Catholic Sovereigns or Catholic Monarchs] to their subjects because of their conquest of Islam. The Spanish Pope, Alexander VI officially recognized their joint designation. While the reconquest of southern Spain certainly added to their domain, the main celebration was in the Church. This secular/ religious frame of reference was a stowaway in the mind of every Spanish passenger headed for the New World. The conquest there extended the front of their Catholic Majesties; it was just as political as religious in the intent of those who achieved it. In order to expedite matters of conversion, the Pope conceded to Ferdinand and Isabella all religious authority in their part of the New World —thereby unifying Church and State throughout the Hispanic domination.

The religious conquest of the Plata environs began in earnest during the rule of Hernandarias. He had been among those trying to enforce the regulations of the encomienda plantations by limiting the workload of the Indians and specifying their benefits. But since the Indians were ineffective in this forced capacity, and not to mention the abuses of their labor and circumstance, Hernandarias appealed to the Church thinking that perhaps missions would be more beneficial for all concerned than the encomienda system. The result was that, while the encomiendas continued, several orders of the Church began to send missionaries to the Indians. The Franciscans and Jesuits became particularly effective in the missionary effort during the colonial period; their work brought significant dialogue between the Spaniards and the natives, thereby easing the cultural clash.

The priests of the *Franciscan Order,* who were already established in Buenos Aires, set up several missions around Asunción and Soriano; the latter was located near the confluence of the Río de la Plata and the Río Negro. Founded about 1624 or later, the settlement of Soriano would remain as the first permanent colonial town of Uruguay (Thomas 1957:59–60).

While these missionary settlements were historically and musically significant, those of the the Jesuits became legendary. They were established by the priests of the *Jesuit Order,* which was especially important to Spain because the order was founded coincidentally by Spanish Saint Ignatius of Loyola in 1539. The community of priests known in Rome as the "Company of Jesus" first came to the Plata in 1585 when the Bishop of Tucumán, Francisco de Victoria, had asked for the help of some missionaries. Several Jesuits arrived in answer to his request from both the territories of Peru and Brazil. However, to avoid conflicts between these powers, the *Jesuit Province of Paraguay* was established in 1607, and their missionary work among the Guaraní and other Indian tribes was begun with the arrival of Diego de Torres (b. Castile, 1550) and a dozen other missionaries (Mörner 1953:59–62).

In order to develop an independent supply of edible products and a livelihood for the Jesuit flock, and while simultaneously avoiding competition with the plantation owners who employed Indians on their encomiendas, Father Torres purchased a ranch in 1609 to be supervised by the fathers in Córdoba, and furnished it with donated cattle. But the results of the arrangement were the opposite of what he intended. Eventually this farm and others operated by the Jesuits competed directly with the privately-owned *encomienda* plantations on the open market. Worse yet, though they were not supposed to, the Jesuit farms provided a ready refuge for the Indian workers who chose to escape from the plantations.

Consequently, from the very beginning, the Jesuits were at odds with the barons of the land-grant estates, the regional aristocrats.

To make matters worse, the Jesuits found themselves in a conflict of interest with the Franciscan missionaries who were already working around their town of Asunción and the area south of there. "San Ignacio Guazú, the first of the reductions which were to form the 'Jesuit State,' was founded on the Paraná River in the spring of 1610. Attempts on the part of the Franciscans who were working in that district to induce the Jesuits to transfer their activities to the territory north of Asunción were in vain (Mörner 1953:66)."

The Jesuits organized the scene of their activities around an independent township under the designation *reduction*. Their way of life included attention to the spiritual as well as the physical and social welfare of the faithful, so every reduction needed not only a church, but houses for priests and Indians, a *cabildo* or town hall from which to govern civil affairs, and nearby farms to make each missionary reduction completely autonomous. By 1706 thirty Jesuit reductions had survived against the illegal slave-trade invasions from São Paolo, and they were populated by a total of 100,000 Indians. By then there were 249 Jesuit priests, 73 of whom were missionaries, and among their flock, including the personnel of the Jesuit college of Córdoba, were 1300 African slaves (Mörner 1953:164–66).

The Jesuit utopia was one of total independence. The priests approached subsistence and economy at the same time: they imported the minimum and exported the maximum. They ate their own produce and foodstuffs with their parishoners, and their exports of livestock and crops became their livelihood. Father José Cardiel singled out their four principal crops: linen, tobacco, sugar, and substantial quantities of yerba for the green herb tea called *mate* (pronounced <u>mah</u>-teh).

> [The fourth and foremost crop is that of Paraguayan yerba, which here and in Chile and in a great part of Peru serves for what chocolate does in Spain; and it is more common than the latter inasmuch as all the rich, poor, and slaves use it] (Cardiel 1747:147).

Regarding the origin and practice of drinking *mate,* as well as its preparation, see Appendix II.

The Indians collected the yerba with the help of mules as beasts of burden which were bred in the missions. In the decade of 1680, over 30,000 head of mules were sold per year. During the same period, the Jesuit college in Buenos Aires exported 20,000 head of cattle every other year (Mörner 1953:167).

In spite of numerous writings about the Jesuits, the success of their century and a half among the Guaraní still awaits comprehensive coverage. Handy short summaries have become available by Mörner and Furlong (1946). The 1986 feature film entitled *The Mission* accurately depicted the level of technical skills that the Guaraní had learned in addition to their love of music. However, their techniques of musical performance and instrument construction, involving the guitar, were so extensive that they require a separate description in Part III, below.

The great humanitarian service of the Jesuits notwithstanding, their survival hinged upon political favors. Unlike the Jesuit administration in Europe, they were governed by bishops who were subject to the king, not the pope. Eventually conflicts with the monarchy, the Spanish plantation owners, Portuguese slave traders, and even other Catholic orders forced the close of the missions by royal decree. Charles III expelled the Jesuit priests from South America, so they fled to Europe, while during the years of 1767 and 1768 their missions were totally evacuated. Their material goods were pillaged or turned over to the rival churches belonging to the other orders. Afterwards some of their converts continued the Christian way of life by migrating into the vast Argentine or Uruguayan rangelands, but many simply went back to nature, as they were. By then even some of the Jesuits had lost faith in their cause: "[A completely Christian life was impossible among the Guaraní] (Cardiel 1758:150)."

During their heyday, the Jesuits proselyted among all the Amerindian tribes that would heed the word, but only the Guaraní were converted in great numbers. Thus, yet another reason that without the Guaraní in the Plata, the European conquest would only have been possible in an era of increased military or spiritual strength.

6. The New Viceroyalty

The centers of colonial administration in the New World were the *viceroyalties*. As implied by their name, they were the autonomous extensions of the royalties they represented, and the viceroy was the king's appointee. Thus, the viceroy held absolute power in his own region, and naturally he modelled his hierarchy of officials on the court of Madrid.

During the entire colonial/viceroyal epoch of Imperial Spain, there were but four permanent viceroyalties in Hispanic America. They were costly and few in number because a viceroyalty was tantamount to a court in residence, with the accompanying entourage of officials and troops for protection. The crown's representatives established a viceroyalty only when communications were already clear, where regional economic independence was sure, and wherever a profit could be shared with the court. The first Viceroy was Columbus himself, who ruled (when overseas) from his settlements in the Caribbean islands.

Once the conquest of New Spain (Mexico and Central America) was underway, the monarchy transferred the general seat of Hispanic colonial government to present-day Mexico City. Thereafter the court created three additional viceroyalties, one in the 16th century and two more in the 18th, as the Hispanic colonization became effective across the Americas. The next large-scale conquest was in Peru, so the second viceroyalty emerged in the 16th century at Lima with the purpose of ruling South America. However, authorities did not subdivide the southern continent until the 18th century. One new viceroyalty extended from the Caribbean islands to present-day Ecuador and the countries between them. Known as New Granada, its viceroyal seat remained at present-day Bogotá in 1740. The other, and last of the four viceroyal courts, was the Viceroyalty of the Río de la Plata.

The late, great gesture of Spanish rule in the Plata was the establishment of its new viceroyal government. All of the territory under discussion had been part of the Viceroyalty of Peru. However, in order to ward off Portuguese settlements that were ever encroaching from the Brazilian side and simultaneously to gain control of the contraband export of cowhides, Charles III created the *Viceroyalty of the Río de la Plata* in 1776. From that moment, henceforth every viceroy in Buenos Aires communicated directly and autonomously with the Spanish court instead of routing all correspondence through Lima. The next step of the plan, the Rule of Free Commerce, became effective only two years later to permit legal export of meat, tallow, and other livestock by-products in addition to the hides (Thomas 1957:102). Now the court could take full, legal advantage of the Plata's major resource for the first time in 240 years.

Despite this progress, the new viceroyalty would not last for long because independence was in the making. The precipitating factor was the threat of a French takeover in Spain. From the beginning of the 19th century, French generals were planning to rule Iberia with a contingent of Napoleon's army. With the imminent French invasion at home, Spain's grip on her possessions weakened because all forces were needed unexpectedly for self-defense. Under these circumstances, Great Britain invaded the Río de la Plata in 1806. Since reinforcements from Spain were unavailable, the citizens of the Plata had to defeat the British unassisted. The army of defense consisted of the peacekeeping force of Spanish soldiers, a cavalry of gauchos, and a spirited contingent of Plata residents who fought from their own rooftops. First they surrounded the British and then forced surrender and an immediate withdrawal. The defenders were filled with the exultant sense of victory over the British. As their morale continued to build, the Argentines severed relations with Spain in 1810, and the Paraguayans, in 1814, if under the imposed dictatorship of José de Francia. The wars against Spain did not last long in the Plata, for the spirit of nationalism was at an all-time high. But the *Banda Oriental* was yet to struggle like the Holy Land or Belgium, between superpowers on either side. The age-old conflict between Spain and Portugal was transferred to Argentina and Brazil, as they continued to harbor troops in the Uruguayan territory lying between them. Its declaration of independence came out in 1825, and finally Argentina and Brazil left the East Bank to its own devices in 1828 when it became the *República Oriental del Uruguay*.

7. References Cited in Part I

Just like the Spanish explorers, we intend to leave a clear path to follow. Owing to the fact that many of the sources cited herein are unknown or scarcely known in the Northern Hemisphere, we digress momentarily to summarize the procedures used in documenting the text and bibliographic citations of this volume. We have chosen the short reference set off in parentheses (the author's last name, the year the work was completed, and the page number) as a basic procedure. In the case of new or recent studies, we have merely cited the most recent date of publication. However, modern editions of works completed before 1900 pose a bit of a problem: the most recent date of publication may be somewhat misleading. In order to avoid creating a false impression on the reader, we have cited the earliest date of <u>completion</u> of such in our text rather than the date of reissue. For example, Ulrich Schmidl's extraordinary diary of the first settlement of Buenos Aires, first published in 1567, bears that date rather than the date of 1980 when Wernicke's translation appeared in its second edition.

Ruy Díaz de Guzmán's history of the conquest is another good example. His *La Argentina* has provided the foundation for our description of the conquest. He completed his manuscript in 1612, making it the first history of the Río de la Plata by a native son—a grandson of Domingo de Irala, no less. Therefore we cite the year of 1612 rather than the date of the modern edition. The complete reference below provides ample information regarding the edition cited in our text. Moreover, in order to facilitate access to other versions of *La Argentina,* we have also cited chapters.

Other editorial procedures are as follows: Archaic spellings remain unchanged, but graphic accents have been added according to modern practice. Capitalization corresponds to the international standard: both the titles of periodicals and the institutions they represent remain capitalized. The precise numbering of periodical issues (whether Arabic or Roman) here conforms to the original edition. Authors such as d'Orbigny or du Biscay are alphabetized under <u>d</u>, but anonymous works appear by title in the references. Brackets indicate either translation or editorial comment.

Azara, Félix de
1801   *Viajes por la América del Sur...desde 1789 hasta 1801.*
        Montevideo: Biblioteca del Comercio del Plata, 1846.

1801 MS *"Memoria rural del Río de la Plata...."* Manuscript, Tomo 375.
        Montevideo: Museo Histórico Nacional.

Barlow, Roger
1541   *A Brief Summe of Geography [Geographia Barlow].* Edited
        with an Introduction and Notes by E.G.R. Taylor. Hakluyt
        Society, Second Series, No. LXIX, 1932. Reprinted. Nendeln,
        Liechtenstein: Kraus Reprint Limited, 1967.

Bougainville, L.A. de
1769   *Viaje alrededor del mundo por la Fragata del Rey la "Boudeuse"
        y la Fusta la "Estrella" en 1767, 1768 y 1769,* Vol. I. Josefina
        Gallego de Dantín, trans. Madrid: Calpe, 1921.

Cardiel, José, S.J.
1741   *Carta-relación de las misiones de la Provincia del Paraguay*
        in Guillermo Furlong, S.J., *José Cardiel, S.J. y su Carta-
        relación* (1747). Buenos Aires: Librería del Plata, 1953.

1758   *Declaración de la verdad: Obra inédita del P. José Cardiel.*
        Introduction by P. Pablo Hernández, ed. Buenos Aires: Juan
        A. Alsina, 1900.

Coni, Emilio A.
1925   "Las siete vacas de Goes," *La Nación* (Buenos Aires), 8 Nov.
        (Sunday), 14.

Díaz de Guzmán, Ruy
1612   *La Argentina.* Introduction and notes by Enrique de Gandia.
        Buenos Aires: Angel Estrada, 1943.

du Biscay, Acarete
1698   *An Account of a Voyage up the River de la Plata, and thence
        over Land to Peru. With Observations on the Inhabitants, as
        well Indians as Spaniards; the Cities, Commerce, Fertility,
        and Riches of that Part of America.* London: Buckley. Facs.
        edition. North Haven, CT: Institute Publishing, 1968.

Falkner, Thomas, S.J.
1774   *A Description of Patagonia, and the Adjoining Parts of South
        America: Containing an Account of the Soil, Produce, Animals,
        Vales, Mountains, Rivers, Lakes, etc. of those Countries...and
        Some Particulars Relating to Falkland's Islands.* Hereford: T.
        Lewis. Republished in facsimile with introduction and notes by
        Arthur E.S. Neumann. Chicago: Armann and Armann, 1935.

Furlong, Guillermo, S.J.
1946   *Los Jesuítas y la cultura rioplatense,* nueva edición corregida
        y aumentada. Buenos Aires: Editorial Huarpes.

Head, Francis Bond
1826   *Rough Notes Taken during Some Rapid Journeys across the
        Pampas and among the Andes.* London: Murray. Reprinted
        with introduction by C. Harvey Gardiner, ed. Carbondale &
        Edwardsville: Southern Illinois University Press, 1967.

Madero, Eduardo
1939   *Historia del puerto de Buenos Aires: Descubrimiento del
        Río de la Plata y de sus principales afluentes, y fundación
        de las más antiguas ciudades, en sus márgenes.* Tercera ed.
        Buenos Aires: Ediciones Buenos Aires.

Mörner, Magnus
1953   *The Political and Economic Activities of the Jesuits in the Plata
        Region: The Hapsburg Era.* Stockholm: Library and Institute
        of Ibero-American Studies.

Mühn, Juan, S.J., ed.
1946   *La Argentina vista por viajeros del siglo XVIII.* Buenos Aires:
        Huarpes.

Musso Ambrosi, Luis Alberto
1976   *El Río de la Plata en el Archivo General de Indias de Sevilla:
        Guía para investigadores.* 2nd ed. Montevideo: Rosgal.

Ramírez, Luis
1528   A report signed *"en este puerto de san zalbador ques en el
        Río de Solís a. diez. días del mes. de. julio de 1528 años."*
        Transcribed in Eduardo Madero, *Historia del Puerto de
        Buenos Aires: Descubrimiento del Río de la Plata y de sus
        principales afluentes....* 3rd ed. Buenos Aires: Ediciones
        Buenos Aires, 1939, Appendix No. 8.

Schmidl, Ulrico (Ulrich or Utz)
1567   *Derrotero y viaje a España y las Indias,* Edmundo Wernicke,
        trans. 2nd ed. Buenos Aires: Espasa-Calpe, 1980.

Thomas, Eduardo
1957   *Compendio de historia nacional.* 4th ed. Montevideo: A.
        Monteverde.

Torre Revello, José
1970   *La sociedad colonial: Páginas sobre la sociedad de Buenos
        Aires entre los siglos XVI y XIX.* Buenos Aires: Ediciones
        Pannedille.

Part II

The Impact of Hispanic Culture

A. The Andalusian Base

Having completed a brief review of the Hispanic conquest and colonization of the Río de la Plata, we may now turn our attention to the culture that the Spaniards brought to the New World. Part II surveys several aspects of Hispanic culture in the Plata region. It emanates from the point of view that initially a mainstream of immigrants and their culture from Andalusia dominated the Plata, as much as they did the other Hispanic American colonies. If such were indeed the case, it is necessary to know first the whereabouts and character of this unique Spanish region as well as how it came to dominate the New World, especially given the fact that Andalusia was far south of the court. This introduction opens the way for a discussion of the mainstream's components which come to bear on guitar history.

The early Spanish immigrants to the New World brought their belongings, of course, but their inherent genetic and cultural traits were infinitely more important. Together, their ancestral heritage and all that they had learned in their environment determined the future of Hispania on American soil. The colonists brought a mixture of isolated, regional traits of Spain to the Americas, but sorting them out has never been easy. Spain's size and its geographical boundaries separated its fourteen regions and maintained its remarkable cultural diversity. Every Spanish region had its own unique characteristics, and some of these would be transferred to America while others would be left behind. But who among the conquerors, despite the patronage of the Catholic Sovereigns, could have enforced the equal representation of every Spanish region in the mass migration? One region dominated. Part II is devoted to the most significant region of all, *la Región de Andalucía,* and especially to the Andalusian cultural traits that the earliest colonists brought to the Americas.

The impact of Andalusian culture—now widely known as *andalucismo* in academic circles—had several specific manifestations in the Río de la Plata. Some of these aspects remain the focus of Part II: first, *Rioplatense,* the spoken language there; second, the nocturnal pleasures of the serenade; and third, popular culture in general. Another Andalusian import, the *fandango,* the wild flamenco dance that guitarists brought to Latin America in the 18th century, is the subject of Part IV. An understanding of these aspects can provide insight into the cultural context of the Rioplatense guitar: where in Spain it came from, the origin and character of the early colonists who played it, and ultimately the social significance of the guitar in the Plata colony.

1. Seville

The most apparent aspect of old Andalusia was its capital, Seville. The world already knows something about it, but the traits of Seville are sometimes mistaken as general characteristics of Spain. For instance, many among the innumerable spectators of the operas *Don Giovanni, Figaro, The Barber of Seville, Carmen, La forza del destino,* or *Fidelio* have come away believing erroneously that they have experienced Spain—to the chagrin of Spaniards outside of Andalusia, for they were all set in Seville. Again, many of those who hear flamenco guitar without knowing much about its development believe that it is a music representing all of Spain— yet not so. These operas and flamenco music portray the character of only one Spanish region. Flamenco guitar is so readily identifiable that a measure of live music or a one-second recorded example would probably be sufficient for most listeners to detect the flamenco style, because it has such an obvious, well-known character from southern Spain.

During Spain's Golden Age, Seville became the literal gateway to the New World. Situated on the Guadalquivir River, it was like Paris, an inland city with direct access to the Atlantic. Already established by empires of the pre-Christian era, the city flourished under the Moorish domination, an era of racial tolerance that lasted for seven centuries. Seville was strategically located and thus over the centuries it had become a major inland port. It was sufficiently populated and diversified at the end of Spain's Reconquest to become the gubernatorial seat of the Hispanic New World. Thus the self-confidence of Seville's citizens grew in proportion to the deliveries of gold and silver that were brought through its harbor (ascending to the lion's share of the world's supply) to usher in an age of incomparable prosperity.

Throughout the Golden Age and beyond, Seville was the most exciting place on earth for many Europeans. They were discovering what in reality had existed there since time immemorial: a unique and exotic local color. It devolved upon the overt extremes of religious piety in contrast with a licentious, secular lifestyle—not to mention the intervening points between them. Examples ranging from the sublime to the brutal that came to the Plata were embodied in *Semana Santa* and the bullfight. For millennia these events attracted tourists to Seville. Holy Week was the devout yet extravagant, period of religious processions that preceded Easter. The bullfight, known as *tauromachia* in the ancient Greek settlement, brought to Seville among other dignitaries not less than Julius Caesar who participated as a matador! (Conrad 1953:14). According to Joseph Blanco White's impressions, his *Letters from Spain* (London, 1822), the city flourished as the focal point of the school of bullfighting:

Seville is acknowledged, on all hands, to have carried these
fights to perfection. To her school of bullfighting that art owes
all its refinements. Bullfighting is considered by many of our
young men of fashion a high and becoming accomplishment;
and mimicking the scenes of the amphitheatre forms the chief
amusement among boys of all ranks in Andalusia (Bennassar
1929:263).

In an age of conquests, moreover, Seville provided the setting for
the infamous, picaresque plays on the amorous conquests of Don
Juan—without doubt Europe's most accomplished if scandalous
lover. Although Tirso de Molina first popularized the Don's legend
on the Golden Age stage as *El burlador de Sevilla* around 1630
(Sloman 1965), it conquered the rest of Europe in the subsequent
romantic versions by Zorilla, Molière, Goldoni, Byron, and finally
Lenau, whose text inspired Richard Strauss's virtuosic symphonic
poem. Then Don Juan came to the musical scenario; Gluck's ballet
and Mozart's *Don Giovanni* remained the classics. Yet Tirso de
Molina's *burlador* reached even more significance when it helped
to motivate Beaumarchais to see Seville for himself and to complete his extraordinary comic trilogy on this same theme. Two
comedies of the trilogy, both situated in Seville, have endured as
operas. Mozart and Lorenzo da Ponte immortalized the first as
The Marriage of Figaro. Then at least a dozen composers of the
19th century set the second, *The Barber of Seville*, to music, though
Rossini's version became best known. Later in the century, it was
Bizet's passionate *Carmen* (Paris, 1875) that again brought
Seville's colorful contrasts to the fore. The conflict in it wavers
between the devout, religious character of Micaela and the sexy,
libertine nature of Carmen over the struggle for Don José's love.

2. Seville vs. Madrid: the Seseo

While Spain, like Flanders, might easily have become fragmented
into different European countries with the march of time, especially given the various nations that entered her shorelines and the
archaic communications that prevailed due to her grandiose size

and several mountain ranges, Spain nevertheless became a major European power during the Golden Age as a result of unification. The country came together under two great gestures of Ferdinand and Isabella. The first of these was their well-publicized betrothal: Fernando of Aragón, of the northeast, married Isabella of Castile, of the central portion of the Iberian peninsula. Then once they were established, their second great gesture was to continue the march on the southern part of the peninsula with the vigor of a medieval crusade to end the Reconquest. They compelled the Mohammedans and Sephardic Jews to elect either conversion to Christianity or exile. Thus in 1492 they completed the second step towards unification with the capture of the Alhambra, the last of the Moorish strongholds of Andalusia, whereupon the unconverted were banished. With the Reconquest out of the way, it was later that year that they became the patrons of the momentous voyages of Columbus, which ultimately added to their domain a continent and a half plus the riches of the New World.

The languages of Spain certainly bear record of its diversity despite its centralized authority in Madrid. With the unification of its fourteen disparate regions under a central command, the Castilian Spanish of Queen Isabella became the official dialect. Even so, in Andalusia, as in most of the other peripheral regions, the local and the official dialects remained polarized. The ambivalence resulted from old regional allegiances, of course, but also from the mixed signal that emanated from the court. It was not only new but in transition. Their Catholic Majesties remained footloose and held court wherever it was convenient to do so. Their grandson, Charles V did likewise. Not until the reign of Philip II was the court moved permanently to Madrid. In 1561 he decided to gather all the bureaus and records from other cities and bring them to one central location (Menéndez Pidal 1962:104). Gradually, in the painstaking process of the move, he consolidated the power of Madrid: its rule and culture, even its language, became politically predominant. Despite its supremacy, however, Madrid could eradicate neither the language of Andalusia nor the style of Seville.

The general response to this state of change varied throughout Imperial Spain in the 16th century. Precisely during the colonization of the Americas, medieval Spanish was on the wane as a result of all the political upheaval, and the dialect of Madrid, even though it would gradually evolve into the modern Spanish that we use today, remained in transition. The reaction in Andalusia, in all but the circles of favored aristocrats, ranged from apathy to resistance. Meanwhile, Andalusia had already become the most prominent Hispanic region among New World colonists. Their complex of social norms and genetic backgrounds were not merely Spanish but rather, Andalusian, a circumstance that contributed to their dissatisfaction with imperial rule and their eventual independence from Spain. The impact became evident immediately in colonial language; the colonists unconsciously maintained the dialect of Andalusia. While the Americas were indeed governed by the imperial court at Madrid and its extensions in the viceroyalties, the settlers—especially the soldiers, sailors, tradesmen, workers, stowaways, and women—were largely Andalusian.

The dissidence of Seville in front of the new authority of Madrid has become a fascinating topic of linguistics. Fortunately the study of language in Spain is facilitated by an abundance of printed and hand-written sources, unlike many cultural phenomena which consist only of oral traditions. The linguistic sources of Seville and Madrid contain evidence of the considerable division between them, particularly in pronunciation. Using the available data on the phonetics of both, Ramón Menéndez Pidal clearly demonstrated their differences, as shown in an example he quoted from Mateo Alemán's *Ortografía,* 1609, a manual on how to spell correctly. Alemán had been in the process of condemning Seville's confusion over the *seseo* (also *ceceo*), the like pronunciation of /ç/, /z/, and /s/. There, he claimed, the residents customarily ruined the spelling of their written communications because of their incorrect pronunciation. Whenever they spoke, they pronounced the letters of the soft /c/, marked in old Spanish with a cedilla under it as /ç/, as well as the /z/ both as an /s/. But their pronunciation was a mistake in the official Castilian dialect, for /ç/ and /z/ were pronounced rather like the sound of our English /th/ in Madrid. Alemán noted the confusion of meanings if the following words were said in precisely the same manner:

casa [house]; caza [hunt]
consejo [advice]; concejo [council; governing board]

But after an erudite presentation of the problem, complete with examples, he confesses that he too falls into the selfsame trap. Although he is a self-proclaimed expert in orthography, he makes the same mistakes in spelling because he was born in Seville!

> ...*en lo que también conosco* [sic] *que yerro algunas vezes* [sic] *con descuido, porque me vuelvo al natural como la gata de Venus, i pecado jeneral en los Andaluzes, de que no se an escapado los castellanos todos, poner /ç/ por /s/, y /z/ por /ç/ o al revez* [sic] (Menéndez Pidal 1962:108).
>
> [...in that which I also know, sometimes I err out of neglect because I turn back to nature like Venus's cat and the universal sin among Andalusians, of which all Castilians have not escaped, of putting /ç/ for /s/, and /z/ for /ç/, or the reverse.]

The Andalusian *seseo* soon appeared in the Americas—and as usual, the American sources shed new light on European practices. During the conquest of Mexican and Caribbean territories, one of its principal chroniclers dilated somewhat upon the personal characteristics of its leaders. In his *Historia verdadera,* Chapter 206, Bernal Díaz del Castillo singled out two of the *conquistadores* and went so far as to describe their pronunciation:

> *E el capitán Gonzalo de Sandoval fue capitán muy esforzado, y sería cuando acá pasó de hasta veinte e cuatro años...y obra de diez meses fue gobernador de la Nueva España...y ceaceaba tanto cuanto* (Díaz del Castillo 1568:II, 544).
>
> *El capitán Luis Marín fue de buen cuerpo e membrudo y esforzado...sería de hasta treinta años cuando acá pasó; era natural de San Lúcar; ceaceaba un poco como sevillano* (Díaz del Castillo 1568:II, 546).

[And Captain Gonzalo de Sandoval was a very courageous captain, and he would be up to twenty-four years (of age) when he spent time here...and for a period of ten months he was governor of New Spain...and he used the *seseo* once in a while.]
[The captain Luis Marín had a good physique, and was husky and courageous...he was as much as thirty when he spent time here. He was a native of San Lúcar; he used the *seseo* somewhat like a man of Seville.]

The *seseo* was of course merely the tip of the proverbial iceberg, a single sound of Andalusian speech. But thanks to the abundant linguistic sources and the light of modern research upon them (Menéndez Pidal 1962, Lincoln Canfield 1981, et al.), it has remained clear that the *seseo* and other habits of Andalusian speech had become the mainstream of communication in the Americas. Even more significant, the *seseo* was symptomatic of a tremendous impact overall. Already in the middle of the 16th century, the norms of Andalusian society were predominating in the Hispanic colonies of the New World.

3. Rioplatense: The Spoken Language

The language and other cultural traits of the first European colonists in the Río de la Plata were not appreciably different from those of the rest of Hispanic America at the outset. The European invasion became permanent first at Asunción; colonists left Asunción to establish Buenos Aires for the second time in 1580; then families migrated from Buenos Aires to build other towns, like Montevideo in 1726, until the shorelines and interior were dotted with settlements as far inland as Salta and Tucumán. As observed previously, the population of the Plata had a mestizo base in its settlements initially, but Plata leaders aimed at Europeanizing the colony during the first centuries of its development. The Plata colony, like other Spanish dominions, maintained a society completely dominated by Hispanic males, so Hispanic culture was critical for upward mobility. In fact, the occasional ships that left Andalusia in order to bring new immigrants, supplies, or aspects of peninsular culture into the Plata region reinforced it:

> [It is evident that the reiterated presence of ships proceeding from Andalusia meant for Buenos Aires an important contact with the speech of the peninsular south, which, in a population of such reduced size as that of Buenos Aires, must have had a decisive significance. This connection must have carried with it as a consequence, moreover, the illegal immigration of new colonists of southern Spanish origin: many of them were

arriving as members of the ships' crews, who would take advantage of landing at Buenos Aires in order to establish themselves in America] (Fontanella de Weinberg 1987:15).

Although it began with the Andalusian base like the rest of the Hispanic American dialects, *Rioplatense* (the spoken dialect of Argentina and Uruguay) developed its uniqueness as a result of regional isolation. The Plata was differentiated from other American regions in that it received shipments of reduced size and quantity, and they arrived either intermittently or illegally. The main Spanish fleet went biannually, laden with European imports to the Viceroyalties of Mexico and Peru with connections in the Caribbean, and naturally it returned with a cargo of American bounty (see map on p. 54). Small shipments were also arriving there regularly with the Columbian Exchange. Notwithstanding, few Spanish ships arrived in the Plata because of its distance from the rest of Hispania and because of its lack of precious metals. Substantial fleets never arrived there because of trade restrictions until the Rule of Free Commerce was established in 1778. This regulation came only two years after the creation of the Viceroyalty of the Río de la Plata, with its center at Buenos Aires. The viceroyalty, full of devoted ministers of the court, permitted the monarchy to control the export of animal by-products. The steady, lucrative shipment of cowhides and tallow had long been a contraband operation out of the Plata ports. But now, having depleted the known supply of silver and gold during two centuries of enterprise in the other viceroyalties, the Spaniards turned their attention to the Plata region with a profit motive. But there was a problem: the creation of the viceroyalty lagged far behind the initial conquest and settlement; exactly 240 years had passed since the first settlement of Buenos Aires in 1536. The original Andalusian colony there and the ensuing two and a half centuries of isolated development within the Plata region had already given Rioplatense culture its archaic uniqueness that has persisted until the present day.

The new viceroyalty, being an extension of the Spanish crown in Buenos Aires, brought with it a new entourage of diplomats, clerks, officials, and soldiers from the Peninsula. The Spaniards were fascinated with the creole culture which they found inexplicably

different from their own except that it was so archaic. To one of the
new arrivals, José de Espinosa, it seemed as if they were discovering a place where time had stood still:

> [Of the customs of the Montevideans, one cannot but praise
> their generosity, hospitality and good disposition that charac-
> terizes them. Among the nobility…they dedicate themselves also
> to the producing of livestock, to the commerce of hides. They
> take considerable delight in horseback riding, both men and
> women; they drink *mate* at all hours, their speech is languor-
> ous, slower here than in other places….
>   It will not be superfluous to expose here the dialogue that is
> customarily presented to the most unfamiliar dwelling. As a
> man approaches any door on horseback, the owner tells him:

—Di-os lo guarde a-a-migo, pro-
nunciado con mucha lentitud.
R.—Y a Vd. lo mis-mo.

—A-pé-ese si gusta.
R.—No hay para que.
—Vaya, no sea son-so [sic].
R. Valdreme de su fa-vor.
—Deje ahí el caballo, no más.
R.—<u>Deo gra-cias</u> (ahora va
entrando)….

    Reinan todavía entre estas
gentes muchos restos de la anti-
gua gallardía española
(Espinosa 1794:560–61).

[—Ma-ay God preserve you my
frie-end, pronounced very slowly.
(The rider {R.} responds)
—And to you (Sir), the sa-ame.

—Dismou-unt if you like.
R.—There's no need.
—Go on, don't be foo-oolish
R.—I would make use of your fa-avor.
—Just leave your horse there.
R.—*I give tha-anks* (now he goes
inside)….

    Many vestiges of old Spanish
gallantry prevail yet among
these peoples.

As revealed here, Espinosa was amused by the speech of the
several Rioplatense classes. In the first case, the hospitable, sport-
ing landowners spoke languorously, and in the second, the typical
dialogue of the horseman was spoken with syllables so drawn out
as to border on comedy. Espinosa explained that these linguistic
norms and other customs were vestiges of an archaic society in the
Banda Oriental. There, people were still giving thanks in liturgical

Latin upon entering a dwelling. They were complying with Paul's admonition to always give thanks as well as the Christian doctrine: "When ye come into an house, salute it (Matthew 10:12)." Espinosa went on to say that over on the west bank, the customs of Buenos Aires were *"como las de Montevideo"* [like those of Montevideo] except that over there the people enjoyed a higher standard of living as a benefit of the new viceroyalty (Espinosa 1794:566). By the time he had come at the end of the 18th century, the Río de la Plata's culture had not only been established, it had become unique, due more to its internal growth than scant immigration. At the same time, Spain's Golden Age had come and gone.

4. The Voseo

In Spain, fundamental linguistic changes resulted from the commerce and remarkable creative impulses of the Golden Age. The Castilian dialect of Queen Isabella finally displaced all others in politics, business, and literature. Its pronunciation became standardized across the empire from top to bottom, from the "received address" of the court down to everyday speech. New word usages gained acceptance and old ones disappeared in the formation of modern Spanish. The most notable change of all was the new syntax: *vos*, the most typical pronoun meaning *you* in old forms of address, had become too volatile and derogatory for everyday speech (Páez Urdaneta). Somehow, only a century after the dignified mandates of the Catholic Sovereigns, the mere use of *vos* had acquired the tone of insult as noted by Lucas Gracián Dantisco in his *Galateo español*, 1593:

> [Whoever calls someone by *vos*, not being very well qualified to do so, scorns him and causes insult in thus naming him because it is understood that they call peons and laborers with such expressions] (Pla Cárceles 1923:246).

The *voseo*, i.e. the use of *vos* and its conjugations, gradually gave way to the use of *usted* and *tú* as personal pronouns for addressing others. *Vuestra merced* [Your Grace!] became the contraction *usted,* abbreviated as *V.M.,* then *Vd.,* and it superseded all other protocol in formal situations. *Usted* also meant *you,* of course, but it showed extraordinary respect through the conjugations of the third person which implied distance. In this environment, *tú* regained its vitality as the typical form of address in intimate or informal circumstances. All of these improvements were set in stone with the formation of the elite *Real Academia Española* [Royal Spanish Academy] which King Philip V established in 1713 in order to set standards for and maintain the purity and elegance of the Castilian language.

Meanwhile, the Plata never absorbed the linguistic innovations of the Iberian Peninsula. Unconsciously the Rioplatenses carefully maintained their pronunciation of Seville, yet they had to add numerous foreign words to describe their new domain, such as its flora and fauna. They added words to their lexicon at first from Amerindian, Portuguese, and African sources. Then in the 19th century, a number of Italian and French words came in with the immigrations. In the 20th, new Anglicisms invaded the vocabulary as a result of the waves of research, technology, and popular culture emanating from the north. Rioplatense syntax, however, remained stable and unchanged from the 16th century: *vos* and its conjugations (now known as the "voseo") once common to both central and southern Spain, endured as the intimate form of address in the Río de la Plata:

> [In extensive reaches of America, separated from the taste of the court and less influenced by the norms that prevailed in the peninsula, mixed paradigms were created with forms proceeding from one pronoun or another, and with singular or plural verb forms. The most frequent type often eliminates the use of *tú, ti, contigo, os* and *vuestro,* and conserves *vos* for functions of subject and prepositional terms, *te* as affixed complement of the verb, and *tu, tuyo* as possessives.... The most vigorous and representative "voseo" (that of the Río de la Plata) is customarily joined to the preservation of the second person plural verb forms without the i of the diphthong (*tomáis* becomes) *tomás, tenés, sos,* which in Spain barely survived to the second third of the 16th century, and of the imperative without -d (*cantad* becomes) *cantá, tené, vení,* which in peninsular usage lasted until

the 17th century. The plebeian character which *tomás, tenés, sos* acquired in Spain has been brought to light, but the loss of prestige of these forms, which before—in a considerable part of the 15th century—had found a place in troubador songbooks, has yet to be explained] (Lapesa 1970:519).

Neither the prestige nor the usage, however, showed any signs of decline in the Río de la Plata. *Vos* remained there prominently as the preferred pronoun of address. Most speakers continued to use *vos* in familiar situations, leaving *tú* and *usted* as alternatives; some situations demanded *tú* or *usted*. The conquerors introduced the voseo, and standardized it in the Americas, but the late-arriving, fancy protocol of a faraway court always seemed too pretentious for universal adoption in the Plata colony, even though simultaneously in Spain the majority had shifted to the preference for *tú* and *usted*. The new preference was so strong that some colonists of the Americas adopted it where contacts were well established, particularly in viceroyal Peru and Mexico. However, *vos* had remained so habitual among the Argentine and Uruguayan colonists, they continued its use in and among all social ranks. The typical chart or paradigm below presents these significant verb forms, with the archaic plural forms for reference:

Fig. 3 The Present Indicative with Vos as the Subject				
infinitive	pronoun	singular	translation	plural
cantar	vos	cantás	(you sing)	cantáis
tener	vos	tenés	(you have)	tenéis
venir	vos	venís	(you come)	venís

Archaic forms persisted also in the preterite indicative (the usual past tense) of Rioplatense, even though today they are used less than those of either the present tense or the emphatic commands. As for historical models of these past forms, they had had been used by Ferdinand and Isabella in their correspondence with Columbus. Since they addressed him as *vos,* their decrees also document the voseo at court. This past tense appeared several times with the voseo in their letter from Barcelona dated 5 September 1493 (emphasis added on the preterite conjugations):

Nosotros mismos y no otro alguno hemos visto algo del libro que nos <u>dejastes</u>.... Y porque para bien entenderse mejor este vuestro libro, habíamos menester saber los grados de las islas y tierra que <u>fallastes</u> y los grados del camino por donde <u>fuistes</u> (Relaciones geográficas 1881:I, xx).
[We ourselves and none other have seen something of the book you *left*.... And in order to better understand this, your book, we need to know the extent of the islands and land that you *found* and the extent of the road where you *went*.]

The following year Ferdinand and Isabella were holding their itinerant court at the picturesque castle of Segovia, not far north of Madrid. From there they wrote again to Columbus because they needed more documentation with regards to the extent, location, and number of his discoveries:

Vimos vuestras letras e memoriales que nos <u>enviastes</u> con Torres. Y visto todo lo que nos <u>escribistes</u>, como quiera que asaz largamente decís todas las cosas, de que es mucho gozo y alegría leerlas; pero algo más queríamos que nos escribiésedes, ansí en que sepamos cuantas islas fasta aquí se han fallado... (16 August 1494, *Relaciones geográficas* 1881:I, xxi).
[We saw your letters and memoirs that you *sent* us with Torres. And on review of all that you *wrote* to us, wanting for completeness as you carefully disclose all things of which it is great joy and happiness to read, we were yet wishing that you would write somewhat more so that we may know how many islands up to now have been found....]

The everyday speech of the Río de la Plata is based on such peninsular models. Plata dialogue in the definite past tense contains precisely the same preterite forms as these proclamations. The singular forms with *vos* are modelled on the plural forms, with the <u>i</u> removed as follows:

Fig. 4 The Preterite Indicative with Vos as the Subject				
infinitive	pronoun	singular	translation	plural
cantar	vos	cantastes	(you sang)	cantasteis
tener	vos	tuvistes	(you had)	tuvisteis
venir	vos	vinistes	(you came)	vinisteis

Fortunately all of the other (indicative and subjunctive) verb forms used with *vos* as the subject pronoun are identical to the forms used with *tú*, as taught in any Spanish textbook and thus, they need not detain us further. However, the imperative forms, as described above by Lapesa, are also archaic, and they soon became evident among the sailors headed for the New World. A 16th-century Castilian diplomat named Eugenio de Salazar was fascinated by the jargon he heard aboard ship during his travel to Mexico. He explained that many sailors were *levantiscos* (they were the lowest-paid rank of seamen, being foreigners from the Syrian or Turkish Levant, or other parts of the Mediterranean), but just the same they were addressed primarily in Andalusian Spanish as they travelled, just like the other sailors. All the Spanish captains and officers managed their ships by making voiced commands. They constantly blurted out changes to be made in the loading, rigging, or steering of the vessel, and naturally these charges were overheard by everyone on the topside, including the passengers. Many of these commands, including the 24 heard and recorded by Salazar, were identical to those of Rioplatense, with vos as the implied subject. A few of these are shown below (underlined), along with the gist of Salazar's argument:

> *Porque si el piloto dice ¿ah de proa? vereislos al momento venir saltando...y él con grande autoridad manda al que gobierna, y dice: botá...gobérná...cargá...meté bien* (c.1573:293).
> [Therefore if the pilot says—"What about the bow?" you should see how they come leaping along...and with great authority he commands those he governs, saying: "shift (that helm)!...get control!...carry this!...set that well!"]

Bernal Díaz del Castillo was Salazar's contemporary, and he too heard these same emphatic commands. In his *Historia verdadera*, Chapter 6, he gives a classic example, for it is a command which also happens to show the placement of pronouns. Díaz del Castillo is enumerating the personal hardships that he and the *conquistadores* experienced in 1527 following their battle on the coastline of Florida. There they had met an Indian ambush as they searched for drinking water. Afterwards, as they languished, he overheard the expression *"Hacételo vos,"* as issued from the lowest rank of the ship's crew (more sailors from the Levant). He recorded their expression in the following passage, which shows the singular command <u>hacé</u> connected to the pronouns <u>te</u> and <u>lo</u>:

> *Traíamos unos marineros levantiscos y les decíamos: "Herma-*
> *nos, ayudad a dar la bomba, pues veis que estamos todos muy*
> *mal heridos y cansados de la noche y del día." Y respondían los*
> *levantiscos: "Hacételo vos, pues no ganamos sueldo* (1568:I, 25)."
> [We were bringing some sailors of the Levant, and we were tel-
> ling them: "Brothers, help out with the bailing (of the ship), for
> you see that we are all very badly wounded and tired from the
> night to the day." And the Levantine sailors responded: "Do it
> yourself, for we are not paid a salary."]

While this may seem a minuscule point of linguistic analysis or indeed a lengthy aside to the history of the guitar, these passages portray exactly the command form of the Rioplatense voseo, as well as the placement of its associated pronouns. Together Salazar and Díaz del Castillo confirm that the voseo was Iberian and that the Hispanic conquerors brought it to the New World long before Philip II could have moved the court to its central location, which equated the "received" dialect of the court with that of Madrid.

The voseo continued in the Plata based on such archaic models. It has remained the preferred form of address for intimate cir-cumstances, yet in others that require an increasing degree of respect, *tú* and *usted* also occur. Therefore, having observed the voseo and the alternatives of *tú* and *usted*, the reader will be able to perceive the shades of meaning between them as they intertwine with the history of the guitar, even when our references contain the mention of *vos*. For when they do, they cannot be regarded as incorrect, but merely archaic because the use of *vos* was the correct form of address in earlier times of the Iberian peninsula, and at the social extremes—from sailors to kings. As for points between them, "In the *Poema del Cid* (1140 A.D.) *vos* is used as the respectful form of address between king and noble, between hus-band and wife, nobleman and nobleman...whereas *tú* is used in addressing persons of inferior rank (Kany 1951:58)." Rioplatense speakers unconsciously maintained the use of *vos* and its meaning despite the linguistic changes of Spain's Golden Age. The formative years of Rioplatense culture were precisely its first two centuries, which happened to overlap with the Golden Age; at the same time, these were the years of the most severe cultural isolation from Spain. The communications between the Iberian peninsula and the Río de la Plata never established a preference for *tú* and *usted*, although these became the usual forms of address in Spain where *vos*, ironically, disappeared once and for all.

The last of the archaic subject pronouns of Rioplatense is *vosotros*. It is the classic form of "you plural" of Spain, as used for instance in the widely circulated Bible translation of Cipriano de Valera (1602), and it is still found in Rioplatense, if considerably less than the other forms meaning you. Today you plural (or you all) is much more often expressed by *ustedes*. However, when used or understood, *vosotros* has its own special conjugations, as shown in Figures 3–5, and as featured in the following sensational news of *La Nación* of Buenos Aires in which the guitar appears (at long last). Carlos Gardel, the great singer and guitarist of the old tango at its apex, has just returned from a triumphal tour of European theatres. The article shows that Gardel has remained unscathed from all the glory (emphasis added):

> ¿*Os* interesa, a los que *habéis oído* alguno de los ciento diez mil discos que vendió en Buenos Aires, solamente al reflejo de sus últimos éxitos de París, saber como vive, como es la casa donde tiene su residencia, aunque sea un poco en el aire, Carlos Gardel? Pues vive de la manera más distinta a como *os imagináis*.... Para alejarse un poco de las admiraciones que enloquecen ha resuelto vivir en una casita de la calle Jean Juarés, cuyo número no damos para evitar que su conocimiento tenga el mismo resultado que si pusiera teléfono.... Pero de lo que hemos visto, *comparad* ¡qué distinto a lo imaginado! Un "hall," más bien patio, grande, amplio, frío, con tres guitarras, dos baúles, un fonógrafo y un par de botas, muy altas, tal vez porque así en Europa parecerán más criollas (30 June 1929).

[Is it of interest *to you*, those of *you* who *have heard* one of his 110,000 recordings which he sold in Buenos Aires, not to mention his latest successes in Paris, to know how Carlos Gardel lives, what his house is like where he resides—be it all a bit up in

the air? Well, he lives in a manner quite different from what
you imagine…. In order to separate himself somewhat from the
bothersome mass-admiration, he has resolved to live on Jean
Juarés Street in a little house whose number we suppress in
order to avoid that its announcement might have the same effect as installing a telephone…. But from what we have seen,
compare how different from what was imagined! A "hall," or
rather a patio, large, wide, cold, with three guitars, two trunks,
a phonograph, and a pair of boots—very tall, perhaps because
thus in Europe they will appear more "creole."]

To sum up, the subject pronouns of current Spanish address, *tú*,
usted, and *ustedes*, reside alongside the archaic forms, *vos* and
vosotros, in the mind of Plata residents with a tenuous balance.
Although the five pronouns translate simply as *you*, they all,
paradoxically, have different meanings. The speaker there unconsciously selects one of the five to show degrees of restraint and
hence varying levels of respect (as in some modern languages but
quite unlike anything in current-day English because our syntax
of *thou* [= tú] died away at around the time of the North American
colonization). *Vos*, being the most archaic, is the most difficult to
understand, for it fell abruptly out of use around 1600 in Peninsular Spanish. Naturally its historical continuity in the Plata
region has come under fire. In fact, some detractors have argued
the gaucho-dictator Juan Manuel de Rosas revitalized the voseo
during his heyday in the middle of the 19th century. While the
proponents of his ruthless dictatorship may have advanced the use
of *vos,* one scholar gathered nine original, pre-Rosas examples of
the voseo from the correspondence of Argentine writers between
the years of 1683 and 1838 (Borello 1969:34–36). An item from
1797 contains the still-current expression, "¡Calláte la boca!"
(requiring a graphic accent) which at the most familiar level
means, "Shut up!" Even so, it would require a different translation
at the level of *tú* or *usted* because in English we only have the
personal pronoun *you* to address others, and we rely on word
usage or tone of voice to express our own levels of respect. Another
chart provided below shows the subtle meanings that these levels
convey within the emphatic commands by varying the semantics
of the translation:

Fig. 5 Forms of the Rioplatense Imperative (with Reflexive Pronouns)		
(vos)	Calláte la boca	(you, very familiar) Shut up.
(tú)	Cállate la boca	(you familiar) Shut your mouth.
(usted)	Cállese la boca	(you, Sir or Ma'am) Quiet, please.
(ustedes)	Cállense la boca	(you all) Quiet, please.
(vosotros)	Callaos la boca	(you all) Be quiet.

Naturally Rioplatense speakers can vary their choice of words, tone of voice, and body language as much as we do, but they have the additional advantage of being able to employ grammatical forms to maintain a particular level of respect or regard for their listeners. Language instruction in Plata public education embodies all of the forms associated with *you* as the subject except for those of the voseo. Even so, teachers have not been able to uproot its hold on the populace: *vos* is still the most popular of all the forms in familiar circumstances, and its forms are easy enough to learn, even for foreign speakers. But the forms of the voseo remain difficult to translate because literal translations, word-for-word, seldom convey the real meaning or the intent of the speaker.

An advanced application of this knowledge to our study of the guitar is also possible, inasmuch as we can now observe the different levels of respect. While the "vigorous forms of the voseo" are apparent in innumerable passages of literature, the following fictional passage by Hilario Ascasubi, an Argentine poet and guitarist of the 19th century, contains the clear contrast of two levels: the dialogue between husband and wife, and their conversation with a stranger. Rufo Tolosa, a man from Santiago, and his wife Juana use the voseo exclusively among themselves; but as they address the infamous gaucho guitarist/balladeer Santos Vega, they only do so with complete veneration by using a contraction of *usted*. In fact, Juana uses the *voseo* with her husband's first name and *usté* with Vega's last to distinguish between the men. But Tolosa, concerned over the rapt attention his wife has been showing to their charming visitor, has just delivered an insult to the musician. Unruffled, Vega remains cool and collected on the exterior by responding with words that momentarily calm the other man while he plans a clever, musical revenge with his guitar:

Ref. 2 *Santos Vega...*   Hilario Ascasubi

<u>Vega</u>   <u>Vega</u>

—*Escuche amigo Tolosa;*   [—Listen my friend Tolosa;
usté nos hace un agravío....   you have offended our intentions....
Para bailar sobra tiempo;   There is plenty of time to dance;
siga nomás su relato,   just continue your ramble
que es lindo, aunque nos contrista. which is nice, though rather sad.
Ansí luego, en acabando,   Then later, when you're done,
usté debe permitirme   you should permit me
él que yo, con el changango,   that I, with my old guitar,
acá con la patroncita   and with the little lady here,
echemos penas a un lado.   that we throw our cares aside.
Con que ansí, amigo Tolosa,   Therefore, my friend Tolosa,
siga el cuento de Monsalbo.   continue the story of Monsalbo.

<u>Tolosa</u>   <u>Tolosa</u>

—*Bueno, amigo, le haré el gusto,*   Well, friend, I'll please you,
seguiré luego; entre tanto   but I'll continue later; now
refrescaré la memoria   I'll refresh my memory
mientras que pito un cigarro.   while I puff on a cigar.

<u>Juana</u>   <u>Juana</u>

—*Justamente—dijo Juana*   —Exactly—said Juana—
—*descansá, Rufo, pitando;*   take a rest, Rufo, by smoking
y usté, don Vega, si gusta   and you, Don Vega, if you like
que bailemos de aquí a un rato,   let's dance here for a while;
cánteme alguna cosita   sing me a little trifle
antes de nuestro malambo.   before our fancy footwork.

<u>Vega</u>   <u>Vega</u>

—*¡Pues no, cielo!, ¡en el momento!* —Well, heck no! Not right now!
—*dijo el cantor; y templando*   —said the singer; and tuning up
la guitarra, se dispuso   his guitar, he decided
a darle un picón amargo   to give first a bitter retort
al santiagueño, en desquite   to the Santiago man to avenge
de aquel brutal lechuzazo.   himself of that brutal wisecrack.

A este fin, cantó en seguida   To this end, he began to sing
las coplas de más abajo   the verses found at length below.]
(Ascasubi 1872:123–24).

5. Rioplatense's Current Status

Isolation had been a key characteristic of the Spanish domain in the Plata region, but nearly the opposite was true of the era following independence. By 1900, Buenos Aires had already become "the Paris of the New World" (Hammerton 1916:126).

If the cultural life of the Plata developed upon the Andalusian base, how then did the capitals of Argentina and Uruguay become so thoroughly cosmopolitan? Buenos Aires evolved far beyond its original function as a port of entry; it connected the republic with the European establishment. By the turn of the century, Buenos Aires was the hub of a rail system that linked the landlocked towns (see map on the following page). The capital's resources brought commerce, banking, and finally the international exchange of other great Western cities. Montevideo gained similar fame, if on a smaller scale. Buenos Aires led Latin America as a publishing center. The pre-eminent performers of the Scala theatre often came to the Plata stages to re-enact their parts with the local orchestra and chorus, and European instrumentalists sought to perform there too. And given the climate of their guitar scene, the capital's stages also served to showcase world-class guitarists.

These dimensions of cosmopolitan life gradually came together in the Plata capitals during the 19th century after independence. The development was far from accidental. At that time, there was a concerted effort to overcome the effects of isolation in the new republics. Typically the new presidents sought to bring their republics into the full flow of the economy afforded by the Atlantic, and using the United States as their model, they opened their doors to accommodate immigration from diverse nations, favoring especially the immigrants of northern Europe. Some leaders even expanded their travels to include the U.S. in order to take note of the material progress there as the gap across the frontier was finally closed. They hoped for industrious settlers who would set new standards of living, education, and culture, whether in the capitals or across the wide-open pampa. Argentine President Domingo F. Sarmiento, famed for his 1845 book entitled *Civilization and Barbarism,* was one of those who visited the United States. Then as

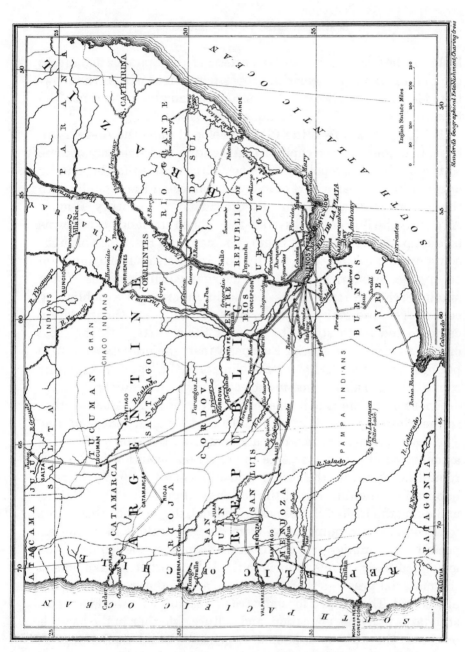

Rail Connections Projected in the 19th C.

a result of the political reform of successive, like-minded presidents, Spanish immigrants were first to respond to the call, but Italians eventually exceeded them in number. Finally prominent minorities of French, British, and other immigrants came in such droves that the old Rioplatense culture was forever levelled and Europeanized—an impact readily apparent in language.

As the modern, cosmopolitan society of the Plata region took shape during the 19th and 20th centuries, *Rioplatense* (the national dialect, as it continued to be spoken) acquired a lowly social status. This was at first a negative reaction to the mid-century regime of gaucho-politician Juan Manuel de Rosas. However, one by one, the presidents who replaced his tyrannical leadership also succeeded in the plan of "modernizing" their countries. During the political environment of modernization, the tide of immigrant foreigners began to fill the cities as well as the countryside. By 1900 the immigrants outnumbered the creoles! As the new, displaced European society became part of the establishment of the land barons, a good many foreigners became institutionalized along with the centers of learning they represented. The obvious experts in language and literature were Spaniards who came to the Plata with ready backgrounds in European philology and the classics. However, as immigrants from another culture, the philologists were quite appalled by the disparity between the spoken language they heard and their own refined Castilian Spanish. So, given the prominent positions in academia which many of them received, they set out upon the considerable project of eliminating all of the divergences between the regional American dialects of Spanish and modern Castilian, inasmuch as they were by then as substantial as those between American and British English. An early, well-known treatise with this purpose was "Advertencias sobre el uso de la lengua castellana..." [Warnings about the use of the Castilian Language...] which Andrés Bello completed in 1834. Some sensed that Spanish, with the decline of Imperial Spain, was on the verge of fragmentation as Latin was after the fall of Rome.

The philologists, as well as the linguists who followed them, remained divided on what to call the spoken language. This was due partly to the fact that many were reluctant even to recognize the spoken language by bestowing upon it the dignity of a name. While there was an effort to study the unique Rioplatense vocabulary as early as the works of Francisco Javier Muñiz (Buenos Aires, 1845) and Daniel Granada (Montevideo, 1890), the philologists were interested in neither the recurring patterns of its archaic syntax nor its Andalusian pronunciation until the 20th century, for they were either unaware of the direct ties between Rioplatense and the ancient peninsular models, or by contrivance, they simply suppressed all mention of them. Whatever their motives, educators of both Argentina and Uruguay brought support to the philological position by attempting to eliminate regionalisms altogether; they taught the Castilian dialect as if it were the only one. But Rioplatense would not die out. Instead, nationalistic surges swept through both the populace and academia that threatened to make it the "national language." Consequently the spoken dialect has ever remained a volatile subject, being charged with political and national overtones. In fact, it has even been called a number of different, pejorative names, as suggested in a short list that goes back only to 1928 (book titles italicized as usual):

Fig. 6   Various Names of the Spoken Dialect
Rossi (1928:49), ...*argentino-uruguayo,* rioplatense
Tiscornia (1930), *La lengua de "Martín Fierro"*
Capdevila (1940), Babel (in *Babel y el castellano*)
Alonso (1943), *Castellano, español, idioma nacional*
Castro (1960), *La peculiaridad lingüística rioplatense*
Borges (1963), El idioma de los argentinos
Rona (1963:102–06), el lenguaje común rioplatense, el español rioplatense, el rioplatense
Malmberg (1966:183), el argentino, el habla popular de Marsilio (1969), *El lenguaje de los uruguayos*
Rosenblat (1971:105), La lengua popular
Malkiel (1972:177), Río de la Plata Spanish (platense)
Guarnieri (1978), *El lenguaje rioplatense*
Pedretti de Bolón (1983), *El idioma de los uruguayos*
Fontanella de Weinberg (1987), *El español bonaerense*

Such a list could be enormous, but the point is sufficiently clear with a few representative examples. Due to the lack of a standardized name for the spoken language, there has been a continuing problem of semantics regarding what to call it. Part of the problem has obviously rested with the political division between Argentina and Uruguay which has inhibited the acknowledgment of pan-linguistic phenomena across the Plata region in the books of some writers. However, most of the confusion has resulted from the extraordinary descriptive vocabulary of the philologists who immigrated to the Plata region and who saw themselves in a prescriptive capacity there. Theirs was a mission of eliminating the "incorrect" speech of the creoles. Consequently in their benevolent tirades against it, they identified the spoken language with countless descriptive adjectives (as our list suggests) and even associated it with occasional metaphors like Capdevila's "Babel"!

The philologists are not entirely to blame, however, for most speakers of Rioplatense still harbor misunderstandings about the language they speak. As Angel Rosenblat and others agree, without doubt, there are indeed two distinct dialects in the Río de la Plata: *"lengua literaria y lengua popular* (1971:105)." Yet ask an informant from that region what is spoken, and the response is always that *castellano* is the language. This is because the speakers of Rioplatense are reluctant to admit to using a different dialect in casual speech. Throughout their education, their teachers have convinced them by quoting philologists (like Bello 1834) that their language habits are absolutely wrong. Their informal speech lacks *cultura,* hence it is crude, undesirable, bad. So in the classroom, as well as in their business and legal documents, even in their personal letters where *tú* is the subject pronoun, the people definitely use only international-style Castilian Spanish that they learn in school. This is about the same as the Spanish taught in the United States, yet without the lingo of the Mexican borderlands. But put two *Porteños* together in Buenos Aires, take "a night out with the boys," live with a family where there are children, go to a movie, to an outlying barrio, or far into the countryside, listen to a popular song, or to the dialogue of literature or of love and the informal dialect is sure to predominate.

The semantic issue ends here: the native speakers of Rioplatense take their language for granted as most people do, and unconsciously they speak what they inherited and share. They are
not concerned about what is and what is not a dialect, and thus,
they care even less about naming it. However, in their personal
communications, they always rely on their own linguistic system
with its archaic syntax, Andalusian pronunciation, and expanded
vocabulary that reflects a synthesis of their myriad cultural experience. These elements come together in intimate surroundings
among speakers of all classes; unavoidably, these same elements of
syntax, pronunciation, and vocabulary impact upon the formal,
Castilian dialect of the Plata region.

With the wisdom of hindsight and using the term Rioplatense
as a noun, Alma Pedretti de Bolón has summed up some recent
developments in the dialect. In one of her books she addresses how
words are added to the vocabulary, as she also reveals how Rioplatense is perceived by both academics and its speakers in general:

> [The middle-class Uruguayan believes that this matter (of
> speaking informally) is a local phenomenon, that it only occurs
> in the Río de la Plata, when actually the branches of linguistic
> science provide ample evidence to demonstrate that the passing
> of words from one language to another is a universal phenom-
> enon and that it has complex motivations which socio-linguists
> can analyze. Spanish, for instance, is indeed receiving exchan-
> ges from other languages which are related to its medieval ori-
> gins, and it has continued to receive foreign terms in spite of the
> so-called "War against Barbarism" which the social elites who
> directed the Spanish linguistic hierarchy of the 18th, 19th, and
> early 20th centuries brought about. Moreover, peninsular
> Spanish in the present is just as plagued with foreign terms,
> particularly Anglicisms, as is *Rioplatense,* and this occurs so
> often that sometimes our language remains more "pure" than
> that of the selfsame peninsular Spaniards] (Pedretti de Bolón
> 1983:117–18).

In the first place, therefore, we would all do well to follow Ms.
Pedretti de Bolón's example of using the term Rioplatense as a
noun in forthcoming references to the spoken dialect of Uruguay

and Argentina. If the dialect were so named, once and for all, some of the foregoing problems could be solved.

In the second place, her perceptive analysis is exemplary of a new school of linguistics. Modern linguists there moved away from the former basis of measuring everything by the standards of literature and the classics; instead they made the scientific method their basis of inquiry. After World War I and during considerable national awareness, Rioplatense's syntax, phonology, and lexicon became the subjects of probing studies in Argentina. After World War II, linguists in Uruguay achieved similar significance with their studies on the voseo (Rona 1967). Scholars are now gathering data in order to identify the speech of the literate class (Siracusa 1977). Prof./Dr. Ana María Barrenechea has continued this pursuit at the National University in a series titled *El habla culta de la ciudad de Buenos Aires*. Multiple volumes are finally available to allow worldwide and simultaneous inquiry on the spoken dialect of Buenos Aires using the same data bank. Dr. Barrenechea's volumes are made up of dialogues that have been carefully transcribed from tape recordings. The last section of the second volume (1987), for example, dedicated to dialogue recorded secretly like "Candid Camera," reveals the voseo as the only form of address in three out of the four interviews.

Now then, with these attitudes and historical developments in mind, we may again apply our understanding of language to the history of the guitar. For the lack of space, let us consider but one example of modern-day familiar speech. The song repertoire remains a wellspring of lyrics worthy of analysis, but among them the language of the tango is notoriously difficult, considering its origins. Its lyrics represent the uneasy mixture of the cosmopolitan vocabulary of around 1900 and regional slang superimposed onto traditional grammatical structures. One example, *¡Che papusa, oí!* even contains slang, a foreign word, and the voseo in its title. Gerardo Matos Rodríguez (composer of *La cumparcita,* a tango well known to us in the north because of its success as an "instrumental") wrote its music. However, Enrique Cadícamo wrote *Che papusa's* lyrics. It was popular on both sides of the Plata, leading to recordings by the likes of Ignacio Corsini, Carlos Gardel, and Julio Sosa. Even so, we shall consider briefly only the 1928,

Odeón recording of Gardel, for it is still available. Odeón released it
again on a cassette entitled *Viejo smoking* [Old Tuxedo] in 1976. It
has Gardel's preferred orchestration; being a guitarist himself, he
sings *Che papusa* as a vocal solo to the accompaniment of his stalwart touring guitarists José Ricardo and Guillermo Barbieri. They
contribute a brilliant introduction, but as usual, they fall into the
background with chordal strumming and motivic fill-ins once the
vocal begins. After the introduction, there are two verses and a
contrasting refrain sung after each one. Here then is the first verse
and refrain from the recording, transcribed with a rhymed translation, to show the Rioplatense dialect of Cadícamo and Gardel:

Fig. 7 *¡Che papusa, oí!*

(Verse 1:) *Muñeca, muñequita, que hablás con zeta*
y que, con gracia posta, batís "mishé";
que con tus aspavientos de pandereta
sos la milonguerita de más chiqué.
Trajeada de bacana, bailás con corte
y por raro snobismo tomás prissé
y que en un auto camba de sud a norte,
paseás como una dama de gran cachet.

(Refrain:) *¡Che papusa, oí! los acordes melodiosos*
que modula el bandoneón.
¡Che papusa, oí! los latidos angustiosos
de tu pobre corazón.
¡Che papusa, oí! como surgen de este tango
los pasajes de tu ayer.
Si entre el lujo del ambiente
hoy te arrastra la corriente,
mañana—te quiero ver.

Hey Papoose, Hear!

(Verse 1:) You're a little babe, so fine, you even say the z;
whenever you put on your wiles, you entice romance.
With all your aspirations, on the tambourine,
you have come to be so chic, in the milonga dance.
When you dress your very best, you dance as if a queen,
though you are a bit aloof, so hasty in your elegance.
When you drive from south to north,
in your plush machine,
you go by to flaunt yourself, as if a dame of confidence.

(Refrain:) Hey papoose, hear! how the tasty chords are sounding
                on the tuneful *bandoneón.*
            Hey papoose, hear! of the restless, anxious pounding
                of your tender *corazón.*
            Hey papoose, hear! just how this tango surges
                to shades of yesterday.
            If among the things you do,
            now the current carries you,
            let me see you—another day.

This is obviously a dancer's monologue directed to his partner; as he sings to her, we cannot help but overhear his impressions. She has so captured his attention that, following his invitation to dance, he gives her the usual shower of compliments (for which Argentines are duly famous) in each verse. In the first, he is impressed with the refinement of her accent: she speaks with the z of Castile rather than with the seseo of Andalusia. *Posta* is Italian, in reference to "putting on" wiles, but most of the classy, complimentary foreign words are either French or Frenchified Spanish variants which rhyme every even line, such as *mishé.* (Mishé= bread loaf in French, but the inside meaning in Plata slang suggests an anxious suitor. Thus "mixing bread" doubles as "stir up a lover.") The others are *chiqué* (= chic), *tomar prissé* (= *tomar prisa,* Sp., to make haste), and *cachet* (*avoir du cachet*= to have distinction).

Che papusa's vocabulary is full of other nuances apart from the French rhymes. *Papusa* and *snobismo* are obviously American-English cognates. Yet *milonguerita* and *bacana* are old Rioplatense slang (meaning, respectively, milonga dancer and ostentatious). *Camba* contains the intentionally reversed syllables of *bacana* (a trick of *lunfardo*—the argot around the port), but the meaning, though coded, is the same. The *bandoneón,* which is mentioned in the refrain, is the button accordion so typical of the tango.

Example 2, below, reveals the musical setting of these lyrics. Although most tango composers notate in 2/4, the transcription casts the many rhythmic subdivisions of *Che papusa* into a more comprehensible appearance in 2/2. After the introduction on the guitars, the melody of the carefree verse remains jovial by leaping on chord tones in the key of C major. Yet as the line develops, the chromatic inflections enhance further its upbeat mood:

Ex. 2 *¡Che papusa, oí!* (Introduction)   Matos Rodríquez/Cadícamo

ñe-ca mu-ñe-qui-ta   q'ha-blás con ze-ta   y   que con gra-cia pos-ta   ba- tís mi-shé

Despite the kaleidoscopic diversity of these lyrics, the verb forms remain consistently uniform, as usual. The conjugations with you as the subject of the verb are in typical dialect: *hablás, batís, sos, bailás, tomás, paseás.* They are all standard forms of the Rioplatense present tense (Fig. 3), and *oí* is the usual imperative (Fig. 5, above). They all imply the use of *vos* as the subject pronoun. Thus, with a single tango verse and its refrain it is possible to reveal some of Rioplatense's widely borrowed vocabulary along with the unerring syntactical forms of the colonial era—those of the archaic voseo—without the infraction of a single rule. The lyrics serve Gardel, the master of emotional expression, as his point of departure, and they serve us as a beginning for understanding the composition. Now to parallel minor and the refrain—an intense, legato entreaty, with a complete change of mood: "Hey papoose, hear!"

Ex. 3 *¡Che papusa, oí!* (Refrain)   Matos Rodríguez/Cadícamo

¡Che pa- pu- sa, oí! los a - cor-des me - lo- dio- sos que mo-du-la'l ban-do-neón

In the rich language of *¡Che papusa, oí!* the pronunciation and syntax are carried over from the colonial epoch, but the polyglot, foreign words are new, owing to the impact of the more recent immigrations to the Plata. Naturally no tango is actual speech, yet this one certainly reflects the two main eras of the spoken dialect. At the same time, this amusing composition and its splendid interpretation would probably meet with immediate rejection on first hearing outside its element. Most Spanish speakers from other parts of the world react negatively to Rioplatense. In this case, they would not take kindly to the mélange of foreign terms they could scarcely understand, and they would dislike Gardel's pronunciation if they were unfamiliar with its origins in Seville. Rioplatense's syntax is of course ridiculous today, sounding like a comedy of errors to foreigners because *vos* was superseded by other forms of *you* some three centuries ago. Worst of all, the good humor, the double meanings, and the character of the slang would be altogether lost on deaf ears. Hence the infamy of Rioplatense, the spoken language in the Paris of the New World:

> *a Buenos Aires, donde es fama universal que se habla el peor*
> *castellano del mundo* (Rosenblat 1971:16)
> [at Buenos Aires, where it is universally known that the worst
> Castilian Spanish in the world is spoken].

But now the reader knows better than to accept such unfounded opinions about Rioplatense, for it is not Castilian. To overcome such mental constructs unfavorably disposed against it, Rioplatense must be defined, and here for the first time in a publication of the Northern Hemisphere: Rioplatense is the widely used but unofficial dialect of the Río de la Plata. It is the same, pre-Golden Age dialect inherited from the predominantly Andalusian conquerors and settlers of that region. The early Rioplatenses were not to be blamed for loyalty or perseverance; despite their initial isolation from Hispania, they preserved their language better than any of their other Hispanic traits—far better than expected for a development of nearly five centuries. To be sure, their language evolved over the course of its existence, but primarily in the aspect of vocabulary, which occurred in two phases. During the colonial era, the lexicon grew with the need to identify the unique elements of their surroundings, so inevitably many of the words came from Amerindian sources. After independence, the vocabulary had to expand again to encompass the cosmopolitan diversity brought by the expatriate Europeans who came into their midst. Yet in spite of this growth in the lexicon, the syntax and pronunciation remained quite constant. Rioplatense thus withstood the infinite transformations imposed upon it by millions of speakers over the course of its history. Therefore, the unofficial dialect of the Río de la Plata can no longer be dismissed in ignorance as "bad Castilian." The spoken language there did not merely stray, uninhibited from the mother tongue like the English of America. It emanated from an earlier source—just like the French of Quebec: it was the language of the conquerors. Since then, without any break in continuity, Rioplatense has remained a viable, expressive, logical dialect of Spanish with wide-ranging levels of respect, a colorful vocabulary, a pronunciation modelled on the Andalusian, and a morphology of historically correct and authentic syntactical forms.

6. Andalusian Culture in the Americas

The implications of this conclusion go well beyond language alone, for, obviously, language is only one of many cultural traits. Ever since the conquest, there were aspects of Andalusian culture in the Río de la Plata, but they were nevertheless difficult to substantiate and to quantify. So for centuries *andalucismo* remained merely an informed opinion that the influence of Andalusia predominated there over that of the other Spanish regions. However, the philologists at Buenos Aires challenged the opinion, and cited linguistic data in support of the opposing view that the Río de la Plata, and indeed the rest of Hispanic America, contained a balanced representation of all fourteen Spanish regions and that one of them could not possibly have predominated such a diverse scenario as the conquest and domination. The fire of the debate was kindled particularly by a student of A. Alonso named Pedro Henríquez Ureña in an article entitled *"El supuesto andalucismo de América (1925)"* [The Alleged *andalucismo* of America]. Naturally this sparked plenty of responses across Hispania, but the debate was never settled until the advent of the extraordinary statistical studies of another of Alonso's students, Peter Boyd-Bowman. He had access to many sources of information, yet paramount among them was the Archive of the Indies in Seville which contained the passport data of all the legal passengers bound for the New World aboard the Spanish fleet. The records bore facts regarding the destination and origin of passengers, their sex, occupation, even the number of children. After decades of painstaking research on the personal data of 40,000 passengers, he concluded that most of the emigrants were indeed Andalusian. The available statistics begin with the period preceding 1519: for example, between 1509 and 1519, precisely 68% of all women in the Spanish fleet were from Andalusia (Boyd-Bowman 1964:Table of Emigration by Regions). For the period of 1520–1539, statistics revealed that 32% of all passengers bound for the Americas were from Andalusia as compared to 16% from Extremadura and 29% from New Castile and Old Castile combined. During the same period, 58.3% of all women emigrating to the Americas were from Andalusia—still more than the total representation of the other thirteen regions put together (Boyd-Bowman 1964:Table VI).

Fortunately Peter Boyd-Bowman was able to focus some of his statistical research directly on the Río de la Plata. By 1539, according to extant documents, a total of 1,088 colonists had arrived there. In fact more than 900 of the total had been a part of Mendoza's original settlement at Buenos Aires. The pioneers of the Plata indeed hailed primarily from Spain, but some came from other parts of Europe. The following summary lists either their native Spanish region or the nationality of the other Europeans:

Andalusia 449 (41.3%), Old Castile 160 (14.7%), New Castile 107 (9.9%), Extremadura 69 (only 6.3%), Portugal 59 (5.4%), Vascongadas 53 (4.9%), León 43 (4.0%), Flanders 25 (2.3%), Italy 25 (2.3%), Galicia 19 (1.7%), Murcia 17 (1.5%), Navarra 10 (0.9%), Asturias 8 (0.7%), Valencia and Baleares 7 (0.6%), France 7 (0.6%), Aragón 6 (0.5%), Catalonia 6 (0.5%), Germany 6 (0.5%), Canary Islands 4 (0.4%), England 4 (0.4%), Greece 2 (0.2%), Córsica 1 (0.1%). Total 1,088, with 130 from outside of Spain or 11.9%! (Boyd-Bowman 1963:188).

Taking Boyd-Bowman's statistics on the Río de la Plata a step further, we could cast them into the typical bar-graph and represent these relative totals visually to emphasize the comparison:

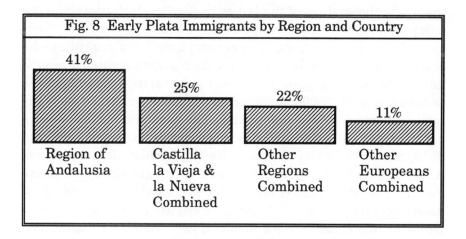

Fig. 8 Early Plata Immigrants by Region and Country

Between 1540 and 1559, 600 new colonists came to the Río de la Plata, and among them were 190 Andalusians. At 31.7% of the total immigration, their numbers still more than doubled the representation of any other Spanish region (Boyd-Bowman 1967:55).

After Boyd-Bowman ended the debate over "the alleged andalucismo," Homero Serís helped to compile its vast bibliography. Therein Serís was able to have the final word. After reviewing and commenting on the literature of *andalucismo,* he suggested the cultural implications of the entire matter:

[Finally, to all of the linguistic discourses adduced by authors in favor of *andalucismo* in America, we will add the following assertion. The traveller that crosses the greater part of the countries of Hispanic America will be able to observe that the Andalusian influence has been exerted, in some measure, not only in the pronunciation, but also in the vocabulary, and moreover in the customs, in the habits, in the whole life. Whoever visits those towns of Hispanic America will contemplate the same houses, the same covered entries, the same patios, the same window grates, the same flat roof, flowerpots, and tiles as in the Andalusian towns, and will notice in the children of the

country the same creative faculty and the same character as
the children of Andalusia] (Serís 1964:688).

To be sure, *andalucismo* also predominated in Rioplatense life,
as many had claimed, but now there was statistical proof of it.
Using Boyd-Bowman's work as a basis, together with the time-
frame provided by the linguistic sources as additional background,
we may begin to consider Argentine and Uruguayan customs well
beyond the linguistic orbit. Significantly, with the heightened perception provided by a sure base of knowledge, we may now regard
the Rioplatense guitar nestled in its proper historical context.

Writers there were already addressing the immense popularity
of the guitar in the 19th century. At that time Domingo Sarmiento
was writing to describe his countrymen of the lower classes as part
of his campaign for the presidency of Argentina. His objective was
to fill the reader with disgust for the despicable cultural habits he
was enumerating, for he was trying to overthrow (with the pen
instead of the sword) the sanguinary dictatorship and methods of
gaucho-politicians the likes of Juan Manuel de Rosas and Juan
Facundo Quiroga. However, as Sarmiento describes the barbarities
of the common man and eventually ties them to these ruthless
leaders, his objective has nearly the opposite effect today than it did
in the 19th century; his detail only sparks our interest and whets
our appetite for more. He likens the guitar player and his milieu to
the *majo* troubador of southern Spain who had been immortalized
in the paintings of Francisco de Goya a generation earlier. At that
time Argentine guitarists possessed both *machismo* and *majismo*
—just like the Andalusian guitarists who were emerging in the
café cantante:

> Guitars are constantly heard at the shop-doors on summer
> evenings; and late in the night, one's sleep is pleasantly dis-
> turbed by serenades and peripatetic concerts....
>   It is well known that the guitar is the popular instrument of
> the Spanish race; it is also common in South America. The *majo*
> or troubadour, the type of a large class of Spaniards, is still found
> there, and in Buenos Ayres especially. He is discoverable in the
> gaucho of the country, and in the townsman of the same class.
> The *cielito,* the dance of the pampas, is animated by the same

spirit as the Spanish *jaleo,* the dance of Andalusia; the dancer makes castanets of his fingers; all his movements disclose the *majo;* the action of his shoulders, his gestures, all his ways, from that in which he puts on his hat, to his style of spitting through his teeth[!], all are of the pure Andalusian type (Sarmiento 1845: 30–31).

B. The Guitar in Popular Culture

Over the Andalusian base, some additional elements of Hispanic culture began to accumulate in the Río de la Plata. The guitar was indeed "the popular instrument of the Spanish race," and it was destined to become the national instrument of the Plata republics, as well. It came initially with the conquerors, and then its presence was reinforced time and again by ties with the rest of Spain as the centuries wore on towards independence.

1. The Serenade

One of the most prominent and delightful uses of the Rioplatense guitar was to accompany the serenade. Even as Sarmiento had claimed in the middle of the 19th century, troubadors still performed widely in the city, towns, or countryside, and their guitars were heard at the shop-doors in the evening or throughout residential areas during the rest of the night. The troubadors, or as he said, *majos* were performing serenades or impromptu concerts. Other Argentines echoed Sarmiento's description, especially inasmuch as the serenade began to show signs of decline by the early 20th century. The ancient serenade had remained typical both as an expression of affection as well as a means of overcoming the boredom associated with the tranquil life of country towns:

[Back then one lived a pristine existence that today can scarcely be imagined....
    Now then, the monotony of that life was only interrupted when several of the young people of the neighborhood would get up a nocturnal procession with the pretense of praising one of the

more celebrated saints, or when some infatuated swain would search for the most effective means of gaining entrance into the home of the object of his amorous intentions.

Thus came the task of looking for the components of the ensemble, which ought to consist of musicians and decisive young men. The former demanded good pay because sometimes they were the ones who suffered abuse as a result of the excursion. For this reason, in order to insure success, young men arranged excursions beforehand. Thus were the serenades organized.

During the remote past in the (Plata) Provinces, the nocturnal visit occurred without prior arrangement; at late hours of the night, one arrived at the selected house, knocked at the door or window, and, once gaining the permission of the owners of the house, began immediately the instrumental part of the performance.

The improvised orchestra consisted of a mandolin and *bandurria* accompanied by the guitar, or sometimes accordion, harp, and violin.

If the family witnessing this special homage accepted it cordially, the serenaders received the most effusive demonstrations of thanks, especially upon the part of the little lady who was the object of the serenade, who also expressed to the swain her amusement or her displeasure. Customarily it happened that the owners of the house would get out of bed and would invite the musicians in for such treats as drinks, *mate,* etc., and finish by returning to bed usually at dawn. This was normal.

Yet sometimes the affair ended in tragedy or in general chaos. (In either case) when the owners of the house did not accept the spontaneous gesture, they made it known immediately to the young men of the musical ensemble by commanding them under threat to go away. If the group did not do so, the residents went on the offensive immediately by throwing as many pieces of junk at them that happened to be close at hand....

This beautiful custom is disappearing in the Provinces. Today, in order to give a serenade, the advance permission must be solicited from the family and then from the police because, if not, all the participants are going to end up in jail] (Contreras 1931:91–92).

In documenting so important and pervasive a practice as the nocturnal serenade in the Argentine Provinces, another reference

is appropriate. What follows is part of an address to the Institute of
Popular Culture in Buenos Aires:

> [The serenade is the nocturnal poem of the interior towns....
> People are sleeping in venturous peace: the young men under
> the vine arbor, as if to find themselves ready to meet the first
> alert of the morning sun; the mother and children inside, but
> with open windows and doors, which liberate the movement of
> the breeze that blows gently against the white sheets, as upon
> the sails of a skiff....
> Then interrupts the nocturnal silence a harmony of strings,
> which, it would seem, is emanating from unknown places and
> is produced by elves with fantastic fingers. The family begins to
> awaken. The music which reaches their ears has such melo-
> dious and penetrating rhythms and the voices are perceived
> with such clarity, that at first it is not possible to identify its
> source because momentarily it is entrancing. It is a serenade
> which appears to conjugate the sounds and essences of the
> night.
> Those who sing, no longer in the stammering manner of surly
> shepherds, but rather in a clear voice and to the steady pattern
> of acoustic instruments, are quite a few young, sun-tanned
> men. They sing as the ancient troubadors, but more than for
> mere delight, they seek the echo of kindred spirits. And at that
> moment, it is said, sometimes a common destiny is begun for
> two lives.
> Once its purpose is completed, the group continues on, with
> uneasy reluctance, ever in search of a dance, a party, an en-
> chantment, of love, and in reality it goes on towards fortune—
> towards glory as an impossible dream.
> The serenade is, above all else, native to Mediterranean cities
> or their environs in some of which remain the archetype of
> customs inherited during the colonial epoch] (Fernández
> 1929:21f).

Although the serenade is often portrayed in the literature about
southern Spain, it would have to date at least as far back as the
troubadors and the minstrels they employed, as well as to either
side of the Pyrenees. But it was an outstanding feature of Golden
Age literature in Spain, which was of course a measure of the lives
and times of its writers.

For Miguel de Cervantes (1547–1616), the serenade and *guitarra* were cohorts in musical persuasion. In his epic *Don Quixote* (Part I, Ch. 51) a certain Vicente de la Roca, a minor protagonist, appeared as a swashbuckling soldier, musician, and poet who improvised poetry to the accompaniment of his guitar. In fact, he strummed it so well that some observers claimed that he made the guitar talk. Most importantly, Vicente gradually conquered his lover's heart by singing lengthy *romances*. As his lady observed them through her open window, night after night, she became convinced to elope with him, to the chagrin of her parents.

In *El celoso extremeño,* Cervantes portrayed another swashbuckling gallant as a musician. This time the guitarist is Loaysa who, among some other pursuits, happens to be a guitar teacher in Seville. One evening he approaches a servant named Luis about taking guitar lessons, but Luis remains indecisive. Loaysa's argument begins with the fact that he has taught many to sing and to dance the divine *zarabanda* to the guitar's accompaniment. But Luis remains reluctant, so Loaysa says—

> *si vos dieseis traza que yo entrase algunas noches a daros lecciones, en menos de quince días os sacaría tan diestro en la guitarra que pudiésemos tañer sin vergüenza en cualquier esquina.*
> [If you would be able to handle my occasional evening visits to give you lessons, in less than fifteen days I would leave you so accomplished on the guitar that we could perform shamelessly on any street corner.]

Loaysa continues the persuasion by comparing the guitar to other instruments of accompaniment. Finally Luis decides to take guitar lessons, after all, in response to the following advice about which instrument to play:

> *El que más a vuestra voz le conviene es el instrumento de la guitarra, por ser el más mañero y menos costoso de los instrumentos.*
> [The most appropriate for your voice is the instrument of the guitar, being both the most clever yet the least difficult of the instruments.]

Cervantes was not the only writer of his day to place the guitar in this context. According to a recent study of some fifty Golden Age *novelas,* the serenade emerged as the foremost characteristic of informal social contact in Spain. According to ancient Spanish customs, a gentleman there was expected to declare his love and prove that it was genuine with an evening serenade:

> It is one o'clock at night. My lady sits at her *reja* [the iron grate covering her window]. Down the street comes a coach containing musicians who have been hired by a gallant *caballero* to entertain his lady. Here begin two torments; first the tuning of the different instruments; and second, the attempt to make them work together in harmony. And more. The music itself may be poor, especially if the musicians have to sing the ballads composed by their employer. If it is a quartette that sings, however, Pedro may excuse himself with Francisco, Francisco with Luis, Luis with Antonio, and Antonio with Domingo. Not only the neighborhood suffered in these serenades. A musician's life was apparently one of very real peril. You could be killed, simply for singing poorly in the street. Or a jealous and temporarily successful rival of your master might charge out of the house at you, madly brandishing his naked sword, and break your guitar. Or another coach with a second musical band might appear if the lady were popular. Should their master attack yours, you were supposed to rally to his defense. You didn't though; you ran. You excused yourself by saying that as your instrument was your means of livelihood, you were leaving to put it in a place of safety....
> What with the late hours, the continuous tuning of instruments, the pitched battles in the street, and the singing of homemade ballads, it would be no wonder if the neighborhood stood solidly for few love affairs. Yet serenades were one of the most acceptable gifts to offer to a lady as a means of winning her favor (Nichols 1952:458–59).

The bibliography on the above-mentioned *novelas,* however, did not include one which had been critical to guitar history—the rather autobiographical *Relaciones de la vida del escudero Marcos de Obregón* [Tales of the Life of Squire Marcos de Obregón] by Vicente Espinel. Although he was born in Ronda, Andalusia in 1550 and educated at Salamanca, Espinel spent most of his life in the larger cities and in the midst of the peninsular ruling class as one of its leading poets and guitarists. He was famed as an innovator: he created the poetic form of the ten-line *espinela;* and the Golden Age poets claimed that it was he who fitted the popular, four-course *guitarra* (a guitar with four pairs of strings) with an extra course. Thus his five-course guitar would reign as the standard guitar of the next two centuries as it surpassed all other plucked strings—most notably the guitarra, vihuela, and lute—in popularity during the Baroque era. But while the *espinela* endured as a poetic medium like the Petrarchan sonnet, whether he actually invented the five-course guitar or not has remained open to question. Miguel de Fuenllana had composed a few pieces with five-line tablature in his monumental vihuela book published in Seville in 1554. The following year Juan Bermudo described several existing tunings for five-course guitar in his Andalusian treatise on the instruments (1555:28v, 97r–98r). Thus, the books of Fuenllana and Bermudo were both published before Espinel had reached his teens and well before he could have invented the five-course instrument destined to cross Europe as the so-called Spanish guitar in the next generation. To make matters worse, some writers for the guitar in the next century, including Nicolão Doizi de Velasco and Gaspar Sanz, were yet perpetuating the myth that Espinel had added the fifth course, in the prefaces of their guitar methods.

> Having taken away from Espinel the honor, as it were, of inventing the instrument, we should not underestimate his role in popularizing it. Cristóbal Suárez de Figueroa, writing in 1615, lists Espinel among the leading performers and composers of the day and particularly associates his name with the guitar and with compositions known as *sonadas* and *cantares de sala.* The second of these terms may simply be a general one, "drawing room songs" perhaps, referring to Espinel's popularity as a composer and performer for musical gatherings in the houses of notables, such as those meetings in Salamanca, Madrid, and Milan mentioned in *Marcos de Obregón* (Heathcote 1977:27).

Repeatedly throughout the book, Marcos de Obregón makes reference to his *sonadas.* In such cases, they were probably mere serenades with an accompanying guitar part for Espinel's elite milieu. In its final section Marcos describes soirées at the residences of Antonio de Londoño in Milan and Bernardo de Clavijo in Madrid. In these he documents interest in the serenade with guitar among the literati and the highest class of his day as he reminds them of the power of music:

> Marcos defends the view that song has lost none of its power to move its hearers to imitate the ideas contained within it. As an example he quotes an incident connected with one of his own *sonadas:* "Break the veins of the passionate breast," which is the first line of Liseo's lament in the "[Monologue Directed to Don Hernando de Toledo]," one of the poems in Espinel's *Diversas rimas.* Such was the intensity of feeling expressed by the performer as he serenaded his beloved that she offered him a dagger to plunge into her breast in imitation of the song. Lope de Vega, in the *Laurel de Apolo,* also pays tribute to effects achieved by Espinel in the performance of the same song. The anecdote may well be apocryphal but it does suggest that many of Espinel's poems were set to music and performed by him in the drawing-rooms—if not beneath the balconies—of the cultured society of the day (Heathcote 1977:28).

2. Music and Conversation: Touchstones of Civilization

The serenade was but one aspect of Spain's popular culture that spread into Europe during the Baroque era. Just as the Italian Renaissance flowed northward into Europe in the 16th century, so did the guitar as an integral component of Spanish culture in the 17th and 18th. What with its near simultaneous consolidation and discovery of America, Spain burst into the limelight as a world power. Then once frequent associations were initiated with Spain during increased international communications beyond the Pyrenees, Europeans inevitably got to know certain aspects of Spanish character. This was a partial result of the new Bourbon dynasty on the Spanish throne, which helped to make fresh ties with central Europe after 1700. The quintessential components of Spain's popular culture were the music and conversation for which Spaniards were best known. In this, the "Spanish guitar," the new fad among all classes of western Europe, was the tangible element, but the intangible involved certain abilities. Back then, elites needed to know the latest games, a little French, how to serenade or dance to the encroaching guitar, and know how to converse on any subject.

In Spain, such specific abilities were evident as far back as the 16th-century courts, for they were certainly associated with the magnificence of the Golden Age. A perfect example was a comedy which was performed before the Queen and Marquis of Valencia in 1524, involving the vihuela. The comedy was a piece by Fernández de Heredia that characterized Valencian social protocol as revealed in its title: *[Colloquium in which is remedied the practice, treatment, and conversations which the ladies of Valencia are accustomed to make, and to have in the visits that they provide one to another]*. The main affair in it has turned out to be rather quiet and uneventful, being limited to petty disputes and preparations until the arrival of a certain Andalusian girl named Catalina and a vihuelist or two:

> She is of a different temperament; she comes from Granada, and is able to restore harmony by her native good-humour and *sal andaluz* [Andalusian salt]. The mistress's hair is done, the reception-room is arranged before the visitors arrive; and then we see the company enter the room and hear their greetings, followed after an interval by the invariable late-comers.
>
> They chatter, play games, dance, and sing *villancicos*. Don Rodrigo, an elegant young man, who speaks Castilian (it is noteworthy that Castilian is already the language of gentlemen), suggests the newest dance, "if only we had a band." Someone offers to play the vihuela, and they begin:

Rodrigo
¿Quieren, pues ay tañedores, que andemos vn contrapás?

[Rodrigo
Would you like, since there are musicians, to go for a *contrapás*?

Señora
¿Contrapás? No per sa fe, que' nell nom se dar maña.

Señora
Contrapás? Not on your life, for I don't know how to manage that one.

Rodrigo
¿Y en la dança de Alemaña?

Rodrigo
And the dance of Germany?

Señora	Señora
Exa, sí.	That one, yes.

Rodrigo	Rodrigo
Pues Ioan, tañe.	Then John, play on.]

So they dance an *Almayne* (as it afterwards came to be called in England) and then arrange to sing in turn—a Portuguese who is present being desperately anxious to show off his powers, which he does at last in a song preserved for us in the [vihuela] book of Luis Milán....

Conversation and music are regarded as the touchstones of civilization; and Juan Fernández de Heredia, the author of this little piece, the friend and contemporary of Luis Milán, has done his best to show, not without a touch of ironic humour, how both the one and the other were made in his time (Trend 1925:9–10).

3. The Spanish Guitar

In 1596 Dr. Joan Carles Amat launched the Baroque guitar officially in a small treatise entitled *Guitarra española....* While his was a five-course, double-strung guitar like Espinel's, Amat set a few precedents of his own. Among them, his book contained the first-published figured bass of the so-called "figured-bass era." He devised or at least notated a numerical system for identifying and performing the twelve major and twelve minor chords, and applied the same theory to some musical examples. He began the examples with a lesson on accompanying the *passeo,* later known as the passacaglia, then continued with the old Renaissance tune *Guárdame las vacas* in all twelve keys by using different combinations of the given chords. Finally he provided a more complex polyphonic example harmonized with the same system (transcribed in Hall 1978). Amat's book was the first of many dedicated to the *Spanish guitar,* so named because the instrument was more popular in Spain than anywhere else.

Meanwhile at the 17th-century court, dancing showed no signs of demise, despite the fact that the Spanish guitar had already replaced the vihuela in the accompaniment. Juan de Esquivel Navarro, a guitarist and dance teacher from southern Spain, went to Madrid in order to study with the best teacher. Yet he claimed to be *vecino y natural de la Ciudad de Sevilla, discípulo de Antonio de Almenda, maestro de dançar de la Magestad de el Rey nuestro* [a citizen and native of the City of Seville, disciple of Antonio de Almenda, dancing master to His Majesty our King].

Esquivel Navarro implied that the guitar was now the typical instrument of the dance studio. The instructor ordinarily taught with it *"llevando la guitarra debaxo del braço (1643:24r)"* [carrying the guitar under his arm], flamenco style. Evidently the guitar was portable enough to be so used in the accompaniment while he played and simultaneously called the steps. He also suggested that two instruments of accompaniment were better than one, even if the two performers happened to be dance instructors:

Y si él que entra es algún maestro, ha de aguardar a que el discípulo acabe de dançar, y luego levantarse y ofrecerle su silla y instrumento, haziendo en ello mucha instancia: lo qual si yo fuera el maestro forastero, no aceptara; y lo que hiziera, fuera sentarme al lado de el maestro, y si hubiera otro instrumento, le tomara y tocara a la par con el otro maestro. Y por esta razón, y por si salta un puente, o cuerda, es mal hecho que el maestro esté en su escuela con un solo instrumento (Esquivel Navarro 1643:32v).
[And if the one who enters is some teacher, he must take care that the disciple first finish dancing, then afterwards rising and offering to (the visiting teacher) a chair and instrument, he is to be treated cordially. If I were the visiting teacher, I would decline this gesture, but what I would do would be to seat myself alongside the teacher, and if another instrument were available, I would take it and play it along with the other teacher. So for this reason, as well as in the case of breaking a bridge or a string, it is a bad thing for a teacher to be in his school with only one instrument.]

Yet even as Esquivel was publishing his book, the guitar was becoming rather well known outside of Spain. The Italians were already using it to accompany their own dances, but they were now taking the trouble of notating some of the new repertoire of *pasacalles* and Spanish plebeian dances that were circulating for the *chitarra spagnola* [Spanish guitar] as they called it. Moreover,

Spanish guitarist Luis de Briceño had found permanent patronage
at Paris. In the preface of his book published there with aristocratic
support in 1626, he summed up the guitar's musical utility and
social significance. Briceño justified the use of the guitar in several
contexts for his patroness as follows:

> *Muchos ay señora mía que se burlan de la guitarra y de su son.*
> *Pero si bien consideran hallaran que la guitarra es un instru-*
> *mento el más fauorable para nuestros tiempos que jamás se bió.*
> *Por que si el día de oy se busca el ahorro de la bolsa y de la pena,*
> *la guitarra es un theatro verdadero deste ahorro. Demás desto*
> *es acomodada y propia para cantar, tañer, dançar, saltar, y*
> *correr, baylar, y zapatear. Ruando con ella cantando y repre-*
> *sentando mil amorosas pasiones con su ayuda.*
> [There are many, My Lady, who make fun of my guitar and its
> sound. Yet if they would but consider carefully, they would find
> that the guitar is the most favorable instrument which has ever
> come to light in our times, because today if one looks for saving
> out-of-pocket expenses and trouble, the guitar is a veritable
> theatre of savings. Besides, in this, it is accommodated and ap-
> propriate for singing, playing, dancing, jumping, running, and
> even the ball or *zapateo;* moreover strolling with it, singing and
> representing a thousand amorous passions with its help.]

Notwithstanding its many strengths, the decisive factor in the
permanence of the guitar at court was Louis XIV's endorsement
of it. He had been a royal amateur of the guitar since youth, so
naturally when he moved into the downtown palace of the Louvre,
he surrounded himself with the best guitarists of the age. Thereafter the guitar was as typical among the royal amateurs as a
minuet was in the symphony. As Louis XV maintained the guitar's prestige at the country residence of Versailles, women took to
it as much as men, to the extent that "you were as sure to see a
guitar on a lady's toilet as rouge or patches," according to the voice
of experience, an attaché of the French court in London (Hamilton
1713:II, 26).

In 18th-century Europe, none of the guitar's social utility was
lost. Amateur musicians, whether in Spain or beyond, continued
their informal study of the guitar because it guaranteed entertainment and social connections. For instance, Don Diego's most

valued skills were learned not in the University of Salamanca's classrooms, but rather (as he was carrying on there after Espinel) in its extra-curricular activities:

> When night fell I would be the first to turn up at dances, weddings or whatever other jollification offered, entertaining the company.... My range of comic and eccentric songs I accompanied on the guitar. I danced trippingly and with an air all the Spanish dances, now with castanets, now again to the guitar, and in others showed my prowess over sword and buckler.... In the end I forgot my Latin, my textbooks, the miserable rudiments of logic I had acquired so stumblingly, a good part of my Christian doctrine and all the modesty and reserve my upbringing had given me. In exchange I turned out a notable dancer, a good *torero,* a tolerable musician, and all in all a polished and daring rascal (Torres Villarroel 1743:72).

During the middle of the 18th century, Beaumarchais went to Seville in order to experience firsthand that same popular culture. As a result, he based both of his comedies, *The Marriage of Figaro* and *The Barber of Seville,* on the legend of the ultimate rascal, Don Juan and his environment which of course had to include the guitar. Mozart and Lorenzo da Ponte saw to it that the guitar's prominence was maintained in their version of *The Marriage of Figaro.* Right from the start—in his opening solo (Act I, Scene 2)—Figaro is portrayed as rather well versed in "the touchstones of civilization." He plans to use his talents in an attempt to beat the Count (the amorous villain) at his own game. Left alone on stage, Figaro devises a clever revenge that will ensnare the Count who has just made a pass at his fiancée Susanna. Before the audience, Figaro rehearses the sub-plot of offering to play his guitar for the Count, or better yet, like Esquivel Navarro (1643:13v), to teach him the *capriole,* the latest, popular dance at his own studio, downtown. He will tempt the Count to hone his skills as a predator:

Se vuol ballare, signor contino,	If you would like to dance my Lord,
il chitarrino le suonerò.	On my guitar, I'll play you a chord.
Se vuol vinire nella mia scola,	If you would come to my dance studio,
la capriola le insegnerò.	I will teach you the *capriole.*

The next appearance of the guitar in *Figaro* is in Act II, Scene 3, but this time it is in the Countess's dressing room, no less! The Countess and her maid Susanna are presently discussing the Count's latest amorous pursuits whereupon the Count's page-boy, Cherubino shows up in order to provide some additional particulars for their case against his master. However—pleasure before business: preceding this inquisition, the Countess asks him to sing his latest composition to the accompaniment of *her* guitar. But the young Cherubino is so shy that he is overcome by reluctance. He is unable to deliver their serenade, so she begs Susanna to accompany him:

> *Prendi la mia chitarra e l'accompagna*
> [Take my guitar and accompany him.]

Encouraged with all their rapt attention, Cherubino finally gives in to the persuasion and reveals his innermost feelings as he sings his naïve little solo which Susanna accompanies:

> *Voi che sapete che cosa e amor...*
> [You who know what love is....]

Naturally the audible accompaniment is played by the orchestra. Just as in Figaro's first solo with pizzicato accompaniment, the orchestral strings imitate the sounds of the guitar, but this time with arpeggios of 16th notes.

Therefore, serenading with the guitar was only part of the social scene that caught on in western Europe during the 17th and 18th centuries. The Spaniards gave the Europeans a different way of getting together, a new pretense for meeting, or as it were, a method for socializing. If they needed to make social contact, then the evening serenade was in order for the initial meeting, but all hoped it would not be the only one. If the serenade went well, music and conversation would continue to be "the touchstones of civilization" in subsequent meetings. For even as Sarmiento and Briceño implied, the serenade synchronized with other "peripatetic concerts," whether indoors or out, including strolling performances, dances, songs, and instrumental pieces all for the entertainment of those present. Music was the conversation-piece in the absence of others, and the mere possession of a guitar was enough of a pretense for meeting. Sarmiento characterized the serenaders as youthful *majos;* they were the amateur musicians or their audience who, often disguised to conceal an aristocratic identity, could masquerade "indiscriminately" and make classless associations in the countryside, detain themselves in secluded areas of the villas or palaces of the elite, or stroll, guitar in hand, through the downtown parks and streets—*ruando* as Briceño called it. This scene was often recorded in the early paintings, especially the cartoons for tapestry, of Francisco de Goya in Spain, or in the landscapes of Louis XV's milieu of Versailles by Jean Antoine Watteau, for the guitar was in vogue, and especially at court. This was all made possible by the fact that there were as many women posing as guitarists as men, so the guitar was a subject that every courtier had to know intimately as an amateur (Pinnell 1980:I, 94, 138–42). With the abundance of European court records and supportive iconographical evidence, it has not been difficult to trace the presence of the guitar among the European aristocracy as a whole. Although the subject of Spanish popular culture inevitably entails the mere personal affairs of the elite (any one of which would be inconsequential) the mass of information focused on the subject is so great and so deep that it has yet to be fathomed, for the guitar at court was an entire movement, a way of life for young aristocrats across western Europe.

On the other hand, the guitar's social utility was not limited to a particular class. Records have indeed remained scarce or at least less accessible for documenting the guitar among the lower classes. Nevertheless, the guitar itself and its repertoire had low-class associations from the beginning. As the guitar acceded to the pinnacle of popularity in Europe, it replaced other, more aristocratic string instruments. During its development in Spain, for instance, the *guitarra* superseded the *vihuela* according to the dictionary that Sebastián de Covarrubias published in 1611:

[*Guitarra*. An instrument well known, and practiced much to the detriment of music; previously the vihuela was played, an instrument of six, and occasionally more courses. The guitar is a small vihuela in size, and in the number of strings because it has

no more than five strings, and some are of only four courses.]
[*Vihuela.* The musical and secular instrument of six courses of
strings.... Up until the present, this instrument has been most
esteemed, and there have been excellent musicians on it; but
after guitars were invented, there are but few who dedicate
themselves to the study of the vihuela. It has been a great loss
because every kind of plucked music was intabulated on it; and
now the guitar is no more than a cowbell, so easy to play, especially in the strummed style, that there is no stable boy who is
not a musician on the guitar.]

With the influx of Spanish popular culture at the British court,
the fashion of the guitar contributed to the demise of the lute, as reported regretfully by William Turner in 1697:

The Lute is not wholly laid aside, but within this 20 or 30 Years
much neglected, to what it was formerly, notwithstanding the
great Improvement of this Instrument among us, within a
hundred Years, by reason of the diversity of Tunings received
from France.... The Fine easie Ghittar, whose Performance is
soon gained, at least after the brushing way, hath at this present
over-topt the nobler Lute. Nor is it to be denied, but that after the
pinching way, the Ghittar makes some good work (Tilmouth
1957:58).

Now then, if the guitar had some low-class appeal, so did its
repertoire, at least among the Spanish dances which the guitarists
exported over the Pyrenees. Lope de Vega summarized the Spanish social context of the repertoire twice in 1621. In two comedies
that year, he mentioned a number of dances as part of the wild,
popular entertainment of his times; accordingly, the following
bailes were often heard in the populace: the *vacas, folías, canario,
villano, Conde de Claro, zarabanda, chacona,* and the *Ay, ay, ay*
(Cotarelo y Mori 1911:180–84). Most of the Italian Baroque guitar
books contained *pasacalles* and such Spanish dances as the *chacona, folía,* or *zarabanda.* The *pasacalle* was a simple theme for
continuous variations. It served guitarists in two ways: either as an
etude for learning to play, or (perhaps originally) as a strolling
piece by name (*pasa*= walking, *calle*= street). Among the many
low-brow dances in Spain, the *chacona, folía,* and *zarabanda* were

those which had considerable impact in the rest of Europe (Hudson 1982). Initially they were all wild, sensual dances, and largely improvised. The guitarists who were accompanying the voice began to develop them into instrumental solos, some of which they notated. Then with the spread of the new repertoire and once guitarists began to perform them north of the Pyrenees, keyboard and ensemble composers also took an interest in them and refined them yet further. As stylized dances, the so-called chaconne, folies, and sarabande, became integral in the era's international suite. By 1700, at least one of the three had to be included in a solo suite to represent Spain. In the 18th century, while the guitar continued unabated in the suite and among courtly dilettantes, the precedent remained for its use among the other classes. Beaumarchais summarized the guitar's social impact in Seville, as staged in Mozart and da Ponte's *Figaro:* to be sure, Figaro had definite upper-class aspirations, though unable to document his parentage, and the Countess had her own guitar; but Susanna and Cherubino performed on it just as well, despite the fact that they were servants.

The impact of Spanish popular culture in Europe must be understood, at least as much as it involved the guitar, because the instrument arrived in the Río de la Plata with all this excess baggage. The guitar was already the national instrument of Spain by 1600 and thereafter known as the "Spanish guitar" throughout most of Europe. Due to its social utility and wide, even aristocratic acceptance, the guitar caused the unfortunate decline of other instruments. It came to the Plata with all of these associations: the Rioplatense guitar emanated from this same genetic and cultural endowment. But in the Plata, there were no other incumbent instruments to "lay aside," to "over-top," or to supersede. Moreover, neither linguistic nor other social barriers impeded the guitar's acceptance. Thus unhampered, the guitar was at once the national instrument of the Rioplatense colonists as well as the tangible component of their social affairs for centuries prior to the advent of a divided musical establishment. The guitar was always appropriate at the social extremes because it commanded dignity and respect. Not until the period of independence did the renowned classical school finally separate from the popular medium, which had given rise to the guitar in the Río de la Plata in the first place.

4. Summary and Conclusions

At a prominent quincentennial conference, the young Mexican musicologist Antonio Corona posed a rhetorical question as his point of departure for a lecture on the guitar music of Veracruz. "Whether you are from Mexico or not, it does not matter; your answer will be the same either way. What popular song is most typical of Mexico? Your answer would have to be *Cielito Lindo;* everybody knows it. But note how the Mariachi version contains a verse about the Sierra Morena [Range of Brown Mountains]."

De la Sierra Morena,	[Down from the Sierra Morena,
Cielito Lindo, vienen bajando	My Dearest, are coming to your land,
un par de ojitos negros,	a pair of dark black eyes,
Cielito Lindo, de contrabando.	which are a shipment of contraband.]

This early 18th-century verse is typical except for the reference to the Sierra Morena: Mexico has none, for it is the mountain range over Andalusia! Thus, a point well taken. In an upbeat, even humorous way, Corona was able to call for an assessment of a very serious matter—Andalusia's impact on the music of Mexico.

Likewise the Andalusian impact is an appropriate point of departure for any study involving the history, culture, or arts of Hispanic America. *Andalucismo* is just as applicable to the Plata as any other part of the Hispanic New World.

Now it is easy to see, from an informed vantage point, that the original cultural mainstream among those pioneering Plata settlers was Andalusian. But for those who lived through the complex of colonial and viceroyal life there, without the benefit of hindsight or retrospect and isolated from the rest of the civilized world, the extent of the Andalusian impact was always taken for granted. On the one hand, nobody—after due consideration—ever doubted the importance of the *Región de Andalucía* in the Hispanic American colonies. After all, somehow Seville, its capital had monopolized both the Columbian Exchange and the gubernatorial seat of the "Indies." However, some authorities insisted, with good reason, that Andalusian culture, despite its importance, was impossible to document or to quantify. On the other hand, there were other authorities who argued the contrary—sometimes to excess, that Andalusia *predominated* over the other thirteen Spanish regions in its social/political impact. As early as 1845 for instance, Domingo Sarmiento, who eventually became the Argentine President, proclaimed that such was indeed the case. His basic political agenda was to suppress the old Andalusian "barbarities" in an attempt to establish a new social order (his own, of course). He described the typical, young Argentine of his times as the perfect likeness, the literal, uncouth, "spittin' image" of the Andalusian *majo:*

> all his ways, from that in which he puts on his hat to his style of spitting through his teeth, all are of the pure Andalusian type.

Such conjecture, no matter how well founded in truth, such excessive, fanatical, or condescending claims led to a long, heated debate on the "supposed" Andalusian predominance. The leadership of the opposition came from Amado Alonso, a Spanish linguist who came first to direct the Institute of Philology at Buenos Aires then to lecture at Harvard University, and from his disciples. Their point of view was that all of Spain was represented in the genetic/ cultural mix of Hispanic America, and that one *Región* could never have predominated over the others in such a complex array of social events. They drew their well-publicized evidence from the divergent linguistic patterns of American Spanish as well as some of the archival documents of Seville in support of their demographic studies. The debate raged on until Peter Boyd-Bowman inherited their project on archival documents led by Pedro Henríquez Ureña. The latter had begun a thorough investigation of all the extant passport data in Seville as Alonso's most outspoken advocate against *andalucismo* (Malkiel 1972:40). Hence, when Boyd-Bowman brought the project to conclusion in the 1960s, the results were all the more shocking. In two separate volumes, he summarized minute statistical data for 40,000 passengers who boarded the Spanish fleet en route to the New World during the 16th century. He documented their backgrounds as well as their New World destinations to settle the issue once and for all. His statistics accounted for the continuous, indisputable Andalusian

predominance in not just one but all the Hispanic colonies of the
Americas. Thus by simple majority alone, the Andalusian provincials set the stage for subsequent developments throughout the
Hispanic New World. Moreover, the Andalusians, notably those of
Seville, had an emotionally charged, assertive style of their own,
and this too became a factor in the beginnings of the Hispanic
settlements, which included such extremes as *Semana Santa* and
the bullfight. The rule of Madrid levelled the *andalucismo,* replacing it with Castilian culture, where the viceroyalties prospered.

To be sure the early settlers of the Plata were predominantly
Andalusian (41.3% by 1539; 31.7% from 1540 to 59), yet as their
colony grew they became more and more independent, if separated from the rest of Hispania, not to mention Western civilization. Lacking the riches of the other parts of America, the citizens
living around the Plata ports suffered neglect and trade restrictions, for they belonged to the southernmost, down-under colony of
the New World. Indeed, it was the farthest from the Columbian
Exchange, and it was ruled from the Viceroyalty of Peru, i.e., from
across the Andes! While the other viceroyalties were beginning to
flourish during the Golden Age, the Plata territory remained insignificant from either political perspective or economic expediency.
Finally by the time the Golden Age had come and gone, the court
designated the Río de la Plata as a viceroyalty unto itself in 1776 in
an attempt to monitor the contraband export of hides and tallow.
For the first time in two and a half centuries of isolated, internalized development, the Plata had direct, regular communication
with Spain. Plata citizens could finally claim their own viceroy as a
representative of the crown and a retinue of specialized officials in
their service. Even so, now that the direct influence of the court
seemed inevitable, it was too late to be of any enduring consequence: the liberation of the Plata republics was only a generation
away. Starting in 1806, British troops invaded Montevideo and
Buenos Aires. An ad-hoc army comprised largely of Plata residents routed first the British insurgence and then, within the
decade, the entire Spanish domination! Thus Latin America's most
Andalusian quarter launched the first successful advances towards independence and eventual liberation from Spain.

*   *   *   *   *

The guitar arrived in the Río de la Plata as part of the Spanish conquest. Thus the guitar's development there cannot be understood outside of the conservative context in which it was the icon of Hispanic identity. Divorced from the ties of this social context, the Rioplatense guitar is incomprehensible; with them, the guitar is the national instrument.

Initially the conquest was military, yet if it was to endure, it also had to be cultural. The ensuing social and political institutions served to reinforce the newly asserted power of Catholic, Imperial Spain. As already demonstrated, the military conquest of the Plata was a powerful one, indeed, if barely won against considerable odds. It was a complex, initial offensive set against innumerable native inhabitants. Like the gradual settlement of the North American frontier, it was centuries in the making. However, the cultural conquest that came with it was not any less significant or enduring; on a daily, hourly basis, the language, religion, point of view, values, and artistic expressions either reaffirmed the military conquest or remained in exile from the dominant society.

Throughout the Golden Age, the Río de la Plata endured as a bastion of conservative Andalusian culture among all classes. The Hispanic identity (in all of its genetic and learned appearances) was of course indispensably prerequisite to social mobility, let alone being part of the ruling class. But Andalusian, not merely Hispanic culture was maintained out of the zeal to conform in the Rioplatense colony. Linguistic research has provided incontrovertible evidence that the other Hispanic colonies gravitated toward the norms imposed by the learning, necessity, and rule of the Golden Age. The better the communications with the Castilian court at Madrid, the more the colonies grew towards the model. However, many of these changes never became effective in the Río de la Plata during the first two and a half centuries of its development because it was so isolated. Indeed, even among the gauchos, the most independent, least educated contingent of the Hispanic population, out on the pampa where the risk of dissolution of the Hispanic character was greatest, it prevailed. F.M. Page, a 19th-century professor at Bryn Mawr College marvelled at how the Spanish character endured over the centuries in the Plata region;

he published the following first-hand observations on the gaucho and his habits:

> Talking and singing are the social pastimes he most delights in. In his conversation he is vivacious and ready, and his language, vivid, voluble and picturesque, borrows similes and metaphors from surrounding life. It is stocked, moreover, with quaint sayings of native origin, and possesses a fair sprinkling of those enchanting Spanish proverbs which the great Sancho Panza employed with such striking effect.... The Gaucho is alert, quick at repartee, and guitar in hand, displays a remarkable ability for improvisation. His crude aesthetic notions and correct ear teach him to detect at once anything like incongruity or discordance. It is probably due to this characteristic that the Spanish language has preserved itself with singular purity over vast regions of territory entirely cut off from educational centres or means of literary perpetuation (1893:22).

Another conservative factor of the region was religion. Unlike its U.S. counterpart, the Plata colony had but one Church, as in medieval Europe. Being Christian was an inseparable component in the Hispanic identity, so every member of Plata society cultivated a devotion to it. Even the less faithful and agnostics were obliged to pay homage at the pantheon for sake of appearance. Although the Catholic orders certainly provided missionaries to proselytize officially as in the Jesuit missions, each and every citizen of the Plata carried the cross to the heathen. Just as in Spain, the infidels had to convert or exile themselves in front of the new order. Obviously the religious conquest continued Ferdinand and Isabella's project of reconquering Spain. The Reconquest came to a close officially in 1492 at Granada, but their project endured (perhaps ingenuously) in the minds of Rioplatense colonists, even across the plains of the interior:

> [They are the descendants of those rough Spanish adventurers who took root on the American plains.... Those who serve today, there in the pampas, fighting against the Indian, in the front line of Argentine civilization, are those who fought upon the mesas of Castile and Aragón against the Moor] (Unamuno 1894:III).

Rioplatense, the living, spoken language of all classes in the Río de la Plata, remains a fascinating microcosm of Plata history. The *lengua nacional* embodies evidence of the Plata culture's development since 1536. Even so, it has only been studied on location with empirically synchronic articles since the middle of the 20th century, enabling diachronic/geographic surveys of it to be published subsequently such as those of the Argentine and Uruguayan references listed below. Thus a precise, uncompromised spectre of what was spoken is finally beginning to take shape. Nevertheless, Rioplatense remains scarcely understood in the north: although its vast literature is taught regularly in our university curricula (one fourth of Englekirk's 1968 textbook), there is not a single complete text on Rioplatense per se published in the Northern Hemisphere.

In the absence of an accessible linguistic study for reference in our midst, we have no remedy but to summarize the main characteristics of the Rioplatense dialect here and now:

1) Its pronunciation, like the *seseo*, conserved the sounds of the Andalusian conquerors more precisely than any other Hispanic American dialect.

2) The once-standard syntax of the *voseo* (the use of *vos* as a pronoun with archaic conjugations, as in Figures 3–5) survived as the main form of address among all people. The voseo's conjugations served millions of speakers since the first settlement of 1536. The grammar of the voseo thus endured innumerable transformations over the course of five centuries without change.

3) Rioplatense's vocabulary was so rich that its new words were adopted but slowly into the lexicon of the Real Academia Española, owing initially to the unique Rioplatense flora, fauna, and other circumstances of its context, then to the Italian words of the immigrants of the 19th century, and finally to the French and English words of imported techno-culture in the 20th century.

4) Despite the enormous front of opposition established by the foreign philologists in the Plata and their followers, Rioplatense has never been an incorrect form of speech but rather the most authentically preserved composite of Hispanic traits to have survived in the region. Neither the prosperous Golden Age of Spain nor its new official dialect were ever experienced in the Plata.

Thus its citizens cannot be blamed, any more than the French of Quebec, for perseverance in maintaining their original language.

5) Rioplatense never was Castilian. The norms and official mandates emanating directly or indirectly from the Castilian court of Madrid were neither successful in levelling the old, original Spanish of the Plata region nor sufficient in replacing it with the newer, official Castilian dialect in everyday speech.

6) Quite simply, Rioplatense has ever remained the pre-Golden Age Hispanic dialect of the Plata with an enriched vocabulary.

Today, examples of Rioplatense can be found in the portrayal of intimate dialogue. Thus, gauchesque poetry and novels provide plenty of fascinating literary sources (de Gregorio de Mac 1967). Song lyrics sometimes contain typical dialogue as well, especially the early tangos. Later on, however, once the new tango began to catch on in Paris, the U.S., and Latin America, its lyricists appealed directly to the international audience by avoiding the voseo and by using the more accessible lyrics of cosmopolitan Spanish. For a movie with obvious Rioplatense syntax at the very beginning, see the 19th-century tragedy called *Camila* (Buenos Aires, 1984). In it a lady descends from a stagecoach after a long overland trip, whereupon she greets her relatives. To her little granddaughter, whom she has not seen for some time, she says in the usual way—

"Yo a vos no te conozco.   "I don't recognize you at all.
¿Cómo te llamás?....   What is your name?....
Decíme...."   Tell me...."

Language was but one, if perhaps the most obvious Andalusian cultural trait brought to the Americas. Toponymy was another. Place-names of a region have often revealed origins or at least cultural ties to an older society, as for example the terms New York or New Jersey. Likewise the conquerors brought Hispanic place-names to Latin America, as in the case of the viceroyalties: New Spain was the designation for the viceroyalty ruled from present-day Mexico City; New Granada, for the one ruled from Bogotá. However, it was the territory of Córdoba, Argentina that was designated the *New Andalusia*:

*En el día 6 de julio de 1573...se fundó la ciudad de Córdoba de la
Nueva Andalucía* (Levillier 1926:II, 396).
[On the day of 6 July 1573...was founded the City of Córdoba of
the New Andalusia.]

      *   *   *   *   *

The conquerors and settlers of the Plata brought along, in the
assortment of their inherited genetic and cultural traits, the guitar. As soon as it arrived, it was the foremost icon of their heritage.
"The Spanish guitar," as it was called simultaneously in Europe,
was already the "national instrument" of the Plata colony.

Music and conversation were traits that had already been "the
touchstones of civilization" amongst the Iberian aristocracy at
least as far back as the 16th century (Trend 1925:10). Aristocratic
music with the vihuela entailed both solo playing and the accompaniment of dance or song. During the next century in Seville,
Cervantine character Loaysa taught guitar and guitarist Esquivel
Navarro taught dancing while the Spanish guitar invaded Europe
along with a new popular culture. In the 18th century, Torres
Villarroel nearly failed at the University of Salamanca because he
became so enmeshed in its popular culture. Ultimately, if Beaumarchais were any judge of Spanish character, he gave the guitar
a prominent position in his comedies set in Seville. Mozart and da
Ponte reaffirmed this prominence in their version of *The Marriage of Figaro.* In fact, Figaro's first aria depicted him as a guitarist, just like Loaysa, and as dance teacher in his own studio, like
Esquivel Navarro—and they all hailed from Seville, of course. Not
less significant in *Figaro,* the female amateur guitarists got equal
billing with their male counterparts, thus equating the opera with
history. The Countess kept her own guitar, as usual, in her dressing room. But since she never actually played it on stage, the
implication was that it was either for her own intimate use or she
kept it there in case of emergency (in order to loan it to unexpected
visitors who came to call on her in the privacy of her bedroom).
Whatever her motives, it was finally her chamber maid (and
Figaro's fiancée) Susanna who had to accompany Cherubino's
tender love song, *Voi che sapete.*

Understandably, then, with this extraordinary pan-social precedent, music and conversation would flow into the Río de la Plata, equally among men or women of the Spanish immigrant population. If the Spanish popular culture was interesting enough to become a musical and social trend in the non-Hispanic courts of western Europe, just imagine how it caught on, during the same time frame, in the Andalusian colony of the Plata! As we shall see in the succeeding parts of our study, the guitar continued to function in the elite salons of the 18th and 19th century, as well as in middle-class entertainments there. It even appealed to the vagabonds of the countryside: "talking and singing" were the preferred social pastimes of the gaucho according to Page. British visitor William MacCann noted that the gaucho's "pleasures consist in visiting amongst friends on the Sabbath-day, together with dancing...(1853:I, 47)."

The serenade and dances of Spain were imported into Europe and America, and guitarists had no small part in the matter. The four-course *guitarra* was the standard popular guitar up to the 16th century, according to Bermudo's Andalusian treatise on the instruments. Yet as he was writing at mid-century, there was already a five-course guitar that was increasing in size and popularity such that it had begun to replace other plucked instruments in its trajectory of becoming the national instrument of Spain for the performance of serenades, songs, and dances. The music and performances of Vicente Espinel were remembered as outstanding examples on the new guitar of the Golden Age. Amat's book was the first written specifically for the "Spanish guitar." As it gained popularity in Paris for accompanying the new popular repertoire according to Briceño, the "serenade and peripatetic concerts" with it were already widespread generally in Hispanic America and specifically in the Plata region, according to Domingo Sarmiento, the eventual president of Argentina. The scenes in the Plata where guitarists introduced these serenades, dances and other pieces were either at the select few aristocratic residences or, for the other classes, at the many local dwellings and sundry shops.

Throughout the Río de la Plata, the guitar was certainly foremost among all of the Hispanic cultural icons in the category of music and entertainment. When the guitar came into the colony, it was just becoming known as the national instrument of Spain. Sarmiento contended, as early as 1845, that this was also its natural legacy in the Plata. Time and again innumerable followers reiterated his claim as, for example, in the words of Juan Rómulo Fernández:

[The guitar is called the national musical instrument...and today it has clear possession of the Argentine soul] (1929:24).

A few years later, Segundo Contreras dedicated his last chapter to the "instrumento nacional: la guitarra (1933:109)."

At the time of these pronouncements, the guitar enjoyed such high esteem in Buenos Aires and Montevideo that it was beckoning the major European classical guitarists. Miguel Llobet, Andrés Segovia, Emilio Pujol, and other notables established themselves there, with residences on either side of the Plata. In fact during his sojourn, Pujol confirmed the former pronouncements regarding the guitar as the national instrument; yet with his characteristic eloquence, he was able to sum up why this was so:

[Without doubt, this must have been what brought the Spanish guitar to its second country. The original Andalusian colony, with its genuine guitar scenes, was spread across all the virgin territory of the Plata, carrying its vihuelas to all parts as well as into the dwellings of Indians and Christians alike. From there was born the fervor which made it the national instrument] (Pujol 1930:39).

These cursory assessments of the Rioplatense guitar compel us to study the nature and the extent of its use in detail. The guitar became, according to European and American authorities, the national instrument there because of its pervasive use in Rioplatense society. Were it not employed by young and old, bond and free, rich and poor, male and female alike, whether for artistic purposes or the rowdiest entertainment and points in between, enfin throughout the entire social spectrum like Rioplatense, the national language, it could scarcely have achieved prominence as the national instrument. What remains now is to probe these specifics and particulars of the guitar's evolution.

5. References Cited in Part II

A. Language and Linguistic Examples

Alonso, Amado
   1943   *Castellano, español, idioma nacional: Historia espiritual de
          tres nombres, cuarta edición.* Buenos Aires: Losada.

Ascasubi, Hilario
   1872   *Santos Vega o los mellizos de La Flor: Rasgos dramáticos de
          la vida del gaucho en las campañas y praderas de la República
          Argentina (1778 a 1808).* Paris: P. Duport. [New edition with
          reviews and biographical notes in two volumes.] Buenos Aires:
          Editorial Sopena, 1939.

Barrenechea, Ana María, ed.
   1987   *El habla culta de la ciudad de Buenos Aires: Materiales para
          su estudio.* Instituto de Filología y Literaturas Hispánicas
          "Dr. Amado Alonso," Tomo 2. Buenos Aires: Facultad de
          Filosofía y Letras, Universidad Nacional de Buenos Aires.

Bello, Andrés
   1834   "Advertencias sobre el uso de la lengua castellana, dirigidas
          a los padres de familia, profesores de los colegios y maestros
          de escuela," *El Araucano* (Santiago, Chile; 13 and 20 Dec. 1833,
          3 and 17 Jan. 1834, 28 Mar. 1834). Republished with prologue,
          notes, and index by Balbanera Raquel Enríquez. La Plata:
          Ministerio de Educación de la Provincia de Buenos Aires, 1956.

Borello, Rodolfo A.
   1969   "Para la historia del voseo en la Argentina," *Cuadernos de
          Filología* (Buenos Aires) III, 25–42.

Borges, Jorge Luis y José Edmundo Clemente
   1963   *El lenguaje de Buenos Aires.* Buenos Aires: Emecé.

Boyd-Bowman, Peter
   1963   "La emigración peninsular a América: 1520 a 1539," *Historia
          Mexicana* (Mexico City) XIII, 165–92.

   1964   *Indice geobiográfico de cuarenta mil pobladores españoles de
          América en el sigo XVI, Tomo I: 1493–1519.* Bogota: Instituto
          Caro y Cuervo.

   1967   "La procedencia de los españoles de América: 1540–1559,"
          Historia Mexicana (Mexico City) XVII, 37–71.

   1968   *Indice geobiográfico de cuarenta mil pobladores españoles
          de América en el siglo XVI, Tomo II: 1520–1539.* Academia
          Mexicana de Genealogía y Heráldica, A.C. Mexico City: Edi-
          torial Jus.

Canfield, D. Lincoln
1981   *Spanish Pronunciation in the Americas.* Chicago and
        London: The University of Chicago Press.

Capdevila, Arturo
1940   *Babel y el castellano,* tercera edición. Buenos Aires: Losada,
        1954.

Castro, Américo
1960   *La peculiaridad lingüística rioplatense y su sentido histórico*
        ...segunda ed. muy renovada. Madrid: Taurus.

de Gregorio de Mac, María Isabel
1967   *El voseo en la literatura argentina.* Cuadernos del Instituto
        de Letras. Santa Fe, Arg.: Universidad Nacional del Litoral.

de Marsilio, Horacio
1969   *El lenguaje de los uruguayos.* Montevideo: Nuestra Tierra.

Díaz del Castillo, Bernal
1568   *Historia verdadera de la conquista de la Nueva España,*
        prólogo de Carlos Pereyra, ed., segunda edición, Tomos I–II.
        Madrid: Espasa-Calpe, 1942.

Donni de Mirande, Nélida Esther
1986   "Problemas y estado actual de la investigación del español de
        la Argentina hasta 1984," *Anuario de Letras* (Mexico City)
        XXIV, 179–236.

Englekirk, John
1968   [with] Irving A. Leonard, John T. Reid, John A. Crow, *An
        Anthology of Spanish American Literature,* 2nd Ed. New York:
        Appleton-Century-Crofts.

Espinosa, José de [et al.]
1794   *Viaje político-científico alrededor del mundo por las corbetas
        Descubierta y Atrevida al mando de los capitanes de navío
        Don Alejandro Malaspina y Don José de Bustamante y Guerra
        desde 1789 a 1794,* publicado con una introducción por Don
        Pedro de Novo y Colson, ed. Madrid: Abienzo, 1885.

"Exitos, recuerdos y discreción de Carlos Gardel,"
1929   *La Nación* (Buenos Aires), 30 Jun., Sect. 3, p. 8.

Fontanella de Weinberg, María Beatriz
1987   *El español bonaerense: Cuatro siglos de evolución lingüística
        (1580–1980).* Buenos Aires: Hachette.

Gardel, Carlos
1928   *¡Che papusa, oí!,* tango by G. Matos Rodríguez and E. Ca-
        dícamo, distributed again on *Viejo smoking.* Cassette, EMI
        20.862. Montevideo: Odeón.

Granada, Daniel
1890   *Vocabulario rioplatense razonado...*2a edición corregida....
        Biblioteca Artigas: Colección de Clásicos Uruguayos, Vols.
        25–26. Montevideo: Imprenta Rural. Republished with prologue
        by Lauro Ayestarán. Montevideo: Ministerio de Instrucción
        Pública, 1957.

Guarnieri, Juan Carlos
1978   *El lenguaje rioplatense.* Montevideo: Ediciones de la Banda
        Oriental.

Henríquez Ureña, Pedro
1925   "El supuesto andalucismo de América," *Cuadernos del
        Instituto de Filología* (Buenos Aires) I, No. 2, 117–22.

Kany, Charles E.
1951   "Chapter III: The Voseo" in *American-Spanish Syntax,* 2nd ed.
        Chicago and London: The University of Chicago Press.

Lapesa, Rafael
1970   "Las formas verbales de segunda persona y los orígenes del
        voseo" in *Actas del Tercer Congreso Internacional de His-
        panistas.* Mexico City: El Colegio de México.

Malkiel, Yakov
1972   *Linguistics and Philology in Spanish America: A Survey
        (1925–1970).* The Hague, Paris: Mouton.

Malmberg, Bertil
1966   *La América hispanohablante: Unidad y diferenciación del
        castellano.* Madrid: Ediciones Istmo, 1974.

Menéndez Pidal, Ramón
1962   "Sevilla frente a Madrid: Algunas precisiones sobre el español
        de América" in *Miscelanea homenaje a André Martinet:
        "Estructuralismo e Historia"* III, Diego Catalán, ed. Canary
        Islands: Universidad de la Laguna.

Muñiz, Francisco Javier
1845   *Voces usadas con generalidad en las Repúblicas del Plata—
        la Argentina, y la Oriental del Uruguay (Montevideo).*
        Buenos Aires. Republished with introduction and notes by
        Milcíades Alejo Vignati, ed. as *El vocabulario rioplatense
        de Francisco Javier Muñiz.* Buenos Aires: Coni, 1937.

Páez Urdaneta, Iraset
1981   *Historia y geografía del voseo.* Colección Hispanoamericana
        de Lingüística. Caracas: La Casa de Bello.

Page, F.M.
1893   "Remarks on the Gaucho and His Dialect," *Modern Language
        Notes* (Baltimore) VIII (1893), 18–27.

Pedretti de Bolón, Alma
1983   *El idioma de los uruguayos: Unidad y diversidad.* Ediciones
        de la Banda Oriental 12. Montevideo: Ediciones de la Banda
        Oriental.

Pla Cárceles, José
1923   "La evolución del tratamiento 'vuestra-merced'," *Revista
        de Filología Española* (Madrid) X, 245–80.

Relaciones geográficas de Indias
1885   Tomo I (1881), Tomo II (1885). Madrid: Ministerio de Fomento,
        Peru.

Rona, José Pedro
1963   "Sobre algunas etimologías rioplatenses," *Anuario de Letras*
        (Mexico City) III, 87–106.

1967   *Geografía y morfología del voseo.* Porto Alegre: Editora
        La Salle.

Rosenblat, Angel
1971   *Nuestra lengua en ambos mundos.* Estella [Navarra]: Salvat
        Editores & Alianza Editorial.

Rossi, Vicente
1928   *Idioma nacional rioplatense (argentino-uruguayo): Primera
        evidencia* [the first of five lexical studies ranging from *Pri-
        mera evidencia* to *Quinta evidencia*]. Folletos Lenguaraces,
        6–10. Río de la Plata [Córdoba, Arg.]: [ImprentaArgentina],
        1928–1929.

Salazar, Eugenio de
c.1573 *Cartas de Eugenio de Salazar, vecino y natural de Madrid,
        escritas a muy particulares amigos suyos* in *Epistolario
        español: Colección de cartas de españoles ilustres antiguos y
        modernos...*D. Eugenio de Ochoa, ed. Tomo segundo, p. 283 ff.
        Biblioteca de Autores Españoles.... Madrid: Hernando, 1926.

Serís, Homero
1964   *Bibliografía de la lingüística española.* Publicaciones del
        Instituto Caro y Cuervo XIX. Bogota: Instituto Caro y Cuervo.

Siracusa, María Isabel
1977   "Morfología verbal del voseo en el habla culta de Buenos Aires"
        in *Estudios sobre el español hablado en las principales
        ciudades de América,* Juan M. Lope Blanch, ed. Mexico City:
        Universidad Nacional Autónoma de México.

Tiscornia, Eleuterio F.
1930   *La lengua de "Martín Fierro".* Facultad de Filosofía y Letras,
        Instituto de Filología, Biblioteca de Dialectología Hispano-
        americana III. Buenos Aires: Universidad de Buenos Aires.

Valera, Cipriano de, ed.
1602   *La Santa Biblia, antiguo y nuevo testamento. Antigua versión
        de Casiodoro de la Reina (1569), revisada por Cipriano de
        Valera (1602) y cotejada posteriormente con diversas traduc-
        ciones, y con los textos hebreo y griego, con referencias.*
        Buenos Aires, Bogota, etc.: Sociedades Bíblicas Unidas, 1957.

Vidal de Battini, Berta Elena
1964   *El español de la Argentina: Estudio destinado a los maestros
        de las escuelas primarias I.* Buenos Aires: Consejo Nacional
        de Educación.

Weber, Frida
1941   "Fórmulas de tratamiento en la lengua de Buenos Aires,"
        Revista de Filología Hispánica (Buenos Aires) III, 105–39.

                    B. Music and Culture in General

Amat, Joan Carles
[1596] *Guitarra española, y vandola en dos maneras de guitarra,
        castellana y cathalana....* Barcelona. [Enlarged ed.] Gerona:
        Joseph Bro, n.d. [London: British Library].

Beaumarchais, Pièrre Augustin Caron de
1799   *Théâtre complète. Lettres relatives a son théâtre.* Paris:
        Gallimard, 1957, 1964.

Bennassar, Bartolomé
1929   *The Spanish Character: Attitudes and Mentalities from the
        Sixteenth to the Nineteenth Century.* Benjamin Keen, trans-
        lator and editor. Berkeley: University of California Press.

Bermudo, Fray Juan
1555   *Declaración de instrumentos musicales.* Osuna, Andalusia.
        Facs., M. Santiago Kastner, ed. Kassel: Bärenreiter, 1957.

Briceño, Luis de
1626   *Método mvi facilíssimo para aprender a tañer la gvitarra
        a lo español,* compuesto por Luis de Briçneo [sic].... Paris:
        P. Ballard. Reprinted in facsimile. Geneva, Switzerland:
        Minkoff, 1972.

Cervantes Saavedra, Miguel de
1616   *Obras completas.* A. Valbuena Prat, ed. Madrid: Aguilar, 1965.

Conrad, Barnaby
1953   *La Fiesta Brava: The Art of the Bull Ring.* Boston: Houghton
        Mifflin.

Contreras, Segundo N.
1931   *Disertaciones musicales.* Buenos Aires: E. Perrot.

Corona, Antonio
  1992   "The Popular Music of Veracruz and the Survival of Instru-
          mental Practices of the Spanish Baroque," unpublished
          lecture delivered 22 May at the conference *After Columbus—
          The Musical Journey*. California Polytechnic State University,
          San Luis Obispo.

Cotarelo y Mori, Emilio
  1911   *Loas, bailes, jácaras, mojigangas desde fines del siglo XVI a
          mediados del XVIII*. 2 vols. Madrid: Bailly-Bailliere.

Covarrubias, Sebastián de
  1611   *Tesoro de la lengua castellana o española*. Madrid: Sánchez.
          Reprinted by Martín de Riquer, ed. Barcelona: Horta, 1943.

Espinel, Vicente
  1618   *Relaciones de la vida del escudero Marcos de Obregón....*
          Madrid: I. de la Cuesta. Barcelona: Biblioteca "Arte y
          Letras," 1910.

Esquivel Navarro, Juan de
  1643   *Discvrsos sobre el arte del dançado, y svs excelencias y primer
          origen, reprobando las acciones deshonestas....* Sevilla: Gómez
          de Blas.

Fernández, Juan Rómulo
  1929   "Aspectos del folklore argentino," *Instituto Popular de Confe-
          rencias* (Buenos Aires) XV, 17–24.

Gardel, Carlos (see references above, Section A: "Exitos" and Gardel.)

Hall, Monica
  1978   "The *Guitarra española* of Joan Carles Amat," *Early Music*
          (London) VI, 362–73, passim.

Hamilton, Anthony
  1713   *Mémoires du Chevalier de Grammont* (Paris: 1773), translated
          by Sir Walter Scott. 2 vols. London: Nimmo, 1885.

Hammerton, J.A.
  1916   *The Argentine through English Eyes, and a Summer in
          Uruguay*. London, New York, Toronto: Hodder and Stoughton.

Heathcote, A. Anthony
  1977   *Vicente Espinel*. Boston: Twayne Publishers.

Hudson, Richard
  1982   *The Folía, the Sarabande, the Passacaglia, and the Chaconne:
          The Historical Evolution of Four Forms that Originated in
          Music for the Five-Course Spanish Guitar*. 4 vols. Musico-
          logical Studies and Documents No. 35, American Institute
          of Musicology. Neuhausen, Stuttgart: Hänssler, 1982.

Levillier, D. Roberto, ed.
1926   *Papeles eclesiásticos del Tucumán: Documentos originales del Archivo de Indias*, Vol. II. Biblioteca del Congreso Argentino: Colección de Publicaciones Históricas. Madrid: Juan Pueyo.

MacCann, William
1853   *Two Thousand Miles' Ride through the Argentine Provinces: Being an Account of the Natural Products of the Country, and Habits of the People; with a Historical Retrospect....* 2 vols. London: Smith, Elder. Facs. ed. New York: AMS Press, n.d.

Mozart, J.C. Wolfgang Amadeus
1786   *Le nozze di Figaro* in *Wolfgang Amadeus Mozart's Werke: Kritisch durchgesehene Gesamptausgabe*, Series 5, No. 17. Leipzig: Breitkopf und Haertel, 1876–1907.

Nichols, Madaline W.
1952   "A Study in the Golden Age" in *Estudios hispánicos, homenaje a Archer M. Huntington.* Wellesley, MA: Wellesley College.

Pinnell, Richard
1980   *Francesco Corbetta and the Baroque Guitar, with a Transcription of His Works.* 2 vols. Studies in Musicology Series No. 25. Ann Arbor: UMI Research Press.

Pujol, Emilio
[1930] *La guitarra y su historia: conferencia* [dada en Londres, París, Barcelona...]. Buenos Aires: Romero y Fernández.

Sarmiento, Domingo Faustino
1845   *Civilización i barbarie: Vida de Juan Facundo Quiroga....* Santiago, Chile: Imprenta del Progreso. *Life in the Argentine Republic in the Days of the Tyrants; Civilization and Barbarism.* From the Spanish of Domingo F. Sarmiento, L.L.D., Minister Plenipotentiary from the Argentine Republic to the United States with a biographical sketch of the author by Mrs. Horace Mann [trans.]. First American from the third Spanish Edition. 1868. Reprinted. New York: Hafner Press. London: Collier-Macmillan, 1974.

Sloman, Albert E.
1965   "The Two Versions of *El burlador de Sevilla*," *Bulletin of Hispanic Studies* (Essex, Eng.) XLII, 18–33.

Tilmouth, Michael
1957   "Some Improvements in Music Noted by William Turner in 1697," *Galpin Society Journal* (Winchester, Eng.) X, 57–59.

Torres Villarroel, Diego de
1743   *Vida, ascendencia...del doctor don Diego de Torres Villarroel....* Valencia and Pamplona. *The Remarkable Life of Don Diego, Being the Autobiography of Diego de Torres Villarroel,*

Translated from the Spanish by William C. Atkinson.... London: The Folio Society, 1958.

Trend, J.B.
1925   *Luis Milán and the Vihuelistas.* [London:] Oxford University Press.

Unamuno, Miguel de
1894   *"El gaucho Martín Fierro," La Revista Española* (Salamanca) I. Republished with notes by Carlos Paz. Montevideo: Ediciones "El Galeón," 1986.

Part III

The Guitar of the Hispanic Domination

"La guitarra es el instrumento musical más nuestro"
[The guitar is the musical instrument most our own]

The Spaniards colonized specific regions of the American continents. Their early activities converged at three locations: first, around the Caribbean as a result of Columbus's initial contacts, next, in Mesoamerica—centered eventually at Mexico City, and finally in South America—focused at Lima. The guitar followed suit: its first appearance was in the invasion of the Caribbean Islands, then Mexico, and finally South America.

The Spanish military presence in the Río de la Plata endured for nearly three centuries. Although the term "conquest" implied an immediate takeover, as in the short-lived invasions of Cortés and Pizarro, the domination of the Plata region was only accomplished over the course of several centuries because it proved more difficult than the previous conquests. The Spaniards came to power there only tenuously at first with the unsuccessful founding of Buenos Aires in 1536. Then, once their presence became firm with another military strategy out of Asunción, the domination lasted until Argentines established their own government in 1810. The Hispanic domination lingered another decade or more in Paraguay and Uruguay, until they too revolted against all other foreign interests and became self-governing republics.

The guitar was established in the Americas during Spain's most prosperous era. The conquerors brought the guitar around 1500, and it remained thereafter as the main instrument of the New World colonists. Simultaneously their colonization was making a tremendous impact back home. Spain's optimism stemming from the Moorish conquest was regenerated over and over again with the affluence and sense of power emanating continuously from the Spanish dominions overseas. The Columbian Exchange provided steady correspondence between these extremes of the empire. The Spanish court amassed a stockpile of precious metals and supplied commodities that soon became necessities to the rest of Europe. The resulting prosperity and self-confidence of the era found expression in the *Siglo de Oro,* Spain's Golden Age of literature and the arts. While the Golden Age blossomed at home, waves of new colonists took ever more *guitarras* and *vihuelas* to the Americas. After 1600, however, the gradual rise of the so-called *guitarra española* enabled it to supersede the older instruments. Presently known as the "Baroque guitar," it became the single predominant plucked instrument throughout peninsular Spain as well as the Americas. Then the Baroque guitar's eventual demise happened to coincide with Spain's loss of power in Latin America. During the stirring of independence around 1800 and the opening of free ports in the Río de la Plata, musicians began to prefer the modern six-string guitar over the Baroque guitar and the smaller folk guitars.

1. Guitarra or Vihuela?

Vicente Espinel (1550–1624), the Andalusian poet and guitarist has already appeared in Part II of this narrative with regard to his guitar and his serenades. But, as a prominent representative of a transitional period between the Renaissance and Baroque eras, he bequeathed yet another aspect of his instrument to subsequent generations and guitar music in general—a change in the name of the instrument. Before Espinel, the bulk of the serious literature for plucked strings in Spain was written for the *vihuela*; after him, the same literature was written specifically for the *guitarra* or the *guitarra española*. Simultaneously it was around 1600 that the guitar's popularity began to spread beyond the Pyrenees; musicians from the other European countries took up an interest in the so-called "Spanish guitar." Therefore, the years of Espinel's maturity at the end of the 16th century coincided precisely with the shift from the Renaissance to the Baroque style and the transition from the vihuela to the five-course Baroque guitar as the main focus of players and composers alike. Unavoidably the terminology with which to distinguish these changes was also in transition. The terms *guitarra* and *vihuela* had become ambivalent; they were no longer exclusive terms.

In the middle of the 16th century Juan Bermudo made clear distinctions between the guitars of several sizes. The *guitarra* was the small, plebeian, strummed guitar of four courses (with strings paired at the unison). The *vihuela* was like it in appearance, except that it was larger, and it came in several of its own configurations. (The *vihuela grande* was even larger than a modern-day Ramírez concert guitar). The vihuela belonged to aristocratic circles, being plucked in the performance of complex, polyphonic music, and it had six courses arranged with one course above and another below the guitarra's strings (Bermudo 1555:28r–28v). Some vihuelas had seven courses, with an extra set of bass strings. Bermudo mentioned a newer, mid-sized, five-course guitar (97r–98v), an instrument of compromise that offered some of the advantages of both of its predecessors. But it did not become popular or widely used until the next generation, the heyday of Vicente Espinel.

The gradual shift to the five-course guitar at the end of the 16th century coincided with the unfortunate decline of its four- and six-course predecessors. This momentous change in Spanish musical practice accompanied alterations in the nomenclature of instruments during the Golden Age. The greatest writers of the age were some of Espinel's most respected acquaintances. Although they may have known him and his music, they were certainly ambivalent on the name of Espinel's instrument: they indiscriminately called it either *guitarra* or *vihuela*.

The extent of this ambivalence is apparent in a few examples by
Claramonte and Cervantes. On the one hand, Claramonte referred repeatedly to Espinel and his instrument, the vihuela:

> That same year [1613], echoes of his fame arrived from Seville
> in Claramonte y Corroy's *Letanía moral* (Sevilla, 1613). In the
> text of the *Letanía* (pp. 383–84) appears the following eulogy:

Pues el gran Padre Espinel	[Thus the great Padre Espinel
en cinco nos la a templado,	in five has attuned us
si al varón diuino y fiel	if to the lad, delightful and faithful
quatro órdenes le an cantado;	they sang on four courses,
cante en cinco órdenes él.	on five he was to sing well.]

> Claramonte explains the meaning of these verses in his *Inqvi-*
> *ridion de los ingenios inuocados,* where he speaks of "El
> Maestro Espinel reformador de las cinco órdenes de la Vigüela,
> y laureado poeta antiguo, famoso en sátiras (fol. LI 4v)" [Maes-
> tro Espinel, reformer of the five courses of the vihuela, old poet
> laureate, famous in satires] (Haley 1959:44–45).

On the other hand, Miguel de Cervantes speaks of his good
friend Espinel in the poem *El viaje del Parnaso* (Ch. II), as well as
his guitarra:

> *es el grande Espinel, que en la guitarra*
> *tiene la prima y en raro estilo*
> [it is the great Espinel, who on the guitar
> has put on the first course and in unique style].

So who was right, Claramonte or Cervantes? Which was the correct Golden Age term for his instrument, guitarra or vihuela?
   Lope de Vega (1562–1635) also made several references to
Espinel but in so doing offered little help to clarify the dilemma
over what to call his instrument:

> The tradition that credits Espinel with having added a fifth
> string to the so-called Spanish guitar has always been con-
> sidered one that Lope began with the following statement in
> the *Dorotea.*...

perdónesele Dios a Vicente Espinel,	[God forgive Vicente Espinel
que nos traxo esta novedad	for bringing us this novelty
y las cinco cuerdas de la guitarra,	and the five (courses) of the guitar
con que ya se van olvidando	with which the noble instruments
los instrumentos nobles....	are being forgotten....]

While this passage refers to the year 1587, approximately, the *Dorotea* did not appear in print until 1632. Before then, Lope had twice mentioned Espinel's supposed reformation of the guitar (Haley 1959:45).

Lope dedicated the *Caballero de Illescas* to Espinel around 1602, though he published it decades later, and praised Espinel as follows:

> *Deve España a v.m. Señor Maestro...*
> *las cinco cuerdas del instrumento,*
> *que antes era tan bárbaro con quatro:*
> *los primeros tonos de consideración*
> *de que aora está tan rica,*
> *y las diferencias....*
> [Spain owes you, Your Grace, Maestro...
> the five (courses) of the instrumentation
> which before was so barbarous with four,
> the first notes of consideration
> of the style just in flower
> and now the variations....]

Lope praised him again in 1630 with the *Laurel de Apolo*. This time he invoked the:

> *inventor suave*
> *De la cuerda que fue de las vigüelas*
> *Silencio más grave....*
> [suave inventor
> of the string which on the vihuelas
> remained in silence most somber...]

Towards the end of the 16th century, during the increasing popularity of the five-course guitar and when Espinel was in his prime, some of the semantic differences between the terms *guitarra* and *vihuela* were lost. Lope was among the worst offenders:

with regard to Espinel's instrument, he used the terms interchangeably! (Pope Conant 1958:135). The greatest writers of the
Golden Age could not have all been confused on a matter of semantics, an integral component of their expertise. The selfsame terms
that had been so clearly distinguished in theory by Bermudo and
Covarrubias were simply no longer exclusive or specific after 1600
in actual practice.

A source in the Baroque guitar literature supports the usage of
the Golden Age poets who knew Espinel and his instrument. One of
the Baroque guitar books, an undated manuscript signed by Antonio de Santa Cruz (Biblioteca Nacional, Madrid), has a curious,
seemingly anachronistic title. It is called "Libro donde se verán
pazacalles de los ocho tonos...para bigüela hordinaria" [Book
wherein will be seen pasacalles of the eight modes...for ordinary
vihuela]. The book is intended for the plucked *vihuela común,* as it
was sometimes called to distinguish it from the less common
bowed viols—which anciently were also designated vihuelas. Notwithstanding, its notation reveals a five-course tablature and the
unmistakably idiomatic style of the late 17th-century guitar books
of Spain. Therefore, the term vihuela has survived, if without the
acute specificity of the past: it is now a generic term, applicable to
the guitar.

This was precisely the word usage taken to Hispanic America
during the colonial era of the 16th and 17th centuries. The conquistadores and settlers used the terms guitarra and vihuela
interchangeably. Nevertheless, later on, the terms regained some
of their specific connotations, as we shall see in forthcoming
sections.

2. The Guitar in Seville

We must stop in 16th-century Seville, but only in passing as a step
towards our goal of reaching America. Despite Seville's popular
culture and the guitarra within it there, as well as the presence of
the classical vihuela among its masters in the heart of Andalusia,
we are tempted to linger and enjoy well beyond a layover. However, Seville must remain a means to an end: being the principal

port of the Atlantic passage to the New World, we must check
through customs and emigration offices just like everyone else in
the migration path.

During the 16th century when the culture of Andalusia was
becoming prominent in the American colonies, the classical tradition of the vihuela was in full bloom at its capital. Representatives
of the guild of *guitarreros* or luthiers had registered their bylaws
among the municipal ordinances of Seville. They had already
drafted their regulations for vihuela construction by 1502. A
journeyman luthier's examination there entailed the construction
of a *vihuela grande,* complete with an appropriate rose carving in
the sound hole and inlays of marquetry. Moreover the instrument
and its trim had to be built as a solo tour de force, without any
assistance (Subirá 1953:219). Soon thereafter vihuela tablatures
began to appear in publication. Several of them were published in
Seville, namely those of Alonso de Mudarra and Miguel de
Fuenllana. Mudarra, after publishing his splendid *Tres libros de
música en cifras para vihuela* [Three Books of Music in Tablature
for the Vihuela] in 1546, spent his next 34 years in the the
production of music for the Seville Cathedral (Stevenson 1980a).
Fuenllana's achievement was even greater: his *Orphénica lyra*
(Seville, 1554) was the longest and what Bermudo perceived as the
best of the vihuela books. Fuenllana's professional service was for
the court of King Philip II, despite the fact that Fuenllana had been
blind from infancy (Ward 1980).

At the end of the century, yet more professional vihuelists of
Seville appeared among the portraits and biographies of the city's
most distinguished sons. Painter Francisco Pacheco, teacher of the
eminent Diego Rodríguez de Silva y Velázquez, published there, in
1599, a handsome, quarto-sized book which featured both his artwork and his writings about famous men of the city. It was entitled
Libro de descripción de verdaderos retratos [Book of Descriptions
of Authentic Portraits]. His book was literally a who's who of the
intelligentsia of Seville: it featured both a biography and an accompanying portrait for the celebrities of Pacheco's era. He showcased,
for instance, a bust of Philip II along with a summary of his
personal achievements. Philip's long, eventful reign had ended
with his death only a year before Pacheco published the book.

Plate IV Pedro de Madrid, Vihuelist in Seville (Pacheco 1599)
After the facsimile edition (Seville: Tarrascó, 1885)

Several of the illustrations feature musicians such as Francisco Guerrero (1527–1599), the outstanding composer of the Cathedral and Manuel Rodrigues, who are both portrayed as vihuelists. Pedro Bravo, *"gran músico de vigüela,"* and Iulio Severino are also listed in passing (even though they lacked a portrait of their own). Most significant for the iconography of the vihuela is Pacheco's portrait of Pedro de Madrid, as shown on the previous page. Don Pedro is shown playing a plain, guitar-like instrument with a single rose, not unlike today's guitars except that it is narrower and strung with double courses. Its strings are arranged in pairs, and it has six courses. This illustration demonstrates that the vihuela was indeed a type of guitar. Plate IV reveals the appearance of a "vihuela" of Seville, precisely at the point of departure for the New World during its era of colonization.

With good reason, the inscription below the portrait contains a flowery eulogy, calculated to honor its subject forevermore:

[For the memory that is justly owed to Pedro de Madrid, who had a place among such excellent men because of his outstanding advocacy of vihuela music, he deserved the designation as the best among those of his epoch.... This illustrious city of Seville is honored with such a son, in whom Nature manifested two extremes (not without great mystery): the one in blessing him with such a unique talent, and the other in leaving him blind.]

3. Music in the Transatlantic Voyage

It was neither new nor unusual to find a Spaniard playing the guitar to help relieve the tedium of a long trip. Voyages at sea, in particular, required frequent musical performances in order to divert the attention of crew and passengers from the boredom and hard work of maintaining the ship. Vicente Espinel left plenty of details on the subject of music in his autobiographical novel entitled *Relations of...Marcos de Obregón*. He told therein of one occasion when he had been captured and taken prisoner aboard a Venetian ship. Marcello Doria was in command of it as they were headed east across the Mediterranean towards the Italian port of Genoa:

Ref. 3 *Relaciones de...Marcos de Obregón*   Vicente Espinel
   As we were proceeding toward Genoa the general [Doria]
   commanded the musicians to sing, and taking up their guitars
   the first piece which they sang was my *octavas* which go thus:
          El bien dudoso, el mal seguro y cierto.
The treble, who was called Francisco de la Peña, began to perform florid vocal passages *(excelentísimos pasajes de garganta)*
for which, since the *sonata* was in a slow tempo, there was
plenty of time—while I punctuated each phrase with a sigh.
They sang all the *octavas* and at the last verse which said:
          El bien dudoso, el mal seguro y cierto,
I could no longer contain myself, and with a thoughtless, impul-
sive movement, exclaimed: "This misfortune still pursues me!"
Peña looked up on hearing me. He had not recognized me before as he was nearsighted and I so disguised in appearance and
dress. On recognizing me, speechless and with tears in his eyes,
he embraced me and turned to the general, saying: "Your excellency, whom do you think we have here?"—"Who?" asked
the general. Peña replied, "the author of these verses and this
sonata which we have sung for your excellency."—"What's
this? Call him hither."—I approached somewhat shamefaced
but a little heartened and the general asked me: "What is your
name?"—"Marcos de Obregón," I replied. Peña, always a
truthful man, said to the general: "So and so [meaning of course
Vicente Espinel] is his true name, but he is concealing it because
of his unfortunate situation (Pope Conant 1958:140–41)."

But this was only the Mediterranean. The Atlantic crossing was
ten times worse in small wooden ships of the same type. The best of
their hulls were no larger than our transcontinental jetliners. The
Atlantic was rough, and the crossing from the Canary Islands (the
only layover) to sight of land in the New World took from four to
ten weeks, depending on weather, morale, and supplies. It took
another four to ten weeks to sail south from point of contact in the
Caribbean to the Río de la Plata, but at least layovers were possible
on the South American coastline.
   The clergy, exhibiting the zeal of religious conquest, followed
along the same route. So as to fulfill their mission, the priests were
subdivided into separate religious orders to address unique problems and special needs. Fortunately many members of the orders
who made the trip lived up to their reputation as men of letters;

they took time to write journals about their early voyages. Some of these have remained available until now, providing sources from which to draw a picture of the Atlantic crossing.

The transatlantic course was so demanding as to humble even the roughest sailors who were accustomed to a life at sea: the harder their trip, the more regular, intense, and musical their devotions became. Ever since the voyages of Columbus, most Atlantic mariners travelled, whether before a gale or becalmed, at the mercy of the elements from their perspective; they always invoked favorable passage with their devotional prayers and music. The sailors prayed and chanted to deity or superstitiously sang their devotions to the constellations or to an evening star, as recalled by Jesuit Father Chome in his crossing to the Plata:

[After they sight it, the sailors sing the Litanies to the Virgin; and finishing them, if the star continues to shine as usual, the Quartermaster salutes it with great whistles, using the pipe with which he orders the movement of baggage] (Chome 1730:138).

Upon arrival in the Plata, Father Chome enumerated the hardships of their voyage, including a hurricane at sea:

[A little while later, our Head Advocate came aboard, overflowing with joy to find his missionaries in perfect health after three months of navigation from the Canary Islands. Out of the 800 persons that were on board the three ships, only one died, a soldier of the (ship) San Francisco at the entrance of the Río de la Plata] (Chome 1730:144).

In addition to the dangers of the trip, the bad food in itself was a trial, not to mention seasickness, according to another Jesuit missionary, Father Anthony Sepp. He went to Paraguay via Buenos Aires, and saw his letters about the trip published in English:

We imbark'd the 17th of January, on St. Anthony's Day at Cádiz, and arriving on the 6th of April at Buenos Ayres, were received with such tremendous demonstrations of joy as is scarce to be express'd; because the inhabitants of this place (which is no bigger than a country town) had not seen any ships

from Spain for three years last past; whereby they were reduced to that extremity, that they had scarce a shirt left to shift
themselves with; so that our vessels sold a yard of linnen cloth at
20 dollars and 25 dollars, etc., a vast profit indeed.... Concerning
my other sufferings in this voyage, I will write more at large
another time. I will only tell you, that without God's peculiar
mercy, out of 40 missionaries that were aboard these vessels, not
half would have reach'd the American shoar [sic], as being altogether unacquainted with such harsh diet as our covetous
Captain was pleas'd to afford us; which was very hard bisket
full of maggots, because it had been bak'd two years before,
about a pint of ill-scented and corrupted water a day, and a
small quantity of flesh; but so full of maggots, that without the
utmost necessity, we could not so much as have look'd upon,
much less have eaten it (Sepp 1697:635).

There were other hardships of the transatlantic voyage: the
sleepless nights due to noise and horrid accommodations, the pests,
and the flaring tempers resulting from the overall coarseness of
the experience along with the other pressures. It was no wonder
that music played such an important part in the voyages as their
main diversion—all the more so with the prohibition of gambling
and drunkenness. According to another Jesuit missionary, Florian
Pauke, his missionary bretheren contributed what they could for
him to purchase a flute for the voyage back to Europe when the
Jesuits were expelled from the Plata region:

[When I was supposed to leave Buenos Aires in 1769, along with
170 Jesuits, they gave me, every one of them from the scarce
money they had at their disposal, enough for a transverse flute
so that we would have a musical pastime, upon the high seas]
(Paucke 1769:I, 143).

Paucke explained further the use of music among passengers,
amidst the inevitable hardships of the crossing back to Europe:

[This French aristocrat was a gentleman in his prime, a musician very adroit on the violin, of which he had two of excellent
quality and goodness. His pastime was to perform music with
me for two or three hours.... I never spoke to the Captain nor

he to me; I would go during the day for one or two hours to the Shipmate's chamber to teach him some on the transverse flute, and then (return) to my place.

I could not stand the unbearable heat in the ship's lower deck during the night; thus I believe that I must have sweated out all the body's vital humours. Yet not only was this the problem, but also the thousands of cockroaches...moreover, the abundance of mice and rats that ran over our cots] (Paucke 1769:III, 123).

One of the most musical of the early chronicles makes specific mention of the guitar. Fray Tomás de la Torre of the Dominican Order left a diary of his difficult, year-long trip from Spain to Mexico in the company of other clergymen. First he recounts the overland trek from Salamanca to the port of Seville in 1544; then he describes the transatlantic voyage and Caribbean jaunts which finally end at Ciudad Real, Chiapas, Nueva España in 1545. He makes a vivid account of the music he heard in his travels, the highlight of which is their glorious landfall at Puerto Rico—at which spontaneously the priests unite in the chant "We praise Thee, God" as the bishop of the island comes out to greet them:

Fig. 9 Music in the Voyage to Mexico, 1544–1545
(de la Torre 1545)

p.71. The first day we sang at compline.

85. We always sang on Sundays and holidays during which there was a sermon witnessed throughout the ship. Every night we sang the *Salve Regina* [Hail Queen of Heaven].

86. Singing the rosary, songs, and hymns, playing the guitar....

93. As we were ending our course, the bishop of Puerto Rico came out to greet us so...we started a *Te Deum laudamus* [We praise Thee, God].

114. On the high seas...during Christmas Eve, we sang vespers with great devotion.... At prime of the night we sang many hymns, then at matins we sang, and finally yet again at the sunrise service.

116. At night we headed into the high seas, and on the following morning (5 Jan.) they recognized the mainland...; with the joy that you can imagine, we sang *Te Deum laudamus*.

120. [In Campeche] we said mass but sang the whole of vespers.

129. [In Villa de Tabasco] we carried many books under cover of luggage as well as bells, clocks, and organs.

139. It was the holiday of St. Thomas's translation so we remembered to sing vespers and compline.

141. With great abundance of tears, we sang a responsory with solemnity

149. We decided to spend the occasion happily by singing the *Te Deum*.

Thus was the importance of music in his daily life. In absolute
compliance with the letter and the spirit, the devout Fray Tomás
was himself a performer in all their musical devotions. It was their
practice to sing the *Te Deum* for expression of joy or thanksgiving;
they sang vespers and compline virtually every day; and of course
they celebrated the mass and certain festivals.

Fray de la Torre witnessed the fact that the ship's crewmen
(and perhaps also some of the laymen on board from among the
passengers) were performing with the guitar out on the high seas.
Their ship was launched on the Atlantic Ocean from 31 July to 25
August of 1544. Father de la Torre heard the guitar then and
made an entry about it in his journal at about halfway between the
Canary Islands and their port of call at Puerto Rico. The laymen
were using the guitar either for solos or to accompany some of
their secular songs, as follows—first in the original Spanish, then
in translation:

> *El día de nuestro Padre (6 de agosto) hicimos gran fiesta y todo
> el navío se alegró.... No es cosa de contar todas estas menuden-
> cias, éstas basten para dar algunos avisos a los que hubieren de
> navegar. Con estas cosas pasamos nuestro camino unas veces
> llorando y otras cantando el rosario, salmos e himnos, aquí tres,
> acuyá seis. Los seglares tañendo guitarra y cantando romances,
> y cada uno a su modo, visitábanos Nuestro Señor con gran con-
> solación y muchos se iban en un rincón en oración, otros leyendo
> en libros y hartos llorando arroyos de lágrimas que Nuestro
> Señor les daba especialmente de noche, cuando el tumulto de la
> gente cesaba* (de la Torre 1545:85–86).

[On the day of Our Father (6 Aug.) we made a grand fiesta and
the entire ship celebrated.... It is not necessary to tell all of the
details; let these be enough to fairly warn those who have to go to
sea. With these things we went our way either crying or sometimes singing the rosary, psalms, and hymns, three here, six
there. The laymen were playing the guitar and singing *romances,* each in his own way; Our Lord visited us with great consolation, and many would go straightaway into a corner to pray;
others were reading books as they tired of crying the rivers of
tears that Our Lord gave them, especially at night when the
tumult of the people ceased.]

4. The Arrival of the Guitar in the Caribbean

The earliest European music in the Americas was undoubtedly a mere extension of what was performed at sea. The men of the Columbian voyages informally took whatever religious and secular music they already knew onto the land. Early on, however, there was also a formal plan to establish music in the colony. Cristoforo Colombo had already made two transatlantic crossings, and each time he had left a settlement in his stead. Now Ferdinand and Isabella needed to fortify his settlements and to improve the quality of life in them. The specific plan to establish music was due largely to their wisdom and foresight: they charged Columbus with the responsibility of including both music and instruments along with the specialists and provisions for an elaborate third journey of exploration and settlement, which was eventually completed in 1498. They mandated the use of music as entertainment for the new settlers in the following royal proclamation:

El Rey é la Reina.
D. Cristóbal Colón, nuestro Almirante del mar Océano, Visorey é Gobernador de la tierra-firme é Islas de las Indias....
Las cosas que nos parece que con ayuda de Nuestro Señor Dios se deben proveer é enviar a las Indias para la gobernación é mantenimiento de las personas que allá están é han de ir para las cosas que allá se han de hacer complideras a servicio de Dios é nuestro, son las siguientes:
Primeramente, en este primer viage, y en tanto que Nos mandamos proveer, hayan de ir a estar en las dichas Indias el número de trescientas é treinta personas de la suerte é calidad é oficios que de yuso serán contenidos...las cuales dichas trescientas é treinta personas han de ser elegidas por vos el dicho nuestro Almirante...é han de ser repartidas en esta manera: cuarenta escuderos, cien peones de guerra, treinta marineros, treinta grumetes, veinte lavadores de oro, cinquenta labradores é hortelanos, veinte oficiales de todos oficios, é treinta mugeres.... Asimismo deber ir un físico é un boticario é un herbolario é algunos instrumentos é músicas [sic] para pasatiempo de las gentes que allá han de estar.... Fecha en la Villa de Medina del Campo a quince días del mes de junio, año del Nacimiento de

*Nuestro Señor Jesucristo de mil é cuatrocientos é noventa é
siete años.—YO EL REY.—YO LA REINA....* (Fernández de
Navarrete 1825:203–06).

[The King and Queen.
Don Christopher Columbus, our Admiral of the high seas, Viceroy and Governor of the mainland and the islands of the Indies....
   The following are the things which appear to us that (with the
help of Our Lord God) ought to be provided and sent to the Indies for the government and maintenance of the people who are
there now and who must go there later, so that what is done
there might be in accordance with the Divine will and our own.
   First of all, the provisions that we recommend for this initial
voyage shall include people who have to go and to stay in the
said Indies in the number of 330 persons constituted according
to the classification and quality of their services...the aforesaid
330 persons ought to be selected by you, the above-named Admiral...and ought to be divided in this manner: 40 shieldbear-
ers, 100 foot soldiers, 30 sailors, 30 cabin boys, 20 gold panners,
50 laborers and gardeners, 20 officials (one of each specialty),
and 30 women.... At the same time must go a physician, a phar-
macist, a botanist, and some instruments and <u>musics</u> for the
pastime of the people who have to be there.... Made at the town
of Medina del Campo on 15 June, year since the birth of Our
Lord Jesus Christ of 1497 (signed)—I THE KING.—I THE
QUEEN...] (my underline).

Thus if European musical instruments had not already been
taken onto American soil at the time of first contact, they certainly
were on subsequent voyages as a direct result of the royal decree of
1497. Notwithstanding, Ferdinand and Isabella left an ambiguous
term in their mandate—the word *músicas*—and here it has been
underlined and translated as <u>musics</u>. The term could refer either
to books and scores of music or to the musicians themselves.
Though the context seems to suggest the former interpretation,
the fact must not escape us that women were taken along on this
voyage, and they became the first European women in the New
World settlements. Columbus may have sought to bring women as
performers, inasmuch as *músico* or *música* could then refer to a
musician in the Castilian dialect. If this were the case, these

women would have to be counted among the first European musicians—perhaps professional musicians—in the Americas.

The same term appeared later during the colonization, and in such cases the word <u>músicas</u> referred to books of music. For example, in the year of 1620, as the Pilgrims were beginning their New England colony, the Hispanic conquest was already more than a century old. That year the high European culture established in Mexico became readily apparent in the inventory of a deceased schoolmaster's library. During his career of teaching in the capital city, Juan García Becerril had amassed a collection of some 55 books of the Golden Age, according to the inventory compiled by a relative (see Leonard 1952). Most important for our consideration, his list of books included four of those published specifically for the vihuela in Spain. The first four items in the inventory were vihuela tablatures—the works of Milán, Enríquez de Valderrábano, Fuenllana, and Narváez. Each tablature book was called specifically a "música de vigüela." Thus in the plural, the <u>músicas</u> had to be books of music, a usage parallel to that of their Catholic Majesties in 1497. Still, any of the thirty women might have been musical.

Only six years after their royal proclamation which mentioned music and instruments, the vihuela was in clear evidence among the *conquistadores*. It appeared in precisely the same sequence as the successive stages of their conquest: first in the Caribbean, then in Mexican territory, and finally in South America. The earliest specific reference to the vihuela was in the *Historia* of Fray Bartolomé de las Casas, wherein he was narrating some details about the invasion of the Caribbean islands. In Book II, Chapter VIII, the soldiers had carried the offensive onto the Island of Hispaniola during the year of 1503. In the very next chapter, the conquest of the Province of Xaraguá within the island was clearly in progress; certain men among the officers who were in charge of it had brought along a vihuela with which to entertain the troops in their off hours:

> *El Comendador Mayor...llevó consigo 300 hombres de pié y 70 de caballo, porque entonces había en esta isla pocas yeguas, y menos caballos, y muy rico había de ser el que alcanzase una yegua en que andar...y aún hombre hobo, de los que vinieron*

en el viaje del Comendador Mayor, que al son de una vihuela,
hacían su yegua bailar ó hacer corvetas ó saltar (de las Casas
c.1530:II, 28).
[The Commanding General...took with him 300 men on foot
and 70 on horseback, because there were few mares on this
island and even fewer stallions, so it was very fortunate to reach
the level of riding cavalry, if only on a mare...and moreover,
there was a man—among those who came along on the trip
with the Commanding General—who made his mare dance,
maneuver around, or jump to the tune of a vihuela.]

Under these circumstances, it seems safe to assume that these
cavalrymen were not performing any studied counterpoint in the
style of a Renaissance mass! They were undoubtedly strumming
the vihuela *rasgueado* style in the accompaniment of a hilarious
popular dance. In other words, with this, the first reference to the
term vihuela on American soil, *vihuela* is already an interchangeable term with *guitarra*.

Bartolomé de las Casas mentioned the vihuela again in Book II,
this time in Chapter LII. The time frame is six years after his first
reference to it: his date of "509" is surely a mere contraction of
1509. However, the two references seem to be related by the context of the Commanding General, his cavalrymen, etc. What is
new is the specific identification of a great vihuelist of that time:

Sucedió luego, en este año de 509, lo siguiente: Hobo un vecino en
esta isla...de que muchas veces habemos a la memoria repetido,
llamado Diego de Nicuesa, que había venido con el Comendador
Mayor, persona muy cuerda y palanciana y graciosa en decir,
gran tañedor de vihuela, y sobre todo gran ginete, que sobre una
yegua que tenía, porque pocos caballos en aquel tiempo aún ha-
bían nacido, hacía maravillas (de las Casas c.1530:II, 116).
[Later in this year of 509, the following occurred: There was a
man hereabouts on the island...whom we have remembered
many times, called Diego de Nicuesa who came with the Commanding General; (he was) a person of good judgement, responsible, and pleasing, which is to say he was a great player of
the vihuela, and more than anything else, a great horseman
upon the mare that he had with which he did marvelous things,
inasmuch as few stallions had been born at that time.]

There were additional, later references to the vihuela in the conquest of the Antilles and around the Caribbean in the chronicles of
Antonio de Herrera and Gonzalo Fenández de Oviedo (see Zavadivker 1982). However, after the troops had cleared the way for
colonization, musical instruments began to appear amidst the
material culture which arrived in support of these settlements.

Guitars were significant imports during Hispanic America's
colonization. Soon after Columbus had established the route to the
New World by running before the Trade Winds and following the
clockwise Atlantic currents, additional fleets were sent laden with
supplies to and from the Americas. The pattern of ships and merchandise across the Atlantic was regular enough to become known
as the *Carrera de Indias* [the Concourse of the Indies] or, later the
"Columbian Exchange." Whatever the terms, it was a bridge of
transatlantic commerce and communication. It was also a money-
maker, for customs officials were set up at departure in Seville and
at ports of call: the officials carefully documented the supplies and
merchandise so that they could be licensed for export and taxed
upon import—hence the painstaking detail in maintaining the
records. The practice paid for itself: customs officials charged 7.5
percent import duty on all merchandise, even the personal items
brought onto the island of Puerto Rico.

The earliest imported guitars arrived at Puerto Rico, according
to surviving documents. Table 1, on the next page, lists eighteen
vihuelas and a guitarra that were imported between 1512 and
1516, already within a decade of Columbus's fourth and final voyage. Both the crewmen and passengers carried these instruments
as part of their cargo for personal use or for resale, inasmuch as
several merchants were already travelling with a handful of instruments in their possession. The Bishop of Puerto Rico had requested the delivery of one vihuela. Another one belonged to a
ship's officer, Alonso de Buenaño, and he probably kept it in his
cabin, or at least sufficiently close at hand to be used for entertainment during the voyage.

The customs officials took care to assess the evaluation of these
instruments along with all the other merchandise of a ship's cargo
—even personal items. In making the assessment they used the
value of both *pesos* and *tomines*. Typically in Imperial Spain, the

peso was equated with a weight of silver, and it was subdivided into eight *reals,* hence the expression "pieces of eight" for pesos. The same applied in this case except that the eighth-part subdivision was called a *tomín,* instead.

Table 1 Guitars Imported in the Columbian Exchange
(Tanodi 1971, my translation)

---

19 Sep. 1512, Alonso de Buenaño, boatswain of the caravel Santiago, brings a small vihuela valued at 1p.2t.
[p.= peso(s), t.= tomín(es)]
25 Dec. 1512, on behalf of Bishop Alonso Manso, who does not pay
import duty, Quintana brings a vihuela.
26 Feb. 1513, merchant Luis de Santisteban brings a vihuela, 2p.4t.
13 May 1513, Fernán Muñiz de Godoy brings a vihuela at 1p.
18 Nov. 1513, merchant Gonzalo de Cea brings 3 vihuelas at 5p.6t.
14 Jun. 1516, Bartolomé Ponce brings an old vihuela valued at 2t.
28 Jun. 1516, merchant Alonso Hernández unloads 6 small vihuelas at 5t. each= 3p.6t.
11 Dec. 1516, Juan Martín, a passenger counts among his personal
belongings a guitarra valued at 3t.
21 Dec. 1516, Antonio Sánchez and Gonzalo Lorenzo bring 4 small
vihuelas at 3t.= 1p.4t.

Compared to the other imports, the guitars were modestly priced. Take for example the shipment which included the six vi-huelas of Alonso Hernández. Also aboard the vessel in which he travelled, the Santa María de la Merced in 1516, were such do-mestic items as scissors, spices, and shirts that suggest the relative value of the imported instruments. A pair of scissors and a pound of cumin spice were both valued at a tomín; frilled linen shirts were worth 5 tomines apiece. At the value of a peso, and thus comparable to the more expensive vihuelas aboard for personal use, were a barrel of 1,000 sardines or a fine hat garnished with velvet, whereas a good horse or a slave was worth 60 pesos in the same shipment. Although several merchants brought along some musical toys and a tambourine in 1516, no other musical instru-ments appeared in the cargo lists at all. Therefore, even though the list of Table 1 represents only the imports sent to Puerto Rico over the course of three years, these items show that affordable guitars were already circulating around the Caribbean. Then, in 1529, the first shipment of musical merchandise between Seville and Venezuelan ports arrived: 15 cheap *vihuelas* (Calzavara 1987:9).

If guitars were reasonably priced, then guitar strings were not. Peninsular gut strings were expensive; they cost, on the average, half as much as an instrument, but they had to be imported for the lack of another alternative. Such strings must have been in high demand around Puerto Rico, as implied in the cargo of the ship's master and man of experience in these convoys, Juan Vizcaíno: he brought along 18 sets on one trip! His supply was either for resale to the highest bidder or for his secluded retirement along some scenic riviera of the West Indies, with all the comforts of home.

Table 2 Vihuela Strings Imported at 16th-Century Puerto Rico
(Tanodi 1971)

---

11 Sep. 1513, Juan Vizcaíno, maestre brings 18 sets at 2p.4t.
18 Nov. 1513, Gonzalo de Cea brings 2 sets at 1p.
17 Mar. 1516, Luis García brings some strings valued at 6t.
03 Apr. 1516, Alonso Alvarez unloaded 2 sets at 3p.3t.
15 May 1516, Martín García brings 6 sets at 1p.4t.
28 Jun. 1516, Alonso Hernández brings 4 sets at 2t. each= 1p.
12 Jul. 1516, Fernando de Avila brings 4 cards of strings at 1p.

---

5. The Guitar in the Conquest of Mexico

After the colonization of the West Indies was well underway, the Spaniards carried their crusade onto the mainland. On his third voyage, during which he bore music and instruments, Columbus made landfall at the Island of Trinidad and then stopped along the coast of "Tierra Firme," present-day Venezuela before returning to known ports. On his fourth and final voyage he made a reconnaissance tour of Central America's Caribbean coastline in which he started on the east coast of Honduras and then sailed south to the Darien Gap. Thereby he left his followers to discover the extent of his initial probe into South and Central America. The Mexican conquest began in earnest with Hernán Cortés who arrived on the mainland in 1519.

Once Cortés assumed the rule and titles of his administration in Aztec territory, he became accustomed to the ovations of pomp and circumstance. A good example happened in June of 1524 or 1525, according to the *Historia* of Bernal Díaz del Castillo, who at the time was one of the young soldiers. On that occasion, Cortés had been as far away as Medellín (that is, the port in Ch. CXC), and on his return, his people scarcely recognized him at first because he had lost so much weight due to the extent and hardships of the journey. Just the same, as he neared present-day Mexico City, the treasurer wrote to him via messengers, requesting him to delay his return by staying overnight at "Tenuztitán," a town lying but several miles away from the capital. Well before his arrival, his subjects wished to have all appropriate celebrations in readiness. The following day, when Cortés marched into the full view of the capital's inhabitants, many of them went out to greet him; the reception included the complete entourage of government officials led by the treasurer himself:

> *Y salido el tesorero con todos los caballeros y conquistadores y cabildo de aquella ciudad, y todos los oficiales en ordenanza, y llevaron los más ricos vestidos y calzas y jubones que pudieron, con todo género de instrumentos…y los que salieron por las calzadas fueron tanto juegos y regocijos que se quedarán por decir, pues en todo el día por las calles de Méjico todo era bailes y danzas; y después que anocheció muchas lumbres a las puertas* (Díaz del Castillo 1568:II, 407).
>
> [The treasurer sallied forth with all of the knights, *conquistadores,* and council of that city, and all of the officials in order, and they wore their best suits and footwear and doublets that they could, bringing all manner of instruments…and those who went out on the sidewalks were playing as much as rejoicing, as yet to be told; thus in all the day long through the streets of Mexico City, there were everywhere all sorts of dancing and many lights at the doorways after sunset.]

Díaz del Castillo eventually found himself among those high enough in the viceroyalty to enjoy the sumptuous lifestyle. Music

accompanied the setting of their greatest feasts. According to
Chapter CCI, they convened the following exemplary celebration
in the fort of Chapultapec:

> *Aunque no vaya aquí escrito por entero, diré lo que se me*
> *acordaré, porque yo fuí uno de los que cenaron en aquellas*
> *grandes fiestas. Al principio fueron unas ensaladas hechas*
> *de dos o tres maneras...y luego cabezas de puercos y de venados*
> *y de terneras enteras, por grandeza, y con ello grandes músicas*
> *de cantares a cada cabecera, y la trompetería y géneros de*
> *instrumentos, harpas, vigüelas, flautas, dulzaínas, chirimías*
> (Díaz del Castillo 1568:II, 490–91).
>
> [Even though I may not make herein a complete written
> account, I will tell as much as I remember because I was one
> of those who dined at those great fiestas. In the beginning there
> were some salads made two or three ways...and later there
> were hogs' heads and deer and whole lambs for the grandeur
> and withal great music performances sung at the head of every
> course, even trumpet fanfares, and the kinds of instruments
> included harps, vihuelas, flutes, dulcians, and shawms.]

In addition to occasional vihuela performances, Díaz del Castillo
also made specific reference to vihuelists. For instance, among the
Hispanic aristocracy was one Luis Ponce, a certain rival of Cortés
mentioned in Chapter CXCII. In the course of Ponce's plans to
overthrow the leadership of the viceroyalty, for which he would
substitute his own, he had become gravely ill. Since Ponce was
himself a musician, it was only natural that he would summon
performances to his bedside in order to raise his spirits:

> *Oí decir a ciertos caballeros que se hallaron presentes cuando*
> *cayó malo, que como el Luis Ponce era músico y de inclinación*
> *de suyo regocijado, que por alegralle que le iban a tañer con una*
> *vigüela y a dar música, y que mandó que le tañesen una baja, y*
> *con los pies estando en la cama hacía sentido con los dedos e pies*
> *y los meneaba hasta acabar la baja* (Díaz del Castillo 1568:II,
> 419–20).
>
> [I heard said among certain gentlemen who were present when
> he fell ill, that inasmuch as Luis Ponce was a musician and of
> the inclination to enjoy music, they would go to play with a vi-
> huela in order to cheer him up, and to perform music; once he

requested of them the performance of a particular bass (tune), and with his feet in the bed, he made gestures with his toes and feet and he tapped them until the bass ended.]

But their performance was of no permanent consequence for he passed away as soon as it had finished.

Díaz del Castillo referred briefly to another vihuelist, this time a dance teacher who had come to the capital as part of the emigration from Cuba to New Spain:

E pasó un Ortiz, gran tañedor de viola e amostraba a danzar; e vino otro su compañero...e fue minero en la isla de Cuba (Díaz del Castillo 1568:I, 74; II, 541).
[And a certain Ortiz, a great vihuela player and dance teacher emigrated; and another came also, his companion...who was a miner on the isle of Cuba.]

Some of these references among the chronicles of New Spain were confirmed in archival studies completed in Mexico City. By citing original documents in his history of colonial music, Gabriel Saldívar identified quite a number of early vihuelists in the new viceroyalty. During the first half of the 16th century, two vihuelists in the capital were "Ortiz el Nahuatlato" and Alfonso Morón (cf. Díaz del Castillo 1568:II, 527), who taught both vihuela and dancing. Saldívar also singled out a certain Risueño who was known for the same activities:

[Of all the instruments, those that prospered most were the vihuela and harp. Coincidentally various musicians there during this period devoted themselves to teaching music.
   Following chronological order in the second half of the 16th century, we find that Diego or Bartolomé Risueño was a music teacher.... A native of Talavera in the kingdom of Spain, he was the son of Hernando Risueño and Catalina de Herrera y Guijosa. At the age of twelve, he learned to play the vihuela in Seville.... His contemporaries were Martín Núñez, a vihuelist, Juan Bautista de Torres, a Spaniard from Toledo, vihuelist and harpist, and Franco, chapel-master at the metropolitan cathedral, all friends of going out on the town in sunrise celebrations and evening serenades] (Saldívar 1934:161–62).

Among the many musicians in 16th-century Mexico, another man of Seville distinguished himself by his performances on the vihuela: "[Antonio López...who plays and sings in the comedies] (Saldívar 1934:161–62)."

Díaz del Castillo's last reference to the vihuela suggested that instrument fabrication had become local, a step which ensured the ready availability and eventually the wide diffusion of musical instruments. He was writing in Chapter CCIX to tell how Indian labor had established many skills and vocations. However, within this context, he explained that his compatriots who were overseeing instrument construction had first learned their trade in Spain, and then came to supervise it among the Indians:

> *Pasemos adelante y digamos cómo todos los más indios naturales destas tierras han deprendido muy bien todos los oficios que hay en Castilla.... Hacen vihuelas muy buenas; pues labradores, de su naturaleza lo son antes que viniésemos a la Nueva España* (Díaz del Castillo 1568:II, 558–60).
> [Let us move forward and say how the rest of the native-born peoples of these lands have learned all of the trades that there are in Castile.... They make very good vihuelas because the artisans of this inclination had it before we ever came to New Spain.]

Luthiers established regulations, like the ordinances of Seville which regulated instrument construction, for the guild of tradesmen in New Spain. The guild obtained viceroyal approval in 1585 for specific examinations to license the makers and repairmen of vihuelas and other instruments (Saldívar 1934:185).

With the availability of locally constructed guitars (or vihuelas as they were still known exclusively in the surviving Mexican sources), there was an early demand for vihuela tablatures. As shown previously in reference to the 1620 inventory of García Becerril's library, Spanish vihuela tablatures were a prized possession in Mexico City. They arrived in New Spain as early as 1576, starting with Miguel de Fuenllana's *Orphénica lyra*, according to records maintained in the customs offices of Seville. Other vihuela tablatures imported to Mexico before 1600 were those of Esteban Daza and Luis de Narváez (Torre Revello 1957:376–80).

Guitar-like instruments had been known only as vihuelas throughout the 16th-century conquest of Mexico and the Caribbean (with only one exception in Table 1). The guitarra did not appear by name until the 17th century: it was so mentioned in some early court proceedings at the Gulf of Mexico's main port, Veracruz. A guitarist there faced prosecution for disturbing the peace in 1606 (Saldívar 1934:300–01).

Decades later, an English friar by the name of Thomas Gage arrived in the missions of New Spain. He took care to keep a diary, and with it he published the first English description of the guitar in Mexican territory. He chanced to travel in the new viceroy's fleet which arrived at the port of Veracruz on 12 September 1625. All the priests of the entourage attended receptions held in their respective cloisters, and Gage, being a Dominican friar, joined the others of his order at a splendid feast. Afterwards their prior, who was in fact a man about town and a capable guitarist, entertained them. Even though Gage was on the receiving end of all these gushing demonstrations of joy and respect, he employed his usual caustic tone of "holier than thou" to criticize the musical activities he observed:

> The Prior of this cloister was no staid, ancient, grey-headed man, such as usually are made Superiors to govern young and wanton friars, but he was a gallant and amorous young spark....
> After dinner he had some of us to his chamber, where we observed his lightness and little favor of religion or mortification in him. We thought to have found in his chamber some stately library, which might tell us of learning and love of study; we found not above a dozen old books, standing in a corner covered with dust and cobwebs, as if they were ashamed that the treasure that lay hid in them should be so much forgotten and undervalued, and the guitar (the Spanish lute) preferred and set above them....
> The discourse of the young and light-headed Prior was nothing but vain boasting of himself, of his birth, his parts, his favor with the chief Superior or Provincial, the love which the best ladies, the richest merchants' wives of the town, bare unto him, of his clear and excellent voice, and great dexterity in music, whereof he presently gave us a taste, tuning his guitar and singing to us some verses—as he said, of his own composing (1644:34–35).

After only two days in Veracruz, Father Gage and the other travelling Dominicans continued on towards their destination in Mexico City. En route they stayed in a town where the Franciscan friars were using the guitar as a means of training the Indian children how to dance:

> The chief town between Puebla and Mexico is called Huejo-tzingo, consisting of some five hundred Indian and one hundred Spaniard inhabitants. Here is likewise a cloister of Franciscans, who entertained us gallantly, and made shew unto us of the dexterity of their Indians in music.... Their greatest glory and boasting to us was the education which they had given to some children of the town, especially such as served them in their cloister, whom they had brought up to dancing after the Spanish fashion at the sound of the guitar. And this a dozen of them (the biggest not being above fourteen years of age) performed excellently for our better entertainment that night. We were there till midnight, singing both Spanish and Indian tunes, capering and dancing with their castanets (Gage 1644:51).

6. The Guitar in Peru

The first mention of the guitar in South American literature appeared in a chronicle of the Peruvian conquest. Francisco Pizarro led the way against the Incas in 1531. Of the remaining chronicles of the colonization, Guamán Poma's left some precedents for the history of the guitar in South America: (1) the earliest appearance of the term "guitarra" in literature, and (2) the first extant drawing of a guitar. Therefore, his chronicle has already come to the attention of guitar specialists (Zavadivker 1977a; Ohlsen 1980).

Felipe Guamán Poma de Ayala was born in Ayacucho, south of Lima, at about the beginning of the Spanish invasion. Inasmuch as he was interested in writing and possessed a singular gift for illustrating, the chronicle which featured both of his abilities was the pet project of his entire life. He finally completed it around 1615 (Pease 1980:I, xi). Being himself a descendant of Andean Indians yet also a Christian, he provided extensive information about both sides of the momentous cultural clash in Peru. In fact, most of his chronicle is an apology for Indian behavior in the wake of the Spanish invasion. He made frequent mention of music, and his drawings of the indigenous instruments were in themselves a substantial survey of the Amerindian musical practices that he knew (Stevenson 1960:140–44; Zavadivker 1977b).

But now to the European instruments. Guamán Poma first mentioned the vihuela within the context of liturgical music. The performers on it were the Indians from around Lima who played the vihuela right along with the other instruments of Catholic ritual and worship:

> *son grandes cantores y múcicos de canto de órgano y llano y de uigüela y de flauta cherimía tronpeta corneta y bigüela de arco, organista* (Guamán Poma c.1615:822).
> [They are great singers and musicians of counterpoint and plainchant and of the vihuela, flute, shawm, trumpet, cornetto, bowed viol, and organ.]

Then he mentioned the guitarra in quite another context. It was part of the wild celebrations of the lowest class, as in—

> *dansas y fiestas y bailes con tanbores y guitaras en todo este rreyno* (Guamán Poma c.1615:890).
> [dances, fiestas, and balls with drums and guitars throughout this kingdom.]

Despite the fact that Guamán Poma is addressing here the extent of the guitar's lower-class impact (to be discussed in Part IV), he also portrays the guitar's place amidst the aristocracy. The American-born Hispanics of Peru, known as the *criollos* [creoles], were the aristocrats of the day; many of them served the viceroyal officials sent directly from Spain. Guamán Poma depicted two of these dilettantes in a marvelous drawing of courtship (on page 856 of the facsimile edition and in Plate V). A young Hispanic man is singing and accompanying himself on the guitar, entreating a young woman of the same class in what Guamán Poma has labelled a "fiesta" among the "criollos." Here the artist portrays a song, albeit with Amerindian lyrics, which the young man sings and accompanies as part of an amorous conquest:

i ŭs

CRIOLLOS · I CRIOLLASIŬS

chipchillunto
chipch. llanto
pacayllanto
maypincaypi ueosastica
maypincaypi chincanuaylla
maypincaypi hamacaylla

fiesta

criollos

Plate V *Fiesta* with Guitar in Peru (Guamán Poma c.1615:856)
After the facsimile edition (Paris: Institut d'Ethnologie, 1936)

Guamán Poma achieved not only outstanding originality but
long-term significance with this portrayal of the guitar. He began
the drawing with a striking caption in the form of a centered
palindrome. It is a statement which reads the same, whether
backwards or forwards like the word rotor:

INS.
CRIOLLOS I CRIOLLAS INS.

[(MALE) INDIAN CREOLES AND CREOLE INDIAN (FEMALES)]

Under the palindrome he placed a short Indian text rhymed a a' a'
b c c, undoubtedly the lyrics of a song. Next, he enhanced the scene
by situating it over a patterned floor of stone or perhaps glazed tile
to make it an indoor scene of some intimacy. Indeed, the couple
may be behind locked doors, inasmuch as the maiden is showing
her keys, though simultaneously she appears to be taken aback by
this serenade. Both the young man and woman are portrayed with
elegant, courtly dress: some of what they wear remains purely
ornamental. The mood is absolutely consistent: the piece flows
diagonally from left to right, from the man's fixed stare, his music,
and even his gait. All of his attention and all of his apparent
gestures—physical, social, and of course emotional—converge
upon the maiden. Here is a conquest in the making over a shy but
submissive beauty. Guamán Poma could not have been more
successful in making a powerful, sensual statement within the
limitations of his medium of line drawing in pen-and-ink.

Given his skill, Guamán Poma was able to provide plenty of detail on the guitar itself. It is a narrow, small guitar with a single,
elaborate rose not inconsistent with European models. The guitar
is held high, almost in the flamenco style of Spanish dance teachers, and the performer's right hand seems positioned for plucking
with the thumb and first two fingers. The bridge suggests that it is
fitted with four strings, but the angled head of the instrument
accommodates enough pegs to allow tuning in courses, perhaps a
single first string, and the rest in pairs. Thus, the first extant
portrayal of the guitar in the Americas was drawn perceptively.

The instrument reveals the continuity between the guitars of the Old and New Worlds, both in appearance and performance practice, and it suggests the importance of the guitar in aristocratic social affairs.

The final stage of the early guitar's impact in Peru was set by its accession to the viceroyal court. From the lofty vantage point of the viceroys of Lima—the potentates who came to rule South America as appointees of the Spanish king, any one of them had ample opportunity to look down upon plebeian music-making with the guitar. Since it was ever a part of Hispanic song, dance, and even some cathedral music, according to Guamán Poma, the viceroy could not help but hear the guitar often. For example, within the first decade following the canonization of guitarist St. Rose of Lima, a celebration was held in her honor. During the festivities the viceroy, in the company of his own family, observed harps and guitars as part of the affair. On that occasion it was Don Melchor de Navarra y Rocafull, Duke of Palata—one of the last appointees of the Spanish branch of the Hapsburg dynasty as the 22nd Viceroy of Peru—who was in attendance:

> *Masquerade of Mulattoes for Saint Rose*
> Saturday, the 9th of August of 1682, at nine at night a masquerade of more than eighty mulattoes in costumes and silly attire set out with two floats. Many of them went dressed as women, dancing with much gaiety to the rhythm of harps and guitars. Bearing many lights, they went completely around the plaza. The viceroy and vicereine with all their family were in the balconies, and all the people were in the plaza and in the streets through which the masquerade passed (Mugaburu 1697:270).

Notwithstanding the color and excitement of such spectacles, neither the viceroy, nor his lady, nor his household were taking the guitar seriously. They were merely passive witnesses of guitar music from afar.

According to surviving evidence, however, some rulers of Peru provided a place for the guitar inside the viceroyal palace (Stevenson 1984:789–91). Don Pedro de Castro, the Count of Lemos took the trouble of bringing a guitarist along for his own chambers. The Hapsburgs appointed the Count of Lemos as the 19th Viceroy of

Peru in 1667, so for his New World sojourn he set about gathering
an appropriate entourage of officials and courtiers. He selected a
chaplain for the viceroyal residence by the name of Lucas Ruiz de
Ribayaz who happened also to be a notable guitarist of his day:

> La lista de los acompañantes del Conde de Lemos, contiene los
> siguientes nombres, con especificación de los cargos que ocu-
> paban en la Casa...entre los Gentiles hombres de la Cámara
> aparecen...el Presbítero D. Lucas Ruiz de Ribayaz (Lohmann
> Villena 1946:30).
> [The list of those who accompanied the Count of Lemos contains
> the following names, along with the specification of the offices
> that they occupied in the palace...among the Gentlemen of the
> Chamber appear(s)...Don Lucas Ruiz de Ribayaz.]

Eventually Ribayaz returned to Spain and earned even more fame
as a guitarist. He published a method-book there in 1677 in which
he included some guitar music of Gaspar Sanz and instructions on
how to play it. If Ribayaz could perform the music he was advocating, the most complex and stylized yet published in Spain for the
guitarra española, he must have been an excellent performer in
his own right. He also confirmed the fact that "the author [i.e.,
Ribayaz himself] has seen different kingdoms, remote and overseas provinces (Strizich 1977:52)."

The guitar's prestige reached its apex during the viceroyal
epoch with the viceroy who was himself a guitarist. For a few
years after 1700 and as the first prince of the Bourbon dynasty, the
youthful Philip V, was coming of age, the viceroy's seat in Lima
remained vacant while lesser officials conducted business and
negotiations. Then in 1707, Philip V appointed Don Manuel de
Oms y Santa Pau, Marqués de Castell dos Ríus (of Valencia) as the
24th Viceroy of Peru. At that moment the guitar was in vogue at
Madrid, for the courtiers of Bourbon France had already embraced the instrument, starting with Louis XIV. Once the French
royalty took to the guitar as practicing dilettantes, it caught on as a
suitable instrument for any courtier. So in a sense, as the guitar
saw revitalization at the court of Madrid under the new Bourbon
dynasty, it was coming full circle—having a bit of a renaissance.
To be sure, the guitar itself was not new there among professionals:

several guitarists had previously served the court in succession, the latest of whom was the pre-eminent Santiago de Murcia of the Chapel Royal. But now the guitar's devotees included not less than the Queen, Marie-Louise-Gabrielle of Savoy, known affectionately to her subjects María Luisa Gabriela. She was taking guitar lessons, herself—a fact confirmed by Murcia, her teacher, and the queen's personal correspondence with her relatives (Lowenfeld 1974:4–5). Therefore it was not so unusual for Don Manuel de Oms to count guitar-playing among the many abilities he brought to his new appointment.

Oms y Santa Pau held the post of viceroy from 1707 to 1710. While in Lima he proved to be a man of great culture and vision: he instituted an academy for the arts and literature in which he was the foremost practicing advocate. It was a Monday-evening social affair with artistic and literary aims. He invited members of his cabinet and other close friends to the weekly meetings with the high humanistic purpose of celebrating music, poetry, and theatre, much like the neo-Platonist academies held at such illustrious Florentine villas as those of Lorenzo de'Medici and Counts Bardi and Corsi in the previous century. The viceroy convened the first session of his academy on 23 September 1709, during which he assigned his cabinet members the task of composing sonnets in a certain way, and then he played the guitar himself for all to behold (Rodríguez de Guzmán 1713:9).

During the century between Guamán Poma and the viceroy-guitarist, therefore, the guitar appeared in every conceivable situation in and around Lima. Its performance contexts ranged from the lowest to the highest class, from the wildest expressions of the "infidels" to the most serene entreaties of cathedral worship. At the same time, the guitar was no mere instrument of passive entertainment before the aristocrats, for sometimes they too were active participants. The dilettantes were merely following suit: what was simultaneously the *royal guitar* of the Bourbon dynasty in the two largest monarchies of Europe (France and Spain) had become the *viceroyal guitar* in South America to begin the 18th century. Thus already during the viceroyal epoch, the guitar was both highly esteemed and appropriate for men and women in every social niche of the Hispanic domination of South America.

7. Guitar Strings and Frets in the Plata

The guitar came to the Plata region with its first European colonists in 1536. It arrived with the pioneer settlers of Buenos Aires
in the company of Pedro de Mendoza. Among them were Juan de
Salazar's sailors who brought a guitar along for entertainment of
the young ladies in the company (Viglietti 1973:109). The guitar
spread from there on the waterways and overland throughout the
greater Plata basin. By the end of the century, with the arrival of
more colonists from Europe, numerous guitars were evident
around the inland city of Córdoba. Court records there indicate
that strings and frets, in appreciable quantities, were already
available in stores in 1597 and 1599 (see Table 3, below).

The strings of the guitarra and vihuela, as well as their tied-on
frets, were made of "catgut." Throughout the Plata region, strings
of local, even home-made fabrication were available, but those
prepared by specialists and marketed in stores were superior and
preferred. The manufacture of gut strings was an old process. For
millennia musicians had made them from the smaller sheep intestine which they stripped to size then twisted, rack-dried, and polished. Strings produced in this way by Old World artisans were
certainly superior to those made from the abundant by-products of
cattle, horses, or sheep of the Plata region. Strings of ram, capon,
ewe, and lamb gut varied in properties of texture, density, and
resilience—hence also musical quality. A guitarist in Minas, Uruguay became known for the strings he fabricated from the tripe of
deer around 1840. That same guitarist, Bernardo Berro, later
ascended to the presidency of the Republic (Viglietti 1973:125).

Musicians made frets of the same gut material as the strings,
and fastened them on the neck, just as in Europe, to keep them in
place. The guitarist wrapped the frets around the neck precisely at
half-step intervals and tied them with a knot on the "north" or
upper side of the fingerboard so as to avoid touching the knots
while performing. The frets remained somewhat movable in the
process, as on most of the early guitars even in the Old World. The
busy player had to change frets occasionally because they were as
fragile as the string material and subject to wear. Throughout the

Plata basin, frets continued to be a typical commodity in general stores and highly valued.

A wealth of archival documentation shows that strings were an expensive but salable commodity. In the first place, gut strings could not last for long. They were consumed like reeds on the woodwinds, so local stores had to have a ready supply. Centuries before the opening of music stores in the Plata, tavern owners sold strings from behind the protective bars of their *pulperías,* the "pubs" of both city and countryside that doubled their service as sundry shops. (Iron bars protected the owners from the impact of brawls and robberies!) Some pulperías were as large and accommodating as the "general stores" of the North American Wild West. The strings marketed in the pulperías appeared extensively throughout the region as part of business transactions and inventories. On an exchange of ownership, whether due to the sale of a business or to the death of a proprietor, strings were always part of the inventory. For instance, an inventory occasioned by a case of insanity in 1773 contained hundreds of items, including two gross of guitar strings (Archivo de la Nación, Bossio 1972:229).

The strings and fret material of the early guitar were valuable, as already suggested in the imports at old Puerto Rico (Table 2). The same was true in Argentine territory. According to the data of Córdoba 1599, Table 3, the strings worth four pesos per set were worth half as much as the median price of the guitars in Table 7, from 1695 to 1786. Upon a person's death, guitar strings were a possession worth itemizing just as much as the lands and personal effects of the deceased. Thus beneficiaries inherited guitar strings along with instruments and the rest of a person's estate, as specified in numerous legal documents.

New World iconographical sources suggested specific stringing, sometimes in courses. Guamán Poma implied string sets or pairs in his drawing of the guitar's headsock (Plate V). Even so, guitars were eventually strung singly, but the date of this transition in America has yet to be ascertained. No doubt availability and price were determining factors.

In the extraordinary tale of the gaucho *Martín Fierro* (1879), the protagonist is a guitarist. In fact, the entire epic consists of lyrical poetry ostensibly recited to the guitar, as set forth from the beginning. In Canto I, as Martín Fierro praises his guitar, he also implies that it is armed with both treble and bass strings:

Con la guitarra en la mano	Whenever I take my guitar in hand,
ni las moscas se me arriman;	even the flies obey my command,
naides me pone el pie encima,	nobody can step on my tail;
y, cuando el pecho se entona,	and when I give my voice a try,
hago gemir a la prima	I make the first string wail
y llorar a la bordona.	and the bass string cry.

Even though many guitars of previous eras had no bass strings, the gaucho epic attests to their use during the 19th century. Additional documentation on the use of bass strings appeared among the judicial records of Córdoba. An extant will there documents the transfer of bass strings in 1792, as shown below in Table 3.

Unfortunately none of these references indicates whether the basses mentioned are "over-spun" or simply thick gut strings. However, a pulpería inventory has survived since the end of the 18th century, and it sheds some light on the question (see Bossio 1972:234, 277–79). The pulpería owned by one Francisco Doldán contained 564 pesos' worth of merchandise that included a guitar and guitar strings, at the following prices:

cuerdas de guitarra, bordonas de plata	*1 peso*
una guitarra	*9 pesos*
[guitar strings, silver basses (at)	1 peso
one guitar	9 pesos]

The inventory implies that bass strings, such as those with a covering of fine silver-plated wire, were available there, just as they were back in the Old World. European guitar construction was in transition at that very moment: the development of a reliable, over-spun bass string was leading to a momentous change in instrument construction. Towards the end of the 18th century, single-strung guitars with over-spun bass strings were superseding the double-strung Baroque guitar. The innovations were so successful that soon thereafter another bass appeared: the 6th or E string, hence the birth of our modern six-string guitar. In the Río de la Plata, these technological advances were already in evidence;

silver plated, over-spun bass strings were in use by the end of the 18th century.

With the availability of fine bass strings by around 1800, the tuning of our modern guitar was made possible in the Plata region. Before then, guitarists must have tuned their four- and five-course guitars according to European practices. All the Spanish Baroque guitar treatises recommended the following tuning as standard: (5)=A (4)=D (3)=G (2)=B (1)=E, even though the actual pitches were only relative. However, the distribution of octaves and unisons remained variable. Sometimes guitarists put a bass string on each of the fourth and fifth courses along with an octave above. Occasionally they replaced one or even both of the bass strings of A and D with strings at the higher octave, a practice which obviously eliminated bass notes altogether (because notes on A and D would be sounding within the range of the other strings). Even so, the European tuning for courses ranging from five to one remained standardized at A D G B E. Four-course guitars had the same tuning but without the A strings. Rioplatense guitar tunings were inherited from Spain, and thus were undoubtedly similar.

Nevertheless, European guitar books sometimes called for a special or an exceptional tuning. In such cases it was called a *scordatura,* and it was specified at the beginning of a piece or at the start of an entire suite of dances. A *scordatura* could provide either a special musical effect or a performer's tour de force, or both. The same was true in the Plata region. Besides the standard, ascending tunings of D G B E, A D G B E, or E A D G B E, special tunings surfaced among the folk. Carlos Vega collected dozens of different *"afinaciones rurales"* [rural tunings] that he found in Argentina (1946a:163–71). Subsequently Alejandro Ayestarán summarized the special folk tunings of the Uruguayan Republic (1980).

The tuning and stringing of the early European guitar remained so complex that not until recent decades have the actual practices become clear. Notwithstanding, these historical practices were the basis for those of the Plata. Table 3, below, shows what remains on the stringing and fretting of the historic Rioplatense guitar around the inland town of Córdoba, Argentina. This information, originally collected by Father Pedro J. Grenón, remains in Córdoba's tribunal and ecclesiastical archives to the present day.

Table 3 Gut Strings and Frets around Córdoba
(Grenón 1929, 1954)

1597. Francisco Nájera has, among the effects received from Domingo Juárez for sale, "82 vihuela frets of gut (A de T, E. 1, P. 1.9, f.1325)." [A de T= Archivo de Tribunales for the Province of Córdoba, Argentina]

1599. In a document, the following were noted: "four sets of vihuela strings, at four pesos per set (A de T, E.1, E.1.9, e.8)."

1604. There were inventoried in a store "100 vihuela strings, at two reals per string (A de T, E.1, P.1.117, f.322)."

1614. Among the effects left in a store were registered "four dozen vihuela strings at three reals apiece (A de T, E.1, P.1.26, f.380)."

1615. In a store were found for sale "several packs of vihuela strings (A de T, E.1, E.1.35, e.2)."

1619. The following belonged to Francisco López Correa of Córdoba: "eight gross vihuela strings (A de T, E.1, P.1.34, f.458)."

1622. On that date the Father General of the Jesuits writes—"I have ordered lute strings to be purchased for Brother Berger" (P. Carlos Leonhardt, "La música en el teatro...de la Provincia de la Compañía de Jesús de Paraguay," *Revista de Estudios* [Buenos Aires] No. 152 [Feb. 1924], p. 129).

1643. Among the personal effects of Andrés de Sosa are listed "two packs of strings for *discante,* and 45 gut frets for guitar...(A de T, E.1, E.1.80)."

1656. In the surrender of the accounts of Gabriel Toro Masote's effects..."Maestro Gregorio Juárez auctioned off 14 and a half sets of guitar strings, I say 20 at 13 reals which come to 32 pesos and 2 reals (A de T, E.1, E.1.110, e.1, f.358)."

1702. According to José Díaz de Casares, owner of an encomienda in Santiago, he has in La Paz: "15 sets of vihuela strings (A de T, E.1, 1.106, e.5, f.13)."

1748. At mid-year, José Rodríguez reported the list of articles in his store which he entrusted to Manuel Castro to sell. Among them were "66 dozens of guitar strings, at five and a half pesos which net nine pesos and a real (A de T, E.1.308, e.1)."

1773. Some of the properties assigned to Andrés Alvarez were, among other things, "a dozen little flutes at five reals each and eleven gross guitar strings at five reals apiece (A de T, E.1, E.1.380, e.7)."

1792. In the balance taken from María Tobares of the effects which Don Lucas Ramírez left her were mentioned "two dozen bass strings for guitar at a real and three pesos...(A de T, E.1, 1.416, e.9, f.2)."

1806. Among the possessions of Antonio Durán in Capilla Rodríguez, are counted "three dozen guitar strings (A de T, Crim., 1.106)."

1814. In the store of Casimiro Pereyra are mentioned "six and a half gross of Chilean guitar strings (A de T, E.1, E.1.445)."

This review of the salient aspects of Rioplatense guitar strings lacks one important detail. The best strings came from Europe to the Americas, according to evidence remaining on both continents. Some of the initial documentation on strings for musical instruments resulted from the careful scrutiny of the ships that were leaving the Spanish mainland in the 16th century. Ship captains had to register their freight just as much as their passengers with the customs offices in Seville. José Torre Revello researched the registers of American-bound ships departing between the years of 1534 and 1586 and discovered among them the specific inclusion of vihuela strings (1943:778, 1948:118).

On the other end of the exchange, American sources confirm the fact that European shipments included strings. An early example (apart from Table 2) is found in an anonymous chronicle of the viceroyal epoch of Peru, entitled "Descripción del Virreinato del Perú" [Description of the Viceroyalty of Peru]. Although it was never published, the manuscript documents events between 1605 and 1615, so it probably dates from the same period. The chronicle

ends with a lengthy appendix. It lists many indispensable articles
of colonial life in Peru that had to be imported from Europe. The
list begins with the following sensational caption:

MEMORIA DE TODOS LOS GENEROS DE MERCADERIAS QUE
SON NECESARIOS PARA EL PERU Y SIN ELLAS NO PUEDEN
PASAR, PORQUE NO SE FABRICAN EN LA
TIERRA, SON LAS SIGUIENTES
(*Descripción* c.1615:124):
[Summary of all the kinds of merchandise that are necessary
in Peru,without which its inhabitants cannot live,
because these items are not made locally,
and they are the following:]

Later, in the same list, p. 133, are:
*Cuerdas de vigüela, finas de Alemania y de Pisa y Florencia y
Roma* [Vihuela strings, fine ones from Germany, Pisa, Florence,
and Rome].

As for the import of guitar strings to the Río de la Plata, Father
Grenón's discoveries included only two items that specified foreign
origins, dated 1622 and 1814 (Table 3). Naturally, when taking
inventory in the pulperías or when enumerating the bequeathed
possessions of an estate, it was impractical to indicate whether
strings were from foreign sources or not, even though they may
have been. The fact that most strings were imported explains why
a set of them cost somewhere between a quarter and half as much
as a guitar. This was the direct consequence of the Río de la Plata's
isolation, and because of the trade restrictions imposed by the Viceroyalty of Peru. Trade was simply not open in the Plata region till
1778 when the Rule of Free Commerce supplanted all previous
restrictions as a benefit of the newly-created, autonomous Viceroyalty of the Río de la Plata. A boom of foreign imports followed the
lifting of trade restrictions, and as a direct result, the customs
offices of Buenos Aires became overburdened with the traffic of
musical merchandise from overseas. This fact is confirmed in the
historic documents published recently by Waldemar Axel Roldán.
Equally important, these same documents show that over-spun
bass strings became widely distributed starting in 1785, as shown
in Table 4, below:

Table 4 The Trade of Guitar Strings in the Plata Viceroyalty
(Documents of the *Archivo General de la Nación,* Colonial
Division, Salon XIII as summarized in Roldán 1987:95–96)

Buenos Aires. Customs Office, 1785 (34.8.2)

Guide No. 2318: Don Mateo Fernández enumerates for the Royal
Aduana (Customs Office) the various products he is removing and
taking to his town, including several "gross guitar strings."
No. 2784: Don Vicente Castes sends, with his cowhand Tobías Del-
gado, some dozens of over-spun guitar strings to Salta.

Buenos Aires. Customs Office, 1786 (34.9.3)

Guide No. 2724: permission is solicited from the Administrator of
the Royal *Aduana,* for authorization to export aboard Don Sebastián Aramburu's ship a used guitar and two gross guitar strings.
No. 2802: permission is solicited from the Administrator of the
Royal *Aduana* to ship two dozen over-spun basses and six gross
guitar strings to Santo Domingo de Soriano [Uruguay].
No. 2834: permission of the Administrator of the Royal *Aduana* is
solicited in order to send two dozen bass strings for the guitar to the
City of Mendoza.

Buenos Aires. Customs Office, 1786 (34.9.4)

Guide No. 3804: Don Francisco Montes is sending eight gross guitar strings to Maldonado [Uruguay].
No. 3930: Don Mariano Tabia writes to the Royal *Aduana* requesting the Administrator's permission to dispatch a vihuela and its
case to him.
No. 3990: Don Gaspar Contreras of the neighboring town of Luján
returns to that town with the effects consigned to him; among
them figure a dozen bass strings for the guitar.
No. 4001: gives permission to the consignee Lucas de Lerma for
him to take ten gross guitar strings to Montevideo [Uruguay].

In conclusion, strings and frets were extremely important on
the Rioplatense guitar. They had their own history in terms of use,
construction, availability, and value, as documented in the region.
Guitarists there followed the European precedent and tied gut
frets on the neck. Pure gut strings were the norm until over-spun
bass strings became widely available with the free trade of the new

viceroyalty (Table 4). Nevertheless, not until the advent of nylon was any other material used generally for treble guitar strings. Some of these references were so early as to shed light on European practices. Even so, the usual historical sequence was the other way around: the Rioplatense guitar's stringing, fretting, and tuning were all a continuation of long-standing tradition. After all, the best guitar strings were European imports, despite the cost.

8. The Vihuela

The great epic poem entitled *El gaucho Martín Fierro,* considered previously in connection with the use of treble and bass strings, has a seemingly unusual beginning, given its subject. It starts out with a reference to the vihuela:

Aquí me pongo a cantar	[Here I sit myself to sing
al compás de la vigüela,	to my vihuela's measure
que el hombre que lo desvela	not to reveal man's treasure
una pena estrordinaria,	but rather extr'ordinary pain,
como la ave solitaria	like a bird in the rain,
con el cantar se consuela.	that only in song reaches pleasure.]

Thus, like the Golden Age poets, Hernández used the terms vihuela and guitar in close proximity, almost interchangeably. However, Esteban Echeverría, the first poet/guitarist of Argentine romanticism, had a more refined style. But like Hernández, he too was ambivalent on the terminology; he put the guitar and vihuela in the same breath:

A mi guitarra	To My Guitar
Tú que has sido siempre	[To you, having always been
Mi fiel compañera,	my companion faithful,
Justo es que te cante,	it is right that I should sing,
Sonora vihuela.	my sonorous vihuela.]

Even though the terms *vihuela* and *guitarra* often appeared interchangeably, some subtle differences between them remained in Plata usage. In the Rioplatense mind's eye, the vihuela is older, being an archaic instrument in remission, so with it Plata poets always evoke the past. This difference occurs in musical sources, as well. For instance, Table 3 shows that all of the strings and frets belong to the vihuela, up until the mention of frets for the guitarra in 1643. Then, references to the guitarra and vihuela overlap, and finally the guitarra replaces the vihuela at the end of the 18th century. The same holds true in Tables 5 through 9: they contain ample data from Córdoba's historical archives to show how the guitarra superseded the vihuela.

Besides being the more archaic of the two instruments, the vihuela was the more traditional and serious. In an example noted earlier, Guamán Poma associated the vihuela with ceremonial church performances and the guitarra with wild secular music during Peru's colonial epoch. The same applied to the Río de la Plata; these serious, even religious connotations carried through Rioplatense life. The vihuela had enough respectability attached to it that women of the upper class or a dignified teacher could play it in 1661, and it was even admissible in church.

The numerous references to the vihuela in Table 5 are no subtle reminder that the history of the guitar will never be complete without the inclusion of the vihuela, and that the American musical sources will ever be a font of information on the subject. To be sure, the vihuela declined among Latin American instruments, but it never died out completely as it did in Europe. In the Plata, it was an instrument of dignity and rather wide distribution in the 17th and 18th centuries:

Table 5 The Vihuela
(Retaining original spellings of the instruments,
from Grenón 1929, 1954)

1609. Doña María Tejeda has in her possession "a good bigüela (A de T, E.1, P.1.21)." [A de T= Archivo de Tribunales, Córdoba]

1633. "Una bigüela" is mentioned in a citation of that year (A de T, E.1, 1.70, e.7).

1636. Diego Páez had "a bigüela without strings" in his possession (A de T, E.1, 1.70, e.7).

1661. Maestro Diego Fernández Sotomayor finished a will on this clause: "Inside of the aforementioned, i.e., my house is my vigüela, my academic hood, and my teacher's tassel (A de T, E.1, E.1.67)."

1687. The historian Francisco Xarque writes that..."an eight-year-old boy can dance fifty variations, without losing the measure (or 'beat') of the vigüela or harp accompaniment, with as much finesse as the most accomplished Spaniard." (F. Xarque, *Insignes misioneros: Vida del Padre Antonio Ruiz de Montoya*. Pamplona: 1687, T. III, p. 23.)

1688. The following is noted in favor of Juan Maldonado in a will: "A used, old vigüela, with the body of a gourd, valued at three pesos (A de T, E.1, 1.164, e.6, f.25)."

1736. [See below, Table 10, in the list pertaining to instruments used in church.]

1761. Pedro Barros Aguilar of Catamarca "had a vihuela and a *rabel* (A de T, E.3, 1.1, e.3)."

1761. [See also below, Table 10, during the same year, a vigüela in the Chapel of Saldán.]

1767. [See below, Table 10, the ten vihuelas in the church of San Javier.]

9. The Discante

The little *discante* was a fashionable 17th-century instrument in Córdoba, Argentina that fell into disuse and obscurity during the period. It was even found among members of the aristocracy. Domingo Prat (1934:405) and the *Real Academia Española* (1950) defined it as a *tiple*, or small guitar. The *Diccionario Kapelusz*, an excellent compendium on the lexicon of Rioplatense (Buenos Aires, 1979) echoed in similar terms:

<u>Discante</u> *s.m. pequeña guitarra de sonido agudo....*
[<u>Discante</u>, masculine noun, small guitar of high pitch....]

Researchers into Rioplatense folklore have confirmed again that the discante was a type of guitar. It was an instrument equated with the *tiple* of four to six courses (Moreno Chá 1980:23 and see Plate 30).

Like the vihuela, the discante was an instrument of serious associations. Despite its small size, it was an expensive instrument for the educated class, suitable for women, and it was acceptable for use in church, according to the data of Table 6.

One of the loveliest tales of Argentine literature involving the guitar-like instruments was also one of the earliest. It was a true story, related by Luis de Tejeda, a priest/poet/guitarist who resided near Córdoba, in his manuscript dated 1663. The story recounted an incident which took place at a hermitage chapel located at Saldán, some ten miles north of the city. The parishoners there constituted only a small congregation, so they had long prayed for a musician who would help embellish their a cappella worship services with an appropriate musical instrument:

Ref. 4 *Coronas líricas*   Luis José de Tejeda
   [One night of tempestuous wind, thunder and lightening, the
parents and children of a devout family were preparing to go to
the chapel in order to comply with their daily devotions, hoping
to calm somewhat the storm. In the worst of it there came some
great knocks against their doors. The owner of the house, who
kept them locked as a precaution, opened the doors to discover a
man that looked rather like a savage, because, although his size,
disposition, and age belonged to a young man, his unkempt, bi-
zarre, and grown-out beard and hair demonstrated that he was
an inhabitant of the deepest woods; his bad, rustic, yet amusing
language revealed that some great misfortune had left him in
that state. He said that he had been headed towards the city, yet
he could not account for the fact that he was thrown off course,
except that the great strikes of lightening had shown him that
stop and the population there near the hermitage. The wind
quieted so the devout family went to the chapel; as they entered
they requested that their unknown guest remain outside. They
had scarcely begun to sing the "Salve" [Hail Mary Queen of
Heaven] when he also entered to hear it, falling to his knees
until the end of it and of their other devotions. After they finished, he took out from beneath his cloak a discante of the usual

small size; he tuned it, and to its accompaniment he sang lyrics
in praise of the Virgin, and many other romances around the
same theme with admirable voice and not a little skill. From
there they went to dine, and they treated him; over the table he
related his story...of living with some uncivilized Indians,
where though his life was also barbarous, he had persevered in
his devotion to Our Lady, to whom among other devotions, he
always sang to the accompaniment of that little discante.... It
seemed to the family in this case a miracle because of their
needs in that moment...] (Tejeda 1663:61–62).

Table 6 The Discante
(Grenón 1929, 1954)

1608. Concerning the tutorial instruction of the young man Martín de Salvatierra, in Córdoba, the following is registered: "Item, 14
pesos of the 26 pesos for the price of the discante which was purchased for the said minor, being a thing of culture (A de T, E.1,
E.1.28)."

1609. Doña Bartola Maldonado has "a discante (A de T, E.1,
P.1.21)."

1611. Francisco Leyton declares among his property "a good discante (A de T, E.1, E.1.24)."

1621. Gaspar López says, "I have a discante; I gave it to D. Domingo de Leiva (A de T, E.1, 1.37)."

1635. María de Sarza was the owner of "a discante (A de T, E.1,
E.1.86)."

1643. [Regarding discante strings, see above, Table 1.]

1645. In María Castro's letter of bequest is included, among the
items, "a discante valued at 12 pesos (A de T, E.1, P.1.55)."

1646. "A discante" is mentioned among the...effects which the deceased María Soria left to her beneficiary (A de T, E.1, E.1.86, e.1).

1649. Angel de Castro, in Córdoba, consigns "a discante (A de T,
E.1, E.1.91)."

10. Sizes and Types of Guitars

In the centuries after the guitar's introduction to the American continents, it evolved considerably beyond its original state. Both the vihuela and guitarra, which Spanish theorists had defined as large and small guitars, came to the Americas in the Columbian Exchange (Table 1). Once in the Americas, these instruments were subject to linguistic trends, such as the semantic shift from vihuela to guitarra. Another trend was the application of the principle, "bigger is better": small guitars were gradually replaced by large ones, and again new semantics came into use to distinguish the various sizes and designs, for they coexisted. For example, a will in Caracas, Venezuela documented the following items in connection with a certain household:

> *1651. Don Manuel Fernández [deja] dos guitarras, una grande, otra pequeña* (Calzavara 1987:221).
> [1651. Don Manuel Fernández (bequeaths) two guitars, one large, the other small.]

In the Río de la Plata, the trend from small to large seems to have commenced with the introduction of guitars from Brazil or even Portugal (coming over the Brazilian border or through the inland, Portuguese port of Colonia, Uruguay). For example, large guitars frequently appeared in the documents of Córdoba, as listed in Table 7, below. In the first three instances (in 1676, 1708, and 1752), the guitars bore the clear designation "Brazilian" or "Portuguese" as well as the label "guitarra grande." While medium-sized guitars also appeared in the documents of Córdoba in 1786 and 1811, large guitars became standardized with the advent of the new viceroyalty. They were specified again in 1793, 1796, 1802, 1806, and 1809 (Table 7, from the archives in Córdoba).

The guitar underwent permanent change with the creation of the Viceroyalty of the Río de la Plata in 1776. The viceroyalty impacted directly on the guitar scene when, after only two years of development, it established the Rule of Free Commerce. The new deregulation of the port sparked the economy for the first time with uninhibited, free trade, so that while large guitars may have been preferred before then, they became widely available as imports after 1778. Another, related factor was the import of overspun bass strings, starting in 1785. The new basses were no doubt better suited to the enhanced resonance and low range of the larger instruments. Over-spun bass strings added richer, louder tone, and improved intonation, as well as lower pitches. Thus the free trade of the viceroyal epoch reinforced the availability and diffusion of the large guitar which used single stringing and overspun basses. Simultaneously the free trade contributed to the decline of the medium-sized Baroque guitar.

A recent scholarly review of the lifestyle during the Plata viceroyalty provided some analytical detail about twenty guitars of the epoch (Porro 1982:180). All the specimens survived as used instruments, in various states of preservation. During the viceroyalty these guitars had ranged in value from one to eight pesos. They all still had friction pegs for tuning, and more: they were all large. However, in spite of the fact that each one was correctly identified as a *guitarra grande*, such instruments were probably no larger than the Panormo or other early 19th-century guitars of Europe.

Table 7 Guitars of Varying Quality and Size
[In all these references, guitar is the translation of *guitarra*.]
(Grenón 1929, 1954)

1676. General Don Gregorio Luna leaves testimony that—"Lieutenant José Sanches de Loria still owes me a large guitar made in Brazil...even though I have asked him for it many times (A de T, E.2, 1.3, e.12)."

1705. Antonio Domínguez bequeaths "two guitars and a *rabel* (A de T, E.1, E.1.210, e.5)."

1708. Antonio Amuchástegui, in Punilla possessed "a large guitar from Brazil, valued at 16 pesos (A de T, E.1, 1.226, e.2, f.36, año 1710)."

1728. José de las Casas manifests the possession of "an old guitar (A de T, E.1, E.1.260, e.5.)."

1732. Mariano Galiano Daroca, a native of Ecija, figures as owner of "seven guitars: four new and three old ones (A de T, E.1, E.1.271, e.6)."

1747. [See in the next table, a fine Portuguese guitar.]

1752. Among the property of Juan José Martínez is mentioned "a large Portuguese guitar (A de T, E.1.314, e.8)."

1754. In the inventory of Amarante is consigned "a small guitar (A de T, Crim.1.9, e.17, f.16)."

1756. Upon his arrest, Anastasio Amarax, a Portuguese silver-smith in Córdoba, made an inventory of his possessions, among which figures "a small guitar (A de T, Crim.)."

1763. [See below, in the list of prices, a large guitar.]

1770. Lorenzo Montenegro, from neighboring Río Seco, Córdoba left among items of his inheritance "a used guitar (A de T, E.1, E.1.367, e.34)."

1773. [See below with regard to the price of two large guitars.]

1776. In the possession of Gerónimo Cortés is noted "an old harp" and "an old guitar" among the properties of his estate (A de T, E.1, E.1.385, e.1).

1776. [See the small guitar in the next table.]

1776. In the accusation against a horse thief named Antonio Areco of Nono (Córdoba) is adduced the robbery of "a guitar and a saddle (A de T, E.3, E.1.27, e.3)."

1777. Pedro Cabrera affirms that he has a guitar (A de T, E.1, E.1.389, e.3).

1780. "Juan Esteban Arias, 30 years of age, was playing the guitar at his brother's home (A de T, Crim. 1.35, e.00, f.4)."

1786. Lorenzo Contrairria appears having among his possessions "a guitar (A de T, E.2, 1.65, 1a, e.10)."

1786. Manuel Ferreyra had, upon his death in los Cocos del Valle, Punilla, "a medium-size guitar (A de T, E.1, 1.405, e.9)."

1788. In the robbery of Francisco Heredia of Río Seco is consigned "a guitar (A de T, Crim., 1.44, e.27)."

1791. In the embargo made for Gaspar Jordán appears "an old guitar (A de T, Crim., 1.54, e.1, f.15.)"

1791. Found guilty of homicide [and subject to incarceration], the Barcelona man Gaspar Jordán had his personal effects confiscated. Among them is enumerated "an old guitar (A de T, Crim., 1.54, e.11)."

1793. Pedro Ahumada recounts among his effects "two large guitars and a harp (A de T, E.3, e.1.43)."

1795. A document says that Antonio Trillo is in possession of "two guitars (A de T, E.2, 1.84, e.21)."

1795. In the will of Juan Ramallo figures "a guitar (A de T, E.1, E.1.424, e.4)."

1796. Regarding "a large guitar in the pulpería...[see below, Table 12]."

1798. José Altamirano relinquishes "a guitar (A de T, E.3, E.1.50, e.6)."

1798. Regarding "a guitar...medium-sized [see the next table]."

1801. José García Pedernera possesses "an old guitar (A de T, E.3, 1.56, e.17)."

1802. Regarding "two large guitars [see below, Table 9 among women and the guitar]."

1805. Miguel Cornejo, native and resident of Río de los Sauces, leaves "an old guitar (A de T, E.4, E.1.26, e.5)."

1806. Francisco Olmedo bequeathed "a new, large guitar (A de T, E.1, 1.433, e.5)."

1809. The beneficiaries of Antonio Pinardel received "a large guitar (A de T, E.1, E.1.437, e.2)."

1811. In Villa Carlota during February of this year, Juan Rodríguez of Seville confirms the possession, among his effects, of "a medium-sized *guitarrita,*" priced at a peso (A de T, E.4, 1.42, e.1).

1813. José Benito Lago, native of Galicia and resident of La Carlota, unmarried, possessed "a much-used guitar (A de T, E.3, 11.61, e.2)."

1826. Among the possessions of Mariana Sánchez figure "an old guitar and a *tiple* valued at three pesos (A de T, E.3, 1.81, e.6, f.49)."

With the standardization of the large guitar, small ones continued to be used, but under specific designations in music sources as well as in the literature of the Plata's viceroyal epoch. The opening of the viceroyalty, the burgeoning legal business of cowhides and animal by-products, and the attraction of a wide-open New World initiated a rediscovery of the Río de la Plata. It became a place to visit or, for the adventurous, a new place to live. Those who came to the Plata as foreign visitors and adventurers left a fascinating literature that often included commentaries about the guitar.

An early Spanish traveller, Alonso Carrió de la Vandera was employed by the monarchy in a high office. Yet he also possessed a gift for picaresque writing, so he posed for both the protection of his position and the liberation of his pen under the extraordinary nom de plume of Concolorcorvo [literally, *with the color of crow*]! His masterpiece was *El lazarillo de ciegos caminantes desde Buenos-Ayres, hasta Lima...desde Montevideo* [Guidebook for Tenderfoot Travellers from Buenos Aires to Lima...out of Montevideo]. With this excellent book, the gauchesque literature found its beginning. Among other matters, Carrió described the gauchos in some detail, calling them by the less-standardized designation of *gauderios.* In a style full of wit and irony, advancing beyond the mere picaresque fiction of the Golden Age, he spoke of the gauchos from first-hand experience. He asserted that they were itinerant cowboys who, with a small guitar, passed away their entire lives as musicians:

Gauderios
Estos son unos mozos nacidos en Montevideo y en los vecinos
pagos. Mala camisa y peor vestido, procuran encubrir con uno
o dos ponchos, de que hacen cama con los sudaderos del caballo,
sirviéndoles de almohada la silla. Se hacen de una guitarrita,
que aprenden a tocar muy mal y a cantar desentonadamente
varias coplas, que estropean, y muchas que sacan de su cabeza,
que regularmente ruedan sobre amores. Se pasean a su albedrío
por toda la campaña y con notable complacencia de aquellos
semibárbaros colonos, comen a su costa y pasan las semanas
enteras tendidos sobre un cuero, cantando y tocando (Carrió de
la Vandera 1776:33–34).

[Gauderios. These are young men born in Montevideo and the
neighboring villages. Dressed in a bad undershirt and worse
clothes, they attempt to cover with one or two ponchos the fact
that their bed is made from the saddle-blankets of their horse,
and the saddle itself serves as their pillow. They make use of a
small guitar, which they learn to play very badly and they sing
out of tune several verses which they ruin; they improvise
many of the lyrics which regularly rotate round the theme of
love. They wander unrestrained about the entire countryside,
yet to the remarkable delight of its semi-barbarous colonists,
the gauderios eat at their expense and spend weeks at a time
stretched out on a cowhide singing and performing.]

The *guitarrita* he mentioned here may have been the usual
designation for the four-course guitar. Such was the case in
Venezuela. There the four-course guitar was usually called the
cuatro, yet historically it was known by other names. According to
Isabel Aretz, the noted ethnomusicologist, the other small, four-
course guitars equated with the cuatro were the following:

guitarrilla, guitarrita, guitarrillo, guitarra pequeña,
discante, y hasta *charanguillo...y requinto* (Aretz 1967b:122).

After introducing the subject, Aretz then offers an explanation
regarding the origins and development of the small, four-course
guitar, similar to the type in use among the gauderios:

[Starting in the 16th century, diverse treatises exist that permit
a detailed understanding of this instrument's evolution. Hence

our affirmation that the Venezuelan *cuatro* is actually the ancient *guitarrilla* of Spain which the musicians of our countryside preserved, changing or enriching its tunings in some cases, adapting it to the performance practices that are typical of Venezuelan music] (Aretz 1967b:147).

In the decade following Concolorcorvo's book, José de Espinosa came to Montevideo and observed music among the same class—the "gauderios," he called them, as well. The small guitar was still in use among them, but this time to accompany some sung dances:

Si es verano se van detrás del rancho a la sombra y se tumban: si invierno, juegan ó cantan unas raras seguidillas, desentonadas, que llaman de Cadena, o el Perico, o Mal-Ambo, acompañándolo con una desacordada guitarrilla que siempre es un tiple. El talento de cantor es uno de los más seguros para ser bien recibido en cualquier parte y tener comida y hospedaje (Espinosa 1794:561).

[If it is summer, they go behind their hut to lie down in the shade; if it is winter, they play or sing some rare, out-of-tune songs that they call the *cadena,* the *pericón,* or the *malambo,* accompanying them with a poorly strung little guitar *(guitarrilla),* which is always a *tiple.* The talent of "singer" is one of the surest ways of being well received anywhere and of obtaining food and lodging.]

The last of the small guitars to come under consideration here is the *charango,* even though it is not authentic to regions around Córdoba or the Plata. In the storehouse of guitar-like instruments belonging to Latin America, the charango and its repertoire have remained the most far-removed from the European mainstream. As a matter of fact it was known to some as a purely autochthonous instrument, invented by South American Indians without any reference to European models. Yet Dale Olsen has disproven this hypothesis by retracing its origins and by examining many historic examples (1980:395). Actually the charango is not unlike the Baroque guitar, though it is smaller (the existing examples averaging only two feet in length): it has the characteristic incurved sides of the figure-eight shape, tied-on frets, and paired gut strings typically arranged in five courses (Vega 1946:149–58). However, the great distinguishing feature of the charango is its body: it is often made from the shell of an armadillo! (see examples in Baumann 1979). Its authentic music originates in the Andean highlands; in it the player strums quickly with the *rasgueado* technique in the accompaniment of unique songs and dances of the region. The charango player adds an inimitable, brisk, high-pitched chord pattern or "layer" to stratified accompaniments. The charango is thus an instrument of the Andean region and associated primarily with present-day Bolivia, although its distribution includes the adjacent provinces of Peru, Chile, and Argentina (Viggiano Esaín 1948; Goyena 1986).

11. Price and Construction of Guitars

Guamán Poma may have made the first American literary reference to the *guitarra* in the chronicle he completed about 1615, but other sources documented its existence a century earlier. The guitarra, so called, was first mentioned amongst the imports entering at Puerto Rico (1516, Table 1), then it appeared in legal documents. The first extant South American reference to it was in Caracas, Venezuela; Francisco Marín mentioned a guitarra in the will that he signed in 1602 (Calzavara 1987:221). The legal documents at Córdoba contain the earliest specific mention of the guitarra in the Plata region: a "guitarra of black ebony" purchased for the boy of an aristocratic family in 1608 (Table 8).

Being an extremely dense, hard wood, ebony was used sparingly in the structural design of European guitars prior to its appearance in fingerboards with metal frets. It was always a difficult wood to bend for the sides, so it had to be applied to the mold slowly and in thin strips to avoid breaking; thus ebony guitars remained for aristocrats. Yet throughout the Baroque era, given its dark black color, ebony appeared often in a guitar's non-functional ornamentation against lighter woods. The same was true of the ornate Hispanic American guitars. An ebony guitar in Caracas, for instance, which was valued at 160 reals or 20 pesos, cost more than any instrument among the historic guitars Father Grenón documented in and around Córdoba in 1929:

*1704. Don Juan de Ascanio [dejó] "una guitarra grande por-
tuguesa embutida de marfil y ébano avaluada a 160 reales*
(Calzavara 1987:221)."
[1704. Don Juan de Ascanio (left) "a large Portuguese guitar
inlaid with ivory and ebony valued at 160 reals."]

The profuse ornamentation of the Baroque style was of course
typical on many old guitars. Antonio Stradivari's guitars, made at
Cremona with intentionally diminished cosmetic ornamentation
around 1700, remained rare in the era. Numerous instruments of
the Plata exhibited fancy decoration, including inlays of contrasting wood or mother-of-pearl, precisely when *rocaille* or decorative
shell work was a lingering fad in Paris (see 1747, 1761 in Table 8).

Apart from the ornamentation of instruments, the type of wood
used in their construction also appeared in some South American
sources. The following remains in evidence at Caracas:

*1759. Don Martín Ramón Isturiz [dejó] "un cinco con la caja y
fondo de madera negra y su tapa de pino, de una vara y sexta de
largo y el brazo perfilado de hueso* (Calzavara 1987:222)."
[1759. Don Martín Ramón Isturiz (left) "a five-course guitar
with the sides and back of black wood and a pine top of a *vara*
and one sixth (about a yard) in length, with bone inlay in the
neck."]

Pine was another wood used in Plata instrument construction,
sometimes for an entire guitar, even though it was far too soft to
provide lasting service for the back and sides. In Soriano, Uruguay
for instance, a pine guitar there was valued at nine reals in 1783
(Ayestarán 1947:44). Some pine guitars existed around Córdoba's
environs in 1695, 1795, 1797, and 1798. Other woods appropriate
for instruments there were jacarandá (the Brazilian rosewood
used until today) in 1796 and willow wood in 1717 (Table 8).

An interesting aspect of a guitar mentioned in 1780 (Table 8)
was its tuning mechanism consisting of both the tuning pegs and
gears of iron, or perhaps even cold-rolled steel. While such mech-
anisms had already existed for the harp, guitarists were slow to
adopt them, and instruments yet today—some of the bowed strings
and of course the flamenco guitar—still have friction pegs.

The price of a guitar during the Plata's colonial era ran anywhere from about a peso to less than twenty. Among the cheapest
guitars was the one there made of willow wood which sold for a
single peso in 1717; another, in 1760, was worth only a few reals.
The most expensive turned out to be the large guitar from Brazil
which was valued at 16 pesos in 1708. These prices were slightly
higher than the assessed values of the guitars imported at Puerto
Rico at the beginning of the 16th century (Table 1) yet still lower
than the Portuguese guitar valued at 160 reals at Caracas in 1704.
According to the thirteen priced items of Table 8, the usual cost of a
guitar ran from three to ten pesos. This conclusion coincides with
the review of twenty Rioplatense guitars of the viceroyal epoch in
which prices ranged as follows (Porro 1982:180):

inexpensive	1-2 pesos
moderate	3-5
expensive	6-8

Table 8 Price and Construction of Guitars
[In all these references, guitar is the translation of *guitarra*.]
(Grenón 1929, 1954)

1608. In that which is spent on behalf of the boy Nicolás García is
enumerated "a guitar of black ebony (A de T, E.1, E.1.18)."

1695. Captain Blas Ferreira declares among the items of his
property "a pine guitar of a hand-span and three quarters in size.
His wife Mariana López has one valued at six pesos (A de T, E.1,
E.1.181, e.5)."

1702. The possessions of poet/priest Luis de Tejeda were subject to
inventory in Saldán, among which were, "a harp at eight pesos
and a strung guitar at twelve pesos...(A de T, E.1, 1.205, e.1, f.48)."

1708. "A large guitar from Brazil, valued at 16 pesos [see previous
list]."

1712. In the letter of bequest favoring Rosa Pacheco, who was recently married to Juan Eusebio Pineiro, is noted "a guitar" valued
at ten pesos (A de T, E.1, P.1.104).

1717. Pedro Guevara disposes of "a guitar of willow wood valued at one peso (A de T, E.1, E.1.238, e.7)."

1745. In Río Segundo, Don José D. de Zeballos is owner of "an old guitar; it was valued at three pesos (A de T, E.1, P.1.28, f.59)."

1747. Juan Farías [of Capiscuchima] left among his personal possessions "a used guitar, but well treated; its inlays were of mother-of-pearl." In another list it is described as "a Portuguese guitar inlaid with mother-of-pearl...(A de T, E.1, E.1.339, e.10)."

1760. There is recorded the exchange of "a guitar worth a few reals" in payment of debt (A de T, Crim. 1.14, e.2).

1760. A creole from Potosí named Hermenegildo Hegiba is selling a guitar to Bruno Fernández in Córdoba (A de T, Crim. 1.11, e.25).

1761. In the book of accounts maintained by the chaplains of Saldán, Córdoba, its administrator and Chaplain-Priest Gabriel Bracamonte records on 15 May in the expenses for the year: "*Item,* I purchased a vihuela adorned with shell inlay for the Chapel so that it might be used to accompany the harp, at seven pesos... (A de C)." [A de C= Archivo Capitular de Canónigos, Catedral]

1763. Don Pedro Fonseca had "a large guitar, well-treated, valued at six pesos (A de T, E.2, 1.32, e.9, f.19)."

1773. Regarding "two large guitars valued at nine pesos [see the next table]."

1776. Juan Mancilla, landowner in Río Cuarto, notes among his properties "a small guitar valued at twelve reals (A de T, E.1, E.1.385, e.2)."

1780. Francisco Batalla recounts among his possessions "an old but well-treated guitar with tuning pegs and gears of iron (A de T, E.1, E.1.393)."

1786. "A guitar and violin...valued at eight reals [see Table 10]."

1795. Juan Luis de Uturbey is owner of "a pine guitar, well-treated (A de T, E.3, 1.50, e.2)."

1796. In the inventory of Don José Bravo of Santiago del Estero is noted "a broken guitar of jacarandá wood (*Revista del Archivo de Santiago del Estero* XIX, p. 26.)"

1797. In that belonging to Bartolomé Carranza is "a guitar of pine stock (A de T, E.3, 1.54, e.6, f.8)."

1798. Francisco J. Carranza possessed "a guitar of pine stock, being medium-sized, flat, without frets, and well used (A de T, E.1, E.1.528, e.10)."

1811. Regarding "a medium-sized guitar valued at a peso [see previous list]."

1823. "Advertisement for music aficionados. Don Mateo and Adam Stodand, who maintain a music store at...Piedad Street No. 98, have received a shipment of pianos and such other instruments as violins, guitars, flutes, drums, etc.... The ladies and gentlemen who would like to see them are welcome at this establishment. There, they also repair and tune pianos (*El Argos de Buenos Aires,* 10 Sep.)."

12. Women and the Guitar

One of the remarkable aspects of the guitar across the Americas is that it has always been an acceptable medium of expression for women. The guitar in Europe attracted women sporadically, yet in Latin America the development was continuous since colonial times. Hispanic women were obviously attracted to the guitar, yet fortunately their performances on it were always socially acceptable, as well. Thus women of all classes and all eras in Hispanic America played the guitar for personal satisfaction, to entertain others, and eventually to interpret the great artistic masterpieces.

Santa Rosa de Lima (1586–1617) was singled out for her exemplary life at Lima. Canonized in 1671 as the first saint of the Americas, she became the patron saint of the New World. She was baptized as Isabel Flores, but because of her beauty, her mother always called her Rosa (Moses 1922:333). She was intensely religious, so her life was marked by miracles, several of which involved the vihuela. Santa Rosa wrote verses for the child Jesus, and then accompanied them on it. Although she had never played a vihuela previously, she found one and put it to use as if she had been an accomplished musician. On another occasion, she played a vihuela without strings, yet it sounded as if it had been perfectly strung (Grenón 1951:20). As the first canonized vihuelist, Santa Rosa de Lima also became the patron saint of Rioplatense guitarists.

Santa Mariana de Jesús (d. 1645) followed Rose's exemplary life during the very next generation at Quito, now Ecuador. Her life confirmed the fact that it was honorable for women to play the vihuela. She owned one, and significantly, it is one of the few surviving instruments of colonial South America. In fact, the vihuela which is preserved up until the present day as a cherished relic of her possession is on continuous display in Quito's Jesuit church. Her vihuela conforms in most respects to the ornate, 17th-century *guitarra española,* except that its headstock is drilled for twelve strings (Ohlsen 1980). Owing to this archaic, improbable stringing, the instrument may have been modified at some point to update it.

While Santa Rosa de Lima and Santa Mariana de Quito were yet living, the vihuela and discante had already been established among women of the Plata. Doña María de Tejeda had "a good vihuela" in her possession in 1609 (Table 5). The discante was as acceptable among women as men, if our data are representative in Table 6; four women and four men owned discantes prior to 1649.

According to surviving documents, women began to play the guitarra (per se) as early as 1686, Table 9. During that year, two teen-age women were out serenading with the guitar past curfew, and thus contracted their own misfortune. After that date, nevertheless, women turned decidedly to the guitar. Thereafter if women played the vihuela at all, it remained undocumented in the evidence proceeding from Córdoba. The nine examples following that of 1686 show that women certainly owned guitars there:

Table 9 Women and the Guitar
(Grenón 1929, 1954)

1609. "Doña María de Tejeda [see Table 5]."

1609. "Doña Bartola Maldonado [see Table 6]."

1635. "María de Sarza [see Table 6]."

1645. "María Castro [see Table 6]."

1646. "María Soria [see Table 6]."

1686. A certain Teresa, daughter of Pascuale Bazán, was the victim of a crime and was involved subsequently in a lawsuit. She indeed suffered disgrace as a result of the crime, but the suit filed for damages on her behalf went unattended and denied. She and another ill-advised girl had put themselves in danger "because they were out making noisy laughter and playing the guitar and dancing without obeying the curfew of the maidens, and because the above-mentioned were out strolling at night apart from the company of their mother...(A de T, E.1, E.1.161, e.11)."

1695. "Mariana López has a guitar valued at six pesos [see above, Table 8]."

1712. "Rosa Pacheco [see Table 8]."

1773. To the young daughter of Josefa Videla...are appropriated "a harp of ten pesos and two large guitars of nine pesos (A de T, E.3, P.1.10, f.300)."

1792. Regarding the bass strings in the possession of María Tobares [see Table 3].

1801. Francisca Romana Carranza is manifested owner of "two guitars (A de T, E.2, E.1.102, e.5)."

1802. In the inventory of Juana de Aguilar there are two large guitars (A de T, E.4, E.1.21, e.20)."

1804. Catalina Miranda is assigned "two guitars (A de T, E.1, E.1.431, e.1)."

1806. Francisco Olmedo and his wife Luisa Quevedo declare in their possession "a new, large guitar (A de T, E.1, 1.433, e.5)."

1826. "Mariana Sánchez has an old guitar and a tiple [see above, Table 7]."

During the 18th century, a French traveller named Antoine
Joseph Pernety was part of an expedition that had a scheduled
layover in Montevideo. Even though it was only a temporary stop
for provisions in the port, he was able to make observations on the
colony while it was yet subject to the Viceroyalty of Peru. He found
some social connections in town by frequenting aristocratic circles,
in the midst of *"les espagnols de Montevideo,"* to the extent that he
was able to report on the guitar. He found it in use, particularly
among women there. In fact he claimed that they were proficient
enough in their social graces and musical accomplishments to
merit comparison to the French women of his times:

> *Les femmes sont chez elles au-moins avec autant de liberté*
> *qu'en France. Elles reçoivent la compagnie de trés-bonne grace,*
> *& ne se sont pas prier pour chanter, danser, jouer de la harpe,*
> *de la guitarre, du tuorbe, ou de la mandoline. Elles sont en cela*
> *beaucoup plus complaisantes que nos Françoises* (Pernety1770:
> 277–78).
> [The women are as much at ease in their homes as in France.
> They receive company very graciously, and they themselves
> never need an invitation to sing, to dance, to play the harp, or
> guitar, or lute, or the mandolin. They are more pleasing in it
> than our French counterparts.]

> *Il est très-rare en général qu'un Espagnol se promene à pied, &*
> *on voit dans les rues, autant de chevaux que d'hommes. Pen-*
> *dant la matinée, les femmes demeurent assises sur un tabouret,*
> *au fond de leur Salle, ayant sous les pieds, d'abord une natte de*
> *roseaux sur le pavé; & par dessus cette natte, des manteaux de*
> *Sauvages, ou des peaux de Tigres. Elles y jouent de la guitarre,*
> *ou de quelque autre instrument en s'accompagnant de la voix,*
> *ou prennent du maté, pendant que les Négresses apprêtent le*
> *dîner dans leur appartement* (Pernety 1770:282–83).
> [It is very rare in general to see a Spaniard about on foot, and
> one sees as many horses as men in the streets. During the
> morning, the women remain seated on a stool, and at the back
> of the room, they have under their feet, first a reed mat over the
> paved floor, then on top of the mat wild animal skins or tiger
> furs. There they play the guitar or some other instrument ac-
> companying themselves with their voice, or they drink their
> *mate* while their negresses prepare dinner in their apartment.]

Plenty of foreign travellers—including other Frenchmen—arrived in the Plata during the 19th century to confirm Pernety's conclusions, starting at about the time of the English invasion. Once independence became a reality, the Plata emerged as a new and interesting place to live. As such, however, the subject must be treated in Part V, below.

*   *   *   *   *

The early iconographical sources of Catholic buildings across Hispanic America provide more evidence linking women and the guitar. When the visual artists of the colonial and viceroyal epochs depicted the guitar in their religious paintings and sculptures, they often portrayed the musicians as women. Men ought to have served just as well, but the consensus of sources indicates that, in the mind's eye of Hispanic artists, women—with guitar in hand—were the ideal angelic musicians.

Fortunately many of the projects of these artists survive yet today in Latin American churches. Their paintings and sculptures not only beautify places of worship and still enhance the intensity of religious sentiment, as intended, they also feature the guitarra or vihuela and provide valuable information about the characteristics or use of the instruments themselves. Typically artists depict the veneration of guitar-like instruments rather than the stigma of secular contexts that one might expect. In such cases, the works of art suggest the possibility of using the guitar in church services. If it were approved for saints and angels, then the guitar might have been as readily used in the celebration of mass, vespers, or at least the singing of hymns. Evidence which supports this hypothesis is substantial across Latin America. Salvador Moreno, for instance, has already studied the musical angels of the early Mexican churches. Although his objective was to identify all of the instruments he saw in these religious artworks, the guitar certainly stands out among them. Given the extent of the coverage he published in 1957 and 1958, we may extract the specific items which depict guitarras and vihuelas. Therefore, what follows is a list of the specific media depicting these instruments and their location in early Mexican churches:

Fig. 10   The Guitar amidst Angels in Old Mexico
16th Century
(location, place.)   (instrument, artistic medium)
Acolmán, iglesia. Guitar sculpted on portal niche, accompanies angels
Epazoyucán, convento, claustro. A guitar is painted among six angels
Meztitlán, iglesia principal. A guitar is sculpted on portal, central niche
Yuriria, Iglesia del Convento. A guitar, sculpted on portal, central niche
17th Century
[M. City= Mexico City, Federal District]
M. City, Catedral. Guitar sculpted on the main portal of the façade, 1687
M. City, Catedral. Vihuelas, sacristy paintings of Correa de Villalpando
Puebla, Iglesia de San Cristóbal. *Guitarrón* in cupola, low-rel. sculpture
18th Century
M. City, Catedral. Guitars among José Naserre's wood sculptures, 1736
M. City, Iglesia de Belén. In the casa-palacio, guitar sculpted in stone
M. City, Basílica de Guadalupe. Guitar in wooden sacristy sculptures
M. City, Mus. Nac. de Historia. Vihuela in Estrada's *Baptism of Christ*
M. City, Mus. Nac. de Historia. Viceroyal guitars in Sala, Arte Popular
M. City, Mus. Nac. de Historia. Painting, *Monja profesa,* violin & guitar
M. City, Iglesia de San Fernando. Guitar sculpted in stone of portal, 1755
M. City, Palace of Santiago Calimalla. Siren with guitar, in stone, 1779
Oxaca, Iglesia de San Agustín. Sacristy, guitar, painting by Luis Juárez
Oxaca, Iglesia, Santo Domingo. Rosary Chapel, guitar in sculpture
Texmelucán, Iglesia del Conv. Franciscano. Vihuela in chapel painting

It is possible to conclude from such extensive coverage that the early guitar was widely accepted in Mexico and held in such high esteem that it may have been used in sacred music, even in church services. In Europe, instruments were rather typical in Catholic services up until the Council of Trent. That 16th-century high council of bishops and cardinals was convened largely in response to the Protestant Reformation which was already well underway. However, the council's net musical impact was to foster serene *a cappella* performances which excluded complex polyphony. All the complexities made the lyrics unintelligible, they felt, and the many instruments, despite the precedent set in the Old Testament, only detracted from the spirit of worship. The council excluded all instruments, except for the organ, as being too reminiscent of the world. The instruments were not reinstated until the concerted masses of the Baroque. Even so, the Council's resolutions did not seem to have had much of an impact on the Mexican artists who portrayed the religious music of their times. They depicted angels with musical instruments—frequently the guitar.

The same was true of South America; angels there were made to sing and to perform on a variety of instruments. The artists usually portrayed them as women, and sometimes they too played guitar-like instruments. In Colombia, Gregorio Vásquez-Ceballos painted a guitar among angels; his painting is now in the Museum of Colonial Art in Bogotá (González 1988:21). In Coro, Venezuela, an 18th-century painting features a musical angel, a young woman painted on a piece of wooden furniture. She is playing a rather large five-course guitar with nine tuning pegs to accommodate a single string on the first course (Ramón y Rivera 1966:64).

Fray Basilio Santa Cruz and his associates completed a series of portraits with angelic musicians in about 1684 for the Franciscan Convent in Santiago de Chile. These oil paintings depict miracles in the life of St. Francis of Assisi. Ever since Giotto's monumental frescoes of the Bardi Chapel of Santa Croce in Florence, the life and especially the miracles of St. Francis had been a favorite subject among painters. One painting of the series in Chile portrays the occasion when Francis happened to fall ill, whereupon he desired to ask an acquaintance to perform vihuela music to raise his spirits. Instead, Francis resisted temptation and decided to deny himself of that luxury, so he went to sleep in torment. God recognizing his need, sent him an angel to play softly to him in order to satisfy his wish. The artists depicted the moment of musical mercy by painting an attractive blonde woman with large wings and sumptuously elegant attire. She looks steadfastly at the beholder as she plays the guitar. Her instrument is a typical, medium-sized, five-course Baroque guitar with elaborate, black filigree decorations inlaid in the top around an ornate rose and bridge, and even on the fingerboard and headstock of the instrument. Its stringing is carefully drawn in several colors to show five double-strung courses and tied-on frets (Zavadivker 1988:15).

Painting and sculpture in the Río de la Plata brought valuable iconographical evidence to the guitar's history, as well. The visual arts of the Jesuit reductions (1607–1767) in particular, often portrayed musical subjects. Musicians were sculpted in rather high relief on sandstone at the Trinity Church of the Misiones Reduction. Although only the ruins remain, some sculptures are intact; they display a guitarist using a five-string or five-course instrument (Furlong 1944a). Another survivor was a cherub painted on wood for the church of San Ignacio Guazú: it featured a similar five-string or five-course guitar (Furlong 1944a).

The outstanding guitar-playing angel of the Río de la Plata is presented in Plate VI, on the next page. The painting embellishes a wooden ceiling, as revealed in its several long cracks. Even so, it has outlasted the era's more fragile paintings on paper, canvas, or plaster. The painting has survived until now in the cupola of the 17th-century Jesuit Church in Córdoba, and probably dates from the time when the church was consecrated. It took more than two decades to build the church: construction began in the middle of the century and ended finally with its consecration in 1671 (Lange 1956:10).

As featured in this plate, an unknown artist of the 17th century has affectionately portrayed a pre-teen girl playing, again, a five-course guitar. In it the girl maintains a perfect state of joy and innocence. She is captured in a transfixed state, with all of her attention focused to the right of the beholder. She ascends upward, gown flowing, in the direction of her unwavering stare, making scant use of her wings.

The angel's guitar is rather typical of both the European high Baroque style and 17th-century instrument construction. The instrument has elegant, unsymmetrical filigree inlays around the bridge, and an ornate rose extended by additional rays of dark inlays around it. The fingerboard shows some ornamentation also, but no attempt has been made to paint strings. The headstock is bent back at a sharp angle (be it more typical of lutes than guitars), and its tuning pegs pierce through it, four to a side, and an additional peg perforates the very top. The nine pegs accommodate five courses, one of which would have been the prima, for the first course was customarily a single string.

Plate VI *Angel* (Female Guitarist) in Córdoba's 17th-c. Jesuit Church

13. The Guitar and Lute in the Jesuit Missions

The missionaries of the Jesuit Order certainly left their mark in Córdoba, developing farms, trade, and even a university there, in addition to their churches. Their achievements were also artistic and intellectual inasmuch as they brought with them the latest trends and discoveries of the European capitals they represented. (In this regard, see especially Furlong, *Los Jesuítas y la cultura rioplatense,* 1946.) However, their main impact in the Plata region was their missionary effort among the Indians far to the northeast of Córdoba, isolated from the other towns of the Argentine interior.

Initially the priests came from other parts of South America to the Plata basin in 1585 to test the feasibility of working the new Jesuit approach among the Indians. As they met with some success, a dedicated missionary effort was established there under the supervision of European priests in 1607, and it lasted until 1767. During that century and a half, the Jesuits organized each unit of their flock into a secluded, independent "reduction." They consecrated all of their time, talent, and resources there; they held all things in common as the highest order of Christian living (Acts 2:44, 2 Cor. 8:14). They made their church the center of economic and social activity; round the hub was a compound that included residences for the priests and other buildings for their teaching, labors, governance, and maintenance. Nearby farms and Indian residences completed the settlement. Little by little, as the Jesuit movement expanded, the priests established a total of thirty such reductions within the region. These were located throughout the east side of present-day Paraguay, *Misiones*, the northeast province of Argentina, and the adjoining borderlands of Brazil.

The earliest Jesuit fathers discovered that certain Indian tribes had prioritized music as their foremost entertainment, whether in native dance or song. (See for instance Padre Bárzana's comment in 1594, as cited below in the conclusions to Part IV.) So the fathers decided to approach their peaceful conquest with the strategy of using European music as the first benefit of conversion. Their approach worked especially well because so many Jesuits were in themselves fine musicians; some had extensive European training.

During the initial phases of colonization, the band of Guaraní Indians had proven to be not only the largest tribe in the region but also the most friendly. Then the Jesuits found in the Guaraní tribe an immediate audience for their work because the Guaraní already had a love of music and a complete veneration for all who practiced it. The Jesuits eventually learned their language, but the language of music allowed them to communicate immediately. Father Pedro Comental was an early musician there, but some priests brought specialized musical training: first among them was the Franco/Belgian Jean Vaiseau (also Juan Vaseo) who arrived in 1616. Their most illustrious exponent was the Italian Domenico Zipoli (1688–1726), who had already established enviable fame in Rome as composer and organist before coming to the reductions (Torre Revello 1944).

Guitarists and lutenists were prominent among the Jesuit missionaries. The earliest string-instrumentalist among them was Father Louis Berger of France who arrived at the port of Buenos Aires in 1616. A man of talent in all of the arts, he was also a musician on several instruments, the favorite of which was the lute he brought from Europe (Furlong 1942:63–64). An item in Table 3, above cites a document requesting lute strings on his behalf in 1622. Notwithstanding, Berger did not introduce the lute into the region. This had been accomplished by an Italian from Genoa, one Bernardo Centurione who, travelling to Peru in the expedition of Leone Pancaldo, chanced to dock at Buenos Aires during a storm in 1538 (Guestrin 1986:14). Centurione stayed on, nonetheless, and soon migrated upriver to Asunción, which at the time was the focal point of the Hispanic insurgence. Despite this appreciable beginning, the lute never flourished in the Plata region beyond the Jesuit domain. (A lute manuscript with more than a hundred Baroque compositions remains in the Biblioteca Nacional, Buenos Aires, but it was imported from Europe—Zavadivker 1974.)

Although the Jesuit lutenists were paramount in the reductions, some of the missionaries were also guitarists. One of them, a German by the name of Johann Wolff, was mentioned in some missionary correspondence. Fray Miguel Herre spoke of him in a report to Provincial Official Francisco Molinder in a description of Buenos Aires dated 1724:

Además de éste, hay otro Hermano del Rhin Superior, de nom-
bre Juan Wolff, quien de oficio es carpintero, y al mismo tiempo
un hábil guitarrista (Mühn 1946:42).
[Besides this one, there is another brother from the Upper
Rhine district named Johann Wolff, who by trade is a carpenter
and at the same time a capable guitarist.]

The most accomplished and best known Jesuit music teacher of
the reductions was Anthony Sepp, another lutenist. He came to his
missionary service there in 1691 as the Jesuits were nearing the
peak of their activity. His published letters revealed the high quality of Jesuit music, whether among the fathers themselves, their
methods of musical instruction, or the performances of the Indians
they trained.

The success of the musical product in the reductions devolved
upon two unique circumstances: the quality of instruction and the
intense emphasis on music among the Indians themselves. The
Jesuits certainly made it seem as though they were perfectly
suited to their calling. Yet the Indians achieved musical excellence
because of their own interest and motivation: the Guaraní
esteemed musical performance as the highest achievement of
their society. Father Sepp became aware of this fact as soon as he
arrived in Buenos Aires:

As for the rest of the inhabitants of Paraquaria they are very
good Christians, and acknowledge no other superiors but the
missionaries.... They make clocks and trumpets, not inferior to
any in Germany; but value music above everything else. When
I shew'd them some of my compositions and musical instruments, I brought along with me out of Europe...they were
ready to adore me (Sepp 1697:637).

Father Sepp witnessed the impressive welcoming reception for
the Jesuits at Buenos Aires. The missionaries were always received
by an orchestra of indigenous instruments, the performers of
which demonstrated their commitment to music:

At the time of our arrival we were met by about 60 Indians
playing upon their pipes and their American horns, one of them
keeping time by the motion of a kind of flag.... I presented these

musicians with some toys, such as looking-glasses, needles, fish hooks and glass beads...which they valued beyond gold and silver (Sepp 1697:637).

According to the usual practice, the new Jesuits arrived at the port of Buenos Aires, but once they had rested, they would have to sail and paddle north with their hosts, up through the waterways to reach Asunción located at the confluence of the Pilcomayo River and the great Paraguay, and to other parts on the rivers where the fathers would take their assignments, as believably portrayed in the 1986 feature film *The Mission (La misión)*. However, before taking his assignment at the Reduction of Yapeyú on the Uruguay River, Father Sepp had to report to the regional Jesuit officials. His reputation had preceded him, so his welcome was not one of celebration. Instead, the mission officials were anxious to verify the extent of Father Sepp's venerable musical abilities; his reception turned out to be more like a performer's audition than an interview for an ecclesiastical appointment:

But the Father Provincial...not thus satisfied, would needs have me make a tryal of my skill in musick; so that to satisfie their curiosity, I was forced to play before them upon the great *theorbe* [lute] which I had bought at Augsburgh, and upon the lesser *theorbe* bought at Genoa; at which they seemed much surprized: Father Anthony Behme and I gave them also a consort of the flute, upon the violin, and a little stroke upon the trumpet marine, which I got made at Cádiz; all which they were much delighted with, tho' I must confess my self but a very indifferent Artist (Sepp 1697:648).

Father Sepp's description of teaching methods in the reductions revealed that the Indians were not merely performing by rote or by ear. First he reviewed the origins of their pedagogy, alluding indirectly to the good teaching of Jean Vaiseau and Luis Berger. But he also complained that subsequently the Indian musicians had regressed, and for a time they lost the ability to read music and reverted back to rote learning. Finally, in his own reduction at Yapeyú, where musical excellence was achieved under his direction, he had to return to the rudiments again before he was able to restore polyphonic mass and vespers celebrations with a full complement of instruments.

> I don't question but that several of our friends...when they hear
> you read this passage will be apt to ask you, who it is that com-
> poses these psalms, litanies, hymns, and masses; who is it that
> has taught the Indians to sing, who to play on the organs, and to
> sound the trumpets and hautboys? Unto which I answer, that
> the same missionaries, who taught these poor wretches the ru-
> diments of the Christian religion, to say Our Father, to take
> bread, to paint, to cast bells, organs and trumpets, and to make
> clock works; the same I say have instructed them in musick,
> which was first introduced here by some Netherland fathers....
> Thus I saw my self obliged to begin with them, quite after
> another and new method, and to teach, old gray hair'd fellows,
> the *ut, re, mi, fa, sol, la,* again. By which means I have (tho' with
> incredible labor) instructed 6 trumpets (of whom each canton
> has 4) 4 organists, 3 theorbists, 30 hautboys and 50 voices
> (besides other instruments) to play and sing most of my compo-
> sitions; which has got me such a reputation with the other mis-
> sionaries, that they send continually to me some of their flocks,
> with presents of hony, preserves, and fruit, to court my friend-
> ship, and to have them introduced in musick, and to speak
> without vanity, this has purchased me the singular esteem
> of the Indians (Sepp 1697:658).

The fact that the Indians could learn music either by note or by
rote was confirmed by Father José Cardiel, a Spaniard who came
at the very end of the Jesuit era in order to dedicate a dozen years'
residence to the Guaraní. Since rote learning (by ear) was the basic
method inherited from their native culture, the tendency to go
back to it was strong, as Father Sepp claimed. Even so, with proper
training, the Indians could perform music of virtually any difficulty from standard notation on the pentagram:

> *Si el cura no pone especial cuidado, visitando frequentemente*
> *esta escuela, no saben cantar sino de memoria en fuerza del*
> *continuo ensayo: y así cantan, y no mal, cuantas Vísperas,*
> *Psalmos y letrillas tienen. Pero si tiene cuidado, aprenden y*
> *cantan como músicos, y cualquiera papel que les den, aunque*
> *sea de difícil composición, en leyéndolo dos o tres veces, lo cantan*

luego (Cardiel 1747:64).
[If the priest is not especially careful, visiting frequently this
school, they will not know how to sing except by rote as a product of continual rehearsal: and thus they sing, and not badly,
as many vespers, psalms, and lesser pieces as they have. But
if the priest takes care, they learn to sing as musicians, and
whatever paper is given to them, though it be a difficult composition, they sing it after reading through it a few times.]

The heyday of the Jesuit reductions coincided precisely with the
Baroque era in Europe. Inasmuch as elaborate improvisation and
ornamentation were both typical of Baroque performances, it was
perhaps curious that the Jesuits did not advocate them in their
teaching. Since Guaraní music had been a product of spontaneous
improvisation in the first place, the priests must have feared that
allowing any form of improvisation within the European music
they were teaching might have contained lapses back to Guaraní
culture. Besides, listening to the European style in the missions was
limited to what the priests themselves could supply. At any rate,
the priests admonished the Indian musicians to perform only note-
for-note, and all unwritten additions, no matter how typical of
Baroque music, were excluded from their performances:

*Ni los que tocan arpas, violines, etc., añaden o mudan alguna
diferencia o trinado, hermosata o cosa equivalente que dé gracia
a su tocata, más que lo que tienen en el papel* (Cardiel 1758:282).
[Not even those who play harps, violins, etc., add or change a
variation or trill, embellishment, or anything like them that
might give gracefulness to their performance; they play no
more than what they have before them on paper.]

Father Sepp's fame spread far and wide in the Jesuit province.
In fact, he became known to his colleagues as soon as they arrived
from Europe. There was the long-standing tradition of welcoming
the fathers when they reached their destination, just as Sepp was.
The tradition dated back at least a century. The Indians would go
to perform for the immigrant missionaries as soon as they disembarked in Buenos Aires at the end of their transatlantic voyage (as
noted below in Table 10, 1628). The Indians also entertained the

priests at Córdoba, according to Father Ripario (Table 10, 1637). The Indians' musical abilities guaranteed them the rewards and recognition of travel within or even beyond their reductions. However, owing to the fact that Yapeyú was the closest reduction to Buenos Aires and that it had river-access to the capital, every maestro of music at Yapeyú was responsible for welcoming the new arrivals. Even after several generations of development in the reductions, this post was still the most visible and prestigious musical appointment among them—precisely the one held by Father Sepp since 2 June 1691 (1697:659). Indian students would drift downstream, meet and entertain the new Jesuits, and then carry them back upstream with the whole entourage to their specific destinations in the reductions, as far as permitted on the waterways. One missionary, Father Matthias Strobel was especially pleased with Father Sepp's group from Yapeyú and its music, which was then at the pinnacle of fame. On 5 June 1729, Father Strobel characterized their reception as a celebration when they arrived at the port of Buenos Aires in a letter addressed to an acquaintance in Vienna:

[One can barely describe the decency or efficacious piety over-all with which the Christian Indians present themselves. A good-sized group from among them has arrived from the reductions along the Uruguay River in twenty boats in order to seek us out, and right away to carry us back, each one to his own destination. The innocence, fear of God, and holiness transcends their countenances in such a manner that, with no more than a look at them, one is buoyed up and filled with overflowing consolation....
A few days ago the Reduction of Yapeyú, which is the nearest, sent musicians in several voices (specifically two sopranos, two contraltos, two tenors, and two basses), accompanied by two harps, two bassoons, two tambourines, with four violins, with violoncellos, and other like instruments, to sing here the vespers, mass, and litanies, together with some other canticles in such a manner, with such art and grace that one not seeing them would believe that they would have come from the best cities of Europe rather than the Indies. Their books of music, brought from Germany and Italy, are partly printed and partly hand-copied. I have observed that these Indians keep the measure

and the beat even more exactly than the Europeans, and also
that they pronounce the Latin lyrics precisely, even though they
are people without formal education. Along with the musicians,
the dancers also came here from Yapeyú. When they are going
to dance, they remove their suit of indigenous cotton in order
to dress up with their rich costumes which are part silk, part
velvet with gold piping; they even have special stockings and
shoes. They cover their heads with a fine hat with borders
garnished in gold. With this beautiful outfit they execute their
dances, accompanied by stringed instruments with such mastery that no European dancing master would be ashamed to
have them recognized as his own students. The Paraguayans do
not owe these arts to any Spaniard or Indian, but rather to the
German, Italian, and Dutch Jesuits, and especially to Reverend
Father Anthony Sepp] (Strobel 1729:60–62).

The year after Father Strobel's arrival in Buenos Aires, an Italian missionary came and matched his description of the music
there. Father Cayetano Cattaneo docked in the port with a new
complement of immigrant missionaries and observed the same
sort of time-honored reception prepared by the Indians of Yapeyú.
However, in one significant detail, his description was better. Father Strobel had mentioned, among glowing superlatives, that the
Indians indeed accompanied their costume dances with stringed
instruments, but failed to specify which ones. Father Cattaneo
explained further, in a letter to his brother dated 20 April 1730,
that some of these instruments were actually the plucked strings,
including the guitar and lute. Moreover, his letters were widely
diffused in French and English translations across Europe. As
revealed in his second letter from the 1759 English edition, the
musicians of Yapeyú enjoyed an excellent reputation for their
public performances as far south as Buenos Aires, where even the
governor of the Río de la Plata attended:

We saw some *Indians* arrive from the *Reductions*. They were
from the *Reduction* of the three Kings, or *Yapejú,* which in the
Indian language signifies the same. Of all the Colonies under
our direction, this is the nearest *Buenos Ayres,* tho' at six hundred miles distance. The Christians of other *Reductions* were

making ready to come and take the Missionaries with them.
Those of *Yapejú* being the nearest got the start, and brought all
sorts of music, to solemnise our arrival. As soon as the *Indians*
landed, they came running to the College, quite impatient to see,
and to be acquainted with us; and went first to father *Herran's*
apartment....

F. Herran sent us notice of their arrival. We came down that
moment into the court, where they had placed themselves in
order to receive us. In the first rank were placed the boys of
twelve or fourteen years old, who sung the treble, and the *Alts*
[sic] who were something older. In the second rank were the
young men, who held the part of *tenors.* Next to them in the
third rank were men who sung the base. The instruments were
placed on both sides. As soon as we appeared, the good *Indians*
intoned the *Te Deum.* I was extremely struck with a scene so
new to me, and particularly with the modesty and zeal of which
they gave such demonstrations....

Several days were spent in feasting and rejoicing. The Gover-
nour frequently honoured their sports and concerts with his
presence; and was so delighted, that he often desired them to be
continued till night. All the town crowded to their performances,
and no one was weary with seeing the *Indians.* One of their
dances was particularly admired, and I believe would not have
displeased the nicest observers in *Europe.* This was formed of
twelve youths, dressed after the manner of the *Incas,* or the
antient nobles of *Peru,* before the *Spanish* conquest. Each had
his musical instrument: four had small *Guitars* that hung from
their necks: four had *Lutes;* and the other four had small *Violins.* They danced and played at the same time, with most surprising exactness. They were also seen performing the exercise
of the bow, and other arms, with very great pleasure to the
spectators.

In the morning they sung several *motets* in our church set to
music, while the Masses were saying [sic]: they were served by
the children in gowns and surplices. Their modesty and exactness in observing the ceremonies that are prescribed, put me
into a rapture. You would have taken the servers at Mass for
two little statues at the foot of each altar, that moved by one and
the same spring. But nothing delighted me more, than to see
them altogether serving at high Mass. Every thing shewed
their respect and devotion, and inspired it (Cattaneo 1759:
242–44).

The Jesuit utopia of total independence came to bear on instrument construction. The Jesuit fathers earned self-respect among their peers and parishoners alike by repairing and maintaining their own instruments, thereby avoiding the necessity of depending on imports from Buenos Aires, the source of the best music supplies. Money that would have gone into repairs became available for more urgent matters—the necessities of life. Thus the Jesuits strengthened their economy while building faith in their talents and abilities. As always, the priests taught by example, whereof the Indians picked up an interest in the luthier's craft. The missionaries began to specialize in instrument construction and repair with their own shops that were soon filled with Indian craftsmen. The Guaraní Indians were at first mere apprentices but then developed journeyman abilities, providing instruments for all occasions in the reductions. If the Indians were producing pneumatic organs, then guitar and lute construction must have been comparatively easy. Their special gift was the ability to copy the exact appearance and detail of European models; then they took great satisfaction in solemnizing their most sacred spectacles by supplying them with replicas of their own manufacture:

En todas las misas de cada día, siempre están tocando y cantando los músicos desde el principio hasta el fin con sumo silencio y veneración del pueblo. Al principio hasta el Evangelio tocan órganos, chirimías, arpas y violines. Desde el Evangelio hasta la Consagración cantan algún salmo de las vísperas con todos los instrumentos juntos. Después cantan algún motete en latín o castellano y tal cual vez en su idioma, o algún himno, variando cada día las letras y las composiciones; y si sobra tiempo hasta el fin, vuelven a tañer los instrumentos. Este divino culto se usa todos los días (Cardiel 1758:280).
[In all the masses of every day, the musicians are always playing and singing from the beginning until the end, to which the people respond with extreme quiet and reverence. At the beginning and up until the gospel, they play organs, shawms, harps, and violins. From the gospel and up until the consecration, they sing some psalm of the vespers along with all the instruments together. Afterwards they sing some motet in Latin, Castilian Spanish, or occasionally in their own language, or a hymn, varying daily the lyrics and the compositions; and if there is any

time left at the end, they play their instruments again. This sacred worship is presented every day.]

The Jesuit musical establishment was a way of life for the Indians who began in it as children. Guaraní boys sang the high parts of the polyphony, and they could also officiate in the ordinances of worship. Like the choirboys in Europe, they had to hold candles, wait on the priests, or run errands, in addition to performing music. Yet like their teachers, they also contributed time to food production and their own maintenance rather than receive special treatment for their talents. Nevertheless, good musicians, including boy sopranos and altos, were always at hand because the missions attracted great activity from the nearby tribal populations. The Jesuit fathers were able to offer auditions to throngs of boys, but with given limitations, they had to skim off only those with the best musical aptitudes. By starting with select talents, the teachers could develop the vocal and instrumental skills of their students for a decade or more in order to produce musicians with a complete formation. Once their voices changed at puberty, the best performers could continue their service on tenor or bass parts or on the instruments. They used quite a variety of instruments, even in sacred services. Indeed, within some reductions, the high mass required the guitar in the company of other instruments (Cardiel 1747:166). In this way the Jesuits trained their performers for mass music or the dignified dances of their religious pageantry as they built their musical establishment over the long term. Father Cardiel summarized these practices as follows:

Y después han venido varios [maestros] muy diestros en esta facultad, y aún los hay ahora. En todos los pueblos hay 30 o 40 músicos. Entran en esta escuela de 9 a 10 años, escogiéndose para ello los de mejor metal de voz, y aunque viven a lo bárbaro, no obstante, en tanta multitud de muchachos, siempre se encuentran buenas voces. Estiman mucho este oficio. La mayor honra que se le puede hacer al hijo del Corregidor o del mayor Cacique es hacerle tiple. Estos son los doctos del pueblo y la oficina de donde salen todos los oficios de Alcaldes, Escribanos, Sobrestantes, etc. Enseñados desde niños con mucha continuación, salen muy diestros. Usan todo género de instrumentos,

órganos, bajones, cornetas, chirimías, espinetas, liras, arpas,
violines y violones, y en algunas danzas, guitarras, cítaras,
bandolas y bandurrias. Yo he atravesado toda España, y en
pocas catedrales he oído músicas mejores que éstas en su
conjunto (Cardiel 1758:280–81).
[And later various (teachers) who are very skilled in this faculty
have come, and there are some yet today. In every one of the
towns there are 30 or 40 musicians. They enter in this school at
nine or ten years of age; those chosen for it have the best quality
of voice, and though they lead a barbarous life, notwithstanding, in such a multitude of boys, good singers are always found.
This vocation is much esteemed among them. The greatest
honor that can come to the son of the Magistrate or the principal chieftain is to cast him as a soprano. These are the enlight-
ened of the town, and the source whence come all the officials,
mayors, accountants, foremen, etc. Taught from childhood with
scrupulous attention, they turn out quite skilled. They use all
kinds of instruments: organs, bajones, cornetti, shawms, spin-
ets, lyres, harps, violins and viols; and in some dances: guitars,
citterns, bandolas, and bandurrias. I have crossed the whole of
Spain, and in few cathedrals have I heard better performances
than these of his ensemble.]

In another book, also an eyewitness account of the Jesuit work
among the Guaraní Indians, Father Cardiel devoted an entire
chapter to liturgical music. There he confirmed that the Jesuits
used guitars, designated *vihuelas*, in church services:

Tienen todo género de instrumentos músicos usados en las
catedrales de Europa, órganos, bajones, chirimías, clarines,
cornetas, arpas, violines y violones; y en algunos pueblos usan
también flautas grandes y lúgubres en tiempo de Cuaresma, y
en otros hay, además de los dichos, liras, trompa marina, vi-
huelas y bandolas y cítaras. Todos estos instrumentos los hacen
ellos (Cardiel 1747:164).
[They have all the types of musical instruments that are used
in the cathedrals of Europe: organs, bajones, shawms, clarin
trumpets, cornetti, harps, violins and viols; in some reductions
they also use flutes both large and lugubrious during the period
of Lent; and besides the aforementioned, there are in other reductions lyres, the tromba marina, vihuelas and bandolas and
lutes. All these instruments are of their own making.]

With all the attention the Indian musicians were receiving, particularly as they performed on occasion in Buenos Aires and Córdoba, the news, to some, seemed almost too good to be true. So secular authorities engaged Fray Joseph Peralta y Barnuevo, then Bishop of Buenos Aires, to visit the Jesuit reductions in order to verify all the superlative reports about them. On 8 August 1740, they charged the bishop, under royal seal, with a complete inspection of the reductions (Peralta 1743:1). Taken from the negative point of view, the court was sending him on a fault-finding mission. Perhaps the priests, coming more often from northern than southern Europe and thus unable to speak Spanish at first, were not paying sufficient respect to Spanish rulers. The Jesuits enjoyed some political and religious favors, also, which irked some of their contemporaries. Besides, the Jesuits did not contribute much to the regional economy: since they were so independent, they took far more in trade and profit than they gave back. Worst of all, they were always at odds with the *encomenderos,* the few rich landowners descended from the *conquistadores,* some of whom used and abused the Indians as virtual slaves. Since the reductions were located in the tropic wilderness with no more access to them than overgrown trails and rivers, it was a tall order to have to visit them all. "When the bishop of Buenos Aires designs to visit the reductions in his diocese, he must lay in provisions to subsist...during a journey of 600 miles...to the first of the Christian colonies of Uruguay (Muratori 1759:123)." But the aging bishop rose to the challenge and visited the seventeen under his jurisdiction, and for good measure, he blessed several of the other thirteen pertaining to the adjacent district of Paraguay with his presence. At the end of several years' labor at this project—travelling, interviewing, and attending services, Bishop Peralta wrote a lengthy report back to the court in order to summarize his findings. He submitted the following assessment of their music of worship:

Y porque no se falte a lo principal, que es el Culto Divino, tienen una escuela separada, donde enseñan los niños del Gremio de Cantores, y los que han de aprender las danzas para las fiestas del Señor, y a los maestros que están ocupados en esta distribución los hacen también aparte sus sementeras. En fin, Señor,

estas Doctrinas, y estos Indios, son una alhaja del Real Patri-
monio de V.M. tan cumplida, y correspondiente a su Real zelo,
y piedad, que si se hallare otra igual, no será mejor (Peralta
1743:4).
[And in order not to fall short of the most important part, i.e.,
Divine Worship, they have a separate school where they in-
struct the children of the Choral Society, as well as attend those
who are to learn the dances of pageantry for the Lord's festival
days and the teachers who are occupied with this assignment—
which they do apart from harvesting their own crops. Enfin,
my Lord, these reductions and these Indians are a jewel of Your
Majesty's Royal Patrimony, so in compliance and so in accord
with your Royal zeal and piety, that if another were found to be
equal, it could not be any better.]

In this same superlative tone, Bishop Peralta went on with his
findings until reaching his final point, which succeeded in dis-
arming some widely held but unfavorable impressions of Jesuit
society. According to his report, some members of his diocese were
complaining that the Jesuits ought to pay tithes, a debt which they
had somehow avoided ever since the foundation of the reductions.
But the Bishop's conclusion was to renew their long-standing
exemption: he recommended that the Jesuits not pay any tithing,
neither in money nor of their crops at all. Even so, perhaps the
greatest value of his assessment was that since he did not belong to
the Jesuit order himself, but rather the *Order of Predicadores,* his
review stood as an external evaluation.

News from this external perspective were also circulating in
Europe. To play the devil's advocate, some detractors were claim-
ing that, for the lack of other reporters, the Jesuits themselves
were merely documenting their own success from a rather biased,
internal perspective. But not so. The Venetian author, Lodovico
Antonio Muratori also wrote of the Jesuits, and like the Bishop of
Buenos Aires, he gave his perspective from outside the Jesuit orbit
(1759:Preface). Although he wrote originally in Italian, he witnessed the diffusion of his book in French and English, as follows:

Besides the natural inclination, which the Indians had for all
kinds of music, the Missionaries discovered that they had

excellent qualifications for their becoming good musicians.
There are very fine voices commonly found among them....
   The Missionaries chuse [sic] among the children those who
appear at that age to be qualified to be formed into musicians.
They teach them to sing and to touch the instruments with so
much exactness and nicety, that their pious concertos are not
less pleasing and affecting than those in Europe. And hence they
have established in each reduction a chapel, as they term it, or a
band of musicians, who equally execute the easiest and the
most composed pieces of music.
   It must no doubt be surprising to hear, that we have scarce any
musical instrument in Europe, that is not in use in the Reductions (Muratori 1759:88).

To be sure, proof of the effectiveness of the Jesuit music teachers
came with the performances of their students. One Indian in particular, Cristóbal Piriobi became a master of instrumental music
in his own right and enjoyed success long after the Jesuits left the
region. Piriobi was born of Guaraní parents at the San Carlos Reduction in 1764 (Monzón 1947:142). He was a child prodigy and
learned to build instruments as well as to play them according to
the Jesuit tradition there. Eventually he went to Buenos Aires and
replaced his first name with a nom de plume, "José Antonio" to become a performer and teacher of renown. His income there enabled him to amass a formidable library featuring symphonies and
chamber music and to collect a broad selection of instruments for
his performances. Although he died at the age of 30, his last will
and testament—presently in the National Archive of Buenos Aires
—left evidence that he was a guitarist. He bequeathed, *"tres guitarras nuevas, dos grandes y una chica"* [three guitars, two large
and one small] to the beneficiaries of his estate (Roldán 1987:45).
   The Jesuit achievements were not entirely musical. The missionaries converted Indians by the thousands to a life of peaceful
separation from their warlike neighbors; they established public
education before it ever emerged among European philosophers;
they taught individual worth by building the dignity and self-
esteem of all who listened; they valued the work ethic and trained
the Indians in specific trades and professions; they helped the Indians to achieve economic independence, whether individually or

as a nation. They reached their goal: there were no poor among them. The Jesuits were thus far ahead of their times, yet simultaneously in their faraway seclusion survived without the least obstruction to the monarchy. In spite of all this splendid success, they encountered serious conflicts with the other institutions of their day. The missionaries and priests of the other orders found the Jesuits in direct conflict with their own objectives. The wealthy oligarchy of *encomenderos,* the owners of sprawling plantations who depended on Indian labor to harvest their crops, livestock, and hides, encountered the Jesuit state competing directly in their own marketplace—indeed, undercutting their prices. Bishop Peralta devoted his closing remarks, an entire page, to the human-rights violations of the encomenderos (1743:8). The missions became the main refuge of the Indians who were able to escape from the *encomienda* farms. But the complaints of religious and secular powers went unresolved, and thus eventually to Madrid where the King traditionally oversaw the administrations of both ecclesiastical and secular affairs. After a century and a half of tremendous growth, thanks to the incalculable personal sacrifices of individual priests, the Jesuit activity was condemned from the Peninsular court. In order to silence the complaints, the loudest of which were emanating from the hierarchy of his richest regional constituents, Charles III, without clear warning, banned the Jesuit presence in Latin America by royal decree in 1767. Soon thereafter the Jesuit priests (probably more than a thousand in the Americas) were removed altogether, by force in some cases, and sent to Spain en route to the continent because they had been exiled from Portugal as well. Overwhelming irony headed the list of injustices inflicted upon the Jesuits with this ban because the Jesuit Order had been initiated by a Spaniard, Ignatius Loyola (1491–1556) during the colonization of the Americas.

It was understandable that some missionaries were reluctant to leave the province they had built over the course of a century and a half. In such cases, pitched battles ensued and the material possessions of the Jesuits were burned along with the buildings of their reductions. However, where they agreed to peaceful acquiescence, their possessions, notably all their music and instruments, were left in the hands of their converts or friends, or in the churches of other religious orders. In some cases, inventories of the musical instruments survive; those that remain reveal the extent of the Jesuit achievement in instrumental music. A handy review of the Jesuit inventories appeared in Vicente Gesualdo's monumental *Historia de la música en Argentina*. In Volume I he lists many of the extant vihuelas found at the reductions and churches towards the end of the Jesuit epoch. Of the instruments numbered specifically in the inventories, there were 1,004 (only a fraction of the total they had actually constructed or imported during their 160-year development), among which were two lutes and fourteen vihuelas (Gesualdo 1961:67–72).

14. The Guitar in Church

The guitar was certainly a part of the myriad musical activities of the Jesuit missions. However, Father Cardiel remained the lone eyewitness to claim that the guitar (whether specified as guitarra or vihuela) played a part in sacred worship of the Catholic faith. In both of his books (1747:164–66; 1758:281) he described the religious music he heard: he listed the instruments in the mass, naming among them the guitar. Thus if caution is the better part of valor, additional confirmation is needed in order to conclude that the Rioplatense guitar was typical of church music.

While working in the Plata region as university professor and musicologist, Francisco Curt Lange implied that the guitar was part of worship services in the early parish churches prior to the purchase of a pipe organ. After the Council of Trent in the 16th century, the organ was of course far more appropriate in Catholic rituals than the guitar. But the organ was obviously an expensive import, and even after its installation, difficult to maintain. Thus parishoners ordinarily put the guitar to use in order to keep the musical portion of the services in tune and agreeable in early Rioplatense churches, sometimes along with the harp or bowed strings, in lieu of the organ. Even so, Lange found it difficult to document this fact because all that has remained in many church archives is scant reference to the purchase of strings for a guitarra or vihuela and some vague explanation as to how they were used:

[It was customary to refer to "several gross of guitar strings to knit together the disciplines of the worship services," as demonstrated in the second book of the Office] (Lange 1956:92).

Lange was both modest and painstaking in documenting this claim. Since he had university affiliations in the interior towns of Argentina, he spent years investigating the subject of ecclesiastical music there. As he visited Andean towns, Lange discovered some valuable data at the parish church of Humahuaca, far to the north, in the Province of Jujuy. The following are the earliest items in the church archive which bear mention of the guitar:

Fig. 11 The Guitar in the Church of Humahuaca (Lange 1954)

Iglesia de Humahuaca

Inventory of 8 Feb. 1743: "A guitar remains in the hands of cantor Francisco Senteno."

Accounts of 1745, folio 32v: "13 reals' worth of strings; another peso's worth of strings."

Accounts of 1769, folio 30: "To repair the church's guitar, on account of its having been treated so poorly, 4 reals.... I purchased guitar strings in the amount of 4 reals."

Several years later, Lange published more information in his quest, but this time regarding the churches in and around Córdoba. There he found numerous references to guitar strings in the 18th-century expense accounts of two churches (as shown in Fig. 12, on the next page).

The same sort of information in favor of using the guitar in church appeared before the years of independence in old Uruguay, then known as the *Banda Oriental* or East Bank. During the 17th century, there was a little Indian town on the east side of the Uruguay River called Santa Cruz in which a guitar used to accompany the church choir on festival days (Viglietti 1973:110–11). Another early town was Santo Domingo de Soriano, located on the Río Negro near present Mercedes. In the archives of its church, four separate items between years of 1769 and 1778 mention the purchase of strings for unspecified *"instrumentos de*

Fig. 12 The Guitar in the Churches of Córdoba (Lange 1956)
Convento de San Francisco de San Jorge
Charged to the Chaplain (13 Jun. 1695): "4 real's worth of guitar strings for the celebration of St. Anthony."
Colegio Máximo de la Compañía de Jesús
Merchandise delivered by Padre Manuel Gonzales (Mar. 1711): "946 strings purchased at 10 reals per gross."
Strings purchased for unspecified musical instruments (1711–1744): 42 separate items.
[Also regarding activities in the Colegio Máximo, the following items appear in *The Book of the Solicitor General's Office,* which was begun in Mar. 1711, Part II:]
"14 reals for guitar strings brought by Molina, and I paid for them," folio 199 (Nov. 1720).
"Two gross vihuela strings to knit together the disciplines," fol. 201 (Jan. 1721).
"Two gross vihuela strings to knit them together," fol. 205 (May 1721).
"About 38 sets of vihuela strings," fol. 213 (Nov. 1721).
"Three gross guitar strings at two pesos per gross," fol. 223 (Nov. 1722).

la iglesia" [instruments of the church]. In yet another reference there, in 1776, the following appeared (Ayestarán 1947:48):

> *El Cabildo de Soriano paga por concepto de cuerdas para arpa y guitarra que se tocan en la Iglesia...*(Cabildo de Soriano, "Libro de Cuentas" No. 69, p. 47).
> [The Municipality of Soriano pays on account for strings of the harp and guitar which are played in the Church....]

Again in Soriano, around 1780, the church musician Maestro Hilario organized an instrumental performance celebrating Santo Patrono using such instrumental musicians as guitarists, harpists, and violinists (Ayestarán 1953:119).

The prominence of the guitar in colonial Soriano was confirmed by external documentation. In 1786 a large shipment of imported guitar strings en route to Santo Domingo de Soriano passed through the port of Buenos Aires. The customs officials there approved the import of two dozen over-spun bass strings and six gross gut strings, all for the guitar (Table 4).

The most extensive evidence supporting the use of the guitar in Argentine churches came to light in Father Grenón's research. For example, he found the guitar mentioned in an episode of Pedro "Inca" Bohorquez's biography. In 1657 a mass was held in his honor at Londres de Tucumán which featured the music of a harp, a large lute, and a guitar (see Table 10, below).

According to surviving documents on the ownership of instruments in the colonial towns of Argentina, it was neither an unusual nor unholy practice to use the guitar in church. Apparently the guitar did not yet have any negative stigma attached to it which would bar the practice. The priests themselves or their delegates purchased vihuelas or guitarras in order to accompany church music, and thereby the instruments remained on hand for any of the services. In Saldán, near Córdoba, for instance, where the discante had been played for worship of the Virgin prior to 1663 (Ref. 4, above), the poet Luis de Tejeda was himself a priest as well as a guitarist. Upon his death in 1702, he bequeathed to his heirs a harp and an expensive guitar (Table 8). Again at Saldán, another priest purchased a fine guitar in 1761 to accompany the harp in the sacred services there (Table 10). The same seemed to be the case at some churches in other interior towns. The most notable references in this regard were those of 1764, 1770, and 1786, every one of which came from the Church of Renca (Table 10). Renca was a small town located in the line between Mendoza and Buenos Aires, near San Luis in the the foothills of the Andes. The church there owned a harp and violin in addition to a guitar. The item of 1770 established the guitar's purpose: it was definitely *"para el culto"* [for the worship service].

Table 10 Stringed Instruments in Church
(Grenón 1929, 1954)

1613. Father Torres says that in Paraguay "the instruments of music made their songs happy, none the least of which were the latest, fashionable dances of the nation" (P. Pedro Lozano, *Historia de la conquista del Paraguay, Río de la Plata y Tucumán*, p. 766).

1626. According to Father Durán..."The Indians, with admirable facility, learned to sing and play instruments—their first teacher being Brother Luis Berger, excellent performer on the chitarrone [cítara]" (Grenón, *Una vida de artista: H. Luis Berger, S.J., 1588–1641*, Córdoba: by the author, 1927). [See also the request for lute strings dated 1622 on behalf of Berger in Table 1, and a description of his background on p. 222, above.]

1628. Don Francisco de Céspedes writes: "The Indians of Uruguay have come here [to Buenos Aires], more than 20 of them, great musicians of organ point, violins, and other instruments in order to officiate in masses and dances" (Enrique Peña, "Don Francisco de Céspedes...[1624–32]," *Anales de la Academia de Filosofía y Letras* [Buenos Aires] V [1916]).

1637. Father Ripario, in his letter written from Córdoba, describes that Indians from the missionary reductions had arrived there to give a concert, those who without any prompting sang from score the entire mass and other motets along with such instruments as violins, harps, cornets, flutes, chitarrones, trombones, trumpets; and others sang a cappella (P. Ripario, *Relación escrita desde Córdoba,* 1637, in P. Antonio Astrain, *Historia de la Compañía de Jesús en el Paraguay,* Tomo I, p. 301, note).

1657. Mr. Enrique Peña...has published an extract from the celebrations realized at Londres de Tucumán on the occasion of Inca Bohorquez's reception in which verses were sung in the Jesuit Church.... The informants Ahumada and Rodríguez declared that they were sung "with harp," but Luis de Hoyos testified that "canzonetas were sung during that mass with the harp, vihuela, and chitarrone (Enrique Peña, *El Inca Bohorquez....* Sevilla, Buenos Aires: 1921)."

1660. [Letter to P. Grenón, Cordoba:] "I received your much appreciated letter on the 20th of the current month. Regarding the citation of the verses which were sung in the Church of Londres de Tucumán, they were accompanied by the harp and guitar. I took this from an item which exists in the Archive of the Indies [of Seville] entitled, "Original decrees pronounced by the Governor of Tucumán, Don Gerónimo Luis de Cabrera...29 Aug. 1659.... (Enrique Peña, Buenos Aires, 24 Oct. 1921)."

1736. In Salta, Father Arteaga, S.J. advises Father Armendia that he has received "a vihuela (*Archivo General de la Nación,* Comp. 1.3)."

1761. [According to the accounts of the Priest, Gabriel Bracamonte of the Chaplaincy of Saldán, Córdoba] "I purchased a vihuela adorned with a shell inlay for the Chapel so that it might be used to accompany the harp [see Table 8, above]."

1764. The following items appear in an inventory taken in the Church of Renca: "a harp and guitar, both in good condition, for the Church (A de G, 1.32, e.28)."

1766. In the Chapel of San Antonio are specified, by inventory, "a large harp and a guitar...(A de T, E.3, E.1.3)."

1767. In two voluminous inventories of ecclesiastical properties that Charles III seized from the Jesuits when he ruined their empire by decree of expulsion, musical instruments figure in greater quantity and quality than any other possession. [The following are those cited for the guitar:]

In Altagracia, there were two violins and two guitars. In 1772, a harp served the Church there.

In San Ignacio de Calamuchita were registered a harp and a guitar.

In Candelaria, a harp, a guitar, and a violin.

In San Javier: six flutes, ten vihuelas, two horns, four large harps (P. Carlos Leonhardt, *Recopilaciones inéditas).*

1770. In the aforementioned sanctuary of Renca, San Luis which touches along the southwest border of Córdoba, figure in the worship service "a violin and a well-used guitar (A de G, L.32, 1.28)." [A de G=Archivo de Gobierno, Archivo Histórico de Córdoba]

1777. Among the furniture of the Chapel of San Bernardo (on the border with Río Cuarto, Arg.), the priest had made an inventory which included "two old guitars (A del O, 1.4, second half)." [A del O=Archivo del Obispado, Diócesis de Córdoba]

1786. In the Church of Renca were inventoried "a guitar and a violin at eight reals apiece (A de G, 1.32, e.28)."

15. Summary and Conclusions

In the middle of the 16th century and during Spain's marvelous Golden Age, Juan Bermudo made clear distinctions between the *guitarra* and *vihuela*. The theorists and composers who were his contemporaries confirmed those distinctions, despite the fact that in literature the terms were becoming less exclusive. The Golden Age poets and playwrights used the terms interchangeably when referring to the music of Vicente Espinel, for in their eyes he was simply what we could call a guitarist.

The non-Spanish audience has always had difficulty in dealing with these terms because they were so archaic and so specialized. The fact that the guitarra and vihuela were both guitars seems to have baffled even a few respectable scholars of our time. Indeed, some early musicologists, when dealing with the vihuela and its literature, went so far as to call it a lute, clouding our perception all the more. (To be sure, the vihuela is basically a long-necked lute in the Hornbostel/Sachs categorization of musical instruments but so is the guitar.) During Spain's Golden Age the guitar was such a diverse phenomenon, so well developed and compartmentalized that guitars of different types, with different names existed for numerous specific purposes. In Spanish society, the guitar was not less common than a television or an automobile is in ours. We designate our cars specifically as "coupe, sedan, roadster, station wagon, van," etc., depending on the type or function of the vehicle. Likewise they unconsciously categorized the diversity of their guitars with special names for which we have no precise English equivalents. Therefore, the specific meanings must be understood if we hope to comprehend the guitar's history in Spain or in the New World where the terminology was even more precise.

The connections between Andalusia and the New World had long been apparent, but some scholars this century took a critical stance and began to doubt the validity of the connections that had already been claimed. Notable scholars began to explore the hypothesis of *andalucismo* in linguistic and demographic sources with the clear intention of disproving it, as explained above in Part II. However, upon the completion of painstaking research, recent scholars have found that Andalusia's genetic and cultural impact in America was even greater than expected at the outset. Thus, the music of Andalusia and its capital, Seville has needed further study in the light of these discoveries.

As for the guitar's early history there (in the briefest of terms), Seville had been paramount in areas of composition, performance, and instrument construction. Such composers as Alonso de Mudarra and Miguel de Fuenllana published their monumental tablature books in Seville, while such performers as Francisco Guerrero (the cathedral's renowned composer of liturgical music), Manuel Rodrígues, Pedro Bravo, Iulio Severino, and Pedro de Madrid were among the notable vihuelists there according to Francisco Pacheco's book of authentic portraits (Seville:1599). Whereas Pacheco sang their praises as among the city's favorite sons, he also provided a full-page, personal portrait of vihuelists Francisco Guerrero and Pedro de Madrid (q.v. Plate IV). Juan Bermudo, born in Ecija (midway between Córdoba and Seville), carefully reviewed the performance practices of the guitarra and vihuela in several parts of his *Declaración,* published in 1555 at Osuna (midway between Seville and Granada).

Whether Spaniards hailed from Seville or not, they had to go through the Andalusian capital en route to the Americas, becoming thus an entity of the Columbian Exchange. Once Columbus had charted the voyage to "the Indies," additional fleets of passengers and supplies could follow in his stead. The well-travelled route of these shipments became known as the *"carrera de Indias."* Like any other Europeans travelling with the Spanish fleet, all passengers had to meet it in Seville. Whatever impression of the guitar they held in their minds as they departed, it was tempered for the last time as they left their lodging and contacts there in preparation for their encounter with emigration officials. Naturally, some passengers and crewmen took along guitars and other instruments with which to lighten the tedium of their voyage and for entertainment in the New World. The first guitars may have arrived in the Americas as early as the voyages of Columbus, inasmuch as the Catholic Monarchs admonished him to include music and instruments among his other provisions in 1497. Even so, the Columbian Exchange, laden with European exports, brought the first guitars and guitar strings for resale to Puerto Rico as early as 1512 (Tables 1 and 2).

Once the crewmen had laden their ships for the transatlantic voyage, they sailed en masse on the first south wind out of the port and onto the Guadalquivir River. The ships left Seville by sailing south on the river, past the port of Cádiz, and then after about a thousand miles south on the Atlantic, they reached the Canary Islands, a Spanish possession along the African coast. The last provisions were taken aboard there for the transoceanic cruise. The passage from the Canaries to landfall in the Caribbean Islands took a month or more of navigation. The cruises were notorious for poor food and accommodations. Whereas gambling and intoxication were prohibited, the main diversion from the boredom and discomfort was music, whether religious, as in the singing of the serene "Te Deum laudamus" to acknowledge or invoke divine intervention in the trip, or secular, to make merry. In one of his Mediterranean crossings during the 16th century, Vicente Espinel mentioned that the guitar had been used effectively in the accompaniment of one of his impassioned songs. More importantly and even earlier, Fray Tomás de la Torre of the Dominican Order made specific mention of the guitar for diversion on the Atlantic. It was used to accompany the popular songs of the laymen on board (de la Torre 1545:85–86). Although more hard evidence remains to be found for this conclusion, one item of circumstantial evidence in support of the guitar's entertainment value in the voyage survived in merchandise arriving at Puerto Rico: a ship's officer who disembarked there in 1512 brought a small vihuela among his belongings (Table 1). Yet another precedent was set with the lute that Bernardo Centurione brought to Buenos Aires when he landed there accidentally during a storm in 1538. In either instance, it was unlikely that the guitar or the lute would have remained locked tightly in its case during the month-long ordeal of crossing the Atlantic.

The guitar appeared frequently in the chronicles of the Hispanic conquest of the 16th century, but only under the designation of *vihuela*. The Spaniards began their process of colonization in the chronological sequence of their discoveries: first amidst the landfalls of Columbus in the Caribbean, second in Mesoamerica under

Cortés, and third in South America, centered at Lima under
Pizarro. Likewise, the appearances of the vihuela followed the
same historical sequence. Fray Bartolomé de las Casas cited recol-
lections of the vihuela in the Caribbean in 1503 and 1509. In the
next decade, the colonists—both individuals and merchants—imported numerous vihuelas and vihuela strings at Puerto Rico (see
Tables 1 and 2 and special mention of the guitarra).

Bernal Díaz del Castillo was the chronicler who in his youth
happened to accompany Cortés in the Mexican conquest. Their
spoils of victory led to a life of luxury which included frequent
musical entertainments. Díaz del Castillo mentioned the vihuela
several times in this context prior to 1568, when his chronicle was
completed. Meanwhile, vihuelists had begun to circulate throughout New Spain (the eventual designation of the Mesoamerican
viceroyalty), as instrument repairmen established guilds (Díaz del
Castillo 1568:II, 541; 560. Saldívar 1934:161; 185). The first mention of the guitarra per se in extant Mexican sources was in the
trial of a guitarist at Veracruz in 1606 (Saldívar 1934:300). After
that, Father Thomas Gage observed the "guitar" at Veracruz and
at Huejotzingo, near Mexico City in 1625 (1644:34, 51).

Upon completion of the conquest of Peru, the vihuela and guitarra began to appear in its literature. Guamán Poma mentioned
them both, if in different contexts. He attested that the vihuela was
used in church ceremonies (c.1615:822), while the guitarra was
the instrument of the wildest entertainments of the laboring class
throughout the kingdom (c.1615:890). Guamán Poma's pen-and-
ink drawing of the guitar also portrayed it amidst a "fiesta" of the
aristocracy (Plate V). The criollos, the American-born Hispanics
were using it in songs of courtship; their guitar was double-strung
with four courses rather like Peninsular models of the Golden
Age. Later in the 17th century, the Conde de Lemos brought along
Lucas Ruíz de Ribayaz, who functioned both as guitarist and chaplain at the viceroyal court. Thereafter, once he had returned to the
Peninsula, Ruiz de Ribayaz published an important guitar method.
But the Viceroy who actually played the guitar, just as had his
Bourbon queen, Marie-Louise-Gabrielle of Savoy, was the Valen-
cian aristocrat Don Manuel Oms...Marqués de Castell dos Ríus.
Thus guitar music graced every conceivable social context of the

century which began with Guamán Poma's chronicle, included Santa Rosa de Lima, and ended with the last-mentioned viceroy of Peru. Between 1615 and 1710, men and women of all social strata in the viceroyalty were using the guitar for religious, secular, and artistic purposes.

*   *   *   *   *

Our understanding of a foreign culture's music may be enhanced if we follow the intended categories of musical production. Composers and performers create different musical expressions for their separate audiences: folk or popular music entertains, artistic music aspires to aesthetic goals, and religious music must obviously enhance worship. These subdivisions may be represented graphically as follows:

Fig. 13 Folkloric, Artistic, and Religious Music

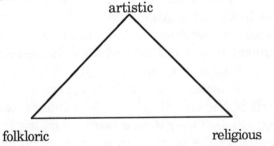

These subdivisions are particularly helpful in considering the history of the Rioplatense guitar, for it had a tripartite existence during the Hispanic domination. Guitarists developed music for all three categories in the Plata, just as they did in Peru. Starting with the Spanish conquest of Buenos Aires in the middle of the 16th century and ending with the declaration of independence from Spain early in the 19th, the early repertoire flourished especially in the categories of popular entertainment and religious ceremonies.

The guitar was popular in the Río de la Plata, as indicated in the sale of "catgut" strings. Whereas Plata musicians fabricated some homemade strings from domestic materials (the small intestine of rams, sheep, lamb, or deer) and prepared them according to old traditions, they nevertheless preferred imported guitar strings. By 1513 both sailors and merchants were carrying marketable quantities of European strings aboard the Spanish fleet, as shown in Table 2. Then, whether by legal commerce or by contraband, they distributed them into the rest of Hispanic America including the Plata region. Tavern owners sold guitar strings over the counter at their local pulperías, the establishments tantamount to the "general stores" of the American Wild West, which sold hard drinks, sundries, and informal social contacts. The pulperías proliferated across South American cities, towns, and countryside.

At first, guitarists put strings on in pairs, and then tuned them with standard European tunings or regional *scordature*. They used frets made from the same gut material as the strings and tied them on the neck (Table 3). Strings and frets were so precious that they were "declared property" in wills and estates as well as in the articles confiscated upon imprisonment. Business owners catalogued them in inventories. Indeed, from among such numerous legal records in Córdoba, Argentina, the inland town founded in the heart of *Nueva Andalucía* in 1573, the presence of the vihuela may be documented back to 1597 and the guitarra back to 1608.

Strings and frets sold at an unusually high price. Whether in the capital, small towns, or out on the lone prairie, pulpería owners supplied strings because they were a standard commodity yet charged for them as if they were a luxury, ranging from a quarter to half as much as the price of an instrument. Imported strings cost more but were nevertheless preferred. At that time, the Peruvian viceroyalty governed the whole of South America for over two centuries as an extension of the crown until the advent of the late viceroyalties at Bogotá and Buenos Aires. The high price of strings resulted from the 7.5 percent import duty and the tight regulation of imported merchandise imposed by the rule of Peru. In 1776, however, the crown established the independent Viceroyalty of the Río de la Plata, and within two years an influx of musical imports began to filter through Buenos Aires which served simultaneously as the viceroyal seat as well as the main port to the Atlantic. Then a legal flow of such items as over-spun bass strings and large guitars from Brazil began to overload the customs offices (Tables 4 and 7).

Large guitars gradually became standardized in the Plata. Initially the vihuela dominated the guitar scene along with the small *discante* (Tables 5 and 6). Then by the middle of the 17th century, the two began to coexist with the influx of a newer type of guitar. Gradually the guitarra (known as the *guitarra española* in Europe) became extremely popular, superseding the discante altogether, and crowding out the vihuela gradually towards the end of the 17th century. As large guitars came into use, smaller ones acquired specific, sometimes obscure names. The *gauderios* or *gauchos* around Montevideo were infamous as vagabond guitarists, for sometimes they would dedicate themselves to nothing but music, besides their immediate necessities, and hang around a settlement for weeks at a time. "Concolorcorvo" [the Spaniard Alonso Carrió de la Vandera] and José de Espinosa, claimed that the musical gauchos lived very modestly but only from the entertainment they would impose on permanent settlers! The gauchos sang improvised verses and at the same time accompanied them on the small *guitarrita* (1776:33). Espinosa described several of their rural dances as accompanied on the *guitarrilla* or *tiple* (1794: 561). Authorities on South American music have equated the guitarrilla and guitarrita with the four-course guitar of Spain or the *cuatro* of Venezuela. For centuries, the *tiple* was identified with these small, four-course guitars. However, in late 19th-century Colombia, where the tiple was already the national instrument, it increased in size as it became a triple-strung, four-course guitar. Nowadays the Colombian tiple even finds a place in formal recitals (Puerta 1988). The *charango* survived as the small, five-course folk guitar of present-day Bolivia and the adjoining parts of Chile, Peru, and Argentina in the Andean highlands.

Starting in 1512, the customs officials at Puerto Rico, assessed the actual cash value of guitars imported there at anywhere from a quarter peso to several pesos. In the Plata, the instruments were worth more, but inflation after a half century may have driven up the entire economy. An early guitar of the Plata sold at a price of about one to ten pesos; occasionally an instrument cost more because of its decoration or materials of construction. Guitars ranged from the very cheapest, made crudely of pine or willow wood, to the most expensive of jacarandá (senna brazilwood or dark rosewood), on the Brazilian imports. Luthiers aspired to leave some as ornately decorated with ebony or mother-of-pearl as those of the Baroque or Rococo courts of Europe. The earliest mention of the "guitarra," per se in Córdoba was in connection with the purchase of an ebony guitar for an aristocratic boy in 1608 (Table 8).

There is ample evidence to show that the guitar was both an artistic and religious instrument in the hands of women. The early exemplars were saints: Santa Rosa de Lima (1586–1617) and Santa Mariana de Quito (d. 1645). Rioplatense women first preferred the smaller discante, but after about 1650, they frequently owned expensive vihuelas and guitars (Table 9). Despite the fact that men published most of the travel memoirs on the Plata, they lavished undiminished, extravagant praise on the women of Buenos Aires and Montevideo. Such literature appeared as early as 1698, when Acarete du Biscay praised the women there for their beauty and devotion to family (see Part I, Section 3). Antoine Joseph Pernety found the Hispanic women of Montevideo to be as charming as any French women he knew. Beyond the cordial manner with which they always received their guests, they delighted them further by singing or performing on the guitar or other instruments: Pernety claimed the Montevidean women "are more pleasing in it than our French counterparts (1770:278)."

Throughout Hispanic America, women also appeared as musical angels in religious artwork, suggesting that the guitar may have been acceptable as a religious instrument. If the guitar were suitable for saints and angels, then why not for church music? This vast religious art-form developed across the Americas precisely at the time when instruments were banned from ceremonial use during the Counter Reformation, and specifically in the Council of Trent. The European bishops working in the Americas were undoubtedly aware of these conservative resolutions, yet they had no choice but to tolerate the ever-present guitar. Once the second practice became well established during the European Baroque, however, guitars probably accompanied the large-scale religious productions, at least in the continuo body of the orchestra.

The foremost technical detail among the angels of the Americas stands out in the stringing of their instruments. The examples cited from Coro, Venezuela, Santiago de Chile, and the three 17th-

century items from the Jesuit era of Argentina and Paraguay provide indispensable iconographical evidence on the Baroque, five-
course *guitarra española*. In the first place, if guitarists performed
in church, more than likely they used the mid-sized Baroque guitar during the 17th century rather than the Renaissance types
because neither the large, six-course vihuela nor the small, four-
course guitarra appeared in the above-named works of art. In the
second place, however, and within the broadest possible implication, these five angels suggest the availability and diffusion of the
Baroque guitar. Despite hundreds of references to guitar strings in
the churches and pulperías of the Rioplatense colony, the data
never specify, even when they mention *bordones* or bass strings,
whether the strings are for four-, five-, or six-course instruments.
However, the five cited examples are invariably consistent in their
manner of stringing: the angels are all playing the five-course
Baroque guitar, identical in each and every instance to European
models, as in Plate VI, representing the 17th-century Jesuit
Church of Córdoba. The angels witness unanimously that the
Baroque guitar, or the so-called *guitarra española* then in use
across the whole of Europe, was also available in South America.
Notwithstanding the irrelevant matter as to whether these Baroque guitars were originally made in Europe or the Americas,
they were used, indeed diffused, across South America.

The guitar and lute were ever present in the musical establishment of the Jesuit missions which dotted the eastern half of present Paraguay at the Brazilian border and the northeast corner of
Argentina. The Jesuit state there lasted officially from 1607 to
1767, during which time the missionaries experienced tremendous material and spiritual growth among their converts, the
Amerindian inhabitants of those regions. The Guaraní tribe in
particular, which had given the conquerors space at the port of
Asunción when it was not available elsewhere, proved over and
again to be the most responsive to Christian ideals and the most
sensitive to European music. Each mission or "reduction" among
them became an intense, self-sufficient module of activity. Since
the missionaries themselves were well-rounded and educated
Europeans, many of them were also fine musicians. All of the
Jesuit priests aspired to musical as well as spiritual and material

self-reliance. They taught, for example, the complete process of instrument construction and repair to the Indians, who in turn built pneumatic organs in the mission luthier shops—so the fabrication of a guitar was but a trifle. The Jesuit fathers taught enough techniques of European performance practice to make music their main diversion. Even so, they did not teach improvisation, probably for fear of introducing an uncontrollable element of performance —whether aspects of the material world or their former "pagan" customs. Anyway, the Indians did not care to become composers or virtuosi; they prided themselves on their ability to duplicate and enjoy European music.

The most notable music teacher among the Jesuits was the Tyrolean lutenist, Anthony Sepp who took an assignment of four decades at the Reduction of Yapeyú. Founded on the Uruguay River, his reduction was the nearest mission settlement to Buenos Aires (at 600 miles, a distance the length of California). Owing to its proximity, the Yapeyú musicians had to cater to the arriving Jesuit fathers from Europe, according to long-standing tradition. The Indians performed for them there because their transatlantic voyage always ended in the port, so Father Sepp's group provided their first brush with the Amerindian natives. Notwithstanding the excellent teaching the Indians received in Yapeyú, the notoriety of their performances, their demand, or travel, or other benefits, the best explanation for musical success among them was their own love of music. Excellence in performance was the paramount achievement of their native culture. So when Charles III proclaimed the irreversible closure of the missions in 1767, many of the Indian musicians migrated south into present Argentina and Uruguay in order to continue their new-found Christian beliefs and their careers. One Cristóbal Piriobi, a guitarist and orchestral musician born in the San Carlos Reduction, went to Buenos Aires to become the best known of the Indian musicians who were taught in the Jesuit tradition (Monzón 1947).

Guitars and lutes were certainly part of the missionary pageants and quasi-entertainment, but far more significant, these instruments were used in their religious ceremonies, as well. On two occasions, eyewitness Father José Cardiel described the music of the Jesuit mass and its instruments—among them, the guitar in certain locations. During the same period outside the missions, many outpost churches throughout the Plata region either owned guitars, or guitarists performed in their sacred music up until pipe organs could be imported and installed in them. The instrument-alists were probably paid in strings instead of cash, because the account books are replete with the regular purchase of strings, often designated as "vihuela strings." Church expense books and accounts remain to document the guitar's use in religious services at the Argentine churches of Humahuaca, the Convento de San Francisco de San Jorge and the Colegio Máximo (both in Córdoba), Londres de Tucumán, Saldán, and Renca. The guitar appeared regularly in the colonial Uruguayan churches of Santa Cruz and Soriano, as well.

In terms of the instrument itself, the early Rioplatense guitar developed in parallel with the so-called "Spanish guitar" of Europe. Already by 1487 Johannes Tinctoris noted the Spanish preference for the vihuela over the lute, documenting the guitar's organic chronology. The guitar of the Renaissance had two roots: the plebeian, strummed, four-course *guitarra* and the aristocratic, plucked, six-course *vihuela,* as described at length by Juan Bermudo (1555), and the two were put to use more pervasively in Spanish society than anywhere else in Europe. During the Golden Age, the guitar was nevertheless in transition: the two roots of the tree or the two branches of the mainstream converged into an instrument of compromise, not only in size and number of strings, but also in technique: the *guitarra española,* was both strummed and plucked. Meanwhile, in consequence of Spain's political, economic, artistic, and literary achievements during the Golden Age, most of Europe developed a taste for Spanish arts and enter-tainment as the Italo-Hispanic Renaissance spread northward. At the start of the 17th century, the guitar was in sudden demand at continental masquerade parties, to accompany the latest dance steps of wild *folías* and *chaconas,* or to interpret lengthy variations on *pasacalles* and sensitive *zarabandas* as guitarists first spread the popular repertoire into all ranks of European society. In the meantime, the small Spanish *guitarrilla,* the Italian *chitarra battente,* or the English *guittar* endured but peripherally to the millennial trajectory of the guitar. The gut-strung, five-course *guitarra española* remained structurally unaltered, even by one Antonio Stradivari, until the end of the Baroque and thus the mainstream or trunk of the tree. Then came the winds of change at the end of 18th-century Europe that wrought innovations in the instrument itself: experiments with over-spun bass strings led to single stringing, the addition of the low E or 6th string, and another increase in size. The last major structural development came with the yet larger, deeply resonant guitar of Antonio Torres, which caught on with the Tárrega technique prior to 1900. Thus, as a product of continual growth up to the present day, the guitar has remained the oldest living instrument of Western civilization, except perhaps the organ or harp, and certainly the most popular instrument ever devised by humankind. The guitar has survived without any interruption in its organology, methods of strummed and plucked performance, or repertoire, at least since Luis Milán's tablature book of 1536, in categories of artistic and popular music.

Inasmuch as the Río de la Plata was a territory of Imperial Spain, established with a predominance of Andalusian culture among its 16th-century colonists, and governed by Spaniards or American-born Hispanics until 1810, it is not surprising to discover that the guitar's history there parallels its development in Spain, particularly with regards to the instrument itself. The guitar arrived with the first European settlers in 1536, the year Milán began the series of publications for the vihuela. The fact that the Plata was isolated from the rest of Hispania was largely compensated in the assiduous cultivation of Hispanic, Roman Catholic ideals, both consciously and unconsciously. The sources of the Rioplatense guitar preserved the fact that "guitarras" gradually superseded "vihuelas" at the middle of the 17th century, soon after the same development in Europe. The guitarra, discante, and vihuela were guitar-like instruments, yet the characteristics of the newer, compromised five-course "guitarra" took over, although lacking the specific European designation of the Baroque guitar— i.e., the *guitarra española*. (The adjective "Spanish" was probably superfluous in a colony where everything they cultivated was Spanish.) Nevertheless, despite the decided switch to the Baroque guitar in actual practice, the term vihuela continued to be used in the Plata. Long after the switch, Rioplatense poets such as Esteban

Echeverría or José Hernández could conjure up associations of somber respectability or nostalgic days of yore by calling an instrument a vihuela. In fact, Hernández's beginning of *Martín Fierro,* "*Aquí me pongo a cantar al compás de la vigüela*," was a mere paraphrase of the standard opening for any gaucho ballad. These usages referred clearly to an instrument of the past. Paradoxically, the archaic, six-course, double-strung, aristocratic vihuela which Bermudo described (Andalusia, 1555) could not possibly have survived up to their times. The same practice of euphemism or wordplay occurred around Rioplatense churches. Priors and prelates purchased "vihuelas" with church funds (Table 10), or they called on "vihuelists" to perform in the ceremony of the mass, but the instruments involved could not have been other than the selfsame guitars of their serenades and dances played only the previous night, despite the careful designation of "vihuelas" over and again in church documents. In other words, Plata word usage was indeed a continuation of that non-restrictive interchangeable usage revealed among the literary geniuses of the Siglo de Oro: in the New World, "vihuela" was simply another way of saying guitar, even when it accompanied the acrobatics of a battle mare used during the conquest of 1503! Yet in Guamán Poma's monumental, illustrated chronicle of 1615, the "vihuela" was played in church, and the "guitarra" accompanied the drums in the wildest secular entertainment in the "kingdom" of Peru. Likewise, the Rioplatense vihuela was ever the older, more respectable, and dignified instrument—indeed, suitable for church; yet the guitarra endured far beyond it in all categories, including also the wildest entertainment of the Rioplatense populace. Therefore, throughout the Plata, the vihuela and early guitarra were the roots of the tree, but the five-course guitar took over the mainstream, just as it did in Europe. The numerous peripherals or branches were the smaller guitars with fewer strings and more limitations; most of them were instruments of momentary but passing significance. Finally with the advent of the new viceroyalty and the abolition of trade restrictions, large guitars and over-spun bass strings flooded the market and inevitably forecast the doom of the five-course Baroque guitar. Thus the guitarists of the Río de la Plata made every effort to stay abreast of the innovations and the main developments of European craftsmen, because in the Plata the guitar itself was the tangible, paramount icon of Spanish civilization. Therefore, no objective consideration of the guitar's history can any longer exclude the Rioplatense guitar, for it had an integral part in the ranging, organic development of this instrument. The the Rioplatense guitar was a direct extension of the guitar's world development as part of the mainstream; it was a significant branch of the tree.

The guitar was used regularly and pervasively throughout the Rioplatense colony, even more so than it was in Spain. Before independence it extended into every category of the society's musical activity, whether folkloric, artistic, or even religious. To be sure, the Rioplatense guitar had yet to ascend to its full artistic glory on the recital stage, but here it is in the making. Here is evidence of the guitar's acceptance and prestige, the regional attitude towards it, the guitar's cultural niche as the standard tool of all forms of musical expression. From this base, the guitarists of Argentina and Uruguay would eventually emerge as world-ranking classical performers; from this base, their folk music of great character and complexity developed, using the foremost icon of Hispanic civilization as their medium of expression, as all of their ancestors had done for centuries. Prior to independence, the guitar was used in church or out: it served for worship, for entertainment of the populace, or in refined artistic performances. Members of every class within the dominant culture played the guitar, whether rich or poor, aristocrats or *gauderios,* bond or free, young or old, and among the three great races of Latin America—the Amerindian natives, the immigrant African blacks, or European whites. Even women were involved in the movement and nearly as often as men; for Pernety, their polite performances excelled any that he had heard by women in his native France.

So far, the greater part of the data under review has been environmental—part of the tangible, quantifiable aspects of life. But now to the delicate matter of *inheritance.* Despite enormous strides in the field of genetics, an explanation of whether there is genetic transfer of musicality or how it is accomplished in the genes has remained wanting. That is, for example, in the case of J.S. Bach, were any of his abilities, talents, or predispositions towards music inherited directly from the musicians of his family tree? Or did he learn everything from an optimal musical environment? Bach's meticulous attention to genealogy suggested his belief in the inheritance factor, although he certainly argued the learning factor as a basis for his achievements. The inheritance factor was evident in the Plata, and from two main sources. The original Andalusian settlers were indeed musical, especially with the guitar. However, the few survivors of Mendoza's original company at the first Buenos Aires had no choice but to take refuge upstream in Asunción (Appendix I), where they were received by the peace-loving Indians, and where the men took the Guaraní women to wife (Part I, Section 3). They too were sensitive to music and inclined towards performance, the highest ideal of their native culture. In the next generation, the mestizo children of this union became the Christian settlers of the downstream Plata towns. Then, gradually, new blood came from Europe, Andalusia still continuing to predominate, to Europeanize the colony. While some intermarriage undoubtedly continued, another large influx of native blood came with the converted Indians who fled to the Hispanic towns at the close of the Jesuit missions in 1767. The Guaraní who had learned the cultural ways of the Hispanic population, like Piriobi, moved south into the Uruguayan and Argentine territories (Part III, Section 13). Since music was the professed specialty of so many converted Guaraní, and since the musicians among them were always culled from the mass population by the process of selection in control of Jesuit missionaries who auditioned all their candidates, the select Amerindian musicians seem to have impacted Rioplatense society. The genetic input of the Guaraní into the posterity of the colonial population did not harm its musicality. If there was any resulting musical impact whatsoever in the Hispanic populace, the racial fusion could only have enhanced its already intense musical predisposition inherited from Spain.

> Guitarra argentina, guitarra española:
> ¡lábaro supremo que feliz tremola
> los regios colores de la patria ideal!
> Suena eternamente...vibra dulcemente,
> ¡hija soberana del pueblo que siente,
> rimando tus sones, la gloria inmortal!

[Guitar of Argentina—guitar of Spain:
supreme symbol of our joy and pain,
regal colors of this ideal nation!
You sound eternally...vibrate so sweetly,
sovereign daughter of those whose destiny
resonates with yours in immortal federation!]
—Ricardo M. Llanes

The Rioplatense guitar was indeed comparable to the European
guitar externally, but internally the guitar was incomparable to
any other aspect of Rioplatense life. The instrument was a unique,
pervasive cultural phenomenon, and thus it came to the attention
of regional experts. Rioplatense musicologists and guitar historians
had no choice but to acknowledge the importance of the guitar in
their own conclusions, for it had already advanced to the status of
"the national instrument," as it had in Spain.

The guitar's universal appeal among the populace set the stage
for its total conquest: it was as if everybody played the same sport!
The guitar became so widely diffused in Argentina that it eventually gained acceptance during the war of independence among
its supreme generals Gregorio de La Madrid and José de San
Martín, and afterwards in the salons of Buenos Aires with Dictator
Juan Manuel de Rosas, his daughter Manuelita, and among founding fathers such as Juan Bautista Alberdi. During the same era,
there was a parallel pattern in Uruguay: liberator José Artigas and
President Bernardo Berro were guitarists. But why? According to
the eminent Argentine musicologist, Carlos Vega (another guitarist), the reasons were both genetic and learned:

[The guitar is our own because of an old predilection of the race.
It came to us with the first singers in the first caravels; it came
to us along with the language and culture of Spain. And justly
so: we needed it that way, small and graceful; we needed it because we inherited the aptitude for song from one of the foremost singing nations of the world—Spain.
    The American pampas did not suppress the Hispanic sensi-
bility. The guitar continued to translate the songs of the plains,
and even before the gaucho war (of independence) there was
scarcely a rancho that did not have a guitar at hand] (Vega
1926:330).

In 1930 Ricardo Muñoz dedicated an entire section of his second volume to the "national instrument." But by then, he had already characterized the guitar around the Argentine capital as unique:

[It can be asserted without fear of mistake that Buenos Aires is by excellence the most important guitaristic city in the world.]

If the guitar were popular in his native Argentina, it came as no surprise to Jesuit historian Guillermo Furlong. Indeed, it was the pre-eminent popular instrument throughout Hispanic America due to the unity and universality of the Spanish inheritance. From his perspective, the guitar was the common property of the folk by total acclamation; it remained unchallenged by any other early instrument:

[Throughout the American continent, the guitar came to be the popular instrument by natural inclination, and in particular it acquired that general and cordial acceptance among all the people in this part of America] (Furlong 1944b:126).

After reviewing and publishing thousands of pages of her own historical and folkloric research, Isabel Aretz came to a capital conclusion about the guitar. It was the only instrument dispersed generally, throughout every niche of the Hispanic population of Argentina (1978:120).

From his vantage point in Uruguay, Cédar Viglietti could see how the guitar came to be so widely accepted in the Río de la Plata. During its first few centuries of development there, it was popular, to be sure, yet it was also an instrument of venerable esteem in every class of society:

[A heartfelt love existed among the people of past centuries towards the instrument itself—at the same time, the ability of knowing how to play it signified something of pride, a lofty privilege at all social ranks—at least in these countries of the Plata region.... For them, those six strings were the equivalent of the sonorous world which envelops us today] (Viglietti 1973: 155–56).

Among many historiographers of the Río de la Plata, it was
Father Grenón who discovered the most data to document the
guitar's early history. Thus, with all due respect, he deserves the
honor of giving the last word here, the final conclusion to Part III.
In the first edition of *Nuestra primera música instrumental* [Our
Earliest Instrumental Music], which covered all the instruments
of the Hispanic domination, Father Grenón singled out one from
all the others. After considering the totality of instrumental music
in Argentina, he claimed that the guitar has always been—

> *el instrumento musical más típicamente nuestro.... La guitarra
> ha sido el instrumento más asequible y usado en nuestra pasada
> vida de sociabilidad y afecto cultural* (Grenón 1929:4).
> [the musical instrument most typically our own.... The guitar
> has been the most accessible and utilized instrument in our past
> social life and cultural inclination.]

In the second edition of the same work, Father Grenón explained and expanded his original conclusion:

> *En esta edición, después de 20 años, me confirmo en la conclu-
> sión de que la guitarra es el instrumento musical más nuestro,
> ya sea por la homogeneidad de la herencia española, ya sea por
> la más manual hechura local y manejo de la guitarra. También
> por ser punteados los sonidos, no se exige el ligado de la armonía.
> Además, los claros del toque punteado de la guitarra se prestan
> para bordar en él el canto flexible como la modulación con-
> natural, a los efectos y expresión nativos nuestros.... Esto así,
> siempre que no se asiente que la guitarra sea autóctona, sino
> española aclimatada a nuestra vida afectiva* (Grenón 1954:26).
> [In this edition, after twenty years, I confirm the conclusion that
> the guitar is the musical instrument most our own, be it due
> either to the universal continuity of our Spanish heritage or to
> the facility with which the guitar is made locally or played. It is
> also due to the fact that, since its sounds are plucked, the guitar
> does not require any complementary harmony. Moreover, its
> transparent, plucked accompaniments lend themselves to the
> embroidery of the most agile song like an indigenous modula-
> tion to our native sentiments and expression.... However, the
> guitar is not to be understood as autochthonous but rather,
> Spanish, acclimated to our own affective life.]

16. References Cited in Part III

Aretz, Isabel
1967a   *Instrumentos musicales de Venezuela*. [Caracas:] Universidad de Oriente.

1967b   "Raíces europeas de la música folklórica de Venezuela: El aporte indígena" in *Music in the Americas*, G. List and J. Orrego-Salas, eds. Bloomington, IN: Indiana University Research Center, 1967.

1978   *La música tradicional de la Rioja*. [Caracas] Venezuela: Biblioteca INIDEF.

Ayestarán, Alejandro
1980   "Uruguay: Folk Music," *The New Grove Dictionary of Music and Musicians*. London: Macmillan.

Ayestarán, Lauro
1947   *Fuentes para el estudio de la música colonial uruguaya* (Apartado de la *Revista de la Facultad de Humanidades y Ciencias* Año I, No. 1). Montevideo: Impresora Uruguaya.

1953   *La música en el Uruguay*, Vol. I. Montevideo: Servicio Oficial de Difusión Radio Eléctrica.

1963   "Folklore musical uruguayo: La guitarra y el acordeón," *La Unión* (Minas, Uruguay) LXXXIII, No. 21811, 24 Aug.

Baumann, Max Peter
1979   "Der Charango—Zur Problemskizze eines akkulturierten Musikinstruments," *Musik und Bildung* (Mainz) XI, No. 10, 603–12.

Bermudo, Fray Juan
1555   *Declaración de instrumentos musicales*. Osuna, Andalusia. Facsimile by M. Santiago Kastner, ed., Documenta Musicológica, Ser. I, Vol. XI. Kassel: Bärenreiter, 1957.

Bossio, Jorge A.
1972   *Historia de las pulperías*. Buenos Aires: Plus Ultra.

Buschiazzo, Mario J., ed., trans.
1941   *Buenos Aires y Córdoba en 1729 según cartas de los padres C. Cattaneo y C. Gervasoni, S.J.* Buenos Aires: Compañía de Editoriales y Publicaciones Asociadas.

Calzavara, Alberto
1987   *Historia de la música en Venezuela: Período hispánico con referencias al teatro y la danza*. [Caracas:] Fundación Pampero.

Cardiel, José, S.J.
1747   *Carta-relación de las misiones de la Provincia del Paraguay*
        in Guillermo Furlong, S.J., *José Cardiel, S.J. y su Carta-*
        relación (1747). Buenos Aires: Librería del Plata, 1953.

1758   *Declaración de la verdad: obra inédita del P. José Cardiel.*
        Introduction by P. Pablo Hernández. Buenos Aires: Juan A.
        Alsina, 1900.

[Carrió de la Vandera, Alonso]
[1776] *El lazarillo de ciegos caminantes desde Buenos-Ayres, hasta*
        Lima...Sacado de las memorias que hizo Don Alonso Carrió
        de la Vandera en este dilatado viage...desde Montevideo. Por
        Don Calixto Bustamante Carlos Inca, alias Concolorcorvo....
        Gijón, Spain [sic]: Rovada [= stolen!], 1773 [sic]. [Lima: c.1776].
        Buenos Aires: Solar, 1942.

Cattaneo, Cayetano, S.J.
1730   "Letters of F.C. Cattaneo" in Lodovico Antonio Muratori, *A*
        Relation of the Missions of Paraguay.... London: J. Marma-
        duke, 1759, letter no. 2. See also the Spanish edition by Mario J.
        Buschiazzo, ed., trans., *Buenos Aires y Córdoba en 1729 según*
        las cartas de los padres C. Cattaneo y C. Gervasoni, S.J. Buenos
        Aires: Compañía de Editoriales y Publicaciones Asociadas, 1941.

Cervantes Saavedra, Miguel de
1616   *Obras completas,* A. Valbuena Prat, ed. Madrid: Aguilar, 1965.

Chome, Padre, S.J.
1730   "Carta del Padre Chome, misionero de la Compañía de Jesús,
        al Padre Vanthiennen, de la misma compañía, en la Ciudad
        de las Corrientes a 26 de septiembre de 1730," in Juan Mühn,
        S.J., ed., *La Argentina vista por los viajeros del siglo XVIII.*
        Buenos Aires: Huarpes, 1946.

de la Torre, R.P. Fray Tomás
1545   *Desde Salamanca, España hasta Ciudad Real, Chiapas: Diario*
        de viaje, 1544–1545. Franz Blom, ed. Mexico City: Editora Central,
        1945.

de las Casas, Fray Bartolomé
c.1530 *Historia de las Indias.* Biblioteca Mexicana, Vol. II. Mexico City:
        Editorial Nacional, 1951.

Descripción del Virreinato del Perú: Crónica inédita de comienzos del siglo
c.1615 *XVII* [anon.]. Edición, prólogo y notas de Boleslao Lewin. Rosario:
        Universidad Nacional del Litoral, Facultad de Filosofía, 1958.

Díaz del Castillo, Bernal
1568   *Historia verdadera de la conquista de la Nueva España,*
        prólogo de Carlos Pereyra, ed., segunda edición, Tomos I–II.
        Madrid: Espasa-Calpe, 1942.

Diccionario Kapelusz
1979   Buenos Aires: Kapelusz.

Echeverría, Esteban
1831   *A mi guitarra* in *Obras completas*...compilación y biografía por
       Juan María Gutiérrez. Buenos Aires: Zamora, 1972.

Espinel, Vicente
1618   *Relaciones de la vida del escudero Marcos de Obregón....* Madrid:
       I. de la Cuesta. Barcelona: Biblioteca "Arte y Letras," 1910.

Espinosa, José de [et al.]
1794   *Viaje político-científico alrededor del mundo por las corbetas
       Descubierta y Atrevida al mando de los capitanes de navío
       Don Alejandro Malaspina y Don José de Bustamante y Guerra
       desde 1789 a 1794,* publicado con una introducción por Don Pedro
       de Novo y Colson, ed. Madrid: Abienzo, 1885.

Fernández de Navarrete, Martín, ed.
1825   *Colección de los viajes y descubrimientos que hicieron por mar
       los españoles, desde fines del siglo XV...Tomo II.* Madrid: Im-
       prenta Nacional.

Furlong, Guillermo, S.J.
1942   "Siete grandes maestros de música colonial rioplatense,"
       Boletín de la Academia Nacional de la Historia (Buenos Aires)
       XVI, 59–76.

1944a "La música en el Río de la Plata con anterioridad a 1810," *Lyra*
       (Buenos Aires) II, No. 11 (May).

1944b *Músicos argentinos durante la dominación hispánica.* Buenos
       Aires: Editorial Huarpes.

1946   *Los Jesuítas y la cultura rioplatense,* nueva edición corregida
       y aumentada. Biblioteca Enciclopédica Argentina, Vol. No. 9,
       Vicente D. Sierra, ed. Buenos Aires: Editorial Huarpes.

Gage, Thomas
1648   *The English-American, His Travail by Sea and Land: or, A
       New Survey of the West-India's, Containing a Journall of Three
       Thousand and Three Hundred Miles within the Main Land of
       America....* London: H. Blunden. J. Eric S. Thompson, ed.
       Norman: University of Oklahoma Press, 1958.

Gesualdo, Vicente
1961   *Historia de la música en la Argentina, 1536–1851,* Vol. I.
       Buenos Aires: Editorial Beta.

González, Francisco
1988   "La guitare en Amérique Latine," *Les Cashiers de la Guitare*
       (Paris) No. 25, 20–22.

Goyena, Héctor Luis
1986   "El charango en el Departamento de Chuquisaca (Bolivia),"
        Temas de Etnomusicología (Buenos Aires) II, 6–28.

Grenón, Pedro J., S.J.
1929   *Nuestra primera música instrumental: Datos históricos.*
        Buenos Aires: Emilio Perrot.

1954   "Nuestra primera música instrumental: Datos históricos,
        segunda edición," *Revista de Estudios Musicales* (Universidad
        Nacional de Cuyo, Mendoza) Año II (1950–51), 11–96; Año III
        (1954), 173–220.

Guamán Poma de Ayala, Felipe
c.1615 *Nueva corónica y buen gobierno: Codex péruvien illustré.* Facs.
        by Université de Paris, Richard Pietschmann, ed. Paris: Institut
        d'Ethnologie, Université de Paris, 1936.

Guestrin, Néstor
1986   "La guitarra en la música suramericana, Capítulo 1: La época
        colonial," *Revista Musical de Venezuela* (Caracas) VIII, No.
        19, 11–22.

Haley, George
1959   *Vicente Espinel and Marcos de Obregón: A Life and Its Liter-
        ary Representation.* Providence, RI: Brown University Press.

Hernández, José
1879   *El gaucho Martín Fierro.* Buenos Aires: Imprenta de la Pampa,
        1872. *La vuelta de Martín Fierro.* Buenos Aires: Librería del Plata,
        1879. [Both republished with "xilografías" by Alberto Nicasio] 9th
        ed. Buenos Aires: Ediciones Peuser, 1960.

Hornbostel, Erich M. von, and Curt Sachs
1914   "Classification of Musical Instruments: Translated from the
        Original German by Anthony Baines and Klaus P. Wachsmann,"
        Galpin Society Journal (Winchester, Eng.) XIV (1961), 3–29.

Lange, Francisco Curt
1954   "La música eclesiástica argentina en el período de la domi-
        nación hispánica (una investigación), primera parte," *Revista
        de Estudios Musicales* (Universidad Nacional de Cuyo, Mendoza)
        III, No. 7, 17–169, passim.

1956   *La música eclesiástica en Córdoba durante la dominación
        hispánica* [reprinted from *Revista de la Universidad Nacional
        de Córdoba*]. Córdoba, Arg.: Imprenta de la Universidad.

Leonard, Irving A.
1952   "One Man's Library, Mexico City, 1620," in *Estudios hispán-
        icos, homenaje a Archer M. Huntington.* Wellesley, MA:
        Wellesley College, pp. 327–34.

Lohmann Villena, Guillermo
 1946   *El Conde de Lemos/Virrey del Perú.* Publicaciones de la Es-
        cuela de Estudios Hispano-Americanos...XXIII (No. General).
        Serie 2a: Monografías, No. 8. Madrid: Universidad de Sevilla.

Lowenfeld, Elena Machado
 1975   "Santiago de Murcia's Thorough-Bass Treatise for the Baroque
        Guitar (1714): Introduction, Translation, and Transcription."
        M.A. thesis, City University of New York. Ann Arbor: Univer-
        sity Microfilms No. M-7910.

Monzón, Antonio
 1947   "Un profesor indígena [Piriobi] de la música en el Buenos Aires
        del siglo XVIII," *Estudios* (Academia Literaria del Plata, Buenos
        Aires) LXXVIII, No. 422 (Sep.), 142–46.

Moreno, Salvador
 1957   *Angeles músicos en México.* Mexico City: Ediciones de la Revista
        Bellas Artes.

 1959   "Angeles músicos en México," *Cuadernos Hispanoamericanos*
        (Madrid) No. 106 (Oct. 1958), 59–70; and No. 115 (Jul. 1959), 4–15.

Moreno Chá, Ercilia, ed.
 1980   *Instrumentos musicales etnográficos y folklóricos de la
        Argentina: Síntesis de los datos obtenidos en investigaciones
        de campo (1931–1980).* Buenos Aires: Instituto Nacional de
        Musicología "Carlos Vega."

Moses, Bernard
 1922   *Spanish Colonial Literature in South America.* London, New
        York: The Hispanic Society of America.

Mühn, Juan, S.J., ed.
 1946   *La Argentina vista por viajeros del siglo XVIII.* Buenos Aires:
        Huarpes.

Mugaburu, Josephe and Francisco
 1697   *Chronicle of Colonial Lima: The Diary of Josephe and Fran-
        cisco Mugaburu, 1640–1697,* translated and edited by Robert R.
        Miller. Norman: University of Oklahoma Press, 1975.

Muñoz, Ricardo
 1930   *Historia de la guitarra.* Buenos Aires: n.p.

Muratori, Lodovico Antonio
 1759   *A Relation of the Missions of Paraguay. Wrote originally in
        Italian by Mr. Muratori, and now done into English from the
        French translation.* London: J. Marmaduke.

Ohlsen, Oscar
 1980   "Antepasados de la guitarra en América Latina," *Revista*

Universitaria (Pontificia Universidad Católica de Chile)
No. 3 (Apr.), 77–86.

Olsen, Dale A.
1980   "Folk Music of South America," in *Musics of Many Cultures,*
        an Introduction, Elizabeth May, ed. Berkeley: University of
        California Press.

Pacheco, Francisco
1599   *Libro de descripción de verdaderos retratos....* Seville. Facs. ed.
        by José M. Asencio, ed. Seville: R. Tarrascó, 1885.

Paucke, Florian, S.J.
1769   *Hacia allá y para acá: Una estada entre los indios mocobíes,*
        1749–1767. Edmund Wernicke, trans. 3 vols. Tucumán,
        Buenos Aires: Universidad Nacional de Tucumán, 1942.

Pease, Franklin, ed., trans.
1980   Felipe Guamán Poma de Ayala, *Nueva corónica y buen*
        gobierno: Transcripción, prólogo, notas y cronología. 2 vols.
        Caracas: Biblioteca Ayacucho.

Peralta, Fray Joseph
1743   *Informe, que remite a S.M. Catholica el illmo. Señor Don Fray*
        Joseph Peralta, Obispo de Buenos-Ayres, de la Orden de Predi-
        cadores: Sobre la Visita, que hizo de todos los Pueblos de las
        Misiones, que están a cargo de los PP. de la Compañía de Jesús,
        y de las otras ciudades, y lugares de su obispado. Buenos-Ayres,
        y enero 8. de 1743. Republished. Havana: O.B. Cintas, n.d.

Pernety, Antoine Joseph
1770   *Histoire d'un voyage aux isles Malouines, fait en 1763 & 1764;*
        avec des observations sur le detroit de Magellan, et sur les
        Patagons. Paris: Saillant & Nyon [etc.].

Pope Conant, Isabel
1958   "Vicente Espinel as a musician," *Studies in the Renaissance*
        (New York) V, 133–44.

Porro, N.R.
1982   [with] J.E. Astiz and M.M. Rospide, *Aspectos del la vida coti-*
        diana en el Buenos Aires virreinal. Buenos Aires: Universidad
        de Buenos Aires.

Prat, Domingo
[1934] *Diccionario biográfico, bibliográfico, histórico, crítico de*
        guitarras (instrumentos afines) guitarristas (profesores,
        compositores, concertistas, lahudistas, amateurs) guitarre-
        ros (luthiers).... Buenos Aires: Romero y Fernández.

Puerta Zuluaga, David
1988   *Los caminos del tiple.* Bogotá: Damel Publishers.

Ramón y Rivera, Luis Felipe
1966 "La música colonial profana," *Revista Nacional de Cultura* (Caracas) XXVIII, Nos. 174–75 (Mar.–Jun.), 62–65.

Real Academia Española
1950 *Diccionario manual e ilustrado de la lengua española,* segunda edición. Madrid: Espasa-Calpe.

Relaciones geográficas de Indias
1885 Tomo I (1881), Tomo II (1885). Madrid: Ministerio de Fomento, Perú.

Rodríguez de Guzmán, Diego
1713 *Flor de academias.* [Manuscript completed at the court of Viceroy Manuel de Oms y Santa Pau in Lima.] Ricardo Palma, ed. Lima: El Tiempo, 1899.

Roldán, Waldemar Axel
1987 *Música colonial argentina: La enseñanza musical.* Buenos Aires: El Ateneo.

Saldívar, Gabriel
1934 [with] Elisa Osorio Bolio, *Historia de la música en México: Epocas precortesiana y colonial.* Mexico City: Editorial "Cvltvra."

Santa Cruz, Antonio de
17thc. "Libro donde se verán pazacalles de los ocho tonos...para bigüela hordinaria," MS Música 2209. [Undated manuscript in five-course tablature, clearly in the style of Spanish guitar books of the century.] Madrid: Biblioteca Nacional.

Sepp, Anthony, S.J.
1697 *An Account of a Voyage from Spain to Paraquaria; Performed by the Reverend Fathers Anthony Sepp and Anthony Behme, Both German Jesuits, the First of Tyrol upon the River Eth, the Other of Bavaria. Containing a Description of All the Remarkable Things and the Inhabitants, as well as of the Missionaries Residing in that Country, Taken from the Letters of Said Anthony Sepp, and Published by His Own Brother Gabriel Sepp. Translated from the High Dutch Original.* Nurenberg: 1697. London: Churchill's Voyages, 1703.

Stevenson, Robert
1960 *The Music of Peru: Aboriginal and Viceroyal Epochs.* Washington, D.C.: Pan American Union, O.A.S.

1980a "Alonso de Mudarra," *The New Grove Dictionary of Music and Musicians.* London: Macmillan.

1980b "Santiago de Murcia: A Review Article," *Inter-American Music Review* (Los Angeles) III (1980), No. 1, 89–101.

1984	"The Music of Colonial Spanish America" in *The Cambridge History of Latin America, Vol. II: Colonial Latin America,* Leslie Bethell, ed. Cambridge: Cambridge Universiy Press.

Strizich, Robert
1974	"A Spanish Guitar Tutor: Ruiz de Ribayaz's *Luz y norte musical* (1677)," *Journal of the Lute Society of America* (Palo Alto) VII (1974), 51–81.

Strobel, Matías
1729	"Carta del Padre Matías Strobel a un padre de Viena" in Juan Mühn, S.J., *La Argentina vista por los viajeros del siglo XVIII.* Buenos Aires: Huarpes, 1946.

Subirá, José
1953	*Historia de la música española e hispanoamericana.* Barcelona: Salvat.

Tanodi, Aurelio, ed.
1971	*Documentos de la Real Hacienda de Puerto Rico, Volumen I (1510–1519).* Buenos Aires: Editorial Nova & Universidad de Puerto Rico.

Tejeda, Luis José de
1663	*Coronas líricas: Prosa y verso por Luis José de Tejeda,* Pablo Cabrera, ed. Córdoba: [La Universidad], 1917.

Tinctoris, Johannes
c.1487	*De inventione et usu musicae.* Naples. Anthony Baines, trans. "Fifteenth Century Instruments in Tinctoris's *De Inventione et Usu Musicae*," *Galpin Society Journal* (Winchester, Eng.) III (Mar. 1950), 19–25.

Torre Revello, José
1943	"Merchandise Brought to America by the Spaniards (1534–1586)," *The Hispanic American Historical Review* (Durham, NC) XXIII, 772–81.

1944	"Músicos coloniales," *Estudios* (Academia Literaria del Plata, Buenos Aires) LXXII, 392–404.

1948	"Mercaderías introducidas por los españoles en América (1534–1586)," *Estudios* (Buenos Aires), Año XXXVIII, Tomo LXXIX, 113–21.

1957	"Algunos libros de música traídos a América en el siglo XVI," *Inter-American Review of Bibliography* (Washington, D.C.) VII, No. 4, 372–80.

Tyler, James
1980	*The Early Guitar: A History and Handbook,* Early Music Series No. 4. London: Oxford University Press.

Vega, Carlos
  1926 "La guitarra argentina," lecture read at the Universidad de la
        Plata, published in Domingo Prat, *Diccionario biográfico,*
        bibliográfico, histórico, crítico de guitarras.... Buenos Aires:
        Romero y Fernández, [1934], pp. 329–30.

  1946a *Los instrumentos musicales aborígenes y criollos de la Argen-*
        tina, con un ensayo sobre las clasificaciones universales, un
        panorama gráfico de los instrumentos americanos.... Buenos
        Aires: Centurión/Hachette.

Vega, Lope de
  1635 *Obras de Lope de Vega...*(nueva edición). Emilio Cotarelo y Mori,
        ed. 13 vols. Madrid: La Real Academia Española, 1916–1930.

Viggiano Esaín, Julio
  1948 *Instrumentología musical popular argentina.* Córdoba: La
        Universidad.

Viglietti, Cédar
  [1973] *Origen e historia de la guitarra.* Buenos Aires: Editorial
        Albatros.

Ward, John M.
  1980 "Miguel de Fuenllana," *The New Grove Dictionary of Music*
        and Musicians. London: Macmillan.

Zavadivker, Ricardo
  1974 "Dos manuscritos musicales de la Biblioteca Nacional," *Notas*
        (Buenos Aires) XVI, 6–7.

  1977a "El primer grabado de la guitarra en América," *The Gendai*
        Guitar (Tokyo) [Vol. XI] No. 124 (Mar.), 69–73.

  1977b "Los instrumentos indígenas en la obra de Guamán Poma,"
        Antiquitas (Universidad del Salvador, Buenos Aires) No.
        24–25 (May–Nov.), 8–35.

  1982 "La guitarra y la vihuela en Hispanoamerica," *Revista de*
        INIDEF (Caracas) V (1981–1982), 44–49.

  1988 "Una guitarra barroca en la iconografía chilena," *El Mundo*
        de la Guitarra (Buenos Aires) No. 4 (Jun.–Jul.), 15.

Part IV

The Infamous Guitar
of
the Fandango and the Pulpería

In the gold mine of American music, there is not a more Andalusian vein than the fandango. As such, the dance certainly connects with the *andalucismo* described in Part II. However, the fandango was a relatively late development of the Hispanic domination: it did not impact upon European society beyond Iberia nor come into the Americas until the 18th century. Furthermore, it is such an exciting, voluminous subject unto itself that it demands its own separate presentation at this point.

In Europe the fandango was already a musical development without parallel, but in the Americas it became even more unique. In the first place, the fandango's musical roots originated in the medieval cultures of Spain. There it must have evolved as a dance for centuries before coming to the notice of the rest of Europe or finally crossing the Atlantic en route to the New World. Second, the *pulpería* tavern was uniquely Latin American, and it preceded the fandango's arrival by a century or more. Even so, the two

271

came together: the South American pulpería shops provided the environment for the fandango, the scene where it was most often danced and celebrated, so the two were wed forever in history. The common denominator between them was the guitar; its worst infamy spread from the fandango at the pulperías.

1. The Early Fandango in Europe

The fandango is certainly one of the oldest living dances in Western civilization. It is found among several traditions, none the least of which is the flamenco repertoire. It belongs thus to the remaining vestiges of the cultural clash that occurred in Andalusia: its music has always been a blending of East and West. Yet due to the fact that fandango variants within that repertoire were created primarily through the method of improvisation and transferred aurally by rote, the fandango's history has heretofore been difficult to track, rather lacking in documented sources before the 19th century. Fortunately, the flamenco fandango is yet a viable form in Andalusia today, so the music itself can be studied, as needed, to fill in historical gaps.

The fandango and its related forms constitute the oldest branch of the flamenco repertoire that was forged in Spain. Centuries ago the fandango was sufficiently popular that it became the parent form of a family of related flamenco dances. The closest and most prominent derivatives bore the names of Andalusian cities where they flourished: Málaga, Ronda, Granada, and Murcia. Even so, the *Malagueña, Rondeña,* the *Granadinas* and *Murcianas* differed but little from the parent form, being either transpositions of the fandango itself or variants on only a few chords of its basic format. Other derivatives like the *jota aragonesa* had historical connections but became separated during recent centuries.

The fandango and its closest derivatives contain a number of common musical characteristics. Since the fandango is usually played with few sharps or flats, some theorists cast it in the key of A minor, even though it always ends on E. However, it is more logical to consider the fandango and its derivatives to be in the Phrygian mode (based on the scale of E F G A B C D). All the fandango variants contain the *falseta,* a short, recurring chord progression that functions as an instrumental refrain or *ritornello.* Using the alternative of modal analysis, the chords of the falseta (iv III II I), as well as the final cadence, end on the tonic. Since the usual mode of the fandango is E Phrygian, the chords of the falseta would compute as triads of A minor, G, F, and E major.

Flamenco, like jazz or the tango, evolved from the fusion of several syncretic musical styles. Flamenco was partially a product of the Moorish occupation of Spain, 711–1492. Even so, some experts have used etymology to argue Afro-<u>American</u> origins for the *fandango,* because, like *tango,* the term has indeed been traced to Africa and to the Americas, whence it supposedly reached Spain. But the argument for that route is flawed, for a sub-Saharan word or style might just as easily have come directly across the Strait of Gibraltar as the Atlantic. Whatever its origins, an American preference for the fandango may have been the precipitating factor for its sudden demand beyond Andalusia about 1700. What remained of the old fandango at the end of the Moorish occupation comprised both Semitic North African and European elements. That repertoire consisted of the fandango dances which blended the melodic traits of the *Hijaz* Arabian mode and the basic chords of E Phrygian:

> It is commonplace to perceive in Renaissance music a coexistence and synthesis of modal and tonal practices. In Spain, the modal practices consisted not only of those inherited from Byzantine and Hellenic systems but also the legacy of Arab music.... The introduction of the major third in the E-Phrygian scale affords the lower tetrachord E-F-G#-A. On the one hand, this can be seen as a means of reconciling the Phrygian scale with an E-major "tonic" chord and, in some contexts, as providing a temporary leading tone to an A-minor chord. On the other hand, the use of the augmented second in this context reflects the clear influence of the Arabian mode *Hijaz,* whose scale is roughly E-F-G#-A-B-C-D. Both Phrygian and *Hijaz* scales have upper rather than lower leading tones to the tonic, and, accordingly, harmony in flamenco and much of Andalusian folk music generally employs the chord progression F–E rather than B7–E or E7–Am as the fundamental cadence (Manuel 1986:50).

Once European modal harmony and Arabian melodic configurations were married in the fandango, a third music culture
came into Andalusia. During the last century of the Moorish occupation, a large band of itinerant Gypsies migrated into southern
Spain. Their vocal practice, identified as *cante jondo,* or deep,
expressive song, along with their own unique repertoire, blended
with the two previously established music cultures to yield the
unlikely tri-cultural combination that has remained the mainstream of flamenco. Yet by the time the Gypsies arrived in Andalusia, the streams of the Arabian-Phrygian fandango had probably
merged at some point of the six centuries prior to their arrival.

The flamenco repertoire has always consisted of dance-songs
sung either unaccompanied or to the accompaniment of the guitar. However, the unique harmonic dissonances, so much a part of
the style, reveal the importance of the guitar in that development.
The accompaniments were, for the most part, strummed. Consequently the most typical dissonances resulted from the inclusion of
strummed open strings which sometimes invaded the triadic
harmony as non-harmonic tones:

> By 1600 in Andalusia the guitar had become the standard in-
> strument for accompanying dance and most kinds of popular
> song in general. Evidence suggests that a standard harmonic
> practice subsequently evolved which came to be adapted to fla-
> menco as that music coalesced in the mid-nineteenth century.
> The guitar has always been the primary, and generally the sole
> non-percussive instrument used for accompanying flamenco.
> The clearest evidence of the guitar's importance in the evolu-
> tion of flamenco harmony lies in the use of altered chords con-
> taining non-triadic tones. These chords tend to occur in the
> Phrygian-based *cantes* or sections of *cantes*...more common
> in the *falsetas* of fandango variants than in the *copla,* which
> employs standard I-IV-V harmonies. A study of flamenco gui-
> tar voicings reveals that in the most typical altered chords, the
> non-triadic tones are generally played on open (unfretted)
> strings (using the standard tuning E-A-D-G-B-E). This phe-
> nomenon is perhaps clearest in the *fandango* family of *cantes.*
> Within this family, the *fandango* proper, the *malagueñas ver-
> diales,* and *fandango de Huelva* are all generally performed in
> the keys of E Phrygian and C major (Manuel 1986:52).

Thus the guitar remained intrinsic to flamenco, at least as an instrument of accompaniment. However, today's recitalists have developed a remarkable and virtuosic repertoire for the guitar soloist in the neo-flamenco style, yet it has drawn sharp criticism for its lack of authenticity. Fandangos often highlight such recitals. The "purists" and those who grew up with the sung dances have never regarded any other interpretations as valid. Their viewpoint was a hotly debated issue during the past half century, and it has remained open to question until now. Should a fandango be removed from its original context of song and dance in order to be played in a guitar recital? Are there historical precedents?

Emilio Cotarelo y Mori summarized the fandango's development between 1700 and 1900. His perspective of its history, enhanced by the 18th-century literature he knows so well, reveals the fandango's riotous social context:

[Fandango (a dance). It is purely Spanish, in three beats per measure and a fast pace.

Under the denomination of fandango are comprised the *Malagueña, Rondeña,* the *Granadinas* and *Murcianas,* not differing from each other more than in the key and a few variations of chords. The instruments that customarily accompany it are the guitar, castanets, or violin and others....

Its introduction took place around the end of the 17th century, and for this reason (the fandango) is mentioned neither among the *entremeses* (the farcical intermezzos) nor the masques (or masquerades) that came before then. In the one called *El novio de la aldeana* (The Boyfriend of the Village Girl), dating from the beginning of the 18th century, "the fandango is played and sung" to some words which begin,

Asómate a esa ventana,	(Lean out of that window,
cara de borrica flaca;	you little burro-face;
a la ventana te asoma	stick your head out of the window,
cara de mulita roma.	you flat-nosed mule face.)

"He quits singing and playing, and they both start yelling and screaming at each other and doing the other things that are customary when the fandangos are sung in an uproar, etc."....

In the masque of *Los sopones* (The Beggars) of Cañizares (1723), it is danced with the following refrain:

> *"Me dice el fandanguillo*
> *¡ay, picarí, picarillo!*
> *Mil finecitas al son."*
> (He calls me *fandanguillo* when I'm around
> —Ah, you tricky little rogue!
> A thousand gestures for every sound.)

Ever since then, it has been extremely popular in Spain, especially in Andalusia, and it is still danced even today] (Cotarelo y Mori 1911:244–45).

In 1767 Casanova saw the fandango in Madrid. Subsequently he described it and certainly confirmed its lurid sensuality:

> Each couple, man and woman, never move more than three steps as they click their castanets with the music of the orchestra. They take a thousand attitudes, make a thousand gestures so lascivious that nothing can compare with them. This dance is the expression of love from beginning to end, from the sigh of desire to the ecstacy of enjoyment. It seemed to me impossible that after such a dance the girl could refuse anything to her partner (Sachs 1963:99).

In *The Marriage of Figaro* (1786), Mozart and da Ponte echoed the debauchery already associated with the fandango. During a comic aria in Act I, Cherubino, the court's page, revealed his infatuation with the Countess; because of this and other capers the Count banished him from the court. Then Figaro obtained a reduced sentence for the poor lad: a tour of military service. Just the same, Figaro reprimanded his youthful ways and then consoled him with the prospects of manly victory and military life:

Non più andrai, farfallone amoroso,   [You can't sow wild oats forever
notte e giorno d'intorno girando   as a butterfly goes from flower to flower
delle belle turbando il riposo,   be no more, as a faithless young rover
Narcisetto, Adoncino d'amor.   Narcissus or Adonis of love.

Non più avrai questi bei pennachini,   You can't have these petty trifles,
quel cappello leggiero e galante,   perfumed hair won't mix with rifles;
quella chioma, quell'aria brillante,   shear your locks and sing a new song,
quel vermiglio, donnesco color.   these pretty flowers won't last for long.

Non più andrai farfallone amoroso...   You can't sow wild oats forever...

Tra guerrieri poffar Bacco!	Now mid warriors, suppress Bacchus!
gran mustacchi, stretto sacco.	formal luggage, great moustaches,
Schioppo in spalla, sciabla al fianco,	shotgun loaded, lined in flanks—
collo dritto muso franco,	you'll be proud to send me thanks.
o un gran casco, un gran turbante	With a great turban and a sash,
molto onor, poco contante,	endless glory, if short of cash,
ed in vece del fandango....	no fandango—it's too rash....]

The Marriage of Figaro begins with a mere introduction of the characters and their social relationships in Seville. In particular, Figaro's opening solo serves to display the very talents he will use to ensnare the Count at his own game:

> *Se vuol ballare, signor contino,*
> *il chitarrino le suonerò...*
> [If you would like to dance, my Lord,
> on my guitar, I'll play you a chord...]

The emphasis here is on humor, characterization, and the plot, so the music itself is no more than a simple, A B A' cavatina. The A' section is a mere shortened statement of A.

To be sure, most of the music of *Figaro* adheres to the central European style, but in the finale to Act III, Mozart employs the striking local color of Seville. The centerpiece of the ensemble finale is an exotic fandango, constituting section B in another A B A' layout. The finale begins with a bold fanfare marked *Marcia* as everyone prepares for a ball. Then two girls sing a pretty duet (theme A) with an Alberti bass in the key of C major, although they are interrupted by a chorus on their theme while motives of the march rhythm are brought back as contrapuntal enhancement in the orchestra parts. Next, for total contrast, the main characters dance the fandango; musically it is an orchestral interlude (theme B) in the key of A minor. Finally the chorus returns to close the scene triumphantly (*alla marcia* on theme A, again in C major) with exultant praises of love and of Count Almaviva.

The fandango, marked only by the tempo of *Andante* and the switch to triple meter, is a monothematic orchestral interlude which is calculated to interrupt the singing. Whether in thematic statements or in the spinning out of motives, most of the material of the fandango comes from the following theme:

Ex. 4 Theme of Figaro's Fandango   Mozart

(strings)

Although Figaro's fandango is monothematic, it too has a layout
in three sections. The theme appears twice in A minor, then again
in E minor before a short development, during which time members of the vocal ensemble dance, and then they leave Figaro to
dance alone. The fandango theme returns in its original key, but in
its last 20 measures, it overlaps dramatic action; it serves as background to the discovery of a love note on stage. Although it is indeed
a stylized rather than authentic fandango, Andalusian character
persists throughout its 42 measures through its own composite
rhythm of steady eighth notes, typical accompaniment patterns,
the second-beat accent in triple meter, the A-minor tonality with
the frequent tonicizing of E, and its peculiar trills and mordents.

Figaro's fandango seems all the more timely and colorful if considered within the historical context of 1786. First of all, Domenico
Scarlatti set the precedent for keyboard around 1740. Up until
now, his reputation has rested solely upon his rather abstract,
early-classic sonatas. However, the recent discovery of a fandango,
complete with a scribal attribution to him, makes his the first extant example for the keyboard (Alvarez Martínez 1984:27–32).
Besides, Mozart may have known this example if not Gluck's
ballet *Don Juan* of 1761 which has a similar theme. Compare
Examples 4 and 5:

Ex. 5 Theme from "Fandango del Signore Scarlate"   Scarlatti

Other composers of significance in the 18th century handed
down isolated examples to us, as well. Scarlatti's pupil, Padre Antonio Soler, took up his model directly. Soler's own harpsichord

fandango was longer, more rhapsodic, and even more technically demanding than his teacher's. The memorable example of chamber music was Luigi Boccherini's *Guitar Quintet No. 4*, G. 448 which ended on the well-known fandango, with castanets obbligato! But these composers lived in Spain decades before writing such pieces—an occasional fandango was expected. However, Figaro's fandango, like Carmen's habanera, composed nearly a century later, was written from afar. While it is not likely that either Mozart or Bizet ever went to Seville, they both paraphrased the popular music of Andalusia in order to add the contrast of exotic local color to their operas.

According to the traditional historical perspective, the fandango found little acceptance at the Spanish court because national expression was held in low esteem. As a matter of fact, the Spanish royalty of this period did not originally hail from Spain. During the 17th century, the Hapsburg lineage of aristocrats favored Flemish and Italian music. In the next century, the Bourbon dynasty replaced the Austrian lineage, so French taste reigned supreme. Obviously the musicians in their service and all others who anticipated the benefit of patronage had to cater to the prevailing taste. The prejudice was clear enough in a guitar method of 1799 by Fernando Ferandiere, a "professor of music in this court":

> *To the Reader....* I am sure that just a good teacher and this
> book, with the seventeen lessons which adorn it, are sufficient
> to learn music and to play a national instrument which is so
> complete and so beautiful that all nations praise it, even without
> knowing just how far the strengths of our guitar go, for some
> people content themselves with strumming the fandango or the
> jota, others with accompanying boleros, and musicians with
> accompanying arias, tonadillas, etc.
> But in truth those are not the merits of the guitar of which I
> speak, for I do not desire merely accompanists, but rather
> players, who will make the instrument sing....

The truth of the matter becomes clear in the catalogue of his compositions at the end of the guitar method. There he lists more than 200 solo and ensemble pieces of which not a single work is a fandango.

Nevertheless, some guitar composers dared to follow their instincts and disregarded aristocratic taste; in so doing they left some early examples of the fandango. Several are found in anonymous manuscript 811 of the Biblioteca Nacional of Madrid (1705:ff. 103, 112–13, 140). The manuscript, entitled *"Libro de diferentes cifras de gitara escojidas de los mejores autores"* [Book of Different Guitar Tablatures Selected from the Best Authors], carries the date of 1705 on its title page, so its fandangos remain the earliest extant examples. Later on Pablo Minguet y Yrol published the basic harmonies of the dance (1774:3). However, neither the fandangos of the manuscript nor those of Minguet are substantial, for their tablatures indicate either intermediate pieces or mere chord progressions. These toys are useful historical documents, but none are worthy of a recital. They reveal the same popular repertoire, virtual accompaniments that Ferandiere had criticized so severely.

These few examples do not indicate the gamut of the early fandango repertoire for the guitar because a great deal of it has failed to survive unto the present day. The disparity between that repertoire and today's is apparent in a bibliography of titles originally published in Madrid; it appeared annually from 1784 to 1791. This *Bibliografía periódica anual...* included the titles of both music and books. The complete six-year run of the bibliography's musical portion came to light again in the *Anuario Musical* (Moll 1969). That secondary source lists 176[!] solo and ensemble compositions, mostly dances, which specify the guitar. Many of these pieces are now lost, but their titles suggest the guitar's importance in this repertoire and imply the extent of its undocumented past. The following titles are all those that bear mention of the fandango:

Table 11 Bibliographic References to the Fandango
in Madrid, 1785–90

Item 8 **[1785]**. *Fandango para clave, compuesto de variaciones de mucho gusto, y que pueden servir para los instrumentos que admiten esta tocata.*

19 **[1785]**. *Diferencias y variaciones del fandango de Cádiz en cifra para guitarra de [5 y 6 órdenes].*

66 [**1787**]. *Seis contradanzas nuevas al estilo portugués, en música y cifra para guitarra, y 48 diferencias del Fandango de Cádiz para 5 y 6 órdenes.*

72 [**1787**]. *Dos Tiranas graciosas a solo, con bajo para guitarra o clave, intituladas: El sudor de la tirana, y El fandango español. Lib. [librería] de Gómez.*

119 [**1789**]. *Seis paspiés con sus minués nuevos: música para bayle a dos violines: el fandango, minués y contradanzas a solo, y a 1.a y 2.a violín: Lib. de Corominas.*

122 [**1789**]. *Tres fandangos nuevos, que son el de Madrid, el de Cádiz y Sevilla, puestos en música y cifra para guitarra de 5 y 6 órdenes, con 40 diferencias cada uno, por JOSEPH AVELLANA. Se hallarán en la calle de Jacometrezo, frente a la del Carbón; también se venden otras composiciones, así de AVELLANA como del PORTUGUES.*

132 [**1789**]. *Una sonata y seis minués del Sr. LAPORTA: otra del Sr. BRITO, Portugués: el fandango, la guaracha, y seis contradanzas, todo con cifra para guitarra: lib. de Correa.*

142 [**1790**]. *Fandango en música por el Señor LAPORTA, un quaderno con seis tiranas a duo y a solo, y dos tonadillas nuevas: librería de Correa.*

Although the items listed here represent but six years of the fandango's development in Madrid, they suggest several conclusions about the dance:
(1) Some items reveal lingering stigma against the dance, such as the first: the "Fandango...variations...that can serve instrumentalists who admit this piece" in their performances. Nevertheless, the many music publications featuring the fandango indicate that by the end of the 18th century, a certain audience in Madrid was enjoying it after all—perhaps the affluent youth.
(2) At some point earlier, possibly with Domenico Scarlatti, the fandango must have become acceptable before the aristocracy.
(3) The fandango was part of the regular fare of solo and light chamber music of the day.

(4) These examples show, like the keyboard and chamber fandangos of Domenico Scarlatti, Soler, and Boccherini, that the dance was appropriate as a recital piece on the guitar.

(5) The fandango, along with the other dances here, may have been intended for dancing as well as listening. The evidence is clear, at least, that these examples were part of the 18th-century entertainments which were reaching several social levels.

2. The Fandango in Hispanic America

After 1700 the fandango came to America. The earliest example among our extant American sources appears in an anonymous guitar manuscript discovered in Mexico earlier this century and that is now known as *Saldívar Codex No. 4.*

The Mexican musicologist Dr. Gabriel Saldívar (1908–1980) discovered the codex in León, Guanajuato, Mexico and purchased it in 1943. It remained thereafter in Dr. Saldívar's private collection as "Codex No. 4." While he hoped to publish a study of the manuscript, he showed it to Robert Stevenson, who was able to bring out a preliminary assessment of it along with its table of contents (1968:235–36). Recently however, Dr. Saldívar's widow, Sra. Elisa Osorio Bolio de Saldívar, published a facsimile edition of Codex No. 4 with the help of Michael Lorimer, who also supplied a thorough introductory study of it. Although the manuscript remains unsigned and undated, and whether composed in the Old World or the New, it is copied in the same hand as Santiago de Murcia's outstanding guitar collection of 1732 that is presently in the British Library.

Indeed, the complementary musical text to Saldívar Codex No. 4 is Murcia's manuscript entitled *"Passacalles y obras de guitarra por todos los tonos...1732"* [Pasacalles and Pieces for the Guitar in All the (Standard) Keys...1732], British Library, Manuscript Add. 31640. Due to the quality of its music, this particular manuscript has attracted more excellent doctoral research during the past decade than the guitar music of any composer—of any era (reviewed in Stevenson 1980b). Manuscript 31640 brings together two basics of the guitarist's Baroque repertoire: in the first half, original Spanish pasacalles that serve as études in all the practical keys; and in the second, collected suites—many of which are in the French style—by other European composers. It contains, for instance, some solo guitar music of Francesco Corbetta (Pinnell 1980:I, 174) and a virtuosic intabulation of certain movements of Corelli's solo violin sonatas Op. 5, Nos. 5 and 8 for guitar solo (Pinnell 1979). Notwithstanding, recent research has traced many of Murcia's pieces to French composers, which has revealed a world of new relationships (Russell 1981:I, 284–309). Yet what has always been lacking in Murcia's output is the music of distinctly Spanish character—the Iberian dances so typical of the other Spanish Baroque guitar books. This void is amply filled with Saldívar Codex No. 4 which supplies in its majority Spanish and even some Latin American popular dances. Therefore, we can concur with the editor of the new edition of Codex No. 4 that Santiago de Murcia is undoubtedly the most likely original owner. It is written in the same hand and in the same musical style as Manuscript 31640, and it must date from the same period—from around 1732.

Saldívar Codex No. 4 contains a marvelous fandango, rather ethnic in character yet certainly recital-worthy. This fandango, perhaps Murcia's own, is the outstanding early guitar composition of its name/category on either side of the Atlantic. The first matter of importance is the dating and context of this piece. Since by his own admission in the preface to his book on accompanying, Murcia was not only in the service of the Queen of Spain, Marie-Louise-Gabrielle of Savoy, he was also her guitar teacher, as confirmed in court documents (Russell 1981:I, 39ff.). Thus, Domenico Scarlatti had not single-handedly obtained the fandango's seal of approval with his example which dated from around 1740 (Alvarez Martínez 1986:5). Instead, Murcia had preceded him at court by a whole generation and had either contributed to or obtained this royal sanction himself. If the aristocratic approval of this wild, plebeian dance were indeed Santiago de Murcia's own doing, then he was following in the footsteps of his guitar-playing predecessors who brought serious interest to the previous Spanish popular idioms of the *pasacalle, zarabanda, folía,* and *chacona.* Surely Santiago de Murcia set the precedent at court with his own fandango.

Ex. 6 "Fandango," Saldívar Codex No. 4

Santiago de Murcia

The preceding note-for-note transcription links with an authentic tuning. Although Murcia certainly wrote for the tuning of A D G B E, the specific stringing of his guitar remains open to question. At least other Baroque guitarists left suitable models for the arrangement of octaves on each pair of strings. Some modern guitarists agree by consensus that the "French tuning" Francesco Corbetta first advocated in 1671 works well for interpreting Murcia's tablatures (Pinnell 1980:I, 152). This tuning is shown below:

Ex. 7 French Tuning, Preface, 1671   Corbetta

(a) actual sound   (b) transcription

The transcription shows the fifth course tuned at the lower octave of the A strings in order to clarify the voicings of the chords and melodies and to minimize the number of position and string markers over the pentagram. (This procedure simplifies the notation and makes it easy to play. It would misrepresent the composer to make the modern notation seem more complex than his original tablature.) The transcription remains playable on any tuning of the guitar, whether historical or modern, provided that the open strings or courses in any octave from five to one correspond to the pitches of A D G B E. However, in recital, the optimal performance would include a close approximation of the Baroque tuning as well as the observation of other authentic performance practices.

Murcia's historic fandango in Ex. 6 is thoroughly modal. It falls naturally within the transposed mode of one flat, which would normally correspond to D minor, given the predominance of C-sharp in the piece. To be sure, notes B and C natural also occur occasionally, depending on the direction of the lines, but they do not disrupt the modal flavor. Its four-measure phrases often begin on the D minor triad; however, they always end on A major (see numbered measures and the last). Thus, like Scarlatti's fandango, it corresponds to the mode of A Phrygian as well as Hijaz Arabian on A (A Bb C# D E F G). In other words, Murcia's fandango duplicates the modality of the traditional flamenco repertoire.

As usual, Murcia is able to get full resonance from the guitar whether in technique or texture. Every 3/4 measure is bristling with rhythmic activity. He alternates full strums (indicated by the single stem joining chord tones) with complex, intricate plucking techniques. Murcia contrasts loud *rasgueado* strumming with quiet, plucked passages at the beginning and end. He effectively syncopates the bass in the middle of the piece, often alternating with measures in which the melody is played off the beat. By harmonizing the melody in thirds or sixths over the bass line, he is able to sustain the texture of two or three lines with a minimum of effort. But the best is saved for last: he subdivides the time into 16ths as the melody notes are intentionally overlapped from course to course. Thereby, with the blurry sustain of unresolved yet cascading, adjacent scale-tones, particularly on open strings, he achieved the most impressionistic effect of Spanish Baroque guitar music—the effect of *campanelas*—to its maximum potential.

*   *   *   *

In the generation after Santiago de Murcia, the New World travellers who published their memoirs began to document the fandango in a number of diverse settings. Early among such travel accounts was *A Voyage to South America*, first published by Jorge Juan and Antonio de Ulloa in 1748. They travelled to several ports and cities in the Americas. Their first stop was the port of Cartagena, in present-day Colombia, and they were able to report on the fandango there in 1735. By then the term fandango had already become more generic than in Spain; sometimes it meant simply a ball or dance, as in the following instances:

> One of the most favorite amusements of the natives here, is a ball, or Fandango. These are the distinguished rejoicings on festivals and remarkable days. But while the galleons, *guarda costas*, or other Spanish ships are here, they are most common and at the same time conducted with the least order—the crews of the ships forcing themselves into their ballrooms. These diversions, in houses of distinction, are conducted in a very regular manner; they open with Spanish dances, and are succeeded by those of the country, which are not without spirit and

gracefulness. These are accompanied with singing, and the parties rarely break up before daylight.

The Fandangos, or balls, of the populace, consist principally in drinking brandy and wine, intermixed with indecent and scandalous motions and gestures; and these continual rounds of drinking soon give rise to quarrels, which often bring on misfortunes (Juan & Ulloa 1748:35).

In Peru, the fandango was part of the Hispanic identity of the Creoles. They contrasted it with the melancholy national airs of the plebeian caste, according to the *Mercurio Peruano* (No. 101, 22 Dec. 1791):

What a contrast with all this sad music does the Spanish *fandango* make, or such derivatives of Spanish dances as we favor here in Peru!
Take, for instance, the *Don Mateo*, the *Punto*, and other joyful dance tunes that abound among us. If not all are as exciting as the *fandango*, they at least show how closely we can approach the gaiety of the Spaniard, and at what an opposite pole our Creole music lives from the melancholy world that gives birth to *yaravíes* (Stevenson 1968:301).

The fandango was foremost among the entertainments observed by Robert L. Vowell during his South American military service which ran from 1817 to 1830. He was among the British soldiers who joined the liberation forces of General Simón Bolívar. Vowell was not merely a mercenary but probably a volunteer, seeking to help a good cause in exchange for travel and adventure, because he was free to come and go as he pleased. He worked primarily in Venezuela but managed to travel to the Guianas as well as the entire west coast of South America. To avoid reprisal during the wars, Vowell published his memoirs anonymously. He first reported on the guitar and fandango in the Guianas where the celebration on behalf of the new British troops had just begun:

The inhabitants of Old Guayana were extremely well pleased at our arrival, as we were among the first English who had arrived to join Bolívar.... After considerable exertion on the part of our host, room was obtained for the dancers, who performed several national fandangos, quite new to us, and, apparently, peculiar to the country; such as the *Bambuco, Zajudina*, and *Marri-marri*. At length, when they began to tire of these, a young Criollo rose, and demanded room. After dancing round the room by himself for a minute or two, he figured up to a lady, to whom he made a bow, and retired. She immediately rose, performed the same evolutions, and stopped opposite to one of our party, curtsying by way of calling on him to exhibit in turn. This caused an universal burst of delight among the spectators, and our companion, after in vain protesting that he knew nothing of the dance, was fairly pushed into the centre of the floor by the laughing brunettes. He was of course obliged to acquit himself as well as he could, amidst shouts of applause, and *"¡Vivan los Inglezes!"* We were all of us called upon in turn to shew our paces, with which we complied, to their great amusement; and were warmly complimented on our readiness to join in their dances, contrary to the fastidious custom of the Spanish officers. The music...consisted of several *vihuelas* (a small kind of guitars) and harps, in time to which half a dozen professed singers screamed some unintelligible couplets at the top of their voices. These minstrels and troubadours were accompanied by rattles, made of hollow calabashes, containing some grains of maiz; with short handles, by which they were shaken; also by several women who, seated round a table, vied with each other in *tamboreando*, or beating time with their open hands (Vowell 1831:I, 24–26).

Vowell next observed the fandango at the village of Los Bagres, a small Venezuelan port. The common people thereabouts were performing it in the *pulperías*. These were taverns which doubled their service as business establishments in the vicinity, supplying food, groceries, and sundries. Just as in Europe, the scene of the fandango there included musicians, dancers, and spectators:

At the farther end of this rancho, was a *pulpería*, or shop for the sale of sundries;—chiefly *aguardiente* and tobacco. In the centre, which was by far the largest compartment, was a crowded assembly surrounding a few dancers, who were amusing themselves and the spectators with a fandango, to the music of a harp, two or three vihuelas, and a choir of singers, partly volunteers, partly hired (Vowell 1831:II, 103).

The common folk of Varinas, Venezuela used the combination of harp and guitar (their favorite instrument) to accompany their dances, as well. On one occasion in the tropical savannas, which contained the tributaries of the Orinoco River, they were preparing for a lovely ball to be held out-of-doors:

> A message shortly after arrived from Doña Rosaura, inviting Páez and his officers to a *fandango*, which the emigrants had prepared near their huts, for the purpose of taking leave of their protectors. An extensive spot of ground had been cleared.... A close, neat screen, of the bright yellow Culegüi cane, completely fenced in this sylvan ballroom; the floor of which was strewed with dry white sand, collected from the banks of the neighbouring lagoon. Lamps, formed of the pink-coloured *caracol* shells found in the savanna, were ranged at short intervals along the screen; and, being fastened round hoops of pliant *bejuco*, [they] were suspended, in lieu of chandeliers, from the branches extending across the salon. There was no want of music; for guitars and vihuelas were as common among the emigrants as in the army. Besides these, two harps, which had been brought by some musicians, who had apparently found more leisure than their neighbours at the time of leaving their homes, added their enlivening strains (Vowell 1831:III, 219).

Beyond its early presence in Mexico, Colombia, Peru, the Guianas, and Venezuela, the fandango was popular in the Republic of Chile. The fandango dates back to 1774 in the police records of San Gerónimo de Alhuí. In two cases there, cited by Pereira Salas (1941:208), the authorities had prohibited,

> *juegos, amancebamiento y fandangos a desoras de la noche...*
> *algunas personas con guitarras en fandangos*
> [games, concubinage, and fandangos at inappropriate times of the night...some persons with guitars in fandangos].

Early in the 19th century, a North American ship captain by the name of Amasa Delano sailed down the South American coastline. Having stopped periodically en route to Chilean ports, he was able to sum up the musical practices he had observed along the way, giving special attention to instruments and dances:

The amusements of the people of the kingdoms of Chili and Peru, as before stated in part, are chiefly music and dancing. The instruments most in use are guitars, which nearly all the ladies play, accompanying them with their voices, which are very melodious. They likewise have harps, spinnets, harpsichords, and piano-fortes, which are very common, and on which they perform extremely well. The gentlemen play on flutes and clarionets. They dance with the most majesty and grace of any people I ever knew. Their dances are minuets, long dances, cotillions, and a very singular kind of dance, called fandango, which is common in old Spain....

When we left this place in February 1806, we steered off to St. Ambrose...(Delano 1817:303).

Vowell's travels took him into Chile, as well. There he witnessed the fandango among the folk. The *huazo* of Chile was the common man of the populace, a cowboy roughly equivalent to the *gaucho* of the Río de la Plata. The *huazas* were their female counterparts:

The Huazas are much fairer in complexion, and smaller in stature, than the men of the same race. They are a cheerful set of women, mild and pleasing in their manners, and very hospitable and attentive to strangers. They form a pleasing contrast to their boisterous, quarrelsome husbands and brothers; not partaking of any of their amusements, except the fandango, of which they are extremely fond. The favourite dances among them are only performed by two, who dance opposite to each other (Vowell 1831:I, 309–10).

The fandango flourished in the Province of Chiloé, which included the southern extreme of Chile's population. Among several references to the fandango, Dr. Gustave Duboc observed the following in 1835 regarding its choreography and accompaniment:

[The most frequent distraction is the dance. Besides the *waltz*, they have many original dances of the country such as the *fandango*, the *pericona*, and the *cuando*. The fandango is a somewhat lascivious dance, without great value, and poor in figures. It is danced between two persons and consists of true piroüttes, jumps, advances, and retreats, with a continuous, deafening heeltap. The woman has a handkerchief in her hand which she

waves sometimes to menace her partner. The instrument used
most often is the guitar of four or five strings played loudly during the entire dance] (Pereira Salas 1941:238).

The fandango's history in the Dominican Republic was similar
to its development in other Hispanic countries. First the populace
took it up as the sensational new Spanish dance, as the travellers
observed; the testimonials of Moreau de Saint Méry in 1783 and
William Walton in 1810 documented it in this case. Then matters
associated with the guitar and music-making at night grew more
and more bothersome until by 1818 the Governor there had to
publish the following edict to ensure peace and order:

> Without a permit from the authorities, *dancing* in the streets
> and squares is prohibited. No *music, serenades or songs to the
> accompaniment of the guitar* will be permitted after ten o'clock
> at night (Coopersmith 1949:16–18).

3. The Infamous Guitar and the Pulpería to 1800

In Part III, all the many faces of the early Rioplatense guitar have
come to light—all except for one, the disreputable side. The Janus
face or the backside of the guitar, the source of the guitar's infamy
in the Old World, has yet to come into focus here. Fortunately this
side is documented better in the Americas than in Europe. It cannot be avoided or simply be dismissed as insignificant; this side
requires full treatment in order to ensure full understanding of the
Rioplatense guitar. With comprehensive coverage, including the
backside, we can consider the complete gamut of guitaristic activity at the social extremes.

The early guitar became infamous across Hispanic America by
association with the most decadent public entertainments. Before
the arrival of the fandango in the Caribbean ports, there was already a wild environment for the pleasure-seeker. In Mexico, the
first mention of the term *guitarra* in print was noted among the
minutes of a trial of sacrilege in 1606, for Alonso de Espinosa of
Veracruz had profaned the songs of the Church by assigning new

lyrics to them. Mexican balls or dances were popular if disorderly affairs, especially at the colonial dance academies. The poorest ranks enjoyed dancing as well. The peasant celebrations were accompanied by such abandon that finally the Viceroy of New Spain, Alonso Pardo had to set a curfew on them, prohibiting any after dark in 1609. But most popular of all in Mexico, throughout the 17th and 18th centuries, were the *oratorios*, despite their religious name. Thus were they called as a pretext for meeting under the guise of a religious purpose. In reality great throngs of the populace gathered on the occasion of an oratorio to dance to the harp and guitar. The Inquisition Section of the National Archive of Mexico City contains an early example of an unruly oratorio held in Los Angeles. On a certain occasion there, a black man named Melchor led a group of harpists and guitarists in the festivities which disturbed the peace of the town in 1669 (Saldívar 1934:221–22). When the fandango became popular during the next century, it was destined to settle into such an environment everywhere south of California.

The excessive oratorios had spread all the way to Guatemala City. In 1704 an officer of the Inquisition there appealed to civil authority for a renewal of the restraining order on such entertainments. On the important festival days of the Church, such as those named for the ancient apostles, people would congregate for worship, as usual. However, once the crowds had assembled for the celebrations, the musicians began to perform, which always gave rise to scandalous dancing and carousing:

[They were accustomed to celebrating with altars, serenades, dances, and indecent balls, with which they were gathering and collecting great concourses of people.... Around here there is no way or sufficient means in order to get them to restrain themselves or to avoid such crowds of people who overstep their limits so much that they even met again to experience such excesses and indecent dances...(offending) the Divine Majesty, whose attention begs reverently to you Sir that your Commission of Guatemala be well served in commanding a renewal of the aforesaid edicts, or in establishing the most convenient remedy.... Guatemala, on 25 February 1704.—Reverend Juan de Cárdenas, B.A.] (Saldívar 1934:305–06).

The guitar often accompanied wild merrymaking in South America, as well. In fact, the earliest mention of the *guitarra* in South American literature was within this context. In his chronicle completed around 1615, Felipe Guamán Poma de Ayala left an elaborate portrayal of life under the Hispanic domination from a native perspective. His description is a product of the conflict he bore within himself: he was both Indian and intensely Christian, so his narrative is laden with frustration. His deep Christian sensibility cringes at both the wanton behavior of his compatriots and the cruelty of the conquerors. Yet he sees great hypocrisy in the new culture as it mixes with the old, even in the performance of music. He describes the fiestas among the idle poor, as filled with gambling, drinking, depraved songs, and other habits of decadence brought in by the Spaniards, to show that Indian life, even amidst the lowest class, had been better before the conquest. He explained this on the page immediately following his splendid sketch of the Hispanic couple with the guitar (Plate V, above):

> *Como los ynos. [e] ynas. criollos y criollas hechos yanaconas y hechas chinaconas son muy haraganes y jugadores y ladrones—que no hazen otra cosa cino borrachear y holgar y tañer y cantar, no se acuerdan de dios ni del rrey.... Anda como rufianes y saltiadores getanos de Castilla* (Guamán Poma c.1615:857).
> [Inasmuch as Indian men and women, and as creole men and women made slaves and maidservants are indeed loafers, gamblers, and thieves—that do nothing more than get drunk, dissipate, play music, and sing, they remember neither their God nor their King.... They go about like ruffians and Gypsy highwaymen of Castile.]

Later on Guamán Poma elaborates on the extent of music in their lives. The poor of Peru use guitars and drums as the feature of most of their social activities, ranging from farm work to their wildest fiestas:

> *Quando hiciere fiestas, minga, sementeras, o algún trauajo, le den esta medida, con esto hagan taquicachaua dansas y fiestas y bayles con tanbores y guitaras en todo este reyno los ynos.* (Guamán Poma c.1615:890).

[Whenever they have a party, a workday, or a sowing, or some
project, they add to it this feature: the Indians do it right along
with the celebration of their dances, fiestas, and balls with
drums and guitars throughout this kingdom.]

Having seen only Guamán Poma's plate and references to the
guitarra and its social context of decadence in Peru, one might be
tempted to dismiss this matter simply on the supposition that such
merrymaking belonged only to the lowest Peruvian caste and to
young aristocrats. But not so—the guitar had already begun to
invade the cloister. Guamán Poma had said also that vihuelas
were used in church (fol. 822). In order to deal with the propriety
of using secular instruments in church and other problems of
frivolity and light-mindedness, a high council of Catholic leaders
convened a meeting in Lima; they met these problems head-on
within their ecclesiastical jurisdiction. Archbishop Bartolomé Lobo
Guerrero was in charge of the august assembly which included
even the viceroy to dignify the ceremonies (Sas 1962:13). They
made definitive resolutions which were published on 27 October
1613 under the title of *Constituciones Sinodales* to stand thence-
forth as ecclesiastical laws. In the resolutions of the "synod," the
clergymen experienced censure. The resolutions advised them to
shun the vihuela, and better yet, to avoid the trappings of popular
culture altogether. The synod resolutions prohibited indecent songs
and dances with the vihuela under severe penalty:

[The clergy...during the night ought neither to play musical
instruments, nor dance, nor sing indecent songs.... (The priest
who) is found at any hour of the night whatsoever with some
musical instruments...will be imprisoned for ten days and fined
another ten pesos...in addition to losing the aforementioned
instruments...to the sheriff or the prosecutor; and upon threat
of the same penalties we prohibit that anyone should dance,
neither should anyone sing indecent songs, nor profane music
in marriages, in new masses, nor in other celebrations, neither
in them play vihuelas nor instruments so that they may sing,
neither that others may dance, nor go about masquerading or
disguised, neither on foot, nor on horseback, neither with whatever suit of clothes...(upon pain of) a universal sentence of total
excommunication] (Sas 1962:13).

Meanwhile, on the other side of the Andes in Tucumán, another synod had already been convened in the previous decade with a similar purpose. The Bishop of Tucumán, Father Fernando de Trejo y Sanabria gathered all the clergymen of the Argentine foothills and called them to order in 1597. Their own resolutions were published in 1601 under the title of *Constituciones y declaraciones aprobadas en el primer Sínodo que hizo celebrar el Obispo de Tucumán*...[Constitutions and Declarations Approved in the First Synod which the Bishop of Tucumán Determined to Convene...]. The bishop and his roundtable of clergymen addressed Number 24 of these declarations to problematic songs and dances:

> [*Constitution 24. That bawdy songs and dances be abolished:* We ordain and command upon penalty of total excommunication that no person dance neither perform nor sing dances nor lascivious, bawdy, nor indecent songs that contain lascivious things or that introduce the devil into the world by causing incurable damage with bawdy sayings and stirrings] (Levillier 1926:I, 41).

Therefore, already by around 1600, the clergy on both sides of the Andes had become painfully aware of the popular culture's negative impact. They opposed it in no uncertain or equivocal terms: they brought maximum penalties onto those subject to condemnation. Under the circumstances, the Church fathers developed an antipathy towards the guitar and vihuela. Yet they were goaded further by the fact that their prohibitions were ineffectual, and that musical instruments continued to flourish among the monastic orders and even among the nuns in the ensuing centuries despite their prohibitions. For instance, three priests at Caracas left guitars in their wills signed between 1608 and 1720 (Calzavara 1987:221). Sisters Santa Rosa de Lima and Santa Mariana de Quito may not have been fully fledged nuns, but they were elevated just the same because of their exemplary lives, even though they had occasional brushes with the vihuela (Part III, above). Moreover, during their lifetime and in simultaneous conflict with the *Constituciones Sinodales* of Lima, the sisters of the Encarnación convent in Lima became widely known for their excellent music which included both guitarras and vihuelas:

Three convent chroniclers—Reginaldo de Lizárraga, 1605;
Antonio Vázquez de Espinosa, 1628; and Antonio de la Calancha,
1631—unite in awarding Encarnación at Lima the palm for
the best music after 1600. Everybody from viceroy to Holy Office goes to hear the music at Encarnación every Saturday, says
Lizárraga. Their music exceeds that of any convent in Spain,
reports Vázquez de Espinosa. Calancha, who gives the most circumstantial account, reports that "their music is the finest in
America and renowned even in Europe; they use nine chests of
viols, and of other instruments they have harps, vihuelas, *bajones* and guitars; more than fifty in the convent make music their
specialty; their voices and instruments make their choir the
most heavenly sounding anywhere" (Stevenson 1960:56–57).

In the Río de la Plata, some of the guitar's boldest infamy spread
from serenades that were performed in either of two ways. First,
privately, a singer expressed his feelings with guitar accompaniment, as under a girlfriend's window, which could get out of hand.
For instance, in 1650, a Sergeant Cubas was arraigned for insult-
ing with his guitar at a wedding in Córdoba. Second, and worse,
guitarists made their instrument the standard tool of public entertainments. Amateur guitarists roamed the streets nightly in
search of social contacts, laughs, or adventure, as did the *majos* of
Spain. This habitual strolling led to boisterous, all-night carousing.
The Rioplatense guitar was such a typical adjunct of leisure time
that it appeared frequently in criminal records, having been an
integral part of the diversions of low-class dandies and felons.
Serenading took place at private residences, of course, yet such
was also the fare of pulpería shops, the scene of both the infamous
guitar and the trouble associated with it since colonial times.
    The pulperías were typical all over South America. As already
observed in Los Bagres, Venezuela, some vihuelas (or small guitars) had been used in the performance of a fandango there, at "a
pulpería, or shop for the sale of sundries;—chiefly *aguardiente*
[rum] and tobacco (Vowell 1831:II, 103)." While the definition was
accurate, it lacked historical perspective, for the pulperías had
preceded the fandango in South America by more than a century.
At the beginning of the 17th century, in fact, the pulpería had
already been defined in the *Descripción del Virreinato del Perú:*

[Throughout the City of Lima, in each of the four cantons or
corners which are formed in the four blocks of all the streets,
there are pulperías, which are both shops for the purchase of
things to eat and taverns for the sale of wine. And they are all
rich because they earn a great deal from what they sell]
(c.1615:74).

Although they were carefully guarded, licensed, and taxed, the
pulperías sometimes functioned as houses of ill repute despite all
the legal supervision. Such was the case in the mining town of
Potosí in Bolivian territory. A half century after the Spaniards had
begun to work the silver mines there, along the "Sierra de la
Plata," Potosí was a boomtown at its peak, as attested in the chronicle *"Descripción de la villa y minas de Potosí, año de 1603"*:

[There are in this place 80 pulperías, according to the book of
the assessor who charges the tax, in which there is extraordinary expense.... There are 120 women of the mantilla and
petticoat, who are well-known in the occupation of prostitution,
and there are great numbers of Indian women in the same
occupation] (*Relaciones geográficas* 1881:I, 124).

The early colony of the Plata region began to spread around the
estuary, and with it the pulperías. The extant legislation dealing
with them specifically in Buenos Aires dates dates back to 1605. As
many of these acquired a diversity of merchandise, they gradually
progressed beyond the lowly status of tavern to that of a corner
market. For instance, they remained the standard outlet for guitar
strings, as explained above in Part III (regarding other merchandise, see Bossio 1972:Ch. XII). Eventually by the last decade of the
18th century, there were hundreds in Buenos Aires alone. In 1793,
due to a revenue shortfall in the capital city, its leaders ordered a
census for those of Buenos Aires that owed back taxes; as a result,
they found 392 pulperías in arrears! (Bossio 1972:305).

In the Rioplatense interior, out on the vast plains, the pulperías
were even more important. They provided the necessities of life
like a general store of the American Wild West, when other dis-
pensaries were lacking, and an oasis for weary travellers. The
pulpería was the single monument to civilization in an otherwise

deserted, wide-open pampa in which the only other sights apparent to the naked eye were small game or livestock along the road and thistles in the sea of tall, blowing grass for hundreds of miles. Being the lone highway establishments, they became the centers for the trade of illicit, contraband merchandise (Slatta 1982). Moreover, they ordinarily maintained a corral of fresh mounts, inasmuch as they doubled their function as outpost mail stops, like the U.S. Pony Express stations, by providing a change of horses for mounted mail carriers at calculated distances of every twelve miles or so across the prairie. Most important, in the absence of other institutions such as churches, schools, clubs, or towns, the pulperías that dotted the interior served as the early social institutions between the pioneer settlements.

Some of the early legislation affecting the pulperías dealt with public disorder, and the guitar was often at the root of the problem. The pulpería was the gathering place, sometimes the only one, where guitarists could congregate and, with them, the crowds. Naturally the problem was not so much the music as the excesses that followed: too much drinking, too much gambling, flaring, daring tempers, too many insults, or simply too much noise. But since guitarists were the main attraction, they certainly drew the lion's share of the blame. The usual remedy was to put a curfew on the pulperías so that the disorder would be nipped in the bud. An early Argentine example appeared in Córdoba's Historical Archive. On 13 January 1690, Don Bartolomé de Olmedo, mayor of Córdoba, imposed a curfew on the pulperías because trouble after dark was the usual result when guitarists began to entertain:

> Por cuanto por diferentes autos está prevenido, por muchos desórdenes que suceden y fracasos, etc., que [en] las pulperías después de dada la Oración, no ayga bullas de gente y en especial con guitarras...(Grenón 1954).
> [Therefore, by different judicial decrees it is prohibited, on account of the many disorders, injustices, and so on that happen, that within the pulperías after the (evening) prayer there be no noisy crowds of people, especially none with guitars....]

The edict goes on to say that, since the pulperías are "una guarida de vagabundos" [a hangout for wanderers], anyone found loitering

around them after a purchase would be subject to prosecution and
fifty lashes of the whip! Furthermore, the proprietor allowing (indeed for good business encouraging) such meetings, fiestas and
conversations, *"más con guitarra"* [more so with the guitar] would
be fined twenty pesos.

Such public disturbances were not limited to outposts of the
interior, however, for civic leaders were having the same trouble
in the capital. On 7 January 1716, José Bermúdez de Castro, Governor of Buenos Aires also prohibited singing and guitar playing at
the pulperías after dark (Rodríguez Molas 1982:63). Yet in 1788,
Governor Don Francisco de Paula Sanz was still trying to contain
the problem for the following reasons:

> *...por las constantes pujas que ocurrían en las pulperías de las*
> *que resultaban muertos y heridos algunas veces y otras, que ser-*
> *vían al mal entretenimiento de esclavos que abandonaban así*
> *el servicio de sus amos, atraídos por la diversión de las guitarras*
> *y el juego de naipes. Preocupado por estos hechos el Síndico so-*
> *licitó al Gobernador que ordenara no se admitiesen reuniones*
> *de gentes ni guitarras* (Bossio 1972:29).
> [...because of the constant fights that were occurring in the pul-
> perías from which sometimes resulted deaths and wounds, and
> because they served as bad entertainment for slaves that aban-
> doned thus the service of their masters, all for the diversion of
> guitars and games of cards. Concerned over these matters, the
> syndicate (of pulpería owners) solicited that the Governor ad-
> vocate the prohibition of such meetings of people and guitars.]

Thus the pulperías had already become a notorious meetingplace, with the guitar and gambling as main attractions. But after
all, these entertainments were not nearly so bad as the consequences associated with them. Guitarists would congregate to
perform, especially insomuch as a guitar was always available.
For many of them, like Santos Vega (Ref. 2, above), music was
their pre-eminent accomplishment, and they dared or insulted
others with their lyrics as they vied for supremacy or spilled their
feelings. After drinking, they too would become involved in the
fighting. To make matters worse, they all carried knives, so duels
were typical and the consequences, all too apparent:

Table 12 The Guitar in the Streets and Pulperías
(Grenón 1929, 1954)

1760. In a summary of proceedings, the following remained: "The witness was in the pulpería of the aforementioned Santiso in the company of Javier Casas and Nicolás Quirós along with the said Santiso; and at that hour the witness went along with the abovementioned cohorts in search of a guitar at the house of Pancho Casas, citizen of this city. From there they searched roundabout until they found a guitar. Then about midnight or later that night, they returned with the guitar that they found—the three named above along with a few others—to Santiso's corner. Upon finding his place closed, they went out again and returned.... Finally from there they left to walk around some more with the same cohorts until morning mass was performed at the Cathedral, where they all congregated to hear it (A de T, Crim. 1.24, e.15, f.119)."

1788. The following complaint was filed with the Bishop: "Representing a business of this [city], and assuming my rights before your Lordship, I, Rosendo Díaz, appear and declare that on the seventh of this month at night, between one and two in the morning a certain Parras, a seminary student and a stepchild of Don Francisco Solares, was, along with some others (whom I cannot identify), going around performing music. Grouped as a gang at this inopportune hour, they came upon the doors of my store to throw rocks and boulders; they left the doors ruined as they remain in evidence. All the while among them, they added insult to injury by ridiculing me personally with the great laughter that they were making."

It appeared to another witness that the protagonist was Don Apolinaro Parras. Among them was..."a pulpería owner named Guerra, who lives next to Saint Teresa...that despite all the beating at the door and the yelling with which they insulted the aforementioned Rosendo, he said he had no part in the affair, for he was merely holding the guitar in his hand when it happened, and that therefore his cohorts had done all the damage (Archivo del Obispado de la Diócesis de Córdoba, 1.34, T.1)."

1796. Santiago Legún owns "a large guitar, presently in the pulpería of Manuel Rodríguez (A de T, E.4, 1.7, e.5)."

The preceding evidence places the guitar in the forefront of low-to middle-class socializing around Córdoba, but it also implies the same might be true in the rest of the Plata region. The pulperías there had an obvious character of their own, part of which was the guitar that was present in most of them. Some of these businesses were quite small and insignificant (the most primitive were called *puestos* or *boliches*) and may not have had an instrument on hand to loan out to entertainers and serenaders, but if there was one, it was certainly the guitar. Far out on the wide-open ranges of the pampa (where documentation has remained scarce) the guitar was probably the only instrument seen or heard for miles around or for years at a time. In towns that dotted the interior, guitarists were involved in obnoxious merrymaking in the pulperías to the extent that their activities were curtailed continuously at least since 1690. Thus, in the light of all this activity involving the guitar, Azara's oft-quoted pronouncement at the end of the 18th century seemed certain (see Pinnell 1984 for the Spanish text and more rationale). Although Azara was not complimentary in his overall assessment, he claimed that every pulpería owned a guitar, even out on the pampa, the domain of the gauchos:

[These cowboys, raised on the uninhabited plains with scarcely any communication, hardly know friendship....
Some owners or overseers of cattle sell at their houses some trinkets—more than anything else rum. Hence these establishments are known by the name of *pulperías,* being the point in the countryside where all of the inhabitants congregate. (The gauchos) do not take any special care of their money; they employ it only for gambling or drinking. Their custom is to invite everybody at the meeting to drink; therefore they fill a great glass with rum (because they do not like wine), and they pass it around from one mouth to the next. They repeat this ceremony down to their last cent, and they feel offended if the invitation is refused. For the purpose of diversion between different rounds of drinks, in every pulpería there is a guitar, and whoever plays it is always flattered and treated at the expense of all who listen.
These musicians never sing more than *yarabís,* which are songs from Peru, the most monotonous, sad songs in the world, for which they are also called *tristes.* The tone is lamentable, and they always deal with ruined love affairs or with lovers

who cry about their pains in the pampas, but never about happy, nor festive, nor even indifferent matters] (Azara 1801:195–96).

The pulpería musicians did sing more than *yarabís!* Even so, though Azara might not have understood much about music—being a Spanish geographer and naturalist, he might have at least noticed some of the more obvious similarities between the pulpería songs and Andalusian folk music in general. For instance, they were both filled with the same sensitive sadness:

[It is often repeated that Argentine music is the product of Andalusian happiness which became diluted with the sadness of the pampa. However, it would be difficult to formulate a less true hypothesis. The Andalusian intonations are not happy either—almost all of them cry about love affairs and wanderings...] (Alvarez 1908:71).

4. The Fandango in the Río de la Plata

In the Old World, the fandango had always been a peasant dance, with roots dating back a millennium to the Moorish occupation of Spain. Yet the fandango was not in evidence beyond its Andalusian birthplace until the 18th century. It began to fill the rest of Spain as a sensational highlight in the theatrical farces that portrayed the adventures of the lower classes. Then footloose guitarists spread it into Europe along with other stylish entertainments of popular culture. With its lurid sensuality, as well as the ruckus associated with the active participation of its spectators, the fandango became the wildest musical sensation in 18th-century Europe. A well-known example during the period of the Enlightenment outside of Spain was that of Mozart and da Ponte; they used the fandango for both humorous and exotic contrast in *The Marriage of Figaro* as they portrayed Seville's garden of delights. In the New World, these associations continued with the fandango, for it spread across the Americas during the 18th century, as well.

The fandango's ports of call included those of the Río de la Plata. However, to facilitate appreciation of its impact there, the fandango requires separate consideration, at first, from the Hispanic

popular culture that had preceded it, because the fandango impacted like a concert to a primed audience. The guitar in the Plata
region was already at the heart of amateur music-making and
entertainment: it was the favorite instrument, even in church
worship preceding the arrival of less portable instruments such as
the harp or pneumatic organ. The guitar was thus in its *segunda
patria*; it had already been standardized as the national instrument. The guitar's conquest in the Plata colony went uncontested,
for it was the tangible component of Hispanic popular culture.
Inevitably, moreover, the Rioplatense guitar had infamous associations with the semi-professional musical entertainments available at the pulperías. After dark, these establishments had always
seemed to breed trouble, whether in the lonesome interior or at the
four corners of every block of the towns and cities. Music and
gambling were already the entertainments there, so the pulpería
provided a rowdy environment for any new Spanish dance. Both
the guitarists and the noisy clientele constituted the primed audience for the fandango. Thus, when it finally arrived as the latest
18th-century dance from Europe, the fandango coalesced with the
earlier popular culture in this nocturnal scene. The new coalition
in popular entertainment brought an immediate threat to what
peace and tranquility the political and religious leaders had institutionalized in the Plata. Consequently they did not know how to
stem the tide of the fandango, which brought increased disorder
and general depravity in its wake, except to fight it head-on with
defiant opposition. The politicians legislated against the new fandango as they had earlier against the guitar in the pulpería, and
religious leaders preached against it from the pulpit.

Documentary evidence in two Uruguayan towns has been cited
to explain how the fandango was received on the Plata's east side
(Ayestarán 1953:474). Musicians in the town of Soriano played it
in a house of ill-repute, which in itself, was insignificant. However,
their performance led to brawling there and eventually to a felony:

> *En una casa de dibirsión de un fandango que hallí había....
> Hallándose en casa de Santos Medina él que declara por haber
> habido un fandango en la expresada casa....*(Expediente No. 2
> del año 1790. *Juzgado Letrado de Soriano.* Mercedes.)

[In a house of diversion, there was a fandango there.... Finding himself in the house of Santos Medina, the witness declares that on account of there being a fandango in the aforementioned house....]

In another Uruguayan town called San Juan Bautista (present-day Santa Lucía), the legislative session of 20 January 1797 prohibited the fandango altogether. The guitarists there had made it a scandalous affair, along with the nightly serenades they were performing in the street. In order to avoid further problems, the Town Council published the following decree:

Mandamos y proivimos que ninguna persona haga fandangos de los que se hacostumbran sin licencia halguna de los Señores Alcs. ni anden por las calles desoras de la noche Con Guitarra cantando versos desonestos (Cabildo de San Juan Bautista, Libro de Acuerdos II, fol. 57. Archivo de la Nación, Montevideo).
[We command and we prohibit any person from having fandangos of those which are customary without the permission of the Town Council, and we prohibit anyone from going around the streets at odd hours of the night With the Guitar singing indecent verses.]

Thus, it became increasingly difficult to maintain law and order in the Plata because of the fandango. It was soon inseparable from the complex of Hispanic popular culture which involved the guitar and late-night serenading at private homes, at the pulpería, and at less respectable establishments. In other words, the fandango and the serenade had joined forces, as it were, against local authority. Together they became the main diversions of the evening—quite especially among the youth whose nocturnal wanderings included stops at these establishments. The serenade and fandango were unruly affairs, they could last the entire night, and worst of all the fandango could lead to drunkenness, brawling, and even manslaughter. The early legal documents and judicial rulings of Córdoba serve to confirm this hypothesis time and time again. The data cited on the following pages comes from both municipal and religious sources, although most of it represents the Criminal Division of the city's Tribunal Archive:

Table 13 The Guitar, Serenade, and Fandango (Grenón 1929, 1954)

1753. In the declaration of one man, "they asked him why he was wearing his sable; he responded that it was to goad some dancers who were attending the celebration of St. Benedict (A de T, Crim. 1.9, e.17, f.16)." [A de T= Archivo de Tribunales, Córdoba]

1756. It is registered in the religious chronicles that "they attended so as to dance the fandango; on account of [Pedro] Mercado's given name, the fandango was arranged that night because it was the celebration of St. Peter which was customarily celebrated in many homes".... The organizing nucleus of the fandango, which ruined the tragic fiesta, was comprised of "three Andalusians: Juan *el gitano* or *Juancito el toreador*, Luis Vega, and Tomás *el herrero armero* (A de T, Crim., E.1, E.1.324)."

1759. Manuel Machado and his companion Fernando were married the same night. [According to one witness,] "On the night that they were married and in the house where they did the fandango, there was a fight between Gaspar (Rojas), deceased, the abovementioned Hermenegildo, who also accompanied on the guitar, and Manuel of Genoa, *padrino* of the aforementioned Manuel of the marriage.... Two of them were shot that night." Days later, the constable Bartolo Molas declares, "that coming from the corner of Apprenticeship Hall...he heard some guitar playing and singing, so he went where they were singing...." It was two o'clock in the morning as they were playing the guitar, and the Genoa man was singing in *Genoese*.... Two constables arrived. They arrested Hermenegildo and put Gaspar between them despite shouts of "Leave that poor man alone!" Manuel, minister of the rounds who was called "Whitey," spoke against Gaspar telling him that he was looking for him and that he was "under arrest." "I'm under arrest, gentlemen," he answered. They raised his cloak to see if he was carrying a pistol. Taking offense, Gaspar stepped back a bit to free himself and resisted arrest. Manuel called out to him: "Help to the King!" Gaspar said: "What King?" The constable Manuel responded with, "You're under arrest, and if not take that!"—and he shot him with a load of buckshot. Gaspar the musician fell with the guitar to the ground, saying—"May God repay it to you, that you have killed me," while Manuel and Fernández got away.

Gaspar, from the ground, cried out to a certain Ortega, present at the musical meeting: *"Compadre,* for God's sake, go to Padre Domingo Bustos so he can confess me, since I'm dying now!"…. "But before the priest arrived, his life was cut short. Don Bruno and Eugenio helped him to die well." A neighbor heard from his bedside that they made him repeat: "Jesus, Jesus." Hermenegildo was carried off to jail and served later to put together the fabric of the story….

The assassin had fled, in spite of being a constable, for his sense of conscience at having abused and over-extended his office, and for having proceeded with vengeance, wounding his own *padrino* of the previous marriage (A de T, Crim. 1.1, e.14).

1759. [On Sunday] 15 April, Félix Acosta of Córdoba asked for lodging at the home of Juana Toledo in the City of Santa Fe. He was admitted so he tied up his horse; he entered. While he was drinking and talking with the lady of the house and with her sister, "they heard Manuel Maciel (of Santa Fe) singing some verses to the sound of his guitar, which they understood as directed toward and to offend the said Acosta by being lewd (injurious, according to yet another witness). [Acosta] being all ears responded to the other man with these words—My *compadre* Maciel, you are looking for me…and you are ridiculing me. At which time, going closer to the referred Maciel, he remained with the same guitar always singing the same verses until, impatient now, Acosta went outside to take on Maciel." The affair ended badly: on the following day, Maciel left his guitar to his heir (A de T, Crim. 1.18, e.13).

1762. A robbery was the subject, realized in October of that year. In order to prove that the robber of that night was neither, as suspected, Marcos Posadas nor Domingo Díaz, this alibi was adduced: Marcos Posadas went out with his guitar with Domingo Díaz and others on some nights singing, dancing, and carousing, playing music. [Domingo Díaz:] "I was involved starting at ten o'clock at night strolling around with the guitar, accompanied by Félix Acosta [et al.] playing music and singing in the home of Margarita Galíndez; and afterwards in that of a lady named Damiana, wife of a man called Montenegro; and finally I went with these cohorts to the home of Ana Lencinas where they were in the said diversion until dawn. It is well known that my part of the night was spent in the three houses of diversion and pleasure." Vicente Acosta posits that "going for a stroll one night, he heard the noise of music in the house of Damiana Zejas at about eleven o'clock...." And Damiana Zejas says in her declaration: "Domingo Díaz was at the home of the witness, singing and dancing until nearly dawn along with Nicolás Pérez and others...(A de T, Crim., 1.16, e.3, f.144)."

1782. Hermenegildo Ferrer...was the brunt of an embarrassing social jest. "Even when Ferrer ought not to have attended the party without having been invited beforehand, [Gregorio] Zamudio, who had been brought up well...should not have harassed the man so much. Wanting to prove his low extraction, he made Ferrer take several ladies out to the dance floor to the last minuet.... Then he asked the musicians to vary the music and to play for him a *fandanguillo* while he was dancing the minuet! (A de T, E.1, E.1.400, e.13)."

1784. Roque Jacinto Juárez, in the shelter of San Pedro upon witnessing against Juan Martín Mesa, exposes that in Tulumba, in the night of 28 August, "he was inside the house of Francisca López in the company of Juan Martín Mesa...[et al.], and he entertained and diverted from Vespers until the morning came with the guitar in no more than dancing with and entertaining the women of the party (A de T, Crim., 1.39, e.23)."

1784. Francisco Fha or Faa was a native of Italy, of 50 years of age, widower, and a "musician by profession, by which he maintains himself." His son was seminary student (*manteísta*) Feliciano Geronimo Faa, also a "musician by profession, that is by which he maintains himself." He was born in Buenos Aires and was 26 years of age, having married in Montevideo. He was asked where he had been that night of the robbery. His father Francisco Faa said that "he passed the night at the home of José de Guzmán, a mulatto slave, organist of the Convent of Santo Domingo, accompanied by his wife and a close friend María Leona...." But Feliciano had been disguised in the cloak of a *manteísta* (the long cape of a seminary student) for reasons which are given below.

The Señora Gregoria Maldonado claims that at seven o'clock she found at her door Feliciano Faa and Antonio Guerrero; she invited them in, but only Guerrero went in, the other excusing himself for the cloak of *manteísta* he was wearing. They passed the guitar to the aforementioned Guerrero, and he was playing it for about half an hour. Later Don José Eugenio Elías arrived, accompanied by yet another lady.... They went back out with the witness (Doña Gregoria), two of her sisters and another woman.... All together they went out to see the fandango at the home of Doña Bernardina Espinosa, where they were until half past ten o'clock.... Then (Feliciano) was asked again regarding his change of clothes for which he was suspected so vehemently since Don Feliciano Faa was not clarifying with respect to what reason or motive that he had gone to the ball with the cloak of a monk.... Just as he said earlier, he insisted that it was because he knew that he told Doña Bernardina Espinosa that they had a ball that night until dawn with the best music of the city: and for this reason the witness asked, in disguise that his father, Mateo, the Cathedral organist, José of Santo Domingo, and Juan José, a bass player, for them not to attend. He was thus disguised in order not to be recognized.... Doña Gregoria manifested, after the aforementioned, on that day with Feliciano, that "they did not speak about anything except regarding whether or not he was going to the fandango of Doña Bernardina...." Meanwhile, during the investigation, the suspects remained under arrest for five days (A de T, Crim., 1.37, e.31).

1792. The Indian was there playing the guitar: "the chieftan of the Indians of Qulino [sic], Joaquín Sayas was treacherously killed by José Francisco, alias Vida (A de T, Crim., 1.55, e.9)."

1793. Antonia Barrientos, married in Catamarca to Santiago Tapia, was involved in an accusation against the Indian witch doctor José Joaquín Coronel. She witnesses that in consequence of "having taken her husband to the fiesta (of the Virgin) of Rosario because he was a harpist and guitarist, she was left alone with her little children (A de T, Crim. 1.58, e.6)."

1798. Mariano Fernández, resident of Río Tercero presents the following.... "And also, after the death of my mother-in-law, I have never been dancing nor played a single [guitar] string, nor even less, acted rowdy nor attended parties or fandangos, as they say in the countryside (A de T, E.3, 1.54, e.7)."

1805. The mulatto Juan, slave of Doña Micaela Peralta, "lives free, without any subjection, such that there is neither party nor meeting in which he is not found because he is a singer and guitar player. He lives in complete freedom.... He has no other life than to

go around to performances and fandangos because he is a guitar
player and singer (A de T, Crim., 1.105, e. 27)."

1806. A witness in a trial posits that "they were on their way to a
serenade at the aforementioned house, during which he was an
accompanist at an odd hour of the night. When they began to sing
at the door, two young men came out of the house into the presence
of the musicians who were with the guitar; then, a moment later,
two young women came out, a mother and her daughter. They
were killed, leaving the serenade without an audience (A de T,
Crim., 1.105, e.4)."

1827. "They went out to fandangos where are frequent both drinking and fighting, as everybody knows (A de T, Crim., 1.161, e.7)."

*   *   *   *   *

Throughout history, dances became popular with repeated exposure in the artistic media. Especially as performers presented a
dance to the concert audience, they were obviously bringing it valuable public exposure. Simultaneously as spectators witnessed a
staged dance in public, they either heard it for the first time or
reinforced their previous knowledge about it. The rise of the plebeian minuet to courtly status was exemplary in Europe: Louis
XIV took a personal interest in it, so then did serious composers,
and finally it became standardized in the late Baroque suite and
the Classic symphony. Both musical concerts and dance recitals
provided similar public exposure for the fandango. In either case,
staged performances helped to maintain it in the social life of the
Río de la Plata.

The fandango came repeatedly to the concerts of the Plata capitals during the 19th century, as documented in the news of the
day. Musicians and dancers performed it in their staged recitals.
Both the fandango and its little descendant, the *fandanguillo* were
part of the concert programs of Montevideo, according to the chronology of Table 14 (on the next page). The evidence cited there,
presently in the collection of Lauro Ayestarán in the Museo Ro-
mántico, appeared in three newspapers of the capital, *El Universal, El Nacional,* and the *Comercio del Plata.*

Table 14 The Fandango in the Concerts of Montevideo (Ayestarán 1953:303–435)

On **23 Oct. 1829,** the fandango was danced by Juana and José Cañete in the Casa de Comedias (*El Universal*, 19 Oct. 1829).

On **24 Sep. 1830,** the fandanguillo was danced by Juan Villarino (*El Universal*, 23–24 Sep. 1830).

On **17 Feb. 1833,** the fandango was danced by Petronilla Serrano and Juan Villarino (*El Universal*, 16 Feb. 1833).

On **25 Feb. 1842,** the guitarist Dr. Nicanor Albarellos [b. Buenos Aires, 1810] gave a recital containing some of his own guitar solos and *Variations on the Cielito* for guitar and orchestra. The concert included *Variations on the Fandango*, his own composition (*El Nacional*, 25 Feb. 1842).

On **3 Aug. 1845,** Dolores de Gambín accompanied herself on guitar in the performance of Andalusian songs (*El Nacional*, 31 Aug. 1845).

On **9 Sep. 1845,** Dolores de Gambín again accompanied herself on the guitar in the performance of some Spanish songs. Among them, she performed, along with another lady, some "boleras afandangadas" (*El Nacional*, 2, 5, 9 Sep. 1845).

On **4 Oct. 1845,** Dolores de Gambín and Fernando Quijano danced the "fandango andaluz" (*Comercio del Plata*, 3 Oct. 1845).

On **20 Dec. 1855,** the ensemble of Sr. Jiménez danced the fandango (*Comercio del Plata*, 20 Dec. 1855).

Scarcely any of this performed music has come down to us in written form because much of it was created and performed without notation. Obviously a substantial number of the fandangos were developed through improvisation, just as they were in Andalusia, and they were retained as memorized music or transmitted only by rote. Nevertheless, there is one extant fandango of the 19th century in the Archive of F.J. Debali, a prominent, foreign-born musician of Montevideo. It had originally been an ensemble piece,

perhaps along the lines of Boccherini's *Quintet No. 4,* G. 448 with
the fandango finale mentioned above (Sect. 1). However, only a
violin part remains in the Archive today as item No. 854. No composer is indicated on the manuscript, but the part is copied in the
hand of Debali (Ayestarán 1953:474). An excerpt from this violin
part appears below to show the typical character of the fandango
and to provide evidence that it was known and heard in Uruguay:

Ex. 8 A Rioplatense Fandango in the Hand of Debali

5. The Fandango in Rioplatense Literature

The trajectory of the Rioplatense fandango lasted a century and a
half. The dance was extremely popular from the time of its introduction around 1740 until the years of independence at the beginning of the 19th century. Then, as the fandango began to decline in
popularity, it lingered nevertheless in Rioplatense literature until
1890 or so. It was usually a part of fictitious works, both theatrical
pieces and gauchesque tales; in either case, it portrayed the merriment or tragedy of life-like situations.

The first secular composition for the Plata theatre was *El amor
de la estanciera* [The Love of the Hacienda Girl]. Appearing
anonymously around the end of the 18th century, it was about the
landowners in the countryside, and not merely a shepherdess, as

implied by its title. Though it was but a modest *sainete*, it ended with an ensemble finale somewhat like the third act of *Figaro*. The bride's father asks a certain musician named Marcos (a Brazilian to add polyglot diversity in Portuguese) to take out his guitar in order to accompany the marriage celebration. In its happy ending (shown below with a rhymed translation), the celebrants dance and sing in turn to the fandango:

Ref. 5 *El amor de la estanciera*							Anon.

Cancho

Traiga su guitarra Marcos
que un fandango hemos de hacer
y ha de bailar Chepa, y Juancho
Cancho, y Pancha su muger
   (Saca la guitarra.)

Marcos

Aquí istá pois ã viola
mui disposta, y encurdada
tein uhas voces galañas
Efica muitu ben temprada

Canta Cancho

Mi yerno Juancho Perucho
con sus lecheras
y sus caallos viva
con su Estanciera....

Canta Cancho y repiten todos

Aquí dio fin el bayle
y el casamiento
viva pues han quedado
todos contentos

Cancho

[Bring here your guitar, Marcos:
we have a fandango to tender
so Chepa and Juancho can fracas,
that Cancho and Pancha can render.
   (He takes out his guitar.)

Marcos

Here's my vihuela and talent:
I'm willing, and it's well strung
to go with the lyrics so gallant
that are yet to be sung.

Cancho sings

What Juancho Perucho endorses,
may he live long and well,
with all his cattle and horses
and with his country belle....

Cancho sings and all repeat

So ends a wonderful dance,
and withal a marriage!
Long live their happy romance,
as they leave in their carriage.]

Starting with the years of independence, the plays developed a more serious, patriotic tone, reminiscent of the European rescue operas which followed the French Revolution. Indeed, Plata

citizens could relate. Once they had thwarted the British invasion
at home in 1806, complete independence was becoming ever more
a possibility with the spread of Napoleon's troops into Spain. A
representative example is *Defensa y triunfo del Tucumán* [De-
fense and Triumph of Tucumán] by Ambrosio Morante. The play
serves to relive heroic steps towards liberation from Spanish rule
in which the victory at Tucumán was decisive. Reference to the
"fandango" appears near the end of the play as a metaphor of this
battle. Here the revolutionary fervor runs high and well rewarded:

Ref. 6 *Defensa y triunfo del Tucumán*   Ambrosio Morante

Cosme
Así en la próxima acción
que por puntos esperamos,
al Soldado, al Oficial,
al Tambor, al Voluntario,
en fin, a cualquier patriota
que en contra de los tiranos
muestre más valor en ella,
le doy de Juana la mano
y también la pulpería.

Cosme
[Thus in the next encounter
for which we all are wary,
to the official or soldier
to the drum or the voluntary,
indeed to any patriot
who against all tyranny
shows most valor in combat,
I'll give'im the hand of my Juana
as well as my store for sundries.

Todos
¡Viva el Patriota!

Everybody
Long live the patriot!

Pierna Santa
Me allano.

Pierna Santa
I'm overwhelmed.

Tambo
Y yo también.

Tambo
Me too.

Churrete
Si no hubiera
esos tropezones malos
también al fandango entrara;
que por la Juana, aunque callo,
el potrillo del amor
suele corcobear a ratos.

Churrete
If there were none
of these fearsome obstacles,
I would go into the fandango;
if only for Juana—I'm holding
on the wild horse of love
which is always bucking.

Juana
¿Y vos, qué decís?

Juana
And you, what do you say?

Malapeste
¿Quién sabe?

Malapeste
Who knows?

Juana
¿Y qué, no entráis en el trato?

Juana
So, aren't you entering into the
agreement (with my father)?

Malapeste	Malapeste
¿Para qué?	What for?

Juana	Juana
¡Nunca creyera que	I would never have thought
me fueses tan ingrato!	you'd be so thankless with me!]

In a considerable portion of the gauchesque poetry, i.e., verse written primarily by men of letters who were exposed to and wrote about the gaucho way of life, there are episodes quite like the misfortunes enumerated in Tables 12 and 13. The writers usually reach the peak of interest at the denouement: the catastrophe where circumstances force the fictional hero into a life of self-imposed exile from society, becoming thus a *gaucho malo.* Of all the gauchesque tales, *Martín Fierro* is the most famous; it contains the confessions of a renegade called Cruz to Martín Fierro. The crux of Cruz's story is his misfortune at a rural dance scene where his renegade life began. At that point, as cited below, he mentions both the fandango and its later variant, the *fandanguillo:*

Ref. 7 *Martín Fierro, Canto XI*   José Hernández

Cruz	Cruz
Ansí andaba como guacho	[I was bouncin' aroun' like an orphan
cuando pasa el temporal.	in the middle of a storm, when
Supe una vez, pa mi mal,	it was my misfortune to happen
de una milonga que había,	upon a fiesta that I found;
y ya pa la pulpería	so I led my horse to the sound,
enderecé mi bagual....	until I was in the tavern....
Con gato y con fandanguillo	With a fast one and *fandanguillo*
había empezao el changango	the gueetar was gittin' quite loud,
y para ver el fandango	I rolled like a ball in the crowd
me colé haciéndomé bola;	to see the fandango and wail,
mas metió el diablo la cola	but the devil stuck in his tail
y todo se volvió pango.	leavin' all confused in a cloud.
Había sido el guitarrero	The guitarist had certainly been
un gaucho duro de boca.	a gaucho with a real big mouth.
Yo tengo pacencia poca	But when made to stomach such clout,

pa'aguantar cuando no debo:	I am a man of short temper;
a ninguno me le atrevo	I don't dare anyone, ever,
pero me halla él que me toca.	but who wants me'll find me about.
A bailar un pericón	So as to dance a *pericón,*
con una moza salí,	I went to the floor with a girl.
y cuanto me vido allí	As soon as he saw our whirl,
sin duda me conoció	he knew me right away
y estas coplitas cantó	'cause these verses he started to say,
como por ráirse de mí:	really mockin' me and the girl:
"Las mujeres son todas	"Women in general
como las mulas;	are rather like mules;
yo no digo que todas,	well if not all, then say I,
pero hay algunas	there are some who, like fools,
que a las aves que vuelan	pull feathers off birds
les sacan plumas."	to make them stick by."
"Hay gauchos que presumen	"There are gauchos who presume
de tener damas;	to have their own bride;
no digo que presumen,	well maybe they assume;
pero se alaban,	but when they're disturbed,
y a lo mejor los dejan	they're always perturbed
tocando tablas."	'cause in this they ever take pride."
Se secretiaron las hembras	So the females all whispered,
y yo ya me encocoré;	but I yelled, man, I'd been had:
volié la anca y le grité,	"Shut up you cricket, stop singin' so bad!"
"Dejá de cantar...chicharra."	While I knew I'd be banished afar
Y de un tajo a la guitarra	in one fell swoop upon his guitar,
tuitas las cuerdas corté.	I cut off his strings and left him so mad.]

Another gauchesque tale worthy of consideration here is actual history, as told by Ricardo Pollo Darraque. It is the literal biography of one Alejandro Rodríguez who, in self defense, caused the death of another man in a duel of daggers. Rodríguez thus became a *gaucho malo*; he eventually took his own life in the prison of Montevideo towards the end of the 19th century. Just like Cruz,

Rodríguez became an outlaw at a musical affair to the accompaniment of the guitar. In Reference 8, below, he responds to the dare of a black singer. Rodríguez spontaneously improvises some verses that end on a double meaning, in which case the fandango is both a dance and a brawl leading to the catastrophe:

Ref. 8 *El Clinudo...*	Ricardo Pollo Darraque
Alejandro Rodríguez	Alejandro Rodríguez
Ni vine a buscar camorra	[I didn't come searchin' for trouble
ni a compadriar en la fiesta,	nor to pal around at the party,
pero sepan los presentes,	but be it known to these people
quien me busca me encuentra.	who's lookin' for me shall find me.
Veré si tiene el moreno	I'll discover if this black man
tanto valor como lengua...	has guts to match his darin'...
Abran cancha las mujeres	Make way, please, my dear women
que ya el fandango comienza.	that the fandango is only startin'.]

Despite the early literary prominence of the fandango, some authors like Florencio Sánchez (b. Montevideo, 1875) began to disregard it. By the end of the century, literary references to the fandango became rare because it was going out of style, perhaps, but also because it was being condemned from the pulpit.

6. The Fandango and the Church in South America

Unfortunately space does not permit an exposé of the controversial fandango in the Viceroyalty of New Spain, as centered at Mexico City, except to say that the dance was causing havoc with polite society. Dancing or performing the fandango or certain other dances like it became an act of indecency, so it was frequently a matter requiring the disciplinary action of the Spanish Inquisition. Typically members of the Inquisition court would gather information from confessions and interviews on social problems before taking action. In the following case near Tulancingo (a town north of Mexico City), a missionary complained about the fandango's consequences to a certain Fray Gabriel of the Inquisition Tribunal:

[Every day I think they invent new songs in the aforementioned
pan de jarabe style so that it will never end, and I think it will
not be uprooted until that Holy Tribunal will take it out by
name.... But this is not all, for there has been no lack of respectable persons to defend the contrary; they are hiring musicians
for public and scandalous fandangos.... Tulancingo, 26 February 1789] (Saldívar 1934:269–70).

The fandango was even more of a nuisance farther south. Ulloa
and Juan captured, in *A Voyage to South America* published in
1748, some lively perspectives of the fandango in Cartagena, as explained above (Section 2). Next they turned their attention towards
a capital if controversial work, not as a sequel to their memoirs, but
rather as an in-depth, candid report to their king in the spirit of the
Inquisition entitled "Discourse and Political Reflections on the
Present State of the Kingdoms of Peru...." It was never printed
during their lifetime, but David Barry brought it out, perhaps un-
scrupulously for the first time in 1826 under his own title, *Noticias
secretas de America* [Secret Information about America]. Born of a
biased viewpoint, its contents have remained polemical, particularly with regard to the activities of the clergy. In fact, it reveals
the fandango in their midst, giving reason to the dauntless clerical
opposition that would eventually curtail the practice of the fandango altogether in South America.

The majority of all excesses committed at the dissolute fandangos in various parts of America, as we have already said in
our *Voyages,* appear to be inventions of the devil himself, who
inspires them in order to find additional slaves among these
people. Yet one finds his choice of instruments for putting them
into effect and giving them direction there terribly strange,
even incredible, and repugnant to all reason. Fandangos or
dances are normally sponsored by members of an order, or to
state it more properly, those nominally called friars. The regular clergy bear the cost, participate themselves, and with their
concubines hold these functions in their own homes. As soon as
the dancing starts, they begin imbibing brandy and anise to
excess. The more drunk they become, the more they translate
their merrymaking into lewd activities, so obscene and lascivious that it would be imprudent to discuss them and defile

the narrative with such obscenity. Leaving them hidden in a veil of silence, we shall be content by saying that all the evil one could imagine, as great as it might be, cannot even permeate the vice in which those perverted souls are wallowing. They are so dissolute and lewd that it is impossible to grasp it fully.

The fact that these fandangos are held in a friar's house is sufficient to prevent civil officials from daring to violate its sanctuary. Although clerical sponsors of these dances masquerade in laymen's clothing, they are so well known that they cannot go unrecognized (Juan & Ulloa 1749:285–86).

Had the fandango remained merely an affair of the common people, local priests might have contained it within their parish churches. But evidently it got out of hand. Certainly neither all of the Catholic clergy nor even significant numbers of priests could have been involved in the fandango's milieu. Yet if only a very few were, if in the most isolated, provincial quarters, the embarrassment would have been sufficient to incite a clerical tirade against the fandango. And thus it happened. The wild fandango, which popular musicians brought directly from Andalusia to the predominantly Andalusian New World colonies and viceroyalties, was gradually stamped out by an affront from the administrative level of the Church. Ironically, the fandango lived on in Andalusia, but across the South American continent, the clergy prohibited both the performance of and dancing to the fandango on threat of total excommunication.

The South American bishops championed the cause against the fandango. They saw it as a scourge that had to be uprooted. In Cartagena, for instance, according to the examples cited there by Ulloa and Juan in their books, the fandango in that port was of sufficient scandal to engage religious condemnation. In the decade following the completion of their second book, Don Diego Peredo, bishop of the same diocese was prohibiting all participation in the fandango. Anyone involved in it was subject to the maximum penalty within his jurisdiction—excommunication from the Church! As a result, the cry of public opposition was so great that the Governor and even the Court of Madrid had to intervene. Secular officials obtained recantation: the Bishop finally had to rescind his order of excommunication.

[Another event that...occurred during this period was the prohibition of the dances called *bundes* or *fandangos*; it was pronounced by the Bishop of the Diocese, Don Diego Peredo under penalty of excommunication because of the many excesses that the dances were causing. As can be imagined, the protest of the people was general, and, foreseeing a delicate situation of public administration, the Governor Don Fernando Morillo y Velarde and the veritable Court of Madrid saw themselves in need of intervening in order to suspend that rigorous measure of Señor Peredo] (Lemaitre 1980:106).

During the same period and within the adjoining diocese, the Bishop of Caracas prohibited the fandango with a similar proclamation. In it he also determined to uproot a few other dances:

[Edict upon the dances commonly called *fandango, zambingue* and *dance of the Moors* and others like them under penalty of excommunication.

As we desire the salvation of souls for all of his subjects, and so that the diabolical injustice of the devil will not beguile them into allowing themselves to be brought into sin, which is facilitated by the occasion of the dances commonly called fandangos, zambingue, dance of the Moors, and others like them in whose practice with great tribulation of men and women in general seriously offends our Lord God...in some towns of this Bishopric where, despising the divine precepts, prohibiting justice, and forgetting the suffering for our predecessors, the dangerous practice has been reintroduced of those dances which are harmful to the spiritual welfare of our flock, and which are offensive to the Divine Majesty..., we command and send to all the faithful of both sexes, residents of the villages, towns, and places where our letters may be published...by virtue of excommunication let sound the canonical admonition...that they abstain from that devious practice of the above-mentioned dances. Caracas, 20 May 1761 (signed) Diego Antonio, Bishop of Caracas] (Calzavara 1987:226).

Precisely a decade after this action, Father Guanare of the same diocese repeated the prohibition of the fandango. Obviously, a renewed prohibition in Caracas implied that the previous one had been ineffective (Calzavara 1987:94).

The situation of the fandango in the Río de la Plata was not unlike its plight in Cartagena or Caracas. The performance of the decadent fandango continued, especially among the middle and lower classes as in other places, and its indecency incited clerical wrath against it from the pulpit. The crimes caused by guitarists or, at least at the scene of their performances (such as those of Table 13) stood to justify the priests' gross religious condemnations. As the Plata clergy spoke against the fandango, however, the secular leaders, some of whom were elected officials, could not give full support to their edicts, despite the fact that the clergymen were backed by other South American bishops. Apparently the governors could not enforce what they believed to be a fanatical view of the fandango.

The high administration of the Church in Buenos Aires had begun to take a dim view of the fandango already around 1740. At that time, the aging bishop of the diocese, Fray José de Peralta y Barnuevo, in the decade after his positive review in favor of the Jesuit missions, took action against the fandango. In counsel with other bishops and archbishops of the church and with local informants, he had determined that certain dances, particularly the fandango, were pernicious and devastating to the soul because of their unbridled social context. Realizing that the guitarists and other musicians who introduced the fandango and performed it were primarily at fault, as in the data of Table 13, he blamed them first. He claimed, as did the Bishops of Cartagena and Caracas, that such dances led to serious sin and they ought not to continue. So Bishop José de Peralta made the following proclamation and saw to its publication:

[Inasmuch as it is our pastoral obligation to look after the health of the souls in our charge, and to uproot the vices and pernicious customs among them, we have recognized that among the dances and balls that are customarily held in private homes to celebrate festivals and holidays, there have originated serious guilt, felonies, and scandals, especially when men and women are in attendance together. Although in real conformity with that required by sacred canons, charged by apostolic, men and practiced in nearly all the bishoprics and archbishoprics, we have prohibited and have admonished the avoidance of such dances and fandangos, we have not been able to obtain their correction. So, desiring for more effective remedies to the problem, making use of appropriate measures, and in order to avoid offenses that they do to our Lord God, bearing in mind that the blame for these disorders rests primarily with persons who put forth their musical instruments in such festivities, we command all the said persons which are accustomed to attending such functions with the musicians that henceforth they not do it any longer upon pain of the universal sentence of total excommunication— let sound the canonical admonition.... And if they do participate, [the musicians] shall lose their instruments...and in consequence we prohibit henceforth the aforementioned balls and dances along with the circumstances of men and women in attendance, and we ordain and command that any person— economic level, character, quality, or condition notwithstanding—that seeks to attend such dances in private homes in any manner is under the same condemnation of excommunication, and a fine of fifty pesos is applicable to those who have applied appropriately for the construction of the Seminary of this Holy Church, Santa Cruzada and to the poor, jail, and to those who are unable being of ordinary means, a fine of ten pesos or a month of prison....

Proclaimed in Buenos Aires on 30 July 1746.—(signed) Fray Joseph, Bishop of Buenos Aires] (Torre Revello 1926:285–86).

Naturally plenty of the faithful parishoners who had attended such affairs were horrified at the thought of severance from the strongest Hispanic institution in the colony! The language and tone of the edict was certain to arouse contempt. Moreover, it had the ring of a secular decree, what with the fines and sentences. For as Bishop José de Peralta devised these punishments, he had stepped into the political arena of the *Cabildo*, the City Council of Buenos Aires, and in so doing he had confronted its leader, none other than the *Procurador General*, the Attorney General of the city.

Despite the power of his words, however, Bishop Peralta was old and incapable of demanding thorough compliance with his decree. In fact no extant document has survived to say that it was even partially effective until the arrival of his replacement. In the new bishop, however, Don Cayetano Marcellano y Agramont who had been transferred from the Bishopric of La Paz, Bishop Peralta's proclamation on the fandango had found a new champion. In spite of the new bishop's motivation and efforts, he too had trouble in his attempt to enforce the ban, for by 1753 he was writing to King Ferdinand VI (no less!) in order to obtain support for the liturgical position. The following excerpt from the Bishop's File in the Archive of the Indies in Seville explains some of Bishop Marcellano y Agramont's predicament:

[Buenos Aires, 20 August 1753....
Lord:
Your Majesty's firm, reverent confidence of Catholic Christian Zeal encourages me to expose to your Royal attention a matter of such depth and weight that it has moved me to carry to your feet and circumstances this most carefully prepared reflection in compliance with my Pastoral Duty.

Maestro, Don, Fray Joseph de Peralta, who was Bishop of this Holy Cathedral Church, finding himself close to death, prohibited on universal sentence of total excommunication, thus withholding absolution to those of sound mind of either sex, who, among the concurrence of men and women, participate in the dances which around these parts are commonly called fandangos by edict of 30 July of the year 1743 which he expedited and commanded to be published in order that it would come to the attention of all of his flock.... These terms, which explain most especially the reckless wanton and inconsiderate liberty of the youth as they are practiced in this garrison, reveal that the dances are indubitably a shipwreck of consciences, the precipitated ruin of souls, in spite of the exhortation and and preaching in these kingdoms by the reverend fathers and Apostolic Missionaries of our Holy Religion who commonly consider these practices next to lewd sins and the gravest of vices: In this regard, the Zealous Prelates have ordained and do not cease to ordain by means of their councils, pastoral letters, and their edicts to their various bishoprics and provinces, the removal of the aforementioned dances....

Moreover, Bishop, Don, Fray Joseph de Peralta had been well informed, during the previous years of his ecclesiastical government, of equal measure concerning the virtue of modest and judicial secular officials and of specific individuals who had seen and witnessed the destruction associated with such diversions: but the denunciation of this is owing mainly to the persuasion of

confessors who with Christian fervor have desired that these
fires be extinguished completely in this capital city because of
the frequent disorders and infamous results, which since the
year 1735 or '36 until '46 were being noticed, and being experienced both inside of this port, with the occasion of the said dances, men and women concurring in the act of the dances and
outside of it, and not only in a room or dwelling but they were
executed in the residential patios because of the throngs of people who at the least rumor would meet by interesting themselves in so licentious an entertainment.... But the *Cabildo,* by
having permitted some dances which admit both sexes on the
condition that they would be practiced with restraint and decency without the character or name of fandangos, to which
there is an open door for all the men and women who wished
to attend them...(such) that simultaneously the vulgar street
people of that example were added to the extent that in order
to continue the dances with intolerable disorder that it was
deemed necessary to call in the said *Cabildo* to vigorously enforce the aforementioned edict, which generally prohibited all
dances that involve both sexes.... Being in these terms...the
satisfaction of the indomitable youth, having before their eyes
the adornment of the maidens, and the married women with
cunning movements of the body, and before their ears the pro-
vocative verses and sayings which turn on the ardor of lust...
thus it regularly attracts vices, and sins reign in one place....

Up to here I have informed your Majesty of the principal matter of this cause, but I have not yet presented for your high consideration the oppression which has resulted from the libertine
and little Christian impudence with which the Attorney General of the City produces in his writings, especially the latest of
which, in speaking of my proposals in confidence, he gives out
the name of attempted (unsuccessful) manifestos.... It was Don
Joseph Antonio de Escurra who acted to suspend and reform
the preceding censure against the dances...which enabled him
to strip me of my jurisdiction.... Your Majesty's Sovereign Aid
is welcomed in which Royal Sanctuary your loyal chaplains and
most faithful bishops always obtain in order that Your Majesty's
powerful shadow might contain the malice....

I hope that Your Majesty's most Religious Zeal may attend
these matters with your Paternal love so that the Spiritual
Government of this Diocese may run without obstacles in the
service of both Majesties....

Buenos Ayres, 20 August 1753 (signed)—Cayetano, Bishop of
Buenos Ayres] (Torre Revello 1926:274–81).

For all his good intentions, the new bishop turned out to be
rather zealous himself. The former Bishop of Buenos Aires, José de
Peralta, had prohibited only the fandango and other scandalous
couple dances like it. Notwithstanding, the new bishop intended to
ban couple dances altogether. Instead of naming specific dances
(except for occasional mention of the fandango), he prohibited
them *all,* making his crusade more straightforward than before
but considerably more difficult to enforce—especially among the
descendants of the light-footed Spaniards of that era who danced
with facility at every social rank. As shown in the underlined
words above, Bishop Marcellano y Agramont exaggerated the
former bishop's original edict.

The Cabildo, in turn, voiced the defensive, opposing view, and
proclaimed another interpretation of the original decree against
the fandango. The Attorney General himself, who was named in
the new bishop's report as Don Antonio de Escurra, responded with
a straightforward rebuttal of the new bishop's complaints. Escurra
wrote directly to the Council of Indies in Seville. In his letter he
never mentions the fandango directly (he does not seem to know
the ecclesiastical edicts except by hearsay!). Perhaps the omission
is intentional and more subtle: he reads his own favorite dances
into his opening reference to Bishop Peralta's proclamation,
thereby making yet another gross exaggeration from the opposing
viewpoint. No stranger to the language of appeals, however, the
Attorney General sprinkles his letter with the usual gushing superlatives so that it cannot offend. Most important and to the point,
he proposes, as a solution for the dilemma over the fandango, two
self-serving recommendations: (1) that the new bishop rescind the
punishment of excommunication for the entire city, and (2) that
all decent dances be allowed to continue, such as the minuet and
contredanse of his initial misquote. The following are portions of
his letter to Seville dated 22 August 1756:

[Joseph de Peralta, the most worthy Bishop who hailed from
this province, prohibited with total excommunication, universal

sentence, the dances of minuets and contredanses [sic!].... And since this is not all in the public interest, whose peace and tranquility are the first obligation of Your Grace, the current, most Illustrious Lord Bishop must be notified, exhorted, and required to absolve the previous sins of the entire city, or all that may be included in the aforesaid excommunication, and it must be removed....

It is indubitable that no dance is intrinsically bad or pernicious, but rather every situation is different, in which there is sufficient proof that it is the universal practice of all Christian people; everyone is accustomed to dancing as a public recreation, either with one sex separately or with both together; in fact none of the superior Tribunals nor the inferiors has ever dreamed of prohibiting them, and much less condemn them as sins. Even the Saints with totally austere lives never reproved them, but held them as useful, and many times as necessary in order to provide recreation for the youth.... There is no doubt that some parties and festivals serve as occasion for sin, but this is not common, nor is there a basis for argument, and since it is not a common vice, it cannot be prohibited generally, especially not with total excommunication.... Who can doubt that in a bullfight there are committed many grave sins? Who can doubt that in the concourse of processions, sermons, Masses of Holidays and other like occasions the lascivious youth unbridles and abuses the holy exercises in working depraved intentions? ....

Enfin, the Holy Mother Church, which gives the best rules and precepts for living well, has not only prohibited dances, but it is allowing them and tolerating them in all the other cities; thus being the case, there is no reason that on this basis that they be prohibited so rigorously here.... I ask Your consideration and beg that you attend to my request...Dr. Orencio Antonio de Escurra] (Torre Revello 1926:281–84).

After the governing Council of Indies in Seville had solicited letters and considerable evidence from both the religious and secular points of view, the Council undoubtedly set the rulings that would remain legal precedents for decades to come. The parties conceded as follows, if in the briefest of terms:

[Around 1746 the dances must have been abundant, as much in private as public places, because the Bishop of that time, Fray José Peralta Barnuevo, prohibited them once and for all. The episcopal resolution was not effective as set forth because a few years later, in 1752, his successor Mons. Cayetano Marcellano y Agramont returned to the subject, threatening the dancers with excommunication. But the City Council (of Buenos Aires) opposed this measure, so the conflict was resolved in the following manner: the Bishop suppressed the order of excommunication and the *Cabildo* or City Council would attempt to eradicate "the dances of the fandango"] (Trenti Rocamora 1948:116).

Thus the bishop faced not only Dr. Antonio de Escurra in the opposition but rather the entire City Council. Initially its members took care to write to the new bishop concerning the impasse. With a tone of unflagging respect for their prelate, they gave him every assurance in their letter that the fandango would be curtailed under their jurisdiction. They even provided some details of the new assignment and the chain of command for its enforcement if only the bishop would recant and rescind his curse on the city:

[The most illustrious Cabildo of Justice and of the Regiment of this most noble and very loyal City of the Holy Trinity, the Port of Saint Mary of Buenos Ayres, etc.
   To the most illustrious Lord, Doctor, Don Cayetano Marcellano y Agramont of His Majesty's most worthy Bishopric of this diocese of the Río de la Plata, etc. Be it known...that it is explained in his charges, principally in the latest ones, the aforementioned fiscal official...which by virtue of communications to Your Most Illustrious Highness that adequate means of enforcing the aforesaid punishment rests with him, with the Royal Justices, and with his other secular ministers to watch over, to exterminate from among the people those dances commonly called fandangos, and to see that there be all due moderation in the other festival dances...in order that the fandangos be stopped inasmuch as they are merely entertainments of the vulgar, ordinary class; and that there be introduced all dutiful moderation in celebrations with dancing when they are attended by men and women of all classes and spheres; therefore, in this case the aforementioned (sacred) censure must be rescinded....
   Buenos Ayres, 13 May 1754 (signed by ten members of the City Council and) By command of the Governing Lords,— Joseph Ferrera Feo, Scribe of the Public and of the Cabildo] (Torre Revello 1926:292–94).

The extermination order on the fandango was now imminent in the hands of secular authority. This was precisely what Bishop Marcellano y Agramont had always wanted, all the more so if it were to be accomplished by another agency. Nevertheless, his battle was not a total victory in the public view. After all, the Council of Indies dictated the outcome. The Council no doubt favored the secular enforcement of the ban on the fandango, ordered that the excommunication of all participants in it be rescinded, and allowed the other couple dances to continue without interruption. Thus the dancers interpreted the result as being in favor of Doctor Antonio de Escurra, the Attorney General. Unfortunately space does not permit exposing all the unfavorable rumblings and retorts sent to the Bishop which amply show that the Bishop never recuperated the loss of respect in the matter. His credibility was ruined in spite of all that happened in his favor.

*   *   *   *   *

As the mid-century clergymen aged, they took heart in the promise of the city officials who had agreed to ban the fandango. Like all citizens, they looked forward to a new generation of leadership and the increased authority of the crown. The new viceroyalty was created at Buenos Aires in 1776. Within two years the fandango was already an issue requiring maximum regional authority under Viceroy Juan José Vertiz. But the leaders were in for a surprise. That the fandango had continued was common knowledge; its infamy had not in the least diminished its practice. The secular leaders were either ineffectual in enforcing the ban or perhaps not even attempting it. So the chronic fandango would inevitably have to come before Viceroy Vertiz for a new ruling. First he had to consider all the previous legal problems with the fandango, the tide of religious proclamations against it, the recommendations of the Council of Indies in Seville, and the current decade of ineffective enforcement of its ban in the hands of city officials; then Vertiz ruled in favor of the dancers! He gave them free license to dance how and when they pleased. Horrified, the clergy would not rest again until they had carried the matter to even higher authority. They assessed the new ruling as follows:

[The moral situation of that epoch in Buenos Aires, which we
know through its chronicles and documents, was at a low level.... This situation reached its lowest ebb with the intent of
Vertiz's authorization which gave permission to dance the
fandango. The opposing view was taken up from the pulpit by
the Franciscan Father, Fray José Acosta who condemned the
procedures of the viceregal mandate] (Millé 1961:318).

During Vertiz's rule as viceroy, he had already provoked conspicuous friction with the new bishop, Dr. Juan Baltazar Maciel.
They were always at odds over certain public entertainments
which Vertiz preferred to ignore and Maciel wanted to ban:

[The dances and public baths gave origin to visible and daily
scandals; but above all, the burials of children which were celebrated at night (with dancing) gave credence to the fact that all
sorts of crimes were being committed against decency. The
scandal, in this case, went so high as to command the attention
of Señor Maciel, who in governing the diocese, prohibited them
categorically] (Cárbia 1914:II, 169).

However, Vertiz's viceroyal policy was to intervene as little as possible in such personal matters as dancing or bathing. So when Father José Acosta publicly opposed his ruling and condemned the
fandango again from the pulpit, the viceroy interpreted his action
as gross insubordination. The viceroy went straightaway to the
clergy and demanded a complete, public apology:

[This one (the viceroy), being offended, obliged Father Acosta's
immediate superior to apologize publicly for the aforementioned
criticism, and to declare that masquerade balls were not immoral, even when the *fandango* was danced in them] (Cárbia
1914:II, 170).

The conflict remained deadlocked. The viceroy and the bishop of
Buenos Aires were not to be reconciled but by the supreme religious and secular authority. The matter finally went to Madrid,
where King Charles III, the same who had expelled the Jesuit
presence in South America, now banned the fandango, once and
for all, on Christmas eve, 1774. In three separate documents that

remain in the Archive of the Indies, he commanded that the fandango and dances like it be prohibited forevermore (Cárbia 1914: II, 170).

In the end, we are reminded of the power of the clergy, particularly in matters of morality. It took more than a century to enforce their ban on the fandango in the Río de la Plata. Yet with the late support of the King and persistent curtailment from the local pulpit, they finally stamped out the fandango. Meanwhile, ironically, it continued on, unchecked in the Region of Andalusia, becoming a main feature in the *café cantante*, where flamenco music gained its wide following. The fandango also worked its way back into the recital repertoire. The result was echoed in the 19th-century memoirs of a certain Italian physician who came to the Río de la Plata. With regard to the fate of the fandango amongst the folk, he concluded on the following nostalgic note:

[The party ends with a ball that is nearly always realized to the jangle of two or three guitars. The most usual dance is the *pericón,* but also the *cielito* in battle or the *cielito* of the pocket, the *gato,* or the *aires* are danced. The *fandanguillo* of Andalusian origin is danced but rarely.... The vivacious and lascivious spark of Andalusian songs has been completely lost on the wide-open Argentine ranges] (Mantegazza 1875:68).

7. Summary and Conclusions

The fandango may be the oldest, most exotic, most widely diffused dance yet remaining in the European repertoire. It has survived in specialized performances of its original medium for voice, guitar, handclap, and castanets in Andalusia. Yet concerts of dance companies and recitals of solo and ensemble arrangements of the fandango have also continued to reinforce its development.

The fandango was a product of the cultural clash that resulted from the Moorish conquest and dominion of the southern third of the Iberian peninsula, which lasted from 711 to 1492. The Moors, or North African Mohammedans, came into Spain's territory and occupied mainly the region below the Sierra Morena range which frames Andalusia, bringing with them a cultural mix of Semitic peoples to what had been the west end of the Holy Roman Empire.

Specific musical traits of the fandango reveal a synergy of East and West, the unlikely combination of both great cultural streams which came together during the period of remarkable cultural synthesis under the Moors. The fandango is characterized by an expressive vocal melody derived from an Arabian mode; it contains an augmented second, corresponding to the Hijaz mode (E F G# A B C D), especially characteristic in the *falseta* or refrain. But other sections of the fandango's verse-like structure correspond to Western modes for contrast, while avoiding the augmented second. Nevertheless, the falseta always returns as the last section of the dance to leave the Arabian melody predominant, indeed triumphant, despite departures away from it. (Murcia emphasized the augmented second between his last two notes of melody as the crux of his example.) The melody of an authentic fandango remains ever modal rather than tonal in its conclusion.

The Moorish/Christian cultural clash endured for more than a millennium in the fandango. Its Arabian melodic characteristics were juxtaposed onto pre-existing harmonic practices of Iberia. The fandango's musical discourse contained the blend of a Near Eastern, Arabian melody superimposed onto the guitar's Western medieval harmony. Both the guitar and its chords were probably present in Iberia prior to the North African invasion. In the first place, the guitar itself was a vestige of Hellenic-Holy Roman culture that remained in Iberia, and it continued as the only chordal instrument of the fandango. The typical Arabian instruments were the *'ud* and *tanbur* (both lute types), but they never endured in Iberia like the guitar. Perhaps the lutes were simply too Arabian to survive during the Mohammedan occupation of Christendom. Moreover, during the occupation, the guitar must have seemed anarchic or at least exotic to the Moors. At any rate, the guitar was standardized as the fandango's accompanying instrument, as its players strummed in 3/4 time with full chords hit with the right-hand fingernails to add color, volume, and rhythmic zest. The chord tones of the accompaniment were derived primarily from the medieval Phrygian mode (E F G A B C D), and triads were built of these tones upon any note of the mode. (Ironically the mode of E F G A B C D, preserved in the fandango, is at once the medieval mode least familiar to our ears, yet the one most highly recommended in Plato's *Republic*.) However, the typical final cadence of the upper leading-tone chord of F resolving to the final chord of E contained a G# (with the Picardy third, making it an E-major chord) in order to resolve the G# tones of the superimposed melody. Transpositions were possible: those of Murcia and Domenico Scarlatti had one flat and ended on A like some of the flamenco variants of the fandango. Both Murcia and Scarlatti remind us, with their frequent cadences on the A major chord, that their fandangos are not poorly conceived pieces in the key of D minor, which never seem to end on the appropriate chord. Instead, their fandangos represent the mix of Hijaz melody over Phrygian harmony. The fandango's blend of East and West always hearkens back to Muslim *al-Andalus* and its era of racial tolerance.

Dissonance was inevitable, particularly in the chord progression of the falseta: paradoxically Am G F E accompanied a melody continuing with the augmented second and of course the G#. In other words, the final cadence on E major reconciled and resolved the melodic tendencies, despite the cross-relation with the root movement of the Am G F E progression. The melodic ambivalence of G-G# particularly following the note of F (resulting in the augmented second) must have created an effect analogous to the ear then as "blue notes" do today. Scarlatti retained precisely such crushed or crunched notes in his many sonatas under the designation of *acciaccatura*. Other dissonances resulted from the guitar's open strings while they were plucked or strummed occasionally as dissonant pedal tones, every one of which belonged to the Phrygian mode on E. All of these developments seem to have been in place prior to the Gypsy invasion into Andalusia during the 15th century, for the fandango lived on and continues apart from *cante jondo,* the Gypsy sub-stream of flamenco. Therefore, the dissonant, bi-modal fandango, the oldest part of the flamenco repertoire of Andalusia was indeed a fusion of Arabian and medieval European practices, and it has remained so up to the present day.

The fandango was a peasant dance of Andalusia until guitarists took a special interest in it. Once they began to perform the fandango regularly outside of its original context, it came to the notice of other musicians, which eventually ensured its viability. It lasted long after the Mohammedans and Sephardic Jews were driven out of Spain. Manuscript examples for guitar date back to 1705. Examples in the theatre repertoire began around then, also, which helped the fandango to invade the strata of European society. At that time the other accepted Spanish dances had begun to decline in popularity across Europe. Previously they had provided musicians, dancers, and audiences the abandon of wild or expressive entertainment: dances such as the folía, zarabanda, and chacona were beginning to lose their flavor. As European keyboard composers of the 18th century manipulated the Spanish Baroque dances according to compositional demands and slowed them down in order to write ever more subdivisions of the beat, the dances lost their vigor and their original cultural associations. Then the stage was set for another upbeat Spanish dance to reveal uninhibited expressions of sexual attraction and, to some extent, social anarchy. Inasmuch as the low-brow Spanish dances of the suite had lost their function in high-brow society, the fandango began to fill the need once satisfied by these other, ironically newer dances from Spain.

The fandango had sensational character because of its sensual choreography and its noisy surrounding nucleus of spectators. Its choreography started with the fixed stare between the dancing partners as they drummed their castanets. Then they enacted a pantomime of intimate love—and who could better witness to the fact than Casanova, the 18th century's Don Juan? Yet besides the lovers' gestures to appropriate music, the scene was completed by the rhythmic hand-clapping and noisy shouts from the crowd of witnesses: they exchanged a volley of insults, back and forth among themselves; or shouted rude compliments for the dancers; the observers induced them to ever more abandon towards the accelerando climax of their dance. The crowd of witnesses is preserved today in the flamenco *tablao*, the group on the raised wooden platform which amplifies the volume and delimits the space of the performance. The fandango was at once the sexiest, most unruly dance of 18th-century Europe—all the more so with the diffusion of its infamy as the spectators learned this active, upbeat participation which even enhanced theatrical versions.

The fandango came out first in Spain's comic farces around 1700, at the time comic operas and plays were emerging elsewhere, and it too eulogized some of the low-class activities that they did. Then the fandango followed the other Spanish dances and the guitar into the court. French music reigned at Madrid's 18th-century court for obvious reasons among the Bourbons. Yet since they revitalized the guitar in Madrid (stemming as they did from the line of guitar-players initiated by Louis XIV), they stimulated a resurgence of guitar practice among courtly dilettantes, starting with Queen Marie-Louise-Gabrielle of Savoy. She was the guitarist who employed Santiago de Murcia as her own instructor and likely the one who granted space to the fandango in the fare of courtly instrumental music. But since she came to her post from Naples, the young Queen may not have known all the infamy of the dance. During the next generation, an apologetic title from among the booksellers of Madrid revealed some of the lingering stigma against it: "**1785:** Fandango for keyboard, composed of tasty variations which can serve instrumentalists who admit this piece."

In Europe beyond the Pyrenees, the fandango never became as well diffused as its Spanish predecessors of the Baroque suite. But just the same, Mozart saw to its inclusion in *The Marriage of Figaro* (1786) which was patterned after the Beaumarchais comedy of the same name for the story and possibly the *"Fandango del Signore Scarlate"* for his musical point of departure. Mozart's fandango was the centerpiece of his ensemble finale to close Act III. He used it to achieve maximum contrast as section B of a ternary form. Sections A and B were made to contrast in key and mode (from C major to A minor), in meter (from 4/4 to 3/4), from a loud chorus to a marked *p* [piano] for instruments, from an exhilarating, populous march to a strangely exotic, solo dance. If contrast were Mozart's secret of success, perhaps it was due to the age in which he lived. Dickens characterized the Enlightenment thus:

> It was the best of times, it was the worst of times, it was the age of wisdom, it was the age of foolishness, it was the epoch of belief, it was the epoch of incredulity, it was the season of Light, it was the season of Darkness, it was the spring of hope, it was the winter of despair.... It was the year of our Lord one thousand seven hundred and seventy-five (Dickens 1859:3)

Whether Mozart orchestrated the fandango from the basis of his own taste and genius, or whether he was merely impelled by the tendency of his times, the contrast was sufficiently clear. Likewise, the fandango's actual history was filled with polar opposites every bit as striking as these while it conquered Hispanic America. There the fandango certainly contained all the bawdy dissolution that it had in Europe, but yet more: some of the clergy may have been associated with it directly. Since the dance represented the opposite pole to the polite, Catholic, conservative Hispanic society of its heyday in South America, the fandango flourished until the clergy had stamped it out with their moral tirades which were eventually reinforced by royal decree.

Santiago de Murcia's outstanding specimen, found in Mexico and only recently published in facsimile, has shown not only that fandangos of quality were known in the Americas, but also that fandangos had been performed as recital-quality guitar solos as far back as the 1730s. What's more, Murcia's fandango, having preceded Domenico Scarlatti's by at least a decade at court, undoubtedly obtained aristocratic acceptance of this dance with his patron, the Queen, so that keyboard composers like José de Nebra, Scarlatti, and his student Padre Antonio Soler, could begin to explore the fandango as an artistic medium with the sanction of their aristocratic supporters. Thereafter, the fandango, with the gradual disappearance of its former low-class stigma, became quite acceptable anywhere. Today's guitarists have long needed this historical precedent, even if it came from the Americas, in order to authenticate and justify their solo recitals.

Whereas Murcia's fandango was an excellent instrumental solo, most of the references to the American fandangos were to the original combination of a vocal solo with guitar accompaniment, marked by occasional hand-clapping or other percussive touches. The fandango was well diffused among the guitar scenes of Hispanic America, for the 18th- and 19th-century travellers there left numerous accounts of it. The fandango appeared in Mexico and Colombia in the 1730s, and within a decade in Peru, Venezuela, the Guianas, Chile, and extensively in the Río de la Plata.

Obviously the fandango did not escape the social forces which hone the history of any major cultural expression. Aristocratic and public acceptance shaped its progress through the hourglass of time. When the fandango came into the Río de la Plata, two special, pre-existing social conditions heightened its impact: (1) the general inclination to dance among the population, and (2) the bawdy environment of the pulpería shops where it was so often performed.

When the fandango arrived, it was certainly not the first dance in the Río de la Plata. The inclination to dance was neither new nor unusual there, for dancing was already a popular pastime for both the native and Hispanic populations. As early as 1594, Father Alonso de Bárzana, an Andalusian priest of the Jesuit Order wrote to describe the music of the Plata Indians:

> [All these nations are given to dancing and singing, and so earnestly that some populations pass the entire night in singing, dancing, and drinking. Among them, the *Lules* are the best musicians from childhood, and with the most entertaining pieces and songs, they not only celebrate all of their festivals by singing, but also their deaths by involving the entire town singing together as well as crying and drinking.... Also, a great part of the people in *Córdoba* are very inclined to sing and dance, and after having worked or walked the entire day, they dance or sing in choirs the greater part of the night] (*Relaciones geográficas* 1885:II, lviii).

As demonstrated in Part II, the Spanish monarchy advocated dancing by example, from the King down through the gamut of his subjects. All levels of Plata society were inclined to dance, as well. The following items show that some dance teachers were already prospering there, just as they were simultaneously in Spain like Esquivel Navarro and Figaro, as specialized professionals:

> [**1605.** The Priest Alonso de Cámara makes mention of "Agustín Mejía, a black, who taught dancing."
> **1608.** In the expense accounts made on behalf of the young Catalina González is read the following: "At that time 50 pesos were spent on Maestro Lázaro López, dance instructor. He taught the girl to dance all of the dances to the extent that she became very proficient in them, which is customary among the daughters of honored men"] (Grenón 1954).

Thus in addition to the importance of dancing among the Indians of the Plata, the aristocrats of the Hispanic colony there were also cultivating the practice. When the fandango arrived it was but a new amusement in an old and well-established repertoire among the black, Hispanic, and Amerindian factions of a society inclined to dance.

Throughout Hispanic America *pulperías,* or shops for sundries and alcoholic beverages, had begun to dot the countryside as well as the corners of the city streets. Pulpería shops preceded the fandango by at least a century and a half in South America. They were known for better or for worse: as the lone establishment out in the countryside, the pulpería was a desert oasis in a sea of waving grass, a postal stop, and a low- to middle-class social institution in the absence of others. Even in town, they provided the necessities of life (like guitar frets and strings). They were also the centers of gambling, contraband, or rarely, prostitution. Thus, well before the fandango arrived around 1730, South America was already full of these infamous taverns that could satisfy all the appetites.

Judicial records show that there was a guitar for general use in at least some of the pulperías (1796, Table 12). In fact the proprietors often hung the guitar conspicuously on the wall of their establishments in order to invite impromptu performances. According to Azara, every pulpería had a guitar, and it was played to excess. Consequently guitarists, entertaining in these rowdy taverns and trying to make their music ever more interesting to the pulpería audience, contributed regularly to the disturbance of the peace. When the fandango arrived, it only introduced more disorder to their unruly entertainments. There was already a primed audience for the fandango among the macho *majos* in the pulperías, and, within that group, a clique of guitar aficionados was waiting to learn the latest dance hit from Spain. Inevitably, then, political and religious leaders had to curtail the excesses in the interest of polite society. The problem was easy to identify but hard to nip in the bud: leaders of both factions prohibited guitar playing at night in order to curtail the disorder, but the enforcement of the ban became a new problem in and of itself. In such cases, colonial administrators imposed curfews repeatedly, over the course of two centuries, in order to ban guitar music after nightfall, as at the locations of Fig. 14:

Fig. 14 Prohibitions against Evening Guitar Music	
Viceroy of New Spain, Mexico City	2 Jan. 1609
Mayor of Córdoba, Argentina	13 Jan. 1690
Gov. Bermúdez de Castro of Buenos Aires	7 Jan. 1716
Police of San Gerónimo de Alhuí, Chile	1774
Gov. Paula Sanz of Buenos Aires	1788
Town Council, San Juan Bautista, Urug.	20 Jan. 1797
Governor of the Dominican Republic	1818

But the curfews were only the capital events, the civil ordinances to deal with the infamous guitar. The specific incidents of Part IV, the individual crimes, lawsuits, complaints, and hearings that implicated the infamous guitar and its players for disturbing the peace, for inciting indecency, drunken brawling, sacrilege, concubinage, homicide, and the like, were far too numerous to mention again in summary. Suffice it to say briefly that the many locations of these incidents ran south from old Los Angeles to Guatemala City, across the Caribbean, and around the complete periphery of Hispanic South America.

The Rioplatense guitar was the common denominator of the serenade, the pulpería, and the fandango. Since the fandango was merely a new dance in the millennial popular culture of Spain, the guitar provided historical continuity to the separate stages of its development. As documented in Table 13, The Guitar, Serenade, and Fandango, these aspects of entertainment were all related and quite popular in the interior towns of Argentine territory. There guitarists regularly used their instrument as a pretense for social encounters. In Córdoba, the guitar in hand after sundown meant that the player was in search of either social contact or diversion: in 1759 guitarists were singing on a street corner at 2:00 A.M.; in 1762 Posadas and Díaz went out strolling one evening with the guitar in hand; in 1784 it was used in entertainment from Vespers until dawn; again in 1784 two young men dropped in for a visit at one lady's house where they were promptly offered a guitar (though only Guerrero played it, for the other was disguised in the habit of a monk!); in 1805 a mulatto slave named Juan led a libertine existence—he had no other life than to circulate around to performances and fandangos because of his stature as a guitar player and singer.

Father Grenón was the foremost researcher of his day in drawing these situations from criminal records in and around Córdoba —both from religious and secular sources. They demonstrated how and to what extent the guitar was used at the bottom ranks of society. The records were extremely valuable (and continue to be so) because they were signed, sworn testimonies, complete with date and place. In most cases, professionals carefully prepared these testimonials for presentation at briefs, trials, or judicial rulings. Thus, under threat of perjury, the witnesses of these papers reliably documented the pervasive impact of the guitar on a branch of society that has previously eluded assessment due to the lack of data.

The tables of Part IV on "The Guitar in the Streets and Pulperías" and "The Guitar, Serenade, and Fandango" demonstrate, beyond the shadow of a doubt the infamy of the guitar. The reader interested in pursuing the matter further, particularly with regard to the guitar in the serenade and fandango, would have to consult Grenón's 1957 article, *"Musicatas episódicas: Antiguas costumbres locales, 1749–1840)"* [Periodic Serenades: Old Local Customs (1749–1840)]. There, as in the tables of Part IV, the sad tales involving domestic disputes, the triangle of lovers battling over a woman they both desire, and drunken, homicidal duels— usually involving the guitar or fandango in one way or another— bring credence to the gauchesque literature. Such writing was a fictional medium that typified the gaucho as one who got into trouble with the guitarists of tavern serenades while in pursuit of adventure. The gauchos always ended up facing one of two difficult situations: either amorous conquests not unlike those of Don Juan, or duels with rivals which finished in bloodshed and left the winner a social outcast. The winner achieved bittersweet victory: as he avenged his pride, honor, and machismo, he also became a *gaucho malo* who had to lead a life of self-imposed exile in order to avoid the pursuit of authorities. Both of José Hernández's notorious characters, Cruz and Martín Fierro are literary types who live on the margins of society as a result of musical encounters turned sour. Yet their experiences are neither more strange nor more colorful than Father Grenón's examples. But Grenón's were not fictitious; they were absolutely true-to-life. As he researched painstakingly during the 1920s, he drew them primarily from the Tribunal Archives of Córdoba—in fact, mostly from the Criminal Division! While they sometimes reveal the best of society, just as often they portray its worst vices and pitiful consequences. Therefore, though he was a Jesuit priest, his writings on the fandango are an uncensored, objective portrayal of music among the dregs of society. For a non-musical comparison, Grenón's collection of documents is not unlike *The Garden of Delights* (the Renaissance painting now in the Prado Museum) by Hieronymus Bosch who was also a priest. Grenón's references are a garden of delights for the early guitar.

The fandango impacted Rioplatense literature of the 18th and 19th centuries. It appeared initially in the first Rioplatense piece for the theatre entitled *El amor de la estanciera,* dating from around 1780. The fandango highlighted the wedding reception at the end of it, to the accompaniment of Marcos's guitar. From then on, the fandango continued prominently in plays, novels, and in the gauchesque poetry that constituted the main literary medium of the 19th century. Its writers simultaneously duplicated history and the *verismo,* true-to-life style. They put a fatal fandango or tavern serenade as the crux of the story, as in fictional examples from the lives of Cruz or Martín Fierro, or in true but romanticized biographies of Santos Vega or Alejandro Rodríguez. In these tales, an author's usual agenda was to justify the actions of the musical gaucho-renegade by revealing the inevitable but picturesque circumstances dictated by his "fate" or the force of destiny. They ended by absolving the gaucho from guilt and responsibility: succeeding admirably at their goal, these authors contributed to his immortalization. Today the guitar-playing gaucho remains a controversial, looming figure over the Plata's historic past.

Throughout its history in the Americas, the term *fandango* underwent an interesting semantic development. While it continued to imply a specific couple dance, just as in Spain, the term expanded in its meaning to encompass references to a low-class

ball. The term eventually became a literary metaphor for a fight in
a play of the revolutionary period of Argentina entitled *Defense
and Triumph of Tucumán* (Morante 1821) and in the biography
of *El Clinudo* published in Uruguay (Pollo Darraque 1884).

During some refined concerts of the 19th century, the fandango
appeared on stage. Musicians performed the fandango in recitals,
as in the case of Argentine guitarist and physician, Dr. Nicanor
Albarellos who interpreted his own version of the fandango for
guitar and orchestra in Montevideo. Women, such as guitarist
Dolores de Gambín, or dance companies armed authentic performances for the recital stage. Thus by this time, a century after
its introduction to the Americas, the fandango had meandered into
two streams—for two separate audiences. Its low-class channel
had gone too far astray as a scene of dissolute orgy to be rescued by
any recitals of polished or authentic models not far removed from
Andalusia. The low-class fandango had become equated with
everything opposed to decency, law, and order: "They went out to
fandangos where are frequent both drinking and fighting, as
everybody knows," according to Córdoba's Tribunal Archive, 1827.

Understandably, then, Church leaders were unanimously opposed to the fandango. Over the course of a century and a half they
thwarted its every aspect from the pulpit. Already in 1743, the
aged Fray José de Peralta, the same Bishop of Buenos Aires who
had visited the Jesuit missions, went so far as to recommend con-
fiscation of the musical instruments used in performances of the
fandango, and excommunication for all who participated in it.
Other bishops joined in his cause by issuing similar canonical ad-
monitions. Peralta's champion was his immediate successor, Don
Cayetano Marcellano y Agramont who had just come from the
Bishopric of La Paz to fill the vacancy. Then the Bishops of Caracas, Venezuela and Cartagena, Colombia lent their simultaneous support by prohibiting the fandango during the 1760s. Again
in Buenos Aires, their front was continued into the new Viceroyalty of the Río de la Plata by Franciscan José Acosta, and into the
new bishopric by Dr. Juan Baltazar Maciel. The clergy made repeated decrees against the fandango with the Latin-language
pronouncement of *excomunion maior, latae sententiae* [universal
sentence of total excommunication], leaving their subjects cut off

from all the Church sacraments, services, and other benefits. The Church officials were absolutely uniform in prohibiting absolution from sin and salvation in the next life—in no uncertain terms—if their parishoners so much as performed or danced the fandango.

Their relentless tirade from the pulpit was not fully understood by secular leaders, however. The politicians also opposed the public disorder caused by the fandango, but some of them were elected officials. In Cartagena and Buenos Aires they regarded the clerical ruling of excommunication as quite overzealous: if implemented, it would have alienated their political constituencies. Thus political leaders could not enforce what they believed to be a fanatical view. One politician in particular, the Attorney General of Buenos Aires, Dr. Orencio Antonio de Escurra argued against Bishop Cayetano y Agramont in respectful but open confrontation. As spokesman of the secular viewpoint, he exaggerated Bishop Peralta y Barnuevo's original proclamation by misquoting and by extending the ban to such newer, polite dances as "minuets and contredanses." His bottom line was a demand for compromise: the new bishop was to respond in an open letter in which he would recant. The Attorney General agreed to restrain the fandango by civil law on the following condition: he would prosecute any participants in the fandango provided that the bishop would simultaneously withdraw the order of excommunication. The bishop rescinded his order of excomunication, as agreed, yet the Attorney General never enforced the law, and thus the indecision on the issue continued to fester. But the religious leaders were not about to let the issue die. They appealed to the King of Spain because the Pope had delegated to him ultimate religious authority in Hispanic America. The Council of the Indies intervened and carefully reviewed the case in the manner of a supreme court; the Council demanded profuse documentation in support of both sides of the issue. The Council also recommended a course of moderation for the bishops. Finally the fandango came before the new Viceroy Vertiz for a definitive judgment, just prior to his inauguration. Even though the viceroy was not an elected official, he wanted to please the masses: Vertiz ruled in favor of the dancers! Never say die: the bishops by-passed all the bureaucracy and intervening authorities until at long last they reached King Charles III, himself. Again they elicited his Royal

Proclamation for prohibiting the South American fandango: once and for all on Christmas Eve, 1774, Charles III banned it, as shown below, along with a summary of its numerous precedents:

| Fig. 15 Religious Edicts against Lascivious Dances ||
authority, title—location—date	purpose
Fernando de Trejo Bishop of Tucumán, 1597	Prohibits the performing and singing of lascivious dances.
Bartolomé Lobo Guerrero Archbishop of Lima, 27 Oct. 1613	Prohibits the vihuela and indecent songs.
Juan Cárdenas Inquisition, Guatemala City, 25 Feb. 1704	Reaffirms ban on indecent dances.
José de Peralta Bishop of Buenos Aires, 30 Jul. 1746	Prohibits the fandango among musicians and dancers alike.
Cayetano Marcellano y Agramont Bishop of Buenos Aires, 20 Aug. 1753	Reaffirms Peralta's prohibition.
Diego Antonio Bishop of Caracas, 20 May 1761	Prohibits the fandango and other dances.
Diego Peredo Bishop of Cartagena, c.1763	Prohibits the fandango and other dances.
Father Guanare Bishop of Caracas, 1771	Reaffirms Bishop Antonio's prohibition of 1761.
José Acosta Franciscan priest of Buenos Aires, 1774	Prohibits the fandango.
Charles III King of Spain, 24 Dec. 1774	Prohibits the fandango and dances like it.
Juan B. Maciel Bishop of Buenos Aires, 1776	Prohibits dances and other vices.
Inquisition letter to Fr. Gabriel Tulancingo, Mexico, 26 Feb. 1789	Suggests ban on scandalous fandangos.

Even though all the religious decrees against the fandango did not take immediate effect, they certainly set in motion its decrescendo. At the same time, as the fandango was losing some of its sensational novelty after several generations, it was becoming less popular. To be sure, some examples of the fandango, whether as a couple dance, a low-class, clamorous ball, or at worst a brawl, continued on into the 19th century after the decrees (the occasion cited by Russian observer Platon Alexandrovich Chikhachev in Part V, is a case in point.) But the surviving examples began to diminish in number, and even the literary references became more and more isolated towards 1900. Uruguayan writer Florencio Sánchez, for instance, did not mention it at all in his popular, turn-of-the-century plays composed and enacted in the capitals.

However, the fandango was a case by itself; within the first decade after its introduction to the Plata region, it became the target of extraordinary, unrelenting religious opposition. In the end, the fandango had withstood more than a century of liturgical cross-fire. But the religious leaders of the Plata, using the maximum penalty at their disposal in conjunction with legal and royal sanctions, finally achieved their coveted goal by 1900. They obliterated the old fandango as a blight of the past.

In retrospect, the lusty enthusiasm with which the populace took up the fandango versus the moral tirades against it point to the extremes of Rioplatense society. The Church fathers represented the devout, law-abiding, conservative faction of a society which was clearly the continued, protracted course inherited from Seville. The wild, opposite extreme, also originating in Seville, dated back to the New World conquest and back to the vihuela and lascivious dances which were condemned at Tucumán and Lima around 1600.

The diametric opposition between the sacred and the secular in Seville was as ancient as *Semana Santa* (the celebration of Holy Week) versus *tauromachia* (the pre-Christian ritual of the bull-fight), and as recent as the operatic dialogue of Micaela versus Carmen. A large part of the opposition was a result of the success and power of the Church in Seville. Its members had developed a conservative pietism not found elsewhere in Europe. The main reasons behind this intense, religious devotion were embedded in 16th-century geographical, racial, and social circumstances:

(1) the Church there was located far below the Pyrenees, leaving it isolated from Rome and central Europe;
(2) Seville was also located below the Sierra Morena, leaving it isolated from Spanish religious centers outside the *Región de Andalucía*;
(3) the Reconquest of Andalusia in 1492 brought the need to eradicate non-Christian values;
(4) the establishment of a rigorous Inquisition insured against failure or regression to Islam;
(5) intense orthodoxy replaced non-Christian beliefs and cultural ways;
(6) the Church's strength was reinforced again in the 16th-c. Council of Trent and the ensuing Counter-Reformation

The fandango in Seville faced an army of opposition: the ortho-
dox Christians, who were inspired by the rigor and strength of the
Church in Andalusia. To the faithful majority, the fandango was
more than a noisy, sensual spectacle: the fandango flaunted social,
political, and even racial anarchy. After all, it was born of an incon-
ceivable, morganatic union of Eastern and Western musical
parents; it was all too reminiscent of the splendor of the North
African occupation. For seven centuries both the Moors and Islam
reigned *al-Andalus*, so, once peace was established with the Reconquest, the Church fathers were partly responsible for overcoming
the former glory and replacing it with the new order:

Fig. 16
Life in Seville after 1492:
Secular versus Sacred

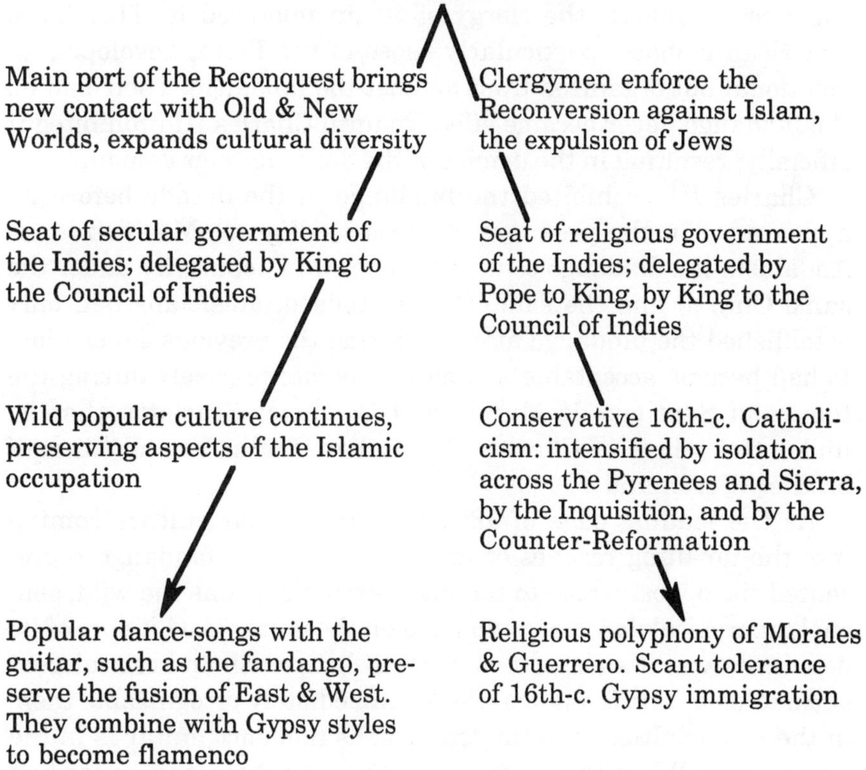

Main port of the Reconquest brings
new contact with Old & New
Worlds, expands cultural diversity

Clergymen enforce the
Reconversion against Islam,
the expulsion of Jews

Seat of secular government of
the Indies; delegated by King to
the Council of Indies

Seat of religious government
of the Indies; delegated by
Pope to King, by King to the
Council of Indies

Wild popular culture continues,
preserving aspects of the Islamic
occupation

Conservative 16th-c. Catholicism: intensified by isolation
across the Pyrenees and Sierra,
by the Inquisition, and by the
Counter-Reformation

Popular dance-songs with the
guitar, such as the fandango, preserve the fusion of East & West.
They combine with Gypsy styles
to become flamenco

Religious polyphony of Morales
& Guerrero. Scant tolerance
of 16th-c. Gypsy immigration

These extraordinary social, religious, and even racial extremes of Seville also framed the background of Rioplatense life, yet additional circumstances there polarized the secular and the sacred even further than before for the colonists. The Plata colony was also isolated from Rome; in order to deal with this fact, the Pope had delegated all religious authority in the vast Hispanic American continents to the Spanish Crown. And the colonists there also faced the compromise of Catholicism in the adoption of pagan gods or ideals, and the dissolution of their European race. After all, the Spanish conquerors had not been successful in overcoming the Amerindian population of the Plata until they had mixed the two races at Asunción. Therefore, under the imminent threat of racial, religious, and political dissolution, the clergy had no greater cause for concern than moral decadence. Their stance against the fandango revealed just how conservative they were; their counterparts, the clergy of Spain tolerated it. The South American bishops, particularly those of the Plata, developed an emotional but organized front against the fandango. Their ban on the fandango never became effective until Charles III prohibited it officially, resulting in the demise of the dance in their domain.

Charles III prohibited the fandango in the decade before its appearance in the première of Mozart's *Figaro*. Meanwhile, in Andalusia the fandango continued to grow in popularity under the same Church and the same Crown. Indeed, musicians had only established the fandango at court during the previous generation. It had become acceptable among aristocrats precisely during the tenure of Santiago de Murcia and Domenico Scarlatti, that is, under the reigns of Charles III's father (Philip V) and his half brother (Ferdinand VI).

As the leading edge of 18th-century popular culture coming into the far-flung reaches of Imperial Spain, the fandango represented the opposite pole to the pious extreme: it was the wild, sensual, anarchical dance accompanied on the guitar. And if part of its popularity was low class, it was intensely Spanish and reminiscent of Andalusia. The fandango was as immediately recognizable then, in the viceroyalties of Latin America, as flamenco guitar is in the world today. When the fandango reached the Plata, the guitar had already been firmly established as the national instrument. In fact, it had grown within a pan-social context for two centuries that even included its ceremonial use in outpost churches! But after the guitar's association with the fandango as its foil, the guitar's life in religious ceremonies could not last for long. From this point forward, the guitar became a totally secular instrument for use in popular or aristocratic circles. In the hands of expert popular or classical performers, the music of the Rioplatense guitar would blossom into ever more refined and specialized styles. The process of this growth in the repertoire continued to evolve until the old Hispanic American version of the fandango had become passé. New, upbeat dances of the Plata replaced the fandango that, at a moment of history, had loomed so important in providing adventure and abandon for all who dared to perform it. Ultimately the South American fandango's 150-year glory was but a season when compared to the millennial trajectory of the guitar and fandango in Europe.

8. References Cited in Part IV

Alvarez, Juan
1908   *Orígenes de la música argentina.* [Rosario: n.p.]

Alvarez Martínez, Rosario
1986   "My Scarlatti Discoveries," *Keyboard Classics* (Paramus, NJ)
        VI, No. 5, 4–5.

Alvarez Martínez, Rosario, ed.
1984   *José Herrando, Doménico Scarlatti, Francisco Courcell, José
        de Nebra y Agustino Massa: Obras inéditas para tecla.*
        Madrid: Sociedad Española de Musicología.

El amor de la estanciera, sainete [anon.].
c.1787 Mariano Bosch, ed. Instituto de Literatura Argentina, Sección
        de Documentos, Tomo IV, No. 1. Buenos Aires: Imprenta de la
        Universidad, 1925.

Ayestarán, Lauro
1953   *La música en el Uruguay,* Volumen I. Montevideo: Servicio
        Oficial de Difusión Radio Eléctrica.

Azara, Félix
1801   *Viajes por la América del Sur...desde 1789 hasta 1801.* Monte-
        video: Biblioteca del Comercio del Plata, 1846.

Beaumarchais, Pièrre Augustin Caron de
1964   *Théâtre complète. Lettres relatives a son théâtre.* Paris:
        Gallimard, 1957, 1964.

Bossio, Jorge A.
1972   *Historia de las pulperías.* Buenos Aires: Plus Ultra.

Calzavara, Alberto
1987   *Historia de la música en Venezuela: Período hispánico con
        referencias al teatro y la danza.* [Caracas:] Fundación
        Pampero.

Cárbia, Rómulo D.
1914   *Historia eclesiástica del Río de la Plata,* Tomos I–II.
        Buenos Aires: Alfa y Omega.

Coopersmith, J.M.
1949   *Music and Musicians of the Dominican Republic.* Washing-
        ton, D.C.: Pan American Union.

Cotarelo y Mori, Emilio
1911   *Loas, bailes, jácaras, mojigangas desde fines del siglo XVI a
        mediados del XVIII,* 2 vols. Madrid: Bailly-Bailliere.

Delano, Amasa
  1817   A Narrative of Voyages and Travels in the Northern and Southern
          Hemispheres: Comprising Three Voyages Round the World....
          Boston: E.G. House. Facs. ed. Upper Saddle River, New Jersey:
          The Gregg Press, 1970.

Descripción del Virreinato del Perú: Crónica inédita de comienzos del
  c.1615 siglo XVII [anon.]. Edición, prólogo y notas de Boleslao Lewin.
          Rosario: Universidad Nacional del Litoral, Facultad de Filosofía,
          Letras y Ciencias... 1958.

Dickens, Charles
  1859   A Tale of Two Cities. London. H.G. Buehler and L. Mason, eds.
          New York: Macmillan, 1922.

Ferandiere, Fernando
  1799   Arte de tocar la guitarra española por música, compuesto
          y ordenado por D. Fernando Ferandiere, Profesor de música
          en esta corte. Madrid: Pantaleón Aznar. Complete facsimile
          edition with an introduction, English translation, and tran-
          scription of the music by Brian Jeffery. London: Tecla
          Editions, 1977.

Grenón, Pedro J., S.J.
  1929   Nuestra primera música instrumental: Datos históricos.
          Buenos Aires: Emilio Perrot.

  1954   "Nuestra primera música instrumental: Datos históricos,
          segunda edición," Revista de Estudios Musicales (Universidad
          Nacional de Cuyo, Mendoza) Año II (1950–51), 11–96; Año III
          (1954), 173–220.

  1957   "Musicatas episódicas: Antiguas costumbres locales (1749–
          1840)," Historia (Buenos Aires) III, No. 9, 33–63.

Guamán Poma de Ayala, Felipe
  c.1600 Nueva corónica y buen gobierno: Codex péruvien illustré. Facs.
          ed. Université de Paris, Travaux et Mémoires de l'Institut
          d'Ethnologie XXIII. Paris: Institut d'Ethnologie, 1936.

Hernández, José
  1879   El gaucho Martín Fierro. Buenos Aires: Imprenta de la Pampa,
          1872. La vuelta de Martín Fierro. Buenos Aires: Librería del
          Plata, 1879. [Both republished with "xilografías" by Alberto
          Nicasio] 9th ed. Buenos Aires: Ediciones Peuser, 1960.

Juan, Jorge and Antonio de Ulloa
  1748   Relación histórica del viaje a la América Meridional...con
          otras varias observaciones. Madrid. A Voyage to South
          America: Describing at Large the Spanish Cities, Towns,
          Provinces; etc.... John Adams, trans. London: 1806. Repub-
          lished by Irving A. Leonard, ed. New York: Knopf, 1964.

1749   *Discourse and Political Refelctions on the Kingdoms of Peru.
        Their Government, Special Regimen of Their Inhabitants, and
        Abuses....* John J. Tepaske, ed. and trans. Norman: Univer-
        sity of Oklahoma Press, 1978.

Lemaitre, Eduardo
1980   *Breve historia de Cartagena, 1501–1901.* Bogotá: Ediciones
        Tercer Mundo.

Levillier, Roberto, ed.
1926   *Papeles eclesiásticos del Tucumán: Documentos originales del
        Archivo de Indias, Volumen I.* Colección de Publicaciones
        Históricas de la Biblioteca del Congreso Argentino. Madrid:
        Juan Pueyo.

"Libro de diferentes cifras de gitara [sic] escojidas de los mejores autores"
1705   (anon.), MS No. 811. Madrid: Biblioteca Nacional.

Mantegazza, Pablo
1876   *Viajes por el Río de la Plata y el interior de la Confederación
        Argentina...*tercera edición corregida por el autor, Milán,
        1876, traducidos por el Consejero de la Universidad, Doctor
        Juan Heller. Buenos Aires: Universidad de Tucumán & Coni
        Hermanos, 1916.

Manuel, Peter
1986   "Evolution and Structure in Flamenco Harmony," *Current
        Musicology* (New York) No. 42, 46–57.

Millé, Andrés
1961   *Crónica de la Orden Franciscana en la conquista del Perú,
        Paraguay y el Tucumán y su convento antiguo de Buenos
        Aires, 1210–1800.* Buenos Aires: Emecé.

Minguet y Yrol, Pablo
1774   *Reglas, y advertencias generales para tañer la guitarra, tiple,
        y vandola.* Madrid: Printed by the author.

Moll, Jaime
1969   "Una bibliografía musical periódica de fines del siglo XVIII,"
        Anuario Musical (Barcelona) XXIV, 1–12.

Morante, Ambrosio
1821   *Defensa y triunfo del Tucumán: Pieza militar en dos actos.*
        Instituto de Literatura Argentina, Sección de Documentos,
        Tomo IV, No. 3. Buenos Aires: Imprenta de la Universidad,
        1926.

Mozart, J.C. Wolfgang Amadeus
1786   *Le nozze di Figaro* in *Wolfgang Amadeus Mozart's Werke:
        Kritisch durchgesehene Gesamtausgabe,* Ser. 5, No. 17.
        Leipzig: Breitkopf und Haertel, 1876–1907.

Murcia, Santiago de
   1732   "Passacalles y obras de guitarra por todos los tonos naturales
           y acidentales...1732," MS Add. 31640. London: British
           Library.

   c.1732 *Saldívar Codex No. 4: Santiago de Murcia Manuscript of
           Baroque Guitar Music (c.1732) Found and Acquired in Septem-
           ber 1943 in León, Guanajuato, Mexico by the Mexican Musicol-
           ogist Dr. Gabriel Saldívar y Silva (1909–1980).* Volume 1, *The
           Manuscript: Complete Facsimile Edition with Commentary*,
           Michael Lorimer, ed. Santa Barbara: Michael Lorimer, 1987.

Pereira Salas, Eugenio
   1941   *Los orígenes del arte musical en Chile.* Santiago: Imprenta
           Universitaria.

Pinnell, Richard
   1979   "Santiago de Murcia's Baroque Guitar Entabulation of
           Corelli's Violin Sonata, Op. 5, No. 8," *Soundboard* (Palo Alto)
           VI, 134–37.

   1980   *Francesco Corbetta and the Baroque Guitar, with a Transcrip-
           tion of His Works.* 2 vols. Studies in Musicology Series No. 25.
           Ann Arbor: UMI Research Press.

   1984   "The Guitarist-Singer of Pre-1900 Gaucho Literature," *Latin
           American Music Review* (Austin, TX) V, No. 2, 243–62.

Pollo Darraque, Ricardo
   1884   *El Clinudo: Un gaucho alzao,* published in installments of
           La Tribuna Popular. Republished as "Dramas de la barbarie en
           el Uruguay: Historia de El Clinudo" in *El País* (Montevideo:
           1924). Republished with commentary by Cédar Viglietti. Minas,
           Uruguay: [By the author] 1955.

Relaciones geográficas de Indias
   1885   Tomo I (1881), Tomo II (1885). Madrid: Ministerio de Fomento,
           Perú.

Rodríguez Molas, Ricardo E.
   1982   *Historia social del gaucho.* "Capítulo," Biblioteca Argentina
           Fundamental...Sociedad y Cultura, No. 11. Buenos Aires:
           Centro Editor de América Latina.

Russell, Craig H.
   1981   "Santiago de Murcia: Spanish Theorist and Guitarist of the
           Early Eighteenth Century." Ph.D. diss., University of North
           Carolina, Chapel Hill. 3 vols. Ann Arbor: University Micro-
           films No. 8211645.

Sachs, Curt
   1963   *World History of the Dance.* New York: Norton, 1937, 1963.

Saldívar, Gabriel
   1934   with Elisa Osorio Bolio, *Historia de la música en México:
           Epocas precortesiana y colonial*. Mexico City: Editorial
           "Cvltvra".

Sas, Andrés
   1962   "La vida musical en la Catedral de Lima durante la colonia,"
           Revista Musical Chilena (Santiago) Año XVI, Nos. 81–82, 8ff.

Slatta, Richard W.
   1982   "Pulperías and Contraband Capitalism in Nineteenth-Century
           Buenos Aires Province," *The Americas* (Washington, D.C.)
           XXXVIII, 347–62.

Stevenson, Robert
   1960   *The Music of Peru: Aboriginal and Viceroyal Epochs*. Wash-
           ington, D.C.: Pan American Union.

   1968   *Music in Aztec and Inca Territory*. Berkeley and Los Angeles:
           University of California Press.

   1980b   "Santiago de Murcia: A Review Article," *Inter-American
           Music Review* (Los Angeles) III, No. 1, 89–101.

Torre Revello, José
   1926   "Un pleito sobre bailes entre el Cabildo y el Obispo de Buenos
           Aires (1746–1757)," *Boletín del Instituto de Investigaciones
           Históricas* (Buenos Aires) V, 274–304.

Trenti Rocamora, J. Luis
   1948   *La cultura en Buenos Aires hasta 1810*. Buenos Aires: Univer-
           sidad de Buenos Aires.

[Vowell, Robert L.]
   1831   *Campaigns and Cruises in Venezuela and New Grenada, and
           in the Pacific Ocean; from 1818 to 1830*. 3 vols. London: Longman.

Part V

Foreign Perspectives of the Guitar in the 19th Century

by

Ricardo Zavadivker

"The whole nation loves gambling, horse-racing, bull-fighting, and even cock-fighting; and their only elegant amusement is playing on the guitar—of which they seem to be fond, though they are not proficient in the art (Scarlett 1839:89)."

1. Introduction

The English diplomat Campbell Scarlett left this extraordinary perspective of the Rioplatense guitar. Likewise many other foreigners went to the Río de la Plata during the 19th century and shared his point of view, even though their travels were motivated by different objectives. If they thought the guitar was the elegant amusement of "the whole nation," it must have had a considerable prior history there, dating back to the era of the Hispanic conquest.

353

At the beginning of the conquest in the 16th century, the guitar was flourishing in Iberia, but it was not yet standardized in terms of its size or number of strings, which varied according to function. The audience of the day reflected the social extremes of the monarchy, from the highest to the lowest class. Performers entertained with the *vihuela* at court or with the *guitarra* at large among the populace. Don Luis Milán, musician at the Valencian court of Germaine de Foix, initiated the published repertoire with his magnificent book of tablatures entitled *Libro de música de vihuela de mano intitulado El Maestro* (Valencia, colophon 1536). His instrument was guitar-like in its appearance, having the figure-eight shape with incurved sides, a flat top and back, ten frets tied on like those of the guitarra, and strings arranged in pairs known as courses. Fray Juan Bermudo, in *Declaración de instrumentos musicales*, confirmed their similarities; the aristocratic six-course vihuela and the popular four-course guitarra had similar tunings:

> *No es otra cosa esta guitarra que una vihuela quitada la sexta y la prima* (1555:28v).
> [This guitarra is nothing more than a vihuela with the sixth and first courses removed.]

He explained that the four courses in the middle of the vihuela were the same as the four courses of the guitarra, and thus implied that their other characteristics were next to identical. Even so, there were some differences between the two instruments. The vihuela was larger and, on its six pairs of strings, it had a range of two octaves plus a seventh; musicians plucked on it the complex, polyphonic style of the Renaissance (Narváez 1538:vii). The popular guitarra had only four courses, and musicians strummed it in the accompaniment of either "romances viejos" or the newer songs of the day (Bermudo 1555:27r–28v).

The contemporary musicologist Isabel Aretz, in *Instrumentos musicales de Venezuela,* has noted some similarities between the guitarra described by Bermudo and the small Venezuelan folk guitar called the *cuatro*. The latter was named for its four strings which replaced the four courses of the Renaissance guitarra, and for its reduced size. As a result of her research, she believes that the earliest guitars in the Americas were probably similar to the popular guitarra (Aretz 1967a:122).

Unfortunately the references to the guitarra and vihuela during the New World conquest were scarce. Bernal Díaz del Castillo was one of the few chroniclers to shed some light on the subject. During his participation in the conquest of New Spain, he made the acquaintance of a leader there named Luis Ponce. Díaz del Castillo heard among "[certain noblemen who were found present when (Luis Ponce) fell ill...that in order to cheer him, they were going to perform on a vihuela and play music] (1568:II, 419)." Nevertheless, the term vihuela was also generic in Spain, and it referred sometimes to the bowed viol. This brief mention of the vihuela did not specify whether the music was bowed or plucked.

We run even worse luck with the first chroniclers of the Río de la Plata. The region of Argentina was conquered gradually on three sides: (a) principally on the east by troops that sailed in directly from Spain, (b) but also from the west, by extension of the Viceroyalty of Peru, from across the Andes, and (c) from the south by Simón de Alcazaba, though the latter region long remained without Hispanic settlers. The writers Ulrich Schmidl, Martín del Barco Centenera, and Ruy Díaz de Guzmán, who were its principal 16th-century historiographers, did not make any mention of the guitar or vihuela at all.

It was not until the spiritual conquest during this age of discovery that musical activities were documented at any considerable length. The Jesuit missionaries converted great numbers of Amerindian natives to the Roman Catholic faith. The priests established the first missions of the Jesuit state among the Guaraní tribe of Paraguay in 1607. Between that year and 1767, when the Jesuits were expelled from their Spanish dominions, the missionaries had established thirty settlements which were distributed as follows: seven in the present-day territory of Brazil, eight in Paraguay and fifteen in Argentina (Busaniche 1955:21). The priests conducted the music, the Guaraní Indians sang and played the instruments, and together they reached excellence in their polyphonic choruses. The Indians also specialized in instrument construction, as suggested in two 18th-century chronicles: the first by Padre Francisco J. Miranda and the second by Padre José Peramás—

[1] [The Jesuit missionary...was the teacher of music as well as the teacher of constructing musical instruments such as organs, clavichords, etc.... But this is to be understood in the infancy or beginnings of the reductions...for after a few years, the same Indians would pass from disciples to masters of their craft] (Furlong 1945:98, 177).

[2] [For those who read this, do not believe that when I say that the Indians were ingenious in making instruments that perhaps these were some shapeless, grotesque apparatuses, for they knew how to make use of tools with the same skill as the most distinguished masters of Europe. Certainly anyone arriving here would marvel to see these superior craftsmen making pneumatic organs and all types of musical instruments] (Furlong 1945:99, 182).

With such skill and ability among the Guaraní craftsmen, the construction of a guitar would have been a comparatively small undertaking. Several guitars remain in the region as iconographical examples from the missionary period. One guitar appears in the ruins of the Reduction of the Santísima Trinidad, founded in 1706 on the Paraguayan side of the Paraná River. There, sculpted in high relief upon blocks of sandstone are eight angels, each playing a musical instrument; one of them is playing a guitar. Another guitar of iconographical significance is that featured amidst the paintings which adorn the cupola of the Jesuit church in Córdoba. A little angel is portrayed there, holding a five-course Baroque guitar with a rose and surface decorations reminiscent of the guitars of the late 17th-century European courts (see Plate VI, above).

In 1945 Padre Guillermo Furlong compiled a considerable part of the accessible information regarding the musical activities of the Jesuits in *Músicos argentinos durante la dominación hispánica*. Therein he provided a superficial overview of the guitar's early history as well as literary and pictorial references to it.

However, the panorama of the early guitar there remains incomplete. We lack specific detail about the guitar, not merely in the Jesuit missions, but in all of the guitar's aspects, whether regarding instrument construction, performance, or repertoire that have evolved since then. Even the guitar's folkloric aspects are of interest, particularly if they have not previously come to light in our times. Moreover, it is still worthwhile to bring historical data to the fore in confirmation of the musical achievements of the Jesuits. Significant information in this regard has survived in the travel account of French scientist Alcide d'Orbigny, even though he went to the Jesuit territory some sixty years after the Jesuit fathers were expelled. While he was in the Argentine Province of Corrientes towards the end of 1827, he visited the town of Itatí and recorded the details of a lovely reception he saw there:

> *Bientôt la musique du lieu, composée de quelques mauvais violons et de harpes, restes de la splendeur musical de Jésuites, et don quelques Indiens jouaient tant bien que mal, vint me donner une sérénade et chanter des couplets en mon honneur* (1835–47:I, 192).
> [Before long the musical group of the place, comprised of some bad violins and harps that remained of the musical splendor of the Jesuits, and whose various Indians play for better or worse, came to give me a serenade and sing verses in my honor.]

Although d'Orbigny did not mention the guitar specifically this time, he noted that a musician of Itatí did play it on another occasion in the accompaniment of some farewell songs (1835–47:I, 468). The two references confirm each other with regards to the farewell song, and the second documents the guitar's function within it. Likewise, many other 19th-century travellers confirmed musical practices in the Plata, especially the use of the guitar. Therefore, the accounts which refer specifically to it demand a careful review. As we focus on them, we shall consider a few plates that lend iconographical evidence to the guitar's history.

Part V contains only external evaluations dating from the 19th century. This restricted scope of firsthand observations of foreigners is not arbitrary, for it coincides with the important historical developments of the region. Independence was born early in the 19th century in all of the Rioplatense republics, and the modern era became established towards the end of it. The foreigners came by invitation to growing towns and cities but preferred to roam the wide-open territories of the Plata. They left a wealth of detail about the guitar, so our focus is not overly delimited or confined. By the time they arrived, the vihuela, whether as a linguistic term or a mental perception, was scarcely used any more, so the foreigners refer only to the guitar. Part V presents their references and then ends on an analysis of the data.

The references presented here in their brevity could not provide the complete panorama of our subject, however. In fact, they remain quite isolated, often concentrated at the humble postal stops —indeed at the far reaches of the interior where the travellers had occasion to rest—rather than amidst the burgeoning affluence of the port cities. Moreover, none of the travellers among our sources claimed to have any musical ability or special interest in the guitar. But this does not detract from the significance of their information, for they were not motivated by any special cause for the guitar. Instead they merely described its function or its cultural context within the circumstances which seemed important enough at the time to be included in their memoirs.

2. Overview of the Foreign Travellers
[by the Editor-translator]

Innumerable foreign travellers came to the Río de la Plata, either to visit or to stay permanently during the 19th century. They came with different motives. Many of them published their travel diaries and memoirs, leaving thereby vivid descriptions of life in the Plata. They mention the guitar often and in variegated contexts and situations. Eventually, their accounts became so well known in Great Britain towards the end of the century that they contributed, along with the rise of interest in folklore and local color, to the creation of the Latin American historical novel of the Victorian era.

The testimony of foreign observers was not new to the guitar's history during the Romantic century. However, the 19th-century foreigners who came to the Plata region were a decidedly new and interesting group. Many were able to publish reports of their travels; those who did were in the majority British, and even a few North Americans published their own essays. Without a doubt, the British were generally the best-informed foreigners on the subject of the Plata. Unpublished travel accounts of the region date back to

Roger Barlow who accompanied Sebastian Cabot's landmark voyage of discovery up the Plata tributaries. Some accounts were published in English as early as du Biscay's of 1698 and Reverend Thomas Falkner's of 1774 (see Part I). Early books on the Plata expeditions also became available in English translation only a few years after publication in other languages, as in the case of Father Anthony Sepp in 1697 or Antoine Pernety in 1770 (Part III)—which brought more evidence of British interest in the Plata.

All foreigners observed largely what they were prepared to see, being guided by their new interests in the territory and its inhabitants. Early in the 19th century, the foreigners came with predominantly imperial motives and stayed only for short periods. But then by mid-century, others arrived with the idea of residing there permanently in order to establish commerce in mining, ranching, or business in the cities. Some came for adventure and found it. Whatever their backgrounds or motives, they were fascinated with Rioplatense folklore, which always included the gaucho and sometimes his guitar.

Around 1800, British observers were keeping a close watch on the impact of Napoleon's army as it spread throughout Europe. He had entrusted his own brother, Joseph Bonaparte with aspects of the invasion of Spain, which they began with the pretense of sending troops by land across the peninsula and into Portugal. Whatever their pretensions, as soon as French troops threatened to cross over the Pyrenees and thus into Spain, the Hispanic yoke began to weaken generally in the Americas and specifically in the Plata. The British seized this opportune circumstance with an attempt to rid the Plata of the Spanish domination and to supplant it with their own. Therefore Commodore Home Popham led his British fleet in an invasion of Buenos Aires and Montevideo in 1806. The result of their attack was a powerful takeover at Montevideo under Samuel Auchmuty who was actually an American royalist with allegiance to Great Britain. The insurgence at Buenos Aires was also successful under William Carr Beresford, but problems ensued, for Beresford was short of troops. After the invasion was underway, the crown left the scarcely experienced Lieutenant-General John Whitelocke in charge of the operation, who proved incapable of developing a successful military strategy. Despite their initial probe into Buenos Aires, Beresford's troops had later been surrounded and taken prisoner. Then due to misinformation and an inappropriate plan of attack, Whitelocke soon faced the loss of thousands of his troops or surrender. He chose the latter, which entailed the gradual removal of all British troops in the process. Once returned to England, Whitelocke endured a military inquisition and tribunal in 1808 for his ineptitude throughout the affair; the trial ended with his court-martial (*Dictionary of National Biography*). The gaucho cavalry and the citizens who fought from their housetops in Buenos Aires deserve credit for the victory because support from Spain consisted only in the peacekeeping militia. The Argentine exhilaration not only led them to sympathy with their northern counterparts at having put down the British invasion, it also gave them a vision of independence from Spain.

Nevertheless some of the best reports on Rioplatense popular and aristocratic music came from the British officers. Although they were at war, somehow the officers received invitations to lavish dinners and upper-middle class socials, and they enjoyed complete acceptance everywhere. Brigadier General Robert Craufurd, for instance, who led the charge of the light brigade at Montevideo, recalled that the women there were excellent dancers:

> [Those of the fair sex waltz exquisitely and many are musicians; frequently one hears, passing by, the sounds of the piano or the guitar] (Craufurd 1807:523).

There remained no choice for the British troops but to obey the mandate of evacuation of the Plata, which some did reluctantly owing to the good times they experienced there. On the eve of their withdrawal, Craufurd witnessed the restoration of music and conversation to their previous importance (1807:526).

After independence in the Plata region, the British could remain there, once divested of their previous military power. Many of them chose to stay on as civilians. Some, like John Miers and Francis Bond Head, were interested primarily in mining. They were quite aware of the potential of mining precious metals thereabouts, as well as the financial basis of Spain's Golden Age. As noted by one U.S. observer of that era, "The quantity of gold and silver

annually sent by the new continent into Europe, amounts to more
than nine-tenths of the produce of the whole mines in the known
world (Brackenridge 1820:I, 3)."

Other Britons, including some Irish and Scottish families, remained in the interior towns of the Plata after the invasion, but
with different motives. They established inland cattle and sheep
ranches, as did Richard Seymour prior to 1869. When they wrote
of their hardships and adventures, the Indian attack was worst of
all. Given Seymour's expertise in ranching, his descriptions of the
livestock and fauna are excellent, but he makes no mention of the
guitar. Likewise, William MacCann shows interest in livestock,
but his focus is on the port where the stakes are higher with the
export of hides and tallow—the crude lard used in manufacturing
soap, candles, cosmetics, and industrial products. With explicit detail, he tells how the cowhides are stripped from the animal and
steeped in brine, while the tallow is extracted by steaming the flesh
and bones overnight. MacCann also provides statistics on rainfall,
mean temperatures, and currency. Yet while he never describes
guitar music in detail, he features the instrument in an illustration
where it is played during supper among the poorer classes (1853:
II, 47). All of the 19th-century British writers, whether curious or
merely appalled by the scenes of abject poverty, give some attention to the lore and lifestyle of the gaucho. On the other hand, few
seem to have mixed with high society, apart from the British officers, for they seldom mention the guitar in that context, though it
was present there, too.

Charles Darwin stayed in Uruguay and Argentina between
July and December of 1832, as narrated in *The Voyage of the
Beagle*. His diary, which contains the foundations of his momentous theory on "the origin of the species," is devoted to Rioplatense
flora, fauna, geology, and rural life in its first half. However, the
terminology he establishes there with regard to the gaucho is
helpful at this point, particularly that for the *pulpería* shops. They
were the first permanent establishments on the pampa, and hence
after the family, its first institution (see Part IV for its early
history). Since the outpost pulpería was at once a general store, a
tavern, and a place to meet, the term has remained without an
English equivalent:

The next day we rode to the village of Las Minas [Uruguay]....
At night we stopped at a pulpería, or drinking-shop. During the
evening a great number of gauchos came to drink spirits and
smoke cigars: their appearance is very striking; they are generally tall and handsome; but with a proud and dissolute expression of countenance. They frequently wear their mous-
taches, and long black hair curling down their backs. With their
brightly-coloured garments, great spurs clanking about their
heels, and knives stuck as daggers (and often so used) at their
waists, they look a very different race of men from what might
be expected from their name of gauchos, or simple countrymen.
Their politeness is excessive; they never drink their spirits without expecting you to taste it; but whilst making their exceedingly graceful bow, they seem quite as ready, if occasion offered,
to cut your throat (Darwin 1839:35–36).

Darwin's expedition pushed on from Minas for several days
through the Uruguayan countryside until the men could go no
further without rest or provisions. En route they spotted a large
cattle ranch, so they decided to make an approach; it belonged to a
certain Don Juan Fuentes. Even though their arrival was not anticipated, Don Juan treated them cordially with supper and the
typical entertainment:

Shortly after our arrival at Don Juan's one of the large herds
of cattle was driven towards the house, and three beasts were
picked out to be slaughtered for the supply of the establishment.... The supper, although several strangers were present,
consisted of two huge piles, one of roast beef, the other of boiled....
The evening was spent in smoking, with a little impromptu
singing, accompanied by the guitar (Darwin 1839:37).

Since the pulperías supplied both drinks and provisions, they
were always the first and sometimes the only meetingplace in
rural areas, and remained so for decades or centuries until towns,
schools, and churches sprang up around them. In order to enhance the social function of the pulperías, the proprietors usually
provided a guitar for use by the clientele. Emeric Essex Vidal's
book of 1820, the best illustrated of the English accounts, contains a
description of the guitar in this context, despite the fact that Vidal

merely paraphrased Azara's account of the previous century without any acknowledgment (as cited in Part IV). Most important, even though he came to the Plata a generation after Azara, Vidal implied that the guitar was still a feature of the pulpería.

Sometimes the pulperías served yet another function out on the pampa. As the they began to dot the plains, some were analogous to U.S. "Pony Express stations" where horses were kept for mail carriers at intervals of every twelve miles or so. They also provided rudimentary accommodations for the occasional traveller who was passing through and would have to spend the night while en route to the larger inland towns. Locally these stops were known as *postas,* and the English called them "post houses" or simply "posts." Vidal found these primitive establishments not unlike the worst low-class inns of Spain, which he seemed to know firsthand:

> After all, these *pulperías,* miserable as they are, are not much inferior to some of the inns, as they are called, in Spain herself. It is very true, that in the larger post-towns improvements have been made of late years in the accommodations for travellers.... As in the pulperías near Buenos Ayres, they are frequently provided with a guitar (Vidal 1820:69–70).

The guitar was found often enough in the post houses to suggest that some of the owners themselves were guitarists. Such was the case at the pulpería/post house of Arecife, yet within the Province of Buenos Aires on the road leading due west of the capital:

> We arrived at the post of Arecife, a pretty good house, having a *pulpería,* or grog-shop, attached to it. The owner, who appeared to be of a sentimental cast, amused himself during the absence of visitors with his guitar; almost all the peasants in this country play on that instrument. The music of the Pampas is dull, melancholy, and monotonous; but its jingle in these wild deserts, in the absence of better sounds, is not unpleasant (Proctor 1825: 11).

Two of the best British writers on the Plata were brothers: J.P. and W.P. Robertson. They wrote two works of capital importance that covered the early 19th century, each of which comprised three volumes. Their first piece was entitled *Letters on Paraguay;* it described their four-year residence in that new republic under the dictatorship of Dr. Gaspar Rodríguez de Francia.

In the first place, the Robertsons had come to the Plata in 1806, landing at Montevideo at the time of the English invasion. Their memoirs reveal many personal anecdotes about the lifestyle of the upper classes they observed as businessmen. They frequented the *tertulias*, the evening socials in which the old Spanish "touchstones of civilization" reigned supreme. Music and conversation were returning to prominence again among social elites, just as Craufurd had claimed from the soldier's perspective. The elites (aristocrats and bourgeoisie) considered Rioplatense popular dances low-class at the time, and, instead, they cultivated European parlor dances performed to the music of a piano-guitar duo. They either hired musicians for the occasion or the elite women in attendance volunteered the performance. Yet beyond these general aspects, the Robertsons observed some regional differences between urban social affairs in Montevideo, Buenos Aires, and Asunción:

[1] I had now, at Montevideo (1807), entered upon the bustle of active life.... Though in an enemy's country, and a fortified town,—under martial law withal,—hostility of feeling between the natives and the English was so far subsiding, that some of the principal families of the place recommenced their tertulias.
I was invited to many of these evening parties; and found them an entertaining *mélange* of music, dancing, coffee-drinking, card-playing, laughter, and conversation.... Every lady that I saw in Montevideo, waltzed and moved through the intricate, yet elegant mazes of the country dance with grace inimitable, because of their natural ease and refinement (Robertson 1839: I, 104–05).

[2] Music is much cultivated at Buenos Ayres. There is always one lady in every house who can furnish a good performance of all the tunes required for the minuet, the waltz, and the country dance. And when the Porteñas *do* dance, it is with a graceful composure and easy elegance (Robertson 1839:I, 179–80).

[3] The amusements of the better classes in Assumption were on an extremely limited scale.... Their tertulias were never

graced by music or dancing; and I believe there were only two or three old jingling pianos in the whole town. For a mere occasional dance they contented themselves with the guitar, accompanied by the voice; and, instead of the minuet and country dance of Buenos Ayres, the *Assumpcianas* indulged in a barbarous movement called the *zarandîg,* or heel-dance. The lower ranks in particular were passionately fond of this dance, and its accompanying music (Robertson 1839:I, 146–47).

The Robertsons also reported objectively on music among the poor. In Asunción, for instance, they attended an outdoor party at the residence of an old friend, a distinguished lady of the town named Doña Juana. Inasmuch as the affair was hosted on her lawn, great numbers of peasants came to celebrate the occasion, led by guitarists to her party:

> By the time the whole party was assembled, the shades of evening were beginning to throw their sombre hues over the scene of the lawn.... What added greatly to the romantic simplicity of the scene was, that, ever and anon, little groups of Paraguayan peasantry, uninvited, except by the report they had heard of the rejoicings that were to take place at Doña Juana's, came through the valley in different directions. They were escorted by one or two *guitarreros* (players on the guitar), who accompanied themselves on that instrument to some plaintive triste, or national ballad (Robertson 1839:I, 325).

Later on the Robertsons made additional mention of the guitar among the folk. One of the musical events they observed was the wake for a deceased child. Customarily wakes were lively parties throughout the countryside, because there the people believed that deceased children went straight to heaven:

> A *paycito* had just finished singing a triste [or sad song], accompanied by his guitar. At the head of the room was a blaze of huge wax lights, in candlesticks of carved wood, gilded all over, and of gigantic dimensions.... Immediately over the head of the coffin was a massive silver figure of our Saviour on the cross; and in the coffin lay dressed out in the most splendid style, *the corpse of my infant god-daughter!* (Robertson 1839:III, 151–52).

The Robertsons titled their second three-volume treatise *Letters on South America* and published it in 1843. It has remained valuable to the history of the guitar ever since. It confirmed Major Alexander Gillespie's account of the English invasion, which documented the guitar at the social extremes, both among the elites in the larger towns and cities as well as among the gauchos out on the pampa. Moreover, apart from the documentary function of their second three-volume set, they surely satisfied their 19th-century audience which was just then acquiring an appetite for the local color of faraway places.

Early in their volumes of 1843, the Robertsons portray the gauchos of the countryside as a lively group in which the guitar held some importance. In one instance, the gauchos were the drivers of a typical pampa caravan. They were leading eighteen enormous ox carts, the equivalent of our prairie schooners except that they had but one axle and two great wheels in order to better ford the lowland creeks and bogs. Thus were they crossing the plains with a cargo of merchandise. Their *capataz*, one Don Manuel, who was in charge of it, saw fit to stop for the usual barbecue supper. [See Plate VII, after a lithograph depicting just such a scene in 1841.] After supper, around the campfire certain members of the group came out to entertain with their guitars until nightfall:

> Where a number of these Gauchos thus congregate, they have generally a select few better adapted than the rest to give hilarity and enjoyment to the evening. They have their *graciosos*,— the Yoricks of the South American peasantry, who are "wont to keep the company in a roar," by their native wit, their drolleries, their stories, and practical jests. They have their vocalists and their never failing *guitarreros*, who blend their music together in the wild *tristes* of the country, or in the *boleros* and other lively songs imported from Spain; to all of which the admiring auditors listen with unfeigned delight, and which they repay with "*¡vivas!*" from the very heart.
>
> The segars smoked,—the *mates* [teas] no longer relished,—the graciosos beginning to yawn,—the singers nodding,—the guitars put away,—sentinels placed to watch the carts and the fires,—and sleep stealing over the senses of the general body— all, save the sentinels, go to rest (Robertson 1843:I, 197).

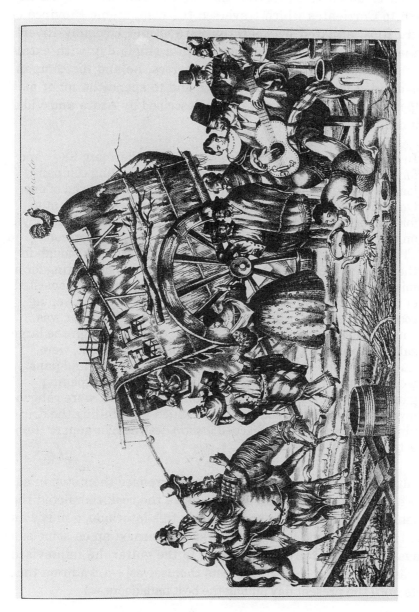

Plate VII *Media caña*, a Country Dance (Julio Daufresne 1841)
Used by permission of Emecé Editores S.A., Buenos Aires

J.P. Robertson provided yet another description of the gauchos in a letter dated 1842. At that time he was reflecting on his trip north to Corrientes which traversed the lush, scenic Province of Entre Ríos, situated between the Paraná and Uruguay Rivers. While he might have made the trip in a single day with extraordinary effort and using numerous horses, he and his companions decided to take a leisurely pace and to spend the night at a pulpería quite like the type already described by Azara and Vidal that doubled as a post house:

> In consideration for George Washington Tuckerman, Esq., and for Philip Parkin, Esq. (both still to be my travelling companions), I consented to take two days to the journey instead of one. On arrival at the half-way post-house, where we were to stop for the night, we found, in consequence of a note sent from Goya on the previous day, everything prepared for our reception.
> The inmates of the hut consisted of a widow, plump, though in the wane of life, of her four daughters (rather good looking for a mixed breed), of two sons, several peons.... The rancho consisted of two apartments, one a large general receiving and sleeping room, with space for half a-dozen hammocks. The other was... without aperture for either light or air, except through the large saloon. Around the walls of this latter mud apartment, were hung calabashes and horse gear; while earthen pots and pans, a copper *mate* pot, two or three spits, a stone for sharpening gauchos' knives, and half a-dozen bullocks' skulls, were ranged around the blazing wood fire, upon which were falling the drippings of the savoury [barbecued] *asado* destined for supper (Robertson 1843:I, 228–29).

Although Robertson and his men had arranged their stop in advance, they experienced a slight delay as the cook completed the finishing touches on their meal. During this interlude, a musician was to entertain the foreigners. First, he warmed up on some sad songs of his repertoire. Then, again to the guitar, he improvised verses which were about the guests themselves!—a tradition that lasts until the present day among the best balladeers:

> Round went the *mate*, and round the paper segars. The *guitarrista* seized his guitar, and accompanied himself to a native

triste. The dogs were stretched out behind the skulls, occupied by the other inmates of the house, and now, too, by ourselves. They lay in sleepy indifference as to the forthcoming meal; for having been satiated with raw beef at the corral, they cared little about having part of the same animal roasted.

George Washington Tuckerman was struck with the rude barbarity of the scene; Don Felipe, less mercurial or less observing...regaled his nostrils with the high-flavoured perfume of the *asado*, and stimulating himself to increasing appetite by eating a few olives...worked his imagination into a lively sense of the savoury substantiality of a tender roast, especially to a hungry traveller. Many a furtive glance he stole at one of the landlady's brunettes. He uttered some uncouth syllables to her in Spanish, and made some awkward attempts at gallantry; but instead of opening up a corner in his fair one's heart, he only elicited laughter from all present.

Being a good-natured man, he laughed loudest himself at the jokes which he did not half understand; and when subsequently the *guitarrista* took him off to admiration in his mode of making love, Don Felipe was the most pleased man in the company. The *guitarreros* of South America, like the Italian buffos of the lower class, have all a facility greater or less, of acting the improvisatore. They have also a good deal of wit, and a perception of character, the more clear in proportion to the elements of contrast to their own of which it may chance to be compounded. Never, in this respect, did so good a subject present himself as Don Felipe to a *guitarrero.* Ours began to scan and draw, in his mind's eye, from the moment of his alighting, rather saddle-sick, from his horse, the character of old Q[uixote]. Having grasped, as he conceived, the whole of my friend's salient traits, and having witnessed his failure in the attempt to attract his Dulcinea, the *guitarrero* broke forth in words, music, and gesticulation, showing himself to be an admirable mimic.

Even George Washington, little as he understood of Spanish verse, rubbed his hands, and forgetting the usual dignity and romance of his character, gave way to unqualified emotions of hilarity, and kissed his fingers, and outstretched his arm, and drew his hand back to his mouth, and pronounced the whole thing "exquisite."

But supper was ready. Some with shells paid their devoirs to the [stew called] *puchero;* but most, with gleaming knives, cut into the *asado* (Robertson 1843:I, 229–31).

Our last reference from this source sheds some light on the upper-class lifestyle in the interior. All those who lived in the countryside were not necessarily employees on the great cattle ranches or the rural poor. Some residents were the employers, the prosperous landowners of the interior estates of the Plata. They inherited magnificent, sprawling pasture lands and villas as descendants of the original *conquistadores*. They ordinarily sent their children to the capital cities for education and refinement, luxuries they could easily afford. In this case, though the Holmos *estancia* or cattle ranch happened to serve as a post house in the countryside, the owner's daughters had no less sophistication than the elite daughters of Buenos Aires: they danced the waltz and minuet, and they entertained on the piano and guitar.

> Our host, at once the *estanciero* and postmaster, was standing at his corral as we came up to the house, and immediately advanced to meet us: he was a fine, hale, yeoman-looking man, and received us with unaffected cordiality, being personally acquainted with us all. Although none of us had met with his family at the estancia on our former journeys, the fame of his daughters' beauty had spread far and near, so that by name, *"las buenas mozas de la posta de Holmos,"*—the pretty girls at the post of Holmos,—were known to every one in the province at large.
>
> When the postmaster, therefore, took us into his *sala,* a plain but neat drawing-room, we were not surprised by the beauty of his three daughters, but we certainly were not prepared for their style. They were fashionable-looking young ladies, who had been brought up in Buenos Ayres, and generally resided there.... Two of them sat sewing beside their mother, a handsome woman of forty; and the third was at a very good piano, playing with no small musical skill! The attractions of the young ladies, both in form and feature, were undeniable; and they lacked none of that grace of motion and polished yet natural and affable manner for which the *Porteñas* [the women of Buenos Aires] are so pre-eminently distinguished.
>
> Instead of being an impatient stoppage, then, for a change of horses, our halt at the post of Holmos turned out to be a fashionable morning visit. We had *mate* handed round to all,—segars to those who liked to smoke,—much animated conversation... some tolerable music; and,—yes, at eleven in the morning,—not

a little dancing. The custom, in those pleasant days, was quite a usual one,—to waltz round the room, or to walk the graceful minuet in boots, at a morning call.... In these agreeable pursuits time fled with a rapidity imperceptible to us all, except to Mr. Fuentes, who, after a considerable absence from home, was on his return to his "dear little wife"...coughed significantly to us when a new minuet, another tune, a song with the guitar, or a fantasia on the piano, was proposed (Robertson 1843:II, 52–55).

Even though the British constituted the majority of those who published the memoirs of their travels around the Plata, the others who did so came from virtually all parts of Europe. For instance, A.Z. Helms, a mining inspector—first in Cracow and then in Lima, published an account of his trip in English translation in 1807. But his references to the guitar were merely undocumented citations from Concolorcorvo and Pernety. Another mining inspector of Polish descent, Ignäcy Domeyko, took careful note of the guitar (as we shall see). Moreover, *Gerstäcker's Travels* were so widely read in German that they too were published in English translation (London, 1854). Even so, he remained a condescending writer for whom the guitar was no more than a distraction of the post office in Buenos Aires (Gerstäcker 1854:64).

The French held a particularly empathetic view of Rioplatense life, as we shall see in the quotes from the voluminous writings of naturalist Alcides d'Orbigny, comparable in his day to Charles Darwin. Moreover, the major illustrator of the Río de la Plata's local color and its guitarists was French—Léon Pallière. While he travelled intermittently in Brazil, Argentina, and Uruguay for two decades, he took a major trek across the pampas and the Andes, from Buenos Aires to Chile and back again in 1860, for which he completed a *Diario de viaje* in 1869. In the "historical present" he narrates an amusing story that shows how the guitar was used in carousing. Leaving Salta on his return to Buenos Aires, he and his group are able to make headway across the pampa by moonlight until reaching a pulpería at a lonesome site called Vipos. Without disturbing the proprietor, they simply unpack nearby and go to sleep on the ground, until they are awakened by surprise:

[I was sleeping, no doubt, when suddenly I heard but three steps

away a guitar played with spirit and the voice of a woman in-
toning improvised verses: "Viva Don Alfonso, that for his love
I'm scrubbin', and I'm walkin', even the ground, waterin',
beautiful girl for his love," etc. and other barbarities of the same
kind, but given the time and place they seemed amusing to me.
Another woman and two gauchos accompany the singer, who is
found seated at a window's opening with protective iron bars. It
is a pulpería from which they demanded service. The interior
light illuminates the scene with sparkles of gold.... The lyrics
and music of the song are sad, which appear adequate for the
medium, contrasting with the conversation at intervals and
with the rum. They are asking the proprietor, "Uh, do you have
any women's pants...?"....With the song of parting finished,
they mount two horses, the women going on the rump; and the
noise of their voices and the hooves of the animals disappear
quickly into the night. The proprietor closes his shutters, and I
get back to my interrupted sleep] (Pallière 1869:230–31).

With such experiences as a basis, Pallière went on to become the
renowned iconographer of the guitar and its folkloric context in
the Plata. He finished at least sixteen art works with the guitar
(listed, 1869:337–44), many of which came out as lithographs in
the 19th century. The following examples with the guitar have
remained readily available because they appeared again, along
with the Spanish translation of his travel diary. With each citation
is Pallière's title, a description, and the medium of the work:

Fig. 17 Iconography of the Guitar in Pallière's Diary, 1869
p. 103 *Gaucho tocando la guitarra* [sketch from 1945 Sp. trans.]
120f. *El payador* [Balladeer with 6-string guitar; lithograph]
155 *La cuna* [The cradle, with mother and 6-string guitar; litho.]
179 *Interior de una pulpería* [guitar hanging on wall; watercol.]
264f. *La posta de Santa Fe* [post house, balladeer in front; litho.]
306 *Guitarist* [sketch from *Diario de viaje*]
322 *Guitarist* [sketch from *Diario de viaje*]

Another distinguished French traveller was Alfred Ebelot. Born
in France during the next generation and educated in Paris as a
civil engineer, he applied his expertise in the capital and countryside of Argentina during most of the decade of the 1870s. He had

an interest in music and a flair for writing about aspects of local color. Ebelot observed the use of the guitar in two rather strange situations. In the first of these, he attended a *velorio*, a wake for a deceased child. As he approached the scene, Ebelot could not explain the fact that he could also hear the merriment of singing and guitar music on that fateful, stormy night:

Ref. 9 *La pampa* Alfred Ebelot

[I penetrated into the main room which was lit by a multitude of candles, indeed those which were being made in this same establishment where the animals were butchered daily.... In the back, at the center of a halo of candles, appeared the cadaver of the boy adorned with his best clothes.

This was the second night he was on exhibition. A light green shadow, like a touch of foliage, grew out of the corner of his lips, and to me—I don't know if it was a figment of my imagination—it seemed that the spots on his flesh were contributing to the stench that impregnated the smells floating in the air. Beside the cadaver was seated a gaucho with white hair and a face the color of *quebracho* [a rugged palm], with the guitar crossed over his knees. On seeing me enter, he had interrupted his music, as the others had their dance. Couples could be discerned amidst the smoke; the young men had their arms wrapped around the slender bodies of the girls and they talked close together: too close for they were somewhat "turned on" by their drinking. The girls laughed with flapping jaws, and threw out noisy compliments, having also brazened their cheekbones with a touch of intemperance. Some old men smoked in the corners and argued about horses.

The mother was on the opposite side of the table from the guitarist. She had a fixed stare and her hands crossed. Some people told her:

—"Your little angel has gone to heaven." "Yes, heaven," she said, as she continued her stare....

Meanwhile the dance continued. Upon passing in front of the dead child, while dancing the *habanera* or *zamacueca*, one or another *bailarina* crossed herself furtively.... Sometimes the thunder covered with its deep, irritated rumblings the melody of the guitar, the murmuring of voices, the measured stamping of feet on the floor, the indiscreet resonance of kisses.

Since that time, I have seen many wakes. What happens with
this practice is the same as with the roads: one finally gets used
to them] (Ebelot 1889:13–15).

In another reference Ebelot demonstrates both his empathy and
his education. He speaks of the guitar in the pulpería with the voice
of experience. For him it is not merely a scene where raw emotions
flow with the liquor at the end of the day; the pulpería is really a
stage which portrays all of the passions of life on the pampas:

Ref. 10 *La pampa*   Alfred Ebelot

[Those in attendance have played the races all day long; they
have won, have lost, have experienced powerful emotions…. At
nightfall they organize a ball. The musicians are nearby. Every
gaucho plays the guitar: be it accompanied by a monotonous
tune on improvised lyrics or not, the guitar is sufficient orchestra for the slow cadence and supple rhythms of the country
dances.

Here we find before us another character worthy of study, and
that would certainly deserve something more than a brief mention in passing: the gaucho balladeer that improvises verses and
sings them with a melancholy tone, accompanying himself on
the guitar…. His songs—rather savage—his rough verses are
laden with nature's lore.

Upon hearing them by the light of the stars in the middle of the
vast melancholy of night, they penetrate the soul with indefin-
able sentiment.

The pulpería should not be judged on the first impression it
provokes. It is merely a shabby rancho, a miserable adobe house.
But, as if theatre were not revealing, the dramas that are enacted in this humble scene do not lack interest. They entail all
the manifestations of pampa life. Its speculations, its commerce,
its poetry, its vices, its passions are resolved in this place. I would
not want you to chide me for being a barfly, but it would be cow-
ardly to deny it: I like the pulpería] (Ebelot 1889:79–80).

Towards the end of the 19th century, the foreign immigrants
had a considerable impact on Rioplatense society; most prominent
among them were the Italians. Between 1869 and 1914 the population of Buenos Aires experienced a growth of over five percent

per year; indeed, during that period it increased from 187,346 inhabitants to 1,576,597 in the capital alone. Among the Plata immigrants on the censuses between 1869 and 1914, the Italians exceeded all others (Baily 1980:36). One of the contributors to this mass migration was Dr. Paolo Mantegazza, who, being a member of both the medical and literary professions, was in a position to extol the benefits of Argentine living to any of his compatriots. His *Viajes por el Río de la Plata y el interior de la Confederación Argentina* [Travels through the Río de la Plata and the Interior of the Argentine Confederation] came out in several editions, first of all in Italian (1867) and then in Spanish (1916). It remains one of the most detailed, factual travel accounts of the 19th century.

Dr. Mantegazza neatly sums up the folk music of the Argentine pampas by contrasting the festive folk dances with the mournful gaucho laments. In either category, the guitar continues as the main or at least the only pitched instrument. However, Dr. Mantegazza cannot help but regret that the dances and gaucho ballads have nearly replaced the once-popular Andalusian style he prefers. Despite his normally empirical methodology of observation, he seems incapable of extricating his emotions and opinions from his perspective of their music:

[The party ends with a ball that is nearly always realized to the jangle of two or three guitars. The most usual dance is the *pericón*, but also the *cielito* in battle or the *cielito* of the pocket, the *gato*, or the *aires* are danced. The *fandanguillo*, of Andalusian origin, is danced but rarely. The Argentine national dances are attractive, tranquil, accompanied by a great deal of mime and often by rhymed responses called "relations" that are directed from one person to the next and that alternate with the clicking of the fingers and the hammering of the dancers' heels.

Between a *pericón* and a *cielito* run copious libations of wine and rum, while the more sober drink *mate*. The poet of the meeting improvises stories and amorous jokes with a nasal if melancholy voice that he accompanies on the guitar. Many times I have admired in those improvisers their great fantasy and spiritual sensitivity, but my ears have always rebelled against that horrible music which is, nevertheless, the only national harmony of the *gaucho*. The vivacious and lascivious spark of Andalusian songs has been completely lost on the wide-open Argentine ranges; the solitary pampa as well as the customs of the savage and independent life have conditioned a sad, monotonous, lugubrious music, which at times juxtaposes lasciviousness with the apathetic, stoic manner of the Indian races] (1876:68–69).

A new literary medium of the Victorian era signalled the close of the 19th century. The British historical novel set in South America grew directly out of the abundant adventures found in the travel accounts, but it drew additional momentum from the appetite for local color that developed in the European audience and from the British folk movement, in particular. Outspoken British advocates nurtured popular and scholarly interest in folklore, like Sir Charles Villiers Stanford: "There is no diet so life-giving and so life-preserving as the natural out-pouring of the songs of the soil (1915:237)."

Meanwhile, as British writers were turning ever more to folk and fiction in the 19th century, South America provided them with a setting and circumstances already well known to their audience. Most of the early European settlements in South America had remained on its periphery, so its vast interior was yet a dark continent. Their novels about South America were spiked with some historical or personal details, especially about the Río de la Plata where a good many earlier writers had travelled, even after the British invasion. Unfortunately, in spite of such an exciting setting, most of these novels did not become classics. They were successful initially yet fell into obscurity because their authors directed them, as is so often the case with the media of entertainment, towards a teenage market and mentality. The authors professed personal as well as historical experience as their basis, but their texts tended to read like the adventures of Gillespie, Seymour, and many others who actually travelled to the Plata region.

G.A. Henty's *Out on the Pampas*, 1871, serves as an example in the medium. Mr. Hardy, a stalwart English father, emigrates with his family to Argentina in order to start a cattle ranch. Soon, with the tremendous effort of the local *guachos* [sic, *orphans?*], they are able to establish a profit in farming and the breeding of livestock. In addition, they meet other Brits there with whom they enjoy lovely parties. Near the end, just as in John Davie's authentic narrative of 1805, the climax of the novel is reached with a bloody Indian attack in which Mr. Hardy proves to be as invincible as he had been infallible. He saves the family and restores order, but they prepare to return to England forever with their new-found riches and tall tales of adventure. Ultimately the advancement of Victorian ideals obscures an accurate perspective of Argentina.

Among the hundred or so novels produced in this medium, there were some that emanated from a more sympathetic viewpoint and a more legitimate basis than others. Occasionally an experienced sage narrated the tales, such as the old gaucho in William Henry Hudson's *El ombú* (a short story published in 1918). A more typical example was Hudson's rather autobiographical novel entitled *The Purple Land that England Lost.* Its enigmatic title refers superficially to the wildflowers that grace the Plata countryside, yet also profoundly to the blood spilt in the 19th-century wars. However, Hudson was not English by birth. His parents had moved from the U.S. to Argentina, where William was born some years later. *The Purple Land* was an early piece which he wrote after trips to Uruguay and the Gran Chaco. A certain Richard narrates it in the first person: it is an account of his experiences in the interior of Uruguay before returning to Argentina at the end. The story is full of fascinating characters, and great affection is displayed between them up to a point—Richard has just recently married. Even the political overtones of the work come across with empathy, for Hudson understands the price of war as well as the necessity of self-defense.

As anticipated, he often mentions the guitar: its performers help to satisfy the British thirst for local color. On one occasion, for instance, Richard has been travelling on horseback out on the Uruguayan pampa. He rested at a pulpería and there chanced to meet a *domador*, a friendly horse-tamer named Lucero. As they became acquainted over drinks, Lucero invited Richard to come to his place, a rancho lying about two miles away on the pampa. Richard gladly accepted, so they rode out to meet the family. They were received in the typical gracious manner, with a round of introductions, whereupon one of Lucero's grandchildren, a boy about the age of twelve, began to give them rapt attention:

Ref. 11 *The Purple Land that England Lost*   William H. Hudson

"Where is your guitar, Cipriano?" said his grandfather, addressing him, whereupon the boy rose and fetched a guitar
which he first politely offered to me. When I had declined it, he
seated himself once more on his polished horse skull and began
to play and sing. He had a sweet boy's voice, and one of his ballads took my fancy so much that I made him repeat the words
to me while I wrote them down in my notebook, which greatly
gratified Lucero, who seemed proud of the boy's accomplishment. Here are the words translated almost literally, therefore
without rhymes, and I only regret that I cannot furnish my
musical readers with the quaint, plaintive air they were sung
to:—

> O let me go—O let me go,
> Where high are born amidst the hills
> The streams that gladden all the south,
> And o'er the grassy desert wide,
> Where slakes his thirst the antlered deer,
> Hurry towards the great green ocean.
>
> The stony hills—the stony hills,
> With azure air-flowers on their crags,
> Where cattle stray unowned by man;
> The monarch of the herd there seems
> No bigger than my hand in size,
> Roaming along the tall, steep summit.
>
> I know them well—I know them well,
> Those hills of God, and they know me;
> When I go there they are serene,
> But when the stranger visits them
> Dark rain-clouds gather round their tops—
> Over the earth goes forth the tempest.
>
> Then tell me not—then tell me not,
> 'Tis sorrowful to dwell alone:
> My heart within the city pent
> Pines for the desert's liberty;
> The streets are red with blood, and fear
> Makes pale the mournful women's faces.
>
> O bear me far—O bear me far,
> On swift, sure feet, my trusty steed:
> I do not love the burial-ground,
> But I shall sleep upon the plain,
> Where long green grass shall round me wave—
> Over me graze wild herds of cattle.
>   (Hudson 1885:26–27)

Subsequently W.H. Hudson published many more books, some of which were born of his interest in ornithology. It was a great loss to the Americas that, after he had initiated such success as novelist and naturalist in South America, that Hudson eventually chose to live in England. At least he left a legacy of the Plata region which has remained perfectly accessible to English readers. The bibliography of his works is but another reminder of the enormous outpouring of English literature that has developed on the Plata over the past four and a half centuries—ever since Roger Barlow's account of how Sebastian Cabot explored the Plata tributaries.

3. Selected Testimonials on the Guitar

The foreigners in the Río de la Plata left many firsthand accounts which document the guitar and its social context. Seen through the eyes of their 19th-century audience, their essays are full of diversity, character, and local color. However, their accounts have also begun to interest a new audience in our own century. Historians and folklorists, in particular, have begun to use the travel accounts as documentation for humanistic studies. For instance, Juan Alfonso Carrizo has reviewed many of their commentaries in *Historia del folklore argentino* (1953). Like most folklorists, he remembers the travellers for their contributions because, as foreigners, they provide observations of phenomena from an external, indeed foreign perspective.

The following accounts of the Rioplatense guitar are presented in chronological order. They remain verbatim citations, except where translated, in which case they appear in brackets. The year alongside each boldface name is the date of the author's arrival in the Río de la Plata.

1796, John Constanse Davie
1. [Convent of St. Dominic, Buenos Aires, Jul. 1797:]
It is not at Buenos Aires as in Old Spain, where none are admitted to an assembly but those of equal rank: here, merchants and their families are invited to the governor's public entertainments;

and though the inhabitants are not so numerous as might be expected in a town so situated at Buenos Ayres, which is in fact the
staple for all the produce of the distant provinces, yet there was at
the last ball given in honour of the governor's birthday a very
numerous and brilliant assembly. The dons were dressed in the
usual Spanish taste, but with a greater variety of colours, and the
ladies' dresses differed very widely from those in Old Spain; their
petticoats were of taffeta, ornamented at the bottom with gold lace,
or fringe, richly tasseled.... I danced a saraband with donna Josefina Theresia Iboriola, a young lady of great beauty and accomplishments; she is a visitor with her father and mother at the
commandant's. They are residents at Córdovo, where Josefina
was born.

Donna Louisa equalled in splendor the richest lady present. She
is the most lively and entertaining female I ever conversed with;
and is, with her husband don Manuel, admired by all their acquaintance.

The paltry distinctions of rank are here laid aside; and from the
freedom of conversation I am inclined to think that French liberty
and equality have stolen into New Spain (Davie 1805:110–11).

2. [Buenos Aires, Jul. 1797:]

The...street of the Holy Trinity, and...the street of St. Benedict,
are by far the handsomest of the whole. The former...runs almost
the whole length of the town, is very regularly built, and occupied
only by the better sort of inhabitants. Almost every house has a
garden both before and behind; and all those that can afford it have
balconies, with sun-shades and lattice-work, adorned with the
most beautiful shrubs and flowers that the earth produces. Here
the families sit the best part of the day, and night too when they are
not visiting, and take their coffee or chocolate, and play on their
guitars and mandolines: most of the ladies have fine voices, so that
the man who strolls about the town in the evening may enjoy the
pleasure of a concert gratis as he passes along (Davie 1805:113 f.).

3. [Convent of St. Dominic, Buenos Aires, Aug. 1797:]

After the hours of sleep, termed the *siesta*, which begins about
two and ends at five—during which time a most profound silence
reigns everywhere around—I dress myself, and pay a visit to some
family or other with whom I have made acquaintance; where I
generally spend three or four hours very pleasantly, in music,
dancing, or conversation (Davie 1805:141).

1806, Major Alexander Gillespie
1. [City of Buenos Aires, Province of Buenos Aires:]
They [the Plata citizens] afforded [to the British troops] many examples of a natural goodness of heart, and they were so often, and so generally exhibited as to convince us that benevolence was a national virtue.... It was winter when we were masters of Buenos Ayres, during which *tertullos*, or dances were given every evening, at one house or another.... Waltzes were the vogue, and the piano, accompanied by the guitar, on which all degrees play, was the music (Gillespie 1818:67).

2. [City of Buenos Aires, Province of Buenos Aires:]
Music was held as a pre-eminent accomplishment, and no expence was spared in that attainment, either as to instruments, or compositions. These articles will always have a ready sale in Buenos Ayres, as they have a partiality for both, when of English manufacture.
Like in all countries bordering on a state of nature, poetry seems the leading genius of the lower classes in this part of South America, for upon any one being asked to play a tune on the guitar, he will always adapt to it a set of extemporaneous and accordant verses, with much facility (Gillespie 1818:68).

3. [City of Buenos Aires, Province of Buenos Aires:]
I received one day an invitation to dinner from a captain of engineers, the particulars of which I will describe, as being probably demonstrative of the general customs on occasions of ceremony. All who sat down to a very long table profusely covered, were three: his wife, Captain Belgrano, and myself. No domestics were present at any time, except when bringing in or carrying away the various courses, which consisted in twenty-four removes.... The wines of St. Juan and Mendoza were circulated freely, and while we were enjoying our segars, the lady of the house, with two others who stepped in, amused us with some pretty English and Spanish airs upon the guitar, accompanied by those female voices. We dined at two, and the party broke up to their siesta at four o'clock (Gillespie 1818:69).

1806, Notes on the Viceroyalty of La Plata (anonymous, London: Stockdale, 1808)
[The author of this splendid work accompanied Brigadier General Samuel Auchmuty and his troops who were sent to the Plata

in late 1806. He remained anonymous so as to comment openly about the weaknesses of their battle plan. The British invaded the city of Montevideo and resided there into 1807, during which time the author became quite attached to the place and its people:]

1. [Montevideo:]
This is the only order of monks in the city.... The guardian of the convent appeared to be, from his countenance, a man of excellent heart, and from his conversation, to possess ideas more enlarged than his brothers.

I once, at the invitation of the superior, dined with a friend at the convent. Their usual hour of dinner was twelve o'clock, but as they wished on this occasion to give an entertainment agreeable to English hours of eating, they fixed it at four. From the specimen which they gave both of their appetites and of their cookery, it does not appear that they endanger their health by fasting, or that they often are guilty of the vice of abstemiousness. There were at least thirty different dishes, or rather different courses, for one dish only was brought in at a time. The entrance of each was welcomed by a shout of joy from the whole table....

They had wines of several sorts, to which they did ample justice. After the [table] cloth was removed, which was not until near seven o'clock, the spirits of these holy men began to rise, and their eyes to sparkle at the brisk circulation of the bottle. They introduced into the apartment which communicated with the dining hall, a musician, who regaled us with a number of songs, which he sung to his guitar. One of the fraternity who had a very good voice, accompanied him. The whole table joined very obstreperously in the chorus. In compliment to their guests, the tune of "God save the King" was played. Several of the songs which they sung were not of the most delicate complexion, nor such as one would expect to hear echoed from the recesses of the cloister by a society of monks. These songs met with the most extravagant applause, and it appeared from the delight which they seemed to communicate, that the thoughts, of these men of holiness, were not always fixed on things above (*Notes* 1808:60–64).

2. [Montevideo:]
The women of Monte Video are generally brunettes. Many of them are very handsome, and though small, elegantly and voluptuously formed. Their carriage is extremely graceful, and they walk with an admirable air. The dress in which they appear

abroad is universally black. They wear the old Spanish habit, to which no modern improvement can add grace or beauty. The fringed satin petticoat...and the black silk mantle...is all the dress consists of....

The Spanish ladies are extremely lively, good-humoured, and witty: their minds, though uncultivated, like the rich soil of their country, have the same luxuriance and fertility....

Their amusements chiefly consist in singing and playing on the guitar, with which they pass many of their hours. They all seem fond of music, and some few of them can touch the piano forte. The airs which they play are mostly love songs, and the melancholy ditties of Peru (*Notes* 1808:83–91).

3. [Montevideo:]
Some may perhaps think these remarks made with too much asperity and warmth; but for their truth I appeal to the world. From the opportunity I had of knowing the sentiments of the people, from the various sources I sought for intelligence and information, and which a knowledge of the language enabled me to attain, I think myself justified in speaking as I do....

It is almost needless to recapitulate the benefits that would be felt by Great Britain from the possession of Río de la Plata. They are so many that their enumeration is difficult, and at the same time so obvious, that it is unnecessary. It will be seen from what we have said, that there can be few spots on the globe where such a variety of advantages are combined, both in a commercial and political view. My words are too feeble to convey a just description of this beautiful country (*Notes* 1808:102–06).

1819, John Miers
1. [Post house of Mercedes, Province of Buenos Aires:]
I could discover no regular employment that any of the people here followed; true it is, this was Sunday; but from all I could see, and all I could learn, there was no sort of regular employment; I could not make out from them how they contrived to live. During by far the greatest part of the day the women were basking in the sun.... The men were equally unemployed, strolling or lying about, hardly desiring to move, having no sort of amusement: one, however, was employed; he was seated on a log near the door of the hut, and played nearly all the day, and all the evening, some wild notes on an old guitar, occasionally singing through his nose a melancholy, barbarous Saracenic air (Miers 1826:44–45).

2. [Las Tunas, Province of Córdoba:]

Lastunas [sic] is a most miserable place.... The people here...are strongly addicted to the use of ardent spirits whenever they can procure them; take great delight in dancing, noise, and revelry.... They displayed great delight in playing the guitar accompanying their rude Moorish canzonets with their voices, singing verses partly extemporaneous. It is, as I have since found, the common practice all over Spanish America, for the people to catch hold of the name of their visitors, and of some circumstance connected with them, and mix them up with their songs, which are expressive of dancing, love, and tender sentiments (Miers 1826:55–57).

3. [City of San Luis, Province of San Luis:]

We had been looking forward with much anxiety to our arrival at *San Luis*, having discovered that one of the iron bolts which carried the whole weight of the coach body had given way.... The coach body being removed, we discovered another broken bolt. I proceeded with them to the only blacksmith in this large town, and requested him to weld them that afternoon if possible.... I went many times in the course of the day to the blacksmith; it was of little avail; the fellow could not be roused from his afternoon's enjoyments, which consisted of smoking cigars with two wretched-looking women, all squatted upon the bare ground of their apartment, alternately playing the guitar, accompanying it with the usual Saracenic minor canzonets, which they bawl forth with nasal discordance. This, indeed, with due intervals of sleep, forms the usual mode of passing away their time. No inducement could urge him to work that night, but he promised to accomplish the job before daylight in the morning (Miers 1826:98–100).

4. [Post house of Tegua, Province of Córdoba:]

I arrived at this post-house of Tegua [sic], in the midst of the celebration of the harvest home; it is the custom in those parts of South America, where corn is grown, during the *trilla*, or thrashing time, to keep open house to all who choose to enter, where they may eat, drink, and be merry to their heart's content. It is a period of great rejoicing throughout the country, and of course produces more of drunkenness than any other period.

In the postmaster's house I met with a number of respectably dressed females from *Córdova* and the neighbourhood, and several persons above the common herd of *gauchos;* outside were above fifty peons dressed in their best *ponchos*, feasting, singing, playing the guitar, and carousing after their own fashion (Miers 1826: 219–20).

1821, Alexander Caldcleugh, Esq.
[Post house of Candelaria, Province of Santa Fe:]

Shortly after my arrival, a man rode up on horseback and came into the house, playing the guitar, and singing an anthem before a figure of our Lady of *Candelaria*, which happened to be in the room; he then turned to me and sang a long song in my praise, my guide having previously given my name (Caldcleugh 1825:I, 250).

1825, Captain Francis Bond Head
[At a post house on the road east to Buenos Aires, after leaving the City of Mendoza:]

[The broken carriage] was not worth more than one hundred dollars; and it would have cost more than that sum to have guarded it, and to have sent a wheel to it six hundred miles from Buenos Aires; so I condemned it to remain where it was, to be plundered of its lining by the gauchos.... The people had now returned from the river, and supper was preparing, when a young Scotch gentleman I had overtaken on the road, and who had ridden some stages with me, asked me to come and sing with the young ladies of the post, who he told me were very beautiful. I knew them very well, as I had passed several times, but I was much too tired to sing or dance. However, being fond of music, I moved my saddle and poncho very near the party, and as soon as I had eaten some meat I again lay down, and as the delightful fresh air blew over my face, I dropped off to sleep just as the *niñas* were singing very prettily one of the *tristes* of Peru, accompanied by a guitar (Head 1826:151–52).

1825, Captain [Joseph] Andrews
1. [Post house of Carmela Achaval, Province of Santiago del Estero:]

The lady of *Atchabal* would have been a fine heroine of a good old Spanish romance.... In person and form, this lady appeared to my fancy a strong resemblance to the handsomer portraits which have been left us of Mary, Queen of Scots. I could not help wishing that the same artist, who had delineated with masterly hand that unfortunate queen's portrait as I have seen it, (be it a resemblance of the unfortunate Mary or not,) with Rizzio seated at her music, could have drawn the lady before us playing on her guitar

(Andrews 1827:139–40)." [Regarding the affair between Queen Mary and her guitarist, David Rizzio, see Conclusion E.10, below.]

2. [City of Santiago del Estero, Province of Santiago del Estero:]
We were now in the city of *Santiago del Estero*, having travelled one hundred and fifteen leagues [some 345 miles] from *Córdova*.... We found, however, that our carriage wanted [needed] some arrangements which would occupy time, and we therefore accepted an invitation to a *bayla del país* in the evening, having nothing better to do. A country ball here is an amusement bearing little resemblance to the *Tertullias* [social gatherings] of *Córdova* and *Buenos Ayres*, where the dancing is for the most part, confined to the graceful Spanish country dance and minuet, which is exceedingly grave and dignified. I had, it is true, seen before occasional specimens of the *Mariquita* and other Gaucho dances, but never in the pure style exhibited here [re. dances, see Vega 1956:112–140]. The airs are played on the guitar, and that of the *Mariquita* is peculiarly expressive of the amatory breathings and incipient advances of lovers to each other, which this dance caricatures. The close of the set is that which excites the most merriment, for then the squeamish and coy fair one, who has kept aloof and hitherto waved her handkerchief as her flag of triumph and independence, now strikes it and yields herself up to the irresistible and overwhelming advances of her amorous swain (Andrews 1827:147ff.).

3. [Post house of Lagunillas, Province of Salta:]
Here we got pretty good accommodation, and were visited in the evening by a group of females from a village, who entertained us with singing and guitar playing (Andrews 1827:277).

1827, Alcide d'Orbigny
1. [Laguna Brava, situated about ten miles northeast of the City of Corrientes, Province of Corrientes:]
[Each farm possesses a certain number of oxen, milking cows, and riding horses because laborers never work on foot. The latter, called in the country *peones* (laborers, day workers), earn monthly five or six *piastres* (25 to 30 francs). They are fed but not lodged, and must furnish their own horses; also, every night or as soon as they have finished their day's work, they return to their homes, or to homes of friends or to neighboring houses to pluck the guitar, sing, dance the *cielito*, or finally, to play which is their favorite activity] (d'Orbigny 1835–47:I, 120). [See Plate VIII.]

Plate VIII *Cielito* near Buenos Aires (Carlos E. Pellegrini c.1831)
Used by permission of Emecé Editores S.A., Buenos Aires

2. [Caacaty, Province of Corrientes:]

[One evening, while I was at the commandant's house, some regional music was presented. I listened to it with real pleasure because of its originality. It was composed by Guaraní Indians. One of them was playing a violin that he had made himself, another plucked a harp made from a single trunk of a hollowed tree on which a soundboard and strings had been fabricated in the village; another plucked the guitar. The harpist's three children composed the serenade: one performed on a tambourine, the other a large drum, the third, a triangle. But what struck me most was a blind Indian who had made a flageolet from a reed, the sounds of which resembled a flute, and on which he executed two octaves of very correct sounds by controlling the intensity of breath. This group of musicians created dance, war, and even church music in Caacaty. Each one was as proud of his talent as if he had been the director of the Pope's music, and each constantly maintained the most imperturbable seriousness, which is, moreover, the general character of the American nations, whose individuals are always very attentive to everything they do. These virtuosos played a few national tunes for us with great precision, and I had difficulty understanding how men without principles of music and having such imperfect instruments, could execute songs and be listened to with such pleasure. They played the accompaniment of the *cielito*; and quickly those present began to dance this joyous dance, always accompanied by songs which retrace, in all its naïveté, the first age of civilization. They continued with a *minué montonero* that is very fashionable in the country, and which joins to the serious character of the ordinary minuet those graceful figures of the steps which the Spaniards know how to execute so well] (d'Orbigny 1835–47:I, 236–37).

3. [City of Corrientes, Province of Corrientes:]

[Nearly all the men are musicians, and they play the guitar and sing *tristes* or sad romances as well as happy songs. But what surprised me on occasion is the facility with which they composed verses. I saw two champions challenge each other with their guitars to a contest to determine who would stop first in alternately singing improvised couplets during which they stayed with only a single subject, and this often continued for hours or even a whole day without a winner. One can sense how much intelligence and ability this kind of contest requires, above all for people who are— so to speak—without formal education. It is right to say, however, that Spanish verses are generally easier to invent than our own because the rhythmic meter alone is required, and there is no rhyme] (d'Orbigny 1835–47:I, 358–59).

(Note: Later d'Orbigny transcribes four strophes in Guaraní that he heard in Corrientes, and then provides the translation in Spanish and French. He clarifies that they are similar to the Peruvian *tristes* or romances "which the inhabitants of Buenos Aires like so much." Contrary to his impression, however, innumerable sources attest to the practice of *rhyming* the Spanish verses, even when they are improvised. —Ed.)

4. [City of Corrientes, Province of Corrientes:]
   [A single room at Corrientes was adorned with a piano; it was the only one which existed in the town; but the walls of the other rooms were garnished with one or several guitars placed at the disposition of amateurs who disdained the harp, violin, oboe, and all other instruments reserved exclusively for professional musicians, which are used only for balls (very rare) and for church music] (d'Orbigny 1835–47:I, 365).

5. [City of Corrientes, Province of Corrientes:]
   [The man of Corrientes is not content to go to just one place. He spends his entire evening either walking about or going from one house to another; he is welcomed everywhere, particularly by the women who are truly extraordinary for the courtesy they show in order to retain the visitor, and for the gaiety they display with him; laughing, even playing, or criticizing their female neighbors with a very particular elegance. If he is a musician, he cannot keep from taking down the guitar hanging in the room, and plucking the accompaniment of the *cielito* or some other dance from the country; or else, he sings about those little trifles which often outline the most coarse intentions, accompanying himself by striking his fingers on the strings of the instrument instead of plucking, and making above all a lot of noise. The *romance* is rare, whereas the merry (or picaresque) song is very common and appreciated by both sexes] (d'Orbigny 1835–47:I, 376).

6. [City of Corrientes, Province of Corrientes:]
   [It is quite usual to see an inhabitant of Corrientes spend the evening in one house or another drinking *mate* and outdoing

others in smoking; but this evening never extends beyond eight
o'clock; for then, he returns home. The doors are closed, the table is
set again, and supper is relished, rather often with something
roasted and something boiled. This meal is eaten like dinner, with
no difference; after which everyone goes to bed. Then sounds the
hour of intrigue: young people begin to run through the streets
with their guitars and give serenades. Thus, during the night, the
streets are less quiet than during the *siesta*] (d'Orbigny 1835–47:I,
378).

7. [City of Corrientes, Province of Corrientes:]
[The young men, who belong to the best families in the city,
spend their life in complete idleness, visiting ladies: plucking the
guitar at the home of this one, all the while singing songs of love or
teasing or courting that one, consuming their time in amorous in-
trigues, turning nights into days, and riding on horseback in the
manner already described] (d'Orbigny 1835–47:I, 378).

8. [City of San Pedro, Province of Buenos Aires:]
[Climbing down to the ground from the Itatí woods, I found at
my house, or rather at our house, a gathering of virtuosos who had
come there with their guitars. I had a great deal of trouble getting
rid of them, which I wasn't able to do until I had listened to several
couplets sung in my honor, and accompanied by the *despedida*
(song of good-byes) often repeated] (d'Orbigny 1835–47:I, 468).

9. [City of Buenos Aires, Province of Buenos Aires:]
[If it is not a private gathering and a visitor arrives—following
the usual compliments to the mother, it is rare that the young
ladies do not stand up on their own to go sit at the piano in order
either to play a few contredances or to accompany themselves
while singing a love song; all of which furnishes the visitor with a
text for conversation. If he is a musician, if he plays the guitar, he is
forced to sing, preferably a *triste* (a languorous love song) which
the ladies like a lot, and which they make him repeat several
times. These friendly evenings are all the more pleasant because
there is much gaiety and the conversation never lags] (d'Orbigny
1835–47:I, 505).

10. [Near Cruz de Guerra, Province of Buenos Aires:]
[The gable, on which the door of the *pulpería* was found, was
sheltered by an overhanging roof, which, extending out four or five

meters, covered the space that the drinkers used when gatherings became too large to be contained indoors. A stone bench stood on either side of the entrance; ordinarily the guitar players and singers, those individuals most important and indispensable to such gatherings, sit there.... The description I have just made of this dwelling, fits, with minor differences, all others like it in the Province of Buenos Ayres] (d'Orbigny 1835–47:I, 620).

1830, Arsène Isabelle
1. [Province of Tucumán:]

[It is fair however to observe that among these herdsmen, those from the Provinces of Buenos Ayres, the Banda Oriental, Entre Ríos, Santa Fe, and even Córdoba, living far from women in the middle of immense loneliness, are the most brutish and the most dissolute. However the peaceful herdsmen of Tucumán and of the entire high country who live together in small groups revealed everywhere, before the wars which desolated these vast plains, and demonstrate still in many places, the innocent customs of ancient Arcadia. "Young couples," a famous geographer wrote, "improvise to the resonance of a guitar, alternating verses in the genre of those that Theocrites and Virgil embellished so very well." For a long time in the factory I formed in Buenos Ayres, I employed two *peones* (day workers) from Tucumán who never sang except in this manner while always accompanying themselves with the guitar] (Isabelle 1835:227). [See Plate IX.]

2. [City of Buenos Aires, Province of Buenos Aires:]

[Nearly all the Spaniards are poets and admirably improvise verses that they sing while accompanying themselves with the guitar or piano] (Isabelle 1835:247).

3. [City of Buenos Aires, Province of Buenos Aires:]

[Do you hear the guitar resonating brilliantly from the rapid vibration of its twelve metal strings? Do you hear inordinate laughter, monotone songs similar to psalmody, interrupted by other songs that hop to a very quick beat? All this commotion, this confusion, this barbaric gaiety comes from the neighboring *pulpería* where a *compadrito* (wily companion), scraping the guitar, makes the Negroes or those of mixed blood perform an immoral dance called the *media caña*, stopping often to swallow a glass of gin or *tafia* (liqueur) as it is passed around the circle] (Isabelle 1835:254).

Plate IX *Payada in the Pulpería* (Carlos Morel c.1842)
Used by permission of Emecé Editores S.A., Buenos Aires

4. [City of Buenos Aires, Province of Buenos Aires:]

[Women from Buenos Aires and Montevideo are as well suited as Italian women for music, but in general they do not bother with studying written music. All they need is to hear a tune once or twice, or a *contredanse*, or even an overture, and they are able to repeat it on either the piano or the guitar with the greatest exactitude. They are particularly fond of Italian and French music, but an irresistible penchant makes them prefer even more the Peruvian *tristes*, Spanish *boleros*, and the national *cielitos* which are not without charm. Nothing is more seductive than a young woman of the port city saying to another in confidence, "This *triste* carries away my soul!"] (Isabelle 1835:257).

1834, The Hon. P. Campbell Scarlett
1. [Republic of Argentina:]
The whole nation loves gambling, horse-racing, bull-fighting, and even cock-fighting; and their only elegant amusement is playing on the guitar—of which they seem to be fond, though they are not proficient in the art (Scarlett 1838:89).

2. [Puente de Márquez, Province of Buenos Aires:]
We have therefore had nothing to do but to eat and drink, and listen all the day long to a poor cracked guitar, on which one of the ladies of our grumbling landlord has been constantly strumming the same air. This tune, if tune it can be called, has very little variety in its composition, but it seems to be the only one known to the simple inhabitants of these regions; as it is played every where, and on all occasions (Scarlett 1838:154).

3. [Province of Tucumán:]
I have been much interested by the perusal of Temple's Travels in *Peru*, from *Buenos Ayres*, which are well worth reading. His description of *Tucumán*, and the *gauchos* of that province, would apply equally well to *Mendoza*, or *Buenos Ayres*. He says if a [man of] *Tucumán* possesses a horse, a knife, a lasso, and a guitar, which they all seem to delight in, he considers himself among the independent sons of earth, and beyond the caprices of fortune (Scarlett 1838:172–73).

1837, Platon Alexandrovich Chikhachev
[On the road from Mendoza to Buenos Aires, at Cabeza del Tigre, Province of Buenos Aires:]

[While at the scene of some cock fights in town,] fatigue, repugnance and, finally, the distant sound of a guitar drew me away from this odious picture. Following the sound, I ended up at home, where Dolorcita was warbling her Buenos Aires songs. Attracted by the same sound, a crowd of young people soon gathered, entering the cabin one after another with no other formality than [the liturgical greeting] *"Ave Maria purissima."* Little by little the conversations died out, and Rodríguez, who never liked to be idle, caught up the last sounds of the guitar with his hoarse voice and sang his favorite song, a popular *fandango.* A group of dancers soon formed, the guitar resounded, and the sharp clicking of the castanets was heard in time with the music. The scene was alive with good-natured and harmless mirth (Chikhachev 1844:58).

1838, Ignácy Domeyko

[The four incidents that follow occurred on the road between Buenos Aires and Mendoza, Province of Mendoza. Domeyko crossed the pampa on horseback in order to travel to Chile by land. He made the trip in the fall, from 29 April to 13 May 1838, and on the way, he had many encounters with the people of the Argentine countryside. En route he was always quick to notice the guitar:]

1. [There was only one pot, one cup, and a couple of spoons for the whole family, and in the house—one table, a guitar, a piece of an old mirror, the sabre, and an old chest covered with a fresh pelt] (Domeyko 1888:II, 103–04).

2. [I saw a sick person. She moved the teapot close to the fire in the middle of the house, and put in a pinch of the herb called *yerba buena,* the effect of which she strongly believed in. There was a crucifix on the wall, a guitar in the corner, there were squashes, and on the only table in the whole house, there was a prayer-book. I looked in the book; it was well written, and it was understandable for the simple people] (Domeyko 1888:II, 113).

3. [The owner asked us to come in. They were expecting the arrival of the village priest—that was why the house was so clean—and on the left hand by the exit was a prepared altar. A large religious icon was hung on the wall; in front of the Holy Mother was a crucifix, two angels made of wood on either side, and two lighted candles. Otherwise the usual order: a guitar on the wall, squashes

and corn in the corner, and hung on the wall, a quarter of fat meat]
(Domeyko 1888:II, 121).

4. [One of the (young ladies), probably the better adjusted, came
nearer, and began a conversation about the weather and parties;
another one, in the yellow coat, sat down farther away, next to
their father. The conversation from this side was with chosen
phrases about politics and trade, sometimes interrupted, but on the
couch it soon came to jokes—merry and innocent—that all the
company enjoyed together. The gentleman wearing the green coat
took the guitar and very politely asked the ladies to play and sing.
The youngest refused because she was still recovering from the
hoarseness she acquired at the last dancing party she had attended, and the oldest—as one could see, did not know music. Then
the owner gave a suggestion that the gentlemen ought to give an
example for the ladies. After this, the one who was sitting by the
ladies turned his eyes on his friend and smiled so that the young
lady just then recognized her cue, whereupon she began to ask
him to sing. He refused for a long time, then took the guitar, low-
ered his eyes, and sat down on the side of a chair, tucked up one
knee, leaving the other leg stretched out, and began with very sad
chords until he found an appropriate one and sang some strange,
pleasant Spanish romance with much emotion, and from time to
time he looked at the ladies. The guests liked the song very much,
and the owner asked for another. The polite guest (who had just
performed) encouraged by the first success, took up the guitar
again, lifted his eyes, straightened up himself, and started a new
song] (Domeyko 1888:II, 122).

1848, Samuel Greene Arnold
1. [Post house of Lobatón, Province of Córdoba:]
[At six o'clock we arrived at Lobatón, a solitary post house like
no other that we have spoken of.... Recuero (Arnold's guide from
Mendoza, Argentina) played the guitar as he does in almost all of
the post houses because there are always guitars] (Arnold 1848
MS:105, but since the MS remains unpublished and in private
custody, our text is taken from the Sp. translation, 1951:191–92).

2. [Cañada de Lucas, Province of Córdoba:]
[Around eight o'clock we arrived at Cañada de Lucas.... This
afternoon we had here a ball. Recuero played the guitar and we
watched two peons dance, with two girls of the post house, the

dance called the *gato* accompanied by the clicking of fingers like castanets, and the rest of the scene—the dirty hut, the glancing looks of the girls, the dim light, and the laughter—all formed a spectacle that reminded me of the dances of *Almeh* in Egypt, except that here the music was different and the dancing was decent] (Arnold 1848:106, 1951:193).

3. [In the Province of Córdoba, the first post house on the west road leaving Cañada de Lucas, situated four leagues or about twelve miles away:]

[Accompanying us was a beautiful young lady with whom Recuero had a long conversation, being a real humming bird (*picaflor*) as they are called here; he played the guitar and courted her energetically for two hours. Then we left at eleven o'clock] (Arnold 1848:107, 1951:194).

4. [Post house of Achiras, Province of Córdoba:]

[At twilight we arrived at Achiras, the last post house of this province. It is a little town of several hundred inhabitants.... The post house is very comfortable. We went about and we stopped at the best hovel where a young woman of simplicity and good manners played the guitar and sang for us. A ball was organized for the night, where the other companions have gone while I write. The ball was in the house of the girl who played the guitar. About 20 persons filled her room. The dirt floor was rough. Some men performed on the guitar while those of our group danced the waltz, minuet, and contredances; I just watched and smoked] (Arnold 1848:108, 1951:196–97).

5. [El Morro, Province of San Luis:]

[Almost the entire day we have been in the Province of San Luis. Here, in Morro, we found the governor of the Province; we visited him.... Soon we said good-bye and we entered into a house where we heard a young woman who played the guitar very well. She was also pretty...she played and sang well so that we might hear her. Recuero broke her guitar by accident so we left. This town has 700 inhabitants] (Arnold 1848:109, 1951:198).

6. [City of San Luis, Province of San Luis:]

[This city has about 5,000 inhabitants, it is the capital of the Province and the best that I have seen lately in the pampas.... This morning, when we went out to walk, we went into a house, we introduced ourselves with complete liberty as is the custom, and soon the young women began to play the guitar] (Arnold 1848:111, 1951:202).

1862, Thomas J. Hutchinson

1. [Tajamares, Province of Córdoba:]

We had been sitting for about an hour outside the house at *Tajamares*, and having just finished our evening meal of *puchero* and *asado* [boiled and baked meat], were talking over the general topics of our journey, when *Don Teodoro*, in a very quiet, slow way of talking he had, told us that his wife and he were going to a ball, and to a house where an infant of only three months old had died yesterday. Thinking this would be an opportunity to witness one of the peculiar customs of the country, I at once acceded to his equally quiet way of hinting to *Don Estevan Rams* and me that we might accompany him.... After about an hour's ride we arrived at the house where the dance was to be.... The foremost scene in the picture was the baby laid out in state on a small table. At its head were two candles, stuck, one in a broken gin, and the other in a damaged beer, bottle. The little defunct seemed but as a dot in the quantity of tinsel and ribbon flowers that swallowed it up. Each of its cheeks was painted with a 'cochineal' daub of about the size of a dollar, and the lips smeared with the same sombre red gave to the rest of its face a very ghastly appearance. An enormous crown was placed above its head, a pair of fragile paper wings fastened to its shoulders, where, I believe, the flying apparatus of cherubims is generally accredited to be, and its little hands were folded over its breast, grasping a cross more than half the size of itself. The rest of the body was covered by a linen wrapper replete with tinsel and spangles. From a branch of one of the large trees near the house was suspended a small cradle of Castile cane. The only light in the place was that from the two candles at the infant's head. As I viewed this scene, and observed a pair dancing when we came up, it occurred to me, how strange would be such a sight to English eyes...[see Plate X].

I saw a woman sitting in the corner strumming a guitar. The tune played for these dances is generally as rapid as that for an Irish jig; but much of its vivacity is diminished by the drawling song with which the player accompanies it. The dances here were *El Gato*, which is performed in conjunction with snapping the fingers to imitate Spanish castanets, *El Escondido*, *Los Aires* [as shown below], and *El Triunfo*, danced in like manner, with *La Mariquita*,

Plate X *My First Ball in Córdova* (Thomas Hutchinson 1865)

which is accompanied by the waving of pocket handkerchiefs. The
guitar was played by two women who relieved each other every
half hour.... Amongst the company were three individuals whom I
deem worthy of a special notice. One...was a *Gaucho* named *José
Vega* who was an 'Improvisatore,' and who chanted, or rather intoned, many plaintive ditties, accompanied by a hornpipe-like harmony on the guitar. My knowledge of the Castilian language did
not enable me to translate any of these effusions; but there seemed
in the mode of reciting them something of the melody and grace of
the natural poet, which had its palpable effect on the audience. For
at the end of each verse was a timid effort at applause by his ad-
mirers. Along with his singing, he was likewise one of the best
dancers in the company.... Thus it went on till near three o'clock in
the morning—dancing, singing, guitar playing, and passing the
gin bottle. As soon as daybreak should appear, the babe was to be
rolled up in a bundle made of that cradle hanging on the tree, and
to be borne by the father on horseback to its last resting-place at the
graveyard of *El Puesto de Castro*, five leagues off (Hutchinson
1865:139–43).

2. Through the kindness of Mr. R.B. Benn, of Rosario, I pro-
cured the following specimen of the songs that are intoned with the
dance [the text of *los Aires* follows with a new, rhymed translation]:

Chorus; [then] the guitar-player chants:

Aires y más aires,   [Airs and gentle breezes
Una vueltita en el aire,   a little turn in the air;
Aires, Aires, Aires,   still more airs and breezes,
Relación para la mujer.   statement from the lady fair.

The woman, dancing, sings:

Son dos hermosos despojos— They are beautiful bounty
  tus ojos,   —your eyes.
Una mis ansias provoca—   What provokes my desires is
  tu boca   —your mouth.
Dos cristales soberanos—   Your hands are like sovereign crystal
  tus manos.   —my prize.
Los tormentos inhumanos   The torments you bring are my
                 commands,
Me sirven de atormentarme; they serve but only to tempt me;
Bastan pues para matarme,   in fact, they're enough to kill me,
Tus ojos, pies, boca y manos. your eyes and feet, your mouth and
                 hands.

General chorus; [then] led off by the man, dancing:

Sois tan bonita y tan fiel You are so pretty and faithful
Como la flor del durazno; like the flower of the peach.
Tú sabes que yo te quiero, You already know that I love you,
¿Qué tienes que andar dudando? Why do you doubt what's in
          reach?

After an interval of dancing...the female again sings:

La alhajita que me disteis, Thank you for the little flower;
Se le cayeron las hojas. already are fallen its leaves.
¿Cómo quieres que te quiera, How can you want me, my lover,
Si tu querida se enoja? if the others are so easily peeved?

To which the man responds:

Las banderillas del fuerte The little flags of the fortress
Se flamean cuando paso, are inflamed with every gesture.
A vos solita te quiero; I love you only, my princess;
De las demás no hago caso. with the others I take no pleasure.]

Altogether the song, in its sentiments as well as performance, has a good deal of the lugubrious about it (Hutchinson 1865:142n).

3. [Candelaria, Province of Córdoba:]

There was a blind boy named *Valentine Viñas* at this station, who got his affliction when at the age of five days he was taken across the country to *Río Seco* to be baptised. He played the guitar with great taste, and sang well; I believe the poor fellow's only accomplishments (Hutchinson 1865:148).

4. [Alderetes, Province of Tucumán:]

At the southern side of the river [*Salí*] is the suburb of *Adirettes*, where (this being carnival time) singing, drinking, and playing the guitar are carried on through the day, while the dancing is put off till night (Hutchinson 1865:186).

5. [Arroyo de la Soledad, Province of Santa Fe:]

Set a *Gaucho* to dance, and he moves as if he were on a procession to his execution; ask him to sing, and he gives utterance to sounds resembling an Irish keen [a lament for the dead], accompanied with nasal drones suggestive of croup; put him to play the guitar, and you feel your flesh beginning to creep (Hutchinson 1865:123).

4. Map References

Most of our illustrious travellers avoided Buenos Aires—at least they did not refer to it as often as they did to the the interior towns. Despite the incomparable satisfaction of cosmopolitan life in the cities, they seemed inclined to find business or adventure in the smaller towns or even in the wide-open spaces of the pampa. For the most part, their official business or personal interests took them into obscure scenes of the countryside, whether north or west of Buenos Aires. In fact, many of the foreigners were only passing through. Some of them, who travelled west on the Plata environs outside of the winter season, went so far as to traverse the plains or scale the Andes en route to Chile. Others crossed Argentina as they headed northwest, towards the highland mines of the Bolivian border or Peru.

The only Plata travellers who numbered extensively in the port cities (of those who managed to publish their memoirs) were the forces of the British invasion that began in 1806. Most of the troops were confined to one side of the Plata or the other. Indeed, thousands never saw the capital; they had to content themselves with having visited only Montevideo or smaller towns on the East Bank that were yet subject to the Buenos Aires viceroyalty during the invasion. British soldiers landed on the Uruguayan shoreline in two large units: Samuel Auchmuty's men, which numbered an estimated 4,000, and Robert Craufurd's infantry, which alone consisted of another 4,000 in reinforcements.

The memoirs of the travellers contain therefore an abundance of burdensome geographical detail regarding tiny country and coastal towns, and even the postal stops between them. In order to deal with this plethora of detail, a map of the Río de la Plata, provided below, documents the major towns and their respective provinces which the travellers observed. However, other places, so obscure that they do not appear on standard maps, are set in **boldface** numbers in order to facilitate reference to them. A chart accompanies the map: the chart serves both as a key to the reference numbers on the map and as a checklist of the locations which the travellers happened to visit during the 19th century.

Location	Map Ref.	Province	Year, Traveller, Account No.
Achiras	13	Córdoba	1848 Arnold, 4
Alderetes	16	Tucumán	1862 Hutchinson, 4
Arroyo de la Soledad	6	Santa Fe	1862 Hutchinson, 5
Buenos Aires, City of		Buenos Aires	1797 Davie, 1–3
" " "		" "	1806 Gillespie, 1–3
" " "		" "	1827 d'Orbigny, 9
" " "		" "	1830 Isabelle, 3–4
Caacaty	20	Corrientes	1827 d'Orbigny, 2
Cabeza del Tigre		[Buenos Aires]	1837 Chikhachev
Candelaria	5	Santa Fe	1821 Caldcleugh
Candelaria	7	Córdoba	1862 Hutchinson, 3
Cañada de Lucas	10	Córdoba	1848 Arnold, 2
Carmela Achaval	15	Santiago del E.	1825 Andrews, 1
Corrientes, City of		Corrientes	1827 d'Orbigny, 3–7
Cruz de Guerra	2	Buenos Aires	1827 d'Orbigny, 10
El Morro	14	San Luis	1848 Arnold, 5
Itatí	19	Corrientes	1827 d'Orbigny, 8
Laguna Brava	18	Corrientes	1827 d'Orbigny, 1
Lagunillas	17	Salta	1825 Andrews, 3
Las Tunas	12	Córdoba	1819 Miers, 2
Lobatón	11	Córdoba	1848 Arnold, 1
Mendoza, City of		Mendoza	1838 Domeyko, 1–4
" "		"	1825 Head
Mercedes	4	Buenos Aires	1819 Miers, 1
Montevideo		Capital, Urug.	1806 anon., 1–3
Puente de Márquez	1	Buenos Aires	1834 Scarlett, 2
San Luis, City of		San Luis	1819 Miers, 3
" " "		" "	1848 Arnold, 6
San Pedro	3	Buenos Aires	1827 d'Orbigny, 8
Santiago del Estero		Santiago del E.	1825 Andrews, 2
Tajamares	8	Córdoba	1862 Hutchinson, 1
Tegua	9	Córdoba	1819 Miers, 4
(unspecified)		Tucumán	1830 Isabelle, 1
"		"	1834 Scarlett, 3

Plata Towns and Posts

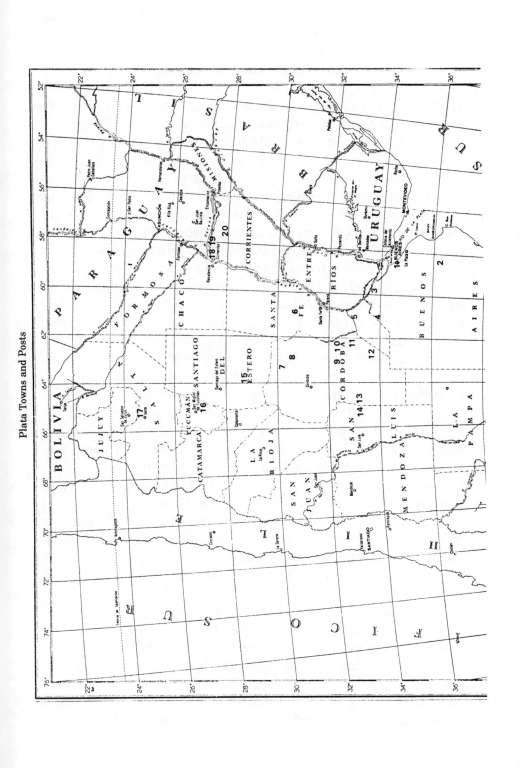

5. Summary and Conclusions

With his customary display of modesty, Francis Bond Head began
his title with *Rough Notes Taken during Some Rapid Journeys...*,
yet it is a beginning that would have suited many of the travel
accounts. It is easy to find fault with them. Their authors were
neither objective nor positive in many cases but naïve and emotional if not altogether biased and condescending instead. Perhaps
the foreigners were overly conscious of the European audience, for
they were superficial and unscientific in their approach. Even so,
empirical writing in the social sciences and humanities was yet in
its infancy because it was still dominated by the philology of classic
literature. Outside of the physical sciences, the scientific method
was yet subservient to philosophical aims. At any rate, the foreigners used a critical tone, and they tended toward overstatement.
Sometimes they even quoted or paraphrased each other without
acknowledgment. Worst of all, they were poorly prepared for their
listening experiences. While music was certainly a highlight of
their narratives, they left no evidence of ever attending a single
concert. Instead, the adventurous travellers were bent on discovering the unknowns of an exotic culture, far indeed from the main
port where there were plenty of classical concerts and opera productions in the Paris of the New World. Even so, they had no prior
frame of reference for appreciating the ethnic music they heard;
they could only relate it to what they already knew. Miers equated
some Argentine folk songs with "barbarous Saracenic airs" or
"rude Moorish canzonets"; Hutchinson, born in Ireland, compared
them to the "Irish keen," a lament for the dead! The Rioplatense
folk dances and the scene of their performance reminded Arnold
of the Egyptian dances of *Almeh!*

Even if the 19th-century travel accounts were not prepared as
scientific essays, they contain a wealth of data on the guitar as well
as a number of authentic characteristics of Rioplatense music. In
order to access this data, we must simply rise above the faults in
the accounts and make conclusions on their similarities. Facts are
verifiable either when they identify acknowledged folkloric traits
and existing musical practices, or when they coincide with another

datum. To be sure, as two or more accounts confirm a single practice at different times and places, their testimonials converge into an incontrovertible proof. Overall, the accounts supply a number of important conclusions about the guitar and how society put it to use.

A. The Guitar in the Entertainment of All Classes

1. The guitar and the piano were equally popular among social elites (d'Orbigny 1835–47:I, 247). This was verified in Buenos Aires (Gillespie 1818:67), at the Holmos estancia in the Argentine interior (Robertson 1843:II, 52–55), and with the youth of the "best families" in the City of Corrientes (d'Orbigny 1835–47:I, 380).

2. The guitar was undoubtedly the favorite and often the only musical instrument of the lower classes in the cities or on the pampa. "The owner [of the pulpería]...amused himself during the absence of visitors with his guitar; almost all the peasants in this country play on that instrument (Proctor 1825:11)." Domeyko observed the guitar repeatedly in the ranchos across the pampa (1888:104, 113, 121, 122). The Robertsons refer to it several times among the peasants in Paraguay (1839:I, 151, 325, 351). Thus the travellers observed the guitar in use at all levels, in fact, repeatedly at the extremes of Hispanic society.

3. By unanimous omission, however, the foreigners surveyed in Part V never mentioned the guitar in the hands of domestic servants. This fact was unusual because unpaid or scarcely paid servants had often specialized in music performance during the colonial epoch, even in church music. For example, as cited above in Table 13, 1805: "The mulatto Juan, slave of Doña Micaela Peralta, 'lives free, without any subjection; such that there is neither party nor meeting in which he is not found because he is a singer and guitar player'."

4. The mere presence of the guitar among Hispanics of the lower classes was a pretense for meeting if not carousing. With it they accompanied their entertainments of song and dance, yet they also played it as a solo instrument (Isabelle 1835:257, Miers 1826:45). The guitar was thus the principal medium of popular entertainment in the 19th century; it was comparable to our mass media of the present day.

5. A man ordinarily employed the guitar as a tool to enhance courtship to a woman in the countryside (Arnold 1848:107; Domeyko 1888:122), and for entertaining or serenading in the town of Corrientes (d'Orbigny 1835–47:I, 376–78).

6. Naturally guitarists were featured on certain holidays and celebrations like the days of St. Peter, St. Benedict (Table 13) or carnival, preceding lent (Hutchinson 1865:186). But during periods of intense work, when friends, relatives, and workers came together, guitarists lightened the burden of shearing time in the spring and the periodic wheat harvest (Miers 1826:219–20).

7. Guitars were widely available. Musicians were always at hand, and virtually all the gauchos played the guitar (Ebelot 1889: 79–80). In the Hispanic sector of the town of Corrientes, Argentina, "Nearly all the men are musicians (d'Orbigny 1835–47:I, 358)." A visit to a cattle ranch in Durazno, Uruguay revealed that "after a plentiful supper we had singing and dancing to the music of the guitar, on which every member of the family—excepting the babies—could strum a little (Hudson 1885:30)."

8. To keep them handy, the guitars of Corrientes were hung on the wall of the home (d'Orbigny 1835–47:I, 358, 365), as they were in the pulpería (Pallière 1869:179). Domeyko observed, in a tidy Argentine house of the interior, "the usual order: the guitar on the wall (1888:121)."

9. Generally the travellers did not specify the technical characteristics of the guitars they observed. However, the iconographical sources reveal a guitar of five double courses, as in the late 17th-century Jesuit church of Córdoba, Argentina (see above, Plate VI), and guitars of six single strings in Pallière's 19th century works representing his trips to Argentina and Uruguay. In other words, their guitars were similar to those of Europe during the same time frame. However, Isabelle had noticed a guitar with twelve metal strings in Buenos Aires (1835:254). Regarding the use of such guitars in Spain, see especially Federico Moretti, *Principios para tocar la guitarra de seis órdenes* [Madrid, 1799].

10. The guitar was taken up by all ages, ranging from the boy of *The Purple Land* (Hudson 1885:26) to the white-haired gaucho of the wake (Ebelot 1889:13–15). Many if not most members of the populace could play the guitar.

11. Nevertheless, there were those who specialized in guitar music (Miers 1826:44–45). Historically the guitarists of folk music (old popular music in the Plata) were called *guitarreros* (Robertson 1839:I, 325; 1843:I, 197). Later on in the Plata, this epithet often applied to guitar makers or luthiers as it did in Spain. The most specialized folk and popular guitarist was the balladeer of the pampas, who was never without his guitar, as portrayed by artist Pallière in *El payador* 1869:120f. (see also C below). Thus anyone in the countryside known as *a musician*, even a singer, was usually a guitarist (This is confirmed by guitarists Hilario Ascasubi in Ref. 2 and Irma Costanzo, below, in Appendix III).

12. Music was welcome anytime. However, the travellers often observed guitar performances around mealtime: before supper (Robertson 1843:I, 229–31), during supper (*Notes* 1808:60–64; see illustration in MacCann 1853:II, 47), or afterwards, especially (Gillespie 1818:69, Darwin 1839:37, d'Orbigny 1835–47:I, 378, and Hutchinson 1865:139–43).

13. In the Río de la Plata, "Nearly all the Spaniards are poets and admirably improvise verses...with the guitar or piano (Isabelle 1835:247)." "Any one being asked to play a tune on the guitar ...will always adapt to it a set of extemporaneous and accordant verses, with much facility (Gillespie 1818:68)."

14. Guitarists continued the two main Renaissance techniques of the right hand in the Río de la Plata: they either plucked the guitar, as in aristocratic Spanish music for the vihuela (d'Orbigny 1835–47:I, 120, 236–37, 376, 380) or strummed after the popular style (Isabelle 1835:254, Hudson 1885:30). However, d'Orbigny's rather elaborate description of strumming was similar to those found in the prefaces of Baroque guitar books:

> Girolamo Montesardo, 1606: *"batter le corde...*[hitting the strings sweetly with three or four fingers]."
> Benedetto Sanseverino, 1620: "[It seems to me that one ought to play the Spanish guitar with full strokes *(botte piene),* and not otherwise] (Pinnell 1980:31–34)."

D'Orbigny also implied strumming with several or all of the right-hand fingertips: the guitarist sang, "accompanying himself by striking his fingers on the strings of the instrument instead of plucking, and making above all a lot of noise (1835–47:I, 376)."

B. The Guitar in Folk Dances

1. The guitar was the typical instrument with which to accompany the 19th-century popular dances of the Plata, now known there as "folk dances."

2. Optimally two or three guitars accompanied these dances, probably in an effort to achieve adequate volume and rhythmic stability in noisy circumstances (Arnold 1848:108, Mantegazza 1876:68–69). Léon Pallière portrayed such a scene in *El gato, baile campestre*, a lithograph in the collection of A. Gonzalo Garano (reprinted in Vega 1946b:97). In it Pallière shows a couple dancing before a crowd of nineteen persons, two of whom are ladies elegantly dressed in the foreground and all the others are young gauchos. Among the latter are two guitarists accompanying the dance.

3. At gatherings in the countryside, a *baile* [ball] with dances was a typical activity before supper (see lithograph by Daufresne, Plate VII), but of course after supper was even better (d'Orbigny 1835–47:I, 378, Arnold 1848:108, Hutchinson 1865:139).

4. Some dances, such as the *malambo*, were instrumental (without singing). The guitarist executed the *malambo,* a short theme and set of continuous variations, as a guitar solo in order to showcase the intricate but virile steps of a man's dance. It was a favorite among the gauchos (according to Espinosa, in Part III, above).

5. However, most of the Rioplatense folk dances were sung dances with guitar accompaniment, and they were intended for couples. The vocals of such dances always involved soloists, yet often the spectators or dancers would join in by singing together in a chorus (Hutchinson 1865:142n).

6. Sometimes, in dances of courtship, the dancers themselves would sing or recite solos of a few lines. In the *aires* they sang some of the responses to each other (Hutchinson 1865:142n). In the *pericón*, which became the national dance of Uruguay (Hudson 1885:30), the dancers recited *relaciones*. These "relations" were improvised verses of four lines, but in reality the dancers might have prepared them beforehand whenever a friendship was well

established. The male sang the four-line verse of entreaty at a given moment before the entire group of dancers; the female had to respond to it immediately with a rhymed verse of equal length which expressed her feelings, without losing the pace of the dance (Mantegazza 1876:68–69; Hernández, Ref.7). Women there were famous for their defensive or witty answers, depending on whether they wanted to discourage or encourage their partners. Either way, they lived by the credo, "He who hesitates is lost." This was a situation in which Plata women always made known their quick wit and spontaneous repartee that so many travellers noticed.

7. None of the folk dances mentioned by the travellers were for close contact. Men could never squeeze their partners in them, as they eventually did in the Viennese waltz or the Rioplatense tango. Singers and guitarists performed the folk dances. Dancers participated as couples, but both the man and the woman danced with some independence (regarding an overview and classification of the folk dances, see Vega 1956:57).

   a. The *cielito* (in Plate VIII and as described by Isabelle and d'Orbigny) and the *media caña* (Isabelle) were both animated dances that required some coordination with other couples, like many stateside folk dances before 1900. Just the same, Isabelle thought the gestures of the *media caña* were immoral.

   b. The *minué montonero* featured a mixture of formal European and upbeat South American steps, hence also varying tempos like the *cuando* (d'Orbigny 1835–47:I, 237).

   c. It was Hutchinson alone among these travellers who witnessed the lively, picaresque dances called the *aires, triunfo*, and the *escondido*, all of which required the spectacular gestures of waving pocket handkerchiefs and the display of fancy footwork.

   d. The *gato* was another fast, syncopated dance in 6/8 (Arnold and Hutchinson; Refs. 1, 7), like the *zamacueca* (Ebelot 1889:15).

   e. The *mariquita* was so sensual that Arnold thought it "peculiarly expressive of the...advances of lovers to each other" (1827: 147–49; Hutchinson 1865:139–43).

   f. The *zarandîg*, an upbeat "heel dance," was popular in Paraguay. Although considered a low-class dance at the time, the *zarandîg* was also prominent at upper-class parties (Robertson 1839:I, 146–47). The travellers did not mention it elsewhere.

8. The dancers often clicked their fingers along with the guitar music in place of castanets (Arnold 1848:106, Hutchinson 1865: 139–43, Mantegazza 1876:68–69, Ebelot 1889:13–15). But Chikhachev actually heard castanets.

9. A *velorio del angelito*, a wake for a deceased child (or little angel), was an elaborate reception for neighbors and friends if the parents of the child could afford it. It was a celebration because any of the baptized Roman Catholic children who died before the age of accountability were thought to be as pure and deserving of heaven as any little angel. The parents displayed the defunct child with religious regalia inside a home or a pulpería in order to dispel the remorse. They organized a ball in conjunction with the showing of the corpse so that young people could attend, dance, and celebrate the child's quick passage into heaven. Guitarists, whether hired or as a service, organized the singing and dancing. An unpretentious funeral and burial followed the wake (see Hutchinson 1865:139–43 and Plate X, "My first ball in Córdova," which shows both the baby and a young woman playing the guitar in the background). The Robertsons witnessed such a wake (1839:III, 151–52) and Ebelot, several (1889:13–15). Regarding the dance for the deceased *angelito*, see Coluccio 1964:II, 482; and the song for the *angelito*, Becco 1960:244–45. While the *canto de velorio* was also sung in colonial Venezuela—clearly suggesting Hispanic origins of the practice—the Rioplatense velorio may date back to indigenous Indian customs. Among the *Lules*, for instance, there were great musicians, and they performed and drank the entire night of the wake in order to celebrate the passing of their dead, according to Father Bárzana in 1594 (see conclusions, Part IV). Starting in 1600 or thereabouts, the Jesuit fathers would attend on these occasions with the purpose of introducing Christian music as part of their religious conquest (Carrizo 1953:47).

C. The Guitar in Gaucho Songs

1. As established in Part III, guitarists performed religious songs which were not intended for dancing. For example in the travel accounts, there were some hymns of praise for "Our Lady of Candelaria (Caldcleugh 1825:250)" and for individuals (d'Orbigny 1835–47:I, 192, 468). A song of *despedida* was a reverent farewell.

2. The gaucho ballads were always lengthy, rhymed narratives, so they were not danced either. The gauchos used only the guitar to accompany their ballads, their "only national harmony (Mantegazza 1876:68–69)." Pallière published lithographs of the gauchos and sketched several with their guitars in his *Diario de viaje* (1869:103, 306, 322). "Of special notice...was a gaucho named José Vega who was...accompanied by a hornpipé-like harmony on the guitar (Hutchinson 1865:139–43)."

3. Some authors, hearkening back to Azara's late 18th-century description, called the gaucho ballad a *yaraví*, an extremely sad song from Peru (Vidal 1820:69). In doing so, they showed that they had been reading in preparation for their travels. Others mentioned the equally sad and perhaps related *triste* from Peru in the same context (Head 1826:152, Isabelle 1835:257, Robertson 1839:I, 325; III, 151; 1843:I, 197). On several occasions d'Orbigny spoke of the *triste*, and treated it as a slow, sad romance or love song (1835–47:I, 358–59, 505). Notwithstanding, the earlier reports may have misled the 19th-century travellers, for the gaucho ballad may not have been so closely related to the yaraví or triste as they thought. (For more on the yaraví and triste, see Aretz 1952:135–38.)

4. The gaucho balladeers were notorious improvisers, and were sometimes likened to "Italian buffos...improvisatore" (Robertson 1843:I, 229–31, Hutchinson 1865:139–43, Mantegazza 1876:68–69, d'Orbigny 1835–47:I, 358–59). To a predictable, repeated musical pattern on the guitar, they would "adapt a set of extemporaneous and accordant verses, with much facility (Gillespie 1818:68)."

5. The gaucho's tour de force was to include the name and circumstances of a visitor of the group into his song, all without losing a beat or the rhyme-scheme (d'Orbigny 1835–47:I, 358–59, 468, Caldcleugh 1825:250, Robertson 1843:I, 229–31). This practice served to prove before his listeners that the performer created the new verses spontaneously. Such was the case for Miers: in his usually caustic, unsympathetic account he claimed, "the people catch hold of the name of their visitors, and of some circumstance connected with them, and mix them up with their songs (1826:55–57)." Yet today the Plata payadors continue this tour de force in their performances. (Hear for instance "Me dicen el Pansa Verde" by Víctor Velázquez on *20 grandes éxitos*, EMI 16236, 1986.)

6. The guitar and the unruly crowds at the pulpería had been prohibited regularly since 1690 (Part III, Sect. 3). This tavern/store continued with the same, unofficial function into the 19th century where singers met and performed (Isabelle 1835:253–54). In the painting by Carlos Morel, *Payada en la pulpería*, Plate IX) two singers compete as they simultaneously play their guitars (d'Orbigny 1835–47:I, 620). Whether in the city neighborhoods, towns, or in the countryside, the pulperías definitely continued to be the local centers of light entertainment: "the guitar players and singers [were] those individuals most important and indispensable to such gatherings (d'Orbigny 1835–47:I, 620)."

7. The proprietor of a pulpería ordinarily enhanced his business potential by providing a guitar in the establishment to loan out to clients. The guitar's easy availability encouraged and facilitated the performances of gaucho sages and other entertainers who in turn always drew large crowds (Part IV, Sect. 3 and Vidal 1820:69; see Pallière, watercolor, 1869:179). In fact, some pulpería owners themselves were guitarists (Table 12; Proctor 1825:105).

8. A guitar was also typical in the wayside *post house,* a pulpería enhanced with extra horses and some makeshift sleeping accommodations for travellers—indeed, the early American motel (Head 1826:151–52; Robertson 1843:II, 52–55; Pallière, lithograph, 1869: 264f.). "Recuero played the guitar as he does in almost all of the post houses, since there are always guitars (Arnold 1848:105)." Vidal likened the rugged post houses of the Argentine frontier to the infamous, low-class *ventas* of Galicia and Catalonia, for also "they are frequently provided with a guitar (1820:69–70)."

9. While Isabelle was merely quoting Concolorcorvo with regard to couples who alternated their spontaneous verses, he said that, at his business in Buenos Aires, he had two laborers from Tucumán who always performed in this manner (1835:227). The pampa balladeers were such experts at singing in improvised dialogue that they would spend long hours at it or even all day, like the Arcadian ancients, to the accompaniment of their guitars (d'Orbigny 1835–47:I, 358–59 and Plate IX).

10. The foreigners often heard the un-danced gaucho ballad, but it was the musical expression that they enjoyed least of all in the Río de la Plata. They complained that it was sad, rather than

upbeat, tragic in subject, and probably in a minor key (Miers 1826: 100; see also *triste* and *yaraví,* above). Yet their commentaries reveal the fact that it was also the musical expression they least understood.

11. The travellers regarded gaucho music as monotonous:

a. The same "tune" or chord progression was repeated continuously on the guitar. According to Scarlett, "We have therefore had nothing to do but to eat, drink, and listen all the day long to a poor cracked guitar, on which one of the ladies of our grumbling landlord has constantly been strumming the same air.... It is played everywhere and on all occasions (1838:154)."

b. Like the medieval troubadors, the gauchos sang each verse to the same melody over and over again as they improvised new words in a continuously unfolding, partly extemporaneous text (Miers 1826:55–57).

c. Some of the songs had such a restricted range that Isabelle called them "psalmodies" (1835:253), like the psalm-singing of church cantors. Gaucho José Vega "chanted or rather intoned" his line (Hutchinson 1865:142–43).

d. The foreigners often missed the point, for they could not always understand the words! (Robertson 1843:I, 229–31). Hutchinson gave the following response to the performance of gaucho José Vega: "My knowledge of the Castilian [sic!] language did not enable me to translate any of these effusions; but there seemed in the mode of reciting them something of the melody and grace of the natural poet, which had its palpable effect on the audience (1865:142–43)." The gaucho dialect was *Rioplatense,* the language they inherited from the original Andalusian colony of the Río de la Plata. The British, like the Spaniards and other foreigners who visited the region, came harboring the same, incorrect assumption that the Castilian dialect was spoken there (see the conclusions of Part II, which define Rioplatense).

D. The Guitar among Social Elites

1. The guitar and piano shared the limelight in the polite salons of Buenos Aires and Montevideo. While guitar solos were indeed performed during the 19th century, musicians in the salon used the guitar most often to accompany dances or songs from Europe,

rather than those of local provenance. They either used the guitar alone or along with the piano in the capital cities (Gillespie 1818: 67). In the interior towns, there were but few pianos, so the guitar was yet their mainstay of accompaniment during the 19th century. In Gillespie's account of an elaborate, 24-course dinner in Buenos Aires, he was entertained by Captain Belgrano's wife and her lady friends, who sang "pretty Spanish and English airs upon the guitar (1818:69)." The Robertsons heard songs in this context (1843:II, 52–55); see also d'Orbigny (1843–47:I, 505) and Isabelle (1835:257). The anonymous author of *Notes from the Viceroyalty* heard guitar songs in the company of monks at a 30-course meal, as well as "God Save the King" during the British occupation of Montevideo! (1808:64).

2. Davie circulated between the elite families (including officials, landowners, and merchants of the capital), among whom music and conversation, "the touchstones of civilization," reigned as the usual pastimes after siesta. In the early evening he would intentionally stroll down the best residential streets of Buenos Aires with the purpose of overhearing serenades, performed to the tune of guitars and mandolins, wafting over their balconies (1805:114–41). Similarly Brigadier-General Robert Craufurd claimed that in Montevideo, "frequently one hears, passing by, the sounds of the piano or guitar (1807:523)." He also claimed that Plata residents reinstated the touchstones of civilization as British troops began to withdraw from the region (Craufurd 1807:526).

3. The piano was yet rare in the countryside. There was but one such instrument in all of Corrientes (d'Orbigny 1835–47:I, 365) and only a few in Asunción (Robertson 1839:I, 146–47). They were not of local manufacture in the 19th century, as in the U.S.; they came from abroad through Buenos Aires (see Table 8:1823). The *British Consular Reports* for 1822 (p. 56) confirmed that only 57 pianos entered the port that year (Jones 1949:30). The mere possession of a piano was a sign of considerable affluence.

4. The social elites of the capitals eschewed the unique popular dances of the Plata region in favor of European imports. In Buenos Aires, perhaps this was due to the old preference for Italian and French music—in archaic imitation of the tastes of the Peninsular court (Isabelle 1835:257; Brackenridge 1820:I, 284–85). Even

in the interior, the elite context emanated from the port because the dancers had to come through the capital cities in order to go to the interior towns, spreading thus the cosmopolitan taste to the distant reaches of the Río de la Plata. The foreigners of the 19th century observed the following European dances in their travels:

a. The *sarabande*, originally the wild 16th-century dance from Latin America, had been standardized in the suite by European guitarists; so by the time Davie danced to its strains in Buenos Aires, it was probably the slow, stately version (1805:111).

b. The *bolero* from Andalusia (Robertson 1843:I, 197, Isabelle 1835:257).

c. The *fandanguillo* and others from Andalusia (Mantegazza 1876:68–69; Table 13:1782). Chikhachev witnessed the *fandango* danced to the accompaniment of guitar and castanets (1844:58; see also Table 13 and Refs. 5–8, above).

d. The *habanera* from Cuba (Ebelot 1889:15).

e. The *contredanse* derived from the English country dance but refined in France (Arnold 1848:108, Isabelle 1835:257, d'Orbigny 1835–47:I, 505, Andrews 1827: 147–49, Robertson 1839:I, 104–05, 179–80).

f. The *minuet* from France (Brackenridge 1820:I, 285, Robertson 1843:II, 52–55, Arnold 1848:108, Andrews 1827:147–49). According to Craufurd, the minuet was danced again with dignity at about the time British troops were evacuating Montevideo (1807:526). The *minué montonero,* however, was more a folk than classical dance (see B.7, above).

g. Other forms mentioned were the *fantasia* on the piano (Robertson 1843:II, 52–55), and the *ouverture* on piano or guitar (Isabelle 1835:257).

5. Certainly the Plata's most notable upper-class dance in the 19th century was the *waltz*. While in Buenos Aires, Gillespie observed that there was already a preference for it during the British invasion (1818:67). The musicians there were performing it on the piano and guitar in 1806. This is surprising for many of the European composers who helped to popularize it were yet in their infancy: Schubert b. 1798, Berlioz b. 1803, Johann Strauss, Sr. b. 1804, Chopin b. 1810. Even Beethoven did not publish the piano variations on Anton Diabelli's waltz until 1823 as Op. 120. Several

Plata travellers witnessed the "natural elegance" or "exquisite manner" of the Rioplatense women whenever they danced the waltz: in Montevideo (Craufurd 1807:523; Robertson 1839:I, 105) and in Buenos Aires (Robertson, 1839:I, 179–80). The dancers waltzed in some smaller towns of the interior, as well (Robertson 1843:II, 52–55 and Arnold 1848:108), yet undoubtedly they had learned the dance beforehand in the capital cities. The waltz continued into the 20th century as a mainstay of tango ensembles in the Plata. (It provided light contrast to their repertoire of impassioned duple-meter tangos and milongas.)

E. Women and the Guitar

1. While men used the guitar directly in their courting to fantasize or to reveal sentiments they could not otherwise express (see A above), women used it indirectly for similar purposes. Women were often found performing to entertain men or to attract attention to themselves: two poor women (Miers 1826:98–100), niñas (Head 1826:151–52), the lady of Achaval (Andrews 1827:139–40), "a group of females...entertained (Andrews 1827: 277)." Arnold observed one "young woman of simplicity and good manners"; another one who "played and sang well so that we might hear her"; and en masse, "soon the women began to play the guitar (1848:108, 109, 111)." As Hudson wrote, "It was noon: the house was quiet.... I was lying on the sofa, smoking a cigarette. Dolores, seating herself near me with her guitar, said, 'Now let me play and sing you to sleep with something very soft.' But the more she played and sang, the further was I from slumber (1885:181)."

2. Just as in North America at the time of Stephen Foster, music was the basic pretense that young women would use to entice young men to visit them at their own home. If the pretense was music, young women could control the situation by practicing. Through their devotion to vocal and instrumental performance, composition, and improvisation, women kept an upper hand in their social affairs. Sensing repeated rewards (a grasp of musical progress in addition to social contact, approval, compliments, recognition, notoriety, etc.) for their efforts, they practiced assiduously to obtain ever more mastery of their notable expertise in music as well as their indoor environment. Since their mothers

generally stayed at home anyway, they encouraged the practice (d'Orbigny 1835–47:I, 365, 376, 380, 505).

3. Already as early as 1770, Pernety had noticed the excellent quality of music emanating from the female guitarists of Montevideo; he compared them to the French women he knew (Part III, Sect. 12). In the next century, during tea time (or as they drank their *mate*—see Appendix III), women invested their leisure hours in guitar practice (*Notes* 1808:35). "The Spanish ladies are extremely lively, good-humored, and witty.... Their amusements chiefly consist in singing and playing on the guitar, with which they pass many of their hours (*Notes* 1808:90–91)." "Women from Buenos Aires and Montevideo are as well suited as Italian women for music (Isabelle 1835:257)."

4. More than for merely attracting men, women could use the guitar in soliciting illicit business (as in Part III, Sect. 3 and in the story of Pallière 1869:230–31). However, this practice was exceptional in the conservative, religious society of the Plata.

5. In aristocratic circumstances, the guitar was still typical among women, for apparently there was no low-class stigma attached to it. Señora de Belgrano sang Spanish and English airs to the guitar in Buenos Aires (Gillespie 1818:69), as did the Holmos daughters in the countryside (Robertson 1843:II, 52–55) and Doña Juana in Asunción (Robertson 1839:I, 308–16).

6. Since the aristocratic dances required guitar accompaniment—whether with the piano or not, women took it upon themselves to perform with the guitar in towns (Arnold 1848:108) or in Montevideo (Craufurd 1807:523). Also, "Music is much cultivated at Buenos Aires. There is always one lady in every house who can furnish a good performance of all the tunes required for the minuet, the waltz, and the country dance (Robertson 1839:I, 179)."

7. On the other hand, women guitarists certainly accompanied folk dances (Plate X, Hutchinson 1865:139–43, Isabelle 1835:257).

8. Women at all social ranks of the Río de la Plata performed on the guitar, just as easily and almost as often as men. They did not compete in the pulpería with the rugged gauchos, but at least they did appear there occasionally as entertainers (Pallière 1869: 230–31; Head 1826:152). Hispanic women specialized primarily in the popular songs of the day which they performed most often in small

gatherings in their own homes or at the *tertulia* of a social acquaintance. In Montevideo, "their amusements chiefly consist in singing and playing on the guitar.... The airs they play are mostly love songs, and the melancholy ditties of Peru (*Notes* 1808:91).

9. By comparing them to Italian musicians, Isabelle equated the women of the capitals in their musical proficiency. On either side of the Plata, they had a gift for performing European and regional styles with *instrumental improvisation* (1835:257; see also Robertson 1843: II, 52–55; d'Orbigny 1835–47:I, 505).

10. Female guitarists of the capital cities were so accomplished musically and otherwise that the foreign observers were hard-pressed for explanations. The foreigners who heard them conjured up the most extreme examples they knew for comparison, starting with Pernety in 1770. Virtually all the foreigners who published their memoirs on the Plata were men. Those who proved capable of seeking out women of their own class found them attractive, especially in Montevideo (*Notes* 1808:83–91) and in Buenos Aires (Bingley 1820:291). Once Darwin's captain asked, "Whether the ladies of Buenos Ayres were not the handsomest in the world," to which Darwin responded, "Charmingly so" (1839:126). According to Davie, "I danced a saraband with Donna Josefina...a young lady of great beauty and accomplishments.... Donna Louisa equalled in splendor the richest lady present. She is the most lively and entertaining female I have ever conversed with (1805:111)." Their singular abilities on the guitar only enhanced them the more. For one traveller, the "lady of Achabal" bore "a strong resemblance to the handsomer portraits which have been left us of Mary, Queen of Scots (Andrews 1827:139–40)." Queen Mary, already known as a beautiful, talented singer and lutenist in her own right, outlived her husband, Francis II of France, as a teenage widow. On her return to Scotland, she entertained her secretary and guitarist David Rizzio, to whom she had given an excellent guitar, until his untimely death (see *Dictionary of National Biography* Vol. XII: 1266 or Schweitzer 1953:409–10). In some cases, at least, it seemed that travellers saw themselves matched to Rioplatense women over the guitar, if only in their fantasies. The evidence remained incontrovertible: even among foreigners in the Plata, women guitarists there were succeeding at their own game.

6. Biographies of Featured Travellers

Andrews, Captain [Joseph], an English sailor and businessman, was known as Captain Andrews because he was owner and commander of the ship "Windham." He arrived at Buenos Aires on 26 March 1825 with interests in the mining explorations of Famatina in the Argentine Province of La Rioja. He also passed through Córdoba, Salta, and Tucumán to take note of local customs and later penetrated into the silver country of Potosí and Arica (Andrews 1827:4, Busaniche 1959:III, 255).

Arnold, Samuel Greene, was born on 12 April 1821 in Providence, Rhode Island, being a descendant of Thomas Arnold, a 17th century colonist of that region. He finished his college education at Brown University in 1841, and then graduated from the Harvard Law School in 1845. At 24 he published his first book, *The Life of Patrick Henry of Virginia*, after which he travelled to Europe and the Near East. In 1847 he embarked for South America, and his travel diary, dedicated to his wife Louisa Gindrat, was completed upon his return to the States in 1848. But he never managed to publish the diary in English (the Spanish translation cited here was drawn from the original manuscript which remains until this day in the hands of Arnold's heirs). Undaunted, Arnold wrote the monumental *History of Rhode Island and Providence Plantation*, and served as the Vice-Governor of Rhode Island as well as the U.S. Senator from his state (Arnold 1848:20–22).

Caldcleugh, Alexander, "[embarked from Plymouth on 9 September 1819, bound for Rio de Janeiro. He was part of the diplomatic entourage that accompanied the English ambassador to that city. After two years there, a Captain Stanhope, commander of the brig 'Alacrity,' offered him the opportunity of visiting Buenos Aires, where he disembarked on 4 February 1821. He was only to remain there briefly, but since he was anxious to cross the Andes, he volunteered for that treacherous trek. He returned at the end of June and embarked again for Rio de Janeiro. Finally on 22 November 1821 he set foot again on English soil] (Cordero 1936:99)."

Chikhachev, Platon Alexandrovich, founder of the Imperial Society of Geography and member of the Society of Minerology of St. Petersburg, was born in Gatchina (near Leningrad). After illustrious service in the Russian army against the Turks, he travelled widely across the Americas. A mountain climber and adventurer, he decided to meet the English steamer which had brought him to Valparaíso, Chile on the other side of the Andes! At midsummer, late in December 1836 he left Chile with a guide, eastbound, and in January 1837 he crossed the Andes and then the Argentine pampa during the usual rigorous passage of some forty days by changing horses several times a day and riding at a full gallop whenever possible. He was delighted to find his English steamer, which had already rounded Cape Horn, awaiting him in the harbor of Montevideo. With it, he soon departed for India, having come to know firsthand both the Plata and its vast adjoining rangelands. Eventually Chikhachev published the diary of his trip across the pampa as "Poezdka cherez buenos-airesskia pampy," *Otechestvennye zapiski* in 1844 (Weiner 1967).

Domeyko, Ignácy, was born of Polish parents in Lithuania in 1802 and died in Santiago, Chile in 1889. He earned a degree in mathematics and then fought in the failed uprising of Lithuania in 1831. He fled to Paris in self-imposed exile to study mining; it was this specialty that would bring him to South America. One of his classmates in Paris was Carlos Lambert, a Chilean student on a government scholarship to study geology. At the end of their course in 1838, they planned to leave France together and to sail to South America. On their departure, the poet Adam Mickiewicz left Domeyko the challenge of writing a journal of the experiences and scenes of his trip. Domeyko complied: he wrote in it from then until his death. Domeyko and Lambert landed at Buenos Aires. Continuing on horseback, they crossed the 900-mile expanse of the pampa and then the Andes en route to Chile. Once established there, Domeyko founded the University of Chile in Santiago with Andrés Bello, and served as its provost from 1867 to 1883. Simultaneously he continued working within his specialty; he identified twenty minerals for the first time and thus helped to reveal the extent of Chile's geological resources. However, though he published many professional papers, his journal was not edited until 1962 in Polish, its original language (Zoltowska 1964).

d'Orbigny, Alcide, the great French naturalist, left the French port of Brest in 1826 and sailed to many parts of the world. Empowered with the title of Travelling Naturalist conferred by the Administration of the Natural Science Museum of Paris, he came to the Río de la Plata as part of an eight-year trip to South America. Then he returned to France, and with governmental support over the course of thirteen years, he completed his multi-volume study. In this vast perspective of his travels, he provides a panoramic, nearly encyclopedic coverage of the countries he visited, supplying not only data for the natural sciences, but also valuable information for the historical and anthropological fields (Cordero 1936:134–35).

Gillespie, Major Alexander, of the British army, led troops in the invasion of Buenos Aires on 26 June 1806 and remained there with the forces of the occupation. Once the city was temporarily taken, he carried the responsibility of Commissioner of Prisoners. He later went into the interior with new orders, "being senior officer of the whole detachment at Salta (Gillespie 1818:175)." However, during the proceedings of the British surrender, he was confined at San Antonio de Areco and Calamuchita, returning at last to England in 1807 (Busaniche 1959:II, 206).

Head, Captain Francis Bond (1793–1879), was the leading horseman of the English travellers. Head had gone to France, Malta, and Greece with the army corps of Royal Engineers, eventually achieving the rank of captain before bringing his family to South America on an assignment for private enterprise. "[He arrived in Buenos Aires and passed through Mendoza in 1825 en route to Chile as Director of the 'Rio Plata Mining Association.' He left us remarkable pages of literature on Argentine folklore unequalled by any other English traveller. Head describes the pampa around Buenos Aires, Córdoba, and Santa Fe, the Indian bandits and the gaucho with admirable mastery; he does the same for the post houses where he slept in his crossing to Mendoza. His descriptions are so tangible that his pages contain first-rate documentation for the study of the socio-political aspects of central Argentina in 1825 and 1826, the year of his return to London] (Carrizo 1953:67–68)."

Hutchinson, Thomas, was born in Stonyford, Ireland in 1802. He finished his general studies then specialized in medicine at the University of Göttingen, finishing in 1832. He relocated in England and ascended until he became surgeon major. Thus he began to travel extensively, taking part in the expedition of the ship "Pleiad" on African rivers in 1854. He remained there for several years on the southwest coast as British Consul. In 1862 Hutchinson went to Argentina to serve as British Consul to Rosario. In 1872 he was transferred from there to Callao, Peru. He died in 1883.

Isabelle, Arsène, born at the French port of Le Havre, felt the urge to travel at an early age, so he decided to go to South America. He arrived in Buenos Aires in 1830 and established there a soap and candle factory that lasted only three years. Even so, he found time to travel to Uruguay and Brazil before returning to France in 1834 (Busaniche 1959:III, 454).

Miers, John, was born in London on 25 August 1789 and died in Kensington on 17 October 1879. He crossed the Argentine pampa in 1819 en route to Chile, where he established a copper refinery. Although he came back momentarily to London in 1825, he returned to Argentina in order to install a coin factory the following year, remaining until 1831. He spent time in Brazil before his trip home in 1838 whence he became an authority on South American flora and fauna in British academic circles (Miers 1826:preface).

Scarlett, P. Campbell, was part of the English diplomatic representation in Rio de Janeiro and neighboring countries. With a colleague of that group, Mr. Hamilton Hamilton [sic], he arrived in Buenos Aires in October of 1834. From there he went to Chile. He established relations with a Mr. Wheelwright, former U.S. Consul to Guayaquil, and provided Wheelwright's newly formed navigation company with data on Callao, Peru, Panama, and other locations. Later he went to Jamaica and finally sailed from there back to England (Cordero 1936:153).

7. References Cited in Part V

Charles Darwin was the early master of the primary sources on the Río de la Plata. He regularly cited Azara, yet referred also to the books of Cuvier, Head, Walkenaer, Schmidl, and d'Orbigny in his own writings. Unlike most of his contemporaries, Darwin was bent on fact-finding exploration, so he must have come prepared with the unusual luxury of bringing his library aboard the "H.M.S. Beagle" in which he travelled the oceans. Dr. Mantegazza followed suit by citing sources: when he came to the effects of drinking *mate,* he listed a page full of references (1876:85). Since then the foreign travellers have become the point of departure for studies on 19th-century Argentina or Uruguay—especially humanistic research. Both Juan Alfonso Carrizo and Carlos Cordero reviewed the foreign literature from the Argentine perspective. But English readers have easy access to the same material. William Bingley published a lively general anthology on South America, as Tom Jones did a century later. In recent decades James Scobie left a checklist of travel accounts which describe Argentina's fascinating history (1971:268–73).

The authors and references cited below appear in two sections: *Section A,* covers the 19th century, *Section B,* the 20th. Section A includes travelogues as well as novels of the 19th century; it represents both the travellers who left firsthand accounts and the novelists they inspired. Naturally not all the 19th-century foreign literature on the Plata is listed here, but rather, only about a third of the travel accounts and a handful of novels—only enough to gain an overview of the guitar and its context from the foreign perspective. Fortunately, by library standards of the present day, these books are merely old and not yet rare. At least some U.S. libraries continue to make them available through the Interlibrary Loan service.

Most of the references of Section B date from the 20th century. They provide either secondary views of the source material or probes into the specific topics discussed in Part V. For instance, Jonathan Nield's book assesses the historical novel of the Victorian era and advances a dozen titles on Latin America.

A. 19th-century Writers on the Río de la Plata

Andrews, Captain [Joseph]
   1827   *Journey from Buenos Aires through the Provinces of Córdoba,*
          Tucumán, and Salta, to Potosí, thence by the Deserts of Ca-
          ranja to Arica, and Subsequently to Santiago de Chili and
          Coquimbo, Undertaken on Behalf of the Perubian Mining
          Association, in the Years 1825–26. Two volumes. London:
          Murray.

Arnold, Samuel Greene
   1848   *Viaje por América del Sur, 1847–1848.* [MS apparently still in
          the hands of the author's descendants in Providence, Rhode
          Island.] Spanish translation by Clara de la Rosa; prologue by
          José Luis Busaniche, preface by David James. Buenos Aires:
          Emecé, 1951.

Bingley, Rev. William
   1820   *Travels in South America, from Modern Writers, with Re-*
          marks and Observations; Exhibiting a Connected View of the
          Geography and Present State of that Quarter of the Globe.
          London: John Sharpe.

Brackenridge, H.M., Esq.
   1820   *Voyage to South America, Performed by Order of the Amer-*
          ican Government in the Years 1817 and 1818, in the Frigate
          Congress. 2 vols. London: Miller.

Caldcleugh, Alexander, Esq.
   1825   *Travels in South America, During the Years 1819–20–21;*
          Containing an Account of the Present State of Brazil, Buenos
          Ayres and Chile. 2 vols. London: Murray.

Chikhachev, Platon Alexandrovich
   1844   *A Trip across the Pampas of Buenos Aires (1836–1837),*
          translated from the Russian by Jack Weiner. Lawrence:
          University of Kansas, 1967.

Craufurd, Robert
   [1807] "Diario de la expedición del Brigadier General Craufurd,"
           Revista Histórica (Montevideo) VIII (1917), 204–12 and 519–27.

Darwin, Charles
   1839   *The Voyage of the Beagle.* London. Reprint by Walter Sullivan,
          ed. New York: Bantam, 1972.

Davie, John Constanse
   1805   *Letters from Paraguay. Describing the Settlements of Monte*
          Video and Buenos Ayres; the Presidencies of Rioja Minor, Nom-
          bre de Dios, St. Mary and St. John, etc. etc. with the Manners,
          Customs, Religious Ceremonies.... London: G. Robinson.

Domeyko, Ignäcy
    1888   *Moje Podróże: Pamietniki Wygnanca*, Elżbieta Helena Nieciowa, ed. Kraków: Zakład Narodowy Imienia Ossolińskich-Wydawnictwo, 1962.

d'Orbigny, Alcide
    1835–47   *Voyage dans l'Amérique Méridionale (le Brésil, la République Orientale de l'Uruguay, la République Argentine, la Patagonie, la République du Chili, la République de Bolivia, la République du Perou), exécuté pendant les années 1826, 1827, 1828, 1829,1830, 1831, 1832 et 1833...*publié sous les auspices de M. le Ministre de l'Instruction Publique. Paris: Pitois-Levrault.

Ebelot, Alfred
    1889   *La Pampa*. Paris: Quantin. Spanish translation by the author. Paris: Escary, 1890. Reprint, Buenos Aires: Editorial Universitaria, 1961.

Gerstäcker, Frederick
    1854   *Gerstäcker's Travels. Rio de Janeiro—Buenos Aires—Ride through the Pampas...California and the Gold Fields.* Translated from the German.... London: Nelson.

Gillespie, Major Alexander
    1818   *Gleanings and Remarks: Collected during Many Months of Residence at Buenos Aires and within the Upper Country... until the Surrender of the Colony of the Cape of Good Hope.* Leeds: Whiteley.

Head, Francis Bond
    1826   *Rough Notes Taken during Some Rapid Journeys across the Pampas and among the Andes.* London: Murray. Reprinted with introduction by C. Harvey Gardiner, ed. Carbondale and Edwardsville: Southern Illinois University Press, 1967.

Helms, Anthony Zachariah
    1807   *Travels from Buenos Aires, by Potosí, to Lima. With notes by the [anon.] translator, containing topographical descriptions of the Spanish possessions in South America, drawn from the last and best authorities.* [Another English translation appeared that same year with a different subtitle.] London: R. Phillips.

Henty, G.A.
    1868   *Out on the Pampas, or The Young Settlers.* Illustrations by J.B. Zwecker. London: Blackie.

Hudson, William H.
    1885   *The Purple Land that England Lost: Travels and Adventures in the Banda Oriental, South America.* London: S. Low, Marston, et al. Republished by the author. London: Duckworth, 1904.

    1918   *Far Away and Long Ago: A History of My Early Life.* New

York: E.P. Dutton. [In 1974, it was made into an Argentine
feature film entitled *Allá lejos y hace tiempo*.]

Hutchinson, Thomas J.
1865 *Buenos Ayres and Argentine Gleanings: with Extracts from a
      Diary of Salado Exploration in 1862 and 1863*. London: Stanford.

Isabelle, Arsène
1835 *Voyage a Buenos-Ayres et a Porto Alegre, par la Banda Oriental,
      les Missions d'Uruguay et la Province de Rio-Grande-do-Sul.
      (De 1830 a 1834)*.... Havre: Morlent.

MacCann, William
1853 *Two Thousand Miles' Ride through the Argentine Provinces.
      Being an Account of the Natural Products of the Country, and
      Habits of the People with a Historical Retrospect of the Río de la
      Plata, Monte Video, and Corrientes*.... 2 vols. London: Smith,
      Elder. Facsimile ed. New York: AMS Press, [c.1969].

Mantegazza, Pablo
1876 *Viajes por el Río de la Plata y el Interior de la Confederación
      Argentina*...tercera edición corregida por el autor, Milán, 1876,
      traducidos por el Consejero de la Universidad, Doctor Juan
      Heller. Buenos Aires: Universidad de Tucumán & Coni, 1916.

Mawe, John
1812 *Travels in the Interior of Brazil...Including a Voyage to the
      Río de la Plata*. London: Longman [et al.].

Miers, John
1826 *Travels in Chile and La Plata, Including Accounts Respecting
      the Geography, Geology, Statistics, Government, Finances,
      Agriculture, Manners, and Customs, and the Mining Opera-
      tions in Chile. Collected During a Residence of Several Years in
      These Countries*. 2 vols. London: Baldwin, Cradock, and Joy.

Notes on the Viceroyalty of La Plata, in South America; With a Sketch
1808 *of the Manners and Character of the Inhabitants*...[anon.]
      London: J.J. Stockdale.

Pallière, Léon
1869 *Diario de viaje*, unpublished manuscript written ca. 1860,
      revised by Pallière in 1869; Spanish translation by Ricardo
      Gutiérrez and Miguel Solá entitled *Diario de viaje por la Amér-
      ica del Sud, con una introducción sobre la vida y la obra del
      artista, ilustrada con acuarelas, grabados y dibujos ejecutados
      en América y en Europa*. Buenos Aires: Peuser, 1945.

Proctor, Robert, Esq.
1825 *Narrative of a Journey across the Cordillera of the Andes and
      of a Residence in Lima, and Other Parts of Peru, in the Years
      1823 and 1824*. London: Archibald Constable.

Robertson, J.P. and W.P. [John Parish and William Parish]
1839   *Letters on Paraguay: Comprising an Account of Four Years'
        Residence in that Republic, under the Government of the
        Dictator Francia....* 3 vols. Second ed. London. Facs. reprint.
        New York: AMS Press, 1970.

1843   *Letters on South America; Comprising Travels on the Banks
        of the Paraná and Río de la Plata....* 3 vols. London: Murray.

Scarlett, P. Campbell
1838   *South America and the Pacific; Comprising a Journey across
        the Pampas and the Andes, from Buenos Ayres to Valparaíso,
        Lima and Panama; With Remarks upon the Esthmus....* 2 vols.
        London: Colburn.

Seymour, Richard Arthur
1869   *Pioneering in the Pampas, or the First Four Years of a Settler's
        Experience in the La Plata Camps.* London: Longmans, Green.

Vidal, Emeric Essex
1820   *Picturesque Illustrations of Buenos Ayres and Monte Video,
        Consisting of Twenty-Four Views: Accompanied with Descrip-
        tions of the Scenery, and of the Inhabitants of Those Cities and
        Their Environs.* London: Ackerman and Strand. Facsimile ed.
        Buenos Aires: Viau, 1943.

                    B. Supplementary References
Aretz, Isabel
1952   *El folklore musical argentino, con 91 ejemplos musicales, 33
        esquemas y 8 láminas.* Buenos Aires: Ricordi.

1967a   *Instrumentos musicales de Venezuela.* Colección La Heredad.
        [Cumaná, Venezuela:] Universidad de Oriente.

Baily, Samuel L.
1980   "Marriage Patterns and Immigrant Assimilation in Buenos
        Aires, 1882–1923," *Hispanic American Historical Review*
        (Durham, NC) LX, 32–48.

Becco, Horacio Jorge
1960   *Cancionero tradicional argentino. Recopilación, estudio prelimi-
        nar, notas y bibliografía....* Buenos Aires: Librería Hachette.

Bermudo, Juan
1555   *Declaración de instrumentos musicales.* Facsimile by M.
        Santiago Kastner, ed., Documenta Musicologica, Ser. I, Vol.
        XI. Kassel: Bärenreiter, 1957.

Busaniche, Hernán
1955   *La arquitectura en las Misiones Jesuíticas Guaraníes.* Santa
        Fe, Argentina: El Litoral.

Busaniche, José Luis
1959   *Estampas del pasado. Lecturas de historia argentina (1527–1910)*. Buenos Aires: Librería Hachette.

Carrizo, Juan Alfonso
1953   *Historia del folklore argentino*. Buenos Aires: Ministerio de Educación.

Coluccio, Félix
1964   *Diccionario folklórico argentino*. Primera edición.... 2 vols. Buenos Aires: Luis Laserre.

Cordero, Carlos J.
1936   *Los relatos de los viajeros extranjeros posteriores a la Revolución de Mayo como fuentes de historia argentina. Ensayo de sistematización bibliográfica*.... Buenos Aires: Coni.

Díaz del Castillo, Bernal
1568   *Historia verdadera de la conquista de la Nueva España*. Carlos Pereyra, ed. 2nd ed. 2 vols. Madrid: Espasa-Calpe, 1942.

Furlong, Guillermo, S.J.
1945   *Músicos argentinos durante la dominación hispánica: Exposición sintética precedida por una introducción por Lauro Ayestarán*. Buenos Aires: Huarpes.

Jones, Tom B.
1949   *South America Rediscovered*. Minneapolis: University of Minnesota Press.

"Mary, Queen of Scots (1542–1587)" [= Mary Stuart]
1917   *Dictionary of National Biography...to 1900* (London: Oxford University Press, 1968) XII, pp. 1258–75.

Moretti, Federico
1799   *Principios para tocar la guitarra de seis órdenes*.... Madrid [London: British Library].

Narváez, Luis de
1538   *Los seys libros del Delphín de Música de cifra para tañer vihuela*. Transcripción y estudio por Emilio Pujol, Monumentos de la Música Española III. Barcelona: Consejo Superior de Investigaciones Científicas, 1945.

Nield, Jonathan
1929   *A Guide to the Best Historical Novels and Tales*. 5th ed. New York: Macmillan.

Pinnell, Richard
1980   *Francesco Corbetta and the Baroque Guitar, with a Transcription of His Works*. 2 vols. UMI Studies in Musicology No. 25. Ann Arbor: UMI Research Press.

Schweitzer, G.
1953   "Die Gitarre Maria Stuarts," *Zeitschrift für Musik* (Leipzig) XIV
       (Jul. 1953), 409–10.

Scobie, James R.
1971   *Argentina: A City and a Nation.* New York: Oxford University
       Press.

Stanford, Charles Villiers
1915   "Some Thoughts Concerning Folk-song and Nationality,"
       Musical Quarterly (New York) I, 232–45.

Vega, Carlos
1946b *Música sudamericana.* Buenos Aires: Emecé

1956   *El origen de las danzas folklóricas.* Buenos Aires: Ricordi.

1944-53 *Bailes tradicionales argentinos. Historia—origen—música—
         poesía—coreografía.* Buenos Aires: Julio Korn.

Velázquez, Víctor
1986   *20 grandes éxitos.* Dolby cassette, EMI 16236. Buenos Aires:
       EMI-Odeón SAIC.

Weiner, Jack
1967   "Platón Alexandrovich Chijachev o Chikhachev (1812–1892):
       Bosquejo biográfico," *Boletín del Instituto de Historia Argentina
       "Dr. Emilio Ravignani"* (Buenos Aires) Año IX, Ser. 2, Nos. 14–
       15, 3–6.

"Whitelocke, John (1757–1833)"
1917   *Dictionary of National Biography...to 1900* (London: Oxford
       University Press, 1968), XXI, p. 119ff.

Zoltowska, Evelina
1964   "Crónica de un viaje por la Argentina en 1838," *La Nación*
       (Buenos Aires), 1 Nov. (Sunday), 4.

Appendices

I. The Conqueror's Rewards

The Spaniards came to the Americas in order to begin, as they believed, a prosperous new life. Their search for gold and silver was of course their foremost objective. Yet inasmuch as they hailed from a Christian monarchy, they also anticipated that as they would help to establish the crown and Christianity in the New World, they would at least become masters of a new domain with a retinue of laborers at their disposal. For instance, in 1536 Melchor Verdugo, *encomendero* and councilman of Trujillo, Peru, wrote back home to assure his mother, Marina de Olivares of Avila, that all was well on his estate: "I live in a place called Trujillo and have my house there and a very good encomienda of Indians, with about eight or ten thousand vassals (Lockhart & Otte 1976:43)."

On 21 May 1534, the King commissioned don Pedro de Mendoza with the conquest of the Río de la Plata, and in return for his considerable efforts, Mendoza was promised the title of "count," his own grand estate, and ten thousand vassals (Madero 1939: 406), though he did not live to see his rewards. While the *conquistadores* established the crown in the Caribbean, Mexico, and Peru within several decades, they scarcely survived in the Río de la Plata during the same period. Therefore, owing to the Plata's difficult conquest, its distance from the 16th-century viceroyalties, and its lack of precious metals, the court turned to more compelling business in the empire. When the Plata conquerors began to submit their petitions for lands, servants, and the building of their estates, the court's ministers could only offer a pittance instead of the usual rewards. Worse yet, they simply ignored some petitions.

As examples of this frustrating predicament, two petitions have survived from old Asunción. They remain in the archives of Seville as part of the administrative correspondence of the "Indies." The writers of these petitions are requesting just remuneration for their services. In the first, a man is applying for the usual grants of lands and servants in lieu of conqueror's treasure; he reviews the

hardships he experienced along with the defeat of Mendoza's
colony at Buenos Aires, since he was among its few survivors. In
the second, a woman, another survivor, files a similar petition:

> To the Council of the Indies
> Very Powerful Lords:
> As a man who has been wronged I cannot refrain from com-
> plaining to your highness as my king. Your highness, I was born
> in the town of Morón, nine leagues from Seville. I came to this
> province of the Río de la Plata twenty-one years ago, with the
> expedition of don Pedro de Mendoza, in which I suffered the
> hardships that your highness doubtless knows all those who
> came in that time have suffered, and I have striven to be first
> in the service of your highness in every way I could, of which I
> would send proof if I were so bold.
> At the end of twenty years the governor of this province gave
> its natives in encomienda to those who are just newly arrived
> and to others who came after we did. Of those who conquered
> the land, some of them losing their sons and some their brothers,
> there remain, from the 1,700 men counted at the muster don
> Pedro de Mendoza held when he landed, about a hundred men,
> and to them the governor gave the worst grants and the most
> distant, from where one can get no service. And so, many have
> not wished to accept the grants, of whom I am one, since he
> gave me sixteen Indians eighty leagues [some 240 miles] from
> where we live, and he gave others fifteen, or twenty, or thirty,
> but for his sons-in-law, and sons-in-law of his sons-in-law, and
> the officials of your highness and for himself, he took the whole
> country, all the best part of it. And when I went to speak to him
> at the time when he was going to make the distribution, I gave
> him a memorandum of the hardships I had undergone, which
> goes along with this letter; he only answered, "How many chil-
> dren do you have?" and said my petition had best be left un-
> made. Seeing how he had treated me, I asked his permission to
> go to the realms of Spain, and he refused me that too. I have said
> this so that your highness will know the treatment that has
> been given to don Pedro's men, and this letter is only to give an
> account of what is going on here and how those who strive are
> treated. From the city of Asunción, the day of St. John, 1556.
>   Your vassal who kisses your royal feet,
>   Bartolomé García
>   (Lockhart & Otte 1976:48–49)

To the most high and powerful Princess Doña Juana
Governor of the Kingdoms of Spain
At her Council of the Indies

Very High and Powerful Princess:
To this province of the River Plate with the first governor of it,
Don Pedro de Mendoza, there came certain women, amongst
whom fortune so willed it that I should be one, and that the fleet
should arrive at the port of Buenos Aires with fifteen hundred
men, and that they all should be in want of food.
So great was the famine that at the end of three months a
thousand perished.... The men became so weak that the poor
women had to do all their work; they had to wash their clothes,
and care for them when sick, to cook the little food they had;
stand sentinel, care for the watch-fires and prepare the cross-
bows when the Indians attacked, and even fire the petronels; to
give the alarm, crying out with all our strength, to drill and put
the soldiers in good order, for at that time we women, as we did
not require so much food, had not fallen into the same state of
weakness as the men.... In the face of such terrible trials, the
few that remained alive determined to ascend the river, weak
as they were, and although winter was coming on, in two brig-
antines, and the worn-out women cared for and looked after
them and cooked their food, bringing the wood for firing into the
vessels on their backs, and cheering them with virile exhorta-
tions...and thus we came to a tribe of Indians who are called
Timbúes, who have good fishings. Then we bestirred ourselves
to find out nice ways of cooking, so that the fish should not disgust them, for they had to eat it without bread and were all very
weak....
Thus they arrived at this city of Asunción, which, though it is
now fertile and full of food, was then in wretchedness, so that it
became necessary that the women should return to their la-
bours, making plantations with their own hands, digging, weed-
ing, and sowing and gathering in the crops without the help of
anyone, until the soldiers recovered from their weakness and
commenced to rule the country and to acquire Indians as their
servants, and so get the land into the state in which it is.
I have wished to write and bring all this before your Highness,
so that you may comprehend the ingratitude that has been
shown me in this country, for at present most of it has been

granted either to the older or the new [colonists] without the
least remembrance either of me or of my hardships, and they
have left me without assigning me a single Indian as my servant. I would much like to have been free to go and put before
your Highness all the services that I have done you and all the
injuries that they are doing me; but this is not in my hands, for I
am married to a gentleman of Seville who is called Pedro de Esquivel, whose services to your Highness have caused mine to be
forgotten. Three times I have saved his life with the knife at his
throat, as your Highness will know.

  Therefore I beseech that you will order that a perpetual [retire-
ment] shall be granted me, and as a payment for my services
that some employment be given to my husband, according to his
quality, for he on his part merits it. May our Lord increase your
royal life and state for many years.

  From this city of Asunción and July the second, 1556.
            Your servant kisses your royal hands,
                  Doña Isabel de Guevara
                  (Graham 1924:281–84)

II. The Origin and Practice of Drinking *Mate*

The *conquistadores* of the Río de la Plata discovered that the natives there generally drank a green-herb tea that was readily
available from a natural resource. The herbs themselves came
from a tree of the holly family eventually named *Ilex paraguayensis,* or literally Paraguayan holly. The tree provided leaves with
the fragrance of mild rosemary spice which the Indians dried and
ground up in their preparations of the drink. Characteristically
they would take a hollow gourd, cut off the top so as to use it as a
cup, and fill it half full of ground herbs. Then they poured small
amounts of hot water over them, and drank the product a sip at a
time as herb tea. The only problem with their rather primitive
method was separating the herbs from the beverage as they drank
it. Using the gourd half full of herbs and sipping the intermittent
spurts of water that the Indians poured over them, the casual or
uninitiated drinker could also take in a mouthful of herbs!

  When the Spaniards arrived, they ignored the outspoken warn-
ings of the clergy who thought of *mate* (mah-teh) as a vice, and

promptly developed a fascination with the beverage because of its taste, its mild effects as stimulant or cathartic, and its extraordinary commercial potential. Ironically the Spaniards named the drink not for its content but rather for its container. Although they followed the practice of the Guaraní Indians in the use of *mate*, the Europeans were uneasy about imitating the Guaraní word for the gourd called caiguá (kaee-<u>gwah</u>) because of its similarity to an unspeakable expletive in their own language. They turned instead to the Quechua equivalent called *matí* (Oberti 1979:8–9). Hispanized it became *mate*, and since the old Spanish verb for making preparations was *cebar*, the expression for pouring the water or serving the tea, *cebando mate,* has endured from then until now.

The early Spanish references to *mate* are mostly concentrated on the commerce of the tree's herb which they called *yerba*. It had commercial value for, being a unique natural resource to the north of the Plata drainage system, its inherent characteristics included a built-in geographical monopoly and a potential downstream market. The large-scale sale of yerba was lucrative: the Spaniards harvested it with the Indian labor of the *encomienda* system, conveyed it inland on locally bred mules, and transported it on rafts. While they shipped some yerba across the Andes to Peru, they exported the greater part by sending it on rafts or barges downstream to Plata ports where sea-going barques awaited to carry it, whether legally or by contraband, to any points on the Atlantic.

When the Jesuits established the Paraguayan missions starting in 1607, they organized their own mass harvest of the yerba, and it became their principal and most profitable export. They poured the profits of their tea back into the missionary reductions, as already observed in Part I, and thus their labors produced enviable prosperity and financial independence. Even so, their project was not at all welcomed by the Spaniards who had vested interests in the same enterprise and competed for sales on the same market.

As *mate* became a staple among Hispanic settlers, they developed various methods of separating the herbs from the brew. At first they inserted a small dam or fence made of twigs into the gourd so as to keep the herbs out of the beverage. However, the Spanish silversmiths fabricated a metal strainer for the same purpose to place inside the gourd. Another solution was simply to cook the herbs in a pot of liquid, to make what is known as *mate cocido*—a process similar to the preparation of oriental tea. But since the herbs were already mild, most people considered *mate cocido* to be too bland or too washed out in its flavor, so they continued to search for a better method of preparing *mate*.

Finally they developed the *bombilla* to be used as a straw, and it became, along with the gourd, the customary utensil associated with the drink. The *bombilla* was simply a narrow pipe about the size of a pencil, with a strainer on one end that could be placed inside the gourd amidst the herbs. Undoubtedly the first bombillas were wooden or cane tubes with a wire strainer or baffle, but the Spaniards invariably used an elegant silver one, closed and flattened on one end with many holes perforated in it to strain the herbs out of the beverage. The bombilla enabled them to drink hotter water than before, which enhanced the effects of the drink, for now they could consume it without burning the lips. While women sometimes added sugar or the flavorings of orange, lemon, or other herbs, men preferred it hot and "black" and called it *mate amargo* or simply *cimarrón*.

Jesuit Father Florian Paucke wrote an early description of the procedures for preparing *mate* which contained the 18th-century sociology of its use in the greater Plata region. Whereas the middle class was yet rather small, he restricted himself to the contrasts between the low and the high social strata. In the former he placed Indians and black slaves; in the latter, the ruling class of Spaniards:

> [The people of humble means take half of a gourd cut in the middle, and this is the vessel from which they drink. Into this half of a gourd, they place a handful of yerba in such a manner as to maintain within it a hollow spot. Then they pour into the opening not boiling but well heated water, and they drink it.... Those who are distinguished Spaniards have their *mate* or half-gourd decorated with silver around the circumference.... But they do not drink after the customary manner in which tea is drunk, but rather they have a small silver straw, a hand-span in length, called the *bombilla* that has a round button on the bottom, which, being hollow, is completely perforated by small holes so that just in case any yerba falls through the above-mentioned grate, it will not go into the little pipe. The water is

sipped up through the little pipe to the mouth, and such is the manner of drinking. When the Spaniards drink this way, one of these drafts of *mate* containing a sixth of water is not enough, but rather they drink two or three of these, or even more] (Paucke 1767:III, 320–21).

Owing to their own wide acceptance of the beverage on account of its stimulating effects, the Spaniards saw to the implementation of *mate* at the scenes of labor. It was as typical in their workplace as the coffeepot is in ours today. Customarily domestic servants were responsible for preparing it at the crack of dawn for their masters. Employers and encomienda barons regularly treated their workers to *mate* breaks throughout the workday. Likewise, they supplied it to slaves to lighten their burden. In the mines of Potosí, the miners found its stimulant useful in dealing with the tedium of their work, but, more important, they also drank *mate* to overcome the deleterious effects of mining itself—the hazards of their employment. Acarete du Biscay wrote in this regard during the 17th century, as he described the region of Paraguay and its natural products:

The land abounds in corn, millet, sugar, tobacco, honey, cattle, oaks fit for shipping, pine-trees for masts, and particularly in that herb, call'd the *herb of Paraguay,* which they drive a great trade in all over the *West Indies;* and this obliges merchants of *Chili* and *Peru,* to hold a correspondence with those of *Paraguay;* because, without that herb (with which they make a refreshing liquor with water and sugar, to be drank lukewarm) the inhabitants of *Peru,* savages and others, especially those that work in the mines, could not subsist, for the soil of the country being full of mineral veins, the vapours that rise out of the ground suffocate them and nothing but the liquor can recover them again, which revives and restores them to their former vigour (du Biscay 1698:10).

Dr. Mantegazza subjected *mate* to rigorous medical testing. He researched the subject, collected data from informants, and drank it himself over a three-year period. He concluded that it heightened emotional sensitivity so he recommended its use for those faced with the long hours of intellectual pursuits (1876:89).

A member of the British invasion summed up the general use of *mate* in Uruguay. The author ensured the confidentiality of his report by remaining anonymous in the *Notes on the Viceroyalty of La Plata* (London: 1808):

> To the use of this herb the inhabitants are universally and immoderately addicted. It is not entirely confined to the natives of the country, but strangers, and those from Old Spain, after living some time among them, become equally fond of it. It serves them for breakfast—the use of tea, coffee, and chocolate, being uncommon in families. They seldom take anything in the morning besides this herb which they drink as soon as they rise, and [then they drink it] at all hours of the day, frequently even at their meals (1808:35–36).

Mate was indeed a beverage for consumption at dawn as well as at mealtime. In the past its water was always heated over the coals in a small metal teapot (affectionately known as the *pavita* or "little turkey" because of its shape), so it was no trouble to heat the water along with a meal cooked over the wood stove or barbecue. For centuries, the typical, minimal supper was beef or mutton, especially out in the countryside with the abundance of livestock and the scarcity of vegetables. The inhabitants ate fresh meat daily and cooked it by boiling or roasting—or both ways as a luxury (Darwin 1839:37). The boiled meat rendered a rich stew called *puchero*, but the preferred meat called *asado* was baked over the coals alongside the teapot (d'Orbigny 1835–47:I, 378; Hutchinson 1865:139). During the 19th century, Robert Proctor was riding out in the Argentine countryside, and on that occasion he observed one of those makeshift suppers near Fraile Muerto:

> The peons in the mean time made themselves comfortable round a fire which they kindled under a tree, where they lay preparing the *asado* and taking their *mate* or Paraguay tea. The method of making and taking this beverage is this: into a small calabash, holding about half a pint, is put the *mate,* which consists of green leaves and small stalks: boiling water is then poured upon it, and sugar added. It is handed round from one to the other, each man taking a suck of it through a small reed; it has a bitter but not a disagreeable flavour (Proctor 1825:30).

Since their arrival in Asunción, virtually starved, the early Hispanic settlers became accustomed to *mate* along with other regional products. Then they institutionalized it due to the abundance and low price of the herb, marketed it with a downstream economy, and continued its use among all classes. By the 17th century, they had begun to export it to other parts of Latin America, as noted by du Biscay. In the 19th, it had even become a standard beverage in Venezuela, according to another traveller:

> They were passing round the *mate;* for the French trader had not forgotten to bring with him an abundant supply of the herb of Paraguay, which is preferred by South American females far above tea, or even chocolate (Vowell 1831:III, 110).

Since then, except for the widely varied silver and gold ornamentation on the gourd or bombilla and the use of a Thermos bottle for the water, the same old tradition of drinking the holly beverage has remained unchanged as the principal hot drink of the Plata.

III. *Mate* and the Guitar

Being the adjuncts of leisure time, *mate,* the *guitar*, and sometimes *cigars* (made from another natural resource) were always found together in the Río de la Plata. In Uruguayan territory, the author of the excellent but anonymous *Notes on the Viceroyalty* observed the typical pastimes during the invasion of Montevideo:

> The court-yards are adorned with tubs and flower-pots filled with the various shrubs and plants of the country. At the sides, raised about two feet from the ground, are beds of earth, in which orange-trees, lemon-trees, and grape-vines are planted. There is usually a frame suspended across the roof for the support of the vine, which gives a shelter, and in the summer season forms a delicious shade with clusters of grapes hanging down. The senses are thus refreshed, and the air delightfully cooled and perfumed by the fragrance. Under this shade the morning and evening is usually passed, and the dinner-table often spread in in sultry weather. Beneath the covert of these

vines the men spend their hours in conversation and smoking.
The women at their needles, thrumming the guitar, or taking
their favourite *mate* (1808:34–35).

Apart from these intimate scenes, *mate,* cigars, and guitars
were also the embellishments of social gatherings, whether among
rich or poor (Gillespie 1818:69, Miers 1826:98–100, d'Orbigny
1835–47:I, 378). Since the colonial epoch, people brought all three
to meetings of small to medium-sized groups, and the vices were
shared with everyone attending, as noted by the Robertsons:

> Round went the *mate,* and round the paper segars. The *gui-*
> *tarrista* seized his guitar, and accompanied himself to a native
> *triste* (1843:I, 229; II, 52–55).

With the sudden, boundless growth of the middle class, starting
in 1776 with the migrations to the Viceroyalty of the Río de la Plata, *mate* and the guitar continued to impact on social gatherings.
Young women of the era were already practicing their guitar
leisurely while taking their *mate* so they could invite young men
over for evening visits (Pernety 1770:277–83). Their pretense for
meeting was exactly the same as in North America at the time of
Stephen Foster: it was their music. Such meetings ranged in size
anywhere from a roomful in a parlor of Corrientes (according to
d'Orbigny) down to the intimacy of a twosome. In groups of all
sizes, everyone took a turn with the guitar as it came around the
room to ensure the presence of entertainment, and the *mate* circulated as a sure sign of fellowship. Women in this—their favorite
social pastime—could be completely confident of their prowess,
having diligently practiced that very day, when it was their turn to
perform. W.H. Hudson described an intimate encounter of this
type in *The Purple Land,* his early and rather autobiographical
novel of the 19th century. Richard, a foreigner and the central
character of the story, narrates the conversation he had with an
Uruguayan woman and her husband at their place:

> [Her husband exclaimed] "*Mate* is the best thing in this country.
> ..."
> "You scarcely do women justice—

"*La mujer es un ángel del cielo*," I returned, quoting the old Spanish song.

He barked out a short little laugh.

"That does very well to sing to a guitar," he said.

"Talking of guitars," spoke the woman, addressing me for the first time; "while we are waiting for the *mate,* perhaps you will sing us a ballad. The guitar is lying just behind you (Hudson 1885:245)."

Whatever the size of the group, everyone present was expected to partake of the beverage and to play the guitar as they came around. Guitarists played solos, singers accompanied themselves, yet non-musical visitors could not hope to escape unscathed from the social pressure. (Ignorance of the law was no excuse!) Some kind of performance was still required, so the non-musical had to comply by relating folk poetry or tall tales to improvised incidental music on the guitar. The stories they told were filled with hilarious, unexpected twists, sad if dealing with death or failed love affairs, or frightening if full of suspense and anticipation of uncanny, super-natural powers. The guitarist's awesome task was to invent music roughly appropriate to each of these textual settings on the spot and perform continuously, without halting the melodrama. Hudson recorded some typical 19th-century stories in the chapter he called "Tales of the Purple Land (1885:210f.)." The practice continued. For examples of 20th-century tall tales and folk poetry with guitar accompaniment, hear the hilarious, heart-wrenching, or totally outlandish stories of Luis Landriscina of Corrientes entitled *Historias de una mateada* on Philips/Aplausos 7126503. Therefore, even today, the Rioplatense arts are still the pretense for social gatherings, and *mate* and the guitar are still passed round the circle, though less now than during the "boom folklórico" of the 1960s.

To sum up, *mate* was not the important thing here but rather the sociability it afforded. To be sure, the beverage was the product of a unique natural resource, inasmuch as the herbs of this particular holly remain unknown in the rest of the world. And though it was originally the drink of Indians, the Hispanics took it up readily in the Rioplatense colony to set a four-century precedent. The use of *mate,* like a performance on the guitar, was considered a sign of cordiality, so either one or both were present when people came together to socialize.

Two Argentine guitarists recently reviewed the combined significance of *mate* and the guitar. The occasion was an interview between Pompeyo Camps (performer, composer, and music critic) and Irma Costanzo (recitalist, eminent teacher, and recording artist); their dialogue on the subject was the following:

[*Mr. Camps*: Now we come to Argentina. How do you feel as an Argentine guitarist in your own country?

Ms. Costanzo: Personally, and my case represents the general sentiment, I feel completely at ease in the presence of any good performer on the instrument, no matter who it is. In Argentina, guitarists are respected. Inclusively, perhaps owing to my own idiosyncrasy, that deference is sometimes exaggerated. I think part of that courtesy is probably linked with the norms of our society.

It is possible that this *auge* [boom] of our instrument in Argentina is partly the fruit of our famous *guitarreadas,* those cordial reunions of our populace which were convened with the purpose of sharing the guitar. Perhaps the aficionados then were the same as those who now want to become acquainted with what happens beyond the practice of music that is both easy and inconsequential.

Camps: We Argentines know that the guitar has a long tradition in our popular music. The instrument had an intrinsic role in the recitation of our Hispanic poetry, in our wars of independence, and in the social life of our people. In this zone of South America, it was habitual that when visitors arrived you were expected to offer them two things: *mate* and the guitar. Then afterwards during the epoch of Domingo Faustino Sarmiento, according to his own testimony in Chile (prior to his 19th-century presidency), the Argentines were already famous for being good "musicians," which back then meant that they were adept guitar players and singers.

Costanzo: Apparently that tradition has been channelled into our official conservatories where half of the student body studies the guitar. In the Conservatory "Juan José Castro" (under my direction) at La Lucila, I have documentation of that enormous statistic] (Camps 1978:77).

IV. Afterword:
Retrospective of the Guitar's Significance

In the dialogue just cited, Pompeyo Camps and Irma Costanzo compel us to ponder the unique excellence of the Rioplatense guitar. In their casual dialogue, they capsulize the early guitar's social significance in the region. Although their exchange is informal—a mere conversation, their approach to the subject at hand is much the same as our procedure throughout this volume. We have focused on the instrument as well as its role in society, humanizing the story wherever possible. In the first place, since the guitar is a social phenomenon, an aspect of the human experience, it remains incomprehensible if divorced from the people who were using it. In the second place, an understanding of its social context can provide answers to some of the most perplexing questions about it. The most important of these is the reason behind the Rioplatense guitar's greatness—herewith our final consideration.

Ms. Costanzo speaks of the *auge* or "boom" of the guitar among her compatriots. Given the recent development of the guitar in the Northern Hemisphere, we might be tempted to equate their boom with the world renaissance of the guitar. But caution: *renaissance* implies a re-birth; there must first be an apostasy before a restoration is possible. The Rioplatense guitar never declined, so we cannot help but respect Costanzo's conclusion: their current boom of the guitar must be founded on past circumstances and achievements. Guitarists there are continuing to ride out the *naissance* of the instrument in their midst. Today it plays on in obvious significance and thrives all the more in its upward, artistic ascendance.

Many social scientists would agree that the environment surrounding the guitarists there made them what they were and what they are today. Undoubtedly the guitarists' social relationships nurtured their progress. The common people thrilled to their entertainments, emoted to the tragic, improvised strains of the gaucho ballad, and danced to the beat of one, two, or three guitars when other instruments were altogether lacking. Young men and women courted each other with the guitar as if it were the only pretense for meeting. Before the early 19th-century independence, the guitar accompanied the mass and lighter church music; afterwards it entertained the heads of state in the new republics, whether in dance or song. The guitar pervaded social gatherings of all sizes and classes, whether among young or old, bond or free, native, white, or black, male or female, and at every social rank in the Río de la Plata. As the experts say there, "The guitar is the musical instrument most our own." History confirmed the fact, over and over again, that those who play the national instrument there have always enjoyed the lion's share of society's rewards.

Now then, if we reflect on the specific achievements of the Rioplatense guitarists, as sketched in the introduction to this volume, we can begin to appreciate the social context in which they performed. At any point in their history, the guitarists' environment stimulated them to excellence with all the rewards at the disposal of society. Their environment was undoubtedly the best of all possible worlds for guitarists, satisfying their every need—already in c.1776 Concolorcorvo [Carrió de la Vandera] was moved to call it "Arcadia." Whether adept at the popular or classical guitar, musicians were compelled to excellence; they saw the goal, envisioned its rewards, and then time and time again they captured both, as a continuous pattern of success developed around their activities. Their notable achievements were as self-reassuring as they were perceptible by all who heard the music. This is not to suggest that somehow the Rioplatense guitarists achieved perfection without effort ("success" comes before "work" only in the dictionary). They built tremendous momentum in their work-success pattern: repeatedly the guitarists practiced long hours, savoured the rewards, and then reinvested themselves in their work. They became jet propelled in the process (as it were) in the continual, regenerating cycle of practice and performance. This cyclical pattern begot intense motivation for the study of the guitar, along with a sense of purpose and indomitable self-confidence. We cannot help but acknowledge the fact that the Plata was indeed a haven for those who played the guitar. At the same time, this concession need not keep us from *re-creating* the same environment for ourselves, our children, or our students.

If we consider the domination of the Argentines in the Alirio Díaz competition in Venezuela during the decade of the 1970s, and the predominance of the Argentine and Uruguayan students of Abel Carlevaro in the Radio France competition at Paris during the following decade, we are left wondering if the environment alone were sufficient in giving these outstanding young guitarists the edge among the virtuosi of the world. Isn't the winning of these competitions tantamount to a blitz of an Olympic category by two countries of relatively few inhabitants? The entire population of Uruguay is only about three million, smaller than downtown Los Angeles; the population of Argentina is about thirty million, comparable to that of California, alone.

This remarkable external recognition of the instrument's significance in the Plata suggests that guitarists there may have enjoyed more than a musician's paradise. It is probable that Plata guitarists have some genetic affinity or predisposition for their instrument. As explained in the conclusions to Part III, the Andalusian progenitors of the Río de la Plata had a demonstrable predisposition towards the guitar, yet the Indian populations with which they at first intermarried also had acute musical sensitivity. They too danced and sang to excess; their excellence in performance was the highest achievement of their aboriginal culture. Sepp claimed, "they...value music above everything else." Then, one by one, from among their best musicians, the priests culled out the top performers by audition and made them the stalwarts of the conversion process and the notables of Christian communities. Indeed the Amerindian converts who continued in Hispanic society could only have enhanced its already acute musicality if they intermarried further. Thereafter for two and a half centuries, ranging from Mendoza's first settlement in 1536 to the advent of the viceroyalty in 1776, the population developed more from within than from European immigration. Though the science of genetics falls short of explaining the organic transfer of musicality, there appears to have been some in the Plata colony, most likely during the 17th and 18th centuries—the era of its severest isolation from Spain and the simultaneous rise and fall of the Jesuit state.

The case of the young classical virtuosi at recent competitions brings to mind the pre-eminent prodigy, Mozart. Certainly, from the very start, the young Wolfgang was couched in the optimal musical environment. He learned from his father and then listened to his older sister practice and perform; soon he was playing everything that she did at a much younger age. Thence to the recital stage and renown. In consequence, Mozart enjoyed the pampering and rewards of the child prodigy to no apparent end. Even so, in response to the many who believed that he had a gift for music, he later claimed that what he accomplished was the product of study and hard work. And thus the continuing debate: his environment was indeed the best of all possible worlds for a musician, yet some of his facility must have stemmed from inheritance, like Bach's—from the line of musicians that preceded him in his family tree.

Thus, like Mozart, Rioplatense guitarists were accorded every benefit of an optimal musical environment, a total support-system at the service of their quest. But the extent of their achievement provokes us to go beyond the current limitations of science and into the realm of inherited musicality in order to explain such success in that part of the world. The only other alternative would be to admit that they have a unique gift for the guitar, but that would not be rational. Mozart's contribution to music seems partly genetic and partly (probably the greater part) learned and conditioned, as a product of an optimal environment. Likewise, musicians of the Río de la Plata were on the receiving end of a similar endowment. Guitarists there either inherited the benefit of both their birthright and their environment, or there is no rational explanation for their undisputed excellence.

References Cited in the Appendices

Camps, Pompeyo
1978   *Reportaje a la guitarra con Irma Costanzo*. Buenos Aires [etc.]: El Ateneo.

[Carrió de la Vandera, Alonso]
[1776]   *El lazarillo de ciegos caminantes desde Buenos-Ayres, hasta Lima...Sacado de las memorias que hizo Don Alonso Carrió de la Vandera en este dilatado viage...desde Montevideo.* Por Don Calixto Bustamante Carlos Inca, alias Concolorcorvo.... Gijón, Spain [sic]: Rovada [sic!], 1773 [sic]. [Lima: c.1776]. Buenos Aires: Solar, 1942.

Darwin, Charles
1839   *The Voyage of the Beagle*. London. Reprint by Walter Sullivan, ed. New York: Bantam, 1972.

d'Orbigny, Alcide
1835–47 *Voyage dans l'Amérique Méridionale (le Brésil, la République Orientale de l'Uruguay, la République Argentine, la Patagonie, la République du Chili, la République de Bolivia, la République du Perou), exécuté pendant les années 1826, 1827, 1828, 1829, 1830, 1831, 1832 et 1833...publié sous les auspices de M. le Ministre de l'Instruction Publique*. Paris: Pitois-Levrault.

du Biscay, Acarete
1698   *An Account of a Voyage up the River de la Plata, and thence over Land to Peru. With Observations on the Inhabitants, as well Indians as Spaniards; the Cities, Commerce, Fertility, and Riches of that Part of America*. London: Buckley. Facsimile ed. North Haven, CT: Institute Publishing, 1968.

Gillespie, Major Alexander
1818   *Gleanings and Remarks: Collected during Many Months of Residence at Buenos Aires and within the Upper Country... until the Surrender of the Colony of the Cape of Good Hope....* Leeds: Whiteley.

Graham, Robert B. Cunninghame
1924   *The Conquest of the River Plate*. Garden City, NY: Doubleday, Page.

Hudson, William H.
1885   *The Purple Land that England Lost: Travels and Adventures in the Banda Oriental, South America*. London: S. Low, Marston, et al. Republished by the author. London: Duckworth, 1904.

Hutchinson, Thomas J.
1865   *Buenos Ayres and Argentine Gleanings: with Extracts from a Diary of Salado Exploration in 1862 and 1863*. London: Stanford.

Landriscina, Luis
1979   *Historias de una mateada.* Stereo cassette, AP 7126503.
        Montevideo: Philips/Aplausos.

Lockhart, James, and Enrique Otte, trans. and eds.
1976   *Letters and Peoples of the Spanish Indies: Sixteenth Century.*
        London, New York, Melbourne: Cambridge University Press.

Madero, Eduardo
1939   *Historia del Puerto de Buenos Aires: Descubrimiento del Río
        de la Plata y de sus principales afluentes, y fundación de las
        más antiguas ciudades, en sus márgenes.* Tercera ed. Buenos
        Aires: Ediciones Buenos Aires.

Mantegazza, Pablo
1876   *Viajes por el Río de la Plata y el Interior de la Confederación
        Argentina...*tercera edición corregida por el autor, Milán, 1876,
        traducidos por el Consejero de la Universidad, Doctor Juan
        Heller. Buenos Aires: Universidad de Tucumán & Coni Her-
        manos, 1916.

Miers, John
1826   *Travels in Chile and La Plata, Including Accounts Respecting
        the Geography, Geology, Statistics, Government, Finances,
        Agriculture, Manners, and Customs, and the Mining Opera-
        tions in Chile. Collected During a Residence of Several Years
        in These Countries.* 2 vols. London: Baldwin, Cradock, and Joy.

Notes on the Viceroyalty of La Plata, in South America; with a Sketch
1808   *of the Manners and Character of the Inhabitants...*[anon.].
        London: J.J. Stockdale.

Oberti, Federico
1979   *Historia y folklore del mate.* Buenos Aires: Fondo Nacional de
        las Artes.

Paucke, Florian, S.J.
1769   *Hacia allá y para acá: Una estada entre los Indios Mocobíes,
        1749-1767.* Edmund Wernicke, trans. 3 vols. Tucumán, Buenos
        Aires: Universidad Nacional de Tucumán, 1942.

Pernety, Antoine Joseph
1770   *Histoire d'un voyage aux isles Malouines, fait en 1763 & 1764;
        avec des observations sur le detroit de Magellan, et sur les
        Patagons.* Paris: Saillant & Nyon [etc.].

Proctor, Robert, Esq.
1825   *Narrative of a Journey across the Cordillera of the Andes and
        of a Residence in Lima, and Other Parts of Peru, in the Years
        1823 and 1824.* London: Archibald Constable.

Robertson, J.P. and W.P.
  1843   *Letters on South America; Comprising Travels on the Banks
          of the Paraná and Río de la Plata....* 3 vols. London: Murray.

[Vowell, Robert L.]
  1831   *Campaigns and Cruises in Venezuela and New Grenada, and
          in the Pacific Ocean; from 1818 to 1830....* 3 vols. London: Long-
          man and Co.

Bibliography

References Cited

Alais, Juan
 n.d.   *La ñatita,* N. Casuscelli [ed.] para una o dos guitarras. B.A.
        9903. Buenos Aires: Ricordi, printed 1957.

 n.d.   *La perezosa,* N. Casuscelli [ed.] para una o dos guitarras. B.A.
        9904. Buenos Aires: Ricordi, printed 1954.

Alonso, Amado
 1943   *Castellano, español, idioma nacional: Historia espiritual de
        tres nombres,* cuarta edición. Buenos Aires: Losada.

Alvarez, Juan
 1908   *Orígenes de la música argentina.* [Rosario: n.p.]

Alvarez Martínez, Rosario
 1986   "My Scarlatti Discoveries," *Keyboard Classics* (Paramus, NJ) VI,
        No. 5, 4–5.

Alvarez Martínez, Rosario, ed.
 1984   *José Herrando, Domenico Scarlatti, Francisco Courcelle, José
        de Nebra y Agustino Massa: Obras inéditas para tecla.* Madrid:
        Sociedad Española de Musicología.

Amat, Joan Carles
 [1596] *Guitarra española, y vandola en dos maneras de guitarra,
        castellana y cathalana....* Barcelona. [Enlarged ed.] Gerona:
        Joseph Bro, n.d. [London: British Library].

El amor de la estanciera, sainete [anon.].
 c.1787 Mariano Bosch, ed. Instituto de Literatura Argentina, Sección
        de Documentos, Tomo IV, No. 1. Buenos Aires: Imprenta de la
        Universidad, 1925.

Andrews, Captain [Joseph]
 1827   *Journey from Buenos Aires through the Provinces of Córdoba,
        Tucumán, and Salta, to Potosí, thence by the Deserts of Ca-
        ranja to Arica, and Subsequently to Santiago de Chili and
        Coquimbo, Undertaken on Behalf of the Perubian Mining
        Association, in the Years 1825–26.* 2 vols. London: Murray.

Aretz, Isabel
 1952   *El folklore musical argentino.* Buenos Aires: Ricordi.

 1967a *Instrumentos musicales de Venezuela.* [Cumaná,Venezuela:]
        Universidad de Oriente.

 1967b "Raíces europeas de la música folklórica de Venezuela: El
        aporte idígena," in *Music in the Americas,* G. List and J.
        Orrego-Salas, eds. Bloomington, IN: Indiana University, 1967.

451

1978   *La música tradicional de La Rioja.* [Caracas] Venezuela:
        Biblioteca INIDEF.

Arnold, Samuel Greene
1848   *Viaje por América del Sur, 1847–1848.* [MS apparently still
        in the hands of the author's descendants in Providence,
        Rhode Island.] Spanish translation by Clara de la Rosa;
        prologue by José Luis Busaniche, preface by David James.
        Buenos Aires: Emecé, 1951.

Ascasubi, Hilario
1872   *Santos Vega o los mellizos de la Flor: Rasgos dramáticos de la
        vida del gaucho en las campañas y praderas de la República
        Argentina [1778 a 1808].* Paris: P. Duport. [New ed. with reviews,
        notes. 2 vols.] Buenos Aires: Editorial Sopena, 1939.

Ayestarán, Alejandro
1980   "Uruguay: Folk Music," *The New Grove Dictionary of Music
        and Musicians.* London: Macmillan.

Ayestarán, Lauro
1947   *Fuentes para el estudio de la música colonial uruguaya*
        [Apartado de la *Revista de la Facultad de Humanidades y
        Ciencias* Año I, No. 1]. Montevideo: Impresora Uruguaya.

1953   *La música en el Uruguay,* Vol. I. Montevideo: Servicio
        Oficial de Difusión Radio Eléctrica.

1963   "Folklore musical uruguayo: La guitarra y el acordeón,"
        La Unión [Minas, Uruguay] LXXXVIII, No. 21811, 24 Aug.

Azara, Félix de
1801   *Viajes por la América del Sur...desde 1789 hasta 1801.*
        Montevideo: Biblioteca del Comercio del Plata, 1846.

1801MS "Memoria rural del Río de la Plata...." Manuscript, Tomo 375.
        Montevideo: Museo Histórico Nacional.

Baily, Samuel L.
1980   "Marriage Patterns and Immigrant Assimilation in Buenos
        Aires, 1882–1923," *Hispanic American Historical Review*
        (Durham, NC) LX, 32–48.

Barlow, Roger
1541   *A Brief Summe of Geography [= "Geographia Barlow"].*
        Edited with introduction and notes by E.G.R. Taylor. The
        Hakluyt Society, Second Series, No. LXIX, 1932. Reprinted.
        Nendeln, Liechtenstein: Kraus Reprint Limited, 1967.

Barrenechea, Ana María, Director, Editor
1987   *El habla culta de la ciudad de Buenos Aires: Materiales para*

su estudio, Instituto de Filología y Literaturas Hispánicas "Dr. Amado Alonso," Tomo 2. Buenos Aires: Facultad de Filosofía y Letras, Universidad Nacional de Buenos Aires.

Barrueco, Manuel
1976   *Heitor Villa Lobos, Camargo Guarnieri, Carlos Chávez....* Stereo, long-play, TV 34676. New York: Turnabout.

Baumann, Max Peter
1979   "Der Charango—Zur Problemskizze eines akkulturierten Musikinstruments," *Musik und Bildung* (Mainz) XI, No. 10, 603–12.

1985   "Saiteninstrumente in Lateinamerika," in *Studia instrumentorum musicae popularis* VIII, Erich Stockmann, ed. Bericht über die 8. Internationale Arbeitstagung der Study Group on Folk Musical Instruments...in Piran, Jugoslavien, 1983. Stockholm: Musikmuseet.

Beaumarchais, Pièrre Augustin Caron de
1799   *Théâtre complète. Lettres relatives a son théâtre.* Paris: Gallimard, 1957, 1964.

Becco, Horacio Jorge
1960   *Cancionero tradicional argentino. Recopilación, estudio preliminar, notas y bibliografía....* Buenos Aires: Librería Hachette.

Beethoven, Ludwig van
1803   *Symphony No. 3 in Eb Major, Op. 55 ("Eroica")* in Paul Henry Lang, ed., *The Symphony, 1800–1900.* New York: Norton, 1969.

Bello, Andrés
1834   "Advertencias sobre el uso de la lengua castellana, dirigidas a los padres de familia, profesores de los colegios y maestros de escuela," *El Araucano* (Santiago, Chile; 13 and 20 Dec. 1833, 3 and 17 Jan. 1834, 28 Mar. 1834). Republished with prologue, notes, and index by Balbanera Raquel Enríquez. La Plata: Ministerio de Educación de la Provincia de Buenos Aires, 1956.

Bellow, Alexander
1970   *The Illustrated History of the Guitar.* Rockville Centre, NY: Franco Colombo, Belwin/Mills.

Benítez, Baltazar
1977   *Latin American Music for the Classical Guitar* [by Manuel Ponce, Agustín Barrios, and Abel Carlevaro: 5 *Preludios americanos.* Recorded in 1976]. Stereo, long-play, H 71349. New York: Nonesuch.

Bennassar, Bartolomé
1929   *The Spanish Character: Attitudes and Mentalities from the Sixteenth to the Nineteenth Century,* Benjamin Keen, trans.

and editor. Berkeley: University of California Press.

Bermudo, Juan
1555   *Declaración de instrumentos musicales.* Facsimile by M. Santiago Kastner, ed., Documenta Musicologica, Ser. I, Vol. XI. Kassel: Bärenreiter, 1957.

Biblioteca Nacional, Madrid
1705   Anon. manuscript (see below, "Libro de diferentes cifras...").

Bingley, Rev. William
1820   *Travels in South America, from Modern Writers, with Remarks and Observations; Exhibiting a Connected View of the Geography and Present State of that Quarter of the Globe.* London: John Sharpe.

Borello, Rodolfo A.
1969   "Para la historia del voseo en la Argentina," *Cuadernos de Filología* (Buenos Aires) III, 25–42.

Borges, Jorge Luis y José Edmundo Clemente
1963   *El lenguaje de Buenos Aires.* Buenos Aires: Emecé.

Bossio, Jorge A.
1972   *Historia de las pulperías.* Buenos Aires: Plus Ultra.

Botet, María Emma
1945   "Apuntes sobre la última visita de Andrés Segovia a La Habana," *Guitarra* (Havana) V (Jul.), 11–12.

Bougainville, L.A. de
1769   *Viaje alrededor del mundo por la Fragata del Rey la "Boudeuse" y la Fusta la "Estrella" en 1767, 1768 y 1769,* Vol. I. Josefina Gallego de Dantín, trans. Madrid: Calpe, 1921.

Boyd-Bowman, Peter
1963   "La emigración peninsular a América: 1520 a 1539," *Historia Mexicana* (Mexico City) XIII, 165–92.

1964   *Indice geobiográfico de cuarenta mil pobladores españoles de América en el siglo XVI, Tomo I: 1493–1519.* Bogotá: Instituto Caro y Cuervo.

1967   "La procedencia de los españoles de América: 1540–1559," *Historia Mexicana* (Mexico City) XVII, 37–71.

1968   *Indice geobiográfico de cuarenta mil pobladores españoles de América en el siglo XVI, Tomo II: 1520–1539.* Mexico City: Jus.

Brackenridge, H.M., Esq.
1820   *Voyage to South America, Performed by Order of the American*

Government in the Years 1817 and 1818, in the Frigate Congress.
2 vols. London: Miller.

Briceño, Luis de
1626   *Método mvi facilíssimo para aprender a tañer la gvitarra a lo
        español, compuesto por Luis de Briçneo* [sic].... Paris: Ballard.
        Facs. reprint. Geneva, Switz.: Minkoff, 1972.

Broqua, Alfonso
1929   *Evocaciones criollas* a María Luisa Anido (*Ecos del paisaje,
        Vidala, Chacarera, Zamba romántica, Milongeos, Pampeana,
        Ritmos camperos*). Edited and fingered by Miguel Llobet and
        Emilio Pujol. Bibliothèque de Musique...pour Guitare Nos.
        1209–15. Paris: Max Eschig.

Busaniche, Hernán
1955   *La arquitectura en las Misiones Jesuíticas Guaraníes.* Santa
        Fe, Argentina: El Litoral.

Busaniche, José Luis
1959   *Estampas del pasado. Lecturas de historia argentina (1527–
        1910).* Buenos Aires: Librería Hachette.

Buschiazzo, Mario J., ed., trans.
1941   *Buenos Aires y Córdoba en 1729 según cartas de los padres
        C. Cattaneo y C. Gervasoni, S.J.* Buenos Aires: Compañía
        de Editoriales y Publicaciones Asociadas.

Cáceres, Oscar
n.d.   *Masters of the Lute and Guitar.* Stereo, long-play, MHS 1055.
        New York: Musical Heritage Society.

1973   *Oscar Cáceres Interprets Leo Brouwer.* Stereo, long-play,
        MHS 3777. New York: Musical Heritage Society.

Caldcleugh, Alexander, Esq.
1825   *Travels in South America, During the Years 1819–20–21;
        Containing an Account of the Present State of Brazil, Buenos
        Ayres and Chile.* 2 vols. London: Murray.

Calzavara, Alberto
1987   *Historia de la música en Venezuela: Período hispánico con
        referencias al teatro y la danza.* [Caracas:] Fundación
        Pampero.

Camps, Pompeyo
1978   *Reportaje a la guitarra con Irma Costanzo.* Buenos Aires,
        [etc.]: El Ateneo.

Canfield, D. Lincoln
1981   *Spanish Pronunciation in the Americas.* Chicago and London:

The University of Chicago Press.

Capdevila, Arturo
1940   *Babel y el castellano,* tercera ed. Buenos Aires: Losada, 1954.

Cárbia, Rómulo D.
1914   *Historia eclesiástica del Río de la Plata,* Tomos I–II. Buenos
        Aires: Alfa y Omega.

Cardiel, José, S.J.
1747   *Carta-relación de las misiones de la Provincia del Paraguay*
        in Guillermo Furlong, S.J., *José Cardiel, S.J. y su Carta-*
        relación (1747). Buenos Aires: Librería del Plata, 1953.

1758   *Declaración de la verdad: Obra inédita del P. José Cardiel.*
        Introduction by P. Pablo Hernández, ed. Buenos Aires: Juan
        A. Alsina, 1900.

Carlevaro, Abel (compositions:)
1958   *Preludios americanos.* B & C 4010–4018, passim.
        1. Evocación, 2. Scherzino, 3. Campo, 4. Ronda, 5. Tamboriles.
        Buenos Aires: Barry.

1978   *Concierto del Plata: para guitarra y orquesta,* reducción
        para guitarra y piano. B & C 4027. Buenos Aires: Barry.

1983   *Introducción y capricho.* Heidelberg: Chanterelle. The
        Introducción, alone appeared in *Guitar Review* (New York)
        No. 62 (summer), 24–26.

1986   *Arenguay...*"identifies the spirit and people of Argentina
        and Uruguay by combining the two names." *Duo Concertante*
        for 2 Guitars. Heidelberg: Chanterelle.

Carlevaro, Abel (didactic works:)
1978   *Escuela de la guitarra: Exposición de la teoría instrumental.*
        Montevideo: Dacisa. Buenos Aires: Barry. English ed. by Jihad
        Azkoul and Bartolomé Díaz, trans. New York: Boosey and
        Hawkes, 1984.

1967–present *Serie didáctica* [with explanations in Eng. and Sp.]:
        No. 1, *Escalas diatónicas,* B & C 4006.
        No. 2, *Técnica de la mano derecha,* B & C 4007.
        No. 3, *Técnica de la mano izquierda,* B & C 4009.
        No. 4, *Técnica de la mano izquierda (conclusión),* B & C 4013.
        Buenos Aires: Barry.

1985–present *Técnica aplicada* [clases magistrales]:
        Vol. 1, *10 estudios de Fernado Sor.*
        Vol. 2, *Sobre 5 Preludios y el Choro No. 1 de H. Villa Lobos.*
        Montevideo: Dacisa.

Carlevaro, Abel (recordings:)
n.d.   *Recital de guitarra* [Manuel Ponce, Moreno Torroba, Isaac
        Albéniz]. Hi-fi, long-play, ALP 1002. Montevideo: Antar.

n.d.   *2o. Recital de guitarra* [J.S. Bach, A. Barrios, Abel Carlevaro,
        Camargo Guarnieri]. Hi-fi, long-play, ALP 4002. Montevideo:
        Antar.

n.d.   *Guitarra: Domenico Scarlatti, Fernando Sor* [respectively,
        sonatas & studies). Long-play, ALP 4014. Montevideo: Antar.

1980   *Compositores americanos del siglo XX.* Stereo, long-play,
        S44-120. Montevideo: Sondor.

1986   *Carlevaro plays Carlevaro [5 Preludios americanos, Intro-
        ducción y capricho, Cronomías (Sonata I)].* Stereo, long-
        play, CR1000. Heidelberg: Chanterelle. The score for the
        Introducción appeared in *Guitar Review* (New York) No. 62
        (summer 1985), 24–26.

Carlevaro, Agustín (arrangements:)
1968   *Serie del ángel: Astor Piazzolla—Milonga del ángel, La muerte
        del ángel, La resurrección del ángel....* Buenos Aires: Lagos.

1970   *4 Estaciones porteñas...música: Astor Piazzolla, arreglo para
        guitarra: Agustín E. Carlevaro.* Buenos Aires: Lagos.

1979   *Album de tangos* [no. 1]: *Griseta, La muela cariada, La copa
        del olvido, El cachafaz.* B.A. 13260. Buenos Aires: Ricordi.

1985   *Adios nonino: Tango by Astor Piazzolla....* Dale Needles, ed.
        San Francisco: Guitar Solo.

1986   *Album de tangos* [no. 2]: *Nunca tuvo novio, La última cita,
        ¡Qué noche!, Gallo ciego, El baquiano.* B.A. 13402. Buenos
        Aires: Ricordi.

Carlevaro, Agustín (recordings:)
1976   *Marrón y azul, Agustín Carlevaro interpreta versiones* [de
        *Marrón y az., Resurrección del angel, Poema valseado, La bor-
        dona, Mi refugio, Copacabana, Loca bohemia, Cartas viejas, La
        muela cariada, Alfonsina y el mar] para guitarra de Agustín
        Carlevaro,* Vol. 3. Stereo, long-play, A/E 8. Montevideo: Ayuí.

1984   *Piazzolla y Gershwin.* Stereo cassette, LBC 026. Montevideo:
        La Batuta.

[Carrió de la Vandera, Alonso]
[1776] *El lazarillo de ciegos caminantes desde Buenos-Ayres, hasta
        Lima...Sacado de las memorias que hizo Don Alonso Carrió
        de la Vandera en este dilatado viage...desde Montevideo.* Por

Don Calixto Bustamante Carlos Inca, alias Concolorcorvo....
Gijón, Spain [sic]: Rovada [sic!], 1773 [sic]. [Lima: c.1776].
Buenos Aires: Solar, 1942.

Carrizo, Juan Alfonso
1953   *Historia del folklore argentino.* Buenos Aires: Ministerio de
        Educación.

Castro, Américo
1960   *La peculiaridad lingüística rioplatense y su sentido histórico...*
        segunda ed. muy renovada. Madrid: Taurus.

Cattaneo, Cayetano, S.J.
1730   "Letters of F.C. Cattaneo" in Lodovico Antonio Muratori, *A
        Relation of the Missions of Paraguay....* London: J. Marma-
        duke, 1759. See also a Spanish edition by Mario J. Buschiazzo,
        ed., trans., *Buenos Aires y Córdoba en 1729 según las cartas
        de los padres C. Cattaneo y C. Gervasoni, S.J.* Buenos Aires:
        Compañía de Editoriales y Publicaciones Asociadas, 1941.

Cervantes Saavedra, Miguel de
1616   *Obras completas,* Angel Valbuena Prat, ed. Madrid: Aguilar,
        1965.

Chikhachev, Platon Alexandrovich
1844   *A Trip Across the Pampas of Buenos Aires (1836–1837),*
        translated from the Russian by Jack Weiner. Lawrence:
        University of Kansas, 1967.

Chome, Padre, S.J.
1730   "Carta del Padre Chome, misionero de la Compañía de Jesús,
        al Padre Vanthiennen, de la misma compañía, en la Ciudad de
        las Corrientes a 26 de septiembre de 1730," in Juan Mühn, S.J.,
        ed., *La Argentina vista por viajeros del siglo XVIII.* Buenos
        Aires: Huarpes, 1946.

Clinton, George
1986   "Jorge Cardoso," *Guitar International* (London—formerly
        Guitar), Dec., 40–43.

Clormann, Jury
1985   "Music from Argentina" [the first of a series dealing with
        traditional folk dances and songs], *Guitar International*
        (London), Dec., 23–26.

Coluccio, Félix
1964   *Diccionario folklórico argentino.* Primera ed.... Buenos Aires:
        Luis Lasserre y Cía.

"Los conciertos de la semana,"
1920   *La Nación* (Buenos Aires), 13 Jun. (domingo).

Coni, Emilio A.
1925   "Las siete vacas de Goes," *La Nación* (Buenos Aires), 8 Nov.
        (domingo), 14.

Conrad, Barnaby
1953   *La Fiesta Brava: The Art of the Bull Ring.* Boston: Houghton
        Mifflin.

Contreras, Segundo N.
1931   *Disertaciones musicales.* Buenos Aires: E. Perrot.

1950   *La guitarra argentina: Apuntes para su historia y otros
        artículos.* Buenos Aires: Castro Barrera.

Coopersmith, J.M.
1949   *Music and Musicians of the Dominican Republic.* Washington,
        D.C.: Pan American Union.

Cordero, Carlos J.
1936   *Los relatos de los viajeros extranjeros posteriores a la Revolu-
        ción de Mayo como fuentes de historia argentina. Ensayo de
        sistematización bibliográfica....* Buenos Aires: Coni.

Corona, Antonio
1992   "The Popular Music of Veracruz and the Survival of Instru-
        mental Practices of the Spanish Baroque," unpublished lecture
        delivered 22 May at the conference *After Columbus—The Musical
        Journey*, California Polytechnic State University, San Luis
        Obispo.

Cotarelo y Mori, Emilio
1911   *Loas, bailes, jácaras, mojigangas desde fines del siglo XVI
        a mediados del XVIII.* 2 vols. Madrid: Bailly-Bailliere.

Covarrubias, Sebastián de
1611   *Tesoro de la lengua castellana o española.* Madrid: Sánchez.
        Reprinted by Martín de Riquer, ed. Barcelona: Horta, 1943.

Craufurd, Robert
[1807] "Diario de la expedición del Brigadier General Craufurd,"
        Revista Histórica (Montevideo) VIII (1917), 204–12; 519–27.

Darwin, Charles
1839   *The Voyage of the Beagle.* London. Reprint by Walter Sullivan,
        ed. New York: Bantam, 1972.

Davie, John Constanse
1805   *Letters from Paraguay: Describing the Settlements of Monte
        Video and Buenos Ayres; the Presidencies of Rioja Minor,
        Nombre de Dios, St. Mary and St. John....* Written during a
        residence of seventeen months.... London: G. Robinson.

de Gregorio de Mac, María Isabel
1967   *El voseo en la literatura argentina.* Cuadernos del Instituto
        de Letras. Santa Fe, Arg.: Universidad Nacional del Litoral.

de la Torre, R.P. Fray Tomás
1545   *Desde Salamanca, España hasta Ciudad Real, Chiapas: Diario
        de viaje, 1544–1545.* Franz Blom, ed. Mexico City: Editora
        Central, 1945.

de las Casas, Fray Bartolomé
c.1530 *Historia de las Indias.* Biblioteca Mexicana. Mexico City: Editorial
        Nacional, 1951.

de Marsilio, Horacio
1969   *El lenguaje de los uruguayos.* Montevideo: Nuestra Tierra.

Delano, Amasa
1817   *A Narrative of Voyages and Travels in the Northern and South-
        ern Hemispheres: Comprising Three Voyages Round the
        World....* Boston: E.G. House. Republished in facsimile. Upper
        Saddle River, New Jersey: The Gregg Press, 1970.

Descripción del Virreinato del Perú: Crónica inédita de comienzos del
c.1615 *siglo XVII* [anon.]. Edición, prólogo y notas de Boleslao Lewin.
        Rosario: Universidad Nacional del Litoral, Facultad de
        Filosofía..., 1958.

Díaz de Guzmán, Ruy
1612   *La Argentina.* Introduction and notes by Enrique de Gandia.
        Buenos Aires: Angel Estrada, 1943.

Díaz del Castillo, Bernal
1568   *Historia verdadera de la conquista de la Nueva España,* prólogo
        de Carlos Pereyra, ed., segunda edición, Tomos I–II. Madrid:
        Espasa-Calpe, 1942.

Díaz Loza, F.M., arr.
n.d.   *La cumparcita, tango de G.H. Matos Rodríguez, arreglo fácil
        para guitarra.* B.A. 6272. Buenos Aires: Ricordi, printed 1963.

Diccionario Kapelusz
1979   Buenos Aires: Kapelusz.

Dickens, Charles
1859   *A Tale of Two Cities.* London. H.G. Buehler and L. Mason, eds.
        New York: Macmillan, 1922.

Domeyko, Ignäcy
1888   *Moje Podróże: Pamietniki Wygnańca,* Elżbieta Helena Nieciowa,
        ed. Kraków: Zakład Narodowy Imienia Ossolińskich—
        Wydawnictwo, 1962.

Donni de Mirande, Nélida Esther
  1986   "Problemas y estado actual de la investigación del español de
          la Argentina hasta 1984," *Anuario de Letras* (Mexico City)
          XXIV, 179–236.

d'Orbigny, Alcide
  1835–47 *Voyage dans l'Amérique Méridionale (le Brésil, la République
          Orientale de l'Uruguay, la République Argentine, la Patagonie,
          la République du Chili, la République de Bolivia, la République
          du Perou), exécuté pendant les années 1826, 1827, 1828, 1829, 1830,
          1831, 1832 et 1833...*publié sous les auspices de M. le Ministre de
          l'Instruction Publique. Paris: Pitois-Levrault.

du Biscay, Acarete
  1698   *An Account of a Voyage up the River de la Plata, and thence
          over Land to Peru. With Observations on the Inhabitants, as
          well Indians as Spaniards; the Cities, Commerce, Fertility,
          and Riches of that Part of America.* London: Buckley. Facs.
          ed. North Haven, CT: Institute Publishing, 1968.

Ebelot, Alfred
  1889   *La Pampa.* Paris: Quantin. [Spanish ed. by the author.] Paris:
          Escary, 1890. Reprint, Buenos Aires: Editorial Universitaria, 1961.

Echeverría, Esteban
  1831   *"A mi guitarra"* in *Obras Completas...compilación y biografía*
          por Juan María Gutiérrez. Buenos Aires: Zamora, 1972.

Englekirk, John
  1968   [with] Irving A. Leonard, John T. Reid, John A. Crow, *An
          Anthology of Spanish American Literature.* 2nd ed. New York:
          Appleton-Century-Crofts.

Escobar, P.C., arr.
  1940   *El Choclo, tango de A.G. Villoldo para guitarra.* Buenos Aires:
          A. Perroti, printed 1962.

Espinel, Vicente
  1618   *Relaciones de la vida del escudero Marcos de Obregón....* Madrid:
          I. de la Cuesta. Barcelona: Biblioteca "Arte y Letras," 1910.

Espinosa, José de [et al.]
  1794   *Viaje político-científico alrededor del mundo por las corbetas
          Descubierta y Atrevida al mando de los capitanes de navío Don
          Alejandro Malaspina y Don José de Bustamante y Guerra desde
          1789 a 1794,* publicado con una introducción por Don Pedro de
          Novo y Colson, ed. Madrid: Abienzo, 1885.

Esquivel Navarro, Juan de
  1643   *Discursos sobre el arte del dançado, y svs excelencias y primer*

origen, reprobando las acciones deshonestas.... Seville: Gómez de Blas [Madrid: Biblioteca Nacional].

"Exitos, recuerdos y discreción, de Carlos Gardel,"
1929   *La Nación* (Aires), 30 Jun., Sect. 3, p. 8.

Falkner, Thomas, S.J.
1774   *A Description of Patagonia, and the Adjoining Parts of South America: Containing an Account of the Soil, Produce, Animals, Vales, Mountains, Rivers, Lakes, etc. of those Countries...and Some Particulars Relating to Falkland's Islands.* Hereford: T. Lewis. Republisihed in facsimile with introduction and notes by Arthur E.S. Newmann. Chicago: Armann and Armann, 1935.

Falú, Eduardo
1962   *Trago de sombra, zamba para guitarra.* B.A. 12200. Buenos Aires: Ricordi.

1977   *Tiempo de partir* [includes V. Sojo/Alirio Díaz, *Cinco temas venezolanos,* A. Chazarreta, arr., *Zamba de vargas,* and five originals]. Stereo cassette, P 7126268. Montevideo: Philips.

1984   *Recuerdos.* Digital stereo, long-play, ACON 5050. Grafenau, Ger.: Aconcagua.

Ferandiere, Fernando
1799   *Arte de tocar la guitarra española por música, compuesto y ordenado por D. Fernando Ferandiere, Profesor de música en esta corte.* Madrid: Pantaleón Aznar. Complete facsimile ed. with an introduction, English translation, and transcription of the music by Brian Jefferey. London: Tecla, 1971.

Fernández, Eduardo
1985   *Legnani, Giuliani, Sor, Diabelli, Paganini.* Digital CD, DH 414-160-2. [London:] Decca. [This and the other CDs listed below are also available on London LP records.]

n.d.   *Rodrigo, Falla, Granados, Albéniz, Turina, Torroba.* Digital CD, DH 414-161-2. Decca.

n.d.   *Villa Lobos: Preludes, Etudes. Ginastera: Sonata.* Digital CD, DH 414-616-2. Decca.

1986   *Rodrigo: Concierto de Aranjuez, Fantasía para un gentil-hombre. Castelnuovo-Tedesco: Guitar Concerto No. 1, Op. 99...* [with the] English Chamber Orchestra, Miguel Gómez Martínez. Digital CD, DH 417-199-2. Decca.

r.1986 *Mauro Giuliani: Guitar Concerto in A Major, Op. 30. Antonio Vivaldi: Concerto in D Major RV93, Concerto for Guitar and*

*Viola d'amore in D Minor RV540, Concerto in A Major RV82
(= Trio Sonata in C Major)....* Norbert Blume, viola d'amore,
English Chamber Orchestra, George Malcom. Digital CD,
DH 417-617-2. Decca.

Fernández, Juan Rómulo
1929 "Aspectos del folklore argentino," *Instituto Popular de Conferencias* (Buenos Aires) XV, 17–24.

Fernández de Navarrete, Martín, ed.
1825 *Colección de los viajes y descubrimientos que hicieron por mar
los españoles, desde fines del siglo XV...*Tomo II. Madrid: Imprenta Nacional.

Fleury, Abel
n.d. *Ausencia, milonga.* Buenos Aires: Antigua Casa Núñez.

1987 *Obras para guitarra,* revisión y digitación: Roberto Lara.
Vol. 1 [contents: *Ausencia, Vidalita, Tonada, A flor de
llanto, La cimarrona, Chamamé, Estilo pampeano, Pegando
la vuelta, Te vas milonga, Milongueo del ayer, Pago largo,
Real de guitarreros, Relato*]. Buenos Aires: Lagos.

Fleury, Abel and Atahualpa Yupanqui
1971 *Guitarras en el tiempo.* Stereo, long-play, DMO 55612, Serie
Azul. Buenos Aires: Odeón.

Fontanella de Weinberg, María Beatriz
1987 *El español bonaerense: Cuatro, siglos de evolución lingüística
(1580–1980).* Buenos Aires: Hachette.

Furlong, Guillermo, S.J.
1942 "Siete grandes maestros de música colonial riplatense,"
Boletín de la Academia Nacional de la Historia (Buenos Aires)
XVI, 59–76.

1944 "La música en el Río de la Plata con anterioridad a 1810,"
Lyra (Buenos Aires) II, No. 11 (May).

1945 *Músicos argentinos durante la dominación hispánica:
Exposición sintética precedida por una introducción por
Lauro Ayestarán.* Buenos Aires: Huarpes.

1946 *Los Jesuítas y la cultura rioplatense,* nueva edición corregida
y aumentada. Buenos Aires: Editorial Huarpes.

Gage, Thomas
1648 *The English-American, His Travail by Sea and Land: or,
A New Survey of the West-India's....* London: H. Blunden.
Edited and with an Introduction by J. Eric S. Thompson.
Norman: University of Oklahoma Press, 1958.

García Martínez, Héctor
  1987   *Abel Fleury: El poeta de la guitarra.* Fasc. No. 1. Buenos Aires:
         by the author.

García Muñoz, Carmen
  1989   "[Review of] Waldemar Axel Roldán, *Música colonial en la Argen-
         tina: La enseñanza musical* (Buenos Aires: El Ateneo, 1987)," in
         Latin American Music Review (Austin, TX) X, 186–87.

Gardel, Carlos
  1928   *¡Che papusa, oí!,* tango by G. Matos Rodríguez and E. Cadícamo,
         redistributed on *Viejo smoking.* Cassette, EMI 20.862. Monte-
         video: Odeón.

  [1970] *Selección 35 aniversario, Carlos Gardel con acompañamiento
         de guitarras.* A re-mastered long-play of old hit recordings with
         José Razzano. P 1065. New York: Parnaso.

Gerstäcker, Frederick
  1854   *Gerstäcker's Travels. Rio de Janeiro—Buenos Aires—Ride
         through the Pampas...California and the Gold Fields.* Tran-
         slated from the German.... London: Nelson.

Gesualdo, Vicente
  1961   *Historia de la música en la Argentina, 1536–1851,* Vol. I. Buenos
         Aires: Beta.

Gil, Martín
  1907   "La guitarra y los doctores" in *Una novena en la sierra.* Buenos
         Aires: Espasa-Calpe, 1944.

Gillespie, Major Alexander
  1818   *Gleanings and Remarks: Collected during Many Months of
         Residence at Buenos Aires and within the Upper Country...
         until the Surrender of the Colony of the Cape of Good Hope....*
         Leeds: Whiteley.

González, Francisco
  1988   "La guitare en Amérique Latine," *Les Cashiers de la Guitare*
         (Paris) No. 25, 20–22.

Goyena, Héctor Luis
  1986   "El charango en el Departamento de Chuquisaca (Bolivia),"
         Temas de Etnomusicología (Buenos Aires) II, 6–28.

Graham, Robert B. Cunninghame
  1924   *The Conquest of the River Plate.* Garden City, NY: Doubleday,
         Page.

Granada, Daniel
  1890   *Vocabulario rioplatense razonado...2a edición corregida....*

Biblioteca Artigas: Colección de Clásicos Uruguayos, Vols. 25–26. Montevideo: Imprenta Rural. Republished with prologue by Lauro Ayestarán. Montevideo: Ministerio de Instrucción Pública, 1957.

Gray, Paul
1988   "Bridge over Cultures: A Translator Gives Latin Writers a New Home," *Time* (New York) CXXXII (11 Jul.), 75.

Grenón, Pedro J., S.J.
1929   *Nuestra primera música instrumental: Datos históricos.* Buenos Aires: Emilio Perrot.

1954   "Nuestra primera música instrumental: Datos históricos, segunda edición," *Revista de Estudios Musicales* (Universidad Nacional de Cuyo, Mendoza) Año II (1950–51), 11–96; Año III (1954), 173–220.

1957   "Musicatas episódicas: Antiguas costumbres locales (1749–1840)," *Historia* (Buenos Aires) III, No. 9, 33–63.

Grunfeld, Frederic
1969   *The Art and Times of the Guitar: An Illustrated History of Guitars and Guitarists.* London: Macmillan, Collier-Macmillan.

Guamán Poma de Ayala, Felipe
c.1615   *Nueva corónica y buen gobierno: Codex péruvien illustré.* Facs. by Université de Paris, Richard Pietschmann, ed. Travaux et Mémoires de l'Institut d'Ethnologie—XXIII. Paris: Institut d'Ethnologie, 1936.

Guarnieri, Juan Carlos
1978   *El lenguaje rioplatense.* Ediciones de la Banda Oriental No. 65. Montevideo: Ed. la Banda Oriental.

Guestrin, Néstor
1986   "La guitarra en la música suramericana, Capítulo 1: La época colonial," *Revista Musical de Venezuela* (Caracas) VIII, No.19, 11–22.

Haley, George
1959   *Vicente Espinel and Marcos de Obregón: A Life and Its Literary Representation.* Providence, RI: Brown University Press.

Hall, Monica
1978   "The *Guitarra española* of Joan Carles Amat," *Early Music* (London) VI, 362–73, passim.

Hamilton, Anthony
1713   *Mémoires du Chevalier de Grammont.* Paris. Sir Walter Scott, trans. 2 vols. London: Nimmo, 1885.

Head, Francis Bond
  1826   *Rough Notes Taken during Some Rapid Journeys across the Pampas and among the Andes.* London: Murray. Reprinted with introduction by C. Harvey Gardiner, ed. Carbondale and Edwardsville: Southern Illinois University Press, 1967.

Heathcote, A. Anthony
  1977   *Vicente Espinel.* Boston: Twayne Publishers.

Heck, Thomas
  1988   "The *Concours International de Guitare:* A View from the Juror's Box," *Soundboard* (Palo Alto) XV, 155–57.

Helms, Anthony Zachariah
  1807   *Travels from Buenos Aires, by Potosí, to Lima. With notes by the translator, containing topographical descriptions of the Spanish possessions in South America, drawn from the last and best authorities.* [Another English translation appeared that same year with a different subtitle.] London: R. Phillips.

Henríquez Ureña, Pedro
  1925   "El supuesto andalucismo de América," *Cuadernos del Instituto de Filología* (Buenos Aires) I, No. 2, 117–22.

Henty, G.A.
  1868   *Out on the Pampas, or The Young Settlers.* Illustrations by J.B. Zwecker. London: Blackie.

Hernández, José
  1879   *El gaucho Martín Fierro.* Buenos Aires: Imprenta de la Pampa, 1872. *La vuelta de Martín Fierro.* Buenos Aires: Librería del Plata, 1879. [Both republished with "xilografías" by Alberto Nicasio, 9th ed.] Buenos Aires: Ediciones Peuser, 1960.

Hodel, Brian
  1985   "Abel Carlevaro: Master Teacher," *Guitar Review* (New York) No. 62 (summer), 20–23.

  1986   "The Guitar in Latin America" [the first in a series of articles on this theme], *Guitar Review* (New York) No. 65 (spring), 27.

Hornbostel, Eric M. von, and Curt Sachs
  1914   "Classification of Musical Instruments: Translated from the Original German by Anthony Baines and Klaus P. Wachsmann," *Galpin Society Journal* (Winchester, Eng.) XIV (1961), 3–29. Originally "Systematik der Musikinstrumente. Ein Versuch," *Zeitschrift für Ethnologie* (Berlin) XLVI (1914), Heft 4–5, 553–90.

Hudson, Richard
  1982   *The Folia, the Saraband, the Passacaglia, and the Chaconne: The Historical Evolution of Four Forms that Originated in*

Music for the Five-course Spanish Guitar. Musicological Studies and Documents 35, American Institute of Musicology, Armen Carapetyan, general ed. 4 vols. Neuhausen-Stuttgart: Hänssler-Verlag.

Hudson, William H.
1885   *The Purple Land that England Lost: Travels and Adventures in the Banda Oriental, South America.* London: S. Low, Marston, [et al.]. Republished by the author. London: Duckworth, 1904.

1918   *Far Away and Long Ago: A History of My Early Life.* New York: E.P. Dutton. In 1974, it was made into an Argentine feature film entitled *Allá lejos y hace tiempo.*

Hutchinson, Thomas J.
1865   *Buenos Ayres and Argentine Gleanings: with Extracts from a Diary of Salado Exploration in 1862 and 1863.* London: Stanford.

Iparraguirre, Pedro A., arr.
[The "Sala Uruguay" of the Biblioteca Nacional, Montevideo maintains copies of the following transcriptions for guitar solo by P.A. Iparraguirre. They are kept with the tangos of other guitarists, including both transcriptions and original compositions. None of the following shows date of copyright or imprint.]

Como te quiero, tango de Francisco Canaro. Buenos Aires: H.N. Pirovano.

Confesión, tango de Enrique S. Discépolo. Buenos Aires: H.N. Pirovano.

Cruz de palo, tango de Guillermo D. Barbieri. Buenos Aires: H.N. Pirovano.

Pelele, tango de Pedro M. Maffia. Buenos Aires: H.N. Pirovano.

Sacudíme la persiana [Shake My Shutter!], *tango de V. Loduca.* Buenos Aires: Núñez.

Sufra, tango de F. Canaro. Montevideo: Editorial Montevideo.

Un tropezón, tango de Raúl de los Hoyos. Buenos Aires: Pirovano.

Irving, Darrel
1985   "Ernesto Bitetti in New York," *Guitar* (London), Apr., 12–15.

Isabelle, Arséne
1835   *Voyage a Buenos-Ayres et a Porto-Alegre, par la Banda Oriental, les Missions d'Uruguay et la Province de Rio-Grande-do-Sul. (De 1830 a 1834)....* Havre: Morlent.

Jones, Tom B.
1949   *South America Rediscovered.* Minneapolis: University of
        Minnesota Press.

Juan, Jorge and Antonio de Ulloa
1748   *Relación histórica del viaje a la América Meridional...con
        otras varias observaciones.* Madrid. *A Voyage to South Amer-
        ica: Describing at Large the Spanish Cities, Towns, Provinces;
        etc....* John Adams, trans. London: 1806. Republished by Irving
        A. Leonard, ed. New York: Knopf, 1964.

1749   *Discourse and Political Reflections on the Kingdoms of Peru.
        Their Government, Special Regimen of Their Inhabitants, and
        Abuses....* John J. Tepaske, ed. and trans. Norman: University
        of Oklahoma Press, 1978.

Kany, Charles E.
1951   "Chapter III: The Voseo" in *American-Spanish Syntax,* 2nd
        ed. Chicago and London: The University of Chicago Press.

Landriscina, Luis
1979   *Historias de una mateada.* Stereo cassette, AP 7126503.
        Montevideo: Philips/Aplausos.

Lange, Francisco Curt
1954   "La música eclesiástica argentina en el período de la domina-
        ción hispánica (una investigación), primera parte," *Revista de
        Estudios Musicales* (Universidad Nacional de Cuyo, Mendoza)
        III, No. 7, 17–169, passim.

1956   *La música eclesiástica en Córdoba durante la dominación
        hispánica* (reprinted from articles published in the *Revista
        de la Universidad Nacional de Córdoba).* Córdoba, Arg.:
        Imprenta de la Universidad.

Lapesa, Rafael
1970   "Las formas verbales de segunda persona y los orígenes del
        voseo" in *Actas del Tercer Congreso Internacional de Hispan-
        istas.* Mexico City: El Colegio de México.

Lara, Roberto
n.d.   *Argentina: Guitar of the Pampas.* Stereo cassette, L 7253. New
        York: Lyrichord. [See also Abel Fleury.]

Lemaitre, Eduardo
1980   *Breve historia de Cartagena, 1501–1901.* Bogotá: Tercer Mundo.

Leonard, Irving A.
1952   "One Man's Library, Mexico City, 1620," in *Estudios hispánicos,
        homenaje a Archer M. Huntington.* Wellesley, MA: Wellesley
        College, pp. 327–34.

Levillier, Roberto, ed.
1926   *Papeles eclesiásticos del Tucumán: Documentos originales del
        Archivo de Indias,* Volumen I. Colección de Publicaciones
        Históricas de la Biblioteca del Congreso Argentino. Madrid:
        Juan Pueyo.

"Libro de diferentes cifras de gitara [sic] escojidas de los mejores autores"
1705   (anon.), MS No. 811. Madrid: Biblioteca Nacional.

Lockhart, James, and Enrique Otte, trans. and eds.
1976   *Letters and Peoples of the Spanish Indies: Sixteenth Century.*
        London, New York, Melbourne: Cambridge University Press.

Lohmann Villena, Guillermo
1946   *El Conde de Lemos / Virrey del Peru.* Publicaciones de la Escuela
        de Estudios Hispano-Americanos...XXIII (No. General), Serie 2a:
        Monografías, No. 8. Madrid: Universidad de Sevilla.

Lowenfeld, Elena Machado
1974   "Santiago de Murcia's Thorough-Bass Treatise for the Baroque
        Guitar (1714): Introduction, Translation, and Transcription."
        Master's thesis, City University of New York. Ann Arbor:
        University Microfilms No. M-7910.

MacCann, William
1853   *Two Thousand Miles' Ride through the Argentine Provinces.
        Being an Account of the Natural Products of the Country,
        and Habits of the People with a Historical Retrospect of the
        Río de la Plata, Monte Video, and Corrientes....* 2 vols. Lon-
        don: Smith, Elder. Facsimile ed. New York: AMS Press, [n.d.].

Madero, Eduardo
1939   *Historia del puerto de Buenos Aires: Descubrimiento del Río
        de la Plata y de sus principales afluentes, y fundación de
        las más antiguas ciudades, en sus márgenes.* Tercera ed.
        Buenos Aires: Ediciones Buenos Aires.

Malkiel, Yakov
1972   *Linguistics and Philology in Spanish America: A Survey
        (1925–1970).* The Hague, Paris: Mouton.

Malmberg, Bertil
1966   *La América hispanohablante: Unidad y diferenciación del
        castellano.* Traducción directa del sueco: Javier López Facal
        y Kristina Lindstrom, revisada por el autor. Tercera ed.
        Madrid: Ediciones Istmo, 1974.

Mantegazza, Pablo
1876   *Viajes por el Río de la Plata y el Interior de la Confederación
        Argentina...*tercera edición corregida por el autor, Milán, 1876,
        traducidos por el Consejero de la Universidad, Doctor Juan

Heller. Buenos Aires: Universidad de Tucumán & Coni, 1916.

Manuel, Peter
1986   "Evolution and Structure in Flamenco Harmony," *Current Musicology* (New York) No. 42, 46–57.

"Mary, Queen of Scots" [= Mary Stuart]
1917   *Dictionary of National Biography...to 1900* (London: Oxford University Press, 1968) XII, pp. 1258–75.

Mawe, John
1812   *Travels in the Interior of Brazil...Including a Voyage to the Río de la Plata.* London: Longman [et al.].

Menéndez Pidal, Ramón
1962   "Sevilla frente a Madrid: Algunas precisiones sobre el español de América," in *Miscelanea homenaje a André Martinet: "Estructuralismo e Historia"* III, Diego Catalán, ed. Canary Islands: Universidad de la Laguna.

Miers, John
1826   *Travels in Chile and La Plata, Including Accounts Respecting the Geography, Geology, Statistics, Government, Finances, Agriculture, Manners, and Customs, and the Mining Operations in Chile. Collected During a Residence of Several Years in These Countries.* 2 vols. London: Baldwin, Cradock, and Joy.

Millé, Andrés
1961   *Crónica de la Orden Franciscana en la conquista del Perú, Paraguay y el Tucumán y su convento antiguo de Buenos Aires. 1210–1800.* Buenos Aires: Emecé.

Minguet y Yrol, Pablo
1774   *Reglas, y advertencias generales para tañer la guitarra, tiple, y vandola.* Madrid: Printed by the author.

Mörner, Magnus
1953   *The Political and Economic Activities of the Jesuits in the Plata Region: The Hapsburg Era.* Stockholm: Library and Institute of Ibero-American Studies.

Moll, Jaime
1969   "Una bibliografía musical periódica de fines del siglo XVIII," *Anuario Musical* (Barcelona) XXIV, 1–12.

Montanaro, Bruno
c.1983   *Guitares hispano-américaines.* Aix-en-Provence: Edisud.

Monzón, Antonio
1947   "Un profesor indígena [Piriobi] de la música en el Buenos Aires del siglo XVIII," *Estudios* (Academia Literaria del

Plata, Buenos Aires) LXXVIII, No. 422 (Sep.), 142–46.

Morante, Ambrosio
1821   *Defensa y triunfo del Tucumán: Pieza militar en dos actos.*
       Instituto de Literatura Argentina, Sección de Documentos, Tomo
       IV, No. 3. Buenos Aires: Imprenta de la Universidad, 1926.

Morel, Jorge
1981   *Virtuoso South American Guitar.* Stereo, long-play, GMR 1002.
       Leeds: Guitar Masters.

1981   *Virtuoso South American Guitar...Guitar Solos* [Morel is com-
       poser of three items]. Gateshead, Eng.: Ashley Mark.

Moreno, Salvador
1957   *Angeles músicos en México.* Mexico City: Ediciones *Bellas Artes.*

1959   "Angeles músicos en México," *Cuadernos Hispanoamericanos*
       (Madrid) No. 106 (Oct. 1958), 59–70; and No. 115 (Jul. 1959), 4–15.

Moreno Chá, Ercilia, ed.
1975   *Documental folklórico de la Provincia de La Pampa,* grabaciones,
       textos y fotografías de Ercilia Moreno Chá. Long-play recording,
       QF 3015/16. Buenos Aires, New York: Qualiton.

1980   *Instrumentos musicales etnográficos y folklóricos de la Argen-
       tina: Síntesis de los datos obtenidos en investigaciones de campo
       (1931–1980).* Buenos Aires: Institiuto Nacional de Musicología
       "Carlos Vega."

Moretti, Federico
1799   *Principios para tocar la guitarra de seis órdenes....* Madrid
       [London: British Library].

Moses, Bernard
1922   *Spanish Colonial Literature in South America.* London, New
       York: The Hispanic Society of America.

Mozart, J.C. Wolfgang Amadeus
1786   *Le nozze di Figaro* in *Wolfgang Amadeus Mozart's Werke:
       Kritisch durchgesehene Gesamtausgabe,* Ser. 5, No. 17.
       Leipzig: Breitkopf und Haertel, 1876–1907.

Mühn, Juan, S.J., ed.
1946   *La Argentina vista por viajeros del siglo XVIII.* Buenos Aires:
       Huarpes.

Mugaburu, Josephe and Francisco
1697   *Chronicle of Colonial Lima: The Diary of Josephe and Francisco
       Mugaburu, 1640–1697.* Robert R. Miller, ed., trans. Norman:
       University of Oklahoma Press, 1975.

Muñiz, Francisco Javier
   1845   *Voces usadas con generalidad en las repúblicas del Plata—
           la Argentina, y la Oriental del Uruguay (Montevideo)*. Buenos
           Aires. Republished with introduction and notes by Milcíades
           Alejo Vignati, *El vocabulario rioplatense de Francisco Javier
           Muñiz*. Buenos Aires: Coni, 1937.

Muñoz, Ricardo
   1930   *Historia de la guitarra*. Buenos Aires: n.p.

Muratori, Lodovico Antonio
   1759   *A Relation of the Missions of Paraguay. Wrote originally in
           Italian by Mr. Muratori, and now done into English from the
           French translation*. London: J. Marmaduke.

Murcia, Santiago de
   1732   "Passacalles y obras de guitarra por todos los tonos naturales
           y acidentales...1732," MS Add. 31640. London: British Library.

   c.1732 *Saldívar Codex No. 4: Santiago de Murcia Manuscript of Baroque
           Guitar Music (c.1732) Found and Acquired in September 1943
           in León, Guanajuato, Mexico by the Mexican Musicologist Dr.
           Gabriel Saldívar y Silva (1909–1980)*. Volume 1, *The Manuscript:
           Complete Facsimile Edition with Commentary*, Michael Lorimer,
           ed. Santa Barbara: Michael Lorimer, 1987.

Musso Ambrosi, Luis Alberto
   1976   *El Río de la Plata en el Archivo General de Indias de Sevilla:
           Guía para investigadores*. 2nd ed. Montevideo: Rosgal.

Narváez, Luis de
   1538   *Los seys libros del Delphín de Música de cifra para tañer
           vihuela*. Transcripción y estudio por Emilio Pujol, Monumentos
           de la Música Española III. Barcelona: Consejo Superior de Inves-
           tigaciones Científicas, 1945.

Nichols, Madaline W.
   1952   "A Study in the Golden Age" in *Estudios hispánicos, homenaje
           a Archer M. Huntington*. Wellesley, MA: Wellesley College.

Nield, Johathan
   1929   *A Guide to the Best Historical Novels and Tales*. 5th ed. New
           York: Macmillan.

Notes on the Viceroyalty of La Plata, in South America; with a Sketch
   1808   *of the Manners and Character of the Inhabitants*...[anon.].
           London: J.J. Stockdale.

Oberti, Federico
   1979   *Historia y folklore del mate*. Buenos Aires: Fondo Nacional de
           las Artes.

Ohlsen, Oscar
1980   "Antepasados de la guitarra en América Latina," *Revista Universitaria* (Pontificia Universidad Católica de Chile) No. 3 (Apr.), 77–86.

Olsen, Dale A.
1980   "Folk Music of South America," in *Musics of Many Cultures, an Introduction,* Elizabeth May, ed. Berkeley: University of California Press.

Oraisón, Jorge
1982   *Castelnuovo Tedesco: Guitar Concerto No. 2, Tarantella, Capriccio, Rondo,* with Adam Gatehouse conducting the Concertgebouw Chamber Orchestra. Stereo, long-play, ETC 1001. Amsterdam: Etcetera: [dist. in New York: Qualiton].

1984   *Astor Piazzolla: Death of the Angel, Songs and Tangos for Guitar.* Stereo, long-play, ETC 1023. Amsterdam: Etcetera.

1987   *Leo Brouwer: Tres apuntes, Elogio de la danza, Canticum, Tarantos, Temas populares cubanos, El decamerón negro, Variaciones sobre un tema de Django Reinhardt.* Digital stereo, long-play, ETC 1034. Amsterdam: Etcetera.

Otero, Corazón
1980   *Manuel Ponce and the Guitar,* John D. Roberts, trans. Shaftesbury, Dorset, Eng.: Musical New Services, 1983.

Pacheco, Francisco
1599   *Libro de descripción de verdaderos retratos....* Seville. Facs. by José M. Asencio, ed. Seville: R. Tarrascó, 1885.

Páez Urdaneta, Iraset
1981   *Historia y geografía del voseo.* Caracas: La Casa de Bello.

Page, F.M.
1893   "Remarks on the Gaucho and His Dialect," *Modern Language Notes* (Baltimore) VIII (1893), 18–27.

Pallière, Léon
1869   *Diario de viaje,* unpublished manuscript written ca. 1860, revised by Pallière in 1869; Spanish translation by Ricardo Gutiérrez and Miguel Solá entitled *Diario de viaje por la América del Sud,* con una introducción sobre la vida y la obra del artista, ilustrada con acuarelas, grabados y dibujos ejecutados en América y en Europa. Buenos Aires: Peuser, 1945.

Paucke, Florian, S.J.
1769   *Hacia allá y para acá: Una estada entre los Indios Mocobíes, 1749–1767.* Edmundo Wernicke, trans. 3 vols. Tucumán, Buenos Aires: Universidad Nacional de Tucumán, 1942.

Pease, Franklin, ed., trans.
1980   Felipe Guamán Poma de Ayala, *Nueva corónica y buen gobierno: Transcripción, prólogo, notas y cronología.* 2 vols. Caracas: Biblioteca Ayacucho.

Pedretti de Bolón, Alma
1983   *El idioma de los uruguayos: unidad y diversidad.* Ediciones de la Banda Oriental 12. Montevideo: Ed. la Banda Oriental.

Peralta, Fray Joseph
1743   *Informe que remite a S.M. Cathólica el illmo. Señor Don Fray Joseph Peralta, Obispo de Buenos-Ayres, de la Orden de Predicadores: Sobre la visita, que hizo de todos los pueblos de las misiones que están a cargo de los PP. de la Compañía de Jesús....* Buenos-Ayres, enero 8. Republished. Havana: O.B. Cintas, n.d.

Pereira Salas, Eugenio
1941   *Los orígenes del arte musical en Chile.* Santiago: Imprenta Universitaria.

Pernety, Antoine Joseph
1770   *Histoire d'un voyage aux isles Malouines, fait en 1763 & 1764; avec des observations sur le detroit de Magellan, et sur les Patagons.* Paris: Chez Saillant & Nyon [etc.].

Piazzolla, Astor
1986   "Agustín Carlevaro," *El País* (Montevideo), 6 Apr. (domingo).

Pierri Sapere, José
1975–86 [Titles in the authentic but easy series for guitar, edited by his daughter Olga Pierri:] *Vidala, Milonga, Rancherita, Estilo No. 8, Gato, Vidalita, Mazurca, Pericón, Milonga No. 3.* Montevideo: Palacio de la Música.

Pinnell, Richard
1979   "Santiago de Murcia's Baroque Guitar Entabulation of Corelli's Violin Sonata, Op. 5, No. 8," *Soundboard* (Palo Alto) VI, 134–37.

1980   *Francesco Corbetta and the Baroque Guitar, with a Transcription of His Works.* 2 vols. UMI Studies in Musicology No. 25. Ann Arbor: UMI Research Press.

1984   "The Guitarist-Singer of Pre-1900 Gaucho Literature," *Latin American Music Review* (Austin, TX) V, No. 2, 243–62.

1992   "La perspectiva norteamericana de la guitarra rioplatense," *El Encordado* (Spånga, Sweden) No.1 (Jan.), 25–27.

Pla Cárceles, José
1923   "La evolución del tratamiento 'vuestra-merced'," *Revista de Filología Española* (Madrid) X, 245–80.

Pollo Darraque, Ricardo
1884   *El Clinudo: Un gaucho alzao,* published in installments of *La Tribuna Popular.* Republished as "Dramas de la barbarie en el Uruguay: Historia de El Clinudo" in *El País* (Montevideo: 1924). Republished with commentary by Cédar Viglietti. Minas, Uruguay: [By the author] 1955.

Pope Conant, Isabel
1958   "Vicente Espinel as a Musician," *Studies in the Renaissance* (New York) V, 133–44.

Porro, N.R.
1982   [with] J.E. Astiz and M.M. Rospide, *Aspectos de la vida cotidiana en el Buenos Aires virreinal.* Buenos Aires: La Universidad.

Prat, Domingo
[1934]   *Diccionario biográfico, bibliográfico, histórico, crítico, de guitarras (instrumentos afines) guitarristas (profesores, compositores, concertistas, lahudistas, amateurs) guitarreros (luthiers)....* Buenos Aires: Romero y Fernández.

Proctor, Robert, Esq.
1825   *Narrative of a Journey across the Cordillera of the Andes and of a Residence in Lima, and Other Parts of Peru, in the Years 1823 and 1824.* London: Archibald Constable.

Puerta Zuluaga, David
1988   *Los caminos del tiple.* Bogotá: Damel.

Pujol, Emilio
[1930]   *La guitarra y su historia: conferencia* [dada en Londres, París, Barcelona...]. Buenos Aires: Romero y Fernández.

[1933]   *Escuela razonada de la guitarra basada en los principios de la técnica de Tárrega.* 4 vols. [Prologue signed by Manuel de Falla in 1933.] Buenos Aires: Ricordi. Eng. trans. of Vols. I and II by Brian Jeffery. Boston & Columbus: Editions Orphée, 1983.

Ramírez, Luis
1528   A report signed *"en este puerto de san zalbador ques en el Río de Solís a. diez. días del mes. de. julio de 1528 años,"* in Eduardo Madero, *Historia del puerto de Buenos Aires: Descubrimiento del Río de la Plata....* 3a ed. Buenos Aires: Ediciones Buenos Aires, 1939, Appendix No. 8.

Ramón y Rivera, Luis Felipe
1966   "La música colonial profana," *Revista Nacional de Cultura* (Caracas) XXVIII, Nos. 174–75 (Mar.–Jun.), 62–65.

Rapat, Atilio, arr.
1954   *La tristecita, zamba de Ariel Ramírez...transcripción para*

guitarra. B.A. 10970. Buenos Aires: Ricordi.

Real Academia Española
1950   *Diccionario manual e ilustrado de la lengua española,* segunda
        edición. Madrid: Espasa-Calpe.

Relaciones geográficas de Indias
1885   Tomo I (1881), Tomo II (1885). Madrid: Ministerio de Fomento,
        Perú.

Robertson, J.P. and W.P. [John Parish and William Parish]
1839   *Letters on Paraguay: Comprising an Account of Four Years'
        Residence in that Republic, under the Government of the
        Dictator Francia....* 3 vols. Second ed. London. Facs. reprint.
        New York: AMS Press, 1970.

1843   *Letters on South America; Comprising Travels on the Banks
        of the Paraná and Río de la Plata....* 3 vols. London: Murray.

Rodríguez de Guzmán, Diego
1713   *Flor de academias,* manuscript completed at Lima. Edited by
        Ricardo Palma. Lima: El Tiempo, 1899.

Rodríguez Molas, Ricardo E.
1982   *Historia social del gaucho.* "Capítulo," Biblioteca Argentina
        Fundamental...Sociedad y Cultura, No. 11. Buenos Aires:
        Centro Editor de América Latina.

Roldán, Waldemar Axel
1987   *Música colonial argentina: La enseñanza musical.* Buenos
        Aires: El Ateneo.

Rona, José Pedro
1963   "Sobre algunas etimologías rioplatenses," *Anuario de Letras*
        (Mexico City) III, 87–106.

1967   *Geografía y morfología del voseo.* Porto Alegre: Ed. La Salle.

Roos, Jaime
1982   *Siempre son las cuatro.* Cassette, SCO 90689. [Montevideo:] Orfeo.

Rosenblat, Angel
1971   *Nuestra lengua en ambos mundos.* Estella [Navarra]: Salvat
        Editores & Alianza Editorial.

Rossi, Vicente
1928   *Idioma nacional rioplatense (argentino-uruguayo): Primera
        evidencia* [one of a total of five lexical studies published as
        "Primera evidencia"–"Quinta evidencia"] Folletos lenguaraces,
        6–10. Río de la Plata [Córdoba, Arg.]: [Imprenta Argentina],
        1928–1929.

Russell, Craig H.
1981   "Santiago de Murcia: Spanish Theorist and Guitarist of the
        Early Eighteenth Century." Ph.D. dissertation, University of
        North Carolina, Chapel Hill. 3 vols. Ann Arbor: University
        Microfilms No. 8211645.

Sachs, Curt
1963   *World History of the Dance.* New York: Norton, 1937, 1963.

Sagregras, Julio S.
1955   *Las primeras lecciones–Las sextas lecciones* [six method-books
        for guitar based on the Tárrega technique yet containing many
        original compositions in the folk style of the Plata]. Buenos Aires:
        Ricordi. Eng. trans. of Vol I. Milwaukee: Hal Leonard.

n.d.   *Don Julio, tango criollo para guitarra.* Buenos Aires: F. Núñez.

Salazar, Eugenio
c.1573 "Cartas de Eugenio Salazar, vecino y natural de Madrid, escritas
        a muy particulares amigos suyos," in Eugenio de Ochoa, ed.,
        *Epistolario español: Colección de cartas de españoles ilustres
        antiguos y modernos,* Tomo segundo. Biblioteca de Autores Es-
        pañoles...Tomo LXII. Madrid: Hernando, 1926.

Saldívar, Gabriel
1934   [with] Elisa Osorio Bolio, *Historia de la música en México:
        Epocas precortesiana y colonial.* Mexico City: Editorial
        "Cvltvra."

Santa Cruz, Antonio de
17th c. "Libro donde se verán pazacalles de los ocho tonos...para bi-
        güela hordinaria," n.d. MS Música 2209. Madrid: Bibl. Nacional.

Santorsola, Guido
1976   *Suite all'antica para 2 guitarras.* Revisión y digitación de Horacio
        Ceballos. Archivo de la Guitarra (Serie Didáctica). B.A. 13172.
        Buenos Aires: Ricordi.

Sarmiento, Domingo Faustino
1845   *Civilización i barbarie: Vida de Juan Facundo Quiroga....*
        Santiago, Chile: Imprenta del Progreso. *Life in the Argentine
        Republic in the Days of the Tyrants: Civilization and Barbarism.*
        From the Spanish of Domingo F. Sarmiento, L.L.D., Minister
        Plenipotentiary from the Argentine Republic to the United States
        with a biographical sketch of the author by Mrs. Horace Mann.
        First American from the third Spanish Edition. 1868. Reprinted.
        New York: Hafner Press. London: Collier Macmillan, 1974.

Sas, Andrés
1962   "La vida musical en la Catedral de Lima durante la colonia,"
        Revista Musical Chilena (Santiago) Año XVI, Nos. 81–82, 8ff.

Scarlett, P. Campbell
  1838   *South America and the Pacific; Comprising a Journey across
          the Pampas and the Andes, from Buenos Ayres to Valparaíso,
          Lima and Panama; With Remarks upon the Esthmus....* 2 vols.
          London: Colburn.

Schmidl, Ulrico (Ulrich or Utz)
  1567   *Derrotero y viaje a España y las Indias,* Edmundo Wernicke,
          trans. 2nd ed. Buenos Aires: Espasa-Calpe, 1980.

Schweitzer, G.
  1953   "Die Gitarre Maria Stuarts," *Zeitschrift für Musik* (Leipzig)
          XIV (Jul. 1953), 409–10.

Scobie, James R.
  1971   *Argentina: A City and a Nation.* New York: Oxford Univ. Press.

Segovia, Andrés
  1973   *Manuel Ponce: Concierto del Sur, Rodrigo: Fantasía para un
          gentilhombre.* Enrique Jordá, conducting. Long-play, MCA 2522.
          Universal City, CA: MCA Records. [The recording originally
          appeared on Decca, DL 710027.]

Sensier, Peter
  1975   "A Gap in the Story of the Guitar," *Guitar* (London), Oct., 16–17.

Sepp, Anthony, S.J.
  1697   *An Account of a Voyage from Spain to Paraquaria; Performed
          by the Reverend Fathers Anthony Sepp and Anthony Behme,
          Both German Jesuits, the First of Tyrol upon the River Eth,
          the Other of Bavaria. Containing a Description of All the
          Remarkable Things and the Inhabitants, as well as of the
          Missionaries Residing in that Country, Taken from the Let-
          ters of Said Anthony Sepp, and Published by His Own Brother
          Gabriel Sepp. Translated from the High Dutch Original.* Printed
          at Nurenberg: 1697. London: Churchill's Voyages, 1703.

Serís, Homero
  1964   *Bibliografía de la lingüística española.* Publicaciones del
          Instituto Caro y Cuervo XIX. Bogotá: Instituto Caro y Cuervo.

Seymour, Richard Arthur
  1869   *Pioneering in the Pampas, or the First Four Years of a Settler's
          Experience in the La Plata Camps.* London: Longmans, Green.

Sinópoli, Antonio, arr.
  n.d.   *Pericón de Gerardo Grasso, transcripción para una o dos
          guitarras.* B.A. 6962. Buenos Aires: Ricordi, printed 1952.

  n.d.   *Pericón de Gerardo Grasso...arreglo fácil para guitarra* [easy
          version]. B.A. 8416. Buenos Aires: Ricordi, printed 1955.

Siracusa, María Isabel
1977   "Morfología verbal del voseo en el habla culta de Buenos Aires"
        in *Estudios sobre el español hablado en las principales ciudades
        de América,* Juan M. Lope Blanch, ed. Mexico City: Universidad
        Nacional Autónoma de México.

Slatta, Richard W.
1982   "Pulperías and Contraband Capitalism in Nineteenth-Century
        Buenos Aires Province," *The Americas* (Washington, D.C.)
        XXXVIII, 347–62.

Sloman, Albert E.
1965   "The Two Versions of *El burlador de Sevilla,*" *Bulletin of
        Hispanic Studies* (Essex, Eng.) XLII, 18–33.

Stanford, Charles Villiers
1915   "Some Thoughts Concerning Folk-song and Nationality,"
        Musical Quarterly (New York) I, 232–45.

Stevenson, Robert
1960   *The Music of Peru: Aboriginal and Viceroyal Epochs.* Wash-
        ington, D.C.: Pan American Union.

1968   *Music in Aztec & Inca Territory.* Berkeley and Los Angeles:
        University of California Press.

1980a   "Alonso de Mudarra," *The New Grove Dictionary of Music and
        Musicians.* London: Macmillan.

1980b   "Santiago de Murcia: A Review Article," *Inter-American Music
        Review* (Los Angeles) III, No. 1, 89–101.

1984   "The Music of Colonial Spanish America" in *The Cambridge
        History of Latin America, Volume II: Colonial Latin America,*
        Leslie Bethell, ed. Cambridge: Cambridge University Press.

Stover, Richard
1982   "Guitarra Americana," [the first installment of a quarterly
        column lasting over two years that featured South America,
        especially the music of Agustín Barrios] *Soundboard* (Palo Alto)
        IX (summer), 150–53.

Strizich, Robert
1974   "A Spanish Guitar Tutor: Ruiz de Ribayaz's *Luz y norte musical*
        (1677)," *Journal of the Lute Society of America* (Palo Alto) VII
        (1974), 51–81.

Strobel, Matías
1729   "Carta del Padre Matías Strobel a un padre de Viena" in Juan
        Mühn, ed., *La Argentina vista por viajeros del siglo XVIII.*
        Buenos Aires: Huarpes, 1946.

Subirá, José
1953   *Historia de la música española e hispanoamericana.* Barcelona: Salvat.

Tanodi, Aurelio, ed.
1971   *Documentos de la Real Hacienda de Puerto Rico,* Volumen I
        (1510–1519). Centro de Investigaciones Históricas.... Buenos
        Aires: Editorial Nova & Universidad de Puerto Rico.

Tejeda, Luis José de
1663   *Coronas líricas: Prosa y verso por Luis José de Tejeda,* Pablo
        Cabrera, ed. Córdoba: [La Universidad], 1917.

Thomas, Eduardo
1957   *Compendio de historia nacional,* 4th ed. Montevideo: Monteverde.

Tilmouth, Michael
1957   "Some Improvements in Music Noted by William Turner in
        1697," *Galpin Society Journal* (Winchester, Eng.) X, 57–59.

Tinctoris, Johannes
c.1487 *De inventione et usu musicae.* Naples. Anthony Baines, trans.
        "Fifteenth-century Instruments in Tinctoris's *De Inventione et
        Usu Musicae," Galpin Society Journal* (Winchester, Eng.) III
        (Mar. 1950), 19–25.

Tirao, Cacho
1975   *Momento musical* [includes A. Piazzolla, *Verano porteño*].
        Stereo cassette, CBS 90.011. Buenos Aires: Discos CBS-SAICF,
        1975–1985.

1981   *La puñalada, milonga tangueada de Pintín Castellanos;
        Derecho viejo, tango de Eduardo Arolas para guitarra.* B.A.
        13300. Buenos Aires: Ricordi.

Tiscornia, Eleuterio F.
1930   *La lengua de "Martín Fierro."* Facultad de Filosofía y Letras,
        Institiuto de Filología, Biblioteca de Dialectología Hispano-
        americana III. Buenos Aires: Universidad de Buenos Aires.

Torre Revello, José
1926   "Un pleito sobre bailes entre el Cabildo y el Obispo de Buenos
        Aires (1746–1757)," *Boletín del Instituto de Investigaciones
        Históricas* (Buenos Aires) V, 274–304.

1943   "Merchandise Brought to America by the Spaniards (1534–
        1586)," *The Hispanic American Historical Review* (Durham,
        NC) XXIII, 772–81.

1944   "Músicos coloniales," *Estudios* (Academia Literaria del Plata,
        Buenos Aires) LXXII, 392–404.

1948   "Mercaderías introducidas por los españoles en América (1534–1586)," *Estudios* (Buenos Aires), Año XXXVIII, Tomo LXXIX, No. 427, 113–21.

1957   "Algunos libros de música traídos a América en el siglo XVI," *Inter-American Review of Bibliography* (Washington, D.C.) VII, No. 4, 372–80.

1970   *La sociedad colonial: Páginas sobre la sociedad de Buenos Aires entre los siglos XVI y XIX.* Buenos Aires: Ediciones Pannedille.

Torres Villarroel, Diego de
1743   *Vida, ascendencia...del doctor don Diego de Torres Villarroel....* Valencia and Pamplona. *The Remarkable Life of Don Diego, Being the Autobiography of Diego de Torres Villarroel Translated from the Spanish by William C. Atkinson....* London: The Folio Society, 1958.

Trend, J.B.
1925   *Luis Milán and the Vihuelistas.* [London:] Oxford Univ. Press.

Trenti Rocamora, J. Luis
1948   *La cultura en Buenos Aires hasta 1810.* Buenos Aires: Universidad de Buenos Aires.

Turnbull, Harvey
1974   *The Guitar, from the Renaissance to the Present Day.* New York: C. Scribner's Sons. Westport, CT: The Bold Strummer, 1992.

Tyler, James
1980   *The Early Guitar: A History and Handbook,* Early Music Series No. 4. London: Oxford University Press.

Unamuno, Miguel de
1894   *"El gaucho Martín Fierro,"* *La Revista Española* (Salamanca) I. Republished with notes by Carlos Paz. Montevideo: Ediciones "El Galeón," 1986.

Valera, Cipriano de, ed.
1602   *La Santa Biblia, antiguo y nuevo testamento. Antigua versión de Casiodoro de la Reina (1569), revisada por Cipriano de Valera (1602), y cotejada posteriormente con diversas traducciones, y con los textos hebreo y griego, con referencias.* Buenos Aires, Bogotá, etc.: Sociedades Bíblicas Unidas, 1957.

Vega, Carlos
1926   "La guitarra argentina," lecture read at the Universidad de la Plata, published in Domingo Prat, *Diccionario biográfico, bibliográfico, histórico, crítico de guitarras (instrumentos afines) guitarristas....* Buenos Aires: Romero y Fernández, [1934], pp. 329–30.

1944–53 *Bailes tradicionales argentinos. Historia—origen—música—poesía—coreografía.* Buenos Aires: Julio Korn.

1946a *Los instrumentos musicales aborígenes y criollos de la Argentina, con un ensayo sobre las clasificaciones universales, un panorama gráfico de los instrumentos americanos....* Buenos Aires: Centurión/Hachette.

1946b *Música sudamericana.* Buenos Aires: Emecé.

1956 *El origen de las danzas folklóricas.* Buenos Aires: Ricordi.

Vega, Lope de
1635 *Obras de Lope de Vega...*(nueva edición). Emilio Cotarelo y Mori, ed. 13 vols. Madrid: La Real Academia Española, 1916–1930.

Velázquez, Víctor
1986 *20 grandes éxitos.* Dolby cassette, EMI 16236. Buenos Aires: EMI-Odeón SAIC.

Vidal, Emeric Essex
1820 *Picturesque Illustrations of Buenos Ayres and Monte Video, Consisting of Twenty-Four Views: Accompanied with Descriptions of the Scenery, and of the Inhabitants of Those Cities and Their Environs.* London: Ackerman and Strand. Facsimile ed. Buenos Aires: Viau, 1943.

Vidal de Battini, Berta Elena
1964 *El español de la Argentina: Estudio destinado a los maestros de las escuelas primarias I.* Buenos Aires: Consejo Nacional de Educación.

Viggiano Esaín, Julio
1948 *Instrumentología musical popular argentina.* Córdoba: La Universidad.

Viglietti, Cédar
[1973] *Origen e historia de la guitarra.* Buenos Aires: Albatros.

Viglietti, Daniel
1973 *Trópicos* [in collaboration with Cuban composer Leo Brouwer]. Stereo cassette, SCO 90.575. [Montevideo:] Orfeo.

Vila, Pablo
1989 "Argentina's *Rock Nacional:* The Struggle for Meaning," *Latin American Music Review* (Austin, TX) X, 1–28.

[Vowell, Robert L.]
1831 *Campaigns and Cruises in Venezuela and New Grenada, and in the Pacific Ocean; from 1818 to 1830.* 3 vols. London: Longman.

Ward, John M.
1980   "Miguel de Fuenllana," *The New Grove Dictionary of Music and Musicians*. London: Macmillan.

Weber, Frida
1941   "Fórmulas de tratamiento en la lengua de Buenos Aires," *Revista de Filología Hispánica* (Buenos Aires) III, 105–39.

Weiner, Jack
1967   "Platón Alexandrovich Chijachev o Chikhachev (1812–1892): Bosquejo biográfico," *Boletín del Instituto de Historia Argentina "Dr. Emilio Ravignani"* (Buenos Aires) Año IX, Ser. 2, Nos. 14–15, 3–6.

"Whitelocke, John"
1917   *Dictionary of National Biography...to 1900* (London: Oxford University Press, 1968), XXI, p. 119ff.

Zavadivker, Ricardo
1974   "Dos antiguos manuscritos musicales en la Biblioteca Nacional," *Notas* (Buenos Aires) XVI, 6–7.

1977a   "El primer grabado de la guitarra en América," *The Gendai Guitar* (Tokyo) [Vol. XI] No. 124 (Mar.), 69–73.

1977b   "Los instrumentos indígenas en la obra de Guamán Poma," *Antiquitas* (Universidad del Salvador, Buenos Aires) Nos. 24–25 (May–Nov.), 8–35.

1979   "Andrés Segovia, entrevista," *Notas* (Buenos Aires) XXII, 50–51.

1982   "La guitarra y la vihuela en Hispanoamerica," *Revista de INIDEF* (Caracas) V (1981–82), 44–49.

1988   "Una guitarra barroca en la iconografía chilena," *El Mundo de la Guitarra* (Buenos Aires) No. 4 (Jun.–Jul.), 15.

Zoltowska, Evelina
1964   "Crónica de un viaje por la Argentina en 1838," *La Nación* (Buenos Aires), 1 Nov. (domingo), 4.

Index

(Italics appear only in titles.)

A mi guitarra 196
Academies of arts and letters:
    Florentine, Neo-Platonist 187
    Bardi, Corsi, de'Medici 187
    Manuel de Oms in Lima 187
    Real Academia Española, La 96
Accompaniments 23, 114, 408, 411ff.
Accordion 121
Achaval, Our Lady of 385
Achiras, Arg. 402
Acosta, Félix 307ff.
Acquisition of lands, vassals
    52, 431ff.
Aduana (see Customs and import...)
Aguado, Dionisio 32
Aires (the dance) 23, 375, 397, 399f., 409
Alais, Juan 10, 26, 32-35
Albarellos, Dr. Nicanor 33, 311
Alberdi, Juan Bautista 22, 258
Alberti bass 132, 277
Alcazaba, Simón 355
Alderetes, Arg. 402
Alemán, Mateo 90
Alexander VI, Pope:
    Concedes religious authority
        in the New World 75
    Designates Catholic Sovereigns 75
    Signs Treaty of Tordesillas 71
Alirio Díaz competition, Caracas 33, 445
Alligator 57
Almaviva, Count 131, 276
Almaviva, Countess 132
Almayne 128
Almenda, Antonio de 129
Alonso, Amado 108, 116ff.
Alvarez Martínez, Rosario 278f.
Amat, Dr. Joan Carles 128
American (U.S.) writers on the Plata
    (see Travellers'...)
Amerindian inhabitants (see Indians...)
Amerindian instruments 182
Amestoy, Juan Carlos 6
Andalucismo 19, 86, 271
    "Alleged" impact 116-18
    Levelled with commerce 97, 138f.
    Statistical data against 116
    Statistical data for 117ff.
    Summarized 136ff.
Andalusian:
    Dialect 88-92

New World colonists 116-18
    Sadness 303
    Stowaways 92
Andean mines (see Mines...)
Andes 59-68, passim
Andrews, Capt. [Joseph] 385ff., 405-19
Angelito, Velorio del (see Velorio...)
Anido, María Luisa 9, 33
Anonymous:
    amor de la estanciera, El 312f.
    "Libro de diferentes cifras," MS 811.
        Madrid: Biblioteca Nacional 280
    Notes on the Viceroyalty (1808) 381f.
    (see also Saldívar Codex No. 4...)
Antola, María H. 35ff.
Anzures, Pedro 65
Aquarachay 57
Aquaraquazú 57
Aragón, Sp. 89
Arcadia (a haven for guitarists, a
    musician's paradise) 4f., 391, 444f.
Arch form 11-13
Archaic liturgical greetings 94, 394
Archbishop of Lima:
    Bartolomé Lobo Guerrero 295
Archivo de Indias 117, 179, 323ff., 330, 431
Archivo de la Nación:
    Buenos Aires 195
    Mexico City 178
Aretz, Isabel 206f., 259, 354f.
Arica, Peru 66
Armado 57
Arnold, Samuel G. 395ff., 405-19
Arpa (see Harp...)
Arroyo de la Soledad, Arg. 402
Artigas, José G. 22, 258
Asado (barbecue) 4, 366f., 369, 438
Ascasubi, Hilario 104
Assisi (see St. Francis...)
Asumpción 64
Asunción, Paraguay:
    Beginnings 64ff., 431
    Equated with the new Buenos Aires 68
    Refuge from first Buenos Aires 64, 432f.
Atlantic crossing, The 164
Auchmuty, Samuel 359
Ausencia (milonga) 28-29
Aussel, Roberto 33, 36
Austrian (see Sepp, Strobel...)
Ayestarán, Alejandro 191

485

Ayestarán, Lauro 18, 311
Ayestarán, Lola 37
Ayestarán, Ramón 35
Ayolas, Juan de 64ff.
Azara, Félix de 70, 302
Bagres, Los, Venez. 289, 297
Baile (dance) 176, 182
Baja (bass theme) 177
Bajón 232, 297
Bambuco (the dance) 289
Banda Oriental:
    (= East Bank, later
        Republic of Uruguay) 73
    Classical guitar school 33ff., 445
Bandola 232
Bandoneón 25, 112f.
Bandurria 121, 232
Barber of Seville 88, 131
Barbieri, Guillermo 112
Barco Centenera, Martín del 355
Bardi, Count Giovanni di (see Academies)
Barlow, Roger 62, 379
Barnuevo (see Peralta y Barnuevo...)
Baroque guitar, 1600-1750: 5-courses
    standard in the Plata 218ff., 250-51
Barrenechea, Ana María 111
Barrios, Agustín 39
Barrueco, Manuel xv
Barry publications (see Abel Carlevaro...)
Bárzana, Alonso de, S.J. 336
Bass strings:
    Early use from 1792, 190
    Over-spun 190-95, 202
    In *Martín Fierro* 190
Baumann, Max P. 18, 208
Beaumarchais, Pièrre A. Caron de 88, 131
Becerril (see García Becerril...)
Beethoven, Ludwig van 12-14
Behme, Anthony, S.J. 224
Bello, Andrés 107ff.
Bellow, Alexander 16
Bells 167, 225
Benítez, Baltazar xv, 36
Beresford, Gen. William Carr
    (Viscount Beresford) 359
Berger, Louis 192, 222
Berlioz, Hector 415
Bermejo River 66
Bermudo, Juan 157, 354
Berro, Pres. Bernardo 22, 188, 258
Bibliografía periódica anual, Madrid 280
bien dudoso, el mal seguro, El 164
Bigüela (see Vihuela...)
Bi-modal fandango 273
Bingley, Rev. William 405-18
Bishop of Buenos Aires (see...):
    Maciel

    Marcellano y Agramont
    Peralta y Barnuevo
Bishop of Caracas:
    Diego Antonio 320
    Padre Guanare 320
Bishop of Cartagena:
    Diego Peredo 319f.
Bishop of Lima (see Archbishop Lobo
    Guerero...)
Bishop of Puerto Rico:
    Alonso Manso, guitarist 174
Bishop of Tucumán:
    Francisco de Victoria 70, 76
    Fernando de Trejo y Sanabria 296
Bitetti, Ernesto 35f.
Bizet, Georges 88, 279
Blanco White, Joseph 87
Blind musicians:
    Indian in Caacaty 388
    Miguel de Fuenllana 161
    Pedro de Madrid 162
    Valentín Viñas 400
Boccherini, Luigi 279ff.
Boga 57
Bohorquez, Inca 241
Bolero (the dance) 279, 393, 415
Boliche 302
Bolio de Saldívar, Elisa O. 282
Bolívar, Gen. Simón 288
Bolivia 55ff., 208, 322
Bonaerense 108
Bonaparte, Joseph 359
Bonaparte, Napoleon 80, 359
Bone inlay 209
Boom folklórico 23, 441
Boom in Latin American fiction 6
Boom of the Rioplatense guitar 483
Bordones, Use of
    (see Bass strings...)
Bosch, Hieronymus 340
Bourbon dynasty:
    In Madrid, Philip V 186, 279f.
    In Paris, Louis XIV 130
    (see also Marie-Louise-Gabrielle...)
Boyd-Bowman, Peter 117f.
Brackenridge, H.M. 361, 405-18
Bravo, Pedro 163
Brazil 56ff.
Brazilwood (see Woods...)
Briçeño, Luis de 130
British invasion of the Plata 359f.
British literature on the Plata:
    Before 1800 (see du Biscay, Falkner,
        Davie...)
    Earliest, 1541, Roger Barlow 62
    Interest in folklore & local color 376
    Travel accounts, 19th century 360ff.

494

Majo 119, 133, 297
Málaga 272
Malagueñas 275
Malambo (the dance) 23, 104, 207
Mandolin 215
Manso (see Bishop of Puerto Rico...)
Mantegazza, Dr. Paolo:
   Analysis of *mate* beverage 437
   Folk dances 375
   Mournful gaucho laments 375f.
Manteísta 308f.
Manuelita (see Rosas...)
Marcellano y Agramont, Bishop
   Cayetano 322-28
Marcos de Obregón 124f., 163f.
Mariachi 136
Mariana (see St. Mariana of Quito...)
Marie-Louise-Gabrielle of Savoy
   187, 283
Mariquita (the dance) 386, 397, 409
Marqués de Castell (see Oms...)
Marquetry:
   Among Seville's luthiers 161
   (see also Inlay...)
Márquez, Pablo 6
Marriage of Figaro, The 131ff., 277ff.
Marri-marri (the dance) 289
Marrón y azul 30
Martín Fierro, El gaucho 189f., 196f., 255
Mary, Queen of Scots 418
Masquerade 133, 185, 295, 308, 319, 329
Mass:
   At sea 167f.
   Guitar in 237-42
   Jesuit Reductions 225ff.
Massini, Esteban 31f., 33
Matador 87
Mate (pronounced mah-teh):
   Bombilla (= straw with strainer) 436
   Harvest and marketing 78, 435
   Indian origin; etymology 434ff.
   Mate and the guitar 439ff.
   Pavita (= small teapot) 438
   Use among Hispanics 215, 436
Media caña (the dance) 391, 409
Melodrama: guitarists improvised the
   background for tales and poetry 441-42
Mendelssohn, Felix 4
Mendoza, City of 75, 402
Mendoza, Pedro de 63ff., 70, 432f.
Menéndez Pidal, Ramón 90
Menotti, Nelly 37
Mercedes, Arg. 402
Merchants with guitars, strings 174f.
Méry (see St. Méry...)
Mesoamerica 155, 245
Mestizaje (see Racial fusion...)

Mexico, Guitar in (see Guitars...)
Miers, John 360, 383ff., 405-22
Milán, Luis 171, 254, 354
Milonga (both a song accompaniment and
   a dance) 27-29, 32, 112, 315
Milongeos (Broqua's) 9
Mines (see Chuquisaca, Potosí, 16th c....)
Mining, 19th-century 360
Minguet y Yrol, Pablo 280
Minué montonero (the dance) 388, 409
Minuet 281, 291, 308, 310, 325f., 364, 371,
   386, 396, 415
Miranda, Francisco J., S.J. 355f.
Misa (see Mass...)
misión, La (see *Mission*...)
Misiones, Arg. 221
Mission, The (feature film) 78, 224
Missions established 75ff.
Mohammedans 89, 273, 330ff.
Molina, Tirso de 88
Molière, Jean Baptiste Poquelin 88
Molinder, Francisco, S.J. 222
Monarchs (see Catholic Sovereigns...)
Monothematic 277f.
Montanaro, Bruno 18
Monte vide eu 59
Montes, Enrique 60ff.
Montesardo, Girolamo 407
Montevideo 402
   Montevideo simpático 40
   Settlement by Canarios out of
     Buenos Aires, 18th c. 71
Monzón, Antonio 235
Moors 89, 140, 330
Morante, Ambrosio 314f.
Mordent 278
Morel, Jorge 8, 35
Moreno, Salvador 216f.
Moreno Chá, Ercilia 18
Moretti, Federico 406
Morphology of Rioplatense verbs
   (see Voseo...)
Morro, El, Arg. 402
Mozart, W.A. 131ff., 276-78, 334, 445f.
Mudarra, Alonso de 161
"Mulatto Juan...lives free...because he
   is a singer and guitar player" 309
Mule breeding and trade 74f.
Mungrullú 57
Muñiz, Javier 108
Muñoz, Ricardo 17, 259
Muratori, Ludovico A. 234f.
Murcia, Andalusia 272
Murcia, Santiago de
   Court guitarist 187, 283
   Courtly sanction of the fandango 283
   Fandango from Saldívar Codex 285f.

"Passacalles y obras...1732" 282ff.
Saldívar Codex No. 4 282ff.
Murcianas 275
Music and conversation 126ff., 143f.
 (see also Touchstones of Civilization...)
Music as the conversation piece or
 pretense for gathering:
 In Spain, 127f.,
 In Europe 130-33
 In the Plata 215, 364, 370, 390, 395,
  416-18, 441f.
Music for the earliest colonists 169f.
Music on the Atlantic 163f.
Músicas (books and scores of music) 171
Musicatas (serenades) 339
Musicology institutes in the Plata
 (see Institutes...)
Muslims (see Mohammedans, Moors...)
Narváez, Luis de 171, 179, 354
National instrument:
 Spain 128, 279
 The Plata 12, 22, 139, 143ff., 258-60, 346f.
National language of the Plata 22, 108, 141
 (see also Rioplatense...)
ñatita, La 34
Nebra, José de 335
Needles, Dale 30
Neo-Platonist academy (see Academies...)
Nicuesa, Diego de 172
Nield, Jonathan 423
Nomenclature of guitar-like
 instruments 156-63, 196-208, 243
"Non più andrai..." 276f.
Nonesuch recordings 36
Novel of the Victorian era, set in South
 America 376ff.
novio de la aldeana, El 275
Núñez Cabeza de Vaca, Alvar 65
Nutria 57
Obispo (see Bishop...)
Oboe (see Shawm, Hautbois...)
Obregón (see Marcos de Obregón...)
Odeón recordings 112
Olmedo, Mayor Bartolomé de, prohibits
 guitar music in Córdoba 299
Olsen, Dale 207
ombú, El 377
Oms y Santa Pau, Manuel de:
 24th Viceroy of Peru 186
 Academy of arts and letters 187
 As guitarist 187
 Marqués de Castell dos Ríus 186
Oraisón, Jorge 30, 37
Oratorio in Mexico and Guatemala 293f.
Orders of Catholic priests 75-78, 164f.
 (see also Dominican, Franciscan,
 Jesuit, Predicadores...)

Organ (church) 167, 182, 225, 230, 232, 356
Organology 17f., 201ff.
Orinoco River 54, 290
Ornamentation of instruments 208ff.
Orphénica lyra 161, 179
Orquesta típica 25
Ortiz el Nahuatlato 178
Ortíz from Cuba 178
Ortografía 90
Osorio (see Bolio...)
Ostrich 57
Osuna, Andalusia 244
Otero, Corazón 41
Out on the Pampas 376f.
Over-spun bass strings
 (see Bass strings...)
Oviedo, Gonzalo Fernández de 173
Oyanguren, Julio M. 34
Pacheco, Francisco 161
Pacu 57
Padrino 306f., 365
Page, F.M. 139f.
Palacios, Leonardo 37
Palindrome 11-12, 184
Pallière, Léon
 Travel diary 371f.
 Iconography of guitar 372, 405-18
Pampa (plains) 53, 57ff.
Pampa Province, La 18
Pan de jarabe (the dance) 318
Panama and the Columbian Exchange 66
Pancaldo, Leone 70, 222
Panormo guitars 202
Paraguay 55ff., 221ff., 355f.
Paraguay River 55ff., 224
Paraná River 55ff.
Paraquaria (= territory of modern
 Paraguay, Misiones, Arg., and Bra-
 zil's southern borderlands) 223, 355
Pardo, Viceroy Alonso 293
Paris of the New World (Buenos Aires) 105
Pasacalle 129, 134, 282ff.
Paseo 128
Paso de los Toros, Urug. xv
Patí 57
Pauke, Florian, S.J. 166f.
Pavita (teapot) 438
Payada 410-13
Payador (gaucho balladeer) 374, 413
Pedrell, Carlos 35
Pedretti de Bolón, Alma 110f.
Pejerrey 57
Pellegrini, Víctor 33
Pensión (hostel) 3
Peralta y Barnuevo, Bishop José 233, 321ff.
Peramás, José, S.J. 355
Peredo, Bishop Diego 319

OTHER MUSIC TITLES AVAILABLE FROM
THE BOLD STRUMMER, LTD.

GUITAR

THE AMP BOOK: A Guitarist's Introductory Guide to Tube Amplifiers *by Donald Brosnac.*

ANIMAL MAGNETISM FOR MUSICIANS: Making a Bass Guitar and Pickup from Scratch *by Erno Zwaan.*

ANTHOLOGY OF FLAMENCO FALSETAS *collected by Ray Mitchell.*

ANTONIO DE TORRES: Guitar Maker—His Life and Work *by José Romanillos. Fwd. by Julian Bream.*

THE ART OF FLAMENCO *by D. E. Pohren.*

THE ART OF PRACTICING *by Alice Arzt.*

THE BURNS BOOK *by Paul Day.*

CLASSIC GUITAR CONSTRUCTION *by Irving Sloane.*

THE DEVELOPMENT OF THE MODERN GUITAR *by John Huber.*

DICCIONARIO ENCICLOPEDIO ILUSTRADO DEL FLAMENCO *by José Blas Vega & Manuel Rios Ruiz.* 2 vols.

THE FENDER GUITAR *by Ken Achard.*

THE FLAMENCOS OF CADIZ BAY *by Gerald Howson.*

THE GIBSON GUITAR FROM 1950 *by Ian C. Bishop.* 2 vols.

THE GUITAR: From the Renaissance to the Present Day *by Harvey Turnbull.*

GUITAR HISTORY: Volume 1—Guitars Made by the Fender Company *by Donald Brosnac.*

GUITAR HISTORY: Volume 2—Gibson SGs *by John Bulli.*

GUITAR HISTORY: Volume 3—Gibson Catalogs of the Sixties *edited by Richard Hetrick.*

GUITAR HISTORY: Volume 4—The Vox Story *by David Petersen & Dick Denney.*

GUITAR HISTORY: Volume 5—The Guild Guitar *by E. G. Beesley.*

GUITAR REPAIR: A Manual of Repair for Guitars and Fretted Instruments *by Irving Sloane.*

GUITAR TRADER'S VINTAGE GUITAR BULLETIN. 6 vols.

OTHER MUSIC TITLES AVAILABLE FROM
THE BOLD STRUMMER, LTD.

BERNARD STEVENS AND HIS MUSIC: A Symposium *edited by Bertha Stevens.*

JANÁCEK: Leaves from His Life *by Leos Janácek. Edited & transl. by Vilem & Margaret Tausky.*

JOHN FOULDS AND HIS MUSIC: An Introduction *by Malcolm MacDonald.*

LIPATTI *(Tanasescu & Bargauanu):* see PIANO, below.

LISZT AND HIS COUNTRY, 1869-1873 *by Deszo Legány.*

MASCAGNI: An Autobiography Compiled, Edited and Translated from Original Sources *by David Stivender.*

MICHAEL TIPPETT, O.M.: A Celebration *edited by Geraint Lewis. Fwd. by Peter Maxwell Davies.*

THE MUSIC OF SYZMANOWSKI *by Jim Samson.*

THE OPRICHNIK: An Opera in Four Acts by Peter Il'ich Tchaikovsky. *Transl. & notes by Philip Taylor.*

PERCY GRAINGER: The Man Behind the Music *by Eileen Dorum.*

PERCY GRAINGER: The Pictorial Biography *by Robert Simon. Fwd. by Frederick Fennell.*

RAVEL ACCORDING TO RAVEL *(Perlemuter & Jourdan-Morhange):* see PIANO, below.

RONALD STEVENSON: A Musical Biography *by Malcolm MacDonald.*

SCHUBERT'S MUSIC FOR PIANO FOUR-HANDS *(Weekly & Arganbright):* see PIANO, below.

SOMETHING ABOUT THE MUSIC 1: Landmarks of Twentieth-Century Music *by Nick Rossi.*

SOMETHING ABOUT THE MUSIC 2: Anthology of Critical Opinions *edited by Thomas P. Lewis.*

A SOURCE GUIDE TO THE MUSIC OF PERCY GRAINGER *edited by Thomas P. Lewis.*

THE SYMPHONIES OF HAVERGAL BRIAN *by Malcolm MacDonald.* Vol. 2: Symphonies 13-29. Vol. 3: Symphonies 30-32, Survey, and Summing-Up.

OTHER MUSIC TITLES AVAILABLE FROM
THE BOLD STRUMMER, LTD

VERDI AND WAGNER *by Erno Lendvai.*

VILLA-LOBOS: The Music — An Analysis of His Style *by Lisa M. Peppercorn.*

THE WORKS OF ALAN HOVHANESS: A Catalog, Opus 1 – Opus 360; with Supplement Through Opus 400 *by Richard Howard.*

XENAKIS *by Nouritza Matossian.*

ZOLTAN KODALY: His Life in Pictures and Documents *by László Eosze.*

GENERAL SUBJECTS

ACOUSTICS AND THE PERFORMANCE OF MUSIC *by Jürgen Meyer.*

AMERICAN MINIMAL MUSIC *by Wim Mertens. Transl. by J. Hautekiet.*

A CONCISE HISTORY OF HUNGARIAN MUSIC, 2ND ENL. ED. *by Bence Szabolozi.*

EARLY MUSIC *by Denis Stevens.*

EXPRESSIVE RHYTHM IN EUROPEAN CLASSICAL MUSIC, 1700-1900: An Annotated Sourcebook and Performance Guide *transl. & edited with commentaries by David Montgomery.*

GOGOLIAN INTERLUDES; Gogol's Story "Christmas Eve" as the Subject of the Operas by Tchaikovsky and Rimsky-Korsakov *by Philip Taylor.*

HISTORY THROUGH THE OPERA GLASS *by George Jellinek.*

JOAN PEYSER ON MODERN MUSIC AND MUSIC MAKING 1: Twentieth Century Music — The Sense Behind the Sound, UPDATED 2ND ED.

JOAN PEYSER ON MODERN MUSIC AND MUSIC MAKING 2: Boulez — Composer, Conductor, Enigma, UPDATED ED.

JOAN PEYSER ON MODERN MUSIC AND MUSIC MAKING 3: The Music of Our Time — Collected Essays and Articles.

MAKING MUSIC GUIDES: Making Four-Track Music *by John Peel.* What Bass, 2ND ED. *by Tony Bacon & Laurence Canty.* What Drum, 2ND ED. *by Geoff Nicholls & Andy Duncan.* What's Midi, 2ND ED. *by Andy Honeybone, Julian Colbeck, Ken Campbell & Paul Colbert.*

THE MUSICAL INSTRUMENT COLLECTOR, REVISED ED. *by J. Robert Willcutt & Kenneth R. Ball.*

OTHER MUSIC TITLES AVAILABLE FROM
THE BOLD STRUMMER, LTD

THE MUSICAL STAMP DATE BOOK: with an Illustrated Guide to the Collecting of Musical Stamps *by Herbert Moore.*

A MUSICIAN'S GUIDE TO COPYRIGHT AND PUBLISHING, ENLARGED ED. *by Willis Wager.*

MUSICOLOGY IN PRACTICE: Collected Essays by Denis Stevens *edited by Thomas P. Lewis.* Vol. 1: 1948-1970. Vol. 2: 1971-1990.

MY VIOLA AND I *by Lionel Tertis.*

THE NUTLEY PAPERS: A Fresh Look at the Titans of Music (humor) *by James Billings.*

PEACE SONGS *compiled & edited by John Jordan.*

PERCUSSION INSTRUMENTS AND THEIR HISTORY, REV. ED. *by James Blades.*

THE PRO/AM BOOK OF MUSIC AND MYTHOLOGY *compiled, edited & with commentaries by Thomas P. Lewis.* 3 vols.

THE PRO/AM GUIDE TO U. S. BOOKS ABOUT MUSIC: Annotated Guide to Current & Backlist Titles *edited by Thomas P. Lewis.* 2 vols.

RAYMOND LEPPARD ON MUSIC: An Anthology of Critical and Personal Writings *edited by Thomas P. Lewis.*

SKETCHES FROM MY LIFE *by Natalia Sats.*

PERFORMANCE PRACTICE / "HOW-TO"
INSTRUCTIONAL

THE BOTTOM LINE IS MONEY: Songwriting *by Jennifer Ember Pierce.*

GUIDE TO THE PRACTICAL STUDY OF HARMONY *by Peter Il'ich Tchaikovsky.*

HOW TO SELECT A BOW FOR VIOLIN FAMILY INSTRUMENTS *by Balthasar Planta.*

IMAGINATIONS: Tuneful Fun and Recital Pieces to Expand Early Grade Harp Skills *by Doris Davidson.*

THE JOY OF ORNAMENTATION: Being Giovanni Luca Conforto's *Treatise on Ornamentation* (Rome, 1593) *with a Preface by Sir Yehudi Menuhin and an Introduction by Denis Stevens.*

MAKING MUSICAL INSTRUMENTS *by Irving Sloane.*

THE MUSICIAN'S GUIDE TO MAPPING: A New Way to Learn Music *by Rebecca P. Shockley.*

OTHER MUSIC TITLES AVAILABLE FROM
THE BOLD STRUMMER, LTD

THE MUSICIANS' THEORY BOOK: Reference to Fundamentals, Harmony, Counterpoint, Fugue and Form *by Asger Hamerik.*

ON BEYOND C *(Davidson):* see PIANO, below.

A PIANIST'S GUIDE TO PRACTICING: see PIANO, below.

THE STUDENT'S DICTIONARY OF MUSICAL TERMS.

TENSIONS IN THE PERFORMANCE OF MUSIC: A Symposium, REV. & EXT. ED. *edited by Carola Grindea. Fwd. by Yehudi Menuhin.*

THE VIOLIN: Precepts and Observations *by Sourene Arakelian.*

PIANO/HARPSICHORD

THE ANATOMY OF A NEW YORK DEBUT RECITAL *by Carol Montparker.*

AT THE PIANO WITH FAURÉ *by Marguerite Long.*

EUROPEAN PIANO ATLAS *by H. K. Herzog.*

FRENCH PIANISM: An Historical Perspective *by Charles Timbrell.*

GLOSSARY OF HARPSICHORD TERMS *by Susanne Costa.*

KENTNER: A Symposium *edited by Harold Taylor. Fwd. by Yehudi Menuhin.*

LIPATTI *by Dragos Tanasescu & Grigore Bargauanu.*

ON BEYOND C: Tuneful Fun in Many Keys to Expand Early Grade Piano Skills *by Doris Davidson.*

A PIANIST'S GUIDE TO PRACTISING *by Zelda Bock.*

THE PIANIST'S TALENT *by Harold Taylor. Fwd. by John Ogdon.*

THE PIANO AND HOW TO CARE FOR IT *by Otto Funke.*

THE PIANO HAMMER *by Walter Pfeifer.*

PIANO NOMENCLATURE, 2ND ED. *by Nikolaus Schimmel & H. K. Herzog.*

RAVEL ACCORDING TO RAVEL *by Vlado Perlemuter & Hélène Jouran-Mor-hange.*

SCHUBERT'S MUSIC FOR PIANO FOUR-HANDS *by Dallas Weekly & Nancy Arganbright.*

THE STEINWAY SERVICE MANUAL *by Max Matthias.*

TECHNIQUE OF PIANO PLAYING, 5TH ED. *by József Gát.*

THE TUNING OF MY HARPSICHORD *by Herbert Anton Kellner.*

ABOUT

THE BOLD STRUMMER, LTD.

AND

PRO/AM MUSIC RESOURCES, INC.

Nicholas Clarke and **Thomas P. Lewis** are the publishers of **THE BOLD STRUMMER** (founded 1974) and **PRO/AM MUSIC RESOURCES** (founded 1982) respectively. While each company maintains its own separate identity, the staffs of the two firms exchange editorial ideas, produce joint advertising and promotion, and share all order fulfillment/warehousing facilities.

THE BOLD STRUMMER is particularly noted for its distinguished books about the guitar — for players, builders and craftspersons, antique guitar enthusiasts, and all school and library music and hobby collections.

PRO/AM MUSIC RESOURCES offers an outstanding list of titles in general music fields — with special attention given to books about the piano, for both professional and amateur performers, and all lovers of the instrument and its repertory.